C: Step-by-Step

C: Step-by-Step

Mitchell Waite, Stephen Prata
The Waite Group

SAMS

A Division of Prentice Hall Computer Publishing
11711 North College, Carmel, Indiana 46032 USA

Dedication

To Benjamin, whose warm and furry four-legged body helped me endure the rigors of writing.

— Mitchell Waite

To my wife, Kathleen.

— Stephen Prata

International Standard Book Number: 0–672–22651–0
Library of Congress Catalog Card Number: 89–60593

From The Waite Group:
Developmental Editor: *Mitchell Waite*
Managing Editor: *Scott Calamar*

From BMR:
Market Research & Editorial Development: *Susan Nelle*
Production: *Jan Granoff*
Interior Design: *Vigne Design*
Illustrations: *Kit Croucher*
Desktop Publishers: *Melanie Field and Lisa Labrecque*

From SAMS:
Acquisitions & Development Editor: *Richard Swadley*
Production Coordinator: *Marjorie Hopper*

Printed in the United States of America

Table of Contents

2   Introducing C   21

3   Data and C   45

Preface

When we wrote *C Primer Plus* in 1984, we aimed to create a friendly, easy-to-use, self-study guide to learning and using the C programming language. The book's subsequent success makes us think we met that goal. However, use of *C Primer Plus* has now moved from self study into the classroom as more institutions offer courses in C. This shift prompted us to develop a new edition of the book, one more directed toward the classroom environment. We surveyed instructors who use our book to find out what features they felt a textbook edition should have. Their advice and our own experiences in teaching C in the classroom have led to this book: *C Step by Step*.

Features

We've retained the major features of the original book, for they are what made the book work for many readers. These features include the following:

- The book is an introduction to programming as well as to C. We don't assume you already are proficient in some other language; however, we do assume you are not a complete computer novice. We don't discuss the history of computing or how computers work.

- We emphasize an interactive approach. In computing, you learn by doing. We often use short, easily typed examples to illustrate just one or two concepts at a time. This gives you quick feedback on how specific concepts work.

- We clarify ideas with figures and illustrations.

- We summarize the main C features in boxes highlighted with a screened background. These boxes simplify finding the summaries when you flip through the text.

- We offer occasional tidbits of information and advice in unscreened boxes.

- Each chapter contains review questions and programming exercises.

- We cover a full range of C topics, including pointers, structures, and bitwise operations.

To this tried and true foundation, we've also added several modifications and features:

- There are many more review questions and exercises. These increase your feedback on concept development and skills comprehension.

- We've increased the emphasis on programming skills by discussing structured programming, step-wise refinement, and top-down programming.

- We've increased the number of programming examples to provide more insight into programming design and analysis.

- More attention is given to developing the skills to find and avoid programming errors.

- We've integrated coverage of the ANSI C standard into the text.

- We cover loops and files earlier than before, and we've augmented the treatment of files.

- We've rewritten and expanded explanations, when necessary, to clarify the subject matter.

- The chapters are structured in a more organized fashion. Each begins with a list of contents and a list of objectives. Each ends with a summary, review questions, and exercises.

- We provide answers for half the review questions at the end of the book.

All in all, we believe we've retained the flavor of the original while adding elements that make this version more suitable for classroom use.

Hardware/Software

Nearly all the examples are "generic" C; that is, they're meant to run on any standard C implementation. We've tested the programs on a VAX 11/750 computer running under BSD 4.3 UNIX and on an IBM AT clone using Microsoft 5.1 C, Microsoft QuickC, and Borland Turbo C, all under MS-DOS. We've pointed out places where the program results may be implementation-dependent, that is, where they may depend on the particular hardware or software in use. Occasionally, we do discuss implementation - dependent matters, although we've confined our remarks to UNIX and DOS (PC-DOS or MS-DOS), which are currently the two most common C environments.

Advice to the Student

In general, learning works best as an active, not a passive process. This is particularly true for programming. Therefore, we encourage you to try out the examples in the book. Such practice will give you a better idea of how C works. If you have questions about a program, you can explore them by modifying the example. Be an active, experimenting learner, and you will learn C more quickly and in greater depth.

We wish you good fortune in learning C. We've tried to make this book meet your needs, and we hope it helps you reach your goals.

Acknowledgements

From Mitchell Waite

I would like to take this opportunity to thank the people who have helped to make *C: Step-by-Step* a reality.

First, I would like to thank Stephen Prata for his continued support and faultless writing, and ability to endure my demands for perfection.

I would like to thank the numerous college professors who responded to the original survey for *C Primer Plus,* and also those who reviewed *C: Step-by-Step's* 1200 manuscript pages. You gave us valuable feedback. Scott Calamar of The Waite Group was critical in pulling the final manuscript together and coordinating with the production company and the author. I would also like to thank Susan Nelle of Business Media Resources for her coordination of the development process and Jane Granoff for managing the production of the book.

Finally I give my thanks to the people behind the scenes at SAMS, who believed in the idea of a college textbook on C: Richard Swadley, who put us in touch with BMR and handled all the pre-sales support for the book, Jim Hill for his faith in the idea, and to all the other people at SAMS who in one way or another are involved in making *C: Step-by-Step* a success.

From Stephen Prata

Many people have helped make this book possible. I wish to thank Susan Nelle of Business Media Resources for surveying what instructors want in a C text and to thank those educators for their responses. I especially wish to thank those who reviewed the first draft: Janet Spears, Myron Kaplan, Kenneth Walker, Eliezer Dekel, David Hale, and Craig Colston. I wish to thank Scott Calamar of The Waite Group, and Jane Granoff of Business Media Resources for guiding the book through production.

Trademarks

All terms mentioned in this book that are known to be trademarks or service marks are listed below. In addition, terms suspected of being trademarks or service marks have been appropriately capitalized. SAMS cannot attest to the accuracy of this information. Use of a term in this book should not be regarded as affecting the validity of any trademark or service mark.

Apple is a registered trademark of Apple Computer, Inc.

IBM is a registered trademark of Interanational Business Machines Corp.

Lifeboat is a trademark of Lifeboat Associates, Inc.

Macintosh is a trademark of McIntosh Laboratory, Inc., and is used by Apple Computer, Inc., with express permission of its owner.

Microsoft is a registered trademark of Microsoft Corporation.

MS-DOS is a registered trademark of Microsoft Corporation.

UNIX is a trademark of AT&T Bell Laboratories.

VAX is a registered trademark of Digital Equipment Corp.

WordPerfect is registered trademark of WordPerfect Corporation.

WordStar is a registered trademark of MicroPro International Corporation.

1

C and Programming

Contents

Objectives

Learning about C's history and features

Understanding the steps to programming

Gaining an overview of structured programming

Learning what compilers and linkers do

Knowing what K & R C and ANSI C are

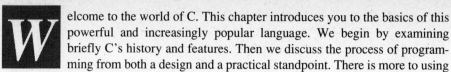

elcome to the world of C. This chapter introduces you to the basics of this powerful and increasingly popular language. We begin by examining briefly C's history and features. Then we discuss the process of programming from both a design and a practical standpoint. There is more to using a computer language than learning the language rules and the mechanics of creating a program, just as there is more to writing a novel than learning grammar and the use of a keyboard. We introduce you to a productive programming style called *structured programming*. Finally, we look at the question of language standards.

1.1 C History

Dennis Ritchie of Bell Labs created C in 1972 as he and Ken Thompson worked on designing the Unix operating system. C didn't spring full-grown from Ritchie's head, however. It came from Thompson's B language, which came from.... But that's another story. The important point is that C was created as a tool for working programmers. Thus, its chief goal is to be a *useful* language.

Most languages, we suppose, aim to be useful, but often they have other concerns. For instance, one of Pascal's main goals is to provide a sound basis for teaching programming principles. BASIC, on the other hand, was developed to resemble English, so that it could be easily learned by students unfamiliar with computers. These are important criteria, but they are not always compatible with pragmatic, workaday usefulness. C's background as a programming tool does, however, support its role as a pragmatic, programmer-oriented language. For example, consider the interface between programs and hardware. Pascal emphasizes general programming principles and attempts to isolate the programmer from hardware considerations. On the other hand, C is designed to work with hardware. So when programmers began using Pascal for real-world programming, Pascal vendors were forced to add many nonstandard extensions to the language, such as the ability to specify hardware addresses. These features often paralleled those already found in C. In addition, C offers many programming shortcuts that reduce your work load.

1.2 C Virtues

During the last decade, C has become one of the most important and popular programming languages. Its use has grown because people try it and like it. As you learn C, you too will recognize its many virtues. Let's mention a few.

Design Features

C incorporates many features that computer science theory and practice find desirable. It has modern control structures: three forms of loops for handling repetitive operations and three structures for choosing alternative paths of action. Through its various types of variables, arrays, and other data structures, C can represent a wide range of information. C encourages you to break down programs into modules (called *functions* in C). It makes it simple for you to document your programs by including explanatory comments. This feature makes it natural for you to use sound programming techniques such as top-down planning, structured programming, and modular design. The result is a more reliable, understandable program. As you master C, you'll come to appreciate all these points more fully.

Efficiency

C is an efficient language. It's a concise language that lets you say what you mean in fewer words. The final code tends to be compact and to run quickly.

Portability

C is a portable language, which means that C programs written on one system can be run with little or no modification on other systems. If modifications are necessary, they often can be made just by changing a few entries in a "header" file that accompanies the main program. Of course, most languages are meant to be portable, but anyone who has converted an IBM PC BASIC program to Apple BASIC or who has tried to run an IBM mainframe FORTRAN program on a VAX computer using the UNIX operating system knows that there can be many troublesome details. C is a leader in portability. C compilers are available for many systems, running from 8-bit microprocessors to 32-bit minicomputers to mighty Cray mainframes.

Power and Flexibility

C is powerful and flexible (two favorite words in computer literature). For example, most of the powerful, flexible UNIX operating system is written in C. (An *operating system* is a set of programs designed to manage a computer and its interactions with hardware and users.) So are many of the supporting programs commonly found on UNIX systems, including text editors and compilers and interpreters for other languages, such as FORTRAN, APL, Pascal, LISP, Logo, and BASIC. When you use FORTRAN on a UNIX machine, ultimately a C program produces the final executable program. C programs have been used for solving physics and engineering problems and even for animating movie sequences.

C exhibits some of the fine control usually associated with assembly language. (Assembly language is a fairly direct representation of the set of instructions built into a particular processor.) If you choose, you can fine-tune your programs for maximum efficiency.

Programmer Orientation

C is oriented toward programmer needs. It gives access to hardware. It lets you manipulate individual bits in memory. It has a rich selection of operators that let you express yourself succinctly. Note: C is less strict than, say, Pascal in limiting what you can do. This freedom is both an advantage and a danger. The advantage is that many operations such as converting forms of data are simpler in C. The danger is that C will allow you to make mistakes that are impossible in some languages. C also has a large library of useful functions that are generally available on most C implementations.

(We include this phraseology for those of you who may have to deal with bureaucratese.) C does have some faults. Often, as with people, faults and virtues are opposite sides of the same feature. For example, we've mentioned that C's freedom of expression requires added responsibility. As a computer preliterate once commented, the price of liberty is eternal vigilance.

C's conciseness combined with its wealth of operators makes it possible to prepare code that is extremely difficult to follow. You aren't compelled to write obscure code, but the opportunity is there. After all, what other language has a yearly "obfuscated code" contest? In addition, C's power, especially its use of pointers, enables you to make programming errors that are quite difficult to trace.

1.3 C Trends

By the early 1980s, C was already a dominant language in the minicomputer world of UNIX systems. Since then, it has spread to personal computers (microcomputers) and to mainframes. Many software houses use C as the preferred language for producing word-processing programs, spreadsheets, compilers, and other large-scale software products. These companies know that C produces compact and efficient programs. More important, they know that these programs are easy to modify and adapt to new computer models.

Many people in computer science learned their field using the UNIX C environment. Their desire to take their C programs and experience home and to new job environments also worked to spread C availability.

What's good for companies and C veterans is good for other users, too. More and more users are turning to C to secure its advantages for themselves, and you don't have to be a computer professional to use this powerful language. See Figures 1.1 and 1.2 for the virtues of C and where it is used.

In short, C is currently one of the most important programming languages and will continue to be so during the next decade. It is used on mainframes, minicomputers, and on personal computers. It is used by software companies, computer science students, and enthusiasts of all sorts. And if you apply for a job writing software, one of the first questions you should be able to answer "yes" to is: "Oh, say can you C?"

1.4 Using C: Seven Steps

C is a *compiled language*. If you are accustomed to using a compiled language such as Pascal or FORTRAN, you are already familiar with the basic steps in putting together a C program. But if your background is in an *interpreted language* such as BASIC or Logo, or if you have no background at all, you must learn how to compile. We soon guide you through the compiling process, and you'll see that it is actually pretty straightforward and sensible.

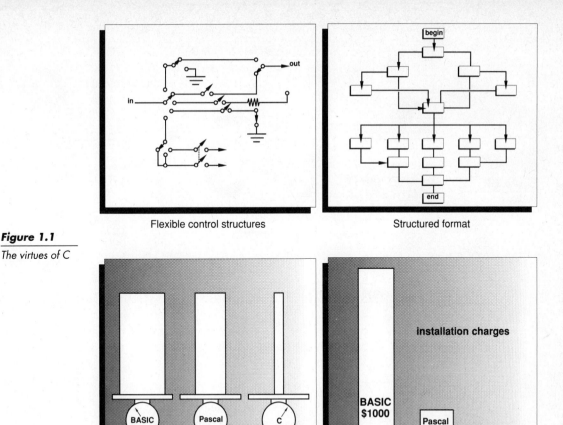

Flexible control structures

Structured format

Figure 1.1

The virtues of C

Compact code—small programs

Portable to other computers

First, to give you an overview of programming, we break down the act of writing a C program into seven steps. We then discuss some of them in more detail.

Step 1: Define the Program Objectives

Naturally enough, you should start with a clear idea of what you want the program to do. Think in terms of what information you need to include in the program, what feats of calculation and manipulation the program must be able to do, and what information the program should report back to you. At this level of planning, you should be thinking in general terms, not in terms of some specific computer language.

Step 2: Design the Program

Once you have a conceptual picture of what the program is to do, you should decide how the program will go about its implementation. What should the user interface be like? How should the program be organized?

Figure 1.2

Where C is used

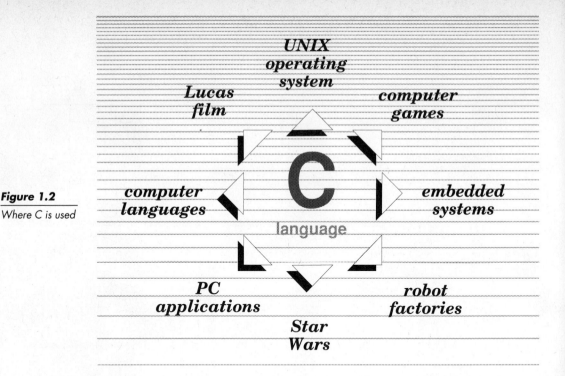

You also need to decide how to represent the data and what methods to use to perform the processing. As you first learn programming in C, the choices are pretty obvious; but as you move on to deal with more complex situations, you will find that such decisions require more thought. Choosing a good way to represent the information often can make the processing much easier. Again, you should be thinking generally, not about code, although some of your decisions may be based on general characteristics of the C language. For example, a C programmer has more options in data representation than, say, a BASIC programmer.

Computer science has developed several principles to guide you toward good program design. We discuss these soon when we go through a short design example.

Step 3: Write the Code

Now that you have a clear idea of what your program will do and how it will do it, you can begin to implement it by writing the code. That is, you translate your program design into the C language. At this stage you put your knowledge of C to work. You can play with your ideas on paper, but eventually you must input your code into the computer. The mechanics of this process depend on your programming environment. We present the details for some common environments shortly. In general, you use a text editor to create what is called a *source code file*. This file contains the C rendition of your program design.

As part of this step, you should document your work. The simplest way is to use C's comment facility to incorporate explanations into your source code.

Step 4: Compile the Code

The next step is to *compile* the source code. Again, the details depend on your programming environment, and we look at some common environments shortly. First, let's take a conceptual look at the task of compiling.

The *compiler* is a program whose job is to convert source code into executable code. *Executable code* is code in the *machine language,* or native language, of the computer on which the final program is to be run. Different computers have different machine languages, and a C compiler translates C into a particular machine language. C compilers also incorporate code from C libraries into the final program. These *libraries* contain a fund of standard routines for your use. (More accurately, a program called a *linker* incorporates the library routines, but on most systems the compiler runs the linker for you.) The end result is an *executable file* containing code the computer understands.

The compiler also checks that your program is valid C. If the compiler finds errors, it reports them to you and doesn't produce an executable file. Understanding a specific compiler's complaints is another skill you will pick up.

Step 5: Run the Program

Traditionally, the executable file is a stand-alone program. To run the program in many common environments, including UNIX and MS-DOS, just type the name of the executable file. Other environments, such as VMS on a VAX, may require a run command or some other mechanism. More recently, integrated environments such as Turbo C and QuickC let you run your executable C program from within the integrated environment by selecting names from a list or by pressing special keys. Again, we provide more details soon.

Step 6: Test and Debug the Program

That your program runs is a good sign, but it's possible that it may run incorrectly. Therefore you should check to see that your program does what it is supposed to do. Some of your programs will have mistakes, called *bugs* in computer jargon (named after the moth that caused the vacuum tubes in an early computer to fail). Making mistakes is a natural part of learning. *Debugging* is the finding and fixing of program mistakes (called *errors*). Since making errors seems inherent to programming in C, you had best prepare yourself to be reminded often of your fallibility. As well, as you become a more powerful and subtle programmer, your errors, too, will become more powerful and subtle.

You have many opportunities to err in making a program. You can make a basic design error. You can implement good ideas incorrectly. You can overlook some unusual input that will confound your program. You can use C incorrectly. You can make typing errors. You can put parentheses in the wrong place. And so on.

Fortunately, the situation isn't hopeless, although there may be times when you feel it is. The compiler catches many kinds of errors, and there are things you can do to help you track down the errors that the compiler doesn't catch. Throughout this book we provide debugging pointers.

Step 7: Maintain and Modify the Program

Once you complete a programming assignment, you may never use that program again. But when you create a program for yourself or for someone else, that program may see extensive use. If it does, most often you'll find reasons to make changes in it. Perhaps there's a minor bug that only shows up when someone enters a name beginning with "Zz." You may think of a better way to do something in the program. You may add a clever new feature. Or, you may adapt the program so that it runs on a different computer system (called "porting"). All these tasks are simplified greatly if you document the program clearly and if you follow sound design practices such as structured programming. Figure 1.3 shows the seven steps of programming in C.

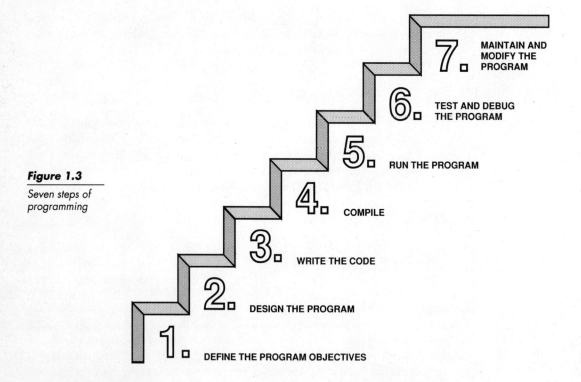

Figure 1.3

Seven steps of programming

7. □ MAINTAIN AND MODIFY THE PROGRAM

6. □ TEST AND DEBUG THE PROGRAM

5. □ RUN THE PROGRAM

4. □ COMPILE

3. □ WRITE THE CODE

2. □ DESIGN THE PROGRAM

1. □ DEFINE THE PROGRAM OBJECTIVES

Commentary for Beginners

Most students tend to neglect steps 1 and 2 (defining program objectives and designing the program) and go directly to step 3 (writing the program). Teachers often see students come into a computer lab, start the editor, and with no particular forethought or plan, start to program. (In fact, most of us have been guilty of this approach ourselves.) One problem is that, at first, it often works. The first programs you write are fairly simple, and it's usually easy to visualize the entire process in your head. As well, if you make a mistake, it's easy to find. But as the programs grow longer and become more complex, mental visualizations begin to fail, and errors become harder to find. Eventually, students who neglect the planning steps are condemned to hours of lost time, confusion, and frustration as they produce dysfunctional and obtuse programs.

The moral: Develop the habit of planning before coding. Use the ancient but honorable "lead-graphite" technology (a pencil) to jot down the program objectives and to outline the design. If you do so, you eventually will reap substantial dividends in time and satisfaction.

Another point is that usually you must go back and forth between steps. For instance, when you are writing code, you may find your plan was impractical or you may see a better way of doing things. Even after you see how a program runs, you may feel motivated to change the design. Documenting your work will help you move back and forth between levels.

Let's take a closer look now at some of these steps in writing a C program. First, we look at an example to illustrate some aspects of design, then we explore the editing and compiling processes in more detail.

1.5 A Design Example

Let's go though some of the design stages with a relatively simple example. Suppose you want a program that figures your United States federal income tax obligation from your taxable income.

Defining the Program Objectives

First, consider the program objectives. Our original statement ("a program that figures your United States federal income tax obligation from your taxable income") is not specific enough. The more vague the objectives are, the harder they are to program. The goal is to specify exactly what information the program needs and how the program is to use the information. It turns out your tax obligation depends on two factors: your taxable income and your filing status. Therefore, the first objective is that the program can read these two facts as input. The second objective is that the program should correctly calculate the tax from this information. Finally, the program should report the calculated tax.

Designing the Program

When it comes to organizing the program, think "modular." Like many programming problems, our tax example falls rather naturally into three tasks: obtaining information, performing some sort of calculation or processing, and reporting information. It makes sense, then, to organize the program into three modules, one devoted to each of these tasks. The modules break down the programming problem into smaller, easier-to-handle parts. If necessary, you can break down a large module into its own separate modules. This process is called *step-wise refinement* or *decomposition*. The idea is that you keep breaking a problem into smaller and smaller subproblems, until you reach a level at which the solution to the subproblem is obvious.

Once you decompose the problem into parts, you consider the parts individually. For our example, the input module involves the most decisions. Should the program be *interactive?* That is, should it be designed so that the program and the user carry on a dialogue? (Program: "What was your taxable income?" User: "10234.34" Program: "My sympathies. Which of the following is your filing status?" And so on.) Or do you want the program to read data from a file or a punched card? Should the program process just one tax case, or should it process a series of cases? If the program is interactive, do you want to use a simple teletype-like display, or do you want boxes, highlighted text, and an active mouse? What should the program do if bad data are entered? Depending on how ambitious your design is, you may have to continue the process of step-wise refinement another level or two. As you can see, designing the interface can be more involved than programming the actual calculations.

The next module is calculating the tax. You can use the instruction book provided by the United States Internal Revenue Service to determine how the tax is calculated. Your task is to devise a method, or algorithm, for reproducing the calculation. (An *algorithm* is a step-by-step recipe for computing a particular result.)

Finally, the third module is reporting the result. You have to decide whether to display the answer on the next line on the screen or to put it into a file, or whatever. This module is the simplest one in this example.

One final element to this stage is deciding what each module should communicate to the others. In this case, the answer is simple. The input module should communicate the taxable income and the filing status to the calculation module, and the calculation module should communicate the tax to the output module. See Figure 1.4.

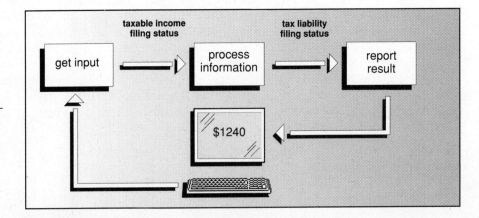

Figure 1.4

Design modules

Now you are ready to implement your work by writing the C code. It's a good idea to have the program reflect the modularity of your design. In fact, C is designed so that you can create complete programs from modules called *functions*. Thus, your main program contains three functions, one for each primary module. If necessary, some of these functions may be decomposed into smaller functions. Also, in C, the main program itself is a function called **main( )**.

Next you write the code for the individual functions. Usually, the best method is first to write the code for **main( )**, the top-level module, then write the codes for the next level of functions, and so on. This process is called *top-down programming*. The opposite process, writing the lowest-level functions first and working your way up, is called *bottom-up programming*. (See Figure 1.5). One advantage of top-down programming is that it is much better at exposing fundamental design flaws in a program, since it deals with broad issues before the details. With bottom-up programming, your programming units may not work together correctly.

Top-down

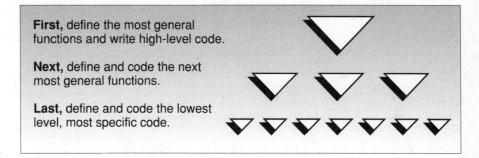

First, define the most general functions and write high-level code.

Next, define and code the next most general functions.

Last, define and code the lowest level, most specific code.

Figure 1.5

Top-down and bottom-up programming

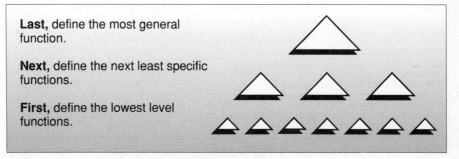

Last, define the most general function.

Next, define the next least specific functions.

First, define the lowest level functions.

Bottom-up

Top-down programming sounds much like step-wise refinement, and the two concepts are closely related. The difference is that step-wise refinement refers more to the conceptual analysis of a problem, and top-down programming refers more to the actual coding process. Step-wise refinement leads to a program's organization. Top-down programming describes the order in which you write the code implementing that organization. In principle, you can use bottom-up programming to implement the same organization, by writing the functions in the opposite order.

Structured Programming

Step-wise refinement, top-down programming, and modularity are all aspects of a programming style called *structured programming*. It evolved in response to the morass in which large programming projects in the 1960s and early 1970s floundered. It aims to produce better designed programs that are completed more quickly and are easier to test, debug, and modify. It's easy to see that this style meets those goals. First, careful planning beats haphazard planning or no planning for complex problems. Second, modularity is quite helpful. Consider our tax example. Suppose you opt for a fancy user interface but have problems with that part of the project. You can temporarily substitute a simpler module and use it to test the rest of the program. Or if you have to modify the program output, you can work just on that one module, leaving the rest alone. Or if your programming for the input module is sufficiently general, you can use it in other programs. Also, you can have different programmers work on different modules. In short, structured programming serves to increase productivity, program reliability, program testing, program debugging, and programming serviceability. We follow the ideals of structured programming throughout the book, especially when the programming becomes more complex.

1.6 Programming Mechanics

The exact steps you must follow to produce a program depend on your computer environment. Currently, the most widespread environments are UNIX C, Microsoft 4.0, 5.0, and 5.1, QuickC, and Borland's Turbo C. We discuss all four environments, filling in some of the details we glossed over when summarizing the programming process. First, however, let's look at some aspects shared by many C environments. You don't really need to know what follows to run a C program, but it's good background, and it may help you understand why you must follow certain steps.

Source Code Files

When you write a program in the C language, you store what you write in a file called a *source code file,* or *source file.* Most C systems, including the ones mentioned previously, require that the name of the source file end in **.c: wordcount.c** and **budget.c,** for example. The part of the name before the period is called the *basename,* and the part after the period is called the *extension.* Thus budget is a basename, and c is an extension. The combination **budget.c** is the *filename.* The name should also satisfy the requirements of the particular computer operating system. For example, PC-DOS and MS-DOS (hereafter simply called DOS) are operating systems for IBM PCs and clones. They require that the basename be no more than eight characters long. Older UNIX systems place a thirteen-character limit on the entire name including the extension; newer systems allow longer names.

Let's assume we have a source code file called **concrete.c** that contains the following C source code:

```
#include <stdio.h>
main()
{
    printf("Concrete contains gravel and cement.\n");
}
```

Don't worry about the details of this program yet. For now, it's enough to have an example of a source code file.

Object Code Files, Executable Files, and Libraries

The basic strategy in C programming is to use programs that convert your source code file to an *executable file,* which is a file containing ready-to-run machine language code. C implementations accomplish this conversion in two steps: compiling and linking. The compiler converts your source code into an intermediate code, and the linker combines this code with other code to produce the executable file. C uses this two-part approach to facilitate the modularization of programs: You can compile individual modules separately, then combine the compiled modules later. Therefore, if you need to alter one module, you don't have to recompile the other ones.

You have several choices for the form of the intermediate files. The most prevalent choice, and the one taken by the implementations we describe, is to convert the source code to machine language code, placing the result in what's termed an *object code file,* or *object file.* (Here we assume that your source code consists of a single file.) Although the object file contains machine language code, it's not ready to run. The object file contains the translation of your source code, but it is not yet a complete program.

What is missing from the object code file is something called the *start-up code,* which is the code that acts as an interface between your program and the operating system. For example, you can run, say, an IBM AT clone under DOS or under XENIX, a UNIX variety. The hardware is the same in either case, so the same object code will work with both. But DOS requires different start-up code than XENIX, since these systems handle programs differently from one another.

Also missing from the start-up code is the code for library routines. Nearly all C programs make use of routines (functions) that are part of the standard C library. For example, concrete.c uses the function **printf( )**. The object code file does not contain the code for this function; it merely contains instructions saying to use the **printf( )** function. The actual code is stored in another file, called a *library,* which contains object code for many functions.

The role of the linker is to bring together the object code, the standard start-up code for your system, and library code into a single file, the executable file. For library code the linker extracts from the library just the code for the functions you use. See Figure 1.6.

In short, an object file and an executable file both consist of machine language instructions. The object file, however, contains the machine language translation only for the

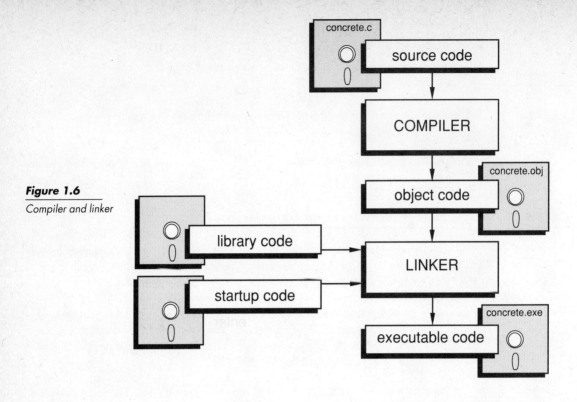

Figure 1.6

Compiler and linker

code you used, whereas the executable file also has machine code for the library routines you use and for the start-up code.

On some systems you must run the compile and the link programs separately. Other systems have the compiler start up the linker automatically, so that you just have to give the compile command. Let's look at some specific systems.

Preparing a C Program on a UNIX System

Because C's popularity began on UNIX systems, we begin here.

Editing on a UNIX System

Unlike BASIC, UNIX C does not have its own editor. Instead, you use one of the general-purpose UNIX editors such as **ed**, **ex**, **edit**, **emacs**, or **vi**. Your two main responsibilities are typing the program correctly and choosing a name for the file that will store the program. Recall that **.c** is the way the name should end. (Note: UNIX distinguishes between uppercase and lowercase letters.) Thus, **budget.c**, **BUDGET.c**, and **Budget.c** are three distinct and valid names for C source files; **BUDGET.C** is not a valid name because it uses an uppercase C instead of a lowercase c.

Let's look at an example. Using the **vi** editor we prepared the following program and stored it in a file called **inform.c**:

```
#include <stdio.h>
main()
{
   printf("A .c is used to end a C program file name.\n");
}
```

The text is the source code, and **inform.c** is the source file. The important point is that the source file is the beginning of a process, not the end.

Compiling on a UNIX System

Our program example is still gibberish to a computer, which can't understand words like **#include** or **printf**. (At this point, you probably don't either.) As discussed earlier, we need the compiler to translate our source code into the computer's machine code. The result is the executable file, which contains all the machine code the computer needs to run the program correctly. See Figure 1.7.

Figure 1.7

Preparing a C program using UNIX

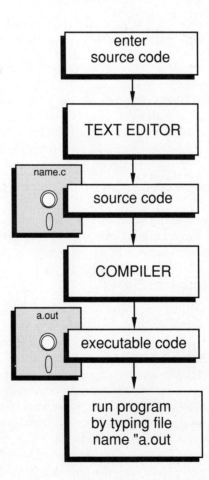

The UNIX C compiler is called **cc**. To compile the program at the UNIX shell prompt (% or $), we type:

```
cc inform.c
```

After a few seconds, the UNIX prompt reappears, telling us the program has been compiled. (Note: If there are any errors, we may get warnings and error messages.) If we use **ls** to list our files, we discover a new file called **a.out**, which is the executable file containing the translation (or compilation) of our program. To run **a.out**, we just type:

```
a.out
```

and the following appears:

```
A .c is used to end a C program filename.
```

If you want to keep the executable file (**a.out**), you should rename it. Otherwise, the file is replaced by a new **a.out** file the next time you compile a program.

What about the object code? The **cc** compiler creates an object code file having the same basename as the source code, but with a **.o** extension. In our example, the object code file is called **inform.o**, although for the linker deletes this file once the executable program is completed. However, if the original program uses more than one source code file, the object code files are saved. When we discuss multiple-file programs later in the text, we describe the usefulness of saving the object code files.

Preparing a C Program on an IBM PC (Microsoft C)

Now let's describe preparing a C program using Microsoft 4.0, 5.0, and 5.1. (QuickC merits a separate discussion.) Note: We assume you are using PC-DOS 3.1 or later or MS-DOS 3.1 or later.

Editing on an IBM PC

First, you need to select a text editor. PC-DOS and MS-DOS come with a rather primitive, although adequate, editor called EDLIN. However, many users probably have access to a word processor such as WordStar, WordPerfect, or Microsoft Word. You can use any of these word processors to write C programs, however you *cannot* use the default file formats normally used by these word processors. The proprietary files contain a lot of text-formatting information in addition to the text you see when writing. This additional information is not understood by the compiler, so you must take care to create simple ASCII files, that is, files containing nothing but text. For example, in WordStar, use the N (non-document) mode for program files. In WordPerfect, use the Text In/Out key to save the file as a DOS file.

A better choice is to use an editor specifically designed for programming. Microsoft, for example, includes a programming editor called the Microsoft Editor (ME) with release 5.1 of the Microsoft C compiler. Similarly, WordPerfect includes its Program Editor in the WordPerfect Library package. Several commercial program editors are available, including Kedit and Brief, as well as ports of the vi and emacs editors to the DOS environment.

Whatever editor you use, you should, as with UNIX, use a filename ending with the **.c** extension. Also, with DOS, recall that the basename (the part of the name preceding the period) is limited to eight characters. Unlike UNIX, DOS does not distinguish between uppercase and lowercase letters, so both **budget.c** and **BUDGET.C** are valid names for the same file.

As an example, use the editor of your choice to create the following file called **inform.c:**

```
#include <stdio.h>
main()
{
   printf("A .c is used to end a C program filename.\n");
}
```

Compiling

Once you have a source code file whose name ends in **.c**, you can invoke the Microsoft C compiler with the command:

```
cl inform.c
```

Like the UNIX **cc** compiler, the Microsoft **cl** compiler first produces an object code file. For DOS systems, the basename of the original file is used, but the **.c** extension is replaced by **.obj**. In our example, the object code file is called **inform.obj**. Next, the compiler requests the system linker to finish compiling the program. On DOS systems, this program is called **link**, and it inputs code from the C library (which comes with the compiler) and adds in the start-up code to produce an executable file called **inform.exe**. In general, the name of the executable file is the basename of the source file with the **.c** extension replaced with **.exe**. Unlike the UNIX compiler, **cl** does not erase the object file when the executable program is completed. See Figure 1.8.

To run the program, type the following command at the DOS prompt (C>):

```
inform
```

Under DOS, this command is equivalent to typing **inform.exe**.

Preparing a C Program on an IBM PC (Turbo C and QuickC)

Both Borland Turbo C and Microsoft QuickC provide low-cost, fast, integrated environments for putting together C programs. The key points are that these two programs have built-in editors that you can use to write a C program. Each program provides menus that allow you to name and save your source code file, and each provides menus that let you compile and run your program without exiting the Turbo C or QuickC environment. Each dumps you back into the editor if the compiler finds any errors, and each identifies

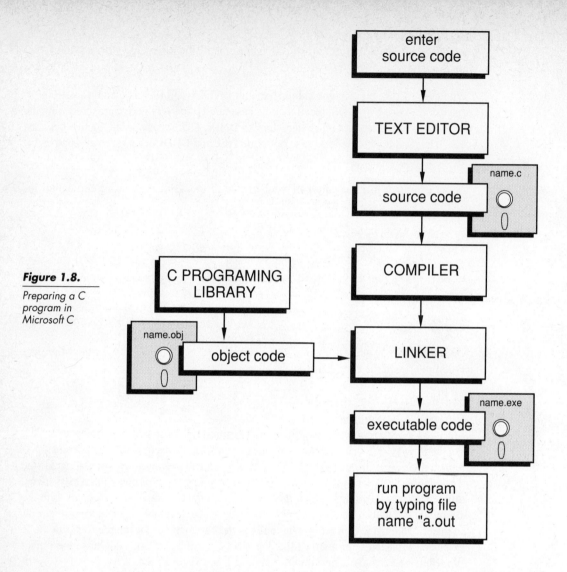

Figure 1.8.

Preparing a C program in Microsoft C

the offending lines and matches them to the appropriate error messages. Each allows you to create object and executable files, so that you can create stand-alone programs that can be run directly from the DOS level. Both follow the standard DOS naming conventions. So source code files should have a **.c** extension. Object files are given the **.obj** extension, and executable files are given the **.exe** extension.

Why Compile?

Those of you who have used BASIC may wonder about going through these steps to run a program. It may seem time-consuming, but once a program is compiled, it will run much faster than a standard BASIC program. You trade some inconvenience in getting a program running for a much swifter final product. As well, if you use an integrated package, the inconvenience is much reduced.

1.7 Language Standards

Currently, many C implementations are available. Ideally, once you write a C program, it should work the same using any implementation, providing it doesn't use machine-specific programming. For this statement to be true in practice, different implementations need to conform to a recognized standard.

In the beginning, there was no official standard for C. Instead, the first edition of *The C Programming Language* by Brian Kernighan and Dennis Ritchie (1978) became the accepted standard. In particular, the *C Reference Manual* in the book's appendix acted as the guide to C implementors. Compilers, for example, would claim to offer a full K & R implementation. However, although the appendix defined the C language, it did not define the C library. More than most languages, C depends on its library, so there was also need for a library standard. In the absence of any official standard, the library supplied with the UNIX implementation became a de facto standard.

As C evolved and as it became more widely used on a greater variety of systems, the C community realized it needed a more comprehensive, up-to-date, and rigorous standard. To meet this need, the American National Standards Institute (ANSI) established a committee (X3J11) in 1983 to develop a new standard. At the time of this writing (1989) the committee has nearly completed its work. This new standard, called *ANSI C,* defines both the language and a standard C library.

For the most part, ANSI C and K & R C are much the same. However, ANSI C supports some extensions and changes. We mention many of these as appropriate throughout this text. Keep in mind, however, that experts expect about a two-year lag between the final acceptance of ANSI C and the full conversion of all implementations to the standard. In the meantime, you may find yourself using implementations that lack some ANSI C features. For that reason, most of our examples avoid ANSI-specific features except where those features are explained.

1.8 Some Typographic Conventions

We are almost ready to begin our study of the C language. Here we mention some conventions we will use in presenting material.

Typeface

For text representing programs, computer input and output, and the names of files, programs, and variables, we use a type font that resembles what you might see on a screen or printed output. We have already used it a few times, for example:

```
#include <stdio.h>
main()
{
   printf("Concrete contains gravel and cement.\n");
}
```

Screen Output

Computer output is indicated with a light grey screen. Where lines of output are interspersed with user input, only the screen output is highlighted. For instance:

```
Please enter the book title.
Press [enter] at the start of a line to stop.
My Life as a Budgie
Now enter the author.
Mack Zackles
```

The lines in light grey screen are program output, and the other lines are user input.

Input and Output Devices

There are many ways that you and a computer can communicate with each other. However, we assume that you type in commands using a keyboard and that you read the response on a screen.

Special Keystrokes

Usually you complete a line of instructions by pressing a key that is labeled "Enter," "c/r," "Return," or some variation of these. In this text, we refer to this key as the Enter key. When showing it as part of input in a program example, we use [enter]. The brackets mean that you press a single key rather than type out the word "enter."

We also refer to control characters such as Control-D. This notation means to press the d key while pressing the key labeled "Control" (sometimes labeled "Ctrl").

Our System

Some aspects of C, such as the amount of space used to store a number, depend on the system. When we give examples and refer to "our system," we speak of a Zenith Z-200 (an IBM AT-compatible) running under MS-DOS 3.21 and using a Microsoft C compiler. We also occasionally refer to running programs on a UNIX system. The one we use is Berkeley's BSD 4.3 version of UNIX running on a VAX 11/750 computer.

1.9 Summary

C is a vigorous, professional programming language. It's popular with those who develop application programs, such as spreadsheets and word processors, because it provides good control over the hardware and because C programs are easier than most to transport from one system to another. Also, C is well-suited for structured programming, which is a collection of techniques that increases the readability, reliability, and maintainability of programs.

C is a compiled language. C compilers and linkers are programs that convert C language source code into executable code.

Programming in C can be taxing, difficult, and frustrating, but it also can be intriguing, exciting, and satisfying. We hope you find it as enjoyable and fascinating as we do.

Review Questions

1. What does portability mean in the context of programming?

2. Distinguish between source code file, object code file, and executable file.

3. What are the seven major steps in programming?

4. What's step-wise refinement?

5. What's top-down programming?

6. What does a compiler do?

7. What does a linker do?

Programming Exercises

We don't expect you to write C code yet, so these exercises concentrate on the earlier stages of the programming process.

1. You have just been employed by MacroMuscle, Inc. (Software for Hard Bodies). The company is entering the European market and wants a program that converts inches to centimeters (1 in = 2.54 cm). The program is to be set up so that it prompts the user to enter an inch value. Your assignment is to define the program objectives and to design the program (steps 1 and 2 of the programming process).

2. Dr. Hunk, MacroMuscle's master physiotheorist, has developed an algorithm that calculates a "fitness level" from a person's weight, sex, age, and pulse rate after a prescribed exercise. He wants this algorithm incorporated into an interactive program that processes just one set of input data. Your assignment is to define the program objectives and to design the program.

3. Handley Bilkem, MegaMuscle's kindly president, has developed an algorithm that calculates a software retail price from a program size and from a "zing" value. He wants a program made from the algorithm. Your job is to define the program objectives and to design the program. Note: as usually is the case in real-life situations, the people requesting the program have been a little vague. Does Bilkem want a program that converts a single set of values provided interactively? Does he want the program to process a file of measurements? Imagine going back to Bilkem and asking for whatever further information you need. Since it's your exercise, you also get to imagine the answers, which are not included at the end of the text.

2

Introducing C

Contents

Objectives

Learning the significance of **main( )**

Understanding the structure of a simple program: header, body, braces, statements

Declaring an integer variable

Assigning a value to a variable

Printing a phrase

Printing the value of an integer variable

Using the newline character: **\n**

Including comments in a program

Writing simple programs

Using more than one function in a program

Debugging simple programs

Understanding and tracing program states

Knowing what keywords are

What does a C program look like? If you scan through this book, you'll see many examples. Quite likely, you'll find C peculiar-looking, sprinkled with symbols like { and ***ptr++**. As you read through this book, you will find that the appearance of these and of other characteristic C symbols grows less strange, more familiar, perhaps even welcome! In this chapter, we begin by presenting a rather simple example program and explaining what it does. We also highlight some of the basic features of C. In the following chapters, we'll elaborate on what we introduce here.

2.1 A Simple Sample of C

Let's look at a simple C program. We have to admit that this example is not very practical, but it serves to point out some of the basic features of a C program. Before you read the line-by-line explanation, read through the program shown in Listing 2.1 to see if you can figure out for yourself what it does.

❖ simple.c

Listing 2.1

```
/*simple.c*/
#include <stdio.h>
main()       /* a simple program */
{
  int num;   /* define a variable called num */

  num = 1;   /* assign a value to num */
  printf("I am a simple ");
          /* use the printf() function */
  printf("computer.\n");
  printf("My favorite number is %d because ");
  printf("it is first.\n",num);
}
```

If you think this program will print some words on the screen, you are right! But exactly what is printed may not be clear, so let's run through the program.

The first step is to use your editor to create a file containing the text from Listing 2.1. You must give the file a name, which should end in .c and meet your local system's name requirements (for example, first.c). Now compile and run the program. If all went well, the output should look like the following:

```
I am a simple computer.
My favorite number is 1 because it is first.
```

This result is not too surprising. But what happened to the **\n**'s and the **%d** in the program? What did some of the strange lines mean?

2.2 The Explanation

We take two passes through the program. The first pass highlights the meaning of each line. The second pass explores some of the implications and details. Refer to Figure 2.1 for the anatomy of a C program.

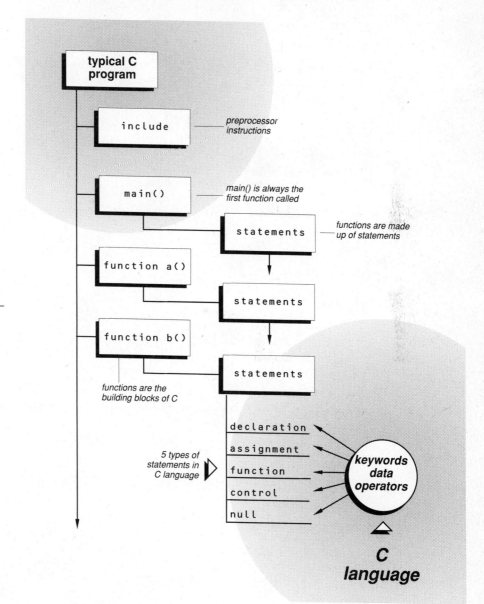

Figure 2.1

Anatomy of a C program

Pass 1: Quick Synopsis

The first line tells the computer to include information found in the file **stdio.h**, which file is part of the C compiler package:

```
#include <stdio.h>
```
⇐ Include another file

C programs consist of one or more functions, which are the basic modules of a C program. This program consists of one function called **main**. The parentheses identify **main( )** as a function name:

```
main()
```
⇐ Function name

You can use the symbols /* and */ to enclose *comments,* which are remarks to help clarify a program. They are intended only for the reader and are ignored by the computer:

```
/* a simple program */
```
⇐ Comment

The opening brace ({) marks the start of the statements that make up the function. The function definition is ended with a closing brace (}):

```
{
```
⇐ Beginning of the body of the function

The declaration statement announces that we will use a variable called **num** and that **num** is an **int**eger:

```
int num;
```
⇐ Declaration statement

The assignment statement assigns the value 1 to **num**:

```
num = 1;
```
⇐ Assignment statement

The following line prints the phrase within the quotation marks (**I am a simple**).

```
printf("I am a simple ");
```
⇐ Print statement

The following line prints the word **computer** to the end of the last phrase printed. The **\n** tells the computer to start a new line:

```
printf("computer.\n");
```
⇐ Another print statement

The following lines print the value of **num** (which is 1) embedded in the phrase in quotation marks. The **%d** instructs the computer where and in what form to print **num**'s value:

```
printf("My favorite number is %d because ");
printf("it is first.\n",num);
```

As noted earlier, the program ends with a closing brace:

```
}
```
⇐ Program end

Let's take a closer look at the program.

#include *Directives and Header Files*

The **stdio.h** file is supplied as part of a C compiler package, and it contains information about input and output functions (such as **printf( )**) for the compiler to use:

```
#include <stdio.h>
```

The name stands for **st**and**ar**d **i**nput/**o**utput header. C users refer to a collection of information that goes at the top of a file as the *header*, and C implementations typically come with several header files. One goal of ANSI C is the standardization of which header files must be provided.

The effect of **#include <stdio.h>** is the same as if we were to copy the entire contents of the **stdio.h** file into our file at the position the line appears. Such **#include** files provide a convenient way to handle information that is required by many programs.

Some programs need to include **stdio.h**; some don't. The documentation for a particular C implementation should describe the functions in the C library and identify which header files are needed. For example, the description for **printf( )** calls for use of **stdio.h**. It may happen that omitting the proper header file may not affect a particular program, but it's best not to rely on that. Because the compiler uses the information in **stdio.h** to build a program, any information that the compiler does not use does not become part of the program. Therefore, including an unnecessary file does not make the final program any longer.

Perhaps you are wondering why something as basic as input and output information isn't included automatically. One answer is that not all programs use this **I/O** (Input/Output) package, and part of the C philosophy is not to carry along unnecessary weight. Incidentally, the **#include** line is not even a C language statement: The # symbol identifies it as a line to be handled by the C preprocessor. The *preprocessor* handles some tasks before the compiler takes over. We discuss more examples of preprocessor instructions later in the text.

The main( ) *Function*

A C program always begins execution with the function called **main( )**:

```
main()
```

We are free to choose names for other functions we may use, but **main( )** must be there to start things off. What about the parentheses? They identify **main( )** as a function. We learn more about functions later. For now, remember that functions are the basic modules of a C program.

The parentheses following a function name generally enclose information being passed along to the function. For our simple example, nothing is passed along with **main( )**, so

The proposed ANSI standard recognizes two kinds of environments in which C programs can run. A *hosted environment* is one in which the C program is run under the management of another program, such as an operating system like DOS, OS/2, or UNIX. A *freestanding environment* is one in which the program may run without the benefit of an operating system. Our comments about **main**() apply to hosted environments, but not to freestanding environments.

the parentheses remain empty. Don't leave them out, but there's no need to worry about them yet.

Comments

Using comments makes it easier for someone (including yourself) to understand your program. One nice feature of C comments is that they can be placed on the same line as the material they explain. A longer comment can be placed on its own line or even spread over more than one line. Everything between the opening /* and the closing */ is ignored by the compiler:

```
/* a simple program */
```

Braces, Bodies, and Blocks

Braces ({,}) mark the beginning as well as the end of the body of a function:

```
{
.
.
.
}
```

(Note: Parentheses and brackets do not serve this purpose.) Braces can also be used to gather together statements inside a program into a *unit* or *block*. If you are familiar with Pascal, Ada, Modula-2, or Algol, you will recognize the braces as being similar to the **begin** and **end** statements in those languages.

Declarations

The *declaration statement* is one of the most important features of C. As noted earlier, our example declares two things:

```
int num;
```

First, somewhere in the function, we use a variable having the name **num**. In C, all variables must be declared, which means you must list all the variables you use in a program, and you must show what "type" each variable is.

Second, **int** proclaims **num** as an *integer*, that is, a whole number without a decimal point. The word **int** is a C keyword that identifies one of the basic C data types. *Keywords* are specific words used to express a language; they may not be usurped for other purposes. For instance, you can't use **int** as a function name or variable name.

The compiler uses the information in the declaration statement to arrange for suitable storage space in memory for the **num** variable. The semicolon at the end of the line identifies the line as a C *statement* or *instruction*. (Note: The semicolon is part of the statement, not just a separator between statements as it is in Pascal.)

At this point, you may have three questions. First, what are data types? Second, what choices do you have in selecting a name? Third, why do you have to declare variables at all? Let's look at some answers.

Data Types

We deal with data types more fully in Chapter 3, but here is a short summary. C deals with several kinds (or types) of data: integers, characters, and "floating point," for example. Declaring a variable to be an integer or a character type makes it possible for the computer to store, fetch, and interpret the data properly.

Name Choice

We suggest that you use meaningful names for variables. The number of characters you can use varies among implementations, but the upper limit is at least 8 characters. The ANSI C standard calls for up to 31 characters, except for external identifiers (Chapter 13), for which only 8 characters need be recognized. Actually, you can use more than the maximum number of characters, but the compiler won't pay attention to the extra ones. Thus on a system with an 8-character limit, shakespeare and shakespencil would be considered the same name, since they have the same first 8 characters. To name variables you may use lowercase letters, uppercase letters, digits, and the underscore (_), which is counted as a letter. The first character must be a letter. The following are some examples:

Valid Names	Invalid Names
wiggles	$Z]**
cat1	1cat
Hot_Tub	Hot-Tub
_kcab	don't

Library routines often use names beginning with the underscore symbol. The assumption is that users are unlikely to choose names beginning with this symbol; thus, there is little chance of a user accidentally using one of these names to mean something else. Resist the temptation to begin names with an underscore symbol, and you will avoid a clash with the library.

Four Good Reasons to Declare Variables

1. Gathering all the variables together in one place makes it easier for a reader to grasp what the program is about. This statement is particularly true if you give your variables meaningful names (such as **taxrate** instead of **r**). If the name doesn't suffice, use the comment facility to explain what the variables represent. Documenting a program in this manner is one of the basic techniques of good programming.

2. Thinking about what to put into the variable declaration section encourages you to plan before you plunge into writing a program. What information will the program need to get started? What exactly do I want the program to produce as output? What's the best way to represent the data?

3. Declaring variables helps prevent one of programming's more subtle and hard-to-find bugs, that of the misspelled variable name. For example, suppose that in some language (not C), you made the statement:

```
RADIUS1 = 20.4;
```

and that elsewhere in the program you mistyped:

```
CIRCUM = 6.28 * RADIUSL;
```

Thus unwittingly, you have replaced the numeral 1 with the letter l. The program would therefore create a new variable called **RADIUSl** and use whatever value it had (perhaps zero, perhaps garbage). **CIRCUM** would be given the wrong value, and you might have a difficult time trying to find out why. (Fortunately, this can't occur in C—unless you had declared two such similar variable names—because the compiler would complain when the undeclared **RADIUSl** was used.

4. Your C program will not run properly if you don't declare your variables.

Assignment

The *assignment statement* is one of the most basic operations, as shown in Figure 2.2. In our example, the assignment statement means "give the variable **num** the value of 1":

```
num = 1;
```

The **int num;** line allotted computer space for the variable **num**, and this line gives it its value. We may assign **num** a different value later if we wish, which is why we call **num**

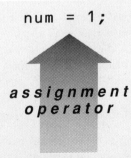

Figure 2.2

The assignment statement is one of the most basic operations.

a variable. Note that the assignment statement, like the declaration statement, is completed with a semicolon.

The printf( ) Function

The following lines all use a standard C function called **printf( )**:

```
printf("I am a simple ");
printf("computer.\n");
printf("My favorite number is %d because it is first.\n",num);
```

The parentheses tell us that we are dealing with a function. The material enclosed in the parentheses is information passed from the **main( )** function to the **printf( )** function. For instance, the first line passes the phrase "I am a simple to the **printf( )** function. Such information is called the *argument* of a function. And what does the function **printf( )** do with this argument? Obviously, it looks at whatever lies between the double quotation marks and prints that on the terminal's screen. See Figure 2.3.

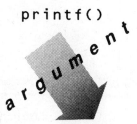

```
printf()
```

argument

```
printf("That's mere contrariness!\n");
```

Figure 2.3

The function **printf( )** with an argument.

The **printf("I am a simple ")** line provides an example of how we *call* or *invoke* a function in C. To do so, we need only type the name of the function and include the desired argument(s) in the parentheses. When your program reaches this line, control is turned over to the named function (**printf()** in this case). When the function is finished, control is returned to the *calling* (original) *program*.

What about the next line? It has the characters **\n** included in the quotation marks, and they didn't get printed. The **\n** is actually an instruction to start a new line. The **\n** combination represents a single character, for which there is no single key representation, called the *newline character*. Its meaning is "start a new line at the far left margin." In other words, this character performs the same function as the Enter key of a typical keyboard, but pressing Enter would be interpreted as an immediate command, not as an instruction to be stored away. In other words, when you press the Enter key, the editor quits the current line on which you are working and starts a new one.

The newline character is an example of an *escape sequence*, which is used to represent difficult- or impossible-to-type characters. Other examples are **\t** for tab and **\b** for backspace. In each case the escape sequence begins with the backslash character (\). We return to this subject in Chapter 3.

That explains why our three print statements produced only two lines; the first print instruction didn't have a newline character in it.

The final **printf( )** line brings up another oddity: What happened to the **%d** when the line was printed? Recall that the output for this line was the following:

```
My favorite number is 1 because it is first.
```

Note that the digit **1** was substituted for the symbol group **%d** when the line was printed, and **1** was the value of the variable **num**. The **%d** is a kind of placeholder to show where the value of **num** is to be printed. This line is similar to the BASIC statement:

```
PRINT "My favorite number is"; num; "because it is first."
```

The C version actually accomplishes a little more than the BASIC version. The **%** alerts the program that a variable is to be printed at that location, and the **d** tells it to print the variable as a digit. The **printf( )** function allows several choices for the format of printed variables. Indeed, the **f** in **printf( )** is there to remind us that this is a formatted print statement.

2.3 The Structure of a Simple Program

Now that you've seen a specific example, you are ready for a few general rules about C programs. A *program* consists of a collection of one or more functions, one of which must be called **main( )**. The description of a *function* consists of a header and a body, as shown in Figure 2.4. The *header* contains any preprocessor statements, such as **#include**, and the function name. You can recognize a function name by the parentheses, which may be empty. The *body* is enclosed by braces and consists of a series of statements, each terminated by a semicolon. Our example had a *declaration statement*, announcing the name and type of variable that we were using. It had an *assignment statement*, giving the variable a value. Finally, there were three *print statements*, each of which called the **printf( )** function. The print statements are examples of *function call statements*.

2.4 Tips on Making Your Programs Readable

Making your programs readable is good programming practice. It makes it much easier to understand the program, which correspondingly makes it easier to correct or modify the program, if necessary. The act of making a program readable also helps clarify your own concept of what the program does. We point out useful techniques as we go along.

We've already mentioned two techniques: choosing meaningful variable names and using comments. Note that these techniques complement each other. For example, if you give a variable the name **width**, you don't need a comment saying that this variable

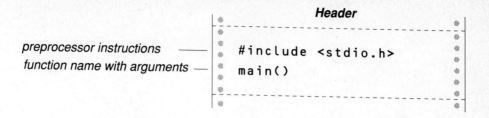

Header

```
#include <stdio.h>
main()
```

preprocessor instructions —
function name with arguments —

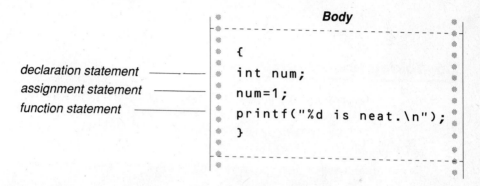

Body

```
{
int num;
num=1;
printf("%d is neat.\n");
}
```

declaration statement —
assignment statement —
function statement —

Figure 2.4

A function has
a header and a
body.

represents a width. But a variable called **video_routine_4** might benefit from an explanation.

Another technique is using blank lines to separate one conceptual section of a function from another. For example, in our simple program, we had a blank line separating the declaration section from the action section (assigning and printing). The blank line is not required by C, but it is part of the C tradition to use it as we did.

A fourth technique is to use one line per statement. Again, this convention is not required by C, as C has a "free-form format." If you wish, you can place several statements on one line or spread one statement over several. The following is legitimate code:

```
main() { int four; four
=
4
;
printf(
   "%d\n",
four); }
```

The semicolons tell the compiler where one statement ends and the next begins, but the logic of a program is much clearer if you follow the one-line-per-statement conventions. Figure 2.5 gives guidelines for writing readable C programs.

Figure 2.5

Making your
program readable

```
main() /* converts 2 fathoms to feet*/  ————— use comments
{
int feet, fathoms;  ————————————————————— pick names
                    ————————————————————————— use space

fathoms=2;
feet=6*fathoms;  ——————————————————— one statement per line
printf("There are %d feet in %d fathoms!\n", feet, fathoms);
}
```

2.5 Taking Another Step

Our next example program isn't much more difficult than our first (Listing 2.2). In this program, we provide a program description, declare multiple variables, perform some multiplication, and print the values of two variables. Let's examine these points in more detail.

❖ **fathm_ft.c**

Listing 2.2

```
/* fathm_ft.c--converts 2 fathoms to feet */
#include <stdio.h>
main()
{
int feet, fathoms;

fathoms = 2;
feet = 6 * fathoms;
printf("There are %d feet in %d fathoms!\n", feet, fathoms);
}
```

Documentation

The program begins with a comment identifying the filename and the purpose of the program. This kind of program documentation takes only a moment and is quite helpful when, at some later time, you browse through several files or print them out.

Multiple Declarations

In this program, we declare two variables instead of just one. All that is necessary is to separate the two variables (**feet** and **fathoms**) with a comma in the declaration statement.

Multiplication

The program performs a calculation: We harnessed the tremendous computational power of our computer system to multiply 2 by 6. In C, as in many languages, the * symbol stands for multiplication. Thus the statement:

```
feet = 6 * fathoms;
```

means "look up the value of the variable **fathoms**, multiply it by 6, and assign the result of this calculation to the variable **feet**."

Printing Multiple Values

This program makes fancier use of **printf( )**. If you run the example, the output should look like the following:

```
There are 12 feet in 2 fathoms!
```

This time we have made *two* substitutions. The first **%d** in the quotation marks is replaced by the value of the first variable (**feet**) in the list following the quoted segment. The second **%d** is replaced by the value of the second variable (**fathoms**) in the list. Note how the list of variables to be printed comes at the tail end of the statement after the quoted portion.

This program is a bit limited in scope, but it can form the nucleus of a program to convert fathoms to feet. All we need is some way to assign other values to **feet**, which we cover later in the text.

2.6 Multiple Functions

Here is one more example (Listing 2.3). So far our programs have used the standard **printf( )** function. In this listing we show how to include and use a function of your own devising.

❖ *two_func.c*

Listing 2.3

```
/* two_func.c--a program using two functions in one file */
#include <stdio.h>
main()
{
   printf("I will summon the butler function.\n");
   butler();
   printf("Yes. Bring me some tea and floppy disks.\n");
}
butler()
{
   printf("You rang, sir?\n");
}
```

The output looks like the following:

```
I will summon the butler function.
You rang, sir?
Yes. Bring me some tea and floppy disks.
```

The function **butler( )** is defined in the same manner as **main( )**, with the body enclosed in braces. The function is called simply by giving its name, including parentheses. When **butler( )** finishes its work, the program moves to the next statement in **main( )**. As you can see, using your own functions can be easy.

Note: It is the location of the **butler( )** call in **main( )**, not the location of the **butler( )** definition in the file, that determines when the **butler( )** function is executed. You can, for instance, put the **butler( )** definition above the **main( )** definition in this program, and the program will still run the same, with the **butler( )** function executed between the two calls to **printf( )** in **main( )**.

Rigorous C usage requires that we declare functions as well as variables. That is, we should assign **butler( )** a type and declare the function before it is used in **main( )**. This convention becomes even more important with ANSI C. We discuss function declarations later in the text when we reach cases in which even nonrigorous C requires them.

2.7 Debugging

Now that you can write a simple C program, you are in a position to make simple errors. For instance, Listing 2.4 presents a program with some errors. See how many you can spot.

❖ *nogood.c*

Listing 2.4

```
/* nogood.c--a program with errors */
#include <stdio.h>
main()
(
    int n, int n2, int n3;
    /* this program has several errors

    n = 5;
    n2 = n * n;
    n3 = n2 * n2;
    printf("n = %d, n squared = %d, n cubed = %d\n",n,n2,n3)
)
```

Syntax Errors

This example contains several syntax errors. You commit a *syntax error* when you don't follow C's rules. It's analogous to a grammar error in English. For instance, consider the following sentence: Bugs frustrate be can. This statement uses valid English words, but doesn't follow the rules for word order, and it doesn't use quite the right words, anyway. C syntax errors use valid C symbols in the wrong places.

Let's now discuss the syntax errors in Listing 2.4. First, we used parentheses instead of braces to mark the body of the function. We used a valid C symbol in the wrong place. Second, the declaration should have been the following:

```
int n, n2, n3;
```

We also used the valid C keyword **int** too often. Next, we omitted the */ code necessary to complete a comment. Finally, we omitted the mandatory semicolon that should terminate the **printf( )** statement.

How do you detect syntax errors? First, before compiling, you can look through the source code and see if you spot anything obvious. Second, part of the compiler's job is to detect syntax errors. If you compile this program, the compiler will report back the errors it finds, identifying their nature and location.

However, the compiler can become confused. A true syntax error in one location may cause the compiler mistakenly to think it has found other errors. For instance, because our example does not declare **n2** and **n3** correctly, the compiler may think it has found further errors when those variables are used. If some of the supposed errors don't make sense to you, first correct the errors before them, recompile, and see if the compiler still complains.

Semantic Errors

Semantic errors are errors in meaning. For instance, consider the following sentence: Furry inflation thinks greenly. The syntax is fine, for adjectives, nouns, verbs, and adverbs are in the right places. But the sentence doesn't mean anything. In C, you commit a semantic error when you correctly follow the C rules to an incorrect end. Our example has one such error:

```
n3 = n2 * n2;
```

Here, **n3** is supposed to represent the cube of **n**, but we've set it up to be the fourth power.

The compiler cannot detect semantic errors, for they don't violate C rules. The compiler has no way of divining your true intentions. Thus, you must find these kinds of errors yourself. One way is to compare what a program does what you expected it to do. For instance, suppose you fix the syntax errors in our example so that it now reads as shown in Listing 2.5.

Its output is the following:

```
n is 5, n squared is 25, n cubed is 625
```

If you are cube wise, you can see that 625 is the wrong value. The next stage is to track down how we wound up with this answer. For this example, you probably can spot the

```
/* stillbad.c--a program with its syntax errors fixed */
#include <stdio.h>
main()
{
    int n, n2, n3;
    /* this program has a semantic error */

    n = 5;
    n2 = n * n;
    n3 = n2 * n2;
    printf("n = %d, n squared = %d, n cubed = %d\n",n,n2,n3);
}
```

Listing 2.5

error by inspection, although in general, you need to take a more systematic approach. One method is to pretend you are the computer and follow the program steps one by one. Let's try this method:

The program body starts by declaring three variables: **n**, **n2**, and **n3**. We can simulate this by drawing three boxes and labeling them with the variable names (see Figure 2.6). Next, the program assigns **5** to **n**. Simulate that by writing **5** into the **n** box. Next, the program multiplies **n** by **n** and assigns the result to **n2**. So we look in the **n** box, see that the value is **5**, multiply **5** by **5** to get **25**, and place **25** in box **n2**. To duplicate the next C statement (**n3 = n2 * n2;**) we look in **n2** and find **25**. We multiply **25** by **25**, get **625**, and place it in **n3**. Aha! We are squaring **n2** instead of multiplying it by **n**.

This method of tracing a program is a bit of overkill for this example, but often going through a program step by step in this fashion is the best way to discover the error.

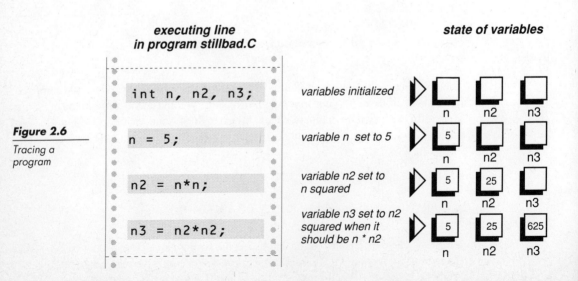

Figure 2.6

Tracing a program

By tracing the program step by step, keeping track of each variable, we monitor the *program state,* which is simply the set of values of all the variables at a given point in program execution. It's a snapshot of the current state of computation.

We just discussed one method of tracing the state: executing the program step by step yourself. In a program that makes, say, 10,000 iterations, you may not feel up to that task. Still, you can go through a few iterations to see if your program does what you meant it to do. However, there is always the possibility that you will execute the steps as you intended them to be rather than as you actually wrote them, so try to be faithful to the actual code.

Another approach is to sprinkle extra **printf( )** statements throughout your program to monitor the values of selected variables at key points. Seeing how the values change can illuminate what's happening. Once you have the program working to your satisfaction, you can remove the extra statements.

A third method for examining the program state is to use a *debugger,* which is a program that let's you run another program step by step and to examine the value of that program's variables. Debuggers come in various levels of ease of use and sophistication. The more advanced debuggers show which line of source code is being executed. This feature is handy for programs with alternative paths of execution, as it makes it easy to see which specific paths are followed.

2.8 Keywords

Keywords are the vocabulary of C. Because they are special to C, you can't use them for variable names. Many of these keywords specify various types, such as **int**. Others such as **if** are used to control the order in which program statements are executed. Table 2.1 lists the keywords recognized by the proposed ANSI C standards.

Table 2.1 ANSI C Keywords

auto	break	case	char	const	continue
default	do	double	else	enum	extern
float	for	goto	if	int	long
register	return	short	signed	sizeof	static
struct	switch	typedef	union	unsigned	void
volatile	while				

2.9 Summary

A C program consists of one or more C functions. Every C program must contain a function called **main( )**, because that is the function called when the program starts up.

A simple function consists of a header, followed by an opening brace, followed by the statements constituting the function body, followed by a terminating closing brace.

Each C statement is an instruction to the computer and is marked by a terminating semicolon. A declaration statement creates a name for a variable and identifies the type of data to be stored in the variable. An assignment statement assigns a value to a variable, or more generally, to a storage area. A function call statement causes the named function to be executed. When the called function is completed, the program returns to the next statement after the function call. The **printf( )** function can be used to print phrases and the values of variables.

The syntax of a language is the set of rules that governs how valid statements in that language are put together. The semantics of a statement is its meaning. The compiler helps you detect syntax errors, but semantic errors only show up in how a program behaves after it is compiled. Detecting semantic errors may involve tracing the program state, that is, the values of all variables, after each program step. Keywords are the vocabulary of a language.

Review Questions

1. What are the basic modules of a C program called?

2. What function should every hosted C program contain? Why?

3. What's a syntax error? Give an example of one in English and of one in C.

4. What's a semantic error? Give an example of one in English and of one in C.

5. Ichabod Bodie Marfoote has prepared the following program and brought it to you for approval. Please help him out.

```
include studio.h
main{} /* this program prints the number of weeks in a year /*
(
int s

s := 56;
print(There are s weeks in a year.);
```

6. In Question 5, which errors are syntax errors and which are semantic errors?

7. Assuming that each of the following examples is part of a complete program, what will each one print?

```
a. printf("Baa Baa Black Sheep.");
   printf("Have you any wool?\n");


b. printf("Begone!\n0 creature of lard!");


c. printf("What?\nNo/nBonzo?\n");


d. int num;

   num = 2;
   printf("%d + %d = %d", num, num, num + num);
```

8. Identify and correct the errors in the following C program:

```
MAIN[]
(
print 'Welcome to error-free programming/n'
)
```

9. Which of the following are C keywords: **main**, **int**, **function**, **char**, =.

10. How would you declare **words** and **lines** to be type **int** variables?

11. How would you print out the values of **words** and **lines** in the form **There were 3020 words and 350 lines.**? Here 3020 and 350 represent values for the two variables.

12. Consider the following program. What is the program state after line 7? line 8? line 9?

```
#include <stdio.h>
main()
{
   int number;


   number = 6;              /* line 7 */
   number = 3 * number;     /* line 8 */
   printf("%d", number + 2); /* line 9 */
}
```

13. Consider the following program. What is the program state after line 6? line 7? line 8?

```
#include <stdio.h>
main()
{
    int a, b;
    a = 5;
    b = 2; /* line 6 */
    b = a; /* line 7 */
    a = b; /* line 8 */
}
```

Programming Exercises

Reading about C isn't enough. You should try writing a simple program or two and see if it goes as smoothly as it looks in this chapter. Here are a few suggestions, but you should also try to think up some problems yourself.

1. Write a program that uses one **printf( )** call to print your first and last name on one line, uses a second **printf( )** call to print your first and last name on two separate lines, and uses a pair of **printf( )** calls to print your first and last name on one line. The output should look like the following:

```
Mae West                        ⇐ First print statement
Mae                             ⇐ Second print statement
West                            ⇐ Still the second print statement
Mae West                        ⇐ Third and fourth print statements
```

2. Write a program to print your name and address.

3. Write a program that converts your age in years to days. At this point, don't worry about fractional years and leap years.

4. Write a program that produces the following:

```
For he's a jolly good fellow!
For he's a jolly good fellow!
For he's a jolly good fellow!
Which nobody can deny!
```

Have the program use two user-defined functions: one that prints the first three lines, and one that prints the final line.

5. Write a program that creates an integer variable called **toes**. Have the program set **toes** to 10. Also have the program calculate what twice **toes** is and what **toes** squared is. The program should print out all three values, identifying them.

6. Write a program that produces this output:

```
Smile!Smile!Smile!
Smile!Smile!
Smile!
```

It should use two user-defined functions (in addition to main( )): one to print **Smile!** once and one to start a new line.

3

Data and C

Contents

Objectives

Learning the basic C data types: **int**, **short**, **long**, **unsigned**, **char**, **float**, **double**, and **long double**

Declaring a variable of any type

Writing integer constants

Writing character constants

Using C escape sequences

Writing floating-point constants

Using some of the **printf( )** format specifiers

Making simple use of **scanf( )**

Knowing what words, bytes, and bits are

Knowing when to use different data types

Programs work with data. We feed numbers, letters, and words to the computer, and we expect it to do something with the data. In the next two chapters we concentrate on data concepts and properties. Following that, we begin examining what we can do with data.

The main topics covered in this chapter are the two great families of data types: integer and floating point. C offers several varieties of these types. We describe what the types are, how to declare them, how to use them, and when to use them. We also discuss the differences between constants and variables.

3.1 A Sample Program

Once again, we present a sample program in Listing 3.1. The program's general intent should be clear, so try compiling and running the source code shown. To save time, you can omit typing the comments. (For reference, we've included a program name as a comment. We will continue this practice with future programs.)

❖ *goldyou.c*

Listing 3.1

```
/* goldyou.c--the worth of your weight in gold */
#include <stdio.h>
main()
{
   float weight, value;    /* 2 floating-point variables */
   char beep;              /*a character variable */
   beep = '\007'; /* assigning a special character to beep */
   printf("Are you worth your weight in gold?\n");
   printf("Please enter your weight in pounds, ");
   printf("and we'll see.\n");
   scanf("%f", &weight);   /* getting input from the user */
   value = 400.0 * weight * 14.5833;
       /* assumes gold is $400 per ounce */
       /* 14.5833 converts pounds to ounces troy */
   printf("%cYour weight in gold is worth $%.2f%c.\n",
       beep,value,beep);
   printf("You are easily worth that! If gold prices drop, ");
   printf("eat more\nto maintain your value.\n");
}
```

When you type in this program, you may wish to change the value **400.00** to the current price of gold. Don't change the **14.5833**, however; it represents the number of troy ounces in a pound. Note that "entering" your weight means to type in your weight and then press the Enter key. (Don't just type your weight and wait.) Pressing Enter informs the computer that you have finished typing your response. When we run the program, the results look like the following:

```
Are you worth your weight in gold?
Please enter your weight in pounds, and we'll see.
175
Your weight in gold is worth $1020831.00.
You are easily worth that! If gold prices drop, eat more
to maintain your value.
```

The program also has a nonvisual aspect. Run the program yourself to find out what that is, but the name of one of the variables should provide a clue.

What's New in This Program

We've introduced several new elements of C in this program:

1. You probably noticed that we use two new kinds of variable declarations. Previously, we used only an integer variable type; now we've added a floating-point variable type and a character variable type so that we can handle a wider variety of data. The **float** type can hold numbers with decimal points. The **char** type can hold characters.

2. We've included some new ways of writing constants. We now have numbers with decimal points, and we have a rather peculiar-looking notation to represent the character named **beep**.

3. To print these new kinds of variables, we use the **%f** and the **%c** codes of **printf( )** to handle floating-point and character values, respectively. We use the **.2** modifier to the **%f** code to fine-tune the appearance of the output so that it displays two places to the right of the decimal.

4. To provide keyboard input to the program, we use the **scanf( )** function. The **%f** instructs the program to read a floating-point number, and the **&weight** tells **scanf( )** to assign the value to the **weight** variable. The **scanf( )** function uses the **&** notation to indicate where it can find the **weight** variable. (We discuss **&** further in the next chapter.)

5. Perhaps the most outstanding new feature is that this program is interactive. The computer asks you for information and then uses the number you type in. This interactive approach lets us create more flexible programs. For instance, our example program can be used for any reasonable weight, not just for 175 pounds. We don't have to rewrite the program every time we want to run it for a new person. The **scanf( )** and **printf( )** functions make possible this two-way communication. See Figure 3.1. The **scanf( )** function reads data from the keyboard and delivers that data to the program; and **printf( )** reads data from a program and delivers that data to your screen.

This chapter discusses the first two items in this list of new features: variables and constants of various data types. Chapter 4 covers the latter three items, although we continue to make limited use of **scanf( )** and **printf( )** in this chapter.

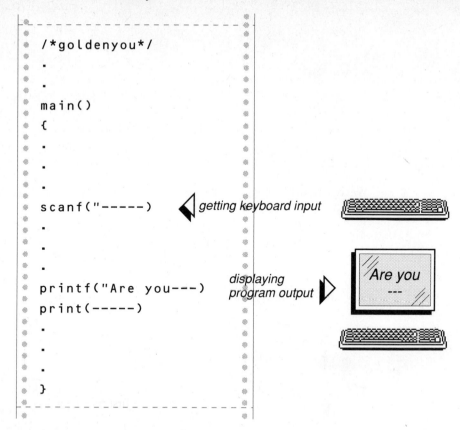

getting keyboard input

displaying
program output

Figure 3.1

The functions
scanf( ) and
printf( ) at work

3.2 Data: Variables and Constants

Under the guidance of a program, a computer can do many things. It can add numbers, sort names, command the obedience of a speaker or video screen, calculate cometary orbits, prepare a mailing list, dial telephone numbers, draw stick figures, draw conclusions, or do whatever else your imagination can create. To accomplish these tasks, the program needs to work with *data,* the numbers and characters that bear the information you use. Some data are preset before a program is used and keep their values unchanged. Such data are called *constants.* Other data may change or be assigned values as the program runs. These data are *variables.* In our sample program, **weight** is a variable and **14.5833** is a constant. The program treats **400.0** as a constant, although the price of gold isn't a constant in real life.

The difference between a variable and a constant is fairly clear: A variable can have its value assigned or changed while the program is running; a constant can't. This difference makes the variables a little tougher and more time-consuming for a computer to handle, but it can do the job.

3.3 Data: Data Types

Beyond the distinction between variable and constant is the distinction between different types of data. Some data are numbers. Some are letters, or more generally, characters. The computer needs a way to identify and use these different kinds of data. C accomplishes this task by recognizing several fundamental *data types*. If a datum is a constant, the compiler usually can tell its type just by the way it looks: **46** is an integer; **46.100** is a floating point. A variable, however, needs to have its type announced in a declaration statement. We describe this procedure as we move through the chapter. First, though, let's look at the fundamental types recognized by standard C. C uses seven keywords to set up the types: **int**, **long**, **short**, **unsigned**, **char**, **float**, and **double**. ANSI C adds four more keywords to the list: **signed**, **void**, **const**, and **volatile**. We now discuss all the data types in the first list and **signed** from the second list.

The **int** keyword provides the basic class of integers used in C. The keywords **long**, **short,** and **unsigned** and the ANSI addition **signed** are used to provide variations of the basic type. We elaborate on our discussion of these data types shortly.

The keyword **char** designates the data type used to represent letters of the alphabet and for other characters such as #, $, %, and &. Finally, **float**, **double**, and the combination **long double** are used to represent numbers with decimal points.

Integer versus Floating-Point Types

The data types created with the keywords can be divided into two families on the basis of how they are stored in the computer. The first five keywords from the pre-ANSI C list create *integer types,* whereas the last two create *floating-point* types. For a human, the difference between an integer and a floating-point number is reflected in the way they can be written. For a computer, the difference is reflected in the way they are stored. Let's look at each of the two classes in turn.

First, if you are unfamiliar with the terms "bits," "bytes," and "words," you may wish to read the box, "Bits, Bytes, and Words," before continuing with the main text. Knowing a little about what goes on inside a computer can occasionally help you use it more effectively.

The Integer

An *integer* is a whole number. It never has a fractional part, and in C it never is written with a decimal point. Examples are 2, –23, and 2456. Numbers like 3.14, ⅔, and 2.000 are not integers. Integers are stored as binary numbers. The integer 7, for example, is written 111 in binary. Thus to store this number in a one-byte word, we set the first five bits to 0 and the last three bits to 1. See Figure 3.2.

The Floating-Point Number

A *floating-point number* more or less corresponds to what mathematicians call a real number. *Real numbers* include the numbers between the integers, for example: 2.75,

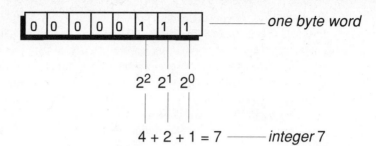

Figure 3.2

Storing the
integer 7 using
a binary code

one byte word

2^2 2^1 2^0

$4 + 2 + 1 = 7$ —— integer 7

▶ Bits, Bytes, and Words

The terms "bit," "byte," and "word" can be used to describe units of computer data or to describe units of computer memory. We concentrate on the second usage here.

The smallest unit of memory is called a *bit*. It can hold one of two values: 0 or 1. (We can also say the bit is set to "off" or "on.") You can't store much information in one bit, but a computer can hold a tremendous number of them. The bit is the basic building block of computer memory.

The *byte* is a more useful unit of memory. For most machines, a byte is 8 bits. Since each bit can be set to either 0 or 1, there are 256 (2) possible bit patterns of 0s and 1s that can fit in a byte. These patterns can be used, for example, to represent the integers from 0 to 255 or to represent a set of characters. Representation can be accomplished using *binary code,* which uses 0s and 1s to represent numbers. (We discuss binary code in Chapter 15, but you can read through the introductory material for that chapter now if you like.)

A *word* is the natural unit of memory for a given computer design. For 8-bit microcomputers, such as the original Apples, a word is just 1 byte. The IBM AT and its clones are 16-bit machines, which means they have a word size of 16 bits, or 2 bytes. Machines like the 80386-based PCs and the Macintosh II have 32-bit words. More powerful computers can have 64-bit words or even larger. Naturally, the larger a word is, the more information it can store. Computers usually can string two or more words together to store larger items, but this process slows down the computer. As an analogy, if you know your multiplication tables up through 20, then 15 x 17 is a single operation. But if you only know the tables through 10, then you have to break up 15 x 17 into smaller operations involving single digits.

We assume a word size of 16 bits for our examples, unless we tell you otherwise.

3.16E7, 7.00, and 2e–8. There are many ways to write a floating-point number. We discuss the "E"-notation more fully later. For now, the notation 3.16E7 means to multiply 3.16 by 10^7, that is, by 1 followed by seven zeros. The 7 is termed the "exponent" of 10.

The key point here is that the scheme used to store a floating-point number is different from the one used to store an integer. Floating-point representation involves breaking up a number into a fractional part and an exponent part and storing the portions separately. Thus, 7.00 in this list is not stored in the same manner as 7, even though both have the same value. The decimal analogy is to write 7.0 as 0.7E1: Here 0.7 is the fractional part, and "1" is the exponent part. Figure 3.3 shows another example of floating-point storage.

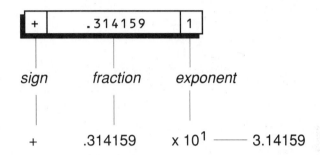

Figure 3.3

Storing the number pi in floating-point format (decimal version)

As noted in the box "Bits, Bytes, and Words," the computer uses binary numbers and powers of two instead of powers of ten for internal storage. You'll find more on this topic in Chapter 15. Here, let's concentrate on the practical differences:

1. Integers are whole numbers, whereas floating-point numbers can represent both whole and fractional numbers.

2. Floating-point numbers can represent a much larger range of values than integers can. See Table 3.1 near the end of this chapter.

3. For some arithmetic operations such as subtracting one large number from another, floating-point numbers are subject to greater loss of precision. See the box "Floating-Point Roundoff Errors."

4. Floating-point operations normally are slower than integer operations. However, microprocessors specifically developed to handle floating-point operations are now available, and they are quite swift.

▶ **Floating-Point Roundoff Errors**

Listing 3.2

Take a number. Add 1 to it, and subtract the original number. What do you get? Answer: 1. But a floating-point calculation, such as in the following listing (Listing 3.2), may give another answer.

```
/* floaterr.c--demonstrates round-off error */
#include <stdio.h>
main()
```

```
{
  float a,b;
  b = 2.0e20 + 1.0;
  a = b - 2.0e20;
  printf("%f \n", a);
}
```

In this case, the output is the following:

```
0.000000                  → VAX  750, UNIX
-13584010575872.000000    → Turbo  C
4008175468544.000000      → QuickC
```

The reason for these odd results is that the computer doesn't keep track of enough decimal places to perform the operation correctly. The number 2.0e20 is 2 followed by 20 zeros, and by adding 1, we are trying to change the 21st digit. To accomplish this task correctly, the program would need to be able to store a 21-digit number. But a **float** number typically is just 6 or 7 digits scaled to bigger or smaller numbers with an exponent. Therefore, the attempt is doomed. On the other hand, if we use, say, 2.0e4 instead of 2.0e20, we get the correct answer; for here we are trying to change the 5th digit, and **float** numbers are precise enough for that operation.

3.4 C Data Types

Now let's look at the specifics of the basic data types used by C. For each type, we describe how to declare a variable, how to represent a constant, and what a typical use would be. Some C compilers do not support all these types, so check your manual to see which ones you have available.

The int Type

C offers a variety of integer data types. They vary in the range of values offered and in whether or not negative numbers can be used. The **int** type is the basic choice, but should you need others to meet the requirements of a particular task or machine, they are available.

The **int** type is a *signed integer,* which means it must be a whole number and can be positive, negative, or zero. The range in possible values depends on the computer system. Typically, **int** uses one machine word for storage. Thus, an IBM PC, which has a 2-byte word, uses 2 bytes (16 bits) to store an **int**. This specification allows a range in values from -32768 to +32767. Other machines may have different ranges. See Table 3.1 near the end of this chapter for examples. ANSI C specifies that the minimum range for **int** should be from -32767 to +32767. Typically, systems represent signed integers by reserving one bit for indicating the sign.

Declaring an int Variable

As we saw in Chapter 2, the keyword **int** is used to declare variables of that type. First comes **int**, then the chosen name of the variable, then a semicolon. To declare more than one variable, you can declare each variable separately, or you can follow the **int** with a list of names in which each name is separated from the next by a comma. The following are valid declarations:

```
int erns;
int hogs, cows, goats;
```

We could have used a separate declaration for each variable, or we could have declared all four variables in the same statement. The effect is the same: Arrange storage space for four **int**-sized variables and associate a name with each one. Declarations that create storage for the variable are termed *definitions* of the variable. So far, all the declarations we've used are definitions, but in Chapter 13 we describe cases in which that is not true. That is, not all declarations cause storage to be set aside for a variable. Some declarations merely announce that you plan to use a variable defined elsewhere. Until Chapter 13, all our declarations will be definitions.

These declarations create variables, but they don't provide values for them. They pick up values in the program, for example:

```
cows = 112;
```

A variable can also pick up a value from a function, for example, from **scanf( )**.

Initializing a Variable

If we know in advance the starting value for a variable, we can initialize that variable. To *initialize a variable* means to assign it an initial value. In C, this task can be accomplished in the declaration statement by following the variable name with the assignment operator (=) and the value you want the variable to have. Here are some examples:

```
int hogs = 21;
int cows = 32, goats = 14;
int dogs, cats = 94;      /* valid, but poor form */
```

Note: In the last line, only **cats** is initialized to **94**. A quick reading may lead you to think that **dogs** is also initialized to **94**, therefore it is best to avoid putting initialized and noninitialized variables in the same declaration statement.

In short, the declaration (when it's a definition) creates and labels the storage. The initialization process then places a value in that storage. See Figure 3.4.

Type int Constants

The various integers (21, 32, 14, and 94) in the last example are integer constants. When you write a number without a decimal point and without an exponent, C recognizes it as an integer. Thus, 22 and −44 are integer constants, and 22.0 and 2.2E1 are not. C treats

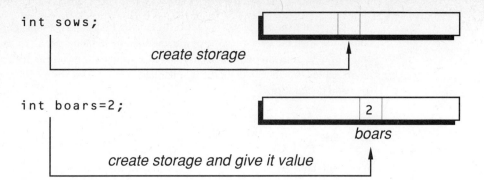

```
int sows;
```
create storage

Figure 3.4

Defining and initializing a variable

```
int boars=2;
```
2

boars

create storage and give it value

most integer constants as type **int**. Very large integers may be treated differently, as we discuss in the section on the **long int** type.

Normally, C assumes you are writing integers as decimal integers, that is, in the base 10 number system. However, octal (base 8) and hexadecimal (base 16) numbers are popular with many programmers. Because 8 and 16 are powers of 2 (and 10 is not), these number systems are more natural for computers to use. For example, the number 65536, which often pops up in 16-bit machines, is simply 10000 in hexadecimal (also called hex). How can the computer tell whether 10000 is meant to be a decimal, hexadecimal, or octal value? In C, special prefixes indicate which number base you are using. A **0** (zero) prefix means you are writing in octal; for example, the decimal value 16 is written as 020 in C octal. Similarly, a prefix of **0x** or **0X** means you are writing in hexadecimal, so 16 is written as 0x10 or 0X10 in hexadecimal. Chapter 15 discusses these alternative number bases more fully.

One important point to realize is that the option of using different number systems is provided as a service for your convenience. It doesn't affect how the number is stored. That is, you can write 16 or 020 or 0x10, and the number will be stored exactly the same way in each case—in the binary code used internally by the computer.

Printing int Values

We can use the **printf( )** function to print **int**s. As we saw in Chapter 2, the **%d** notation is used to indicate just where in a line the integer is to be printed. The **%d** is an example of a format specifier, for it indicates the format used to display a value. Each **%d** must

❖ *print1.c*

Listing 3.3

```
/* print1.c--displays some properties of printf() */
#include <stdio.h>
main()
{
    int ten = 10;

    printf("%d minus %d is %d\n", ten, 2, ten - 2 );
}
```

be matched by an **int** value, which can be an **int** variable, an **int** constant, or any other expression having an **int** value. Listing 3.3 presents a simple program that initializes a variable and prints some values.

Compiling and running the program produces the following output:

```
10 minus 2 is 8
```

Thus, the first **%d** represents the **int** variable **ten**, the second **%d** represents the **int** constant **2**, and the third **%d** represents the **int** expression **ten – 2**.

Just as C lets you write a number in any one of three number systems, it also lets you print a number in any of these systems. To print an integer in octal notation instead of decimal, use **%o** instead of **%d**. To print an integer in hexadecimal, use **%x**. Listing 3.4 shows a short example.

Listing 3.4

```
/* bases.c--prints 100 in decimal, octal, and hex */
#include <stdio.h>
main()
{
   int x = 100;

   printf("dec = %d; octal = %o; hex = %x\n", x, x, x);
}
```

Compiling and running this program produces the following output:

```
dec = 100; octal = 144; hex = 64
```

We see the same value displayed in three different number systems; the **printf( )** function makes the conversions. Note that the **0** and the **0x** prefixes are not displayed in the output. ANSI C provides that the specifiers **%#o**, **%#x**, and **%#X** will generate the **0**, **0x**, and **0X** prefixes, respectively.

Other Integer Types

When you are first learning the C language, the **int** type is probably the only integer type you will need. But let's also look at the other forms. If you like, you can skim over this section to the discussion of the **char** type and return here when you have the need.

C offers three *adjective keywords* to modify the basic integer type: **unsigned**, **long**, and **short**.

1. The type **short int**, or **short**, may use less storage than **int**, thus saving space when only small numbers are needed. Like **int**, **short** is a signed type.

3.4 C Data Types **55**

2. The type **long int**, or **long**, may use more storage than **int**, thus allowing larger integers to be used. Like **int**, **long** is a signed type.

3. The type **unsigned int**, or **unsigned**, shifts the range of numbers that can be stored. For example, a two-byte **unsigned int** allows a range from 0 to 65535 in value instead of from –32768 to +32767. The bit used to indicate the sign of signed numbers now becomes another binary digit, allowing the larger number.

4. ANSI C and many pre-ANSI C compilers also recognize **unsigned long int**, or **unsigned long**, and **unsigned short int**, or **unsigned short**, as valid types.

Why do we say **long** and **short** types "may" use more or less storage than **int**? Because all that C guarantees is that **short** is no **long**er than **int** and that **long** is no shorter than **int**. The idea is to fit the types to the machine. On an IBM PC, for example, an **int** and a **short** are both 16 bits, whereas a **long** is 32 bits. On a VAX 750, however, a **short** is 16 bits, and both **int** and **long** are 32 bits. The natural word size on a VAX is 32 bits. Since this capacity allows integers in excess of two billion (see Table 3.1), the implementors of C on the VAX did not see a necessity for anything larger; thus, on the VAX **long** is the same as **int**. But for many VAX uses, integers of that size are not needed, so a space-saving **short** was created. The IBM PC, on the other hand, has only a 16-bit word, which means that a larger **long** was needed.

The most common practice today is to set up **long** as 32 bits, **short** as 16 bits, and **int** to either 16 bits or 32 bits, depending on the machine's natural word size. In principle, however, these three types can represent three distinct sizes.

ANSI C provides guidelines that specify the minimum allowable size for each basic data type. The minimum range for both **short** and **int** is –32767 to 32767, corresponding to a two-byte unit; the minimum range for **long** is –2147483647 to 2147483647, corresponding to a four-byte unit. For **unsigned short** and **unsigned int**, the minimum range is 0 to 65535, and for **unsigned long** the minimum range is 0 to 4294967295.

Let's now discuss the uses of the various **int** types. First, let's consider **unsigned** types. It is natural to use these for counting, since you don't need negative numbers and the unsigned types let you reach higher positive numbers than the signed types.

You use the **long** type if you need to use numbers that **long** can handle and that **int** cannot. However, on systems for which **long** is bigger than **int**, using **long** may slow down calculations. Therefore, it's a good idea not to use **long** if it is not essential. One further point: If you are writing code on a machine for which **int** and **long** are the same size, and if you need 32-bit integers, you should use **long** instead of **int**, so that the program will function correctly if transferred to a 16-bit machine.

You use **short** to save storage space or if, say, you need a 16-bit value on a system in which **int** is 32 bits. Saving storage space usually is important only if your program uses large arrays of integers.

What happens if an integer gets too big for its type? Let's now set an integer to its largest possible value, add to it, and see what happens (Listing 3.5 below). The behavior described is not mandated by the rules of C, but it is the typical implementation.

Listing 3.5

```
/* toobig.c--exceeds maximum int size on our system */
#include <stdio.h>
main()
{
    int i = 32767;

    printf("%d %d %d\n", i, i+1, i+2);
}
```

Here's the result for our system:

```
32767 -32768 -32767
```

The integer **i** is acting like a car's odometer. When it reaches its maximum value, it starts over at the beginning, in this case at –32768. Notice that you are not informed that **i** has exceeded ("overflowed") its maximum value. You would have to include your own programming to keep tabs on that.

Declaring Other Integer Types

Other integer types are declared in the same manner as the **int** type. The following list shows several examples, although not all pre-ANSI C compilers can recognize the last two:

```
long int estine;
long johns;
short int erns;
short ribs;
unsigned int s_count;
unsigned players;
unsigned long headcount;
unsigned short yesvotes;
```

Type long Constants

Normally, when you use a number like 2345 in your program code, it is stored as an **int** type. But what if you use a number like 1000000 on a system in which **int** cannot hold such a large number? Then the compiler treats your number as a **long int**, assuming that type is large enough. If the number is larger than the **long** maximum, C treats it as **unsigned long**.

Sometimes you may need to store a small number as a **long** integer. Programming that involves explicit use of memory addresses on an IBM PC, for instance, can create such a need. Also, some standard C functions require type **long** values. To cause a constant to be stored as type **long**, you can add an **l** or **L** as a suffix. We recommend the second form, since it looks less like the digit 1. Thus on a system with a 16-bit **int** and a 32-bit **long**, the integer 7 is stored in 2 bytes, and the integer 7L is stored in 4 bytes. The **l** and **L** suffixes also can be used with octal and hex integers.

Printing long, short, and unsigned Types

To print an **unsigned int** number, use the **%u** notation. To print a **long** value, use the **%ld** format specifier. If **int** and **long** are the same size on your system, **%d** will suffice, but your program will not work properly when transferred to a system on which the two types are different. You can also use the **l** prefix for **x** and **o**; thus, **%lx** means to print a **long** integer in hexadecimal format.

ANSI C provides several additional forms. First, you can use an **h** prefix for **short** types. Thus, **%hd** displays a **short** integer in decimal form, and **%ho** displays a **short** integer in octal form. Both the **h** and **l** prefixes can be used with **u** for unsigned types. For instance, you can use the **%lu** notation for printing **unsigned long** types. Listing 3.6 provides a sample.

❖ *print2.c*

Listing 3.6

```
/* print2.c--more printf() properties */
#include <stdio.h>
main()
{
   unsigned un = 40000;
   long ln = 2000000000;
   unsigned long uln = 2 * 2000000000; /* or 4000000000 */
   short sn = 200;

   printf("un = %u and not %d\n", un, un);
   printf("ln = %ld and not %d\n", ln, ln);
   printf("uln = %lu and not %u\n", uln, uln);
   printf("sn = %hd and, on this system, %d\n", sn, sn);
}
```

The output is as follows:

```
un = 40000 and not -25536
ln = 2000000000 and not -27648
uln = 4000000000 and not 10240
sn = 200 and, on this system, 200
```

This example points out that using the wrong specification can produce unexpected results. It also points out that you should be wary of implementation differences. For instance, we use **2 [*] 2000000000** instead of **4000000000** because one of our implementations does not recognize written decimal integers beyond the **long** limit. In this respect, it falls short of the ANSI C standard. Also, because we ran this program on a system in which **int** and **short** are the same size, both the **%hd** and the **%d** produced the same result.

Using Characters: Type char

As we've said, the **char** type is used for storing characters such as letters and punctuation marks, although technically it is an integer type because it actually stores integers, not characters. After all, a computer can only store a pattern of 1s and 0s. To handle characters, the computer uses a numerical code in which certain integers represent certain characters. The most commonly used code is the ASCII code given in Appendix E, and it is the code we assume for this book. In it, for example, the integer 65 represents the uppercase letter A. Thus to store the letter A, we actually need to store the integer 65. (Many IBM mainframes use a different code called EBCDIC, but the principle is the same.)

The standard ASCII code runs numerically from 0 to 127. The numbers are small enough that seven bits can hold the largest code value. The **char** type typically is defined as a one-byte (or eight-bit) unit of memory, so it is more than large enough to encompass the standard ASCII code. Many systems such as the IBM PC and the Apple Macintosh offer extended ASCII codes (not the same for both systems) that also remain within an eight-bit limit. More generally, C guarantees that the **char** type will be large enough to store the basic character set for the system on which C is implemented.

Declaring Type char Variables

As you may expect, **char** variables are declared in the same manner as other variables. Here are some examples:

```
char response;
char itable, latan;
```

This program creates three **char** variables: **response**, **itable**, and **latan**.

Signed or Unsigned?

Some C implementations make **char** a **signed** type, which means it can hold values typically in the range −128 through +127. Other implementations make **char** an **unsigned** type, which provides a 0 through 255 range. Your compiler manual should tell you which type **char** is.

ANSI C and many newer implementations allow you to use the keywords **signed** and **unsigned** with **char**. Then regardless of what **char** is, **signed char** is signed, and **unsigned char** is unsigned.

Character Constants and Initialization

Suppose you want to initialize a character constant to the letter A. You can use the following numerical code:

```
char grade = 65;
```

In this example, **65** is type **int**, but since the value is smaller than the maximum **char** size, it can be assigned to **grade** without any problems.

On the other hand, computer languages are supposed to make tasks easier for us to accomplish. We shouldn't have to memorize the ASCII code to initialize a character constant to the letter A. We can assign the character A to **grade** with the following initialization:

```
char grade = 'A';
```

A single letter contained between single quotation marks is a C character constant. When the compiler sees **'A'**, it converts it to the proper code value. For example, on an EBCDIC system, the compiler uses the EBCDIC code for the letter A. The single quotation marks are essential:

```
char broiled;      /* declare a char variable */
broiled = 'T';     /* OK */
broiled = T;       /* NO! Thinks T is a variable */
broiled = "T";     /* NO! Thinks "T" is a string */
```

If you leave them off, the compiler in this case thinks T is the name of a variable. If you use double quotation marks, the compiler thinks you are using a "string." A string (Chapter 4) is a sequence of characters treated as a unit.

Nonprinting Characters

The single-quotation technique is suitable for use with characters, digits, and punctuation marks, but if you look through Appendix E, you will see that some of the ASCII characters are designated as nonprinting. For example, some represent actions such as backspacing, going to the next line, or making the terminal bell ring (or speaker beep). C offers three ways to represent nonprinting characters.

The first way we have already mentioned: just use the ASCII code. For example, the ASCII code for the beep character is 7, thus:

```
char beep = 7;
```

The second method is to use a special form of the ASCII code. To do so, take the octal ASCII code, precede it with a backslash (\), and place the entire statement within single quotation marks. We followed this in Listing 3.1 at the beginning of this chapter:

```
beep = '\007';
```

You can omit the leading zeros, so **'\07'** or even **'\7'** will work. This notation causes numbers to be interpreted as octal even if there is no initial **0**. Note: Using **'\007'** is different from using **7**. One difference is that **'\007'** can be incorporated into a string, whereas **7** cannot.

ANSI C and many new implementations accept a hexadecimal form for character constants. In this case, the backslash is followed by an **x** or **X** and one to three hexadecimal digits. For example, the Control-P character has an ASCII hex code of 10

Figure 3.5

Writing constants within the **int** *family*

Int Family Constants			
member	hex	octal	decimal
char	N.A.	'\034'	N.A.
short	±0X23	±078	±92
unsigned short	0X23	078	92
long	±0X23L	±078L	±92L

(16, in decimal), so it can be expressed as `'\x10'` or `'\X010'`. Figure 3.5 summarizes the representation of integer constants.

When you use ASCII code, note the difference between numbers and number characters. For example, the character 4 is represented by ASCII code value 52. This code represents the symbol "4" and not the numerical value 4.

The third method to represent certain nonprinting characters in C is to use special symbol sequences, which are called *escape sequences:*

```
\a alert (ANSI C)
\b backspace
\f form feed
\n newline
\r carriage return
\t horizontal tab
\v vertical tab (ANSI C)
\\ backslash(\)
\' single quote(')
\" double quote(") (ANSI C)
```

These, too, are enclosed in single quotation marks when assigned to a character variable. For example, we can make the statement:

```
nerf = '\n';
```

and then print the variable **nerf** to advance the printer or screen one line.

Let's take a closer look at what each escape sequence does. The alert character (\a), added by ANSI C, produces an audible or visible alert. The nature of the alert depends on the hardware; at present, the beep is the most common alert. The ANSI standard states that the alert character shall not change the *active position,* which is the location on the display device (screen, teletype, printer, and so on) at which the next character output will appear. In short, the active position is a generalization of the screen cursor you probably are accustomed to. Therefore, using the alert character in a program using a screen display should produce a beep without moving the screen cursor. If you have a compiler that supports this escape sequence, you can use it instead of `'\007'` in Listing 3.1.

Next, the **\b**, **\f**, **\n**, **\r**, **\t**, and **\v** escape sequences are common output device control characters. They can be described in terms of how they affect the active position. A backspace (**\b**) moves the active position back one space on the current line. A form feed (**\f**) advances the active position to the start of the next page. A newline (**\n**) sets the active position to the beginning of the next line. A carriage return (**\r**) moves the active position to the beginning of the current line. A horizontal tab (**\t**) moves the active position to the next horizontal tab stop; typically, these are found at character positions 1, 9, 17, 25, and so on. A vertical tab (**\v**) moves the active position to the next vertical tab position.

These escape characters do not necessarily work with all display devices. For instance, the form feed and vertical tab characters produce odd symbols on a PC screen rather than any cursor movement, although they work as described if sent to a printer instead of to the screen.

The last three escape sequences (\\, \', and \) let you use \, ', and as character constants. (Because these symbols are used to define character constants as part of a **printf( )** command, the situation could become confusing if you use them literally.) If you want to print the line:

```
Gramps sez, "a \ is a backslash."
```

use:

```
printf("Gramps sez, \"a \\ is a backslash.\"\n");
```

At this point you may have two questions. (1) Why didn't we enclose the escape sequences in single quotation marks in the last example? (2) When should you use the ASCII code, and when should you use the escape sequences? The answers:

1. When a character, be it an escape sequence or not, is part of a string of characters enclosed in double quotation marks, don't enclose it in single quotation marks. Notice that none of the other characters in this example (G,r,a,m,p,s, and so on) are marked off by single quotation marks.

2. If you have a choice between using one of the special escape sequences, say **'\f'**, or an equivalent ASCII code, say **'\014'**, use the **'\f'**. First, the representation is more mnemonic. Second, it is more portable. For example, if you have a system that doesn't use ASCII code, the **'\f'** will still work.

Printing Characters

The **printf( )** function uses **%c** to indicate that a character should be printed. Recall that a character is stored as an integer; so if we print the value of a **char** variable, we should get an integer. The **%c** format specifier tells **printf( )** to convert the integer to the corresponding character. The program in Listing 3.7 takes both uses of a character, as the sample run that follows the listing shows.

Listing 3.7

```
/* charcode.c--displays code number for a character */
#include <stdio.h>
main()
{
  char ch;

  printf("Please enter a character.\n");
  scanf("%c", &ch);     /* user inputs character */
  printf("The code for %c is %d.\n", ch, ch);
}
```

```
Please enter a character.
C
The code for C is 67.
```

When you use the program, remember to press Enter after typing the character. **Scanf( )** then fetches the character you typed, and the ampersand (**&**) sees to it that the character is assigned to the character variable **ch**. **Printf( )** then prints out the value of **ch** twice, first as a character (prompted by the **%c** code), then as a decimal integer (prompted by the **%d** code). Note that the **printf( )** specifiers determine how data is displayed, not how it is stored. See Figure 3.6.

Types **float** *and* **double**

The various integer types serve well for most software development projects. However, mathematically oriented programs often make use of floating-point numbers. In C, such numbers are called type **float**; they correspond to the real types used in FORTRAN and Pascal. The floating-point approach, as already mentioned, allows you to represent a much greater range of numbers, including decimal fractions. Floating-point numbers

Figure 3.6

Data display versus data storage

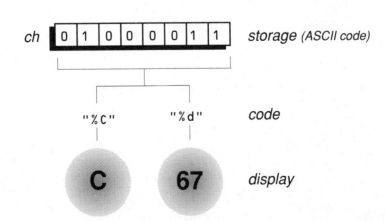

representation is similar to scientific notation, a system used by scientists to express very large and very small numbers.

In scientific notation, numbers are represented as decimal numbers multiplied by powers of ten. Here are some examples:

Number	Scientific Notation	Exponential Notation
1,000,000,000	$= 1.0 \times 10^9$	$= 1.0e9$
123,000	$= 1.23 \times 10^5$	$= 1.23e5$
322.56	$= 3.2256 \times 10^2$	$= 3.2256e2$
0.000056	$= 5.6 \times 10^{-5}$	$= 5.6e-5$

The first column shows the common notation, the second column scientific notation, and the third column exponential notation, which is the way scientific notation is usually written for and by computers, with the "e" followed by the power of ten.

Often, 32 bits are used to store a floating-point number: Eight bits are used to give the exponent its value and sign, and 24 bits are used to represent the nonexponent portion. This produces a digit precision of six or seven decimals and a range of 10^{-37} to 10^{+38}. Such a range is handy if you like to use numbers such as the mass of the sun (2.0e30 kilograms), the charge of a proton (1.6e-19 coulombs), or the national debt.

C also has a **double** (for double precision) floating-point type. Although it is not required to be any more precise than **float** (just as **long** is not required to be larger than **int**), **double** usually uses twice as many bits, typically 64. Some systems use all 32 additional bits for the nonexponent portion to increase the number of significant figures and reduce roundoff errors. Other systems use some of the bits to accommodate a larger exponent, which increases the range of numbers that can be accommodated. See Figure 3.7.

ANSI C allows for a third floating-point type, called **long double**, whose intent it is to provide for even more precision than **double**. However, all that ANSI C guarantees is that **long double** is at least as precise as **double**.

Declaring Floating-Point Variables

Floating-point variables are declared and initialized in the same manner as their integer cousins, for example:

```
float noah, jonah;
double trouble;
float planck = 6.63e-34;
long double gnp;
```

Floating-Point Constants

We have many choices when we write a floating-point constant. The basic form is a signed series of digits including a decimal point, then an **e** or **E**, then a signed exponent indicating the power of 10 used. Two examples are

−1.56E+12   2.87e −3

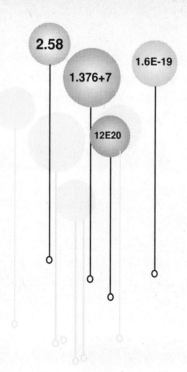

Figure 3.7

Some floating-point numbers

You can omit positive signs. You can also omit a decimal point (2E5) or an exponential part (19.28), but not both simultaneously. Also, you can omit a fractional part (3.E16) or an integer part (.45E– 6), but not both. Some valid floating-point constants follow:

3.14159   .2   4e16   .8E–5   100

You cannot use spaces in a floating-point constant, such as

1.56   E+12   (Wrong)

Floating-point constants are taken to be double precision. Suppose, for example, that **some** is a **float** variable, and that you have the statement:

```
some = 4.0 * 2.0;
```

Then the **4.0** and **2.0** are stored as **double**, using (typically) 64 bits for each. The product is calculated using double-precision arithmetic, and only then is the answer trimmed down to regular **float** size. This procedure ensures greater precision for your calculations.

ANSI C lets you specify how a floating-point constant is stored. An **f** or **F** suffix on a floating-point number makes it type **float**: Examples are 2.3f and 9.11E9F. An **l** or **L** suffix makes it type **long double**: Examples are 54.3l and 4.32e4L. Note that **L** is much less likely to be mistaken for a **1** than is **l**. If the floating-point number has no suffix, it's type **double**.

Printing Floating-Point Values

The **printf( )** function uses the **%f** format specifier to print type **float** and **double** numbers using decimal notation, and it uses **%e** to print them in exponential notation. See Listing 3.8.

❖ *showf_pt.c*

Listing 3.8

```
/* showf_pt.c--display float value two ways */
#include <stdio.h>
main()
{
   float value = 32000.0;
   printf("%f can be written %e\n", value, value);
}
```

The output is the following:

```
32000.000000 can be written 3.200000e+004
```

Listing 3.8 illustrates the default output. The next chapter discusses how to control the appearance of this output by setting field widths and the number of places to the right of the decimal. Those implementations that support the new ANSI C **long double** type use the **%Lf** and **%Le** specifiers to print that type.

Other Types

That finishes our list of fundamental data types. C does have other types derived from the basic types. These types include arrays, pointers, structures, and unions. Although these are subject matter for later chapters, we already have smuggled some pointers into this chapter's examples. See Figure 3.8. (A pointer "points to" the location of a variable or other data object. The **&** prefix we used with the **scanf( )** function creates a pointer telling **scanf( )** where to place information.)

▶ *Floating-Point Overflow and Underflow*

What happens if you try to make a **float** variable exceed its limits? For example, suppose you multiply 1.0e38 by 100 (overflow) or divide 1.0e-37 by 1.0e8 (underflow)? The result depends on the system. With Microsoft C on an IBM PC, any number that overflows will cause the program to abort and print a "runtime error" message; any number that underflows will be replaced by 0. Turbo C, on the other hand, aborts a program for both overflow and underflow. Other systems may not issue warnings or may offer you a choice of responses. If this matter concerns you, check out the rules on your system. If you can't find the information, don't be afraid to try a little trial and error.

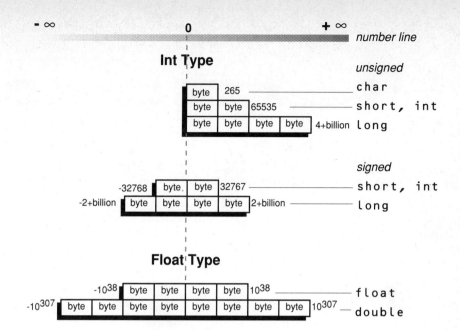

Figure 3.8

C data types for a typical system

Derived Types

- arrays
- pointers
- strings
- structures
- unions

Type Sizes

Table 3.1 shows type sizes for some common C environments.

Table 3.1 Type Facts for Representative Systems

	DEC PDP-11	DEC VAX	IBM PC (Microsoft and Turbo C)	ANSI C Minimum
char	8	8	8	8
int	16	32	16	16
short	16	16	16	16
long	32	32	32	32
float	32	32	32	6 digits*
double	64	64	64	10 digits*
Exponent range (double)	–38 to 38	–38 to 38	–307 to 308	–37 to 37

*Decimal digits of precision

What is your system like? Try running the program in Listing 3.9 to find out. C has a built-in operator called **sizeof** that gives the size of things in bytes.

❖ *typesize.c*

Listing 3.9

```
/* typesize.c--prints out type sizes */
#include <stdio.h>
main()
{
    printf("Type int has a size of %d bytes.\n",sizeof(int));
    printf("Type char has a size of %d bytes.\n",sizeof(char));
    printf("Type long has a size of %d bytes.\n",sizeof(long));
    printf("Type double has a size of %d bytes.\n",
      sizeof(double));
}
```

Our output from this program is the following:

```
Type int has a size of 2 bytes.
Type char has a size of 1 bytes.
Type long has a size of 4 bytes.
Type double has a size of 8 bytes.
```

We found the size of just four types, but you can easily modify the program in Listing 3.9 to find the size of any type. Incidentally, notice in the last line how we spread the **printf( )** statement over two lines. This format is okay as long as the break does not occur in the section in quotation marks or in the middle of a word.

▶ Summary: The Basic Data Types

Keywords. The basic data types are set up using the following eight keywords: **int, long, short, unsigned, char, float, double, signed** (ANSI C).

Signed integers. These can have positive or negative values:

int: the basic integer type for a given system.

long or **long int**: can hold an integer at least as large as the largest **int** and possibly larger.

short or **short int**: the largest **short** integer is no larger than the largest **int** and may be smaller. Typically, **long** is larger than **short**, and **int** is the same as one of the two. For example, Turbo C and Microsoft C for the IBM PC provide 16-bit **short** and **int** and 32-bit **long**. Other systems may vary.

Unsigned integers. These have zero or positive values only, and extend the range of the largest possible positive number. Use the keyword **unsigned** before the desired type: **unsigned int**, **unsigned long**, **unsigned short**. A lone **unsigned** is the same as **unsigned int**.

Characters. These are typographic symbols such as A, &, and +. Typically, they use one byte of memory.

char: the keyword for this type. Some implementations use a signed **char;** others use an unsigned **char**. ANSI C allows you to use the keywords **signed** and **unsigned** to specify which form you want.

Floating point. These can have positive or negative values:

float: the basic floating-point type for the system.

double: a (possibly) larger unit for holding floating-point numbers. It may allow more significant figures and perhaps larger exponents than **float**.

long double: a (possibly) even larger unit for holding floating-point numbers. It may allow more significant figures and perhaps larger exponents than **double**.

▶ *Summary: How to Declare a Simple Variable*

1. Choose the type you need.

2. Choose a name for the variable.

3. Use the following format for a declaration statement: *type-specifier variable-name*. The type-specifier is formed from one or more of the type keywords. Examples are: **int erest**; and **unsigned short cash**.

4. You may declare more than one variable of the same type by separating the variable names with commas, for example, **char ch, init, ans;**.

5. You can initialize a variable in a declaration statement, for instance, **float mass = 6.0E24;**.

3.5 Using Data Types

When you develop a program, take note of the variables you need and of what type they should be. Most likely you can use **int** or possibly **float** for the numbers and **char** for the characters. Declare them at the beginning of the function that uses them, and choose a name for the variable that suggests its meaning. When you initialize a variable, match the constant type to the variable type:

```
int apples = 3;      /* RIGHT */
int oranges = 3.0;   /* WRONG */
```

C is more forgiving about type mismatches than, say, Pascal. Most compilers will pass the second initialization, but they may complain, particularly if you have activated a higher warning level. It is best not to develop sloppy habits.

3.6 I/O Arguments and Pitfalls

As you may recall, the items of information passed to a function are termed arguments. For instance, the function call **printf("Hello, pal.")** has one argument: **"Hello, pal."**. A series of characters in quotes, such as **"Hello, pal."**, is called a string. One string, even one containing several words and punctuation marks, counts as one argument.

Similarly, the function call **scanf("%d", &weight)** has two arguments: **"%d"** and **&weight**. C uses commas to separate arguments to a function. The **printf( )** and **scanf( )** functions are unusual in that they aren't limited to a specific number of arguments. For instance, we've used calls to **printf( )** with one, two, and even three arguments. For a program to work properly, it needs to know how many arguments there are. **Printf( )** and **scanf( )** use the first argument to indicate how many additional arguments are coming. The trick is that each format specification in the initial string indicates an additional argument. For instance, the statement:

```
printf("%d cats ate %d cans of tuna\n", cats, cans);
```

has two format specifiers: **%d** and **%d**. These specifiers tell the program to expect two more arguments: **cats** and **cans**.

It's the programmer's responsibility to make sure the number of format specifications matches the number of additional arguments. The new ANSI standard provides a mechanism *(function prototyping)* for checking whether a function call has the correct number of arguments, but it doesn't work with **printf( )** and **scanf( )** because they take a variable number of arguments.

What happens if you don't live up to the programmer's burden? Suppose, for example, you write a program like that of Listing 3.10. None of the four compilers we tried raised any objections to this code. Nor were there any complaints when we ran the program.

❖ *pitfalls.c*

Listing 3.10

```
/* pitfalls.c */
#include <stdio.h>
main()
{
    int f = 4;
    int g = 5;

    printf("%d\n", f, g);   /* too many arguments */
    printf("%d %d\n",f);    /* too few arguments */
}
```

All four versions printed **4** for the first line. For the second line we got **4 5** (twice), **4 130**, and **4 936**. As you can see, the computer doesn't catch this kind of error during run time. And because the program may even run correctly, you may not notice the errors, either. But if a program doesn't print the expected number of values or if it prints unexpected values, check the **printf( )** arguments.

3.7 One More Example

Let's run one more printing example, one that makes use of some of C's special escape characters. In particular, the program in Listing 3.11 shows how backspace (**\b**), tab (**\t**), and carriage return (**\r**) work.

❖ *escape.c*

Listing 3.11

```
/* escape.c--use escape characters */
#include <stdio.h>
main()
{
   float salary;

   printf("Enter your desired monthly salary:"); /* 1 */
   printf(" $_____\b\b\b\b\b\b\b");             /* 2 */
   scanf("%f", &salary);
   printf("\n\t$%.2f a month is $%.2f a year.", salary,
      salary * 12.0);                             /* 3 */
   printf("\rGee!\n");                            /* 4 */
}
```

What Happens

Let's walk through this program step by step as it would work under an ANSI C implementation. The first **printf( )** statement (the one we've numbered 1), prints the following:

```
Enter your desired monthly salary:
```

Because there is no **\n** at the end of the string, the cursor is left positioned after the colon.

The second **printf( )** statement picks up after the first stops, so after it's finished, the screen looks like the following:

```
Enter your desired monthly salary: $_____
```

The space between the colon and the dollar sign occurs because the string in the second **printf( )** statement begins with a space. The effect of the seven backspace characters is to move the cursor seven positions to the left, which backs the cursor over the seven underline characters, placing the cursor directly after the dollar sign. Note that backspacing does not erase the characters that are backed over.

At this point, you type in your response, say **2000.00**. Now the line looks like the following:

```
Enter your desired monthly salary: $2000.00
```

The characters you type replace the underline characters, and when you press Enter to enter your response, the cursor moves to the beginning of the next line.

The third **printf( )** statement begins with \n\t. The newline character moves the cursor to the beginning of the next line. The tab character moves the cursor to the next tab stop on that line, typically to column 9. Then the rest of the string is printed. After this statement, the screen looks like the following:

```
Enter your desired monthly salary: $2000.00
    $2000.00 a month is $24000.00 a year.
```

Because the **printf( )** statement doesn't use the newline character, the cursor remains after the final period.

The fourth **printf( )** statement begins with \r, which positions the cursor at the beginning of the current line. Then **Gee!** is displayed, and the \n moves the cursor to the next line. The final appearance of the screen is the following:

```
Enter your desired monthly salary: $2000.00
Gee! $2000.00 a month is $24000.00 a year.
```

A Possible Problem

Some older C implementations do not work as we've just described. The problem lies in when **printf( )** actually sends output to the screen. In general, **printf( )** statements send output to an intermediate storage area called a *buffer*. Every now and then, the material in the buffer is sent on to the screen. Under ANSI C, the rules for when output is sent from the buffer to the screen are clear: It is sent when the buffer becomes full, when a newline character is encountered, or when there is impending input. (This clearing of the buffer is called *flushing the buffer*.) For instance, the first two **printf( )** statements don't fill the buffer and don't contain a newline, but they are immediately followed by a **scanf( )** statement asking for input. This statement forces the **printf( )** output to be sent on to the screen.

Some older C implementations, however, do not invoke the third condition (impending input) for flushing the buffer. If you run Listing 3.11 with one of these compilers, the output of the first two **printf( )** statements remains in the buffer. If you type in a response anyway and then press Enter, the newline generated by the return key flushes the buffer. Therefore, you have to type your answer before you see the question! The solution to this awkward situation is to use a newline at the end of the **printf( )** statement preceding the input. That newline will flush the buffer. To accomplish this task, the code can be changed to look like the following:

```
printf("Enter your desired monthly salary:\n");
scanf("%f", &salary);
```

This code works whether or not impending input flushes the buffer. However, it also places the cursor on the next line, preventing you from entering data on the same line as the prompting string. A sample run follows:

```
Enter your desired monthly salary:
2000.00
```

To maintain greater portability, we follow this model (response on the line following the prompt) for the rest of the book.

3.8 Summary

C has a variety of data types, but the basic types fall into two categories: integer types and floating-point types. The two distinguishing features for integer types are the amount of storage allotted to a type and whether it is signed or unsigned. The smallest integer type is **char**, which may be either signed or unsigned, depending on the implementation. ANSI C allows you to use **signed char** and **unsigned char** to specify explicitly which you want to use. The other integer types include **short**, **int**, and **long**. C guarantees that each of these types is at least as large as the preceding type. All three of these are signed types, but with ANSI C you can use the **unsigned** keyword to create the corresponding unsigned types: **unsigned short**, **unsigned int**, and **unsigned long**. K & R C recognizes only **unsigned int**.

The three floating-point types are **float**, **double**, and, new with ANSI C, **long double**. Each is at least as large as the preceding type.

Integers can be expressed in decimal, octal, or hexadecimal form. A leading **0** indicates an octal number, and a leading **0x** or **0X** indicates hexadecimal numbers. For example, 32, 040, and 0x20 are decimal, octal, and hexadecimal representations of the same value. An **l** or **L** suffix indicates a **long** value.

Character constants are represented by placing the character in single quotation marks: `'Q'`, `'8'`, **and** `'$'` for example. C escape sequences such as `'\n'` represent certain nonprinting characters. You can use the form `'\007'` to represent a character by its ASCII code. Floating-point numbers can be written with a fixed decimal point, as in 9393.912, or in exponential notation, as in 7.38E10.

The **printf( )** function lets you print various types of values by using conversion specifiers that, in their simplest form, consist of a percent sign and a letter indicating the type, as in **%d** or **%f**.

Review Questions

1. Which data type would you use for each of the following kinds of data?

a. The population of Rio Frito

b. The average weight of a Rembrandt painting

c. The most common letter in this chapter

d. The number of times that letter occurs

2. Identify the type and meaning, if any, of each of the following constants:

a. '\b'

b. 1066

c. 99.44

d. 0XAA

e. 2.0e30

3. Virgila Ann Xenopod has concocted an error-laden program. Help her find the mistakes:

```
#include <stdio.h>
main
(
   float g; h;
   float tax, rate;

   g = e21;
   tax = rate*g;
)
```

4. Identify the data type (as used in declaration statements) and the **print( )** format specifier for each of the following constants:

Constant	Type	Specifier
a. 12		
b. 0X3		
c. 'C'		
d. 2.34E07		
e. '\040'		
f. 7.0		
g. 6L		

5. Identify the data type (as used in declaration statements) and the **printf( )** format specifier for each of the following constants:

Constant	Type	Specifier

a. 012

b. 2.9e05L

c. '?'

d. 100000

e. '\n'

f. 20.0f

g. 0x44

6. Suppose that **ch** is a type **char** variable. Show how to assign the carriage return character to **ch** by using an escape sequence, a decimal value, an octal character constant, and a hex character constant.

7. Correct this silly program (the / in C means division):

```
main() / this program is perfect /
{
  cows, legs integer;

  printf("How many cow legs did you count?\n);
  scanf("%c", legs);
  cows = legs / 4;
  printf("That implies there are %f cows.\n", cows)
}
```

8. Identify what each of the following escape sequences represents:

a. \n

b. \\

c. \"

d. \t

Programming Exercises

1. Find out what your system does with integer overflow, floating-point overflow, and floating-point underflow by using the experimental approach (that is, write programs having these problems).

2. Write a program that asks you to enter an ASCII code value (such as 66) and prints out the character having that ASCII code.

3. Write a program that sounds the alert and then prints the following text:

```
Startled by the sudden sound, Sally shouted, "By the Great
Pumpkin, what was that!"
```

4. Write a program that reads in a floating-point number, then prints it in decimal-point notation, then in exponential notation. Have the output use the following format:

```
The input is 21.290000 or 2.129000e+001.
```

5. There are approximately 3.156×10^7 seconds in a year. Write a program that requests your age in years and then displays the equivalent number of seconds.

6. The mass of a single molecule of water is about 3.0×10^{-23} grams. A quart of water is about 950 grams. Write a program that requests an amount of water, in quarts, and displays the number of water molecules in that amount.

4

Character Strings and Formatted Input/Output

Objectives

Understanding the character string

Writing character strings

How strings are stored

Using an array to hold a string

Using the **strlen( )** function

Using **scanf( )** to read in a string

Learning the preprocessor **#define** directive

Using **printf( )** and **scanf( )** conversion specifications

Fine-tuning output formats

Creating variable-width formats

Skipping over input

*I*n this chapter we concentrate on input and output. Programs are more interesting when they can deal with text, so we begin our study of character strings and how to handle them interactively. We also take a more detailed look at **printf( )** and **scanf( )**. These two important C I/O functions give you the tools to communicate with a C program and to format output to meet your needs and tastes. We also discuss the C preprocessor, an important C facility, and learn how to define and use symbolic constants.

4.1 Introductory Program

Listing 4.1 presents a program that engages in a dialogue with the user.

❖ *talkback.c*

Listing 4.1

```
/* talkback.c--nosy, informative program */
#include <stdio.h>
#define DENSITY 62.4 /* human density in lbs per cu ft */
main()
{
   float weight, volume;
   int size, letters;
   char name[40];

   printf("Hi! What's your first name?\n");
   scanf("%s", name);
   printf("%s, what's your weight in pounds?\n", name);
   scanf("%f", &weight);
   size = sizeof name;
   letters = strlen(name);
   volume = weight/DENSITY;
   printf("Well, %s, your volume is %2.2f cubic feet.\n",
      name, volume);
   printf("Also, your first name has %d letters,\n",
      letters);
   printf("and we have %d bytes to store it in.\n",  size);
}
```

Running the program produces results such as the following:

```
Hi! What's your first name?
Angelica
Angelica, what's your weight in pounds?
102.5
Well, Angelica, your volume is 1.64 cubic feet.
Also, your first name has 8 letters,
and we have 40 bytes to store it in.
```

The following are the main new features of this program (the terms used are defined and described throughout this chapter).

1. We have used an array to hold a character string, in this case, someone's name.

2. We used the **%s** conversion specification to handle the input and output of the string. Note that **name**, unlike **weight**, does not use the **&** prefix when used with **scanf( )**. (As we will see later, both **&weight** and **name** are addresses.)

3. We used the C preprocessor to define the symbolic constant **DENSITY**.

4. We used the C function **strlen( )** to find the length of a string.

The C approach may seem a little complex compared to the input/output modes of, say, BASIC. However, this complexity buys a finer control of I/O and greater program efficiency.

4.2 Character Strings—An Introduction

A *character string* is a series of one or more characters, for example:

```
"Zing went the strings of my heart!"
```

The double quotation marks are not part of the string. They are there to mark off the string, just as single quotation marks are used to mark off a character.

Type char Arrays and the Null Character

C has no special variable type for strings. Instead, strings are stored in an *array* of **char** type. More exactly, an array is an ordered sequence of data elements of one type. Therefore, you can think of the characters in a string as being stored in adjacent memory cells, one character per cell. See Figure 4.1.

Note in the figure that we show the character **\0** in the last array position. This character is the *null character,* and C uses it to mark the end of a string. The null character is not

Figure 4.1

A string in an array

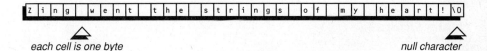

each cell is one byte   null character

the digit zero; it is the nonprinting character whose ASCII code number is 0. Strings in C are always stored with this terminating null character. The presence of the null character means that the array must have at least one more cell than the number of characters to be stored.

We can think of an array as several memory cells in a row. In Listing 4.1, we create an array of 40 memory cells, each of which can store one **char**-type value. We accomplish this array with the declaration:

```
char name [40];
```

The brackets identify **name** as an array, **[40]** indicates the number of elements in the array, and **char** identifies the type of each element. Also see Figure 4.2

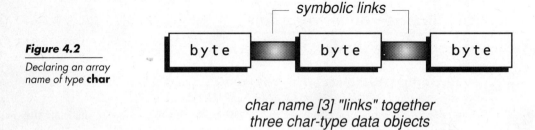

Figure 4.2

Declaring an array name of type **char**

char name [3] "links" together three char-type data objects

One compiler we've used in the past required the following declaration instead:

```
static char name[40];
```

Here **static** is a *storage class specifier* (discussed in Chapter 14). The difference between the two declarations was due to a bug in the **scanf( )** function for the second implementation. That bug has since been fixed, but we mention this difference to point out that there may be discrepancies between C as we describe it and C as it exists on your system.

Using Strings

Using character strings may sound a bit complicated, but fortunately the computer can take care of most of the details itself. Try the program in Listing 4.2 to see how easily using strings can be in practice:

The **%s** tells **printf( )** to print a string. We use **%s** twice because we print two strings: the one stored in the name array and the one represented by **PRAISE**.

Listing 4.2

```
/* praise1.c--use an assortment of strings */
#include <stdio.h>
#define PRAISE "My sakes, that's a grand name!"
main()
{
    char name[50];

    printf("What's your name?\n");
    scanf("%s", name);
    printf("Hello, %s. %s\n", name, PRAISE);
}
```

Running this program should produce output similar to the following:

```
What's your name?
Elmo Blunk
Hello, Elmo. My sakes, that's a grand name!
```

Note: We do not have to put the null character into the array **name** ourselves. That task is done for us by **scanf( )** when it reads the input. Nor do we include a null character in the character string constant **PRAISE**. We discuss the **#define** statement soon; but for now, you should know that the double quotation marks that enclose the phrase following **PRAISE** identify it as a string and take care of putting in the null character.

Note: **Scanf( )** reads only Elmo Blunk's first name. After this function starts to read input, it stops at the first *whitespace* (blank, tab, or newline) it encounters. Thus, it stops scanning for **name** when it reaches the blank between "Elmo" and "Blunk." In general, **scanf( )** used with **%s** reads just single words, not whole phrases as a string. C has other input-reading functions such as **gets( )** for handling general strings. We explore strings more fully later in Chapter 11.

Strings Versus Characters

The string **"x"** is not the same as the character **'x'**. One difference is that **'x'** is a basic type (**char**), and **"x"** is a derived type, an array of **char**. A second difference is that **"x"** consists of two characters: **'x'** and the null character. See Figure 4.3 for the differences.

String Length — strlen( )

In the last chapter we described the **sizeof** operator, which gives us the size of things in bytes. The **strlen( )** function gives us the length of a string in characters. Since it takes one byte to hold one character, you may suppose that both will provide the same result when applied to a string—but they don't. Let's add a few lines to our example and see why. (See Listing 4.3.) If you are using an ANSI C compiler, you should add the line:

```
#include <string.h>
```

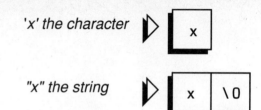

'x' the character

"x" the string

null character ends string

Figure 4.3

The character 'x' and the string "x"

after the first **#include** line. Although not necessary, this addition will make the program more harmonious with the ANSI spirit. We discuss this file more fully in Chapter 12.

❖ *praise2.c*

```
/* praise2.c */
#include <stdio.h>
#define PRAISE "My sakes, that's a grand name!"
main()
{
   char name[50];

   printf("What's your name?\n");
   scanf("%s", name);
   printf("Hello, %s. %s\n", name, PRAISE);
   printf("Your name of %d letters occupies %d memory cells.\n",
      strlen(name), sizeof name);
   printf("The phrase of praise has %d letters ",
      strlen(PRAISE));
   printf("and occupies %d memory cells.\n", sizeof  PRAISE);
}
```

Listing 4.3

Incidentally, note that we have used two methods to handle long **printf( )** statements. (Remember: we spread one print statement over two lines. We can break a line between arguments but not in the middle of a string.) Then we used two **printf( )** statements to print just one line. We accomplished this task by using the newline character (**\n**) only in the second statement. Running the program can produce this interchange:

```
What's your name?
Perky
Hello, Perky. My sakes, that's a grand name!
Your name of 5 letters occupies 50 memory cells.
The phrase of praise has 30 letters and occupies 31 memory cells.
```

The array **name** has 50 memory cells, which is what the **sizeof** operator reports to us. But only the first 5 cells are needed to hold **Perky**, which is what **strlen( )** reports. The 6th cell in the array **name** contains the null character, and its presence tells **strlen( )** when to stop counting. See Figure 4.4.

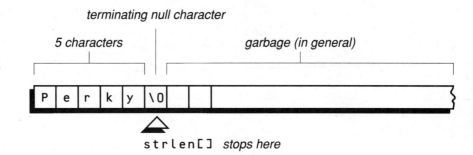

When we move on to the **PRAISE** statement, we find that **strlen( )** again gives us the exact number of characters (including spaces and punctuation) in the string. The **sizeof** operator gives us a number one larger, for it also counts the null character used to end the string. We don't tell the computer how much memory to set aside to store the phrase; it counts the number of characters between the double quotation marks itself.

One other point: In the preceding chapter we used **sizeof** with parentheses, and in this chapter we didn't. Whether or not you use parentheses depends on whether you want the size of a type class or the size of a particular quantity. Parentheses are required for type classes, but they are optional for specific quantities. That is, you use **sizeof(char)** or **sizeof(float)**, but **sizeof name** or **sizeof 6.28**.

In Listing 4.3, our use of **strlen( )** and **sizeof** was not crucial, although they are important programming tools. **Strlen( )**, for example, is useful in all sorts of character string programs, as we'll see in Chapter 11.

4.3 Constants and the C Preprocessor

Sometimes we need to use a constant in a program. For example, we can give the circumference of a circle as follows:

```
circ = 3.14 * diameter;
```

Here we use the constant **3.14** to represent the famous constant pi. To use a constant, we simply type in the actual value, as we did here. However, there are good reasons to use a *symbolic constant* instead. That is, we can use a statement like the following:

```
circ = pi * diameter;
```

and have the computer substitute in the actual value later.

Why is this method better? First, a name tells us more than a number does. Compare these two statements:

```
owed = 0.015 * housevl;
owed = taxrate * housevl;
```

If we are reading through a long program, the meaning of the second version is plainer.

Second, suppose we have used a constant in several places and it becomes necessary to change its value. After all, tax rates do change, and a state legislature once passed a law stating that the value of pi would henceforth be a simple 3 1/7. (Presumably many a circle became a fugitive from justice.) In this case, we need merely alter the definition of the symbolic constant rather than find and change every occurrence of the constant in the program.

How do we set up a symbolic constant? One way is to declare a variable and set it equal to the desired constant, for example:

```
float taxrate;
taxrate = 0.015;
```

This method works well for a small program, but it is a little wasteful because the computer has to check into the **taxrate** memory location every time it is used. It is an example of *execution time substitution,* for the substitutions take place while the program is running.

The C preprocessor provides a better method. In Chapter 2 we saw how the preprocessor uses **#include** to include information from another file. The preprocessor also lets us define constants. For example, all you have to do is add a line like the following at the top of the file containing your program:

```
#define TAXRATE 0.015
```

When your program is compiled, the value **0.015** is substituted everywhere you have used **TAXRATE**. This method is called a *compile time substitution*. By the time you run the program, all the substitutions already have been made. Such defined constants often are termed *manifest constants.*

Note the format. First comes **#define**. In older implementations, the # should be in the leftmost column; ANSI C removes this restriction. Next comes the symbolic name for the constant, then the value for the constant:

```
#define NAME value
```

No semicolon is used, since this is not a C statement. Also note that it is a sensible C tradition to type constants in all uppercase letters; for example **TAXRATE**. Then when you come across one in a program, you know at once that it is a constant and not a variable. This convention is another example of trying to make programs readable. Your programs will still run if you don't capitalize the constants, but capitalizing them is a good habit to cultivate.

Listing 4.4 provides a simple example. The **%1.2f** in the **printf( )** statement causes the printout to be rounded to two decimal places.

Listing 4.4

❖ *pizza.c*

```c
/* pizza.c--used defined constants in a pizza context */
#include <stdio.h>
#define PI 3.14159
main()
{
   float area, circum, radius;

   printf("What is the radius of your pizza?\n");
   scanf("%f", &radius);
   area = PI * radius * radius;
   circum = 2.0 * PI * radius;
   printf("Your basic pizza parameters are as follows:\n");
   printf("circumference = %1.2f, area = %1.2f\n", circum,
      area);
}
```

Here is a sample run:

```
What is the radius of your pizza?
6.0
Your basic pizza parameters are as follows:
circumference = 37.70, area = 113.10
```

See Figure 4.5 for the difference between what you type and what is compiled.

The **#define** statement can be used for both character and string constants: Use single quotation marks for the former and double quotation marks for the latter. Thus, the following examples are valid:

```c
#define BEEP '\007'
#define TEE 'T'
#define ESC '\033'
#define OOPS "Now you have done it!"
```

Remember that everything following the symbolic name is substituted for it. Don't make this common error:

```c
/* the following is wrong */
#define TOES = 20
```

If you do so, **TOES** is replaced by **= 20**, not just **20**.

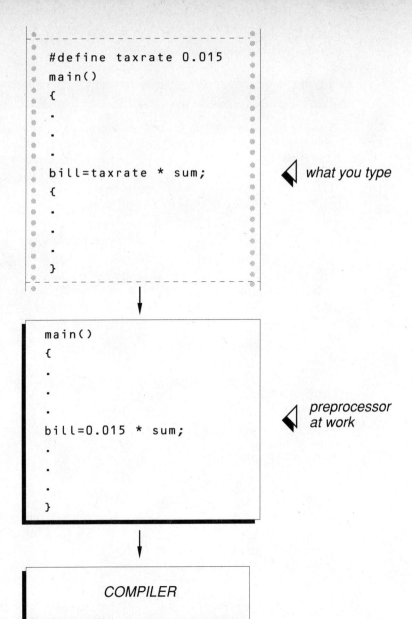

Figure 4.5

What you type versus what is compiled

```
#define taxrate 0.015
main()
{
    .

    .

    .

bill=taxrate * sum;
{
    .

    .

    .

}
```
◁ *what you type*

```
main()
{
    .
    .
    .

bill=0.015 * sum;
    .

    .

    .

}
```
◁ *preprocessor at work*

COMPILER

Using #define and #include *Together*

Suppose you develop a whole packet of programs that use the same set of constants. You can do the following:

1. Collect all your **#define** statements in one file; call it, say, **const.h**.

2. At the head of each file of programs, insert the statement **#include "const.h"**.

Then when you run the programs, the preprocessor will read the file **const.h** and use all the **#define** statements contained with it. The **.h** at the end of the filename is a reminder to you that the extra file is a header. The preprocessor itself doesn't care if you use this naming convention or not.

Note that we used **"const.h"** and not **<const.h>**. The difference lies in where the compiler first looks for the include file and is implementation dependent. On UNIX systems, placing the filename in angle brackets causes the preprocessor to look in specific system directories for the files. Placing the filename in quotation marks causes the preprocessor to look in the current directory first, then in the system directories. You can also specify a full pathname, as in **"/usr/tiger/myincludes/bar.h"**, in which case just the indicated directory (**/usr/tiger/myincludes**) is searched. Microsoft C and Turbo C follow similar conventions in the DOS environment. Microsoft C has you set an environmental variable called **INCLUDE** to the system directory you use for the standard include files, and Turbo C uses an environment menu to identify the standard include directory. For both programs, using angle brackets means to search the standard include directory first, and quotation marks mean to search the current directory first.

C—A Master of Disguise: Creating Aliases

The capabilities of **#define** go beyond the symbolic representation of constants. Consider, for instance, the program in Listing 4.5. This listing looks a little like Pascal, and it doesn't seem to be C. The secret is in the file **alias.h**:

```
/* alias.h--a silly abuse of preprocessing power */
#define program main( )
#define begin {
#define end }
#define then ;
#define takein scanf
#define spitout printf
#define TWO 2
#define times *
#define whole int
```

The example illustrates how the preprocessor works. Your program is searched for items defined by **#define** statements, and its finds are then replaced. In our example, all **thens** are rendered into semicolons at compilation. The resulting program is identical to

❖ *alias.c*

Listing 4.5

```
/* alias.c--uses alias.h */
#include <stdio.h>
#include "alias.h"/* see below for more on this file */
program
  begin
    whole yours, mine then
    spitout("Give me an integer, please.\n ") then
    takein("%d", &yours) then
    mine = yours times TWO then
    spitout("%d is twice your number!\n", mine) then
  end
```

what we would have received by typing in the usual C terms. (Note: This example is meant to be an entertaining illustration of how the preprocessor works; it is not intended to be a model to emulate.) This powerful defining facility also can be used to define a macro, which we discuss in Chapter 16.

The define feature does have limitations. For example, parts of a program within double quotation marks are immune to substitution. For instance, the following combination doesn't work:

```
#define MN "mimimifidianism"
printf("He was a strong believer in MN.\n");
```

The printout will read:

```
He was a strong believer in MN.
```

because **MN** is enclosed in double quotation marks in the **printf( )** statement. However, the statement:

```
printf("He was a strong believer in %s.\n", MN);
```

produces:

```
He was a strong believer in minimifidianism.
```

In this case, the **MN** was outside the double quotation marks and is therefore replaced by its definition.

The C preprocessor is a useful, helpful tool. We'll show you more applications as we move along.

4.4 Exploring and Exploiting printf( ) and scanf( )

The functions **printf( )** and **scanf( )** let us communicate with a program. We call these functions *input/output functions,* or *I/O functions.* They are not the only I/O functions we can use with C, but they are the most versatile. Historically, like all other functions in the C library, these functions were not part of the definition of C. C originally left the implementation of I/O to the compiler writers, which made it possible to match I/O better to specific machines. In the interests of compatibility, various implementations all came with versions of **scanf( )** and **printf( )**. However, there were occasional discrepancies between implementations. The ANSI C standard describes standard versions of these functions, and we follow that standard. The discrepancies should disappear as the standard is implemented. Generally, **printf( )** and **scanf( )** work much the same, each using a control string and a list of arguments.

The instructions we give **printf( )** when we ask it to print a variable depend on what type the variable is. For instance, we have used the **%d** notation when printing an integer and the **%c** notation when printing a character. These notations are called *conversion specifications,* for they specify how the data are to be converted into displayable form. We list the conversion specifications that the ANSI C standard provides for **printf( )**, and the type of output they cause to be printed in Table 4.1 (those in boldface did not appear in the first edition of Kernighan and Ritchie, and they are not yet commonly found in all implementations).

Table 4.1 ANSI C Conversion Specifications

Conversion Specification	Output
%c	Single character
%d	Signed decimal integer
%e	Floating-point number, e-notation
%E	Floating-point number, E-notation
%f	floating-point number, decimal notation
%g	Use %f or %e, whichever is shorter
%G	Use %f or %E, whichever is shorter
%i	Signed decimal integer
%o	Unsigned octal integer
%p	Pointer
%s	Character string
%u	Unsigned decimal integer
%x	Unsigned hexadecimal integer, using hex digits a–f
%X	Unsigned hexadecimal integer, using hex digits A–F

Using printf( )

Let's now show how to use the more common conversion specifications. Listing 4.6 contains a program that uses some of the examples we will discuss.

The output is the following:

```
The 5 women drank 13.500000 glasses of ouzo.
The value of pi is 3.141593.
Farewell! thou art too dear for my possessing,
$62000
```

The format for using **printf( )** follows:

```
printf(Control-string, item1, item2,...);
```

Listing 4.6

```
/* printout.c--use conversion specifiers */
#include <stdio.h>
#define PI 3.141593
main( )
{
  int number = 5;
  float ouzo = 13.5;
  int cost = 3100;

  printf("The %d women drank %f glasses of ouzo.\n",number,
     ouzo);
  printf("The value of pi is %f.\n", PI);
  printf("Farewell! Thou art too dear for my possessing,\n");
  printf("%c%d\n", '$', 2 * cost);
}
```

Item1, **item2**, and so on are the items to be printed. They can be variables, constants, or even expressions that are evaluated first before the value is printed. **Control-string** is a character string describing how the items are to be printed. As mentioned in Chapter 3, the control string should contain a conversion specifier for each item to be printed. For example, in the following statement:

```
printf("The %d women drank %f glasses of ouzo.\n", number, ouzo);
```

the control string is the phrase in double quotation marks. It contains two conversion specifiers that correspond to **number** and **ouzo**, which are the two items to be displayed. See Figure 4.6 for arguments for **printf( )**.

Figure 4.6

Arguments for
printf( )

Here is a another line from our example:

```
printf("The value of pi is %f.\n", PI);
```

This time, the list of items has just one member, the symbolic constant **PI**.

Therefore, we see that **control-string** contains two distinct forms of information:

1. Characters that are actually printed

2. Conversion specifications

See Figure 4.7 for control strings.

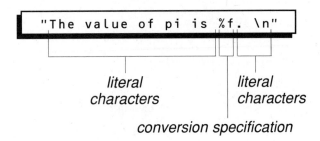

Figure 4.7

Anatomy of a control string

"The value of pi is %f. \n"

literal characters   *literal characters*

conversion specification

Also, don't forget to use one conversion specification for each item in the list following **control-string**. Don't do the following:

```
printf("The score was Squids %d, Slugs %d.\n", score1);
```

Here, there is no value for the second **%d**. The result will depend on your system, but at best you will get nonsense.

If you just want to print a phrase, you don't need any conversion specifications, and if you just want to print data, you can dispense with the running commentary. Thus, each of the following statements from Listing 4.6 is acceptable:

```
printf("Farewell! Thou art too dear for my possessing,\n");
printf("%c%d\n", '$', 2 * cost);
```

In the second statement, note that the first item on the print list is a character constant rather than a variable and that the second item is a multiplication. The statement illustrates that **printf( )** uses values, be they variables, constants, or expressions.

Since the **printf( )** function uses the % to identify the conversion specifications, there is a slight problem if you wish to print the % sign itself. If you use a lone % sign, the compiler will think you have bungled a conversion specification. The way out is simple. Just use two % symbols:

```
pc = 2*6;
printf("Only %d%% of Sally's gribbles were edible.\n", pc);
```

The following output then results:

```
Only 12% of Sally's gribbles were edible.
```

We can modify a basic conversion specification by inserting modifiers between the **%** and the defining conversion character. Tables 4.2 and 4.3 list the symbols you can place there legally. If you use more than one modifier, they should be in the same order as they appear in Table 4.2. Not all combinations are possible. The tables reflect the ANSI C standard; your implementation may not yet have all the options shown.

Table 4.2 Conversion Specification Modifiers

Modifier	Meaning
flag	The five flags (−, +, *space*, #, and **0**) are described in Table 4.3. Zero or more flags may be present. *Example:* **%-10d**
digit-string	The minimum field width. A wider field is used if the printed number or string won't fit in the field. *Example:* **%4d**
.digit-string	Precision. For **e**, **E**, and **f** conversions, the number of digits to be printed to the right of the decimal. For **g** and **G** conversions, the maximum number of significant digits. For **s** conversions, the maximum number of characters to be printed. For integer conversions, the minimum number of digits to appear; leading zeros are used if necessary to meet this minimum. Using **.** (period) alone is the same as using **.0**. *Example:* **%5.2f** (two decimal places in a field five characters wide)
h	Used with an integer conversion to indicate a **short int** or **unsigned short int** value. *Examples:* **%hu**, **%hx**, **%6.4hd**
l	Used with an integer conversion to indicate a **long int** or **unsigned long int**. *Examples:* **%ld**, **%8lu**
L	Used with a floating-point conversion to indicate a **long double value**. *Examples:* **%Lf**, **%10.4Le**

Table 4.3 Conversion Flags

Flag	Meaning
–	The item is left-justified; that is, it's printed beginning at the left of the field. *Example: %–20s*
+	Signed values are displayed with a plus sign if positive and with a minus sign if negative. *Example: %+6.2f*
space	Prepends a space to positive signed quantities when no plus sign is used; a space overrides a + flag. For instance, **printf("$% 6.2f",10)** prints as $ 10.00. *Example: % 6.2f*
#	Use an alternative form for the conversion specification. Produces an initial **0** for the **o** form, an initial **0x** or **0X** for the **x** and **X** forms. For all floating-point forms, guarantees a decimal point character is printed, even if no digits follow. For **g** and **G** forms, prevents trailing zeros from being removed. *Examples: %#o, %#8.0f, %+#10.3E*
0	For numeric forms, pad the field width with leading zeros instead of with spaces. This flag is ignored if a – flag is present or if, for an integer form, a precision is specified. *Examples: %010d, %08.3f*

One point you may notice in the tables is that although there are provisions for printing floating types **double** and **long double**, there is no specifier for **float**. The reason is that under K & R C, **float** values were automatically converted to type **double** before being used in an expression or as an argument. In general, ANSI C does not call for automatic conversion of **float** to **double**, but to protect the enormous number of existing programs that use **printf( )**, **float** arguments to **printf( )** are still automatically converted to **double**. Thus under either K & R C or ANSI C, no conversion specifier is needed for type **float**.

❖ *width.c*

Listing 4.7

```
/* width.c--field widths */
#include <stdio.h>
main( )
{
   printf("/%d/\n", 336);
   printf("/%2d/\n", 336);
   printf("/%10d/\n", 336);
   printf("/%-10d/\n", 336);
}
```

Examples

Let's put these modifiers to work. We begin by looking at the effect of the field width modifier on printing an integer. See Listing 4.7. This program prints the same quantity four times, using four different conversion specifications. We use a slash (/) to let you see where each field begins and ends.

The output follows:

```
/336/
/336/
/        336/
/336        /
```

The first conversion specification is **%d** with no modifiers, which is the so-called *default option,* that is, what occurs automatically if you don't give further instructions. Here we see that **%d** produces a field with the same width as the integer being printed. The second conversion specification is **%2d**, which should produce a field width of 2, but since the integer is three digits long, the field is automatically expanded to fit the number. The next conversion specification is **%10d**, which produces a field 10 spaces wide. Indeed, there are 7 blanks and 3 digits between the /'s, with the number tucked into the right end of the field. The final specification is **%-10d**. It also produces a field 10 spaces wide, and the − puts the number at the left end of the field. Once you are used to it, this system is easy to use and gives you nice control over the appearance of your output.

Now let's look at some floating-point formats. See Listing 4.8.

❖ *floats.c*

Listing 4.8

```
/* floats.c--some floating-point combinations */
#include <stdio.h>
main( )
{
  printf("/%f/\n", 1234.56);
  printf("/%e/\n", 1234.56);
  printf("/%4.2f/\n", 1234.56);
  printf("/%3.1f/\n", 1234.56);
  printf("/%10.3f/\n", 1234.56);
  printf("/%10.3e/\n", 1234.56);
  printf("/%+4.2f/\n", 1234.56);
  printf("/%010.2f/\n", 1234.56);
}
```

This time the output is as follows:

```
/1234.560000/
/1.234560e+003/
/1234.56/
```

```
/1234.6/
/ 1234.560/
/1.235e+003/
/+1234.56/
/0001234.56/
```

Again we begin with the default version, **%f**. In this case, there are two defaults: the field width and the digits to the right of the decimal. The second default is six digits, and the field width is whatever it takes to hold the number.

Next is the default for **%e**. We can see that it prints one digit to the left of the decimal point and six places to the right. We seem to be getting a lot of digits, and the cure is to specify the number of decimal places to the right of the decimal. The next four examples in this segment accomplish this task. Notice how the fourth and the sixth examples cause the output to be rounded off.

Finally, the + flag causes the result to be printed with its algebraic sign, which is a plus sign in this case. The **0** flag produces leading zeros to pad the result to the full field width. Note that in the specifier **%010** the first **0** is a flag and the remaining digits (**10**) specify the field width.

Listing 4.9 demonstrates a few more combinations.

❖ **flags.c**

Listing 4.9

```
/* flags.c--illustrates some flags */
#include <stdio.h>
main( )
{
   printf("%x %X %#x\n", 31, 31, 31);
   printf("**%d**% d**% d**\n", 42, 42, -42);
   printf("**%5d**%5.3d**%05d**%05.3d**\n", 6, 6, 6, 6);
}
```

On a system that conforms to the ANSI C standard, the output looks like the following:

```
1f 1F 0x1f
**42** 42**-42**
**    6**  006**00006**  006*
```

First, **1f** is the hex equivalent of 31. The **x** specifier yields a **1f**, and the **X** specifier produces **1F**. Using the # flag provides an initial **0x**.

The second line illustrates how using a space in the specifier produces a leading space for positive values but not for negative values. This result means that positive and negative values with the same number of significant digits occupy the same field widths.

The third line illustrates how using a precision specifier with an integer form produces enough leading zeros to pad the number to the minimum value of digits. Using the **0** flag, however, pads the number with enough leading zeros to fill the entire field width. If you provide both the **0** flag and the precision specifier, the **0** flag is ignored.

Let's now examine some of the string options. See Listing 4.10.

❖ *strings.c*

Listing 4.10

```
/* strings.c--string formatting */
#include <stdio.h>
#define BLURB "Outstanding acting!"
main()
{
  printf("/%2s/\n", BLURB);
  printf("/%22s/\n", BLURB);
  printf("/%22.5s/\n", BLURB)
  printf("/%-22.5s/\n", BLURB);
}
```

Here's the output:

```
/Outstanding acting!/
/ Outstanding acting!/
/                Outst/
/Outst                /
```

Notice how the field is expanded to contain all the specified characters. Also notice how the precision specification limits the number of characters printed. The **.5** in the format specifier tells **printf( )** to print just five characters.

Applying Our Knowledge

How would you set up a statement to print something having the following form?

```
The NAME family just may be $XXX.XX dollars richer!
```

Here **NAME** and **XXX.XX** represent values that will be supplied by variables in the program, say, **name[40]** and **cash**.

Here is one solution:

```
printf("The %s family just may be $%.2f richer!\n",name,cash);
```

The Meaning of Conversion

A conversion specification converts a value stored in the computer in some binary format to a series of characters (a string) to be displayed. For example, the number 76 may be stored internally as 01001100. The **%d** conversion specifier converts this internal number to **7** and **6**, displaying **76**. The **%x** conversion converts the same value (01001100) to the hexadecimal representation **4c**. The **%c** conversion converts the same value to the character representation **L**.

The term "conversion" probably is somewhat misleading, since it wrongly suggests the original value is replaced with a converted value. Conversion specifications really are translation specifications; for example, **%d** means translate the given value to a decimal integer representation and print the translation. Yet conversion is the term used in the literature, so we use it, too.

Mismatched Conversions

Naturally, you should match the conversion specification to the type of value being printed. Often, you have choices. For instance, if you want to print a type **int** value, you can use **%d**, **%x**, or **%o**. All these specifiers assume you are printing a type **int** value; they merely provide different representations of the value. Similarly, you can use **%f**, **%e**, or **%g** to represent a type **double** value.

But what if you mismatch the conversion specification to the type? Listing 4.11 shows some examples within the integer family.

Listing 4.11

❖ *intconv.c*

```
/* intconv.c--some mismatched integer conversions */
#include <stdio.h>
main()
{
   int num = 336;
   int mnum = -336;

   printf("%d %u %d %u\n", num, num, mnum, mnum);
   printf("%d %c\n", num, num);
   printf("%ld %d\n", 65616, 65616);
}
```

Our system produces the following results:

```
336 336 -336 65200
336 P
65616 80
```

Looking at the first line, we see that both **%d** and **%u** produce **336** as output, which presents no problem. But the **%u** (unsigned) version comes out as **65200**, not as the 336 you may have expected. This result occurs because of the way signed integers are represented on our reference system. This system uses a method called the *two's complement*, in which the numbers 0 to 32767 represent themselves, and the numbers 32768 to 65535 represent negative numbers, with 65535 being –1, 65534 being –2, and so on. Thus, **–366** is represented by 65536–336, or **65200**. Therefore **65200** represents **–336** when interpreted as a signed **int** and represents **65200** when interpreted as an **unsigned int**; one number can be interpreted as two different values. Not all systems use this method to represent negative integers. Nonetheless, don't expect a **%u** conversion simply to strip the sign from a number.

The second line shows what happens if you try to convert a number larger than 255 to a character. On our system, an **int** is two bytes, and a **char** is one byte. When **printf( )** goes to print **336** using **%c**, it looks at only one byte out of the two bytes used to hold **336**. This truncation amounts to dividing the integer by 256 and keeping just the remainder. See Figure 4.8. In this case, the remainder is 80, which is the ASCII decimal code for the character **P**. More technically, we can say the number is interpreted modulo 256, which means using the remainder when the number is divided by 256.

Finally, we tried printing an integer (**65616**) larger than the maximum **int** (32767) allowed on our system. This time, the computer interprets the number as modulo 32768. Because of its size, the number **65616** is stored as a four-byte **long** value on our system. When we print it using the **%d** specification, **printf( )** only uses the last two bytes, which corresponds to using the remainder after dividing by 65536. In this case, the remainder is **80**. A remainder between 32767 and 65536 would be printed as a negative number because of the way negative numbers are stored. Systems with different integer sizes have the same general behavior, but with different numerical values.

When you start mixing integer and floating-point types, the results are even more bizarre. Consider, for example, Listing 4.12.

❖ *floatcnv.c*

Listing 4.12

```
/* floatcnv.c--mismatched floating-point coversions */
#include <stdio.h>
main ()
{
    float n1 = 3.0;
    double n2 = 3.0;
    long n3 = 2000000000;
    long n4 = 1234567890;

    printf("%.1e %.1e %.1e %.1e\n", n1, n2, n3, n4);
    printf("%ld %ld\n", n3, n4);
    printf("%ld %ld %ld %ld\n", n1, n2, n3, n4);
}
```

On our system, it produces the following output:

```
3.0e+000 3.0e+000 3.1e+046 3.1e+046
2000000000 1234567890
0 1074266112 0 1074266112
```

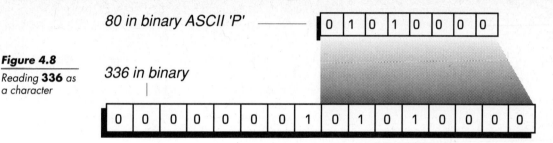

Figure 4.8

*Reading **336** as a character*

80 in binary ASCII 'P' ——— | 0 | 1 | 0 | 1 | 0 | 0 | 0 | 0 |

336 in binary

| 0 | 0 | 0 | 0 | 0 | 0 | 0 | 1 | 0 | 1 | 0 | 1 | 0 | 0 | 0 | 0 |

The first line of output shows that using a **%e** specifier does not convert an integer to a floating-point number. Consider, for example, what happens when we try to print **n3** (type **int**) using the **%e** specifier. First, the **%e** specifier causes **printf( )** to expect a type **double** value, which is an eight-byte value on our system. So when **printf( )** looks at **n3**, which is a four-byte value on our system, it also looks at the adjacent four bytes. Thus, it looks at an eight-byte unit in which the actual **n3** is embedded. Second, it interprets the bits in this unit as a floating-point number. Some bits, for example, are interpreted as an exponent. Thus even if **n3** had the correct number of bits, they would be interpreted differently under **%e** than under **%ld**. The net result is nonsense.

The first line also points out what we mentioned earlier: **Float** is converted to **double** when used as arguments to **printf( )**. On our system, **float** is four bytes, but **n1** was expanded to eight bytes so that **printf( )** would display it correctly.

The second line of output shows that **printf( )** can print **n3** and **n4** correctly if the correct specifier is used. The third line of output shows that even the correct specifier can produce false results if the **printf( )** statement has mismatches elsewhere. As you may expect, trying to print a floating-point value with a **%ld** specifier fails. But here, trying to print a type **long** using **%ld** also fails. The problem lies with how C passes information to a function. The exact details of this failure are implementation-dependent, but they are representative of what can go wrong. Let's take a look.

Passing Arguments

The mechanics of argument passing depend on the implementation. On our system, argument passing works in the following manner. We used the following function call.

```
printf("%ld %ld %ld %ld\n", n1, n2, n3, n4);
```

This tells the computer to give the values of the variables **n1**, **n2**, **n3**, and **n4** to the computer. The computer accomplishes this by placing them in an area of memory called the *stack*. When the computer puts these values in the stack, it's guided by the types of the variables, not by the conversion specifiers. So for **n1**, the computer places eight bytes in the stack (**float** is converted to **double**). Similarly, it places eight more bytes for **n2**, followed by four bytes each for **n3** and **n4**. Control then shifts to the **printf( )** function, which reads the values off the stack. But when it does so, it reads them according to the conversion specifiers. The **%ld** specifier indicates that **printf( )** should read four bytes. So **printf( )** reads the first four bytes in the stack as its first value, which is only the first half of **n1**, and this value is interpreted as a **long** integer. The next **%ld** specifier reads four more bytes, which is the second half of **n1**, and this value is interpreted as a second **long** integer. Similarly, the third and fourth instances of **%ld** cause the first and second halves of **n2** to be read and interpreted as **long** integers. Therefore, although we have the correct specifiers for **n3** and **n4**, **printf( )** is reading the wrong bytes.

The Return Value of printf( )

In general, a C function has a *return value,* which is a value the function computes and returns to the calling program. For example, the C library contains a **sqrt( )** function that takes a number as an argument and returns its square root. The return value can be assigned to a variable, used in a computation, passed as an argument, and so on. In other words, the return value can be used like any other value. The **printf( )** function also has a return value: It returns the number of characters it printed. If there is an output error, **printf( )** returns a negative value.

The return value for **printf( )** is incidental to its main purpose of printing output, and it usually isn't used. One reason to use the **printf( )** value is to check for output errors, although this task is more commonly performed when writing to a file rather than to a screen. For example, if a full floppy disk prevents writing from taking place, you can then have the program take some appropriate action, such as beeping for 30 seconds. But you first must know about using the If statement. Let's look at a simple example. See Listing 4.13.

❖ *prntval.c*

Listing 4.13

```
/* prntval.c--finding printf( )'s return value */
#include <stdio.h>
main()
{
   int n = 212;
   int rv;

   rv = printf("%d F is water's boiling point.\n", n);
   printf("The printf() function printed %d characters.\n",
          rv);
}
```

The output is as follows:

```
212 F is water's boiling point.
The printf() function printed 32 characters.
```

First, we use the form **rv = printf(...);** to assign the return value to **rv**. Therefore, this statement performs two tasks: printing information and assigning a value to a variable.

Second, note that the count includes all the printed characters, including the spaces and the unseen newline character.

Printing Long Strings

Occasionally, **printf( )** statements become too long to put on one line. Because C ignores whitespace (spaces, tabs, newlines) except when used to separate elements, you can spread a statement over several lines, as long as line breaks are placed between elements. For instance, in Listing 4.13, we use two lines for a statement:

```
printf("The printf() function printed %d characters.\n",
      rv);
```

As you can see, the line is broken between the comma element and **rv**. To show you that we are continuing the line, we indent the **rv**. Again, note that C ignores the extra spaces.

However, you cannot break a string in the middle. For example, if you use the following statement:

```
printf("The printf() function printed %d
        characters.\n", rv);
```

C will complain that you have used an illegal character in the string. You can use **\n** in a string to symbolize the newline character, but you can't have the actual newline character generated by the return key in a string.

If you must split a string, you have three choices, as shown in Listing 4.14.

❖ *longstrg.c*

Listing 4.14

```
/* longstrg.c--printing long strings */
#include <stdio.h>
main()
{
   printf("Here's one way to print a ");
   printf("long string.\n");
   printf("Here's another way to print a \
     long string.\n");
   printf("Here's the newest way to print a "
     "long string.\n");                     /* ANSI C */
}
```

The output follows:

```
Here's one way to print a long string.
Here's another way to print a long string.
Here's the newest way to print a long string.
```

The first method is to use more than one **printf( )** statement. Since the first string printed doesn't end with a **\n** character, the second string continues where the first ends.

The second method is to terminate the end of the first line with a backslash-return combination. This procedure causes the text on the screen to start a new line but without including a newline character in the string. The effect is to continue over the string to the next line. However, the next line must start at the far left, as shown in the example. If we indent that line, say, five spaces, then those five spaces become part of the string.

The third method, new with ANSI C, is *string concatenation*. If you follow one quoted string with another, separated only by whitespace, C treats the combination as a single string. The following three forms are therefore equivalent:

```
printf("Hello, young lovers, wherever you are.");
printf("Hello, young " "lovers", " wherever you are.");
printf("Hello, young lovers"
       ", wherever you are.");
```

Note: When using any of these methods to split a string, you should include any required spaces in the strings. For example, "Jim"   "Smith" becomes "JimSmith", but the combination "Jim ""Smith" is "Jim Smith".

Using scanf( )

Let's move from output to input and examine the **scanf( )** function. The C library contains several input functions, and **scanf( )** is the most general of them, for it can read a variety of formats. Of course, input from the keyboard is text because the keys generate text characters: letters, digits, and punctuation. When we desire to enter, say, the integer 2002, we type the characters **2**, **0**, **0**, and **2**. If we want to store those characters as a numerical value rather than as a string, our program has to convert the string input to a numerical value—which is the job of **scanf( )**. **Scanf( )** converts string input into various forms: integers, floating-point numbers, characters, and C strings. It's the inverse of **printf( )**, which converts integers, floating-point numbers, characters, and C strings to text to be displayed on the screen.

Like **printf( )**, **scanf( )** uses a control string followed by a list of arguments. The control string indicates into which formats the input is to be converted. The chief difference between these two functions is in the argument list. **Printf( )** uses variable names, constants, and expressions. **Scanf( )** uses pointers to variables. Fortunately, we don't have to know anything about pointers to use the function. Just remember these two rules:

1. If you wish to read in a value for one of the basic variable types discussed, precede the variable name with **&**.

2. If you wish to read in a value for a string variable, don't use **&**.

Listing 4.15 illustrates these rules.

```
/* input.c--when to use & */
#include <stdio.h>
main()
{
   int age;
   float assets;
   char pet[30];

   printf("Enter your age, assets, and favorite pet.\n");
   scanf("%d %f", &age, &assets); /* use the & here */
   scanf("%s", pet);               /* no & for char array */
   printf("%d $%.0f %s\n ", age, assets, pet);
}
```

Listing 4.15

The following is a sample exchange:

```
Enter your age, assets, and favorite pet.
82
8345245.19 rhino
82 $8345245 rhino
```

Scanf( ) uses whitespace (blanks, tabs, and spaces) to decide how to divide the input into separate fields. It matches up consecutive conversion specifications to consecutive fields, skipping over the whitespace in between. Note how we spread our input over two lines. We could just as well have used one or five lines, as long as we had at least one newline, space, or tab between each entry. The only exception to this rule is when using the **%c** specification, which reads the very next character, even if it is whitespace. We return to this topic shortly.

The **scanf( )** function uses pretty much the same set of conversion-specification characters as **printf( )** does. Table 4.4 lists the main conversion specifiers as described in ANSI C. You can also use modifiers in these conversion specifiers. These modifiers go between the percent sign and the conversion letter, and if you use more than one in a specifier, they should appear in the same order as shown in Table 4.5.

Table 4.4 ANSI C Conversion Specifiers for scanf( )

Conversion Specifier	Meaning
%c	Interpret input as a character
%d	Interpret input as a signed decimal integer
%e, %f, %g	Interpret input as a floating-point number
%E, %G	Interpret input as a floating-point number
%i	Interpret input as a signed decimal integer
%o	Interpret input as a signed octal integer
%p	Interpret input as a pointer

%s	Interpret input as a string; input begins with the first non-whitespace character and proceeds to the first whitespace character
%u	Interpret input as an unsigned decimal integer
%x, %X	Interpret input as a signed hexadecimal integer

Table 4.5 scanf( ) Conversion Modifiers

Modifier	Meaning
*	Suppress assignment (see rest of chapter for fuller description). *Example:* **%*d**
integer-string	The maximum field width. Input stops when the maximum field width is reached or when the first whitespace character is encountered, whichever comes first. *Example:* **%10s**
h, l, or **L**	**%hd** and **%hi** indicate the value will be stored in a **short int**. **%ho**, **%hx**, and **%hu** indicate the value will be stored in an **unsigned short int**. **%ld** and **%li** indicate the value will be stored in a **long**. **%lo**, **%lx**, and **%lu** indicate the value will be stored in **unsigned long**. **%le**, **%lf**, and **%lg** indicate the value will be stored in type **double**. Using **L** instead of **l** with **e**, **f**, and **g** indicates the value will be stored in type **long double**. In the absence of these modifiers, **d**, **i**, **o**, and **x** indicate type **int**; **e**, **f**, and **g** indicate type **float**.

As you can see, the use of conversion specifiers can become involved, and there are other features that we have omitted. Such features primarily facilitate reading selected data from highly formatted sources, such as punched cards or other data records. Since we use **scanf( )** here primarily as a convenient means for feeding data interactively to a program, we don't discuss these features.

The scanf( ) *View of Input*

Let's look in more detail at how **scanf( )** reads input. Suppose you use a **%d** specifier to read an integer. **Scanf( )** begins reading input one character at a time. As mentioned, it skips over whitespace characters (spaces, tabs, and newlines) until it finds a non-whitespace character. Because it is attempting to read an integer, **scanf( )** expects to find digit characters or, perhaps, a sign. If it finds a digit or a sign, it saves it and then reads the next character. If that next character is a digit, it saves it and reads the next character. **Scanf( )** continues reading and saving characters until it encounters a non-digit. It then concludes it has reached the end of the integer. **Scanf( )** then places the nondigit back into the input. This means the next time the program goes to read input, it will start at that character. Meanwhile, **scanf( )** computes the numerical value that corresponds to the digits it read and places that value in the specified variable. If you use a field width, **scanf( )** halts at the field end or at the first whitespace, whichever comes first.

What if the first non-whitespace character is, say, an **A** instead of a digit? Then **scanf( )** stops and places the character back into the input. No value is assigned to the specified variable, and the next time the program reads input, it begins at the **A** again. If all your program has are **%d** specifiers, **scanf( )** will never get past that **A**. Also, if you use a **scanf( )** statement with several specifiers, ANSI C requires the function to stop reading input at the first failure.

Reading input using the other numeric specifiers works much the same as the **%d** case. The main difference is that **scanf( )** may recognize more characters as being part of the number. For instance, the **%x** specifier requires that **scanf( )** recognize the hexadecimal digits **a–f** and **A–F**. Floating-point specifiers require **scanf( )** to recognize decimal points and E-notation.

If you use a **%s** specifier, any character other than whitespace is acceptable. So **scanf( )** skips whitespace to the first non-whitespace character, then saves up non-whitespace characters until encountering whitespace again. Therefore, **%s** results in **scanf( )** reading a single word, that is, a string with no whitespace in it. If you use a field width, **scanf( )** stops at the end of the field or at the first whitespace. You can't use the field width to make **scanf( )** read more than one word for one **%s** specifier. One final point: When **scanf( )** places the string in the designated array, it adds the terminal **'\0'** to convert the input to a C string.

If you use a **%c** specifier, all input characters are fair game. If the next input character is a space or a newline, then a space or a newline is assigned to the indicated variable; whitespace is not skipped. One subtle point: If **%c** is preceded by a space in the format string, **scanf( )** skips to the first non-whitespace character. Thus, the command **scanf(" %c", &ch)** reads the first character encountered in input, and **scanf(" %c", &ch)** reads the first non-whitespace character encountered.

Actually, **scanf( )** is not the most commonly used input function in C. It is featured here because of its versatility; it can read all the different data types. C has several other input functions such as **getchar( )** and **gets( )** that are better suited for specific tasks, for example, reading single characters or reading strings containing spaces. We cover some of these functions in Chapters 7, 11, and 12. In the meantime, if we need an integer or decimal fraction or a string, we can use **scanf( )**.

The scanf( ) Return Value

The **scanf( )** function returns the number of items it successfully reads. If it reads no items, which occurs if you type in a nonnumeric string when the function expects a number, then **scanf( )** returns the value 0. It returns **EOF** if it detects the condition known as *end of file*. EOF is a special value defined in the **stdio.h** file. Typically, a **#define** directive gives EOF the value -1. We discuss **EOF** in Chapter 6 and make use of the return value later in the book.

The * Modifier with printf( ) and scanf( )

Both **printf( )** and **scanf( )** can use * to modify the meaning of a specifier, but they do so in dissimilar fashions. First, we examine * with **printf( )**.

Suppose that you don't want to commit yourself to a field width in advance but that you want the program to specify it. You can accomplish this task by using * instead of a number for the field width, although you also have to use an argument to tell what the field width should be. That is, if you have the conversion specifier %*d, the argument list should include a value for * and a value for **d**. The technique also can be used with floating-point values to specify the precision as well as the field width. Listing 4.16 is a short example.

❖ *varwid.c*

```
/* varwid.c--uses variable-width output field */
#include <stdio.h>
main()
{
    unsigned width, precision;
    int number = 256;
    double weight = 242.5;

    printf("What field width?\n");
    scanf("%d", &width);
    printf("The number is :%*d:\n", width, number);
    printf("Now enter a width and a precision:\n");
    scanf("%d %d", &width, &precision);
    printf("Weight = %*.*f\n", width, precision, weight);
}
```

Listing 4.16

The variable **width** provides the **field width**, and **number** is the number to be printed. Because the * precedes the **d** in the specifier, **width** comes before **number** in the argument list. Similarly, **width** and **precision** provide the formatting information for printing **weight**. Here is a sample run:

```
What field width?
6
The number is : 256:
Now enter a width and a precision:
8 3
Weight = 242.500
```

In this run we answered the first question with 6, so that was the field width used. Similarly, our second reply produced a width of 8 with 3 digits to the right of the decimal. More generally, a program can decide on values for these variables after looking at the value of **weight**.

The * serves quite a different purpose for **scanf( )**. When placed between the % and the specifier letter, it causes that function to skip over corresponding input. Listing 4.17 provides an example. This **scanf( )** instruction says, "Skip two integers and copy the third into **n**."

Listing 4.17

```
/* skip2.c--skips over first two integers of input */
#include <stdio.h>
main()
{
   int n;

   printf("Please enter three integers:\n");
   scanf("%*d %*d %d", &n);
   printf("The last integer was %d\n", n);
}
```

Here is a sample run:

```
Please enter three integers:
445 345 1212
The last integer was 1212
```

This skipping facility is useful, for example, if a program needs to read just certain items from a file that has data arranged in a standard format.

4.5 Usage Tips

Specifying fixed field widths is useful when you want to print columns of data. Since the default field width is simply the width of the number, the repeated use of, for example:

```
printf("%d %d %d\n", val1, val2, val3);
```

produces ragged columns if the numbers in a column have different sizes. For example, the output may look like the following:

```
12 234 1222
4 5 23
22334 2322 10001
```

(This output assumes that the value of the variables has been changed between print statements.)

The output can be cleaned up using a sufficiently large fixed field width. For example:

```
printf("%9d %9d %9d\n", val1, val2, val3);
```

yields:

12	234	1222
4	5	23
22334	2322	10001

Leaving a blank between one conversion specification and the next ensures that one number will never run into the next, even if it overflows its own field. This situation occurs because the regular characters in the control string, including spaces, are printed out.

On the other hand, if a number is to be embedded in a phrase, it often is convenient to specify a field as small or smaller than the expected number width. This situation makes the number fit in without unnecessary blanks. For example:

```
printf("Count Beppo ran %.2f miles in 3 hours.\n", distance);
```

may produce:

```
Count Beppo ran 10.22 miles in 3 hours.
```

On the other hand, changing the conversion specification to **%10.2f** gives:

```
Count Beppo ran      10.22 miles in 3 hours.
```

4.6 Summary

A string is a series of characters treated as a unit. In C, strings are terminated by the null character, which is the character whose ASCII code is 0. Strings can be stored in character arrays. An array is a series of items, or elements, all of the same type. To declare an array called **name** and having 30 elements of type **char**, use:

```
char name[30];
```

Be sure to allot a number of elements sufficient to hold the entire string, including the null character. String constants are represented by enclosing the string in double quotation marks, for example: **"This is an example of a string."**

The **strlen( )** function can be used to find the length of a string (not counting the terminating null character). **Scanf( )**, when used with the **%s** specifier, can be used to read in single-word strings.

The C preprocessor searches a source code program for preprocessor directives, which begin with the # symbol, and acts on these directives before the program is compiled. The **#include** directive causes the processor to add the contents of another file to your file at the location of the directive. The **#define** directive lets you establish manifest constants, that is, symbolic representations for constants.

The **printf( )** and **scanf( )** functions provide versatile support for input and output. Each uses a control string containing embedded conversion specifiers that indicate the number and type of data items to be read or printed. Also, you can use the conversion specifiers to control the appearance of the output: field widths, decimal places, and placement within a field.

Review Questions

1. Run Listing 4.1 again, but this time give your first and last name when it asks you for your first name. What happens? Why?

2. Assuming that each of the following examples is part of a complete program, what will each one print?

a. `printf("He sold the painting for $%2.2f.\n", 2.345e2);`

b. `printf("%c%c%c\n", 'H', 105, '\41');`

c. `#define Q  His Hamlet was funny without being vulgar.`
   `printf("%s\nhas %d characters.\n", Q, strlen(Q));`

d. `printf("Is %2.2e the same as %2.2f?\n", 1201.0, 1201.0);`

3. In Question 2c, what changes can we make so that string **Q** is printed out enclosed in quotation marks?

4. Find the errors in the following program:

```
define B booboo
define X 10
main()
{
   int age;
   char name;

   printf("Please enter your first name.");
   scanf("%s", name)
   printf("All right, %c, what's your age?\n", name);
   scanf("%f", age);
   xp = age + X;
   printf("That's a %s! You must be at least %d.\n", B, xp);
}
```

5. Suppose a program starts like the following:

```
#define BOOK "War and Peace"
main()
{
float cost =12.99;
float percent = 80.0;
```

Now construct a **printf( )** statement that uses **BOOK** and **cost** to print the following:

```
This copy of "War and Peace" sells for $12.99.
That is 80% of list.
```

6. What conversion specification can you use to print each of the following?

  a. A decimal integer with a field width equal to the number of digits

  b. A hexadecimal integer in the form 8A in a field width of 4

  c. A floating-point number in the form 232.346 with a field width of 10

  d. A floating-point number in the form 2.33e+002 with a field width of 12

  e. A string that is left-justified in a field of width 30

7. What conversion specification can you use to print each of the following?

  a. An **unsigned long** integer in a field width of 15

  b. A hexadecimal integer in the form 0x8a in a field width of 4

  c. A floating-point number in the form 2.33E+002 that is left-justified in a field width of 12

  d. A floating-point number in the form +232.346 in a field width of 10

  e. The first eight characters of a string in a field eight characters wide

8. What conversion specification can you use to print each of the following?

  a. A decimal integer having a minimum of four digits in a field width of 6

  b. An octal integer in a field whose width will be given in the argument list

  c. A character in a field width of 2

  d. A floating-point number in the form +3.13 in a field width equal to the number of characters in the number

  e. The first five characters in a string that is left-justified in a field width of 7

9. For each of the following input lines, provide a **scanf( )** statement to read it. Also declare any variables or arrays used in the statement.

  a. **101**

  b. **22.3 28.34E-09**

  c. **Chelsea**

  d. **catch 22**

  e. **catch 22** (but skip over **catch**)

10. What is whitespace?

11. Suppose you would rather use parentheses than braces in your programs. How well do the following statements work?

```
#define ( {
#define ) }
```

Programming Exercises

1. Write a program that asks for your first name, then your last name, and then prints the names in the format last, first.

2. Write a program that requests your first name and does the following with it:

a. Prints it enclosed in double quotation marks

b. Prints it in a field 20 characters wide, with the entire in quotation marks.

c. Prints it at the left end of a field 20 characters wide, with the entire field enclosed in quotation marks.

d. Prints it in a field 3 characters wider than the name.

3. Write a program that reads in a floating-point number, then prints it in decimal-point notation, then in exponential notation. Have the output use the following formats:

a. `The input is 21.3 or 2.1e+001.`

b. `The input is +21.290 or 2.129E+001.`

4. Write a program that requests your height in inches and your name, and then displays the information in the following form:

`Dabney, you are 6.208 feet tall.`

Hint: Use type **float**, and use / for division.

5. Write a program that requests the user's first name and last name. Have it print the entered names on one line and the number of letters in each name on the following line. Have each letter count aligned with the end of the corresponding name, as in the following:

```
Melissa Honeybee
      7        8
```

Then have it print the same information, but with the counts aligned with the beginning of each name:

```
Melissa Honeybee
7       8
```

5

Operators, Expressions, and Statements

Contents

Objectives

Understanding what operators and operands are

Learning several basic operators

Understanding C expressions

Evaluating C expressions: operator precedence

Learning what a C statement is

Using a **while** loop

Forming a compound statement, or block

Learning about automatic type conversions

Using type casts

Defining a function that uses an argument

I n Chapters 3 and 4 we talked about the kinds of data that C recognizes and about data input/output. Now we look at ways to process the data. C offers many possibilities. We start with basic arithmetic: addition, subtraction, multiplication, and division. To make our programs more interesting and useful, we first look at loops.

5.1 Introducing Loops

Listing 5.1 calculates the length in inches of a foot that wears a men's size 9 shoe. The program uses multiplication and addition. It takes your shoe size (if you wear a size 9) and tells you how long your foot is in inches. You may say to yourself that you could solve this problem by hand more quickly than you could type the program. That's a

❖ shoes1.c

Listing 5.1

```
/* shoes1.c--converts a shoe size to inches */
#include <stdio.h>
#define OFFSET 7.64
#define SCALE 0.325
main()
{
   float shoe, foot;

   shoe = 9.0;
   foot = SCALE*shoe + OFFSET;
   printf("Shoe size (men's)      foot length\n");
   printf("%10.1f %15.2f inches\n", shoe, foot);
}
```

❖ shoe2.c

Listing 5.2

```
/* shoe2.c calculate foot lengths for several sizes */
#include <stdio.h>
#define OFFSET 7.64
#define SCALE 0.325
main()
{
   float shoe, foot;

   printf("Shoe Size (men's)    Foot Length\n");
   shoe = 3.0;
   while (shoe < 18.5)/* starting the while loop */
   {                  /* start of block */
     foot = SCALE*shoe + OFFSET;
     printf("%10.1f %15.2f inches\n", shoe, foot);
     shoe = shoe + 1.0;
   }                  /* end of block */
   printf("If the shoe fits, wear it.\n");
}
```

good point. It is a waste of time and effort to produce a one-shot program that calculates only one shoe size. We could make this program more useful by writing it as an interactive program, but that still barely taps the computer's potential.

What we need is some way to instruct the computer to perform repetitive calculations for a succession of shoe sizes. C offers several methods to accomplish this, and we outline one here. This approach, called a **while** loop, enables us to make a more interesting exploration of operators. Listing 5.2 presents our improved shoe-sizing program.

Here is a condensed version of the output:

```
Shoe Size (men's)     Foot Length
       3.0             8.61 inches
       4.0             8.94 inches
       ...             ...
       ...             ...
      17.0            13.16 inches
      18.0            13.49 inches
If the shoe fits, wear it.
```

(Incidentally, the constants for this conversion were obtained during an incognito visit to a shoe store. The only shoe-sizer left lying around was for men's sizes. Those of you interested in women's sizes will have to make your own visit to a shoe store.)

The following is how the **while** loop works. When the program first reaches the **while** statement, it checks to see if the condition within parentheses is true or not. In this case, the expression is the following:

```
shoe < 18.5
```

The < symbol means "less than." The variable **shoe** was initialized to **3.0**, which certainly is less than **18.5** — therefore the condition is true. In this case the program proceeds to the next statement, which converts the size to inches. Then it prints out the results. The set of braces ({ }) delimits the **while** loop. The statements between the two braces are the ones that may be repeated. The section of program between and including the braces is called a *block*. The next statement:

```
shoe = shoe + 1.0;
```

increases **shoe** by **1.0**, making it **4.0**. At this point the program returns to the **while** portion to check the condition because the closing brace (}) marks the end of the loop. The value **4** is less than **18.5**, so the **while** loop cycle is repeated. (In computerese, the program is said to *loop* through these statements.) This activity continues until **shoe** reaches a value of **19.0**, at which time the condition

```
shoe < 18.5
```

becomes false, since **19.0** is not less than **18.5**. When this situation occurs, control passes to the next statement following the **while** loop, in this case, the final **printf( )** statement.

You can modify this sample program to perform other conversions. For example, if you change **SCALE** to **1.8** and **OFFSET** to **32.0** and alter the printed message, you have a program that converts Centigrade to Fahrenheit. If you change **SCALE** to **0.6214** and **OFFSET** to **0** and alter the printed message, you convert kilometers to miles. And so on.

The **while** loop provides a convenient, flexible means of controlling a program. Let's now turn to the fundamental operators that we can use in our programs.

5.2 Fundamental Operators

C uses *operators* to represent arithmetic operations. For example, the + operator causes the two values flanking it to be added together. Let's look at operators you can use for basic arithmetic: =, +, −, *, and /. (Note: C does not have an exponentiating operator. In Chapter 9, we present a function to accomplish this task.)

Assignment Operator: =

In C, = does not mean "equals." Instead, it is a value-assigning operator and is called the *assignment operator*. The statement

```
bmw = 2002;
```

assigns the value **2002** to the variable named **bmw**. That is, the item to the left of the = sign is the *name* of a variable, and the item on the right is the *value* of the variable. Again, don't think of the line as saying, "**bmw** equals **2002**." Instead, read it as "assign the value **2002** to the variable **bmw**." The action reads from right to left for this operator.

Perhaps this distinction between the variable name and the variable value seems like hair-splitting, but consider the following common type of computer statement:

```
i = i + 1;
```

As mathematics, it makes no sense. If you add one to a finite number, the result isn't equal to the number you started with. But as a computer assignment statement, it is perfectly reasonable: "Find the value of the variable whose name is **i**; to that value, add **1**, then assign this new value to the variable whose name is **i**." See Figure 5.1.

A statement such as

```
2002 = bmw;
```

Figure 5.1

The statement
i = i + 1;

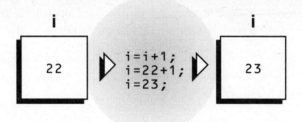

makes no sense in C because **2002** is just a number. You can't assign a value to a constant; it already *is* its value. Therefore, remember that the item to the left of an = must be the variable name. Actually, the lefthand side must refer to a storage location. The simplest method is to use the name of a variable, but as we discuss later, a "pointer" can be used to point to a location. More generally, ANSI C uses the term *modifiable lvalue* to label those entities to which you can assign values. "Modifiable lvalue" is not, perhaps, the most intuitive phrase you've encountered, so let's look at some definitions.

Some Terminology: Objects, Lvalues, and Operands

An *object* is a general term for a region of data storage that can be used to represent values. For instance, the data storage used to hold a variable or an array is an object. ANSI C uses the term *lvalue* to mean a name or expression that identifies a particular object. The name of a variable or an array, for instance, is an lvalue. Therefore, object refers to the actual data storage, and lvalue is a label used to identify, or locate, that storage.

Not all objects can have their values changed, so ANSI C uses the term *modifiable lvalue* to identify objects whose values can be changed. Thus, the lefthand side of an assignment operator should be a modifiable lvalue. Indeed, the *l* in *lvalue* comes from *l*eft, for modifiable lvalues can be used on the lefthand side of assignment operators.

❖ *golf.c*

Listing 5.3

```
/* golf.c--golf tournament score card */
#include <stdio.h>
main()
{
    int jane, tarzan, cheeta;

    cheeta = tarzan = jane = 68;
    printf("                    cheeta   tarzan   jane\n");
    printf("First round score %4d %8d %8d\n",cheeta,tarzan,
           jane);
}
```

The proper term for what we have called an "item" (as in "the item to the left of the =") is the *operand,* which are what operators operate on. For example, you can describe eating a hamburger as applying the "eat" operator to the "hamburger" operand. Or you can say the left operand of the = operator shall be a modifiable lvalue.

The basic C assignment operator is a little flashier than those of most other programming languages. Try the short program in Listing 5.3.

Many languages would balk at the triple assignment made in this program, but C accepts it routinely. The assignments are made right to left; first **jane** gets the value **68**, then **tarzan** does, and finally **cheeta** does. Thus, the output is the following:

```
                  cheeta   tarzan   jane
First round score   68       68      68
```

C has several other assignment operators that work differently from the one described here; we discuss these in Chapter 6.

Addition Operator: +

The *addition operator* (+) causes the two values on either side of it to be added together. For example, the following statement:

```
printf("%d", 4 + 20);
```

causes the number **24** to be printed, not the expression **4 + 20**.

The operands can be variables as well as constants. Thus, the statement:

```
income = salary + bribes;
```

causes the computer to look up the values of the two variables on the right, add them, and assign this total to the variable **income**. The + operator is termed a *binary* or *dyadic operator,* meaning that it takes two operands.

Subtraction Operator: –

The *subtraction operator* (–) causes the number after the – sign to be subtracted from the number before the sign. The following statement:

```
takehome = 224.00 - 24.00;
```

assigns the value **200.0** to **takehome**.

Sign Operators: – and +

The – sign is also used to indicate or change the algebraic sign of a value. For instance, the following sequence:

```
rocky = -12;
smokey = -rocky;
```

gives **smokey** the value **12**. When – is used in this manner, it is called a *unary operator,* meaning that it takes just one operand. See Figure 5.2.

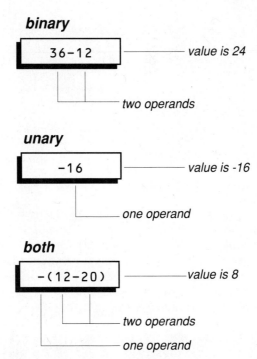

Figure 5.2

Unary and binary operators

The ANSI standard adds a unary + operator to C. It doesn't alter the value or sign of its operand; it simply lets you use statements such as the following:

```
dozen = +12;
```

without getting a compiler complaint. Formerly, this construction was not allowed.

Multiplication Operator: *

The *multiplication operator* is indicated by the * symbol. The statement

```
cm = 2.54 * in;
```

multiplies the variable **in** by **2.54** and assigns the answer to **cm**.

C doesn't have a squaring function, but as shown in Listing 5.4, we can use multiplication to calculate squares.

```
/* squares.c--produces a table of first 20 squares */
#include <stdio.h>
main ()
{
  int num = 1;

  while ( num < 21)
  {
    printf("%10d %10d\n", num, num * num);
    num = num + 1;
  }
}
```

Listing 5.4

This program prints out the first 20 integers and their squares, as you can verify for yourself.

Exponential Growth

You probably have heard the story of the powerful ruler who seeks to reward a scholar who has done him a great service. When the scholar is asked what he would like, he points to a chessboard and says, "Just one grain of wheat on the first square, two on the second, four on the third, eight on the next, and so on." The ruler, lacking mathematical erudition, is astounded at the modesty of this request, for he had been prepared to offer great riches. The joke, of course, is on the ruler, as the program in Listing 5.5 shows.

```
/* wheat.c--exponential growth */
#include <stdio.h>
#define SQUARES 64             /* squares on a checkerboard */
#define CROP 7E14              /* US wheat crop in grains */
main( )
{
  double current, total;
  int count = 1;

  printf("Square    Grains Added    Total Grains   ");
  printf("Fraction of \n");
  printf("                                        ");
  printf("US Total\n");
  total = current = 1.0;       /*start with one grain */
  printf("%4d %15.2e %13.2e %13.2e\n", count, current,
    total, total/CROP);
  while ( count < SQUARES )
  {
    count = count + 1;
    current = 2.0 * current; /*double grains on next square*/
```

Listing 5.5

**Listing 5.5
(cont'd.)**

```
        total = total + current; /* update total */
        printf("%4d %15.2e %13.2e %13.2e\n", count, current,
           total, total/CROP);
    }
}
```

This program calculates how many grains go on each square and keeps a running total. Since you may not be up-to-date on wheat crops, we also compare the running total to a rough estimate of the annual wheat crop in the United States.

The output begins innocuously enough:

Square	Grains Added	Total Grains	Fraction of US Total
1	1.00e+000	1.00e+000	1.43e-015
2	2.00e+000	3.00e+000	4.29e-015
3	4.00e+000	7.00e+000	1.00e-014
4	8.00e+000	1.50e+001	2.14e-014
5	1.60e+001	3.10e+001	4.43e-014
6	3.20e+001	6.30e+001	9.00e-014
7	6.40e+001	1.27e+002	1.81e-013
8	1.28e+002	2.55e+002	3.64e-013
9	2.56e+002	5.11e+002	7.30e-013
10	5.12e+002	1.02e+003	1.46e-012

After 10 squares, the scholar acquires just a little over a thousand grains of wheat. But look what happens by square 50:

50	5.63e+014	1.13e+015	1.61e+000

The haul has exceeded the total U.S. annual output! If you want to see what happens by the 64th square, you will have to run the program yourself. This example illustrates the phenomenon of exponential growth.

Division Operator: /

C uses the / symbol to represent the *division operator*. The value to the left of the / is divided by the value to the right, for example:

```
four = 12.0/3.0;
```

gives **four** the value of **4.0**. Division works differently for integer types than it does for floating-point types. Floating-point type division gives a floating-point answer; integer division yields an integer answer. An integer has to be a whole number, which makes dividing 5 by 3 awkward, since the answer isn't a whole number. In C, any fraction resulting from integer division is discarded. This process is called *truncation*.

❖ *divide.c*

Listing 5.6

```
/* divide.c--divisions we have known */
#include <stdio.h>
main()
{

   printf("Integer division: 5/4 is %d \n", 5/4);
   printf("Integer division: 6/3 is %d \n", 6/3);
   printf("Integer division: 7/4 is %d \n", 7/4);
   printf("Floating division: 7./4. is %1.2f \n", 7./4.);
   printf("Mixed division: 7./4 is %1.2f \n", 7./4);
}
```

Try the program in Listing 5.6 to see how truncation works and how integer division differs from floating-point division.

Note that we also include a case of "mixed types" by having a real number divided by an integer. C is a more forgiving language than some and will let you get away with this activity, although normally you should avoid mixing types. The results follow:

```
Integer division:      5/4 is 1
Integer division:      6/3 is 2
Integer division:      7/4 is 1
Floating division:     7./4. is 1.75
Mixed division:        7./4 is 1.75
```

Notice how integer division does not round to the nearest integer but always truncates. Also notice that when we mix integers with floating-point numbers, the answer is the same as the floating-point answer. When a calculation mixes both integer and floating-point types, the integer is converted to floating point before division.

The properties of integer division are quite handy for some problems. We present an example shortly; first we must discuss what happens when you combine more than one operation into one statement.

Operator Precedence

Consider the following line:

```
butter = 25.0 + 60.0 * n / SCALE;
```

This statement includes addition, multiplication, and division. Which operation takes place first? Is **25.0** added to **60.0**, the result of **85.0** then multiplied by **n**, and that result then divided by **SCALE**? Or is **60.0** multiplied by **n**, the result added to **25.0**, and that answer divided by **SCALE**? Or is it some other order? Let's take **n** to be **6.0** and **SCALE** to be **2.0**. If you work through the statement using these values, you find that the first approach yields a value of 255, and the second approach gives 192.5. A C program, on the other hand, gives a value of **205.0**.

Clearly the order of executing the various operations can make a difference, so C needs unambiguous rules for choosing which to perform first. Therefore, C assigns each operator a precedence level. Multiplication and division have a higher precedence than addition and subtraction, so they are performed first. If the operators of equal precedence share an operand, they are executed according to the order in which they occur in the statement. For most operators, the order is from left to right. (The = operator is an exception.) Therefore, in the statement:

```
butter = 25.0 + 60.0 * n / SCALE;
```

the order of operations is the following:

60.0 * n	The first * or / in the statement, then (assuming **n = 6** so that **60.0 * n = 360.0**)
360.0 / SCALE	The second * or / in the statement, and finally (since **SCALE = 2.0**)
25.0 + 180	The first + or − in the statement to yield **205.0**

Many people like to represent the order of evaluation with a type of diagram called an *expression tree*. Figure 5.3 is an example of such a diagram, and it shows how the original expression is reduced by steps to a single value.

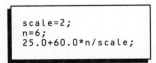

Figure 5.3

Expression trees showing operators, operands, and order of evaluation

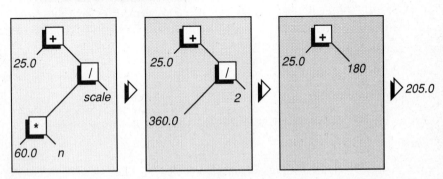

If you want, say, an addition to take place before a division, then you can modify the statement by adding parentheses:

```
flour = (25.0 + 60.0 * n) / SCALE;
```

Whatever is enclosed in parentheses is executed first. Within the parentheses, the general rules hold. For this example, the multiplication takes place first, then the addition. Only then is the result divided by **SCALE**.

Table 5.1 summarizes the rules for operators we've used so far. (Appendix B contains a table covering all operators.) Notice that the two uses of the minus sign have different precedences, as do the two uses of the plus sign. The associativity column tells us how an operator associates with its operands. For example, the unary minus sign associates with the quantity to its right, and in division the left operand is divided by the right.

Table 5.1 Operators in Order of Decreasing Precedence

Operators	Associativity
( )	Left to right
+, – (unary)	Left to right
*, /	Left to right
+, – (binary)	Left to right
=	Right to left

Precedence and the Order of Evaluation

Operator precedence provides vital rules for determining the order of evaluation in an expression, but it doesn't necessarily determine the complete order. C leaves some choices up to the implementor. Consider this statement:

```
y = 6 * 12 + 5 * 20;
```

Precedence tells us how to establish the order of evaluation when two operators share an operand. For example, the **12** is an operand for both the * and the + operators, and precedence tells us multiplication comes first. Similarly, precedence tells us that the **5** is to be multiplied, not added. In short, the multiplications **6 * 12** and **5 * 20** take place before any addition. What precedence does not establish is which of these two multiplications occurs first. C leaves that choice to the implementor, because one choice may be more efficient for one kind of hardware, and the other choice may work better on another kind of hardware. In either case, the expression reduces to **72 + 100**, so the choice doesn't affect the final value for this particular example.

"But," you say, "multiplication associates from left to right. Doesn't that mean the leftmost multiplication is performed first?" Let's discuss it. The association rule applies for operators that share an operand. For instance, in the expression **12 / 3 * 2** the / and * operators, which have the same precedence, share the operand **3**. Thus the left-to-right rule applies in this case, so the expression reduces to **4 * 2**, or **8**. (Going from right to left

gives **12 / 6**, or **2**. Here the choice does matter.) In the previous example, the two *****
operators did not share a common operand, so the left-to-right rule did not apply.

Trying the Rules

Let's try out these rules on a more complex example. See Listing 5.7.

❖ rules. c

Listing 5.7

```
/* rules. c--precedence test */
#include <stdio.h>
main()
{
    int top, score;
    top = score = -(2 + 5) * 6 + (4 + 3 * (2 + 3));
    printf("top = %d \n", top);
}
```

What value will this program print out? Figure it out, then run the program or read the
following description to check your answer.

First, parentheses have the highest precedence. Whether the parentheses in **–(2 + 5) * 6**
or in **(4 + 3 * (2 + 3))** are evaluated first depends on the implementation, as just
discussed. Either choice leads to the same result for this example, so let's take the left
one first. The high precedence of parentheses means for the subexpression **–(2 + 5) * 6**,
we evaluate **(2 + 5)** first, obtaining **7**. Next, we apply the unary minus operator to **7** to
obtain **–7**. The expression now reads as follows:

```
top = score = -7*6 + (4 + 3*(2 + 3))
```

The next step is to evaluate **2 + 3**. The expression then becomes:

```
top = score = -7*6 + (4 + 3*5)
```

Since ***** has priority over **+**, the next expression becomes the following:

```
top = score = -7*6 + (4 + 15)
```

and then:

```
top = score = -7*6 + 19
```

Multiply **–7** by **6**, and you get this expression:

```
top = score = -42 + 19
```

Addition makes it:

```
top = score = -23
```

Now **score** is assigned the value –23, and finally, **top** gets the value –23. Remember that the = operator associates from right to left.

5.3 Some Additional Operators

C has about 40 operators, but some are used much more than others. The ones just covered are the most common, and here we add four more useful operators to the list.

The sizeof Operator

We've used this operator already in Chapter 3. To review, **sizeof** returns the size, in bytes, of its operand. The operand can be a specific data object such as the name of a variable, or it can be a type. If it is a name type, the operand should be enclosed in parentheses. For instance, the example in Listing 5.8 shows both forms.

❖ *sizeof.c*

Listing 5.8

```
/* sizeof.c--size of operator */
#include <stdio.h>
main()
{
    int n;

    printf("n has %d bytes; all ints have %d bytes.\n",
        sizeof n, sizeof (int) );
}
```

Modulus Operator: %

The *modulus operator* (%) is used in integer arithmetic. It gives the remainder that results when the integer to its left is divided by the integer to its right. For example, **13 % 5** (read as "13 modulo 5") has the value **3**, since **5** goes into **13** twice, with a remainder of **3**. Note: This operator does not work with floating-point numbers.

At first glance, the % operator may strike you as an esoteric tool for mathematicians, but actually it is rather practical and helpful. One common use is to help you control the flow of a program. Suppose, for example, you are working on a bill-preparing program that is designed to add in an extra charge every third month. To accomplish this task, simply have the program evaluate the month number modulo 3 (that is, **month % 3**) and use an "if statement" (Chapter 9) to check to see if the result is 0. If so, add in the extra charge.

Listing 5.9 shows another use for %.

```
/* min_sec.c--converts seconds to minutes and seconds */
#include <stdio.h>
#define SEC_PER_MIN 60    /* seconds in a minute */
main()
{
   int sec, min, left;

   printf("Convert seconds to minutes and seconds!\n");
   printf("Enter number of seconds you wish to convert.\n");
   scanf("%d", &sec); /* number of seconds is read in */
   min = sec / SEC_PER_MIN;
                             /* truncated number of minutes */
   left = sec % SEC_PER_MIN;
                             /* number of seconds left over */
   printf("%d seconds is %d minutes, %d seconds.\n", sec,
      min, left);
}
```

Listing 5.9

Here is a sample output:

```
Convert seconds to minutes and seconds!
Enter number of seconds you wish to convert.
234
234 seconds is 3 minutes, 54 seconds.
```

One problem with this interactive program is that it processes just one input value. Can you figure out a way to have the program prompt you repeatedly for new input values? We return to this problem in this chapter's "Review Questions" (Question 4).

❖ *add_one.c*

```
/* add_one.c--incrementing: prefix and postfix */
#include <stdio.h>
main()
{
   int ultra = 0, super = 0;

   while (super < 5)
   {
      super++;
      ++ultra;
      printf("super = %d, ultra = %d \n", super, ultra);
   }
}
```

Listing 5.10

The *increment operator* (++) increments (increases) the value of its operand by one. The operator comes in two varieties: The ++ may come before the affected variable, which is the *prefix mode;* the ++ may come after the affected variable, which is the *postfix mode.* The two modes differ with regard to the precise time the incrementing takes place. We look at the similarities first and then return to the difference. The short example in Listing 5.10 shows how the increment operators work. A sample run produces the following:

```
super = 1, ultra = 1
super = 2, ultra = 2
super = 3, ultra = 3
super = 4, ultra = 4
super = 5, ultra = 5
```

In this program we count to 5 twice and simultaneously. We confess we could have achieved exactly the same results by replacing the two increment statements with the following:

```
super = super + 1;
ultra = ultra + 1;
```

These are simple enough statements. Why bother creating one, let alone two, abbreviations? One reason is that the compact form makes your programs neater and easier to follow. These operators give your programs an elegant gloss that cannot fail to please the eye. For instance, we can rewrite part of Listing 5.2:

```
shoe = 3.0;
while (shoe < 18.5)
{
   foot = SCALE*size + OFFSET;
   printf("%10.1f %20.2f inches\n", shoe, foot);
   ++shoe;
}
```

But we still haven't taken full advantage of the increment operator. We can shorten the fragment this way:

```
shoe = 2.0;
while (++shoe < 18.5)
{
   foot = SCALE*shoe + OFFSET;
   printf("%10.1f %20.2f inches\n", shoe, foot);
}
```

Here we have combined the incrementing process and the **while** comparison into one expression. This type of construction is so common in C that it merits a closer look. First, how does it work? Simply. The value of **shoe** is increased by one, then compared to **18.5**. If **shoe** is less than **18.5**, the statements between the braces are executed once. Then **shoe** is increased by one again, and the cycle is repeated until **shoe** exceeds **18.5**.

Note: We changed the initial value of **shoe** from **3.0** to **2.0** to compensate for **shoe** being incremented before the first evaluation of **foot**. See Figure 5.4.

The incrementing process also makes your programs more compact, and more important, it gathers in one place the two processes that control the loop. The first process is the test: do we continue or not? In this case, the test is checking to see if the shoe size is less than **18.5**. The second process changes an element of the test; in this case, the shoe size is increased.

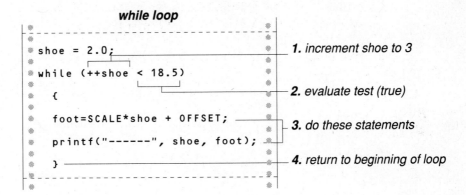

while loop

```
shoe = 2.0;
while (++shoe < 18.5)
    {
    foot=SCALE*shoe + OFFSET;
    printf("------", shoe, foot);
    }
```

1. *increment shoe to 3*

2. *evaluate test (true)*

3. *do these statements*

4. *return to beginning of loop*

Figure 5.4

Through the loop once

Now suppose we forget to change the shoe size. Then **shoe** is always less than **18.5**, and the loop never ends. The computer churns out line after identical line, caught in an infinite loop. Eventually, you will have to halt the program execution. Having the loop test and the loop change at one place instead of at separate locations makes it easier to remember to include a loop change.

Another advantage of the increment operator is that it usually produces slightly more efficient machine language code, since it is similar to actual machine language instructions. However, as implementers produce better C compilers, this advantage may disappear; a smart compiler will recognize that **x = x + 1** can be treated the same as **++x**.

Finally, the prefix and postfix increment operators have an additional feature. Try running the program in Listing 5.11.

❖ *post_pre.c*

Listing 5.11

```
/* post_pre.c--postfix vs prefix */
#include <stdio.h>
main()
{
    int a = 1, b = 1;
    int aplus, plusb;
    aplus = a++;                    /* postfix */
    plusb = ++b;                    /* prefix */
    printf("a    aplus  b    plusb \n");
    printf("%1d %5d %5d %5d\n", a, aplus, b, plusb);
}
```

You should get the following result:

a	aplus	b	plusb
2	1	2	2

Both **a** and **b** are increased by **1**, as promised. However, **aplus** has the value of **a** *before* **a** changed, and **plusb** has the value of **b** *after* **b** changed. The following is the difference between the prefix and the postfix forms:

```
aplus = a++; /* postfix: a changed after its value is used */
plusb = ++b; /* prefix: b changed before its value is used */
```

See Figure 5.5.

Figure 5.5

Prefix and postfix forms

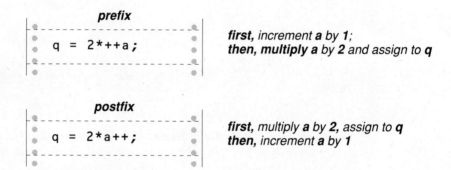

When one of the increment operators is used by itself, as in a solitary **ego++;** statement, it doesn't matter which form you use. The choice does matter, however, when the operator and its operand are part of a larger expression, as in the assignment statements just shown. In this kind of situation, you must give some thought to the result you want. For instance, recall our use of the following:

```
while (++shoe < 18.5)
```

This statement produced a table up to men's size 18 shoes. But if we had used **shoe++** instead of **++shoe**, the table would have gone to size 19, since **shoe** would be increased after the comparison instead of before. (Of course, you can always fall back on the less subtle **shoe = shoe + 1;** statement, but then no one will believe you are a true C programmer.) We suggest that you pay special attention to the examples of increment operators as you read through this book. Ask yourself if we could have used either one or if circumstances dictated a particular choice.

Counting Sheep

Do computers ever sleep? Listing 5.12 reveals what really goes on.

```
/* sheep.c--using the ++ operator in a loop */
#include <stdio.h>
#define MAX 40
main ()
{
  int count = 0;

  printf ("I count sheep to go to sleep.\n");
  while ( ++count < MAX )
    printf("%d million sheep and still not asleep...\n",
      count);
  printf("%d million sheep and zzzzzz....\n",count);
}
```

Listing 5.12

What would be the effect of replacing the prefix form of the increment operator with the postfix form? Note: When you have just one statement in a **while** loop, you don't need to enclose it in braces; with two or more statements, you need braces.

The Decrementing Operator: --

For each increment operator, there is a corresponding decrement operator. Instead of ++, we use --.

```
--count;   /* prefix form of decrement operator */
count --;  /* postfix form of decrement operator */
```

Listing 5.13 illustrates that computers can be accomplished lyricists. Note: The > operator stands for "is greater than." Like <, it is a "relational operator," which is described in Chapter 6.

❖ bottles.c

```
/* bottles.c--counting down */
#include <stdio.h>
#define MAX 100
main()
{
  int count = MAX + 1;

  while ( &count > 0) {
  printf(
    "%d bottles of beer on the wall, %d bottles of beer!\n",
    count, count);
  printf("Take one down and pass it around,\n");
  printf("%d bottles of beer!\n\n", count-1);
  }
}
```

Listing 5.13

The output begins as follows:

```
100 bottles of beer on the wall, 100 bottles of beer!
Take one down and pass it around,
99 bottles of beer!
```

```
99 bottles of beer on the wall, 99 bottles of beer!
Take one down and pass it around,
98 bottles of beer!
```

It ends this way:

```
1 bottles of beer on the wall, 1 bottles of beer!
Take one down and pass it around,
0 bottles of beer!
```

Apparently our program has a problem with plurals, but that can be fixed by using the conditional operator discussed in Chapter 7.

Precedence

The increment and decrement operators have a high precedence of association: Only parentheses are ranked higher. Thus, **x*y++** means **(x)*(y++)**, not **(x*y)++**. (This situation is fortunate because the latter statement is meaningless. The increment and decrement operators affect a variable (or more generally, a modifiable lvalue), and the combination **x*y** is not itself a variable, although its parts are.)

Don't confuse precedence of these two operators with the order of evaluation. Suppose we have the following:

```
y = 2;
n = 3;
nextnum = (y + n++)*6;
```

What value does **nextnum** have? Substituting in values yields the following:

```
nextnum = (2 + 3)*6 = 5*6 = 30
```

Only after **n** is used is it increased to **4**. Precedence tells us that the **++** is attached only to **n**, not to **2 + n**. It also tells us when the value of **n** is used for evaluating the expression, but the nature of the increment operator determines when the value of **n** is changed.

When **n++** is part of an expression, you can think of it as meaning "use **n**; then increment it." On the other hand, **++n** means "increment **n**; then use it."

You can get fooled if you try to do too much at once with the increment operators. For example, you may think that you can improve on our program to print integers and their squares (Listing 5.4) by replacing the **while** loop with this one:

```
while ( num < 21)
  {
  printf("%10d %10d\n", num, num*num++);
  }
```

In this case, we print the number **num**, multiply it by itself to get the square, and then increase **num** by one. In fact, this program may even work on some systems—but not all. The problem is that when **printf( )** retrieves the values for printing, it may evaluate the last argument first and increment **num** before getting to the other argument. Thus, instead of printing, say:

```
5        25
```

it may print:

```
6        25
```

C gives the compiler the freedom to choose which arguments in a function to evaluate first; this freedom increases compiler efficiency but can cause trouble if you use an increment operator on an argument.

Another possible source of trouble is a statement like the following:

```
ans = num/2 + 5*(1 + num++);
```

Again, the problem is that the compiler may not perform operations in the same order you have in mind. You may think that it will find **num/2** first, then move on. But it may find the last term first, increase **num**, and use the new value in **num/2**. There is no guarantee.

A third troublesome case is the following:

```
n = 3;
y = n++ + n++;
```

Certainly, **n** winds up larger by two after the statement is executed, but the value for **y** is ambiguous. A compiler can use the old value of **n** twice in evaluating **y**, then increment **n** twice. This procedure gives **y** the value **6** and gives **n** the value **5**. Or it can use the old value once, increment **n** once, use that value for the second **n** in the expression, then increment **n** a second time. This procedure gives **y** the value **7** and **n** the value **5**. Either choice is allowable.

It is easy enough to avoid these problems:

1. Don't use increment or decrement operators on a variable that is part of more than one argument of a function.

2. Don't use increment or decrement operators on a variable that appears more than once in an expression.

5.4 Expressions and Statements

We have been using the terms "expression" and "statement" throughout these first few chapters, and now the time has come to study their meanings more closely. Statements form the basic program steps of C, and most statements are constructed from expressions.

Expressions

An *expression* consists of a combination of operators and operands. (An operand, recall, is what an operator operates on.) The simplest expression is a lone operand, and you can build in complexity from there. Here are some expressions:

```
4
-6
4+21
a*(b + c/d)/20
q = 5*2
x = ++q % 3
q > 3
```

As you can see, the operands can be constants, variables, or combinations of the two. Some expressions are combinations of smaller expressions, which we can call *subexpressions*. For instance, **c/d** is a subexpression of the fourth example.

Every Expression Has a Value

An important property of C is that every C expression has a value. To find the value, we perform the operations in the order dictated by operator precedence. The value of the first few expressions is clear, but what about the ones with = signs? Those expressions simply have the same value that the variable to the left of the = sign receives. Thus, the expression **q = 5*2** has the value **10**. Such relational expressions as **q > 3** have the value **1** if true and **0** if false. Here are some expressions and their values:

Expression	Value
$-4 + 6$	2
$c = 3 + 8$	11
$5 > 3$	1
$6 + (c = 3 + 8)$	17

The last expression looks strange, but it is perfectly legal in C, for it is simply the sum of two subexpressions, each of which has a value.

Statements are the primary building blocks of a program. In other words, a *program* is a series of statements with punctuation. A statement is a complete instruction to the computer. In C, statements are concluded by a semicolon. Thus:

```
legs = 4
```

is an expression (which may be part of a larger expression). But

```
legs = 4;
```

is a statement.

A complete instruction concludes an action. The following expression:

```
2 + 2
```

is not a complete instruction. It tells the computer to add **2** and **2**, but it fails to tell the computer what to do with the answer. However, if we say:

```
kids = 2 + 2;
```

we are telling the computer to store the answer (**4**) in the memory location labeled **kids**. With the number **4** thus disposed of, the computer can move on to the next task.

Although a statement is a complete instruction, not all complete instructions are statements. Consider the following statement:

```
x = 6 + (y = 5);
```

In it, the subexpression **y = 5** is a complete instruction, but it is only part of the statement. Because a complete instruction is not necessarily a statement, a semicolon is needed to identify instructions that truly are statements.

So far we have encountered four kinds of statements. Listing 5.14 gives a short sample that uses all four.

Let's discuss the example. By now you are pretty familiar with the declaration statement. Nonetheless, we remember that it establishes the names and types of variables and causes memory locations to be set aside for them.

The assignment statement is the workhorse of most programs; it assigns a value to a variable. It consists of a variable name, followed by the assignment operator (=), followed by an expression, followed by a semicolon. Note that the **while** statement includes an assignment statement within it.

A function statement causes the function to do whatever it does. In our example, the **printf( )** function is invoked to print out some results.

Listing 5.14

```
/* addemup.c--four kinds of statements */
#include <stdio.h>
main()      /* finds sum of first 20 integers */
{
   int count, sum;               /* declaration statement */

   count = 0;                    /* assignment statement */
   sum = 0;                      /* ditto */
   while ( count++ < 20 )        /* while */
      sum = sum + count;         /* statement */
   printf("sum = %d\n", sum);    /* function statement */
}
```

A **while** statement has three distinct parts: (1) the keyword **while**, (2) a test condition in parentheses, and (3) the statement that is performed if the test is met. See Figure 5.6. Only one statement is included in the loop. It can be a simple statement, as in this example, in which case no braces are needed to mark it off. Or the statement can be a compound statement, like some of our earlier examples, in which case braces are required. We discuss compound statements in the next section.

The **while** statement belongs to a class of statements sometimes called *structured statements,* because they possess a structure more complex than that of a simple assignment statement. In later chapters we encounter many other kinds of structured statements.

Compound Statements (Blocks)

A *compound statement* is two or more statements grouped together by enclosing them in braces. It is also called a block, as was mentioned with regard to the **while** statement that

Figure 5.6

*Structure of a simple **while** loop*

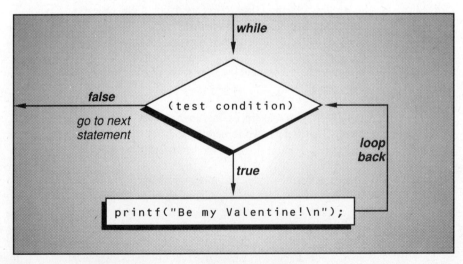

encompassed several statements in Listing 5.2. Compare the following program fragments:

```
/* fragment 1 */
index = 0;
while (index++ < 10 )
   sam = 10*index + 2;
printf ("sam = %d\n", sam);

/* fragment 2 */
index = 0;
while (index++ < 10 )
   {
   sam = 10*index + 2;
   printf ("sam = %d\n", sam);
   }
```

In fragment 1, only the assignment statement is included in the **while** loop. (In the absence of braces, a **while** statement runs from the **while** to the next semicolon.) The printout will occur just once, after the loop has been completed.

In fragment 2, the braces ensure that both statements are part of the **while** loop, and a printout is made each time the loop is executed. The entire compound statement is considered to be the single statement in terms of the structure of a **while** statement. See Figure 5.7.

Figure 5.7

While *loop with a compound statement*

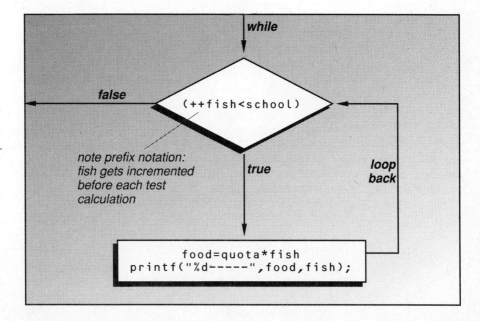

Look again at the two **while** fragments described in the section "Compound Statements (Blocks)" and notice how indentations mark off the body of the **while** loops. The indentation makes no difference to the compiler, which uses the braces and its knowledge of the structure of **while** loops to decide how to interpret our instructions. The indentation is there so that we can see at a glance how the program is organized.

We have shown one popular style for positioning the braces for a compound statement. Another common style is the following:

```
while (index++ < 10) {
    sam = 10*index + 2;
    printf("sam = %d \n", sam);
    }
```

This style highlights the attachment of the block to the **while** loop; the other style emphasizes that the statements form a block. Again, as far as the compiler is concerned, both forms are identical.

To sum up, use indentation as a tool to point out the structure of a program to the reader.

5.5 Type Conversions

Statements and expressions normally use variables and constants of just one type. If, however, you mix types, C doesn't complain the way, say, Pascal does. Instead, it uses a set of rules to make type conversions automatically. This can be a convenience, but it can also be a danger, especially if you are mixing types inadvertently. (The lint program found on many UNIX systems checks for type "clashes." Many non-UNIX C compilers report possible type problems if you select a higher "error level.") It is a good idea to have at least some knowledge of the type conversion rules:

1. When appearing in an expression, **char** and **short**, both signed and unsigned, automatically are converted to **int**, or if necessary, to **unsigned int**. (If **short** is the same size as **int**, then **unsigned short** is larger than **int**; in that case, **unsigned short** is converted to **unsigned int**.) Because these are conversions to larger types, they are called *promotions*.

2. In any operation involving two types, both values are converted to the "higher" ranking of the two types.

3. The ranking of types, from highest to lowest, is **long double**, **double**, **float**, **unsigned long**, **long**, **unsigned int**, and **int**. One possible exception is if **long** and **int** are the same size; in this case, **unsigned int** outranks **long**. The **short** and **char** types don't appear in this list because they would have already been promoted to **int** or perhaps **unsigned int**.

4. In an assignment statement, the final result of the calculations is converted to the type of variable that is being assigned a value. This process can result in promotion, as described in item 1, or *demotion,* in which a value is converted to a lower-ranking type.

> ## Summary: Expressions and Statements

Expressions. An expression is a combination of operators and operands. The simplest expression is a constant or a variable with no operator, such as **22** or **beebop**. More complex examples are **55 + 22** and **vap = 2 * (vip + (vup = 4))**.

Statements. A statement is a command to the computer. There are simple statements and compound statements. Simple statements terminate in a semicolon, such as:

Declaration statements: **int toes;**

Assignment statements: **toes = 12;**

Function call statements: **printf(" %d\n", toes);**

Control statements: **while (toes < 20)**
                        toes = toes + 2;

Null statement: **;**   **/* does nothing */**

Compound statements, or blocks, consist of one or more statements (which themselves can be compound) enclosed in braces. The following **while** statement contains an example:

```
while ( years < 100 )
  {
  wisdom = wisdom + 1;
  printf("%d %d\n", years, wisdom);
  years = years + 1;
  }
```

Promotion to higher-ranking type values usually is a smooth, uneventful process, but demotion can lead to trouble. The reason: The lower-ranking type may not be large enough to hold the complete number. For example, **char** variable can hold the integer **101** but not the integer **22334**. When floating-point types are demoted to integer types, they are truncated (rounded) toward zero; thus **23.12** and **23.99** are both truncated to **23** and **–23.5** is truncated to **–23**.

Listing 5.15 illustrates how these rules work.

```
/* convert.c automatic type conversions */
#include <stdio.h>
main()
{
    char ch;
    int i;
    float fl;

    fl = i = ch = 'A';              /* line 8 */
    printf("ch = %c, i = %d, fl = %2.2f\n", ch, i, fl);
    ch = ch + 1;                    /* line 10 */
    i = fl + 2*ch;                  /* line 11 */
    fl = 2.0*ch + i;                /* line 12 */
    printf("ch = %c, i = %d, fl = %2.2f\n", ch, i, fl);
    ch = 5212205.17;                /* line 14 */
    printf("Now ch = %c\n", ch);
}
```

Listing 5.15

The output follows:

```
ch = A, i = 65, fl = 65.00
ch = B, i = 197, fl = 329.00
Now ch = -
```

This is what happens on our system:

Lines 8 and 9: The character **'A'** is stored as a one-byte ASCII code in **ch**. The integer variable **i** receives the integer conversion of **'A'**, which is **65** stored as two bytes. Finally, **fl** receives the floating-point conversion of **65**, which is **65.00**.

Lines 10 and 13: The character variable **'A'** is converted to the integer **65**, which then is added to **1**. The resulting two-byte integer **66** is truncated to one byte and stored in **ch**. When printed using the **%c** specifier, **66** is interpreted as the ASCII code for **'B'**.

Lines 11 and 13: The value of **ch** is converted to a two-byte integer (**66**) for multiplication by **2**. The resulting integer (**132**) is converted to floating point to be added to **fl**. The result (**197.00**) is converted to **int** and stored in **i**.

Lines 12 and 13: The value of **ch** (**'B'**, or **66**) is converted to floating point for multiplication by **2.0**. The value of **i** (**197**) is converted to floating point for addition, and the result (**329.00**) is stored in **fl**.

Lines 14 and 15: Here we try a case of demotion, setting **ch** equal to a rather large number. After truncation takes place, **ch** winds up with the ASCII code for the hyphen character. One other promotion may take place: To preserve numerical accuracy, K & R C converts *all* **float** values to **double** when arithmetic calculations are performed. This conversion greatly reduces roundoff error. The final answer, of course, is converted back to **float** if the result is assigned to a **float** type. ANSI C drops this conversion as a requirement, but it doesn't prohibit it from taking place.

Usually it is best to steer clear of type conversions, especially of demotions. But sometimes it is convenient to make conversions, providing you exercise care in what you do. The type conversions we've discussed so far are done automatically. It is also possible for you to give instructions for the precise type conversion you want. The method is called a *cast,* and it consists of preceding the quantity with the name of the desired type in parentheses. The parentheses and type name together constitute a *cast operator.* The general form follows:

```
(type)
```

in which the actual type desired is substituted for the word *type.*

Consider the following two lines, in which **mice** is an int variable:

```
mice = 1.6 + 1.7;
mice = (int) 1.6 + (int) 1.7;
```

The first example uses automatic conversion. First, **1.6** and **1.7** are added to yield **3.3**. This number is then converted through truncation to the integer **3** to match the **int** variable. The second line contains two casts to type **int**. Here, **1.6** is converted to an integer (**1**) before addition, as is **1.7**, so that **mice** is assigned the value **1 + 1**, or **2**.

▶ Summary: Operating in C

Assignment Operator.

=   Assigns value at its right to the variable at its left.

Arithmetic Operators.

+   Adds value at its right to the value at its left.

−   Subtracts value at its right from the value at its left.

−   As a unary operator, changes the sign of the value at its right.

*   Multiplies value at its left by the value at its right.

/   Divides value at its left by the value at its right. Answer is truncated if both operands are integers.

%   Yields the remainder when the value at its left is divided by the value to its right (integers only).

++   Adds 1 to the value of the variable to its right (prefix mode) or of the variable to its left (postfix mode).

Miscellaneous Operators.

sizeof   Yields the size, in bytes, of the operand to its right. The operand can be a type specifier in parentheses, as in **sizeof (float)**, or it can be the name of a particular variable, array, and so on, as in sizeof foo.

(type)   Cast operator: converts following value to the type specified by the enclosed keyword(s). For example, **(float) 9** converts the integer **9** to the floating-point number **9.0**.

5.6 Function Arguments and Type Conversions

Automatic type conversions may also take place in the arguments to a function call. By default, type **char** and **short** values (signed or unsigned) are promoted to type **int** (or **unsigned int** if **int** is not large enough) when used as an argument. Similarly, **float** is promoted to **double**. The **char** and **short** promotions are the same as the promotions that occur when these types appear in expressions elsewhere. However, whereas the promotion of **float** to **double** is a general requirement under K & R C, it is required by ANSI C only when the **float** value is a function argument.

While we are discussing function arguments, let's preview how to write a function that uses an argument. (At this point, you may wish to review the **butler( )** function example near the end of Chapter 2; it shows how to write a function without an argument.) Listing 5.16 includes a **pound( )** function that prints a specified number of pound signs (#s). The example also illustrates some points about type conversion.

❖ *pound.c*

Listing 5.16

```
/* pound.c--defines a function with an argument */
#include <stdio.h>
main()
{
   int times = 5;
   char ch = '!';   /* ASCII code is 33 */
   float f = 6.0;

   pound(times);    /* int argument */
   pound(ch);       /* char automatically -> int */
   pound((int) f);  /* cast forces f -> int */
}
   pound(n)         /* old-style function header */
   int n;      /* says pound( ) takes one type int argument */
{
   while ( n-- > 0 )
     printf("#");
     printf("\n");
}
```

Running the program produces this output:

```
#####
###############################
######
```

First, let's examine the function heading:

```
pound(n)
int n;
```

If the function took no arguments, then the parentheses would be empty. Since the function takes one argument, we include one variable name: **n**. You can use any name consistent with C's naming rules. Next, on the following line, we declare the type of **n**. This declaration is like other declarations we've made, except it precedes the opening brace. Argument declarations come between the function name and opening brace.

Declaring an argument creates a variable called the *formal argument,* or the *formal parameter*. In this case, we've created a type **int** variable called **n**. Making a function call like **pound(10)** acts to assign the value **10** to **n**. Or in the case of our program, the call **pound(times)** serves to assign the **times** value of **5** to **n**. We say the function call passes a value, and this value is called the *actual argument,* or the *actual parameter*. Therefore the function call **pound(10)** passes the actual argument **10** to the function, where **10** is assigned to the formal argument. Variable names are private to the function, which means that a name defined in one function doesn't conflict with the same name defined elsewhere. For example, if we use **times** instead of **n** in **pound( )**, that creates a variable distinct from the **times** in **main( )**. That is, we may have two variables with the same name, and the program keeps track of which is which.

Let's look at the function calls. The first one is **pound(times)**, and as we said, it causes the **times** value of **5** to be assigned to **n**. This action causes the function to print five pound signs and a newline. The second call is **pound(ch)**. Here **ch** is type **char**. It is initialized to the **!** character, which on ASCII systems, means **ch** has the numerical value **33**. The automatic promotion of **char** to **int** on our system converts **!** from **33** stored in one byte to **33** stored in two bytes. So the value **33** now is in the correct form to be used as an argument to this function. The last call, **pound((int) f)**, uses a type cast to convert **f** to the proper type for this argument.

Suppose we omit the type cast. Then the default promotion converts **f** to type **double**. On our system, the function call then places an eight-byte value into the stack, a temporary storage area. Then the **pound( )** function, expecting type **int**, reads only two of those eight bytes. The result bears little resemblance to the original value. In short, using a **float** or **double** argument when a function expects type **int** does not lead to an automatic type conversion, which is why we use an explicit type cast to convert **f** to the proper type.

ANSI C introduces a new feature called *function prototyping* that can force automatic type conversions to take place when the types appearing in a function call don't match the function's argument types. ANSI C also provides an alternative form for declaring function variables. We discuss these points in Chapter 9.

5.7 An Example Program

Listing 5.17 illustrates several of the ideas in this chapter. It appears lengthy, but all the calculations are performed in six lines near the end. The bulk of the program relays information between the computer and the user. We've tried using enough comments to make it nearly self-explanatory.

❖ running.c

Listing 5.17

```
/* running.c--A useful program for runners */
#include <stdio.h>
#define S_PER_M  60         /* seconds in a minute */
#define S_PER_H  3600       /* seconds in an hour */
#define M_PER_K  0.62137    /* miles in a kilometer */
main()
{
  float distk, distm;   /* distance run in km and in miles */
  float rate;         /* average speed in mph */
  int min, sec;       /* minutes and seconds of running time */
  int time;           /* running time in seconds only */
  float mtime;        /* time in seconds for one mile */
  int mmin, msec;     /* minutes and seconds for one mile */

  printf(
    "This program converts your time for a metric race\n");
  printf(
    "to a time for running a mile and to your average\n");
  printf("speed in miles per hour.\n");
  printf("Please enter, in kilometers, the distance run.\n");
  scanf("%f", &distk);
  printf("Next enter the time in minutes and seconds.\n");
  printf("Begin by entering the minutes.\n");
  scanf("%d", &min);
  printf("Now enter the seconds.\n");
  scanf("%d", &sec);
  time = S_PER_M * min + sec;
                   /* converts time to pure seconds */
  distm = M_PER_K * distk;
                   /* converts kilometers to miles */
  rate = distm / time * S_PER_H;
                   /* miles per sec X sec per hour = mph */
  mtime = (float) time / distm;
    /* time/distance = time per mile */
  mmin = (int) mtime / S_PER_M; /* find whole
            minutes */
  msec = (int) mtime % S_PER_M; /* find remaining
            seconds */
  printf("You ran %1.2f km (%1.2f miles) in %d min, %d
    sec.\n",
  distk, distm, min, sec);
  printf("That pace corresponds to running a mile in %d min,"
        mmin);
  printf("%d sec.\nYour average speed was %1.2f mph.\n",msec,
        rate)
```

In this listing we utilize the same approach we used in Listing 5.9 to convert the final time to minutes and seconds, but this program also requires some type conversions. Why? Because we need integer arguments for the seconds-to-minutes part of the program, but the metric-to-mile conversion involves floating-point numbers. We have used the cast operator to make these conversions explicit.

Actually, it should be possible to write the program using just automatic conversions. In fact, we did so, using **mtime** of type **int** to force the time calculation to be converted to integer form. However, that version failed to run on one of the five systems that we tried. Using casts makes your intent clearer not only to the reader but perhaps to the compiler as well.

Here's a sample output:

```
This program converts your time for a metric race
to a time for running a mile and to your average
speed in miles per hour.
Please enter, in kilometers, the distance run.
10.0
Next enter the time in minutes and seconds.
Begin by entering the minutes.
36
Now enter the seconds.
23
You ran 10.00 km (6.21 miles) in 36 min, 23 sec.
That pace corresponds to running a mile in 5 min, 51 sec.
Your average speed was 10.25 mph.
```

5.8 Summary

C has many operators. In general, operators operate on one or more operands to produce a value. Operators that take one operand such as the − sign and **sizeof** are termed unary operators. Operators that require two operands such as + and * are called binary operators.

Expressions are combinations of operators and operands. In C, every expression has a value, including assignment expressions and comparison expressions. Rules of operator precedence help determine how terms are grouped when expressions are evaluated.

Statements are complete instructions to the computer and are indicated in C by a terminal semicolon. So far we have worked with declaration statements, assignment statements, function call statements, and control statements. Statements included with a pair of braces constitute a compound statement, or block. One particular control statement is the **while** loop, which repeats statements as long as a test condition remains true.

In C, many type conversions take place automatically. The **char** and **short** types are promoted to type **int** whenever they appear in expressions or as function arguments. The **float** type is promoted to type **double** when used as a function argument. Under K & R C (but not ANSI C), **float** also is promoted to **double** when used in an expression. When a value of one type is assigned to a variable of a second type, the value is converted to the same type as the variable. When larger types are converted to smaller types (**long** to **short** or **double** to **float**, for example), there may be a loss of data. In the case of mixed arithmetic, smaller types are converted to larger types following the rules outlined in this chapter.

When you define a function that takes an argument, you declare a variable, or formal argument, in the function definition. Then the value passed in a function call is assigned to this variable, which then can be used in the function.

Review Questions

1. Assume all variables are of type **int**. Find the value of each of the following variables:

    a. x = (2 + 3) * 6;

    b. x = (12 + 6)/2*3;

    c. y = x = (2 + 3)/4;

    d. y = 3 + 2*(x = 7/2);

2. Assume all variables are of type **int**. Find the value of each of the following variables:

    a. x = (**int**) 3.8 + 3.3;

    b. x = (2 + 3) * 10.5;

    c. x = 3 / 5 * 22.0;

    d. x = 22.0 * 3 / 5;

3. Fine the errors in the following program:

```
main( )
{
   int i = 1,
   float n;
   printf("Watch out! Here comes a bunch of fractions!\n");
   while (i < 30)
   n = 1/i;
   printf(" %f", n);
   printf("That's all, folks!\n");
}
```

4. Here's a first attempt at making Listing 5.9 interactive. The program is not satisfactory. Why not? How can it be improved?

```
#include <stdio.h>
#define S_TO_M 60
main( )
{
   int sec, min, left;

   printf("This program converts seconds to minutes and");
   printf("seconds.\n");
   printf("Just enter the number of seconds.\n");
   printf("Enter 0 to end the program.\n");
   while ( sec > 0 ) {
     scanf("%d", &sec);
     min = sec/S_TO_M;
     left = sec % S_TO_M;
     printf("%d sec is %d min, %d sec. \n", sec,
     min, left);
     printf("Next input?\n");
     }
   printf("Bye!\n");
}
```

5. What will this program print?

```
#include <stdio.h>
#define FORMAT "%s is a string\n"
main( )
{
   int num = 0;

   printf(FORMAT,FORMAT);
   printf("%d\n", ++num);
   printf("%d\n", num++);
   printf("%d\n", num--);
   printf("%d\n", num);
}
```

6. What will this program print?

```
#include <stdio.h>
main( )
{
   char c1, c2;
   int diff;
   float num;

   c1 = 'D';
   c2 = 'A';
   diff = c1 - c2;
   num = diff;
   printf("%c%c%c:%d %3.2f\n", c1, c2, c1, diff, num);
}
```

7. What will this program print?

```
#include <stdio.h>
#define TEN 10
main( )
{
   int n = 0;

   while (n++ < TEN)
   printf("%5d", n);
   printf("\n");
}
```

8. Modify the program in Question 7 so that it prints the letters **a** through **g** instead.

9. If the following fragments were part of a complete program, what would they print?

a.
```
int x = 0;

while ( ++x < 3 )
   printf("%4d", x);
```

b.
```
int x = 100;

while ( x++ < 103 )
   printf("%4d\n",x);
   printf("%4d\n",x);
```

c.
```
char ch = 's';
while (ch < 'w')
   {
   printf("%c", ch);
   ch++;
   }
printf("%c\n",ch);
```

10. What will the following program print?

```
#define MESG "COMPUTER BYTES DOG"
#include <stdio.h>
main( )
{
   int n = 0;

   while ( n < 5 )
   printf("%s\n", MESG);
   n++;
   printf("That's all.\n");
}
```

11. Construct statements that do the following:

a. Increase the variable **x** by 10

b. Increase the variable **x** by 1

c. Assign twice the sum of **a** and **b** to **c**

d. Assign **a** plus twice **b** to **c**

12. Construct statements that do the following:

a. Decrease the variable **x** by 1

b. Assign to **m** the remainder of **n** divided by **k**

c. Divide **q** by **b** minus **a** and assign the result to **p**

d. Assign to **x** the result of dividing the sum of **a** and **b** by the product of **c** and **d**

Programming Exercises

1. Use a **while** loop to convert time in minutes to time in hours and minutes. Use **#define** and a sensible method of ending the loop.

2. Write a program that asks for an integer and then prints out all the integers from (and including) that value up to (and including) a value larger by 10. (That is, if the input is 5, the output runs from 5 to 15.)

3. Write a program that asks you to enter the number of days and converts that value to weeks and days. For example, it must convert 18 days to 2 weeks, 4 days.

4. Review Listing 5.14, which found the sum of the first 20 integers. (If you prefer, you can think of it as a program that calculates how much money you get in 20 days if you receive $1 the first day, $2 the second day, $3 the third day, and so on.) Modify it so that you can tell it interactively how far the calculation should go; that is, replace the **20** with a variable that is read in.

5. Modify Listing 5.14 so that it computes the sum of the squares of the integers. (Or if you prefer, how much money you receive if you get $1 the first day, $4 the second day, $9 the third day, and so on.) C doesn't have a squaring function, but you can use the fact that the square of **n** is **n** * **n**.

6. Modify Listing 5.14 so that when it finishes a calculation, it asks you for a new limit so that it can repeat the process. Have the program terminate when you enter a **0**. (Hint: Use a loop within a loop. Also, see Review Question 4 and its answer.)

7. Write a program that requests a floating-point number and prints the value of the number cubed. Use a function of your own design to cube the value and print it. The **main( )** program should pass the entered value to this function.

6

C Control Statements: Looping

Objectives

Learning to use C's loop forms: **while, for**, and **do while**

Understanding the difference between entry-condition and exit-condition loops

Using the relational operators (<, >, >=, <=, !=, and ==) in relational expressions

Learning the other assignment operators: +=, −=, *=, /=, and %=

Using the comma operator

Knowing what an array is and how to declare one

Using the return value for **scanf**( ) to control an input loop

Defining and using a function with a return value

f you want to create powerful, intelligent, versatile, and useful programs, then you need a language that provides the three basic forms of program "flow" control. According to computer science, a good language should provide these three forms of program flow:

1. Executing a series of statements

2. Repeating a sequence of statements until some condition is met (looping)

3. Using a test to decide between alternative actions (branching)

You already know the first four; all our programs have consisted of a sequence of statements. The **while** loop is one example of the second form. We take a closer look at the **while** loop along with two other loop structures, the **for** and **do while** loops, in this chapter. The final form, choosing between different possible courses of action, makes a program much more "intelligent" and increases enormously the usefulness of a computer. We discuss this form in Chapter 7, although in this chapter we look at the varieties of relational expressions and operators that are used both with loop structures and branching structures. In this chapter, we also talk a bit about arrays, which are often used with loops. Finally, we take a first look at functions that return values.

6.1 An Initial Example

We have used the **while** loop a few times, but let us review it with a program that sums integers entered from the keyboard. See Listing 6.1. This example makes use of the **scanf( )** return value to terminate input.

❖ *summing.c*

Listing 6.1

```
/* summing.c--sum integers entered interactively */
#include <stdio.h>
main()
{
   long num;
   long sum = 0L;         /* initialize sum to zero */
   int status;

   printf("Please enter an integer to be summed. ");
   printf("Enter q to quit.\n");
   status = scanf("%ld", &num);
   while ( status == 1) /* == means "is equal to" */
   {
      sum = sum + num;
      printf("Please enter next integer to be summed. ");
      printf("Enter q to quit.\n");
      status = scanf("%ld", &num);
   }
   printf("Those integers sum to %ld.\n", sum);
}
```

We use type **long** to allow for larger numbers. For consistency, we initialize **sum** to **0L** (type **long** zero) rather than to **0** (type **int** zero), even though C's automatic conversions allow us to use a plain **0**. Here is a sample run:

```
Please enter an integer to be summed. Enter q to quit.
20
Please enter next integer to be summed. Enter q to quit.
5
Please enter next integer to be summed. Enter q to quit.
30
Please enter next integer to be summed. Enter q to quit.
q
Those integers sum to 55.
```

Program Comments

Let's look at the **while** loop in Listing 6.1. The test condition for this loop is the following expression:

```
status == 1
```

The == operator is C's equality operator; that is, this expression tests to see if **status** is equal to **1**. Don't confuse this expression with **status = 1**, which *assigns* **1** to **status**. With the **status == 1** test condition, the loop repeats as long as **status** is **1**. During each cycle, the loop adds the current value of **num** to **sum**, so that **sum** maintains a running total. Once **status** receives a value other than **1**, the loop terminates, and the program reports the final value of **sum**.

For the program to work properly, it should read a new value of **num** during each loop cycle, and it should reset **status** during each cycle. We accomplish this task by using two distinct features of **scanf( )**. First, we use **scanf( )** to attempt to read a new value for **num**. Second, we use the **scanf( )** return value to report on the success of that attempt. Recall that **scanf( )** returns the number of items successfully read. If **scanf( )** succeeds in reading an integer, it places the integer in **num** and returns the value **1**, which is assigned to **status**. (Note that the input value goes to **num**, not to **status**.) This action updates both **num** and the value of **status**, and the **while** loop goes through another cycle. If you respond with nonnumeric input, such as **q**, no items are read, so the return value and **status** are **0**, and the loop terminates.

This dual use of **scanf( )** gets around a troublesome aspect of interactive input to a loop: how to tell the loop when to stop. Suppose, for instance, that **scanf( )** does not have a return value. Then all that can change each loop is the value of **num**. In this case we can use the value of **num** to terminate the loop, using, say, **num > 0** (**num** greater than 0) or **num != 0** (**num** unequal to 0) as a test condition, but this prevents us from entering certain other values such as –3 or 0 as input. We can also add new code to the loop to instruct the program when to terminate, such as asking "Do you wish to continue? <y/n>" on each cycle and testing if the user enters a **y**. This method is a bit clunky and slows down input. Using the **scanf( )** return value avoids both of the preceding problems.

To return to the **while** loop in Listing 6.1, we insert a **scanf( )** before we get to the loop to obtain the input and check the value of **status** before we get to the body of the loop. But for the loop to continue, we have to insert a read statement inside the loop so that it can find out the **status** of the next input. Therefore, we also have a **scanf( )** statement at the end of the loop to ready the program for the next iteration.

> ### Pseudocode
>
> Let's take a closer look at the program structure in Listing 6.1. We can summarize it thus:
>
> *initialize sum to 0*
> *prompt user*
> *read input*
> **while** *the input is an integer,*
>   *add the input to sum,*
>   *prompt user,*
>   *then read next input*
>
> Such *pseudocode* is the art of expressing a program in simple English that parallels the forms of a computer language. Pseudocode is useful for working out program logic. Once the logic seems correct, you then can attend to the details of translating the pseudocode into the actual programming code. The advantage of pseudocode is that it lets you concentrate on the logic and organization of a program while sparing you the effort of simultaneously worrying about how to express the ideas in a computer language.

C–Style Reading Loop

The last example could be written in Pascal, BASIC, or FORTRAN using the same design displayed in the box "Pseudocode." C, however, offers a short-cut. The original construction looks like this:

```
status = scanf("%ld", &num);
while ( status == 1)
{
  /* loop actions */
  status = scanf("%ld", &num);
}
```

We can replace it with the following:

```
while ( scanf("%ld", &num) == 1)
{
  /* loop actions */
}
```

This form uses **scanf( )** in two different ways simultaneously. First, the function call, if successful, places a value in **num**. Second, the function's return value (which is 1 or 0 and not the value of **num**) controls the loop. Since the loop condition is tested during each iteration, **scanf( )** is called during each iteration, providing a new **num** and a new test.

6.2 The while *Statement*

Let's now take a more formal look at the **while** statement. The general form is the following:

while (*expression*)
   statement

Our examples so far have used *relational expressions* for the expression part; that is, *expression* has been a comparison of values. More generally, you can use any expression. The statement portion can be a simple statement with a terminating semicolon, or it can be a compound statement enclosed in braces. If *expression* is true (or more generally, nonzero), the statement is executed once, and then the expression is tested again. This cycle of test and execution is repeated until *expression* becomes false (or more generally, zero). Each cycle is called an *iteration*. See Figure 6.1.

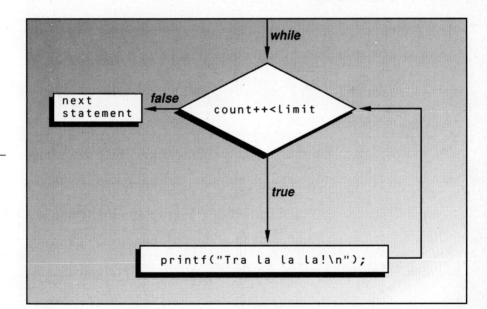

Figure 6.1

Structure of the **while** *loop*

Terminating a while *Loop*

Important note: When you construct a **while** loop, it must include something that changes the value of the test expression so that the expression eventually becomes false.

Otherwise, the loop will never terminate. (Actually, you can use the **break** and an **if** statement to terminate a loop, and we discuss these later in the text.) Consider this example:

```
index = 1;
  while ( index < 5 )
    printf("Good morning!\n");
```

This fragment prints its cheerful message indefinitely, for nothing in the loop changes the value of **index** from its initial value of **1**.

The following fragment isn't much better:

```
index = 1;
  while ( --index < 5 )
    printf("How are the old atoms vibrating!\n");
```

It changes the value of **index**, but in the wrong direction! At least this version will terminate eventually when **index** drops below the most negative number the system can handle.

When a Loop Terminates

It's important to realize that the decision to terminate or continue the loop takes place only at the time the test condition is evaluated. For instance, consider the program shown in Listing 6.2.

❖ *when.c*

Listing 6.2

```
/* when.c--when a loop quits */
#include <stdio.h>
main()
{
  int n = 5;

  while ( n < 7)                /* line 7 */
  {
    printf("n = %d\n", n);
    n++;                        /* line 10 */
    printf("Now n = %d\n", n);
  }
}
```

This produces the following output:

```
n = 5
Now n = 6
n = 6
Now n = 7
```

The variable **n** first assumes the value **7** on line 10 during the second cycle of the loop. But the program only quits the loop when the test condition on line 7 is evaluated for the third time. (The variable **n** was **5** on the first test and **6** on the second test.)

while: *An Entry–Condition Loop*

The **while** loop is a conditional loop using an entry condition. It is called a *conditional loop* because the execution of the statement portion depends on the condition we describe through the expression portion. Is **index** less than **5**? Is the last character read as **n**? The expression is an *entry condition* because the condition must be met before the body of the loop is entered. In a situation like the following, the body of the loop is never entered because the condition is already false:

```
index = 10;
   while ( index++ < 5 )
      printf("Have a fair day or better.\n");
```

If we change the first line to the following:

```
index = 3;
```

the loop will execute.

Syntax Points

Keep in mind when using the **while** loop that only the single statement, simple or compound, following the test condition is part of the loop. Indentation is an aid to the reader, not the computer. Listing 6.3 illustrates what can happen if you forget this important point.

❖ *while1.c*

Listing 6.3

```
/* while1.c--watch your braces */
#include <stdio.h>
main()
{
   int n = 0;

   while (n < 3 )
      printf("n is %d\n", n);
      n++;
   printf("That's all this program does\n");
}
```

Running this program produces the following output:

```
n is 0
n is 0
n is 0
n is 0
 ...
```

Although we indent the **n++;** statement, we didn't include it and the preceding statement in braces. So only the single statement immediately following the test condition is part of the loop. Thus **n** is never updated, the condition **n < 3** remains eternally true, and the loop prints **n is 0** until you kill the program. Listing 6.3 is an example of an *infinite loop,* which is one that does not quit without outside intervention.

Another point is that the **while** statement itself, even if it uses compound statements, counts syntactically as a single statement. The statement runs from the **while** to the first semicolon, or in the case of using a compound statement, to the terminating brace.

In addition, be careful where you place your semicolons. For instance, consider the program in Listing 6.4.

❖ *while2.c*

Listing 6.4

```
/* while2.c--watch your semicolons */
#include <stdio.h>
main()
{
    int n = 0;

    while (n++ < 3 );              /* line 7 */
        printf("n is %d\n", n);    /* line 8 */
    printf("That's all this program does.\n");
}
```

This program has the following output:

```
n is 4
That's all this program does.
```

As noted earlier, in the absence of a compound statement, the loop ends at the first semicolon. Since a semicolon immediately follows the test condition on line 7, the loop ends there; the print statement on line 8 is thus not part of the loop. Therefore, **n** is incremented each loop, but it's printed only after the loop is exited.

In this example, the test condition is followed by a lone semicolon, which represents the null statement. Occasionally, programmers use the **while** statement with a null statement either to create a time delay or because all the work is done in the test. For example, suppose you want to skip over input to the first character that isn't whitespace or a digit. You can use a loop like the following:

```
while ( scanf("%d", &num) == 1 )
    ;           /* skip integer input */
```

As long as **scanf( )** reads an integer, it returns **1**, and the loop continues. Note that in this example we put the semicolon on the following line instead of immediately after the test condition. This placement makes it easier to pick out when you read a program and also reminds you that it is there deliberately.

6.3 Which Is Bigger: Using Relational Operators and Expressions

While loops often rely on test expressions that make comparisons, which we have already termed relational expressions. The operators that appear in them are called *relational operators*. Table 6.1 lists all of the C relational operators.

Table 6.1 Relational Operators

Operator	Meaning
<	is less than
<=	is less than or equal to
==	is equal to
>=	is greater than or equal to
>	is greater than
!=	is not equal to

That pretty much covers all the possibilities for numerical relationships. (Numbers, even complex ones, are less complex than humans.) Caution: Do not use = for ==. Some computer languages (BASIC, for example) use the same symbol for the assignment operator as for the relational equality operator, but the two operations are quite different. As noted in Chapter 5, the assignment operator assigns a value to the lefthand variable. The relational equality operator, however, checks to see if the lefthand and righthand sides are already equal. It doesn't change the value of the lefthand variable, if one is present. For example, **canoes = 3** assigns the value **3** to **canoes**; **canoes == 5** checks to see if **canoes** has the value **5**. Also see Figure 6.2. Some care is needed, for a compiler will let you use the wrong form in some cases, yielding results other than what you expect. We show an example shortly.

The relational operators are used to form the relational expressions used in **while** statements and in other C statements we discuss later. These statements check to see if the expression is true or false. Here is a trio of examples:

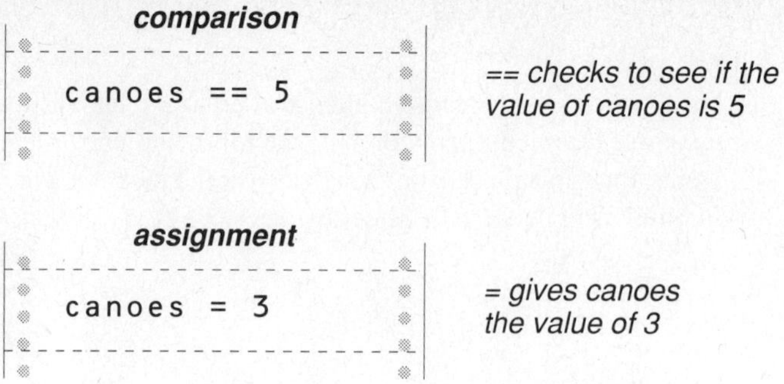

Figure 6.2

*The relational
operator == and
the assignment
operator =*

comparison

```
canoes == 5
```

*== checks to see if the
value of canoes is 5*

assignment

```
canoes = 3
```

*= gives canoes
the value of 3*

```
while ( number < 6)
{
    printf("Your number is too small.\n");
    scanf("%d", &number);
}

while ( ch != '$')
{
    count++;
    scanf("%c", &ch);
}

while ( scanf("%f", &num) == 1)
    sum = sum + num;
```

Note that the relational expressions can also be used with characters. The machine code (which we have been assuming is ASCII) is used for the comparison. However, you can't use relational operators to compare strings; in Chapter 11 we discuss how to handle strings.

The relational operators can be used with floating-point numbers, too. However, you should limit yourself to using only < and > in floating-point comparisons because roundoff errors can prevent two numbers from being equal even though logically they should be. Consider, for example, the following decimal system analog: Certainly the product of 3 and ⅓ is 1.0, but if we express ⅓ as a six-place decimal fraction, the product is .999999, which is not quite equal to 1.

What Is Truth?

Each relational expression is judged to be "true" or "false," which raises an interesting question. The answer, at least as far as C is concerned, is to recall that an expression in C always has a value. This situation is so even for relational expressions, as the example in Listing 6.5 shows. In it we assign the values of two relational expressions, one true and one false, to two variables. We assigned **true** as the value of a true expression, and **false** as the value of a false expression.

```
/* t_and_f.c--true and false values in C */
#include <stdio.h>
main()
{
   int true, false;

   true = ( 10 > 2);    /* value of a true relationship */
   false = ( 10 == 2); /* value of a false relationship */
   printf("true = %d; false = %d \n", true, false);
}
```

Listing 6.5

Running the program produces the following simple output:

```
true = 1; false = 0
```

Note: In C, a true expression has the value **1**; a false expression has the value **0**. Indeed, some C programs use the following construction:

```
while (1)
{
   ...
}
```

for loops meant to run forever.

So What Else Is True?

If we can use a **1** or a **0** as a **while** statement test expression, can we use other numbers? If so, what happens? Let's experiment by trying the program in Listing 6.6.

```
/* truth.c--what values are true? */
#include <stdio.h>
main()
{
   int n = 3;
   while ( n )
      printf("%d\n", n--);
   n = -3;
   while ( n )
      printf("%2d\n", n++);
}
```

Listing 6.6

The results follow:

```
3
2
1
-3
-2
-1
```

The first loop executes when **n** is **3**, **2**, and **1**, but it terminates when **n** is **0**. Similarly, the second loop executes when **n** is **–3**, **–2**, and **–1**, but it terminates when **n** is **0**. More generally, all nonzero values are regarded as "true," and only **0** is recognized as "false." C is quite tolerant of the notion of truth!

Alternatively, we can say a **while** loop executes as long as its test condition evaluates to nonzero values and that relational expressions evaluate to **1** if true and to **0** if false. This situation places test conditions on a numerical basis instead of a true/false basis.

Many programmers make use of this property of test conditions, for example:

```
while (goats != 0)
```

can be replaced by the following:

```
while (goats)
```

since the expression (**goats != 0**) and the expression (**goats**) both become **0** (false) only when **goats** has the value **0**. We think the second form is not as clear in meaning as the first, but many C programmers prefer the second form. The popular lore has been that the second form is more efficient, for it requires fewer processing operations for the computer when the program runs. But some compilers are clever enough to use the same efficient code for either form. The current tendency is to try for clear code and leave it to clever compilers to maximize the efficiency.

Troubles with Truth

C's tolerant notion of truth can lead to trouble. For example, let's make one small change in the program in Listing 6.1, producing the program in Listing 6.7.

```
/* trouble.c--misuse of = */
#include <stdio.h>
main()
{
  long num;
  long sum = OL;
  int status;

  printf("Please enter an integer to be summed. ");
  printf("Enter q to quit.\n");
  status = scanf("%ld", &num);
  while ( status = 1)
  {
    sum = sum + num;
    printf("Please enter next integer to be summed. ");
    printf("Enter q to quit.\n");
    status = scanf("%ld", &num);
  }
  printf("Those integers sum to %ld\n", sum);
}
```

Listing 6.7

Running this version produces output like the following:

```
Please enter an integer to be summed. Enter q to quit.
20
Please enter next integer to be summed. Enter q to quit.
5
Please enter next integer to be summed. Enter q to quit.
30
Please enter next integer to be summed. Enter q to quit.
q
Please enter next integer to be summed. Enter q to quit.
Please enter next integer to be summed. Enter q to quit.
Please enter next integer to be summed. Enter q to quit.
Please enter next integer to be summed. Enter q to quit.
...
```

The modification replaces **status == 1** with **status = 1**. The second statement is an assignment statement, so it gives **status** the value **1**. Furthermore, the value of an assignment statement is the value of the left side, so **status = 1** has the numerical value **1**. For all practical purposes, our **while** loop is the same as using **while(1)**; that is, it is a loop that never quits. We enter **q**, and **status** is set to **0**, although the loop test resets **status** to **1** and starts another cycle.

You may wonder why, since the program keeps looping, the user doesn't get a chance to type in any more input after entering **q**. When **scanf( )** fails to read the specified form of input, it leaves the nonconforming input in place to be read the next time. So when **scanf( )** tries to read the **q** as an integer and fails, it leaves the **q** there. During the next loop cycle, **scanf( )** attempts to read where it left off last time, which is at the q. Once again, **scanf( )** fails to read the **q** as an integer.

To sum up, the relational operators are used to form relational expressions. Relational expressions have the value **1** if true and **0** if false. Statements such as **while** and **if** that normally use relational expressions as tests can use any expression as a test, with nonzero values recognized as true and zero values recognized as false.

Precedence of Relational Operators

The precedence of the relational operators is lower than that of the arithmetic operators, including **+** and **−**, and greater than that of assignment. For example:

```
x > y + 2
```

means the same as the following:

```
x > (y + 2)
```

Also:

```
x = y > 2
```

means the following:

```
x = (y > 2)
```

That is, **x** is assigned **1** if **y** is greater than **2** and **0** otherwise; **x** is not assigned the value of **y**.

The relational operators are themselves organized into two different priorities. The higher-priority group are the following: **<**, **<=**, **>**, and **=>**. The lower-priority group are the following: **==** and **!=**.

Like most other operators, the relational operators associate from left to right. Thus:

```
ex != wye == zee
```

is the same as the following:

```
(ex != wye) == zee
```

First C checks to see if **ex** and **wye** are unequal. Then the resulting value of **1** or **0** (true or false) is compared to the value of **zee**. This sort of construction is uncommon, but it is good to know that it is possible in C. (Note: Appendix B contains a complete precedence ranking of all operators.)

Keyword: while

General comments. The **while** statement creates a loop that repeats until the test expression becomes false, or zero. It is an entry-condition loop, which means that the decision to go through one more pass of the loop is made before the loop is traversed. Thus, it is possible that the loop is never traversed. The statement part of the form can be a simple statement or a compound statement.

Form.

while (*expression*)
  statement

The *statement* portion is repeated until the *expression* becomes false, or zero.

Examples.

```
while ( n++ < 100 )
printf(" %d %d\n",n, 2*n+1 );

  while ( fargo < 1000 )
  {
  fargo = fargo + step;
  step = 2 * step;
  }
```

Relational operators. Each of these operators compares the value at its left to the value at its right:

<	Is less than
<=	Is less than or equal to
==	Is equal to
>=	Is greater than or equal to
>	Is greater than
!=	Is unequal to

Relational expressions. A simple relational expression consists of a relational operator with an operand on each side. If the relation is true, the relational expression has the value **1**. If the relation is false, the relational expression has the value **0**.

Examples.

      5 > 2 *is true and has the value* **1**
      (2 + a) == a *is false and has the value* **0**

6.4 Indefinite Loops and Counting Loops

Some of our **while** loop examples have been *indefinite loops,* which means that we don't know in advance how many times the loop will be executed before the expression becomes false. For instance, when we use an interactive loop to sum integers, we don't have prior knowledge of how many integers will be entered. Other of our examples have been *counting loops,* which means that they execute a predetermined number of repetitions. Listing 6.8 is a short example of a **while** counting loop.

❖ *sweetie1.c*

Listing 6.8

```
/* sweetie1.c--a counting loop */
#include <stdio.h>
#define NUMBER 22
main()
{
   int count = 1;                          /* initialization */

   while ( count <= NUMBER )               /* test */
   {
      printf("Be my Valentine!\n");        /* action */
      count++;                             /* increment count */
   }
}
```

Although this form works fine, it is not the best choice for this situation, since the actions defining the loop are not all gathered together. Let's elaborate on this point.

Three actions are involved in setting up a loop that is to be repeated a fixed number of times: A counter must be initialized; it must be compared with some limiting number; and it must be incremented each time the loop is traversed. In Listing 6.8, the initialization of the counter is performed outside the loop, which makes it possible to forget to initialize a counter. The **while** loop condition takes care of the comparison. And at the end of the loop, the increment operator takes care of the incrementing, which makes it

❖ *sweetie2.c*

Listing 6.9

```
/* sweetie2.c--a counting loop using for */
#include <stdio.h>
#define NUMBER 22
main()
{
   int count;

   for ( count = 1; count <= NUMBER; count++)
      printf("Be my Valentine!\n");
}
```

possible to omit the incrementing accidentally. It would be better to combine the test and update actions into one expression by using **count++ <= NUMBER**.

6.5 The for Loop

Let's look at a control statement that avoids these problems. The **for** loop gathers all three actions into one place. By using this construction, we can replace the preceding program with the one shown in Listing 6.9.

The parentheses following the keyword **for** contain three expressions separated by semicolons. The first expression is an initialization, and it is performed once, when the **for** loop first starts. The second expression is a test condition; it is evaluated before each potential execution of a loop. When the expression is false (when **count** is greater than **NUMBER**), the loop is terminated. The third expression is evaluated at the end of each loop. We use it here to increment the value of **count**, but it needn't be restricted to that use. The **for** statement is completed by following it with one simple or compound statement. Figure 6.3 summarizes the structure of a **for** loop.

To show another example, Listing 6.10 uses a **for** loop in a program that prints a table of cubes. Looking at the first line of the **for** loop tells us immediately all the information about the loop parameters: the starting value of **num**, the final value of **num**, and the amount that **num** increases each looping.

❖ for_cube.c

Listing 6.10

```
/* for_cube.c--using a for loop to make a table of cubes */
#include <stdio.h>
main()
{
   int num;

   printf("     n   n cubed\n");
   for ( num = 1; num <= 6; num++)
     printf("%5d %5d\n", num, num*num*num);
}
```

The program prints the following output:

```
n    n cubed
1    1
2    8
3    27
4    64
5    125
6    216
```

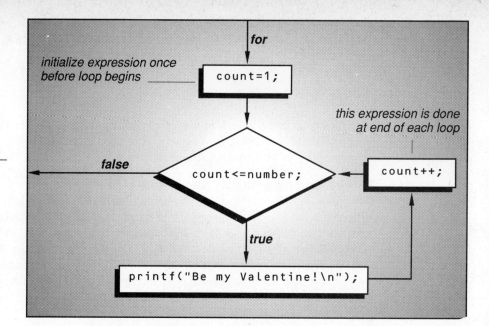

Figure 6.3

Structure of a
for *loop*

One common use of a **for** loop is to have the computer mark time, slowing its responses down to human levels. For example:

```
for ( n = 1; n <= 10000; n++)
  ;
```

instructs the computer to count to **10000**. The lone semicolon on the second line is the null statement. One problem with this delay loop is that it depends on the processor speed. A VAX or a 386 machine counts to **10000** much faster than, say, an Apple or the original IBM PC. Some implementations provide library functions that enable you to specify delays in terms of time instead of counts. The ANSI C library, for example, has a **clock( )** function that can be used to create a delay function.

Using for for Flexibility

Although the **for** loop seems similar to the FORTRAN DO loop, the Pascal FOR loop, and the BASIC FOR...NEXT loop, it is much more flexible than any of these. This flexibility stems from how the three expressions in a **for** specification can be used. So far we have used the first expression to initialize a counter, the second expression to express the limit for the counter, and the third expression to increase the counter by 1. When used in this fashion, the C **for** statement is indeed much like the others. But many other possibilities exist.

1. To count down instead of up, use the decrement operator:

```c
#include <stdio.h>
main()
{
    int n;

    for ( n = 5; n > 0; n--)
        printf("%d seconds!\n", n);
    printf("We have ignition!\n");
}
```

The output follows:

```
5 seconds!
4 seconds!
3 seconds!
2 seconds!
1 seconds!
We have ignition!
```

2. You can count by twos, tens, and so on:

```c
#include <stdio.h>
main()
{
    int n;

    for ( n = 2; n < 60; n = n + 13)
        printf( "%d \n", n);
}
```

This program increases **n** by **13** during each cycle, printing the following:

```
2
15
28
41
54
```

Note: C also offers a shorthand notation for incrementing a variable by a fixed amount. Instead of the following:

```
n = n + 13
```

we can use:

```
n += 13
```

The += is the *additive assignment operator,* and it adds whatever expression is at its right to the variable name at its left. See the boxes "More Assignment Operators" and "Summary: New Operators" for more details.

3. You can count by characters instead of by numbers:

```c
#include <stdio.h>
main()
{
  char ch;

  for ( ch = 'a'; ch <= 'z'; ch++)
      printf("The ASCII value for %c is %d.\n", ch, ch);
}
```

The abridged output follows:

```
The ASCII value for a is 97.
The ASCII value for b is 98.
...
The ASCII value for x is 120.
The ASCII value for y is 121.
The ASCII value for z is 122.
```

The program works because characters are stored as integers.

4. You can test some condition other than the number of iterations. In Listing 6.10, we can replace the following:

```c
for ( num = 1; num <= 6; num++)
```

with

```c
for (num = 1; num*num*num <= 216; num++)
```

if we are more concerned with limiting the size of the cube than in limiting the number of iterations.

5. You can let a quantity increase geometrically instead of arithmetically. That is, instead of adding a fixed amount each time, you can multiply by a fixed amount:

```c
#include <stdio.h>
main()
{
  float debt;

  for ( debt = 100.0; debt < 150.0; debt = debt*1.1 )
    printf("Your debt is now $%.2f.\n", debt);
}
```

This program fragment multiplies **debt** by **1.1** each cycle, increasing it by 10 percent. The output follows:

```
Your debt is now $100.00.
Your debt is now $110.00.
Your debt is now $121.00.
Your debt is now $133.10.
Your debt is now $146.41.
```

Note: There is also a shorthand notation for multiplying **debt** by **1.1**:

```
debt *= 1.1
```

The *= operator is the *multiplicative assignment operator,* and it multiplies the variable to its left by whatever is to its right. See the boxes "More Assignment Operators" and "Summary: New Operators" for more details.

6. You can use any legal expression you want for the third expression. Whatever you put in is updated during each iteration:

```
#include <stdio.h>
main()
{
   int x;
   int y = 55;

   for ( x = 1; y <= 75; y = ++x*5 + 50)
     printf("%10d %10d\n", x, y);
}
```

This loop prints out the values of **x** and of the algebraic expression **5 * x + 50**. The output follows:

```
       1          55
       2          60
       3          65
       4          70
       5          75
```

Notice that the test involves **y** and not **x**. Each of the three expressions in the **for** loop control can use different variables. (Note that although this example is valid, it does not show good style. The program would be clearer if we didn't mix the updating process with an algebraic calculation.)

7. You can even leave one or more expressions blank (but don't omit the semicolons). Just be sure to include within the loop itself some statement that will eventually cause the loop to terminate:

```
#include <stdio.h>
main()
{
   int ans, n;

   ans = 2;
```

```
       ans = 2;
       for (n = 3; ans <= 25;)
         ans = ans*n;
       printf("n = %d; ans = %d.\n", n, ans);
    }
```

The output follows:

```
n = 3; ans = 54
```

The loop keeps the value of **n** at **3**. The variable **ans** starts with the value **2**, then increases to **6, 18**, and obtains a final value of **54**. (The value **18** is less than **25**, so the **for** loop goes through one more iteration, multiplying **18** by **3** to get **54**.)

The following loop:

```
for ( ; ; )
  printf("I want some action\n");
```

goes on forever, since an empty test is considered to be true.

8. The first expression need not initialize a variable. Instead, it can be a **printf( )** statement of some sort. Just remember that the first expression is evaluated or executed only once, before any other parts of the loop are executed:

```
#include <stdio.h>
main()
{
  int num;

  for ( printf("Keep entering numbers!\n"); num != 6; )
    scanf("%d", &num);
  printf("That's the one I want!\n");
}
```

This fragment prints the first message once, then keeps accepting numbers until you enter a **6**:

```
Keep entering numbers!
3
5
8
6
That's the one I want!
```

9. The parameters of the loop expressions can be altered by actions within the loop. For example, suppose you have the loop set up like the following:

```
for ( n = 1; n < 10000; n += delta)
```

If after a few iterations your program decides **delta** is too small or too large, an **if** statement inside the loop can change the size of **delta**. (**If** statements are discussed in Chapter 7.) In an interactive program, **delta** can be changed by the user as the loop runs.

In short, the freedom you have in selecting the expressions that control a **for** loop makes this loop able to do much more than just perform a fixed number of iterations. The power of the **for** loop is enhanced further by the operators we will discuss shortly.

▶ Summary: The **for** statement

Keyword: for

General comments. The **for** statement uses three control expressions, separated by semicolons, to control a looping process. The initialize expression is executed once, before any of the loop statements are executed. If the test expression is true (or nonzero), the loop is cycled through once. Then the update expression is evaluated, and the test expression is checked again. The **for** statement is an entry-condition loop, which, as noted earlier, means that the decision to go through one more pass of the loop is made before the loop is traversed. Thus, it is possible that the loop is never traversed. The statement part of the form can be a simple statement or a compound statement.

Form.

for (*initialize; test; update*)
   statement

The loop is repeated until *test* becomes false, or zero.

Example.

```
for ( n = 0; n < 10 ; n++ )
   printf(" %d %d\n", n, 2*n+1 );
```

▶ More Assignment Operators

In Chapter 5 we mentioned that C has several assignment operators. The most basic one, of course, is =, which simply assigns the value of the expression at its right to the variable at its left. The other assignment operators update variables: +=, -=, *=, /=, %=. Each is used with a variable name at its left and an expression at its right. The variable is assigned a new value equal to its old value adjusted by the value of the expression at the right. The exact adjustment depends on the operator. For example:

Scores += 20	Is the same as	**Scores = scores + 20**
Dimes –= 2	Is the same as	**Dimes = dimes – 2**
Bunnies *= 2	Is the same as	**Bunnies = bunnies * 2**
Time /= 2.73	Is the same as	**Time = time / 2.73**
Reduce %= 3	Is the same as	**Reduce = reduce % 3**

Here we used simple numbers on the right, but we could have used more elaborate expressions:

x *= 3*y + 12   Is the same as   **x = x * (3*y + 12)**

These assignment operators have the same low priority that = has, that is, less than that of + or –. This precedence is reflected in the preceding example.

There is one difference between using a combination assignment operator and writing out the code the long way. C guarantees that the object to the left of a combination assignment operator is evaluated only once.

Note: You are not required to use these forms. They are, however, more compact, and they may produce more efficient machine code than the longer form. They are particularly useful if you are trying to squeeze something into a **for** loop specification.

The Comma Operator

The comma operator extends the flexibility of the **for** loop by allowing you to include more than one initialization or update in a **for** loop specification. For example, Listing 6.11 shows a program that prints out first class postage rates. (At the time of this writing, the rate is 25 cents for the first ounce and 20 cents for each additional ounce.)

❖ *postage.c*

Listing 6.11

```
/* postage.c--first-class postage rates */
#include <stdio.h>
#define FIRST 25
#define NEXT 20
main()
{
   int ounces, cost;

   printf("Ounces Cost\n");
   for ( ounces=1, cost=FIRST; ounces<= 16; ounces++,
       cost += NEXT)
     printf("%d %7d\n", ounces, cost);
}
```

The first four lines of output look like the following:

```
Ounces     Cost
   1        25
   2        45
   3        65
```

We use the comma operator in the first and the third expressions. Its presence in the first expression causes **ounces** and **cost** to be initialized. Its second occurrence causes **ounces** to be increased by **1** and **cost** to be increased by **20** (the value of **NEXT**) during each iteration. All the calculations are done in the **for** loop specifications. See Figure 6.4.

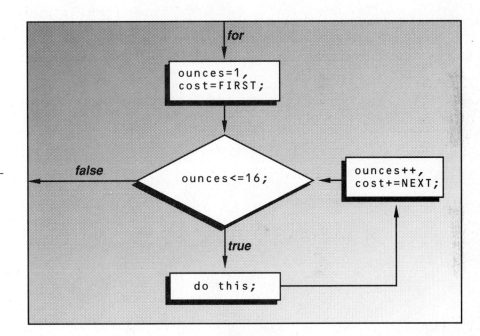

Figure 6.4

*The comma operator and the **for** loop*

The comma operator is not restricted to **for** loops, but that is where it is most often used. The operator has two further properties. First, it guarantees that the expressions it separates will be evaluated in a left-to-right order. Thus, **ounces** is initialized before **cost**. This ordering is not important for the example, but it would become important if the expression for **cost** contained **ounces**. Second, the value of the entire comma expression is the value of the righthand member. Therefore the effect of the following statement:

```
x = (y = 3, (z = ++y + 2) + 5);
```

is to first assign **3** to **y**, then increment **y** to **4**, then add **2** to **4** and assign the resulting **6** to **z**, then add **5** to **z** and assign the resulting value of **11** to **x**. Note, however, that the reasons for such usage are beyond the scope of this book.

The comma is also used as a separator. Thus, the commas in the following:

```
char ch, date;
```

and

```
printf("%d %d\n", chimps, chumps);
```

are separators, not comma operators.

▶ **Summary: New operators**

Assignment operators. Each of these operators updates the variable at its left by the value at its right, using the indicated operation (we use r-h for righthand, and l-h for lefthand).

+=	Adds the r-h quantity to the l-h variable
−=	Subtracts the r-h quantity from the l-h variable
*=	Multiplies the l-h variable by the r-h quantity
/=	Divides the l-h variable by the r-h quantity
%=	Gives the remainder from dividing the l-h variable by the r-h quantity

Example.

Rabbits *= 1.6;   Is the same as   **Rabbits = rabbits * 1.6;**

Miscellaneous: The comma operator. This operator links two expressions into one and guarantees that the leftmost expression is evaluated first. It is typically used to include more information in a **for** loop control expression.

Example.

```
for ( step = 2, fargo = 0; fargo < 1000; step *= 2)
    fargo += step;
```

Zeno Meets the for Loop

Let's see how the **for** loop and the comma operator can help solve an old paradox. The Greek philosopher Zeno once argued that an arrow would never reach its target. First, he said, the arrow had to cover half the distance to the target, then it had to cover half of the remaining distance, then it still had half of what was left to cover; and so forth. Since the journey had an infinite number of parts, Zeno argued, it would take the arrow an infinite amount of time to reach its journey's end. (We doubt, however, that Zeno would have volunteered to be a target just on the strength of this argument.)

Let's take a quantitative approach and suppose that it takes the arrow 1 second to travel the first half. It then takes $\frac{1}{2}$ second to travel half of what is left, $\frac{1}{4}$ second to travel half of what is left next, and so on. We can represent the total time by the infinite series $1 + \frac{1}{2} + \frac{1}{4} + \frac{1}{8} + \frac{1}{16} + \ldots$

Listing 6.12 finds the sum of the first few terms.

❖ zeno.c

Listing 6.12

```
/* zeno.c--series sum */
#include <stdio.h>
#define LIMIT 15
main()
{
   int count;
   float time, x;

   for ( time=0.0, x=1.0, count=1; count <= LIMIT; count++,
      x *= 2.0)
   {
      time += 1.0/x;
      printf("time = %f when count = %d.\n", time, count);
   }
}
```

The following gives the sum of the first 15 terms:

```
time = 1.000000 when count = 1.
time = 1.500000 when count = 2.
time = 1.750000 when count = 3.
time = 1.875000 when count = 4.
time = 1.937500 when count = 5.
time = 1.968750 when count = 6.
time = 1.984375 when count = 7.
time = 1.992188 when count = 8.
time = 1.996094 when count = 9.
time = 1.998047 when count = 10.
time = 1.999023 when count = 11.
time = 1.999512 when count = 12.
time = 1.999756 when count = 13.
time = 1.999878 when count = 14.
time = 1.999939 when count = 15.
```

We can see that although we keep adding more terms, the total seems to level out. Indeed, mathematicians have proven that the total approaches 2.0 as the number of terms approaches infinity, just as our program suggests. For instance, suppose $S = 1 + 1/2 + 1/4 + 1/8 + ...$ Then dividing by 2 gives $S/2 = 1/2 + 1/4 + 1/8 + 1/16 + ...$ Subtracting the second expression from the first gives $S - S/2 = 1 + 1/2 - 1/2 + 1/4 - 1/4 + ...$, which is $S/2 = 1$, or $S = 2$.

The program also shows that we can use more than one comma operator in an expression. We initialize **time**, **x**, and **count**. Once we set up the conditions for the loop, the program itself is extremely brief.

6.6 An Exit-Condition Loop: do while

The **while** loop and the **for** loop are both entry-condition loops. C also has an *exit-condition loop,* in which the condition is checked *after* each iteration of the loop. This variety is called a **do while** loop, Listing 6.13 shows an example.

❖ do_while.c

Listing 6.13

```
/* do_while.c--exit-condition loop */
#include <stdio.h>
main()
{
   char ch;

   do
   {
     scanf("%c", &ch);
     printf("%c", ch);
   } while ( ch != '#')
}
```

The program reads input characters and reprints them until the # character appears. How is this program different from a **while** loop version such as that shown in Listing 6.14?

❖ entry.c

Listing 6.14

```
/* entry.c--entry condition loop */
#include <stdio.h>
main()
{
   char ch;

   scanf("%c", &ch);
   while ( ch != "#");
   {
     printf("%c", ch);
     scanf("%c", &ch);
   }
}
```

The behavioral difference appears when the # is read. The **while** loop prints out all the characters *up to* the first #; the **do while** loop prints out all the characters *up to and including* the #. Only after it has printed the # character does the **while** loop check to see if a # character appears; in a **do while** loop, that action precedes the test condition.

The general form of the **do while** loop follows:

do
>*statement*
>**while** (*expression*)**;**

The statement can be simple or compound. Note that the **do while** loop itself counts as a statement and therefore requires a terminating semicolon. Also see Figure 6.5.

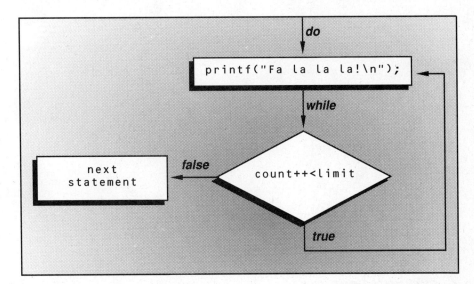

Figure 6.5

Structure of a **do while** *loop*

A **do while** loop always is executed at least once, since the test is made after the body of the loop is executed. On the other hand, a **for** loop or a **while** loop may be executed zero times, since the test is made before execution. You should restrict your use of **do while** loops to cases that require at least one iteration. For example, a password program can include a loop along these lines:

do
{
>*prompt for password*
>*read user input*
} **while** (*input not equal to password*)**;**

You should avoid a **do while** structure of the type shown in the following pseudocode:

ask user if he or she wants to continue
do
some clever stuff
while (*answer is yes*)**;**

After the user answers "no," "some clever stuff" is performed anyway because the test follows the body of the loop.

Keywords: do, while

General comments. The **do while** statement creates a loop that repeats until the test expression becomes false, or zero. The **do while** statement is an exit-condition loop, which means that the decision to go through one more pass of the loop is made after the loop is traversed. Thus, the loop must be executed at least once. The statement part of the form can be a simple statement or a compound statement.

Form.

do
    statement
       while (*expression*);

The *statement* portion is repeated until the *expression* becomes false, or zero.

Example.

```
do
  scanf("%d", &number);
    while( number != 20 );
```

6.7 Which Loop?

Once you decide you need a loop, which one should you use? First, you must decide whether you need an entry-condition loop or an exit-condition loop, although your answer should usually be an entry-condition loop. There are several reasons why computer scientists consider an entry-condition loop superior. One is the general principle that it is better to look before you leap (or loop) than after. A second reason is that a program is easier to read if the loop test is found at the beginning of the loop. Finally, in many uses, it is important that the loop be skipped entirely if the test is not initially met.

Let's assume you need an entry-condition loop. Should it be a **for** loop or a **while** loop? Your decision is partly a matter of taste, since what you can accomplish with one loop, you can also accomplish with the other. To make a **for** loop like a **while** loop, you can omit the first and third expressions:

for (*;test;*)

is the same as the following:

while (*test*)

To make a **while** loop like a **for** loop, preface it with an initialization and include update statements:

```
initialize;
while ( test )
{
    body;
    update;
}
```

is the same as the following:

```
for ( initialize; test; update )
    body;
```

In terms of style, it seems appropriate to use a **for** loop when the loop involves initializing and updating a variable and to use a **while** loop when the conditions are otherwise. Thus, **while** is natural for the following idiom:

```
while (scanf("%ld", &num) == 1)
```

The **for** loop is a more natural choice for loops involving counting with an index:

```
for ( count = 1; count <= 100; count++)
```

6.8 Nested Loops

A *nested loop* is a loop that is inside another loop. One common context for nested loops is displaying data in rows and columns. One loop can handle, say, all the columns in a row, and the second loop can handle the rows. Listing 6.15 shows a simple example.

❖ *rows1.c*

Listing 6.15

```
/* rows1.c--uses nested loops */
#include <stdio.h>
#define ROWS 6
#define CHARS 6
main()
{
    int row;
    char ch;

    for (row = 0; row < ROWS; row++)           /* line 10 */
    {
        for (ch = 'A'; ch < 'A' + CHARS; ch++)   /* line 12 */
        printf("%c", ch);
            printf("\n");
    }
}
```

Running the program produces this output:

```
ABCDEF
ABCDEF
ABCDEF
ABCDEF
ABCDEF
ABCDEF
```

Discussion

The **for** loop beginning on line 10 is called the outer loop, and the loop beginning on line 12 is called an inner loop because it is inside the other loop. The outer loop starts with **row** having a value of **0** and terminates when **row** reaches **6**. Thus it goes through six cycles, with **row** having the values **0** through **5**. The first statement in each cycle is the inner **for** loop. This loop also goes through six cycles, printing the characters **A** through **F** on the same line. The second statement of the outer loop is **printf("\n");**, which starts a new line so that the next time the inner loop is run, the output is on a new line. Note that with a nested loop the inner loop runs through its full range of iterations each single iteration of the outer loop. So in the last example, the inner loop prints six characters to a row, and the outer loop creates six rows.

A Nested Variation

In the last example, the inner loop performed the same activity each cycle of the outer loop. But you can also instruct the inner loop to behave differently each cycle by making part of the inner loop depend on the outer loop. Listing 6.16, for example, alters the last program slightly by making the inner loop starting character depend on the cycle number of the outer loop.

❖ *rows2.c*

Listing 6.16

```
/* rows2.c--using dependent nested loops */
#include <stdio.h>
#define ROWS 6
#define CHARS 6
main()
{
   int row;
   char ch;

   for (row = 0; row < ROWS; row++)
   {
     for (ch = 'A' + row; ch < 'A' + CHARS; ch++)
       printf("%c", ch);
     printf("\n");
   }
}
```

This time the output is as follows:

```
ABCDEF
BCDEF
CDEF
DEF
EF
F
```

Because **row** is added to **A** during each cycle of the outer loop, **ch** is initialized to one character later in the alphabet on each row. The test condition, however, is unaltered, so each row still ends on **F**, which results in one less character being printed for each row.

6.9 Arrays

Arrays are important features in many programs. They let you store several items of related information in a convenient fashion. We devote all of Chapter 10 to arrays later, but because arrays often are used with loops, we introduce them now.

An *array* is a series of data objects of the same type, such as 10 **char**s or 15 **int**s, stored sequentially. The entire array bears a single name, and the individual data objects, or *elements*, are accessed by using an integer index. For instance, the following declaration:

```
float debts[20];
```

announces that **debts** is an array with 20 elements. The first element is called **debts[0]**; the second element is called **debts[1]**; and so on up to **debts[19]**. Note that the numbering of array elements starts with 0 and not 1. Because we declare the array to be type **float**, each element can be assigned a **float** value, for example:

```
debts[5] = 32.54;
debts[6] = 1.2e+21;
```

An array can be of any data type:

```
int nannies[22]; /* an array to hold 22 integers */
char alpha[26];  /* an array to hold 26 characters */
long big[500];   /* an array to hold 500 long integers */
```

For example, in Chapter 4 we discussed strings, which are a special case of **char** arrays. (In general, a **char** array is one whose elements are assigned **char** values. A string is a **char** array in which the null character, `'\0'`, is used to mark the end of the string. See Figure 6.6.)

The numbers used to identify the array elements are called *subscripts* or *indices*. The subscripts must be integers, and as mentioned the subscripting begins with 0. The array elements are stored next to each other in memory. See Figure 6.7.

character array but not a string

Figure 6.6

Character arrays and strings

character array and a string

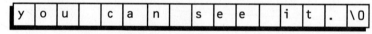

null character

Using a for Loop with an Array

There are many, many uses for arrays. Listing 6.17 is a relatively simple one. It's a program that reads in 10 scores that are to be processed later. By using an array, we avoid inventing 10 different variable names, one for each score. Also, we can use a **for** loop to do the reading. The program goes on to report the sum of the scores and their average.

❖ *scores_in.c*

Listing 6.17

```
/* scores_in.c--use loops for array processing */
#include <stdio.h>
#define SIZE 10
main()
{
    int index, score[SIZE];
    int sum = 0
    float average;

    printf("Enter %d scores:\n", SIZE);
    for (index = 0; index < SIZE; index++)
        scanf("%d", &score[index]); /* read in the ten scores */
    printf("The scores read in are as follows:\n");
    for (index = 0; index < SIZE; index++)
        printf("%5d", score[index]);  /* verify input */
    printf("\n");
    for (index = 0; index < SIZE; index++)
        sum += score[index];          /* add them up */
    average = (float) sum / SIZE;  /* time-honored method */
    printf("Sum of scores = %d, average = %.2f\n", sum,
        average);
}
```

Let's check to see if it works; then we can make a few comments. The output follows:

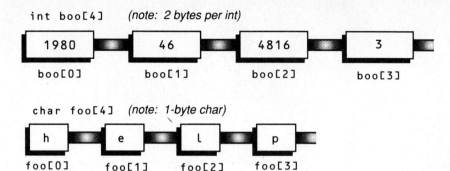

Figure 6.7

The **char** *and* **int** *arrays in memory*

```
int boo[4]    (note: 2 bytes per int)
```

1980	46	4816	3

  boo[0]   boo[1]   boo[2]   boo[3]

```
char foo[4]   (note: 1-byte char)
```

h	e	l	p

  foo[0]   foo[1]   foo[2]   foo[3]

```
Enter 10 scores:
76 85 62 48 98 71
66 89 70 77 99
The scores read in are as follows:
   76 85 62 48 98 71 66 89 70 77
Sum of scores = 742, average = 74.20
```

It works, so let's analyze some of the details. First, note that although we typed 11 numbers, only 10 were read, for the reading loop reads just 10 values. Also, remember that because **scanf( )** skips over whitespace, we can type all 10 numbers on one line or spread them over several lines.

Next, using arrays and loops is much more convenient than using 10 separate **scanf( )** statements and 10 separate **printf( )** statements to read in and verify the 10 scores. The **for** loop provides a simple and direct way to utilize the array subscripts. Notice that an element of an **int** array is handled like an **int** variable. To read an int variable **fue**, we would use **scanf("%d", &fue)**. Here we are reading an **int** element **score[index]**, so we use **scanf("%d", &score[index])**.

This example illustrates several style points. First, we use a **#define** directive to create a manifest constant (**SIZE**) to specify the size of the array. We use this constant in defining the array and in setting the loop limits. If we need to expand the program to handle 20 scores, we simply redefine **SIZE** to be **20**, and we don't have to change every part of the program that uses the array size.

Second, the following idiom:

```
for (index = 0; index < SIZE; index++)
```

is a handy one for processing an array of size **SIZE**. It's important to use the correct array limits. The first element has index **0**, and the loop starts by setting **index** to **0**. Because the numbering starts with **0**, the element index for the last element is **SIZE – 1**. That is, the 10th element is **score[9]**. The test condition **i < SIZE** accomplishes this task, for the last value of **index** used in the loop is **SIZE – 1**. You can also use the test **index <= SIZE – 1**, although this statement is more awkward-looking.

Third, it is good practice to have a program repeat, or *echo*, the values it has just read in. It helps ensure that the program is processing the data you think it is.

Finally, note that we use three separate **for** loops. You may wonder if this step is really necessary. Can we have combined some of the operations in one loop? The answer is that we could have done so, and the program would have been more compact. However, we were swayed by the *principle of modularity*. The idea behind this phrase is that a program should be broken into separate units with each unit having only one task to perform. Modularity makes it easier to read a program. Perhaps even more important, it makes it much easier to update or modify a program if different parts of it are not intermingled. Once we know enough about program functions, we can also make each unit into a function, enhancing the program modularity.

6.10 A Loop Example Using a Function Return Value

For our last example in this chapter, let's design a function that calculates the result of raising a number to an integer power. The three main tasks in this exercise are devising the algorithm for calculating the answer, expressing the algorithm in a function that returns an answer, and providing a convenient way of testing the function.

First, let's look at an algorithm. We keep the function simple by restricting it to positive integer powers. If we want to raise **a** to the **b** power, we multiply **a** by itself **b** times. This type of task is natural for a loop. We can set a variable **pow** to **1**, then multiply it by **a** repeatedly:

```
for (i = 1; i <= b; i++)
    pow *= a;
```

Recall that the *= operator multiplies the lefthand side by the righthand side. So after the first loop cycle, **pow** is **1*a**, or **a**. After the second cycle, **pow** is its previous value (**a**) multiplied by **a**, or **a** squared, and so on. Once **b** is known, the **for** loop is natural in this context because the loop is executed a predetermined number of times.

Now that we have an algorithm, we should decide on what data types to use. The exponent **b**, being an integer, should be type **int**. To allow maximum range in values for **a** and its power, we make **a** and **pow** type **double**.

Next let's consider how to put the function together. We need to give the function two values, and the function should give back one. To get information to the function, we can use two arguments, one **double** and one **int**, specifying which number to raise to what power. But how do we arrange for the function to return a value to the calling program? To write a function with a return value, do the following:

1. When you define a function, state the type of value it returns.

2. Use the keyword **return** to indicate the value to be returned.

For example:

```
double power(a,b)/* power( ) returns type double */
double a;
int b;
{
  double pow = 1;
  int i;

  for (i = 1; i <= b; i++)
    pow *= a;
  return pow;     /* return the value of pow */
}
```

To declare the function type, we preface the function name with the type, just as we do when declaring a variable. The keyword **return** causes the function to return the following value to the calling variable. Here we return the value of a variable, but you can return the value of expressions, too. For instance:

```
return 2 * x + b;
```

is a valid statement. The function then computes the value of the expression and returns it. In the calling program, the return value can be assigned to another variable, be used as a value in an expression, or be used as an argument to another function, as in **printf(" %f", power(6.28, 3))**. The return value also can be ignored.

Now let's use the function in a program. To test the function, it is convenient to be able to feed several values to the function, which suggests setting up an input loop. The natural choice for this operation is the **while** loop. We can use **scanf( )** to read in two values at a time. If successful in reading two values, **scanf( )** returns the value **2**, so we can control the loop by comparing the **scanf( )** return value to **2**. One more point: To use the **power( )** function in our program, we need to declare it, just as we declare variables that the program uses. Listing 6.18 shows the program.

❖ *power.c*

Listing 6.18

```
/* power.c--using return values */
#include <stdio.h>
main()
{
  double x, xpow;
  double power();            /* a function declaration */
  int n;

  printf("Enter a number and the positive integer power");
  printf(" to which\n the number will be raised. Enter q");
  printf(" to quit.\n");
  while ( scanf("%lf%d", &x, &n) == 2)
  {
    xpow = power(x,n);    /* function call */
    printf("%.3e to the power %d is %.3e\n", x, n, xpow);
  }
}
```

Listing 6.18
(cont'd.)

```
double power(a,b)       /* function definition */
double a;
int b;
{
  double pow = 1;
  int i;

  for (i = 1; i <= b; i++)
    pow *= a;
  return pow;            /* return the value of pow */
}
```

The following is a sample run:

```
Enter a number and the positive integer power to which
the number will be raised. Enter q to quit.
2.2 5
2.200e+000 to the power 5 is 5.154e+001
8.0
8
8.000e+000 to the power 8 is 1.678e+007
144 2
1.440e+002 to the power 2 is 2.074e+004
q
```

Program Discussion

The **main( )** program is an example of a *driver*, which is a short program designed to test a function. The **while** loop is a generalization of a form we've used before. Entering **2.2 5** causes **scanf( )** to return **2**, and the loop continues. Because **scanf( )** skips over whitespace, input can be spread over more than one line, as the sample output shows. But entering **q** produces a return value of **0**, because **q** can't be read using the **%lf** specifier. Entering **q** therefore terminates the loop. Similarly, entering **2.8 q** produces a return value of **1**, which also terminates the loop.

Let's look at the function-related matters. The **power( )** function appears three times in this program. The first appearance:

```
double power( ); /* a function declaration */
```

declares that the program will be using a function called **power( )**. The parentheses following **power** indicate that **power( )** is the name of a function, much as brackets indicate an array name. The keyword **double** indicates that the **power( )** function returns a type **double** value. The compiler needs to know what kind of value **power( )** returns so that it will know how many bytes of data to expect and how to interpret them (which is the reason why we have to declare the function).

The second appearance:

```
xpow = power(x,n);    /* function call */
```

calls the function, passing it two values. The function calculates the **nth** power of **x** and returns it to the calling program, where the return value is assigned to the variable **xpow**.

The third appearance is in the head of the function definition:

```
double power(a,b)    /* function definition */
double a;
int b;
```

Here we find that **power( )** takes two arguments: a **double** and an **int.** Note that **power( )** is not followed by a semicolon when it appears in a function definition, although it is followed by a semicolon when in a function declaration. After the function heading is the code that specifies what **power( )** does.

Recall that the **power( )** function uses a **for** loop to calculate the value of **a** to the **b** power and assign it to **pow**. The following line:

```
return pow; /* return the value of pow */
```

makes the value of **pow** the function return value.

Using Functions With Return Values

Declaring the function, calling the function, defining the function, and using the **return** keyword are the basic elements in defining and using a function with a return value. Our example follows traditional K & R C practices in performing these steps. In Chapter 9, we look at the new, more powerful ANSI C techniques.

At this point, you may have some questions. For example, since our definition of **power( )** says it is type **double**, why do we have to declare it separately? Or, if we are supposed to declare functions before we use their return values, why did we use the **scanf( )** return value without declaring **scanf( )**?

We answer the first question first. The compiler needs to know what type **power( )** is when it first encounters it in the program. At this point, the compiler has not yet encountered the definition of **power( )**, so it doesn't know that the definition says the return type is **double**. To help the compiler, we preview what is to come by using what is termed a *forward declaration,* which informs the compiler that **power( )** is defined elsewhere and that it will return type **double**. If we place the **power( )** function definition ahead of **main( )** in the file, we can omit the forward declaration, for in this case, the compiler will know all about **power( )** before reaching **main( )**. However, such a format is not standard C style: Since **main( )** usually provides the overall framework for a program, it's best to show it first. Also, functions are often kept in separate files, so that a forward declaration is essential.

Next, why didn't we declare **scanf( )**? Well, we did. The **stdio.h** header file has in it function declarations for **scanf( )**, **printf( )**, and several other I/O functions. The **scanf( )** declaration states it returns type **int**. However, if you forget to include **stdio.h**, the program will still run, because C assumes that if you don't declare the function type it is type **int**. Early C programming often relied heavily on this assumption, but modern practice is to declare the function type even if it is **int**.

6.11 Summary

This chapter described program control. C offers many aids for structuring your programs. The **while** and **for** statements provide entry-condition loops. The latter are particularly suited for loops that involve initialization and updating. The comma operator lets you initialize and update more than one variable in a **for** loop. For the rare occasion when an exit-condition loop is needed, C provides the **do while** statement.

All these loops use a test condition to determine if another loop cycle is to be executed. In general, the loop continues if the test expression evaluates to a nonzero value and terminates otherwise. Often, the test condition is a relational expression, which is an expression formed using a relational operator. Such an expression has a value of 1 if the relation is true and a value of 0 otherwise.

In addition to the relational operators, the chapter discussed several of C's arithmetic assignment operators such as += and *=. These operators modify the value of the lefthand operand by performing an arithmetic operation on it.

We also discussed arrays further. These are declared in the same fashion as ordinary variables, but they contain a number in brackets to indicate the number of elements. The first element of an array is 0, the second is 1, and so on. The subscripts used to number arrays can be manipulated conveniently by using loops. Finally, we showed how to write and use a function with a return value.

Review Questions

1. Find the value of **quack** after each line:

```
int quack = 2;
quack += 5;
quack *= 10;
quack -= 6;
quack /= 8;
quack %= 3;
```

2. What output does the following loop produce?

```
for ( value = 36; value > 0; value /= 2)
  printf("%3d", value);
```

3. Represent each of the following test conditions:

a. **x** is greater than **5**

b. **Scanf( )** attempts to read a single **double** and fails

c. **x** has the value **5**

4. Represent each of the following test conditions:

a. **Scanf( )** succeeds in reading a single integer

b. **x** is not **5**

c. **x** is **20** or greater

5. Find the errors in the following program:

```
main()                        /* Line 1 */
{                             /* Line 2 */
   int i, j, list(10);        /* Line 3 */

   for (i = 1, i <= 10, i++)  /* Line 5 */
   {                          /* Line 6 */
      list[i] = 2*i + 3;      /* Line 7 */
      for (j = 1, j > = i, j++)   /* Line 8 */
        printf("%d\n", list[j]); /* Line 9 */
   }                          /* Line 10 */
```

6. Use nested loops to write a program that produces the following pattern:

```
$$$$$$$$
$$$$$$$$
$$$$$$$$
$$$$$$$$
```

7. What does each of the following programs print out?

a.
```
#include <stdio.h>
...
main()
{
  int i = 0;
  ...
  while ( ++i < 4)
    printf("Hi! ");
  do
     printf("Bye! ");
  while ( i++ < 8);
}
```
b.
```
#include <stdio.h>
main()
{
   int i;
   char ch;
```

```
        for (i = 0, ch = 'A'; i < 4; i++, ch += 2 * i)
            printf("%c", ch);
    }
```

8. Given the input "Saddle up my horse!," what do each of the following programs produce for output? (Note: the ! follows the space character in the ASCII sequence.)

   a.
```
#include <stdio.h>
main()
{
    int ch;

    scanf("%c", &ch);
    while ( ch != 'o' )
    {
        printf("%c", ch);
        scanf("%c", &ch);
    }
}
```

   b.
```
#include <stdio.h>
main()
{
    int ch;

    scanf("%c", &ch);
    while ( ch != 'o' )
    {
        printf("%c", ++ch);
        scanf("%c", &ch);
    }
}
```

   c.
```
#include <stdio.h>
main()
{
    int ch;

    do {
        scanf("%c", &ch);
        printf("%c", ch);
    } while ( ch != 'o' );
}
```

   d.
```
#include <stdio.h>
main()
{
    int ch;

    for ( ch = '!'; ch != 'o'; scanf("%c", &ch) )
        putchar(ch);
}
```

9. What does the following program print?

```c
#include <stdio.h>
main()
{
    int n, m;

    n = 10;
    while ( ++n <= 13 )
      printf("%d",n);
    do
      printf("%d",n);
    while ( ++n <= 12);

    printf("\n***\n");

    for ( n = 1; n*n < 60; n +=3)
      printf("%d\n", n);

    printf("\n***\n");

    for ( n = 1, m = 5; n < m; n *= 2, m+= 2)
      printf("%d %d\n", n, m);

    printf("\n***\n");

    for ( n = 4; n > 0; n--)
    {
      for ( m = 0; m <= n; m++)
        printf("+");
      printf("\n");
    }
}
```

10. Consider the following declaration:

```c
double mint[10];
```

a. What is the array name?

b. How many elements does the array have?

c. What kind of value can be stored in each element?

d. Which of the following is a correct usage of **scanf( )** with this array?

(a) **scanf("%lf", mint)**

(b) **scanf("%lf", mint[2])**

(c) **scanf("%lf", &mint[2])**

(d) **scanf("%lf", &mint)**

11. Mr. Noah likes counting by twos, so he's written the following program to create an array that is filled with the integers 2, 4, 6, 8, and so on. What, if anything, is wrong with this program?

```
#include <stdio.h>
#define SIZE 8
main()
{
    int by_twos[SIZE];
    int index;

    for ( index = 1; index <= SIZE; index++)
        by_twos[index] = 2 * index;
    for ( index = 1; index <= SIZE; index++)
        printf("%d ", by_twos);
    printf("\n");
}
```

12. You want to write a function that returns a **long** value. What should your definition of the function include?

13. Define a function that takes an **int** argument and returns, as a **long**, the square of that value.

14. What does the following program print?

```
#include <stdio.h>
main()
{
    int k;

    for (k = 1, printf("%d: Hi!\n", k); printf("k = %d\n",k),
        k*k < 26; k+=2, printf("Now k is %d\n", k) )
            printf("k is %d in the loop\n",k);
}
```

Programming Exercises

1. Write a program that creates an array with 26 elements and stores the 26 lowercase letters in it. Also have it show the array contents.

2. Use nested loops to produce the following pattern:

```
$
$$
$$$
$$$$
$$$$$
```

3. Use nested loops to produce the following pattern:

```
F
FE
FED
FEDC
FEDCB
FEDCBA
```

4. Write a program that prints a table with each line giving an integer, its square, and its cube. Ask the user to input the lower and upper limits for the table. Use a **for** loop.

5. Write a program that reads a single word into a character array and then prints the word backward. Hint: Use **strlen( )** to compute the index of the last character in the array.

6. Consider the following two infinite series:

```
1.0 + 1.0/2.0 + 1.0/3.0 + 1.0/4.0 + ...
1.0 - 1.0/2.0 + 1.0/3.0 - 1.0/4.0 + ...
```

Write a program that evaluates running totals of these two series up to some limit of number of terms. Have the user enter the limit interactively. Examine the running totals after 20 terms, 100 terms, and 500 terms. Does either series appear to be converging to some value? Hint: −1 multiplied by itself an odd number of times is −1, and −1 multiplied by itself an even number of times is 1.

7. Write a program that requests two floating-point numbers and prints the value of their difference divided by their product. Have the program loop through pairs of input values until the user enters nonnumeric input.

8. Modify Question 7 so that it uses a function to return the value of the calculation.

9. Write a program that creates an eight-element array of type **int**, sets the elements to the first eight powers of 2, and then prints out the values. Use a **for** loop to set the values, and for variety, use a **do while** loop to display the values.

10. Write a program that reads eight integers into an array and then prints them out in reverse order.

11. Write a program that reads in a line of input and then prints out the line in reverse order. Recall that you can use **scanf( )** with the **%c** specifier to read characters and that the newline character (**\n**) is generated when you press the Enter key.

12. Daphne invests $100 at 10 percent simple interest. That is, every year, the investment earns an interest equal to 10 percent of the original investment. Deirdre invests $100 at 5 percent interest compounded annually. That is, interest is 5 percent of the current balance, including previous addition of interest. Write a program that finds out how many years it takes for the value of Deirdre's investment to exceed the value of Daphne's investment. Also show the two values at that time.

7

C Control Statements: Branching and Jumps

Contents

Objectives

Using the **if** statement to execute statements selectively

Using **if else** to choose between two alternatives

Using **if else if else** or **switch** to choose among multiple alternatives

Learning the logical operators: **&&**, **||**, and **!**

Using the conditional operator: **?:**

Using the jump commands: **break**, **continue**, and **goto**

Using the **getchar( )** and **putchar( )** functions

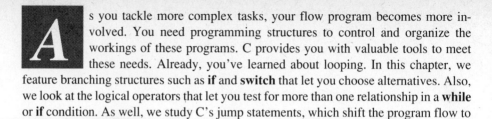

As you tackle more complex tasks, your flow program becomes more involved. You need programming structures to control and organize the workings of these programs. C provides you with valuable tools to meet these needs. Already, you've learned about looping. In this chapter, we feature branching structures such as **if** and **switch** that let you choose alternatives. Also, we look at the logical operators that let you test for more than one relationship in a **while** or **if** condition. As well, we study C's jump statements, which shift the program flow to another part of a program.

7.1 The if Statement

Let's start with a simple example of an **if** statement. See Listing 7.1. This program reads in a list of daily low temperatures (in Celsius) and reports back the total number of entries and the percent that are below freezing. We use **scanf( )** in a loop to read in the values. During each loop cycle, we increment a counter to keep track of the number of entries. An **if** statement detects temperatures below freezing and keeps track of their number.

❖ *colddays.c*

Listing 7.1

```c
/* colddays.c--find fraction of days below freezing */
#include <stdio.h>
#define SCALE "Celsius"
#define FREEZING 0
main()
{
   float temperature;
   int freezing = 0;
   int days = 0;

   printf("Enter the list of daily low temperatures.\n");
   printf("Use %s, and enter q to quit.\n", SCALE);
   while( scanf("%f", &temperature) == 1)
   {
     days++;
     if ( temperature < FREEZING )
       freezing++;
   }
   if ( days != 0 )
     printf("%d days total: %.1f%% are below freezing.\n",
         days, 100.0 * (float) freezing / days);
   if ( days == 0 )
     printf("No data entered!\n");
}
```

Here's a sample run:

```
Enter the list of daily low temperatures.
Use Celsius, and enter q to quit.
20 11 3 -4 -6 -10 -2.5 10 8 -5 q
10 days total: 50.0% are below freezing.
```

The **while** loop test condition uses the return value of **scanf( )** to terminate the loop when **scanf( )** encounters nonnumeric input. By using **float** instead of **int** for **temperature**, the program is able to accept input like **–2.5** as well as **8**.

The new statement in the block is the following:

```
if ( temperature < FREEZING )
   freezing++;
```

This **if** statement instructs the computer to increase **freezing** by **1** if the value just read (**temperature**) is less than zero. If **temperature** is not less than zero, then the **freezing++;** statement is skipped, and the **while** loop moves on to read the next temperature value.

We use the **if** statement two more times to control the output. If there are data, the program prints the results. If there are no data, the program reports that fact. (Soon we describe a more elegant way to handle this part of the program.)

We use a cast to **float** in finding the percent to avoid integer division. Strictly speaking, the cast is superfluous, for in the expression **100.0 * freezing / days**, the subexpression **100.0 * freezing** is evaluated first and is forced into floating point by the automatic type conversion rules. We use the type cast to document our intent and to protect the program from faulty compilers.

if Basics

The **if** statement is called a branching statement because it provides a junction at which the program has to select which of two paths to follow. The general form follows:

if (*expression*)
   statement

If *expression* is true (or more generally, nonzero), the *statement* is executed; otherwise, it is skipped. As with a **while** loop, *statement* can be a single statement or a single block, or compound statement. The **if** structure is similar to a **while** statement. The chief difference is that in an **if** statement, the test and (possibly) the execution are performed just once; but in the **while** loop, the test and execution may be repeated several times.

Normally *expression* is a relational expression; that is, it compares the magnitude of two quantities (**x > y** or **c == 6**, for example). If the expression is true (**x** is greater than **y** or **c** equals **6**), then the statement is executed. Otherwise, it is ignored. More generally, any expression can be used, and an expression with a 0 value is taken to be false.

The statement portion can be a simple statement, as in Listing 7.1, or it can be a compound statement or block, marked off by braces:

```c
if ( score > big)
    printf("Jackpot!\n");            /* simple statement */

if ( joe > ron)
{
    joecash++;
    printf("You lose, Ron.\n");   /* compound statement */
}
```

The entire **if** structure counts as a single statement, even when it uses a compound statement.

7.2 Adding else to the if Statement

The simple form of an **if** statement gives you the choice of executing a statement (possibly compound) or skipping it. C also lets us choose between two statements by using the **if else** structure.

We can use **if else** to fix an awkward segment from Listing 7.1:

```c
if ( days != 0 )
    printf("%d days total: %.1f%% were below freezing.\n",
        days, 100.0 * (float) freezing / days);
if ( days == 0 )
    printf("No data entered!\n");
```

If the program finds that **days** is not unequal to **0**, it should know that **days** must be **0** without retesting. With **if else**, we can rewrite the fragment:

```c
if ( days != 0 )
    printf("%d days total: %.1f%% were below freezing.\n",
        days, 100.0 * (float) freezing / days);
else
    printf("No data entered!\n");
```

With this revised code, one test is made. If the test expression is true, the temperature data are printed. If it's false, the warning message is printed.

Note the general form of the **if else** statement:

if (*expression*)
   statement1
else
   statement2

If *expression* is true, or nonzero, *statement1* is executed. If *expression* is false, or zero, the single statement following the **else** is executed. The statements can be simple or compound. The indentation is not required by C, but it is the standard style. It shows at a glance those statements whose execution depends on a test.

You must use braces to create a single block if you want to insert more than one statement between the **if** and the **else**. The construction:

```
if ( x > 0)
   printf("Incrementing x:\n");
   x++;
else
   printf("x < 0 \n");
```

is not valid. Instead, use:

```
if ( x > 0)
{
   printf("Incrementing x:\n");
   x++;
}
else
   printf("x < 0 \n");
```

The **if** statement lets us choose whether or not to do one action. The **if else** statement lets us choose between two actions. See Figure 7.1.

Another Example: Introducing getchar( ) and putchar( )

Most of our examples have been using numeric input. To provide some variety and practice with other types, let's look at a character-oriented example. We can, of course, use **scanf( )** and **printf( )** with the **%c** specifier to read and write characters, but C also provides a pair of functions specifically designed for character I/O: **getchar( )** and **putchar( )**.

The **getchar( )** function takes no arguments, and it returns the next character from input. For instance:

```
ch = getchar();
```

reads the input character and assigns it to the variable **ch**. The **putchar( )** function prints its argument. For example:

```
putchar(ch);
```

prints out the character previously assigned to **ch**.

Because these functions only deal with characters, they are faster and more compact than the more general **scanf( )** and **printf( )** functions. Also, for the same reason, they don't need to be provided with format specifiers. Both functions typically are defined in

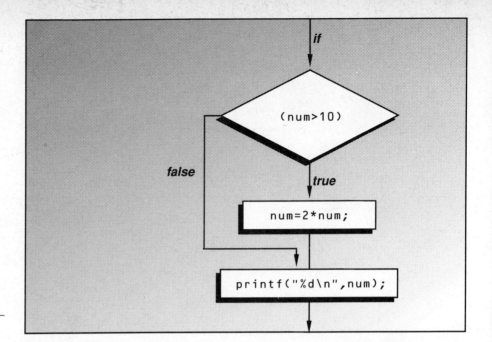

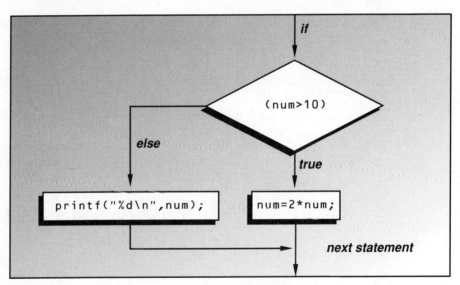

Figure 7.1

The **if** versus
the **if else**

the **stdio.h** file. (Typically, they are preprocessor macros rather than true functions. We discuss functionlike macros in Chapter 16.)

To see how these functions work and to see another example of **if else**, let's write a program that repeats an input line but replaces each nonspace character with the character that follows it in the ASCII code sequence, except that spaces will be reproduced as spaces. We can state the desired response this way: *If* the character is a space, print it, *else* print the next character in the ASCII sequence. The C code looks much like this statement. See Listing 7.2.

```
/* cypher1.c--alter input, preserving spaces */
#include <stdio.h>
#define SPACE ' '
main()
{
  char ch;

  ch = getchar();           /* read a character */
  while (ch != '\n')        /* while not end of line */
  {
    if (ch == SPACE)        /* leave the space */
      putchar(ch);          /* character unchanged */
    else
      putchar(ch + 1);      /* change other characters */
    ch = getchar();         /* get next character */
  }
}
```

Listing 7.2

A sample run follows:

```
CALL ME HAL.
DBMM NF IBM/
```

One point to notice is how this loop compares to the one in Listing 7.1. On the one hand, Listing 7.1 uses the status returned by **scanf( )** rather than the value of the input item to determine when to terminate the loop. On the other hand, Listing 7.2 uses the value of the input item to decide when to terminate the loop. This difference results in a slightly different loop structure for Listing 7.2, with one read statement before the loop and one read statement at the end of each loop. C's flexible syntax, however, lets us emulate Listing 7.1 by combining reading and testing into a single expression. Listing 7.3 presents Listing 7.2 rewritten in a more typically C style:

❖ *cypher2.c*

```
/* cypher2.c--alter input, preserving spaces */
#include <stdio.h>
#define SPACE ' '
main()
{
  char ch;

  while ((ch = getchar()) != '\n')
  {
    if (ch == SPACE)     /* leave the space */
      putchar(ch);       /* character unchanged */
    else
      putchar(ch + 1);   /* change other characters */
  }
}
```

Listing 7.3

The critical line in Listing 7.3:

```
while ( (ch = getchar() ) != '\n')
```

demonstrates a characteristically C programming style: combining two actions in one expression. The actions are assigning a value to **ch** and comparing this value to the newline character. The parentheses around **ch = getchar( )** make it the left operand of the != operator. To evaluate this expression, the computer must call the **getchar( )** function and assign its return value to **ch**. The value of an assignment expression is the value of the left member, so the value of **ch = getchar( )** is simply the value of **ch**. After ch is read, the test condition is thus **ch != '\n'**, that is, **ch** not being the newline character.

This idiom is common in C programming. All the parentheses are necessary. Suppose instead we used:

```
while ( ch = getchar() != '\n' )
```

The != operator has higher precedence than =, so the first expression to be evaluated is **getchar( ) != '\n'**. Because this expression is relational (is the return value not a newline character?), its value is **1** or **0** (true or false). This value is then assigned to **ch**. Therefore, omitting the parentheses means **ch** is assigned **0** or **1** rather than the return value of **getchar( )**, which is not desirable.

Multiple Choice: else if

Life often offers us more than two choices. We can extend the **if else** structure with **else if** to accommodate this fact. Let's look at an example. Utility companies often charge depending on the amount of energy you use. Here are the rates we are charged for electricity, based on kilowatt-hours (kWh):

First 240 kWh: $0.06898 per kWh

Next 300 kWh:$0.12032 per kWh

Over 540 kWh: $0.14022 per kWh

If you worry about your energy management, you may wish to prepare a program to calculate your energy costs. The program in Listing 7.4 is a first step in that direction.

❖ *electric.c*

Listing 7.4

```
/* electric.c--calculate electric bill */
#include <stdio.h>
#define RATE1 0.06898    /* rate for first 240 kwh */
#define RATE2 0.12032    /* rate for next 300 kwh */
#define RATE3 0.14022    /* rate for over 540 kwh */
#define BREAK1 240.0     /* first breakpoint for rates */
#define BREAK2 540.0     /* second breakpoint for rates */
```

```
#define BASE1 RATE1 * BREAK1  /* cost for 240 kwh */
#define BASE2 BASE1 + RATE2 * (BREAK2 - BREAK1)
                            /* cost for 540 kwh */
main()
{
  float kwh;                 /* kilowatt-hours used */
  float bill;                /* charges */

  printf("Please enter the kwh used.\n");
  scanf("%f", &kwh);
  if (kwh <= BREAK1)
    bill = RATE1 * kwh;
  else if (kwh <= BREAK2) /* kwh between 240 and 540 */
    bill = BASE1 + RATE2 * (kwh - BREAK1);
  else                       /* kwh above 540 */
    bill = BASE2 + RATE3 * (kwh - BREAK2);
  printf("The charge for %.1f kwh is $%1.2f.\n", kwh, bill);
}
```

**Listing 7.4
(cont'd.)**

We have used symbolic constants for the rates, therefore our constants are gathered in one place. If the power company changes its rates, having the rates in one place makes it less likely that we will fail to update a rate. We also have expressed the rate breakpoints symbolically. They too are subject to change. **BASE1** and **BASE2** are expressed in terms of the rates and breakpoints. Then if the rates or breakpoints change, the bases are updated automatically. You may recall that the preprocessor does not perform calculations. Where **BASE1** appears in the program, it is replaced by **0.06898 * 240.0**. The compiler, however, does evaluate this expression to its numerical value (**16.56**), so the program code uses this final value.

The flow of the program is straightforward, with the program selecting one of three formulas, depending on the value of **kwh**. Figure 7.2 illustrates the flow. We should point out that the only way the program can reach the first **else** is if **kwh** is equal to or greater than **240**. Thus, the **else if (kwh <= BREAK2)** line really is equivalent to demanding that **kwh** be between **240** and **540**, as we noted in the program comment. Similarly, the final **else** can be reached only if **kwh** equals or exceeds **540**. Finally, note that **BASE1** and **BASE2** represent the total charges for the first 240 and 540 kilowatt-hours, respectively. Thus, we need only add on the additional charges for electricity in excess of those amounts.

Actually, the **else if** is just a variation on what we already know. For example, the core of our program is another way of writing the following:

```
if ( kwh <=BREAK1 )
  bill = RATE1 * kwh;
else
  if ( kwh <=BREAK2 )
    bill = BASE1 + RATE2 * (kwh - BREAK1);
  else
    bill = BASE2 + RATE3 * (kwh - BREAK2);
```

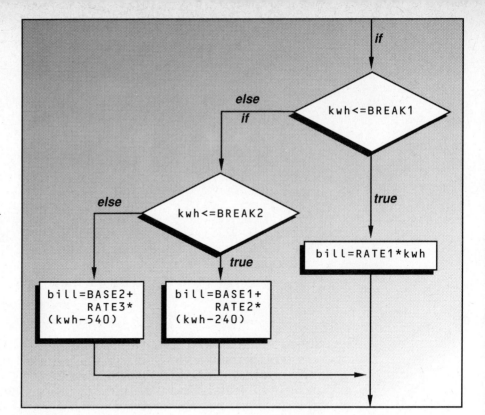

Figure 7.2

Program flow for Listing 7.4

That is, the program consists of an **if else** statement for which the statement part of the **else** is another **if else** statement. The second **if else** statement is said to be nested in the first. (Recall that the entire **if else** structure counts as a single statement, which is why we don't have to enclose the nested **if else** in braces.)

These two forms are equivalent. The only differences are in where we put spaces and newlines, and these are ignored by the compiler. Nonetheless, the first form (Listing 7.4) is preferred, for it shows more clearly that we are making a three-way choice. This form makes it easier to scan the program and see what the choices are. The nested forms of indentation should be used, for instance, when you must test two separate quantities. An example would be if there were a 10 percent surcharge for kilowatt-hours in excess of 540 during the summer only.

You may string together as many **else if**s as you need (within compiler limits, of course), as illustrated by this fragment:

```
if (score < 1000)
   bonus = 0;
else if (score < 1500)
   bonus = 1;
else if (score < 2000)
   bonus = 2;
else if (score < 2500)
   bonus = 4;
else
   bonus = 6;
```

(This fragment could be part of a game program, in which **bonus** represents how many additional photon bombs or food pellets you get for the next round.)

Pairing elses with ifs

When you have many **if**s and **else**s, how does the computer decide which **if** goes with which **else**? For example, consider the following program fragment:

```
if ( number > 6 )
  if ( number < 12 )
    printf("You're close!\n");
else
  printf("Sorry, you lose a turn!\n");
```

When is "Sorry, you lose a turn!" printed: When **number** is less than or equal to **6**, or when **number** is greater than **12**? In other words, does the **else** go with the first **if** or the second? The answer: when **number** is greater than **12**. That is:

Number	Response
5	(None)
10	You're close!
15	Sorry you lose a turn!

The rule is that an **else** goes with the most recent **if** unless braces indicate otherwise. See Figure 7.3. We indent our example to make it look as if the **else** goes with the first **if**, but remember that the compiler ignores indentation. If we really want the **else** to go with the first **if**, we can write the fragment as follows:

```
if ( number > 6 )
{
  if (number < 12 )
    printf("You're close!\n");
}
else
  printf("Sorry, you lose a turn!\n");
```

Now we get these responses:

Number	Response
5	Sorry you lose a turn!
10	You're close!
15	(None)

More Nested ifs

We've already seen that the **if else if else** sequence is a form of nested **if**s, one that selects from a series of alternatives. Another kind of nested **if** is used when choosing a particular selection leads to an additional choice. For example, a program can use an **if else** to select between males and females. Each branch within the **if else** then can contain another **if else** to distinguish between different income groups.

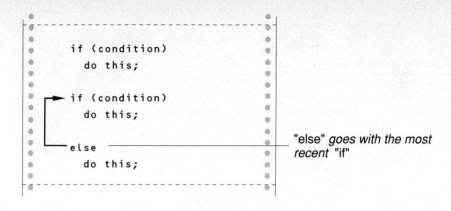

```
      if (condition)
         do this;

      if (condition)
         do this;

      else
         do this;
```

"else" *goes with the most recent* "if"

Figure 7.3

The rule for **if else** pairings

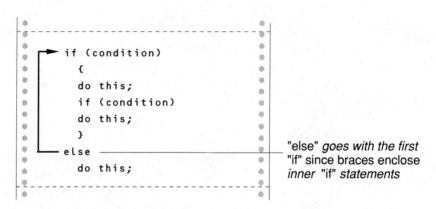

```
      if (condition)
      {
      do this;
      if (condition)
      do this;
      }
      else
         do this;
```

"else" *goes with the first* "if" *since braces enclose inner* "if" *statements*

Let's apply this form of nested **if** to the following problem: Given an integer, print out all the integers that divide into it evenly; if there are no divisors, report that the number is prime. This problem requires some forethought. First, we need an overall design for the program. For convenience, the program should use a loop to let us input numbers to be tested; that way, we don't have to run the program again each time we want to examine a new number. We've already developed a model for this kind of loop:

prompt user
while *the* **scanf( )** *return value is 1*
   analyze the number and report results
   prompt user

Recall that by using **scanf( )** in the loop test condition, we attempt to read in a number and also check to see if the loop should be terminated.

Next we need a plan for finding divisors. Perhaps the most obvious approach is something like the following:

```
for ( div = 2; div < num; div++)
   if ( num % div == 0)
     printf("%d is divisible by %d\n", num, div);
```

The loop checks all the numbers between **1** and **num** to see if they divide evenly into **num**. However, this approach is quite wasteful of computer time. We can do much better. Consider, for example, finding the divisors of 144. We find that 144 **%** 2 is 0, meaning 2 divides evenly into 144. If we then actually divide 2 into 144, we get 72, which also is a divisor. So we can get two divisors instead of one out of a successful **num % div** test. The real payoff, however, comes in changing the limits of the loop test. To see how this procedure works, let's look at the pairs of divisors we get as the loop continues: 2,72; 3,48; 4,36; 6,28; 8,18; 9,16; 12,12; 16,9; 18,8.... Note: Once we get past the 12,12 pair, we start getting in reverse order the same divisors that we already found. So, instead of running the loop to 143, we can stop after reaching 12. That saves a lot of cycles!

Generalizing this discovery, we see that we only have to test up to the square root of **num** instead of to **num**. For numbers like 9, there is no big savings, but the difference is enormous for a number like 10,000. Rather than messing with square roots, however, we can express the test condition as follows:

```
for ( div = 2; div * div <= num; div++)
   if ( num % div == 0)
     printf("%d is divisible by %d and %d.\n",
         num, div, num / div);
```

If **num** is **144**, the loop runs through **div = 12**. If **num** is **145**, the loop runs through **div = 13**. (The reason for using this test instead of the square root test is that integer multiplication is much faster than extracting a square root.)

We need to address two more problems, and then we'll be ready to create the program. First, what if the test number is a perfect square? Reporting that 144 is divisible by 12 and 12 is a little clumsy. But we can use a nested **if** to test if **div** equals **num** / **div**. If so, the program will print out just one divisor instead of two:

```
for (div = 2; div * div <= num; div++)
{
   if (num % div == 0)
   {
     if ( div * div != num)
       printf("%d is divisible by %d and %d.\n",
           num, div, num / div);
     else
       printf("%d is divisible by %d.\n", num, div);
   }
}
```

(Note: Because the **if else** statement counts as a single statement, the braces around it are not needed. The outer **if** is also a single statement, so the braces around it are not needed. But when statements get long, the braces make it easier to see what is happening in the program. In addition, they offer protection if you later add another statement to an **if** or to the loop.)

Second, how do we know if a number is prime? If **num** is prime, then program flow never gets inside the **if** statement. To solve this problem we can set a variable to some value, say 1, outside the loop and reset the variable to 0 inside the **if** statement. Then after the loop is completed, we can check to see if the variable is 1. If it is, the **if** statement was never entered, and the number is prime. Such a variable often is called a *flag*.

Listing 7.5 incorporates all the ideas we've discussed. Note that to extend the range, we switch to type **long**. Also notice that we use the comma operator in the **for** loop control expression to let us initialize **prime** to **TRUE** for each new input number.

❖ *divisors.c*

Listing 7.5

```
/* divisors.c--nested ifs display divisors of a number */
#include <stdio.h>
#define NO 0
#define YES 1
main()
{
   long num;          /* number to be checked */
   long div;          /* potential divisors */
   int prime;

   printf("Please enter an integer for analysis; ");
   printf("enter q to quit.\n");
   while ( scanf("%ld", &num) == 1)
   {
      for (div = 2, prime = YES; div * div <= num; div++)
      {
         if (num % div == 0)
         {
            if ( div * div != num)
               printf("%ld is divisible by %ld and %ld.\n",
                  num, div, num / div);
            else
               printf("%ld is divisible by %ld.\n", num, div);
            prime = NO;  /* number is not prime */
         }
      }
      if (prime == YES)
         printf("%ld is prime.\n", num);
      printf("Please enter another integer for analysis; ");
      printf("enter q to quit.\n");
   }
}
```

A sample run follows:

```
Please enter an integer for analysis; enter q to quit.
36
36 is divisible by 2 and 18.
36 is divisible by 3 and 12.
36 is divisible by 4 and 9.
36 is divisible by 6.
Please enter another integer for analysis; Enter q to quit.
149
149 is prime.
Please enter another integer for analysis; enter q to quit.
30077
30077 is divisible by 19 and 1583.
Please enter another integer for analysis; enter q to quit.
q
```

▶ Summary: Using **if** Statements for Making Choices

Keywords: if, else

General comments. In each of the following forms, the statement can be either a simple statement or a compound statement. A true expression, more generally, means one with a nonzero value.

Form 1.

if (*expression*)
   statement

The *statement* is executed if the *expression* is true.

Form 2.

if (*expression*)
   statement1
else
   statement2

If the *expression* is true, *statement1* is executed; otherwise *statement2* is executed.

Form 3.

if (*expression1*)
   statement1
else if (*expression2*)
   statement2
else
   statement3

If *expression1* is true, then *statement1* is executed. If *expression1* is false but *expression2* is true, *statement2* is executed. Otherwise, if both expressions are false, *statement3* is executed.

Example.

```
if (legs == 4)
   printf("It might be a horse.\n");
else if (legs > 4)
   printf("It is not a horse.\n");
else     /* case of legs < 4 */
   {
   legs++;
   printf("Now it has one more leg.\n")
   }
```

7.3 Let's Get Logical

We've seen how **if** and **while** statements often use relational expressions as tests. Sometimes it is useful to combine two or more relational expressions. For instance, suppose we want a program that counts only nonwhitespace characters in an input sentence. That is, we wish to keep track of characters that are not spaces, not newline characters, and not tab characters. We can use *logical operators* to meet this need. And we can use the period character (.) to identify the end of a sentence. Listing 7.6 presents a short program illustrating the method.

❖ *chcount.c*

Listing 7.6

```
/* chcount.c--counts nonwhitespace characters */
#include <stdio.h>
#define PERIOD '.'
main()
{
   int ch;
   int charcount = 0;

   while ((ch = getchar()) != PERIOD)
      if( ch != ' ' && ch != '\n' && ch != '\t')
         charcount++;
   printf("There are %d non-whitespace characters.\n",
         charcount);
}
```

Here's a sample run:

```
Logical     operators
combine relationships.
There are 36 non-whitespace characters.
```

The action begins as the program reads a character and checks to see if it is a period, since the period marks the end of a sentence. Next comes something new, a statement using the logical "and" operator **&&**. We can translate the **if** statement thus: If the character is not a blank, and if it is not a newline character, and if it is not a tab character, then increase **charcount** by one.

All three conditions must be true if the entire expression is to be true. The logical operators have a lower priority than the relational operators, so it is not necessary to use additional parentheses to group the subexpressions. There are three logical operators in C:

Operator	Meaning
&&	And
||	Or
!	Not

Suppose **exp1** and **exp2** are two simple relational expressions like **cat > rat** or **debt == 1000**. Then we can state the following:

1. **exp1 && exp2** is true only if both **exp1** and **exp2** are true.

2. **exp1 \|\| exp2** is true if either or both of **exp1** and **exp2** are true.

3. **!exp1** is true if **exp1** is false.

Here are some examples:

```
5 > 2 && 4 > 7       is false because only one subexpression is true.
5 > 2 || 4 > 7       is true because at least one of the subexpressions is true.
!(4 > 7)             is true because 4 is not greater than 7.
```

Note: The last expression is equivalent to the following:

```
4 <= 7
```

If you are unfamiliar or uncomfortable with logical operators, remember:

```
(practice && time) == perfect
```

Precedence

The **!** operator has a very high precedence, higher than multiplication, the same as the increment operators, and just below that of parentheses. The **&&** operator has higher precedence than **\|\|**, and both rank below the relational operators and above assignment in precedence. Thus, the following expression:

```
a > b && b > c || b > d
```

is interpreted as:

```
((a > b) && (b > c)) || (b > d)
```

That is, **b** is between **a** and **c**, or **b** is greater than **d**.

Order of Evaluation

Aside from those cases in which two operators share an operand, C ordinarily does not guarantee which parts of a complex expression will be evaluated first. For example, in the statement:

```
apples = (5 + 3) * (9 + 6);
```

the expression **5 + 3** may be evaluated before **9 + 6** or it may be evaluated afterward. This ambiguity was left in the language to enable compiler designers to make the most efficient choice for a particular system. One exception is the treatment of logical operators, for which C guarantees that logical expressions are evaluated from left to right. Furthermore, C guarantees that as soon as an element is found that invalidates the expression as a whole, the evaluation stops.

Such guarantees make it possible to use constructions like the following:

```
while((c = getchar()) != ' ' && c != '\n')
```

This sets up a loop that reads characters up to the first space or newline character. The first subexpression gives a value to **c** which then can be used in the second subexpression. Without the order guarantee, the computer may try to test the second expression before finding out the value of **c**.

Another example is:

```
if ( number != 0 && 12/number == 2)
    printf("The number is 5 or 6.\n");
```

If **number** has the value **0**, the expression is false, and the relational expression is not evaluated any further. This spares the computer the trauma of trying to divide by zero. Many languages do not have this feature; after seeing that **number** is 0, they still move on to check the next condition.

► Summary: Logical Operators and Expressions

Logical operators. Logical operators normally take relational expressions as operands. The **!** operator takes one operand. The rest take two: one to the left, one to the right. The logical operators are the following:

&&	**And**
||	**Or**
!	**Not**

Logical expressions.

expression1 && expression2 is true if both expressions are true.
expression1 || expression2 is true if either one or both expressions are true.
!expression is true if the expression is false.

Order of evaluation. Logical expressions are evaluated from left to right. Evaluation stops as soon as something is discovered that renders the expression false.

Examples.

```
6 > 2 && 3 == 3        is true.
! ( 6 > 2 && 3 ==3 )   is false.
x != 0 && 20/x < 5     The second expression is evaluated only if x is nonzero.
```

7.4 A Word–Count Program

Now we have the tools to make a word-counting program, that is, a program that reads input and reports the number of words it finds. We may as well also count characters and lines. Let's discuss what such a program involves.

First, it should read input character by character, and it should have some way of knowing when to stop. Second, it should be able to recognize and count the following units: characters, lines, and words. Here's a pseudocode representation:

read a character
while *there is more input*
    increment character count
    if *a line has been read, increment line count*
    if *a word has been read, increment word count*
    read next character

We already have a model for the input loop:

```
while ( (ch = getchar()) != STOP)
{
   ...
}
```

Here **STOP** represents some value for **ch** that will signal the end of the input. So far we have used the newline character and a period for this purpose, but neither is satisfactory for a general word-counting program. For the present, we'll choose a character (|) that is not common in text. In Chapter 8, we present a better solution that also allows the program to be used with text files as well as keyboard input.

Now let's consider the body of the loop. Since the program uses **getchar( )** for input, it can count characters by incrementing a counter during each loop cycle. To count lines, the program can check for newline characters. If a character is a newline, then the program should increment the line count.

The trickiest part of the program is identifying words. First, we have to define what we mean by a word. We take a relatively simple approach and define a word as a sequence of characters that contains no whitespace. Thus, "glymxck" and "r2d2" are words. A word starts, then, when a program first encounters nonwhitespace, and it ends when the next whitespace character appears. To keep track if a nonwhitespace character is the first character in a word, we can set a flag (call it **wordflag**) to **1** when the first character in a word is read. We also can increment the word count at that point. As long as **wordflag** remains **1**, subsequent nonwhitespace characters don't mark the beginning of a word. At the next whitespace character, we reset the flag to **0**, and the program is ready to find the next word. Let's look at the pseudocode:

if c *is not whitespace and* **wordflag** *is* **0**
    set **wordflag** *to* **1** *and count the word*
if c *is whitespace and* **wordflag** *is* **1**
    set **wordflag** *to* **0**

This approach sets the flag to **1** at the beginning of each word and to **0** at the end of each word. Words are counted only at the time the flag setting is changed from **0** to **1**.

Listing 7.7 translates these ideas into C.

❖ *wordcnt.c*

Listing 7.7

```
/* wordcnt.c--counts characters, words, lines */
#include <stdio.h>
#define STOP '|'
#define YES 1
#define NO 0
main()
{
    char c;                /* read in character */
    long n_chars = 0L;     /* number of characters */
    int n_lines = 0;       /* number of lines */
    int n_words = 0;       /* number of words */
    int wordflag = NO;     /* ==YES if c is in a word */

    while(( c = getchar()) != STOP)
    {
        n_chars++;             /* count characters */
        if (c == '\n')
            n_lines++; /* count lines */
        if (c != ' ' && c != '\n' && c != '\t' && wordflag == NO)
        {
            wordflag = YES;  /* starting a new word */
            n_words++;       /* count word */
        }
```

**Listing 7.7
(cont'd.)**

```
    if(( c == ' ' || c == '\n' || c == '\t') &&
        wordflag == YES)
      wordflag = NO;    /* reach end of word */
  }
  printf("characters = %ld, words = %d, lines = %d\n",
      n_chars, n_words, n_lines);
}
```

Here is a sample run:

```
Reason is a
powerful servant but
an inadequate master.
|
characters = 55, words = 9, lines = 3
```

Since there are three different whitespace characters, we use the logical operators to check for all three possibilities. Consider, for example:

```
if( c != ' ' && c != '\n' && c != '\t' && wordflag  == NO)
```

It says: "If **c** is not a space and not a newline and not a tab, and if we are not in a word." (The first three conditions together ask if **c** is nonwhitespace.) If all four conditions are met, then we must be starting a new word, and **n_words** is incremented. If we are in the middle of a word, then the first three conditions hold, but **wordflag** will be **YES**, and **n_words** is not incremented. When we reach the next whitespace character, we set **wordflag** equal to **NO** again. Check the coding to see whether or not the program gets confused if there are several spaces between one word and the next. In the next chapter, we show how to modify this program to count words in a file.

7.5 The Conditional Operator: ?:

C offers a shorthand way to express one form of the **if else** statement. It is called a *conditional expression* and uses the **?:** conditional operator. This operator is a two-part operator that has three operands. Here is an example that yields the absolute value of a number:

```
x = ( y < 0 ) ? -y : y;
```

Everything between the = and the semicolon is the conditional expression. The meaning of the statement is this: If **y** is less than zero, then **x = −y**; otherwise, **x = y**. In **if else** terms:

```
if (y < 0)
  x = -y;
else
  x = y;
```

The general form of the conditional expression follows:

expression1 ? *expression2* : *expression3*

If *expression1* is true (nonzero), then the entire conditional expression has the same value as *expression2*. If *expression1* is false (zero), the entire conditional expression has the same value as *expression3*.

You can use the conditional expression when you have a variable to which can be assigned two possible values. A typical example is setting a variable equal to the maximum of two values:

```
max = (a > b) ? a : b;
```

Usually, an **if else** statement can accomplish the same end as the conditional operator. The operator versions, however, are more compact, and they usually lead to more compact machine language code.

Let's look at a paint program example, one that calculates how many cans of paint are needed to paint a given number of square feet. The basic algorithm is simple: Divide the square footage by the number of square feet covered per can. But suppose the answer is 1.7 cans. Stores sell whole cans, not fractional cans, so you must buy 2 cans to paint such a surface. Therefore, the program should round up to the next integer when a fractional can is involved. The conditional operator can handle this task. Also, we use the conditional operator to print **cans** or **can**, as appropriate. See Listing 7.8.

❖ *paint.c*

Listing 7.8

```
/* paint.c--use conditional operator */
#include <stdio.h>
#define COVERAGE 200 /* square feet per paint can */ main()
{
   int sq_feet;
   int cans;

   printf("Enter number of square feet to be painted:\n");
   while (scanf("%d", &sq_feet) == 1 )
   {
      cans = sq_feet / COVERAGE;
      cans += (sq_feet % COVERAGE == 0) ? 0 : 1;
      printf("You need %d %s of paint.\n", cans,
          cans == 1 ? "can" : "cans");
   }
}
```

Here's a sample run:

```
Enter number of square feet to be painted:
200
You need 1 can of paint.
210
You need 2 cans of paint.
q
```

Because we're using type **int**, the division is truncated, that is, **210/200** becomes **1**; so **cans** is rounded down to the integer part. If **sq_feet % COVERAGE** is **0**, then **COVERAGE** goes into **sq_feet** evenly, and **cans** is left unchanged. Otherwise, there is a remainder, so **1** is added. The following statement accomplishes this task:

```
cans += (sq_feet % COVERAGE == 0) ? 0 : 1;
```

It adds the value of the expression to the right of += to **cans**. The expression to the right is a conditional expression having the value **0** or **1**, depending on whether or not **COVERAGE** goes into **sq_feet** evenly.

The final argument to the **printf( )** function also is a conditional expression:

```
cans == 1 ? "can" : "cans");
```

If the value of **cans** is **1**, then the string **"can"** is used; otherwise **"cans"** is used. This line demonstrates that the conditional operator can use strings for its second and third operands.

▶ Summary: The Conditional Operator

The conditional operator: ? This operator takes three operands, each of which is an expression. They are arranged as follows:

expression1 ? expression2 : expression3

The value of the entire expression equals the value of *expression2* if *expression1* is true; it equals the value of *expression3* otherwise.

Examples.

```
( 5 > 3 ) ? 1 : 2        has the value 1
( 3 > 5 ) ? 1 : 2        has the value 2
( a > b) ? a : b         has the value of the larger of a or b
```

7.6 Multiple Choice: switch and break

The conditional operator and the **if else** construction make it easy to write programs that choose between two alternatives. Sometimes, however, a program needs to choose among several alternatives. To accomplish this task, we can use **if else if else**, but in many cases it is more convenient to use the C **switch** statement. Listing 7.9 shows how the **switch** structure works. This program reads in a letter, and then responds by printing an animal name that begins with that letter.

❖ *animals.c*

Listing 7.9

```
/* animals.c--use a switch statement */
#include <stdio.h>
main()
{
  char ch;

  printf("Give me a letter of the alphabet; I will give ");
  printf("an animal\nname beginning with that letter.\n");
  printf(
    "Please type in a letter; type a # to end my act.\n");
  while((ch = getchar()) != '#')
  {
    if ( ch >= 'a' && ch <= 'z')  /* lowercase only */
      switch (ch)
      {
        case 'a' :
          printf("argali, a wild sheep of Asia\n");
          break;
        case 'b' :
          printf("babirusa, a wild pig of Malay\n");
          break;
        case 'c' :
          printf("coati, racoonlike mammal\n");
          break;
        case 'd' :
          printf("desman, aquatic, molelike critter\n");
          break;
        case 'e' :
          printf("echidna, the spiny anteater\n");
          break;
        default :
          printf("That's a stumper!\n");
      }                           /* end of switch */
    else
      printf("I only recognize lowercase letters.\n");
    while( getchar() != '\n')
      ;                           /* skip rest of input line */
    printf("Please enter another letter or a #.\n");
  }                               /* while loop end */
{
```

A sample run follows:

```
Give me a letter of the alphabet; I will give an animal
name beginning with that letter.
Please type in a letter; type a # to end my act.
a [return]
argali, a wild sheep of Asia
Please enter another letter or a #.
dab [return]
desman, aquatic, molelike critter
Please enter another letter or a #.
r [return]
That's a stumper!
Please enter another letter or a #.
Q [return]
I only recognize lowercase letters.
Please enter another letter or a #.
# [return]
```

(Note: we use [**return**] to indicate that you press the Enter key.)

The program's two main features are its use of the **switch** statement and its handling of input. We look first at how **switch** works.

Using the switch Statement

The expression in the parentheses following the word **switch** is evaluated. In this case, it has whatever value we last entered for **ch**. Then the program scans a list of *labels* (**case 'a' :**, **case 'b' :**, and so on, in this instance) until it finds one that matches that value. The program then jumps to that line. If there is no match, the program moves to the line labeled **default :**. Otherwise, the program proceeds to the statement following **switch**.

The break statement causes the program to break out of the **switch** and skip to the next statement after the **switch**. See Figure 7.4. Without the **break** statement, every statement from the matched label to the end of the **switch** will be processed. For example, if we remove all the **break** statements from our program and then run the program using the letter **d**, we have the following exchange:

```
Give me a letter of the alphabet; I will give an animal
name beginning with that letter.
Please type in a letter; type a # to end my act.
d [return]
desman, aquatic, molelike critter
echidna, the spiny anteater
That's a stumper!
Please enter another letter or a #.
# [return]
```

In this situation, all the statements from **case 'd' :** to the end of the **switch** are executed.

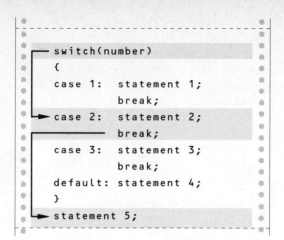

```
switch(number)
{
case 1:    statement 1;
           break;
case 2:    statement 2;
           break;
case 3:    statement 3;
           break;
default:   statement 4;
}
statement 5;
```

```
switch(number)
{
case 1:    statement 1;
case 2:    statement 2;
case 3:    statement 3;
default:   statement 4;
}
statement 5;
```

Figure 7.4

Program flow using the **switch** *statement, with and without* **break**s

in each case, number has the value 2

If you are familiar with Pascal, you will recognize the **switch** statement as being similar to the Pascal case statement. The most important difference is that the **switch** statement requires the use of a **break** if you want only the labeled statement to be processed.

The **switch** labels must be type **int** (including **char**) constants or constant expressions (expressions containing only constants). You can't use a variable for a label. The expression in the parentheses should be one with an integer value (again, including type **char**). The structure of a **switch** follows:

switch (*integer expression*)
   {
  case *constant1* :
    statements; *(optional)*
  case *constant2* :
    statements; *(optional)*
     . . .
  default : *(optional)*
    statements; *(optional)*
  }

The other new feature incorporated into Listing 7.9 is how it reads input. As you may have noticed in the sample run, when **dab** was entered, only the first character was processed. Often this behavior is desirable in interactive programs looking for single-character responses. The code responsible for this behavior follows:

```
while( getchar() != '\n')
    ;    /* skip rest of input line */
```

This loop reads characters from input up to and including the newline character generated by the Enter key. Note that the function return value is not assigned to **ch**; thus the characters are merely read and discarded. Because the last character discarded is the newline character, the next character to be read will be the first character of the next line. This new character is read by the **getchar( )** and assigned to **ch** in the outer **while** loop.

If we omit this loop, the program runs into a bit of trouble. Suppose, for instance, you respond with the letter **a**. Entering it involves pressing Enter, so you actually send the sequence **a** followed by the newline character. After the program processes the **a**, it reads the newline character and prints the "I only recognize lowercase letters." message. Thus each letter entered causes the program to run through the outer **while** loop twice, which is disconcerting to the user. Later in this chapter we discuss the **continue** statement, which offers another way to handle the intrusive newline character.

Multiple Labels

We can use multiple labels for a given statement. For instance, consider the example in Listing 7.10.

Listing 7.10

```
❖ vowels.c

/* vowels.c--use multiple labels */
#include <stdio.h>
main()
{
   char ch;
   int a_ct, e_ct, i_ct, o_ct, u_ct;

   a_ct = e_ct = i_ct = o_ct = u_ct = 0;

   printf("Enter some text; enter # to quit.\n");
   while((ch = getchar()) != '#')
   {
      switch (ch)
      {
         case 'a' :
         case 'A' :    a_ct++;
                       break;
```

Listing 7.10
(cont'd.)

```
          case 'e' :
          case 'E' :    e_ct++;
                        break;
          case 'i' :
          case 'I' :    i_ct++;
                        break;
          case 'o' :
          case 'O' :    o_ct++;
                        break;
          case 'u' :
          case 'U' :    u_ct++;
                        break;
          default : break;
      } /* end of switch */
 } /* while loop end */
 printf("number of vowels: A  E  I  O  U\n");
 printf("                  %4d %4d %4d %4d %4d\n",
     a_ct, e_ct, i_ct, o_ct, u_ct);
 }
```

If **ch** is, say, the letter **i**, the **switch** statement goes to the location labeled **case 'i'**. Because there is no **break** associated with that label, program flow continues to the next statement, which is **i_ct++;**. If **ch** is **I**, program flow continues directly to that statement. In essence, both labels refer to the same statement. Here's a sample run:

```
Enter some text; enter # to quit.
I see under the overseer.#
number of vowels:   A E I O U
                    0 7 1 1 1
```

▶ Multiple Choice with **switch**

Keyword: switch

General comments. Program control jumps to the statement bearing the value of the expression as a label. Program flow then proceeds through the remaining statements unless redirected again. Both the expression and the labels must have integer values (type **char** is included), and the labels must be constants or expressions formed solely from constants. If no label matches the expression value, control passes to the statement labeled **default**, if present. Otherwise, control passes to the next statement following the **switch** statement.

Form.

```
switch (expression)
  {
  case label1 : statement1
  case label2 : statement2
```

```
    default : statement3
    }
```

There can be more than two labeled statements, and the **default** case is optional.

Example.

```
switch (letter)
   {
   case 'a' :
   case 'e' : printf("%d is a vowel\n", letter);
   case 'c' :
   case 'n' : printf("%d is in \"cane\"\n", letter);
   default  : printf("Have a nice day.\n");
   }
```

If **letter** has the value 'a' or 'e', all three messages are printed; 'c' and 'n' cause the last two to be printed. Other values print only the last message.

switch *and* if else

When should you use a **switch** and when should you use an **if else** construction? Often you don't have a choice. You can't use a **switch** if your choice is based on evaluating a **float** variable or expression. Nor can you conveniently use a **switch** if a variable must fall into a certain range. For example, it is simple to write the following:

```
if (integer < 1000 && integer > 2 )
```

but covering this possibility with a **switch** involves setting up case labels for each integer from 3 to 999. However, if you can use a **switch**, often your program will run a little faster and require less code.

7.7 Other Control Statements: break, continue, goto

The branching and looping statements we have discussed are the most important control mechanisms in C. They should be used to provide the overall structure of a program. The three statements we discuss next should be used much more sparingly. Using them excessively will make a program harder to follow, more error-prone, and harder to modify.

The break *Statement*

The most important of these three control statements is **break**, which we encountered when studying **switch**. It can be used with **switch**, where often it is necessary, and also with any of the three loop structures. When encountered, **break** causes the program to break free of the **switch, for, while,** or **do while** that encloses it and to proceed to the next stage of the program. If the **break** statement is inside nested structures, it affects only the innermost structure containing it.

Sometimes **break** is used to leave a loop when there are two separate reasons to leave. Here's an echo loop that stops when it reads either a newline character or a tab character:

```
while ( ( ch = getchar()) != '\n' )
{
   if (ch == '\t')
     break;
   putchar(ch);
}
```

However, we can make the logic clearer if we put both tests in one place:

```
while ( ( ch = getchar() ) != '\n' && ch != '\t' )
   putchar(ch);
```

Note: If you find that you have used a **break** as a part of an **if** statement, see if you can express the condition differently (as we did in the preceding fragment), so that there is no need for the break.

The continue *Statement*

This statement can be used in the three loop forms but not in a **switch**. Like **break**, **continue** interrupts the flow of a program. Instead of terminating the entire loop, however, **continue** causes the rest of an iteration to be skipped and the next iteration to be started. See Figure 7.5.

Let's replace the **break** in the preceding fragment with a **continue**:

```
while ( ( ch = getchar() ) != '\n')
{
   if ( ch == '\t' )
     continue;
   putchar(ch);
}
```

The **break** version quits the loop entirely when a tab character is encountered. The **continue** version merely skips over the tabs and quits only when a newline character is encountered.

Of course, this fragment can be expressed more economically as follows:

```
while ( ( ch = getchar() ) != '\n' )
   if ( ch != '\t')
     putchar(ch);
```

Often, as in this case, reversing an **if** test eliminates the need for a **continue**.

```
    while ( (ch = getchar() ) !=EOF)
    {
        blahblah(ch);
        if (ch == '\n')
            break;
        yakyak(ch);
    }
    blunder(n,m);
```

```
    while ( (ch = getchar() ) !=EOF)
    {
        blahblah(ch);
        if (ch == '\n')
            continue;
        yakyak(ch);
    }
    blunder(n,m);
```

Figure 7.5
break and
continue

On the other hand, the **continue** statement can shorten some programs, especially if they involve long **switch** or nested **if else** statements. For example, recall that in Listing 7.9 we used an inner **while** loop to discard extra characters on the input line, particularly the newline character:

```
while ((ch = getchar()) != '#')
{
  if ( ch >= 'a' && ch <= 'z') /* lowercase only */
    switch (ch)
    {
      case 'a' :
        ...
    }                           /* end of switch */
  else
    printf("I only recognize lowercase letters.\n");
  while ( getchar() != '\n')
    ;                           /* skip rest of input line */
  printf("Please enter another letter or a #.\n");
}
```

A different approach uses the **continue** statement. It doesn't discard extra characters on a line, but it does skip over the troublesome newline character:

```
while ((ch = getchar()) != '#')
{
  if ( ch == '\n')
    continue;                    /* skip newline characters */
  if ( ch >= 'a' && ch <= 'z') /* lowercase only */
    switch (ch)
    {
      case 'a' :
        ...
    }                            /* end of switch */
  else
    printf("I only recognize lowercase letters.\n");
  printf("Please enter another letter or a #.\n");
}
```

The goto Statement

The **goto** statement, the bulwark of BASIC and FORTRAN, is available in C. However, unlike those two languages, C can get along quite well without it. Kernighan and Ritchie refer to the **goto** statement as "infinitely abuseable" and suggest that it "be used sparingly, if at all." First let's look at how to use the **goto** statement in C; then let's show why you don't need it.

The **goto** statement has two parts: the **goto** and a label name. Naming a label follows the same conventions used in naming a variable, for example:

```
goto part2;
```

For this statement to work, there must be another statement bearing the **part2** label. This other statement begins with the label name followed by a colon:

```
part2: printf("Refined analysis:\n");
```

Avoiding the goto

In principle, you never need to use the **goto** in a C program. But if you have a background in FORTRAN or BASIC, both of which require its use, you may have developed programming habits that depend on using the **goto**. To help you get over that dependence, we outline some familiar **goto** situations and then show you a more C-like approach.

1. Handling an **if** situation that requires more than one statement:

```
if ( size > 12)
  goto a;
goto b;
a: cost = cost * 1.05;
   flag = 2;
b: bill = cost * flag;
```

In old-style BASIC and FORTRAN, only the single statement immediately follow-ing the **if** condition is attached to the **if**; no provision is made for blocks or compound statements. We have translated that pattern into the C equivalent. The standard C approach of using a compound statement or block is much easier to follow:

```
if (size > 12)
   {
   cost = cost * 1.05;
   flag = 2;
   }
bill = cost * flag;
```

2. Choosing from two alternatives:

```
if ( ibex > 14)
   goto a;
sheds = 2;
goto b;
a: sheds = 3;
b: help = 2 * sheds;
```

Having the **if else** structure available allows C to express this choice much more cleanly:

```
if ( ibex > 14)
   sheds = 3;
else
   sheds = 2;
help = 2 * sheds;
```

Indeed, newer versions of BASIC and FORTRAN have incorporated the **else** into their syntax.

3. Setting up an indefinite loop:

```
readin: scanf("%d", &score);
if( score < 0)
   goto stage2;
lots of statements;
goto readin;
stage2: more stuff;
```

C uses a **while** loop instead:

```
scanf("%d", &score);
while( score >= 0)
   {
   lots of statements;
   scanf("%d", &score);
   }
more stuff;
```

4. Skipping to the end of a loop. C uses **continue** instead.

5. Leaving a loop. C uses **break** instead. (Actually, **break** and **continue** are specialized forms of a **goto**. The advantages of using them are that their names tell you what they are supposed to do and that, since they don't use labels, there is no danger of putting a label in the wrong place.)

6. Leaping madly about to different parts of a program: *DON'T!*

There is one use of **goto** that is tolerated by many C practitioners: getting out of a nested set of loops if trouble begins:

```
while ( funct > 0 )
  {
  for (i = 1; i <= 100; i++)
    {
    for ( j = 1; j <= 50; j++)
      {
      statements galore;
      if ( big trouble)
         goto help;
      statements;
      }
    more statements;
    }
  yet more statements;
  }
and more statements;
help : bail out;
```

(A single **break** gets you out of only the innermost loop.)

As you can see, the alternative forms are clearer than the **goto** forms. This difference grows even greater when you mix several of these situations together: Which **goto**s are helping **if**s? Which are simulating **if else**s? Which are controlling loops? Which are just there because you have programmed yourself into a corner? And so on. Using **goto** excessively lets you create a labyrinth of program flow. If you aren't familiar with **goto**, keep it that way. If you are used to using it, try to train yourself not to. Ironically, C, which doesn't need a **goto**, has a better **goto** than most languages, because it lets you use descriptive words for labels instead of numbers.

▶ *Summary: Program Jumps*

Keywords: break, continue, goto

General comments. These three instructions cause program flow to jump from one location of a program to another location.

The break command. The **break** statement can be used with any of the three loop forms (**while**, **do while**, and **for**) and with the **switch** statement. It causes program control to skip over the rest of the loop or **switch** containing it and to resume with the next command following the loop or switch.

Example.

```
switch ( number )
  {
  case 4:  printf("That's a good choice.\n");
         break;
  case 5:  printf("That's a fair choice.\n");
         break;
  default: printf("That's a poor choice.\n");
  }
```

The **continue** command. The **continue** statement can be used with any of the three loop forms but not with a **switch**. It causes program control to skip the remaining statements in a loop. For a **while** or **for** loop, the next loop cycle is started. For a **do while** loop, the exit condition is tested, and then if necessary, the next loop cycle is begun.

Example.

```
while ( (ch = getchar()) != EOF)
   {
   if ( ch == ' ' )
      continue;
   putchar(ch);
   chcount++;
   }
```

This fragment echoes and counts nonspace characters.

The **goto** command. A **goto** statement causes program control to jump to a statement bearing the indicated label. A colon is used to separate a labeled statement from its label. Label names follow the same rules that apply to variable names. The labeled statement can precede or follow the **goto**.

Form.

goto *label*;
  . . .
label : *statement*

Example.

```
top : ch = getchar();
   . . .
if ( ch != 'y' )
  goto top;
```

7.8 Summary

The **if** statement uses a test condition to control whether or not a program executes the single simple statement or block following the test condition. Execution occurs if the test expression has a nonzero value; it doesn't occur if the value is zero. The **if else** statement lets you select from two alternatives. If the test condition is nonzero, the statement before the **else** is executed; if the test expression evaluates to zero, the statement following the **else** is executed. By using another **if** statement immediately following the **else**, you can set up a structure that chooses between a series of alternatives.

The test condition often is a relational expression, that is, an expression formed using one of the relational operators discussed in Chapter 6. By using C's logical operators, you can combine relational expressions; for example, you can test to see if x is greater than 0 and less than 20.

The conditional operator (**?:**) creates an expression whose value is governed by its first operand and is given by one of the next two operands. If the first operand is nonzero, the entire expression has the value of the second operand; otherwise, the value is that of the third operand.

The **switch** statement lets you select from a series of statements labeled with integer values. If the integer value of the test condition following the **switch** keyword matches a label, execution continues at the statement bearing that label. Execution then proceeds through the statements following the labeled statement unless you use a **break** statement.

The **break**, **continue**, and **goto** instructions are jump statements that cause program flow to jump to another location in a program. They are not as important control mechanisms as are the branching and looping statements discussed in Chapters 5 and 6, and they should be used more sparingly. A **break** statement causes the program to jump to the next statement following the end of the loop or **switch** containing the **break**. The **continue** statement causes the program to skip the rest of the containing loop and to start the next cycle.

Review Questions

1. Determine which expressions are true and which are false.

a. `100 > 3 && 'a' > 'c'`

b. `100 > 3 || 'a' > 'c'`

c. `!(100 > 3)`

2. Construct an expression to express the following conditions.

a. **number** is equal to or greater than 1 but smaller than 9

b. **ch** is not a q or a k

c. **number** is between 1 and 9 but is not a 5

d. **number** is not between 1 and 9

3. The following program has unnecessarily complex relational expressions as well as some errors. Simplify and correct it:

```
#include <stdio.h>
main()                                          /* 1 */
{                                               /* 2 */
   int weight, height; /*weight in lbs, height in inches */
                                                /* 4 */
   scanf("%d, weight, height);                  /* 5 */
   if ( weight < 100)                           /* 6 */
     if ( height >= 72 )                        /* 7 */
       printf("You are very tall for your weight.\n");
     else if ( height < 72 && > 64)             /* 9 */
       printf( "You are tall for your weight.\n");
   else if ( weight > 300 && !(weight <= 300) )/* 11 */
     if ( !(height >= 48)                       /* 12 */
       printf( " You are quite short for your weight.\n");
   else                                         /* 14 */
     printf("Your weight is ideal.\n");         /* 15 */
                                                /* 16 */

}
```

4. What is the numerical value of each of the following expressions?

a. 5 > 2

b. 3+4 > 2 && 3 < 2

c. x >= y || y > x

d. d = 5 + (6 > 2)

e. 'X' > 'T' ? 10 : 5

f. x > y ? y > x : x > y

5. What will the following program print?

```
#include <stdio.h>
main()
{
   int num;
   for ( num = 1; num <= 11; num++)
   {
     if (num % 3 == 0)
```

```
            putchar('$');
        else
            putchar('*');
            putchar('#');
        putchar('%');
    }
    putchar('\n');
}
```

6. What will the following program print?

```
#include <stdio.h>
main()
{
    int i = 0;
    while ( i < 3) {
        switch(i++) {
            case 0: printf("Merry");
            case 1: printf("Merr");
            case 2: printf("Mer");
            default: printf("Oh no!");
        }
        putchar('\n');
    }
}
```

7. What's wrong with this program?

```
#include <stdio.h>
main()
{
    char ch;
    int lc = 0;  /* lowercase char count
    int uc = 0;  /* uppercase char count
    int oc = 0;  /* other char count

    while ( (ch = getchar()) != '#')
    {
        if ('a' <= ch >= 'z')
            lc++;
        else if ( !(ch < 'A') || !(ch > 'Z')
            uc++;
        oc++;
    }
    printf(%d lowercase, %d uppercase, %d other, lc, uc, oc);
}
```

8. What will the following program print?

```
/* retire.c */
#include <stdio.h>
main()
{
    int age = 20;
    while (age++ <= 65)
    {
        if (( age % 20) == 0) /* is age divisible by 20? */
            printf("You are %d. Here is a raise.\n", age);
        if (age = 65)
            printf("You are %d. Here is your gold watch.\n", age);
    }
}
```

9. What will the following program print when given this input?

Input:

```
q
c
g
b
```

Program:

```
#include <stdio.h>
main()
{
    char ch;

    while ( (ch = getchar() ) != '#')
    {
        if (ch == '\n')
            continue;
        printf("Step 1\n");
        if (ch == 'c')
            continue;
        else if (ch == 'b')
            break;
        else if ( ch == 'g')
            goto laststep;
        printf("Step 2\n");
    laststep: printf("Step 3\n");
    }
    printf("Done\n");
}
```

10. Rewrite the program in Question 9 so that it exhibits the same behavior but does not use a **continue** or a **goto**.

Programming Exercises

1. Write a program that reads input until encountering the # character and that reports back the number of spaces read, the number of newline characters read, and the number of all other characters read.

2. Write a program that reads input until encountering #. Have the program print out each input character and its ASCII decimal code. Print eight character-code pairs per line. Suggestion: Use a character count and the modulus operator (%) to print a newline character every eight cycles of the loop.

3. Using **if else** statements, write a program that reads input up to #, replaces each period with an exclamation mark, replaces each exclamation mark initially present with two exclamation marks, and reports at the end the number of substitutions it has made.

4. Rewrite the program in Exercise 3, using a **switch**.

5. Write a program that reads input up to # and reports back the number of times that the sequence "ei" occurs. Note: The program will have to "remember" the preceding character as well as the current character. Test it with input like "Receive your eieio award."

6. Write a program that requests the hours worked in a week and then prints the gross pay, the taxes, and the net pay. Assume the following:

   Basic pay rate = $10.00/hour

   Overtime (in excess of 40 hours) = time and a half

   Tax rate =15 percent of the first $300

   20 percent of the next $150

   25 percent of the rest

   Use **#define** constants, and don't worry if the example does not conform to current tax law.

7. Modify the basic pay rate in Exercise 6 so that the program presents a menu of pay rates to choose from. Use a **switch** to select the pay rate. The beginning of a run should look something like the following:

   ```
   Enter the number corresponding to the desired pay rate or action:
   1) $8.75/hr    2) $9.33/hr
   3) $10.00/hr  4) $11.20/hr
   5) quit
   ```

   If choices 1–4 are selected, then the program should request the hours worked. The program should recycle until choice 5 is entered. If something other than choices 1–5 is entered, the program should remind the user what the proper choices are, and then recycle. Use **#define** constants.

8. Write a program that accepts an integer as input and displays all the prime numbers smaller than or equal to that number.

9. The 1988 United States Federal Estimated Tax Schedule is the simplest in recent times. It has four categories, and each category has two rates. Here is a summary (dollar amounts are taxable income):

Category	Tax
Single	15 % of first $17,850 plus 28 % of excess
Head of household	15 % of first $23,900 plus 28 % of excess
Married, joint	15 % of first $29,750 plus 28 % of excess
Married, separate	15 % of first $14,875 plus 28 % of excess

For instance, a single wage earner with a taxable income of $20,000 dollars owes 0.15 x $17,850 + 0.28 x ($20,000 – $17,850). Write a program that lets the user specify the tax category and the taxable income and then calculates the tax. Use a loop so that the user can enter several tax cases.

8

Character Input/Output and Redirection

Contents

Objectives

Learning the difference between buffered and unbuffered input

Understanding how C treats I/O devices as files

Learning how to detect the end of a file

Learning how to simulate the end-of-file condition from the keyboard

Using input and output redirection

Learning how to handle input better

Checking input for validity

*T*he words *input* and *output* have more than one use in computing. We can talk about input and output devices such as keyboards, disk drives, and dot-matrix printers. We can talk about the data that are used for input and output. And we can talk about the functions that perform input and output. Our main intent in this chapter is to discuss input and output functions.

By *I/O functions,* we mean functions that transport data to and from your program. We've used several already: **printf( )**, **scanf( )**, **getchar( )**, and **putchar( )**. In this chapter we take a closer look at the conceptual basis for these functions. Also, we describe how to improve the program-user interface.

Input and output functions originally were not part of the definition of C; their development was left to implementors. In practice, the UNIX implementation of C has served as a model for these functions. The ANSI C standard library, recognizing past uses, contains a large number of these I/O functions, including the ones we've used. Such standard functions must work in a wide variety of computer environments, so they don't take advantage of features peculiar to a particular system. Thus, many C implementors supply additional I/O functions that do make use of special features, such as the 8086 microprocessor I/O ports. These functions let you write programs that utilize a specific computer more effectively, but often they can't be used on other computer systems. We concentrate on the standard I/O functions available on all systems, for they allow you to write portable programs that can be moved easily from one system to another.

8.1 Single-Character I/O: getchar( ) and putchar( )

As we saw in Chapter 7, **getchar( )** and **putchar( )** perform input and output one character at a time. Such a system may strike you at first as rather silly. After all, you and I easily read groupings larger than a single character. But this method well suits the ability of a computer. Furthermore, this approach is the heart of most programs that deal with text, that is, with ordinary words. To remind you how **getchar( )** and **putchar( )** work, Listing 8.1 shows a simple example that fetches characters from keyboard input and sends them to the screen. We call this type of activity *echoing the input.* We use a **while** loop that terminates when the # character is encountered.

❖ *echo.c*

Listing 8.1

```
/* echo.c--repeat input */
#include <stdio.h>
main()
{
   char ch;

   while ( (ch = getchar() ) != '#')
     putchar(ch);
}
```

On most systems the definitions of **getchar( )** and **putchar( )** are found in the system file **stdio.h**, which is why we include that file in the program. (Typically, these functions are not true functions but are defined using preprocessor "macros," which we cover in Chapter 16.) Using this program produces exchanges such as the following:

```
Hello, there. I would[return]
Hello, there. I would
like a #3 bag of potatoes.[return]
like a
```

Remember: The **[return]** is our way of indicating that you press the Enter key.

The program raises two questions. First, why do you have to type a whole line before the input is echoed? Second, is there a better way to terminate input? Using a specific character such as # to terminate input, prevents us from including that character in the text. To answer these questions, we must look at how C programs handle keyboard input. In particular, we need to examine buffering and the concept of a standard input file.

8.2 Buffers

When you run Listing 8.1 on some systems, the text you input is echoed immediately. That is, a sample run looks like the following:

```
HHeelloo,, tthheerree.. II wwoouulldd[return]

lliikkee aa #
```

The immediate echoing is an instance of *unbuffered,* or *direct,* input, meaning that the character you type is immediately made available to the waiting program. On most systems, nothing happens until you press Enter, as in the example we showed first. This delayed echoing illustrates *buffered input,* in which the characters you type are collected and stored in an area of temporary storage called a *buffer.* Pressing Enter then causes the block of characters (or single character, if that is all you typed) to be made available to your program. See Figure 8.1.

Why have buffers? First, it is much less time-consuming to transmit several characters as a block than one by one. Second, if you mistype, you can use your keyboard correction facilities to fix your mistake. When you finally press Enter, the corrected version can be transmitted. Unbuffered input, on the other hand, is desirable for some interactive programs. In a word processor, for instance, you would like each command to take place as soon as you press a key. Therefore, both buffered and unbuffered input have their uses.

We can distinguish between fully buffered I/O and line-buffered I/O. If input is *fully buffered,* it's not sent on to the program until the buffer is full. Sending the buffer contents on is called flushing the buffer, as we mentioned in Chapter 3. Since C typically sets up 512-byte buffers, fully buffered input requires a lot of typing before anything is sent on to a program. With *line buffered I/O,* the buffer is flushed whenever

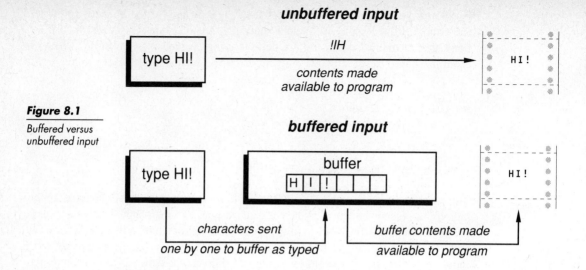

Figure 8.1

Buffered versus unbuffered input

a newline character is used. Keyboard input normally is line-buffered, so that pressing Enter flushes the buffer.

Which do you have: buffered or unbuffered? You can find out by running the program in Listing 8.1 and seeing which behavior results. Some C compilers give you your choice. On our microcomputer system, for example, **getchar( )** provides buffered input, and **getche( )** gives direct input. Also, some operating systems provide a choice. On UNIX, for instance, the **stty** command and the **ioctl( )** function let you specify the type of input that you want. In ANSI C, the **setbuf( )** and **setvbuf( )** functions supply some control over buffering, but the inherent limitations to some systems can restrict the effectiveness of these functions. (We discuss **setbuf( )** and **setvbuf( )** in Chapter 12.) In this book, we assume that you are using buffered input.

8.3 Terminating Keyboard Input

The program in Listing 8.1 terminates when # is entered, which is convenient as long as we exclude that character from normal input. What is the ideal character for program termination? It should be one that normally does not show up in text. That way, it won't pop up accidentally in the middle of some input, stopping the program before we want it to stop. C has an answer to this need, but to understand it, we need to know how C handles files.

Files, Streams, and Keyboard Input

A *file* is a block of memory in which information is stored. Normally a file is kept in some sort of permanent memory, such as on a floppy disk, a hard disk, or tape. You probably are aware of the importance of files to computer systems. For instance, your C programs are kept in files. And programs used to compile your programs are kept in files. This last example points out that some programs need to be able to access particular files. When you compile a program stored in a file called **echo.c**, the compiler opens the **echo.c** file and reads its contents. When the compiler finishes, it closes the file. Other programs, such as word processors, not only open, read, and close files, they also write to them.

C, being powerful, flexible, and so on, has the capacity to open, read, write to, and close files. On one level, it can deal with files using the basic file tools of the host operating system. This feature is called *low-level I/O*. Because of the wide differences among computer systems, it is impossible to create a standard library of universal low-level I/O functions, and ANSI C does not attempt to do so. But C also deals with files on a second level called the *standard I/O package,* which involves creating a standard model and a standard set of I/O functions for dealing with files. Differences between systems are handled by the C implementation so that you deal with a uniform interface.

What are these differences? Different systems store files differently. Some store the file contents in one place and information about the file elsewhere. Some build a description of the file into the file. In dealing with text, some systems use a single newline character to mark the end of a line; others may use the combination of the carriage return and linefeed characters to represent the end of a line. Some systems measure file sizes to the nearest byte; some measure in blocks of bytes.

When you use the standard I/O package, these differences are hidden. Thus to check for a newline, you can use **if (ch == '\n')**. If the system uses the carriage return and linefeed combination, the I/O function automatically translates back and forth between the two representations.

Conceptually, the C program deals with a stream instead of directly with a file. A *stream* is an idealized flow of data to which the actual input or output is mapped. Therefore, various kinds of input with differing properties are represented by streams with more uniform properties. The process of opening a file then becomes one of associating a stream with the file, and reading and writing take place via the stream.

We discuss files in general in Chapter 12. The relevance here is that C treats input and output devices the same as it treats regular files on storage devices. In particular, the keyboard and display device are treated as files that are opened automatically by every C program. Keyboard input is represented by a stream called **stdin**. Output to the screen (or teletype, or other output device) is represented by a stream called **stdout**. The **getchar( )**, **putchar( )**, **printf( )**, and **scanf( )** functions all are members of the standard I/O package, and they deal with these two streams.

One implication of C's treatment of input and output is that we can use the same techniques with keyboard input as we do with files. For example, a program reading a file needs a way to detect the end of the file so that it knows where to stop reading. Therefore C input functions come equipped with built-in end-of-file detectors. Since keyboard input is treated like a file, we should be able use the end-of-file detector to terminate keyboard input. Let's explore the end-of-file concept, beginning with files.

A computer operating system needs some way to tell where each file begins and ends. One method to detect the end of a file is to place a special character there, which is the method used, for example, by CP/M, IBM-DOS, and MS-DOS text files. These operating systems use (or once used) the Control-Z character to mark the ends of files; Control-Z is the character generated by holding the Control key down while pressing the z key. Figure 8.2 illustrates this approach.

prose:

Ishphat the robot
slid open the hatch
and shouted his challenge.

Figure 8.2

A file with an end-of-file marker

prose in a file:

Ishphat the robot\n slid open the hatch\n and shouted his challenge.\n ^Z

A second approach is for the operating system to store information on the size of the file. If a file has 3000 bytes and a program has read 3000 bytes, then it has reached the end of the file. MS-DOS and its relatives use this approach for binary files, since it allows the files to hold all characters, including Control-Z. Newer versions of DOS also use this approach for text files. UNIX uses this approach for all files.

C uses the **getchar( )** function to return a special signal when the end of a file is detected, regardless of the method actually used to find the end of the file. The name given to this signal is **EOF** (end of file). Thus, the return value for **getchar( )** when it detects an end of file is **EOF**. The **scanf( )** function also returns **EOF** on detecting the end of file.

Typically, **EOF** is defined in the **stdio.h** file as follows:

```
#define EOF (-1)
```

Why -1? Normally, **getchar( )** returns a value in the range 0 through 127, since those values correspond to the standard character set. It may return values from 0 through 255 if the system recognizes an extended character set. In either case, the value -1 does not correspond to any character, so it can be used as a signal.

Some systems may define the **EOF** constant with a different numerical value, but any value chosen always is different from a return value produced by a legitimate input character. If you include the **stdio.h** file and use the **EOF** symbol, you don't have to worry about the numerical definition. The important point to keep in mind is that **EOF** represents a signal from **getchar( )** that it found the end of a file; it is not a symbol actually found in the file.

To use **EOF** in a program, we compare the return value of **getchar( )** with **EOF**. If they are different, we have not yet reached the end of a file. In other words, we can use an expression like the following:

```
while ( (ch = getchar() ) != EOF)
```

What if we are reading keyboard input and not a file? Most systems provide a way to simulate an end-of-file condition from the keyboard. Therefore, we can rewrite our basic read-and-echo program (Listing 8.1) as shown in Listing 8.2.

Listing 8.2

❖ *echo_eof.c*

```
/* echo_eof.c--repeat input to end of file */
#include <stdio.h>
main()
{
   int ch;

   while ( (ch = getchar() ) != EOF)
     putchar(ch);
}
```

Note these points:

1. We don't have to define **EOF**; **stdio.h** takes care of that detail.

2. We don't have to worry about the actual value of **EOF**, for the **#define** statement in **stdio.h** lets us use the symbolic representation **EOF**.

3. We change **ch** from type **char** to type **int**. We do so because **char** variables may be represented by unsigned integers in the range 0 to 255, but **EOF** may have the numerical value –1. Such a value is an impossible value for an unsigned **char** variable, but it is not for an **int**. Fortunately, **getchar( )** is actually of type **int** itself, so it can read the **EOF** character. Implementations that use a signed **char** type may get by with declaring **ch** as type **char**, but it is better to use the more general form.

4. The fact that **ch** is an integer doesn't bother **putchar( )**, which still prints out the character equivalent.

5. To use this program on keyboard input, we need a way to type the **EOF** character. You can't just type the letters E-O-F or the value –1. (Typing –1 in fact transmits two characters: a hyphen and the digit 1.) Instead, you have to find out what your system requires. On most UNIX systems, for example, typing Control-D at the beginning of a line causes the end-of-file signal to be transmitted. Many microcomputing systems recognize a Control-Z typed anywhere on a line as an end-of-file signal.

Here is a buffered example of running Listing 8.2:

```
She walks in beauty, like the night
She walks in beauty, like the night
  Of cloudless climes and starry skies...
  Of cloudless climes and starry skies...
  Lord Byron
  Lord Byron
[control-d]
```

Each time we press Enter, the characters stored in the buffer are processed, and a copy of the line is printed out. This pattern continues until we simulate the end of file UNIX-style.

Let's consider the possibilities for Listing 8.2. It copies onto the screen whatever input we feed it.

1. Suppose we can somehow feed a file to it: Then it will print the contents of the file onto the screen, stopping when it reaches the end of the file, because it will have encountered an **EOF** signal.

2. Suppose instead that we can find a way to direct the program's output to a file: Then we can type data on the keyboard and use Listing 8.2 to store what we type.

3. Suppose we can simultaneously direct input from one file into Listing 8.2 and send the output to another file: Then we can use Listing 8.2 to copy files.

Therefore, such a program has the potential to look at the contents of files, to create new files, and to make copies of files. The key is to control the flow of input and output.

8.4 Redirection and Files

Input and output involve functions, data, and devices. For instance, Listing 8.2 uses the input function **getchar( )**. The input device (we have assumed) is a keyboard, and the input data are individual characters. Let's now consider keeping the same input function and the same kind of data and changing where the program looks for data. A good question to ask is: "How does a program know where to look for its input?"

By default, a C program using the standard I/O package looks to the standard input as a source for input, which is the stream we earlier identified as **stdin**. This source is whatever has been set up as the usual way for reading data into the computer. It can be magnetic tape, punched cards, a teletype, or (as we continue to assume) a video terminal. A modern computer is a suggestible tool, however, and we can influence it to look elsewhere for input. In particular, we can instruct a program to seek its input from a file instead of from a keyboard.

There are two methods to instruct a program to work with files instead of the keyboard. One way is to use explicitly special functions that open files, close files, read files, write in files, and so forth (which we discuss in Chapter 12). A second way is to use a program designed to work with the keyboard and the screen but to *redirect* input and output along different channels, for example, to and from files. In other words, we reassign the **stdin** stream to the file. The **getchar( )** program continues to receive its data from the stream, not really caring from where the stream gets its data. This approach is more limited in some respects than the first one, but it is much simpler to use, and it is the one we use in this chapter.

One major problem with redirection is that it is a feature of the operating system, not of C. But the most popular C environments (UNIX and DOS 2.0 and later) allow for redirection, and some C implementations simulate it on systems lacking the capacity.

UNIX and DOS Redirection

UNIX and current DOS versions let you redirect both input and output. Redirecting input enables you to use a file instead of the keyboard for input. Redirecting output enables you to use a file instead of the screen for output.

Redirecting Input

Suppose you have compiled the program in Listing 8.2 and placed the executable version in a file called **echo_eof** (or **echo_eof.exe** on DOS systems). To run the program, you just type the filename:

```
echo_eof
```

and the program runs as described earlier, taking its input from what you type at the keyboard.

Now suppose you wish to use the program on a text file called **words**. A *text file* is one that contains text, that is, data stored as characters. This file can be an essay or a program in C, for example. A file that contains machine language instructions such as the file holding the executable version of a program is not a text file. Since our program works with characters, it should be used with text files. All you need to do to run the file called **words** is enter the following command:

```
echo_eof < words
```

The < symbol is a UNIX redirection operator. (Note: The spaces on either side of the < are optional for UNIX.) It causes the **words** file to be associated with the **stdin** stream, channeling the file contents into **echo_eof**. The **echo_eof** program itself doesn't know (or care) that the input is coming from a file instead of the keyboard. All it knows is that a stream of characters is being fed to it, so it reads them and prints them one character at a time until the end-of-file symbol appears. Because C regards files and I/O devices on the same basis, the file is now the I/O "device."

The following is a sample run for a specific **words** file:

```
$ echo_eof < words
To see a World in a grain of sand,
And a Heaven in a wild flower,
Hold Infinity in the palm of your hand,
And Eternity in an hour.
$
```

The $ is one of the two standard UNIX prompts. On a DOS system, you will see the DOS prompt, perhaps an **A>** or **C>**.

Redirecting Output

Now suppose that you wish to have the words you type sent to a file called **mywords**. Then you can enter:

```
echo_eof > mywords
```

and begin typing. The > is a second redirection operator. It causes a new file called **mywords** to be created for your use, and then it redirects the output of **echo_eof** (that is, a copy of the characters you type) to that file. The operator reassigns **stdout**, so that it is associated with the **mywords** file instead of with the display screen. If you already have a **mywords** file, normally it is erased and replaced with the new version. (Note: Some UNIX systems give you the option of protecting existing files, however.) All that appears on the screen are the letters you type, and the copies go to the file instead. To end the program on a UNIX system press Control-D at the beginning of a line; on a DOS system press Control-Z. The following example uses the UNIX prompt:

```
$ echo_eof > mywords
You should have no problem recalling which redirection
operator does what. Just remember that each operator points
in the direction the information flows. Think of it as a
funnel.
[control-d]
$
```

Remember: Each line must end with a **[return]** to send the buffer contents to the program. Once Control-D or Control-Z is processed, the program terminates and returns control to the UNIX or DOS operating system, as is indicated by the return of the prompt. To find out if the program copied the text to the **mywords** file, first use the UNIX **ls** command or DOS **dir** command, which lists filenames, to show that the **mywords** file exists. Then use the UNIX **cat** or DOS **type** command to check the contents. As well, you can run **echo_eof** again and redirect the file to the program:

```
C> echo_eof < mywords
You should have no problem recalling which redirection
operator does what. Just remember that each operator points
in the direction the information flows. Think of it as a
funnel.
C>
```

This time, we show the DOS **C>** prompt.

Combined Redirection

Now suppose you want to make a copy of the file **mywords** and call it **savewords**. Issue the following command:

```
echo_eof < mywords > savewords
```

and the deed is done. The command:

```
echo_eof > savewords < mywords
```

can serve as well, since the order of redirection operations doesn't matter.

Note: Don't use the same filename for both input and output in one command:

```
echo_eof < mywords > mywords    ⇐Wrong
```

Remember that **> mywords** causes the original **mywords** to be erased before it is ever used as input.

In brief, the following rules govern the use of the two redirection operators **<** and **>**:

1. A redirection operator connects an executable program (including standard UNIX commands) with a file. It cannot be used to connect one file with another file or one program with another program.

2. Input cannot be taken from more than one file, nor can output be directed to more than one file using these operators.

3. Normally, the spaces between the names and operators are optional, except occasionally when some characters with special meaning to the UNIX shell or DOS are used. For example, in general we can use **echo_eof<words**.

We have already given several proper examples. Here are some incorrect examples (**addup** and **count** are executable programs; **fish** and **stars** are text files):

fish > stars Violates Rule 1

addup < count Violates Rule 1

addup < fish < stars Violates Rule 2

count > stars fish Violates Rule 2

UNIX and DOS also feature a **>>** operator, which lets you add data to the end of an existing file, and the pipe operator (**|**), which lets you connect the output of one program to the input of a second program. See a UNIX book such as *UNIX Primer Plus* (Waite, Prata, and Martin, Indianapolis: Howard W. Sams, 1987) for more information on all these operators.

Comment

Redirection enables us to use keyboard-input programs with files. But for this process to work, the program has to test for end of file. For example, in Chapter 7 we presented a word-counting program that counted words up to the first | character. If we change **ch** from type **char** to type **int** and replace '|' with **EOF** in the loop test, we can use the program to count words in text files.

▶ **Summary: How to Redirect Input and Output**

With most C systems you can use redirection, either for all programs through the operating system or else just for C programs, courtesy of the C compiler. In the following, let **prog** be the name of the executable program and let **file1** and **file2** be names of files.

Redirecting output to a file: >

prog > file1

Redirecting input from a file: <

prog < file2

Combined redirection:

prog < file2 > file1
prog > file1 < file2

Both forms use **file2** for input and **file1** for output.

Spacing. Some systems require a space to the left of the redirection operator and no space to the right. Other systems (UNIX, for example) will accept either spaces or no spaces on either side.

8.5 A Graphic Example

We can use **getchar( )** and **putchar( )** to produce geometric patterns using characters. See Listing 8.3. This program reads a character and then prints it a number of times, the number depending on the ASCII value. It also prints a sufficient number of leading spaces to center each line.

The program uses nested loops. The outer **while** loop gathers input characters. The first inner **while** loop prints spaces to center the following text, and the second **while** loop prints the character. The number of the character printed is determined from the numeric code for the character.

```
/* patterns.c--produces a symmetric pattern of
     characters */
#include <stdio.h>
main()
{
  int ch;              /* read character */
  int index;
  int chnum;

  while ((ch = getchar()) != '\n') {
    chnum = ch % 26; /* produces a number from 0 to 25 */
    index = 0;
    while (index++ < (30-chnum))
      putchar(' '); /* spaces to center pattern */
    index = 0;
    while (index++ < (2*chnum + 1))
      putchar(ch);  /* print ch several times */
  putchar('\n');
  }
}
```

Listing 8.3

Your printout depends on the data you input. If, for example, you type:

What's up?

then the response is the following:

```
                WWWWWWWWWWWWWWWWW
                        h
    aaaaaaaaaaaaaaaaaaaaaaaaaaaaaaaaaaaaaaa
        ttttttttttttttttttttttttttt
            ''''''''''''''
          sssssssssssssssssssssss
        uuuuuuuuuuuuuuuuuuuuuuuuuuu
            ppppppppppppppppp
          ?????????????????????????
```

With this program, you can combine input characters into patterns. For example, the following input:

hijklmnopqrstuiii

produces:

```
                h
               i i i
              j j j j j
             k k k k k k k
            l l l l l l l l l
           m m m m m m m m m m m
          n n n n n n n n n n n n n
         o o o o o o o o o o o o o o o
        p p p p p p p p p p p p p p p p p
       q q q q q q q q q q q q q q q q q q q
      r r r r r r r r r r r r r r r r r r r r r
     s s s s s s s s s s s s s s s s s s s s s s s
    t t t t t t t t t t t t t t t t t t t t t t t t t
   u u u u u u u u u u u u u u u u u u u u u u u u u u u
               i i i
               i i i
               i i i
```

8.6 Creating a More Friendly User Interface

Sometimes programmers, especially beginning ones, neglect the interface between the program and the user. It is often possible to facilitate data entry and smooth over the effects of faulty input. Let's look at some typical input problems and solutions.

Working with Buffered Input

Although buffered input often is a convenience to the user, it can be bothersome to the programmer when character input is used. The problem, which we've seen in some examples earlier in this book, is that buffered input requires the user to press Enter to transmit input. This action also transmits a newline character, which the program must handle.

Let's review this problem with a guessing program. We pick a number, and the computer tries to guess it. The method is a plodding one, but we are concentrating on I/O here, not algorithms. The program has input problems in addition to handling newlines; let's solve them, too. See Listing 8.4 for the starting version of the program.

❖ *guess.c*

Listing 8.4

```
/* guess.c--an inefficient number-guesser */
#include <stdio.h>
main()
{
    int guess = 1;
    char response;

    printf("Pick an integer from 1 to 100. I will try to ");
```

Listing 8.4
(cont'd.)

```
    printf("guess it.\nRespond with a y if my guess is right");
    printf("and with\nan n if it is wrong.\n");
    printf("Uh...is your number %d?\n", guess);
    while((response = getchar()) != 'y')   /* get response */
    printf("Well, then, is it %d?\n", ++guess);
    printf("I knew I could do it!\n");
}
```

Here's a sample run:

```
Pick an integer from 1 to 100. I will try to guess it.
Respond with a y if my guess is right and with
an n if it is wrong.
Uh...is your number 1?
n
Well, then, is it 2?
Well, then, is it 3?
n
Well, then, is it 4?
Well, then, is it 5?
y
I knew I could do it?
```

Out of consideration for the program's pathetic guessing algorithm, we choose a small number; fortunately, it was odd. What's happening is that the program reads our **n** response as a denial that the number is **1**, then reads the newline character as a denial that the number is **2**.

One solution is to use a **while** loop to discard the rest of the input line, including the newline character. This method has the additional merit of treating responses such as **no** or **no way** the same as a simple **n**. The original version treats **no** as two responses. Here is the revised loop:

```
while((response = getchar()) != 'y') /* get response */
{
   printf("Well, then, is it %d?\n", ++guess);
   while ( getchar() != '\n')
      ;                        /* skip rest of input line */
}
```

Using this loop produces responses like the following:

```
Pick an integer from 1 to 100. I will try to guess it.
Respond with a y if my guess is right and with
an n if it is wrong.
Uh...is your number 1?
```

```
n
Well, then, is it 2?
no
Well, then, is it 3?
no sir
Well, then, is it 4?
forget it
Well, then, is it 5?
y
I knew I could do it!
```

We therefore have solved the problem with the newline character. But as a purist, you may not like **f** being treated as meaning the same as **n**. To eliminate this defect, we can use an **if** statement to screen out other responses:

```
while((response = getchar()) != 'y') /* get response */
{
  if ( response == 'n')
    printf("Well, then, is it %d?\n", ++guess);
  else
    printf("Sorry, I only understand y or n.\n");
  while ( getchar() != '\n')
    ;                          /* skip rest of input line */
}
```

Now the program response looks like the following:

```
Pick an integer from 1 to 100. I will try to guess it.
Respond with a y if my guess is right and with
an n if it is wrong.
Uh...is your number 1?
n
Well, then, is it 2?
no
Well, then, is it 3?
no sir
Well, then, is it 4?
forget it
Sorry, I only understand y or n.
n
Well, then, is it 5?
y
I knew I could do it!
```

When you write interactive programs, you should try to anticipate ways in which users will fail to follow instructions. Then you should design the program to handle these user failures gracefully. Tell them when they are wrong, and give them another chance.

Sometimes we use **getchar( )** to read input a character at a time, and sometimes we use **scanf( )** to read numbers or strings. This mixture can create problems because **getchar( )** **reads every character, including spaces, tabs, and newlines, whereas scanf( )**, when reading numbers, skips over spaces, tabs, and newlines. (However, when reading characters using the **%c** specifier, **scanf( )** behaves like **getchar( ).**)

To illustrate a representative problem, Listing 8.5 presents a program that reads in a character and two numbers as input. It then prints the character using the number of rows and columns specified in the input.

❖ *showchar.c*

```
/* showchar.c--program with an I/O problem */
#include <stdio.h>
main()
{
   int ch;            /* character to be printed */
   int rows, cols;    /* number of rows and columns */
   void display();    /* print ch as directed */

   while( (ch = getchar()) != EOF)
   {
      scanf("%d %d",&rows, &cols);
      display(ch, rows, cols);
   }
}

void display(c, n, m)
char c;
int n,m;
{
   int row, col;

   for ( row = 1; row <= n; row++)
   {
      for ( col = 1; col <= m; col++)
         putchar(c);
      putchar('\n'); /* end line and start a new one */
   }
}
```

Listing 8.5

We've set up the program so that **main( )** reads the data and **display( )** does the printing. Note the new keyword **void**. Modern C usage calls for declaring functions without return values as type **void**. Here **void** indicates emptiness, the absence of a return value. Our emphasis, however, is on the input process. Let's look at a sample run and see what the problem is:

```
a 2 3
aaa
aaa
b 1 2
```

```
bb
```

```
[control-z]
[control-z]
```

The program works well at first: We enter **a 2 3**, and the program prints two rows of three **a** characters, as expected. Then we enter **b 1 2**, and the program prints one row with two **b** characters. But in between the program prints eight blank lines! The newline character is at fault again. The first newline character immediately follows the **3** on the first input line. Since **getchar( )** doesn't skip over newline characters, this newline character is read by **getchar( )** during the next cycle of the loop and becomes the character to be displayed.

Our **scanf( )** statement also adds to our problems. Because **getchar( )** reads the newline, the next input is the **b** character, which **scanf( )** attempts to read as an integer and fails. Therefore, **rows** retains its previous value of **2**, and **scanf( )** tries to read the **cols** value. Input remains stuck on the **b**, so that read also fails, and **cols** remains at **3**. The net result is that the program instructs **display( )** to print two rows of three newline characters. Because each newline character generates a new line, the program prints a total of eight blank lines. The next loop cycle then begins, and **getchar( )** finally is able to read the **b**, which allows **scanf( )** to read the next two numbers. Similarly, the newline following this line results in our having to enter Control-Z twice to end the program (assuming the program is run on a DOS system).

To clear up this problem, the program has to skip over any newlines or spaces between the last number typed for one cycle of input and the character typed at the beginning of the next line. Also, it would be nice if the program could be terminated at the **scanf( )** stage in addition to the **getchar( )** test. Listing 8.6 updates our program to accomplish this task.

❖ *showchar.c*

Listing 8.6

```
/* showchar.c--print chars in rows and columns */
#include <stdio.h>
main()
{
    int ch;          /* character to be printed */
    int rows, cols;  /* number of rows and columns */
    void display();  /* print ch as directed */
```

```
    while( (ch = getchar()) != EOF)
    {
        if ( ch != '\n' && ch != ' ' && ch != '\t')
        {
                if (scanf("%d %d",&rows, &cols) != 2)
            break;
          display(ch, rows, cols);
        }
    }
}

void display(c, n, m)
char c;
int n,m;
{
    int row, col;

    for ( row = 1; row <= n; row++)
    {
        for ( col = 1; col <= m; col++)
            putchar(c);
        putchar('\n'); /* end line and start a new one */
    }
}
```

Listing 8.6 (cont'd.)

The **if** statement causes the program to skip over the **scanf( )** and **display( )** instructions if **ch** is whitespace. Thus we can now enter data fairly freely:

```
a 2 3
aaa
aaa
b 1 2 c 3 5
bb
ccccc
ccccc
ccccc
[control-z]
```

By using an **if** statement with a **break**, we terminate the program if the return value of **scanf( )** is not **2**. This situation occurs if one or both input values are not integers or if the end-of-file marker is encountered. The **if** statement also allows the program to skip over spaces as well as newlines. Therefore, the program can handle the second input line. If we omit the space-skipping, the input line will have to look like the following:

```
b 1 2c 3 5
```

Otherwise, a space between the **2** and **c** will be read into **ch**, and **scanf( )** will try to read **c** as an integer.

8.7 Character Sketches

Let's now create a program that draws rough, filled-in figures using characters. Each line of output consists of an unbroken row of characters. We choose the character and the starting and stopping positions for printing the character in the row. The program keeps reading our choices until it finds **EOF**. See Listing 8.7. The program illustrates several programming techniques, which we discuss shortly.

❖ *sketcher.c*

Listing 8.7

```
/* sketcher.c--this program makes solid figures */
#include <stdio.h>
#define TRUE 1
#define FALSE 0
#define MAXLENGTH 80
main()
{
    int ch;            /* character to be printed */
    int start, stop;   /* starting and stopping points */
    int badlimits();   /* returns TRUE for bad limits */
    void display();    /* print ch as directed */

    while((ch = getchar()) != EOF)  /* read in character */
    {
        if ( ch == '\n' || ch == ' ' || ch == '\t')
            continue;      /* skip newlines, spaces */
        if (scanf("%d %d", &start, &stop) != 2)
                        /* read limits */
            break;
        if( badlimits(start, stop, MAXLENGTH) )
            printf("Inappropriate limits were entered.\n");
        else
            display(ch, start, stop);
    }
}
int badlimits(begin, end, limit)
int begin, end, limit;
{
    if (begin > end || begin < 1 || end > limit)
        return TRUE;
    else
        return FALSE;
}

void display(c, n, m)
char c;
int n,m;
{
    int column;  /* position counter */
```

**Listing 8.7
(cont'd.)**

```
for ( column = 1; column < n; column++)
    putchar(' ');   /* print blanks to starting point */
for ( column = n; column <= m; column++)
    putchar(c);     /* print char to stopping point */
putchar('\n');      /* end line and start a new one */
}
```

The general structure is similar to that of Listing 8.6, with three main differences:

1. Instead of running the main part of the program as a part of an **if** statement that tests to see if **ch** is not whitespace, we use a **continue** statement to skip to the end of the loop if **ch** is whitespace.

2. The **display( )** function is rewritten to display the character in a different manner. Now **n** represents the first column for displaying the character, and **m** represents the last column for displaying the character. Previously they represented the number of rows and columns.

3. We've added a **badlimits( )** function to screen out bad input values.

Suppose we call the executable program **sketcher**. To run the program, we type its name. Then we enter a character and two numbers. The program responds, we enter another set of data, and the program responds again until we provide an **EOF** signal. On a UNIX system using the % to prompt an exchange can look like the following:

```
% sketcher
B 10 20
         BBBBBBBBBBB
Y 12 18
           YYYYYYY
[control-d]
%
```

The program prints out the character **B** in columns 10 to 20, and it prints **Y** in columns 12 to 18. Unfortunately, when we use the program interactively, our commands are interspersed with the output. A much more satisfactory way to use the program is to create a file containing suitable data and then to use redirection to feed the file to the program. Suppose, for example, the file **fig** contains the following data:

```
_ 30 50
| 30 50
| 30 50
| 30 50
| 30 50
| 30 50
```

```
= 20 60
: 31 49
: 30 49
: 29 49
: 27 49
: 25 49
: 30 49
: 30 49
/ 30 49
: 35 48
: 35 48
```

Then the command **sketcher < fig** produces the output shown in Figure 8.3. (Note: Printers and screens have different values for the vertical-to-horizontal ratio for characters, and this discrepancy causes figures of this sort to look more compressed vertically when printed than when displayed on a screen.)

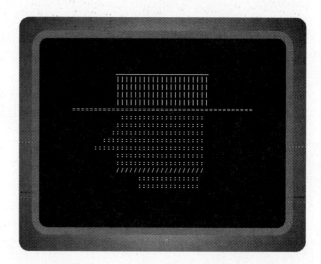

Figure 8.3

Output of character sketch program

Analyzing the Program

The program in Listing 8.7 is short, but it is more involved than the examples we have given previously. Let's look at some of its elements.

Line Length

We limit the program to print no farther than the 80th column, since 80 characters is the standard width of many video monitors and of normal-width paper. However, you can redefine the value of **MAXLENGTH** if you wish to use the program with a device having a different output width.

Program Structure

We follow the modular approach, using functions to verify input and to manage the display. The **main( )** function handles data acquisition:

```
while ( (ch = getchar()) != EOF)
{
  if ( ch == '\n' || ch == ' ' || ch == '\t')
    continue;                    /* skip newlines, spaces */
  if (scanf("%d %d", &start, &stop) != 2)  /* read limits */
    break;
    ...
}
```

With Listing 8.6, we already discussed the rationale for reading in data the way we do, skipping over whitespace. One more point is that separating the character input from the numeric input lets the program decide whether or not to read numbers based on the character value. Note, however, that this situation wouldn't be true if we used something along the following lines:

```
while ( scanf("%c%d%d", &ch, &start, &stop) == 3 )
```

Next the program checks to see if the input makes sense:

```
if( badlimits(start, stop, MAXLENGTH) )
  printf("Inappropriate limits were entered.\n");
else
  ...
```

The purpose of this **if else** statement is to let the program skirt around values of **start** and **stop** that lead to trouble. We discuss the details of the **badlimits( )** function later in the next section. The important point here is that **badlimits( )** returns a value of **TRUE** if the data fail to pass the testing procedure. In that case, the computer prints a message and skips over the **else** portion, which is the display output.

The **display( )** function uses one **for** loop to print spaces up to where the character is first to appear. The second **for** loop then prints the character from the start column to the end column. Finally, the **display( )** function prints a newline to end the line:

```
void display(c, n, m)
char c;
int n,m;
{
  int column;      /* position counter */

  for ( column = 1; column < n; column++)
    putchar(' ');  /* print blanks to starting point */
  for ( column = n; column <= m; column++)
    putchar(c);    /* print char to stopping point */
  putchar('\n');   /* end line and start a new one */
}
```

Error-Checking

The problem of getting the user to input data that the computer can use properly is a pervasive one. One technique is to use *error-checking*, which means having the computer check the data to see if it is okay before using it. We have included a beginning effort at error-checking in this program with the **badlimits( )** function:

```
int badlimits(begin, end, limit)
int begin, end, limit;
{
   if (begin > end || begin < 1 || end > limit)
     return TRUE;
   else
     return FALSE;
}
```

What are we protecting against? First, it makes no sense for the starting position to follow the final position; terminals normally print from left to right, not vice versa. The expression **begin > end** checks for that possible error. Second, the first column on a screen is column **1**; we can't write to the left of the left margin. The **begin > 1** expression guards against making that kind of error. Finally, the expression **end > limit** checks to see that we don't try to print beyond the right margin.

Are there any other erroneous values we could give to **begin** and **end**? Well, we could try to make **begin** greater than **limit**. Our program doesn't check for this error directly. However, suppose **begin** is greater than **limit**. Then, either **end** is also greater than **limit**, in which case the error is caught, or **end** isn't greater than **limit**. If **end** is less than **limit**, it must also be less than **begin**, so this error is caught by the first test. Another possible error is that **end** is less than **1**. We leave it to you to make sure that this error doesn't sneak through.

Out test is pretty simple. If you design a program for serious use, you should put additional effort into this part of the program. For instance, you should put in error messages to identify which values are wrong and why. You can also inject more personality into the messages, for example:

```
Your value of 897654 for stop exceeds the screen width.
Oh my! Your START is bigger than your STOP. Please try again.
THE START VALUE SHOULD BE BIGGER THAN 0, HONORED USER.
```

Another potential input problem is having letters appear when **scanf( )** expects numbers. As the program is set up, such a situation causes the program to terminate, which is preferable to it getting stuck or misinterpreting input. It's also possible to have **scanf( )** skip over data it can't read; we discuss this technique in Chapter 9.

8.8 Menu Browsing

Many computer programs use menus as part of the user interface. Menus make programs easier for the user, but they pose some problems for the programmer. Let's see what's involved.

A menu offers the user a choice of responses. Here's a hypothetical example:

```
Enter the letter of your choice:
a. advice    b. bell
c. count     d. quit
```

Ideally, the user then enters one of these choices, and the program acts on that choice. As a programmer, you want this process to go smoothly. Your first subgoal is for the program to work well when the user follows instructions. Your second subgoal is for the program to work well when the user fails to follow instructions. As you may expect, the second goal is the more difficult, for it's hard to anticipate the possible mistreatment that users may invent.

Tasks

Let's look specificaly at the tasks the program needs to perform. It needs to obtain the user's response, and it needs to select a course of action based on that response. Also, the program should allow the user to return to the menu for further choices. C's **switch** statement provides a natural vehicle for choosing actions, for each user choice can be made to correspond to a particular **case** label. We can use a **while** statement to provide repeated access to the menu. In pseudocode, we can describe the process this way:

> *get choice*
> **while** *choice is not 'd'*
>   **switch** *to desired choice and execute it*
>   *get next choice*

Toward a Smoother Execution

Program smoothness comes into play when we decide how to implement our goals. One thing we can do, for example, is have the "get choice" segment screen out inappropriate responses so that only correct responses are passed on to the **switch**. This idea suggests representing the input process by a function that can only return correct responses. Combining this screening procedure with a **while** loop and a **switch** leads to the following program structure:

```
#include <stdio.h>
main()
{
   int choice;
   int getchoice();
   void count();
```

```
while ( (choice = getchoice()) != 'd')
{
  switch (choice)
  {
    case 'a' : printf("Buy low, sell high.\n");
       break;
    case 'b' : putchar('\a'); /* ANSI */
       break;
    case 'c' : count();
       break;
    default  : printf("Program error!\n");
       break;
  }
}
}
```

The **getchoice( )** function is defined so that it can return only the values '**a**', '**b**', '**c**', and '**d**'. We use it much as we use **getchar( )**: obtaining a value and comparing it to a termination value, '**d**', in this case. We've kept the actual menu choices simple, so that we can concentrate on the program structure; we discuss the **count( )** function in greater detail shortly. The **default** case is handy for debugging. If our **getchoice( )** function fails to limit its return value to the intended values, the **default** case lets us know we've run into a problem.

The getchoice( ) *Function*

Here, in pseudocode, is one possible design for this function:

show choices
get response
while *response is not acceptable*
    prompt for more response
    get response

The following is a simple, but awkward, implementation:

```
int getchoice()
{
  int ch;

  printf("Enter the letter of your choice:\n");
  printf("a. advice  b. bell\n");
  printf("c. count   d. quit\n");
  ch = getchar();
  while ( ch < 'a' || ch > 'd')
  {
    printf("Please respond with a, b, c, or d.\n");
    ch = getchar();
  }
  return ch;
}
```

The problem is that with buffered input, every newline generated by the Enter key is treated as an erroneous response. To make the program interface smoother, the function should skip over newlines.

There are several ways to implement this feature. One is to replace **getchar( )** with a new function, call it **getfirst( )**, that reads the first character on a line and discards the rest. This new function also has the advantage of treating an input line consisting of, say, **advice**, as being the same as a simple **a**, instead of treating it as one good response followed by **d** for **quit**. With this goal in mind, we can reprogram the input function as follows:

```
int getchoice()
{
   int ch;
   int getfirst();

   printf("Enter the letter of your choice:\n");
   printf("a. advice   b. bell\n");
   printf("c. count    d. quit\n");
   ch = getfirst();
   while ( ch < 'a' || ch > 'd')
   {
      printf("Please respond with a, b, c, or d.\n");
      ch = getfirst();
   }
   return ch;
}

int getfirst()
{
   int ch;

   ch = getchar();     /* read next character */
   while (getchar() != '\n')
      ;                /* skip rest of line */
   return ch;
}
```

Mixing Character and Numeric Input

As we saw in Listing 8.7, mixing character and numeric input poses problems, and that is true with our menu example, too. Suppose, for instance, the **count( )** function (choice **c**) looks like the following:

```
void count( )
{
   int n,i;
   printf("Count how far? Enter an integer:\n");
   scanf("%d", &n);
   for (i = 1; i <= n; i++)
      printf("%d\n", i);
}
```

If you then respond by entering **3**, **scanf( )** will read the **3** and leave a newline character as the next character in the input queue. The next call to **getchoice( )** will then result in **getfirst( )** returning this newline character, leading to undesirable behavior.

One way to fix the problem is to rewrite **getfirst( )** so that it returns the next non-whitespace character rather than just the next character encountered. We leave this task as an exercise (Programming Exercise 7).

A second approach is to have the **count( )** function tidy up and clear the newline itself:

```
void count()
{
  int n,i;

  printf("Count how far? Enter an integer:\n");
  if (scanf("%d", &n) != 1)
  {
    printf("Please use digits next time; this time");
    printf(" I'll use the integer 5.\n");
    n = 5;
  }
  for (i = 1; i <= n; i++)
    printf("%d\n", i);
  while ( getchar() != '\n')
    ;        /* clear newline, bad input */
}
```

We also use the return value of **scanf( )** to detect nonnumeric input. To simplify matters, we have the program substitute a default value for **n** if the input is bad. Also, in that case, the **while** loop at the end of the function disposes of the bad input. If you are more ambitious, you can have the function prompt for new input instead of using a default value. We show an example in Chapter 9.

Listing 8.8 shows the final menu program.

❖ *menu.c*

Listing 8.8

```
/* menu.c--a menu example */
#include <stdio.h>
main()
{
  int choice;
  int getchoice();
  void count();

  while ( (choice = getchoice()) != 'd')
  {
    switch (choice)
    {
      case 'a' : printf("Buy low, sell high.\n");
        break;
```

```
                case 'b' : putchar('\a'); /* ANSI */
                    break;
                case 'c' : count();
                    break;
                default  : printf("Program error!\n");
                    break;
            }
        }
}

void count()
{
    int n,i;

    printf("Count how far? Enter an integer:\n");
    if (scanf("%d", &n) != 1)
    {
        printf("Please use digits next time; this time");
        printf(" I'll use the integer 5.\n");
        n = 5;
    }
    for (i = 1; i <= n; i++)
        printf("%d\n", i);
    while ( getchar() != '\n')
        ;
}

int getchoice()
{
    int ch;
    int getfirst();

    printf("Enter the letter of your choice:\n");
    printf("a. advice      b. bell\n");
    printf("c. count       d. quit\n");
    ch = getfirst();
        printf("Please respond with a, b, c, or d.\n");
        ch = getfirst();
    }
    return ch;
}

int getfirst()
{
    int ch;

    ch = getchar();
    while (getchar() != '\n')
        ;
    return ch;
}
```

Listing 8.8
(cont'd.)

Here is a sample run:

```
Enter the letter of your choice:
a. advice      b. bell
c. count       d. quit
a
Buy low, sell high.
Enter the letter of your choice:
a. advice      b. bell
c. count       d. quit
count
Count how far? Enter an integer:
two
Please use digits next time; this time I'll use the integer 5.
1
2
3
4
5
Enter the letter of your choice:
a. advice      b. bell
c. count       d. quit
q
Please respond with a, b, c, or d.
d
```

It can be hard work getting a menu interface to work as smoothly as you may want, but once you develop a viable approach, you can reuse it in a variety of situations.

8.9 Summary

Many programs use **getchar( )** to read input character by character. Typically, systems use line-buffered input, meaning input is sent on to the program when you press Enter. This action also transmits a newline character that may require programming attention.

C features a family of functions, called the standard I/O package, that represents different file forms on different systems in a uniform manner. The **getchar( )** and **scanf( )** functions belong to this family. Both functions return the value **EOF** (defined in the **stdio.h** header) when they detect the end of a file. UNIX systems let you simulate the end-of-file condition from the keyboard by typing Control-D at the beginning of a line; DOS systems use Control-Z for the same purpose.

Many operating systems, including UNIX and DOS, feature redirection, which lets you use files instead of the keyboard and screen for input and output. Programs that read input up to **EOF** can be used either with keyboard input with simulated end-of-file signals or with redirected files.

Review Questions

1. The expression **putchar(getchar( ))** is a valid expression. What does it mean? Is **getchar(putchar( ))** also valid?

2. What will each of the following statements accomplish?

   a. **putchar('H');**

   b. **putchar('\007');**

   c. **putchar('\n');**

   d. **putchar('\b');**

3. Suppose you have a program named **count** that counts the characters in its input. Devise a command that counts the number of characters in the file **essay** and stores the result in file **essayct**.

4. Given the program and files described in Question 3, which of the following are valid commands?

   a. **essayct <essay**

   b. **count essay**

   c. **essay >count**

5. What is **EOF**?

6. What is the output of each of the following fragments for the indicated input (assume that **ch** is type **int** and that the input is buffered):

   a. The input:

   ```
   If you quit, I will.[return]
   ```

   The fragment:

   ```
   while (( ch = getchar() ) != 'i' )
   putchar(ch);
   ```

b. The input:

```
Harhar[return]
```

The fragment:

```
while ( ( ch = getchar() ) != '\n' )
    {
    putchar(ch++);
    putchar(++ch);
    }
```

7. How does C deal with the fact that different computer systems have different file and newline conventions?

8. What potential problem do you face when intermixing numeric input with character input on a buffered system?

Programming Exercises

1. Produce the program described in "Review Questions," Question 3. That is, devise a program that counts the number of characters in its input up to the end of the file.

2. Modify the program in Exercise 1 so that it beeps each time it counts a character. Insert a short delay loop (a loop that does nothing but increment a counter) to separate one beep from the next. (Note: Do not use this program for long files.)

3. Write a program that reads input until it encounters **EOF**. Have the program print out each input character and its ASCII decimal code. Note that characters preceding the space character in the ASCII sequence are nonprinting characters; give them special treatment. If the nonprinting character is a newline or tab, print \n or \t, respectively. Otherwise, use control character notation. For instance, ASCII 1 is Control-A, which can be displayed as ^A. Note that the ASCII code for **A** is simply the code for Control-A plus 64. A similar relation holds for the other nonprinting characters. Print ten pairs of input characters and their ASCII decimal codes per line, except start a fresh line each time a newline character is encountered.

4. Write a program that reads input until it encounters **EOF**. Have it report the number of uppercase letters and the number of lowercase letters in the input. Assume the numeric code for the lowercase letters is sequential; assume the same for uppercase letters.

5. Write a program that reads input until it encounters **EOF**. Have it report back the average number of letters per word. Don't count whitespace as being letters in a word. Note: Punctuation shouldn't be counted either, but don't worry about that now.

6. Modify the guessing program of Listing 8.4 so that it uses a more intelligent guessing strategy. For example, have the program initially guess 50, and have it ask the user whether the guess is high, low, or correct. If, say, the guess is low, have the next guess be halfway between 50 and 100, that is, 75. If that guess is high, let the next guess be halfway between 75 and 50, and so on. Using this *binary search strategy,* the program quickly zeros in on the correct answer, at least if the user does not cheat.

7. Modify the **getfirst( )** function in Listing 8.8 so that it returns the first nonwhitespace character encountered. Test it in a simple program.

8. Modify Programming Exercise 7 in Chapter 7 so that the menu choices are labeled by characters instead of by numbers.

Functions

Objectives

Learning to define a function

Using arguments to communicate values from the calling function to the called function

Understanding the difference between a formal argument and an actual argument

Knowing where to declare arguments and where to declare the other local variables in a function

Using **return** to communicate a value from the called program to the calling program

Learning when and how to use addresses and pointers for communication

Understanding function types and knowing when and where to declare functions

Using ANSI C function prototyping

Knowing when to use the **void** type

Learning about recursion

*T*he C design philosophy is based on using functions. We have used several functions already: **printf( )**, **scanf( )**, **getchar( )**, **putchar( )**, and **strlen( )**. These functions come with the system, but we also created several functions of our own. Most of them have been called **main( )**, for programs always start by executing the instructions in **main( )**; after that, **main( )** can call other functions such as **printf( )** or ones of our own design into action. We've already previewed several aspects of creating your own functions. In this chapter we consolidate and expand on this information. We also look at the new ANSI C methods for defining and using functions.

9.1 Review

First, what is a function? A *function* is a self-contained unit of program code designed to accomplish a particular task. A C function plays the same role that functions, subroutines, and procedures play in other languages, although the details may be different. Some functions cause action to take place; for example, **printf( )** causes data to be printed on your screen. Some functions find a value for the program to use; for instance, **strlen( )** tells a program how long a certain string is. In general, a function can both produce actions and provide values.

We use functions to save us from repetitious programming. If we have to perform a certain task several times in a program, we write an appropriate function once, then have the program use that function wherever needed. We can use the same function in different programs, just as we use **putchar( )** in many programs. As well, even if we perform a task only once in just one program, it is worthwhile to use a function because functions make a program more modular, hence easier to read and easier to change or fix. Suppose, for example, we want to write a program that does the following:

> Reads in a list of numbers
> Sorts the numbers
> Finds their average
> Prints out a bar graph

We can use this program:

```
#include <stdio.h>
#define SIZE 50
main()
{
   float list[SIZE];

   readlist(list, SIZE);
   sort(list, SIZE);
   average(list, SIZE);
   bargraph(list, SIZE);
}
```

Once we have the basic program design, we can write the four functions: **readlist( )**, **sort( )**, **average( )**, and **bargraph( )**. By using descriptive function names, we can make it quite clear what the program does and how it is organized. We then can work with each function separately until it performs its job correctly. An added benefit is that if we make the functions general enough, they can prove useful in other programs.

Many programmers like to think of a function as a "black box" defined in terms of the information that goes in (its input) and of what it produces (its output). What goes on inside the black box is only of concern to those who write the functions. For example, when we use **printf( )**, we know we have to give it a control string and, perhaps, some arguments. We also know what output **printf( )** should produce. We never had to think about the programming that went into creating **printf( )**. Thinking of functions in this manner helps us concentrate on the overall design of the program rather than on the details. Before writing and code, you should consider what the function should do and how it relates to the program as a whole.

What do we need to know about functions? We need to know how to define them properly, how to call them up for use, and how to set up communication between a function and the program that invokes it. We begin with a simple review example and then elaborate on it, adding more features.

Creating and Using a Simple Function

Our modest first goal is to create a function that types 65 asterisks in a row. To give our function a context, we include it in a program that prints a simple letterhead. See Listing 9.1. The program consists of the functions **main( )** and **starbar( )**. See Figure 9.1.

❖ lethead1.c

Listing 9.1

```
/* lethead1.c */
#include <stdio.h>
#define NAME "MEGATHINK, INC."
#define ADDRESS "10 Megabuck Plaza"
#define PLACE "Megapolis, CA 94904"
#define LIMIT 65
main()
{
   void starbar();  /* declare the function */
   starbar();
   printf("%s\n", NAME);
   printf("%s\n", ADDRESS);
   printf("%s\n", PLACE);
   starbar();
}

/*define the starbar() function */
void starbar()
{
   int count;
   for ( count = 1; count <= LIMIT; count++)
     putchar('*');
   putchar('\n');
}
```

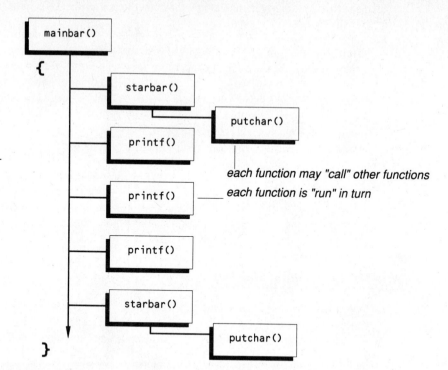

Figure 9.1

Control flow for
Listing 9.1

each function may "call" other functions

each function is "run" in turn

Here is the output:

```
*************************************************************
MEGATHINK, INC.
10 Megabuck Plaza
Megapolis, CA 94904
*************************************************************
```

There are several major points to note about this program:

1. We *call* (invoke, summon) the function **starbar( )** from **main( )** by using just its name. We follow the name and parentheses with a semicolon, creating a statement:

```
starbar();
```

Whenever the computer reaches a **starbar( )** statement, it looks for the **starbar( )** function and follows the instructions there. When finished, it returns to the next line of the *calling program,* **main( ),** in this case. (This method is only one way to call up a function.)

2. We follow the same form in writing **starbar( )** as we do in **main( ):** First the name, then the opening brace, then a declaration of variables used, then the defining statements of the function, then the closing brace. See Figure 9.2.

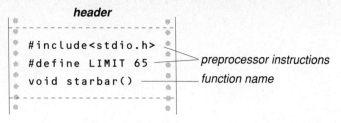

header

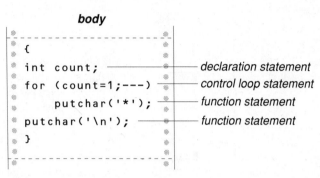

body

Figure 9.2

Structure of a simple function

3. We include **starbar( )** and **main( )** in the same file, although we can use two separate files. The single-file form is slightly easier to compile, but two separate files make it simpler to use the same function in different programs. If we place the functions in separate files, then we also must place the necessary **#define** and **#include** directives in those files. We discuss using two or more files later in the chapter. For now, we keep all our functions together. The closing brace of **main( )** tells the compiler where that function ends. The parentheses in **starbar( )** tell the compiler that **starbar( )** is a function. Note that this instance of **starbar( )** is not followed by a semicolon, which tells the compiler that we are defining **starbar( )** rather than using it.

4. The variable **count** in **starbar( )** is a *local variable,* which means it is a variable known only to **starbar( )**. You can use the name **count** in other functions, including **main( )**, and there is no conflict. In this case, you simply wind up with separate, independent variables having the same name. Internally, the program uses different identifiers for these name twins, so there is no confusion.

5. Like variables, functions have types. The type **void** is used for functions without return values. The type appears in the function definition. (The **void** type is part of ANSI C and is not part of K & R C. However, most C implementations added the **void** type prior to the ANSI standard.)

6. Programs that use a function should declare the type before the function is used. Therefore, **main( )** contains this declaration:

```
void starbar();
```

The parentheses indicate that **starbar( )** is a function name. The **void** indicates the type. The semicolon indicates that we are declaring the function, not defining it.

That is, we are announcing that the program uses a type **void** function called **starbar( )** and that the compiler should expect to find the definition for this function elsewhere. We return to function types again when we review return values.

7. If we think of **starbar( )** as a black box, its action is the line of asterisks that is printed. It doesn't have any input because it doesn't need to use any information from the calling program. This function doesn't require any communication with the calling program.

Function Arguments

Let's create a case where communication is needed. The letterhead will look a little nicer if the text is centered. We can center the text by printing the correct number of spaces before the rest of the line is printed. This action sounds similar to the **starbar( )** function that printed a certain number of asterisks, except now we want to print a certain number of spaces. Rather than writing separate functions for each task, we follow C philosophy and write a single, more general function that performs both tasks. We call the function **n_chars( )**. Instead of having the display character and number of repetitions built into the function, we use function arguments to indicate the character to be displayed and the number of times it's to be printed.

Let's look at the details. Our bar of stars is 65 characters wide, and the function call **n_chars('*', 65)** should print these specifications. To center the letterhead, we first note that **MEGATHINK, INC.** is 15 spaces wide. Thus in our first version, there were 50 spaces following the heading. To center it, we should lead off with 25 spaces, which will result in 25 spaces on either side of the phrase. We can therefore use the call **n_chars(' ', 25)** to accomplish this task.

Aside from using arguments, the **n_char( )** function is quite similar to **starbar( )**, although one difference is that it won't add a newline the way **starbar( )** does. This difference allows us to print other text on the same line if we wish. Listing 9.2 shows the new program. To emphasize how arguments work, the program uses a variety of argument forms.

❖ *lethead2.c*

Listing 9.2

```
/* lethead2.c */
#include <stdio.h>
#define NAME "MEGATHINK, INC."
#define ADDRESS "10 Megabuck Plaza"
#define PLACE "Megapolis, CA 94904"
#define LIMIT 65
#define SPACE ' '
main()
{
   int spaces;
   void n_char();
```

```
/* minimum value function, third version */
imin(n,m)
int n,m;
{
    if ( n < m)
        return (n);
    else
        return (m);
}
```

It is generally better to use **return** just once in a function to make it easier for someone to follow the control flow through the function. However, it's no great sin to use multiple **returns** in a function as short as this one. In any case, all three versions are the same to the user, since all take the same input and produce the same output. Just the innards are different. Even this fourth version works the same:

```
/* minimum value function, fourth version */
imin(n,m)
int n,m;
{
    if ( n < m )
        return(n);
    else
        return(m);
    printf("Professor Fleppard is a fopdoodle.\n")
}
```

The **return** statements prevent the **printf( )** statement from ever being reached. Professor Fleppard can use the compiled version of this function in his own programs and never learn the true feelings of his student programmer.

You can also use a statement like

```
return;
```

which causes the containing function to terminate and return control to the calling function. Because no expression is included in parentheses, no value is given to the function, so this form is used in a type **void** function.

Function Types

Functions should be declared by type. A function with a return value should be declared to be the same type as the return value. Functions with no return value should be declared as type **void.** If no type is given for a function, C assumes the function is type **int**. In the early days of C, most functions were type **int**, so defaulting to **int** was convenient.

The type declaration is part of the function definition. Keep in mind that the declaration refers to the return value, not to the function arguments. For instance, the function heading

```
double klink(a,b)
int a,b;
```

indicates that we are defining a function that takes two type **int** arguments but that returns a type **double** value.

To use a function correctly, a program needs to know the function type. The compiler must have this information at hand before the function is used for the first time. One way to accomplish this task is to place the function definition ahead of its first use, although such placement may make the program harder to read. Also, the functions may be part of the C library or in some other file. So most often we inform the compiler about functions we will use by declaring them in advance. For example, the **main( )** function in Listing 9.3 contains these lines:

```
#include <stdio.h>
main()
{
   int evil1, evil2, lesser;
   int imin();
```

The statements establish that **imin** is the name of a function that returns a type **int** value. The compiler therefore knows how to treat **imin( )** when it appears later in the program.

So far we've placed the function declarations inside the function using them. They also can be placed outside the function. For instance, we can rewrite the beginning of Listing 9.3 as follows:

```
#include <stdio.h>
int imin();  /* imin() declaration */
main()
{
   int evil1, evil2, lesser;
```

The chief concern is that the function declaration appear before the function is used.

The ANSI C standard library groups functions into families each having its own header file. The header files contain, among other things, the declarations for the functions in the family. For instance, the **stdio.h** header file contains function declarations for the standard I/O library functions such as **printf( )** and **scanf( )**. The **math.h** header file contains function declarations for a variety of mathematical functions. For example, **math.h** may contain the declaration

```
double sqrt();
```

(or the ANSI equivalent) to tell the compiler that the **sqrt( )** function returns a type **double** value. Don't confuse these declarations with definitions. A function declaration tells the program what type the function is, but the function definition supplies the actual code. In other words, the **math.h** header tells the compiler that **sqrt( )** returns type **double**, but the code for **sqrt( )** resides in a separate file of library functions.

9.2 ANSI C Function Prototyping

The traditional C scheme for declaring functions is deficient in that it declares the function but not its arguments. For instance, the declaration

```
int imin();
```

informs the compiler that **imin**( ) returns a type **int** value. But, it says nothing about the number or type of arguments that this function requires. Thus if you use **imin**( ) with the wrong number or type of arguments, the compiler doesn't catch the error.

The Problem

Let's look at some examples involving **imax**( ), a close relation to **imin**( ). Listing 9.4 shows a program that uses **imax**( ) incorrectly.

❖ *misuse.c*

```
/* misuse.c--use a function incorrectly */
#include <stdio.h>
int imax();
main()
{
   printf("The maximum of %d and %d is %d.\n",
          3, 5, imax(3) );
   printf("The maximum of %d and %d is %d.\n",
          3, 5, imax(3.0, 5.0) );
}

int imax(n,m)
int n,m;
{
   int max;

   if ( n > m)
      max = n;
   else
      max = m;
   return max;
}
```

Listing 9.4

The first call to **printf**( ) omits an argument to **imax**( ), and the second call uses floating-point arguments instead of integers. Despite these errors, the program compiles and runs. QuickC gave us the following output:

```
The maximum of 3 and 5 is 130.
The maximum of 3 and 5 is 0.
```

But Turbo C outputs values of 273 and 0. Both compilers are functioning fine; they merely are following the older C standards.

The actual mechanics may differ among systems, but let's describe here what goes on with an IBM PC or VAX. The calling function places its arguments in a temporary storage area called the stack, and the called function reads arguments off the stack. These two processes are not coordinated with one another: The calling function decides what type to pass based on the actual arguments in the call; the called function reads values based on the types of its formal arguments. Thus, the call **imax(3)** places one integer on the stack. When the **imax( )** function starts up, it reads two integers off the stack. Only one integer is actually placed on the stack; the second value read is simply whatever value is in that memory location.

The second time we call up **imax( )** in the example program results in the calling function placing two **double** values on the stack. On our system, these values are 8 bytes each, so 16 bytes of data are placed on the stack. Then **imax( )** reads two **int**s from the stack, which are the first two bytes on the stack. In this case, they are zeros, so **imax( )** sets **n** and **m** to **0**.

The ANSI Solution

The ANSI standard's solution to the problems of mismatched arguments is to permit the function declaration also to declare the variable types. The result is a *function prototype*, a declaration that states the return type, the number of arguments, and the type of arguments. For example, to indicate that **imax( )** requires two **int** arguments, we can declare it using either of the following ways:

```
int imax(int, int);
int imax(int a, int b);
```

The first form uses a comma-separated list of types. The second also uses variable names. These names are dummy names and don't have to match the names used in the function definition.

With this information, the compiler can check to see if the function call matches the prototype: Are there the correct number of arguments? Are they the correct type? If there is a type mismatch, the compiler performs a type cast to convert the actual arguments to the same type as the formal arguments. For instance, **imax(3.0,5.0)** becomes **imax ((int) 3.0, (int) 5.0)**.

Listing 9.5 is a modification of Listing 9.4 that uses a function prototype.

We attempted to compile this program on two separate implementations. One compiler gave an error message stating that the call to **imax( )** had too few parameters. A second compiler gave a warning to the same effect. (The difference between an error and a warning is that an error prevents compilation, whereas a warning permits compilation.) In both cases, the compiler now checked to see that the correct number of arguments was present.

```
/* proto1.c--use a function prototype */
#include <stdio.h>
int imax(int, int); /* prototype */
main()
{
  printf("The maximum of %d and %d is %d.\n",
        3, 5, imax(3) )
; printf("The maximum of %d and %d is %d.\n",
        3, 5, imax(3.0, 5.0) );
}

int imax(n,m)
int n,m;
{
  int max;

  if ( n > m)
    max = n;
  else
    max = m;
  return max;
}
```

Listing 9.5

To investigate the type errors, we replaced **imax(3)** with **imax(3,5)** and tried compilation again. This time there were no messages, and we ran the program, which produced the following output:

```
The maximum of 3 and 5 is 5.
The maximum of 3 and 5 is 5.
```

Note: Both of our sample compilers automatically convert the **3.0** and **5.0** of the second call to **3** and **5** so that the function can handle the input properly. However, by resetting the warning level features, we can instruct them to warn us whenever they have to make a type conversion.

No Arguments and Unspecified Arguments

Suppose you input a prototype such as the following:

```
void print_name();
```

An ANSI C compiler assumes that you have decided to forego function prototyping, and it therefore does not check arguments. To indicate that your function really has no arguments, use the keyword **void** within the parentheses. That is, ANSI C interprets

```
void print_name(void);
```

to mean that **print_name( )** takes no arguments. It then checks to see that you, in fact, do not use arguments when calling this function.

A few functions such as **printf( )** and **scanf( )** take a variable number of arguments. In **printf( )**, for instance, the first argument is a string, but the remaining arguments are fixed neither in type nor number. ANSI C allows partial prototyping for such cases. For instance, we can use the following prototype for **printf( )**

```
int printf(char *, ...);
```

that says that the first argument is a string and that there may be further arguments of an unspecified nature. (Chapter 11 discusses strings in detail.)

ANSI-Style Function Definitions

The ANSI standard allows us to use the same form for function definitions as we do for prototypes. The old-style function used the following form:

```
int imax(n,m)
int n, m;
```

Under the ANSI standard, we can use this setup instead:

```
int imax( int n, int m)
```

Eventually, the ANSI version will become the standard way to head a function definition, and the old way will be phased out. At the present, your compiler may allow both forms, or if it is not yet fully compliant with the new standard, it may only recognize the older form. Note that we use the older style version in this text because it is more widely accepted at this time. But if you are using a compiler that implements ANSI-style declarations, use the newer standard to avoid obsolescent code.

9.3 Finding Addresses: The & Operator

Some functions assign values to variables in the calling program. These functions, such as **scanf( )**, use the address operator (**&**) in arguments. The **&** operator gives us the address at which a variable is stored. For example, if **pooh** is the name of a variable, then **&pooh** is the address of the **pooh** variable. We can think of the address as a location in memory, but we also can think of it as the label the computer uses to identify a variable. Suppose we have the following statement:

```
pooh = 24;
```

Also suppose that the address where **pooh** is stored is 12126. Then the statement

```
printf("%d %u\n", pooh, &pooh);
```

produces this output:

Furthermore, the machine code for the assignment statement is something like "store 24 in location 12126."

Listing 9.6 uses the **&** operator to see where variables of the same name, but in different functions, are kept.

❖ loccheck.c

Listing 9.6

```
/* loccheck.c--check where variables are stored */
#include <stdio.h>
void mikado(); /* declare function */
main()
{
   int pooh = 2, bah = 5;

   printf("In main(), pooh = %d and &pooh = %p\n",
          pooh, &pooh);
   printf("In main(), bah = %d and &bah = %p\n",
          bah, &bah);
   mikado(pooh);
}
void mikado(bah) /* define function */
int bah;
{
   int pooh = 10;

   printf("In mikado(), pooh = %d and &pooh = %p\n",
          pooh, &pooh);
   printf("In mikado(), bah = %d and &bah = %p\n",
          bah, &bah);
}
```

Here we use the **%p** format for printing the addresses. This format is used for displaying addresses but is not available on some systems. If your system lacks **%p**, try **%u**. On our system, the output is the following:

```
In main(), pooh = 2 and &pooh = FFD8
In main(), bah = 5 and &bah = FFDA
In mikado(), pooh = 10 and &pooh = FFD0
In mikado(), bah = 2 and &bah = FFD6
```

The manner in which **%p** represents pointers varies between implementations. This one, Turbo C on a PC, displays the address in hexadecimal form.

What does this output show? First, the two **pooh**s have different addresses. The same is true of the two **bah**s. Thus, the computer considers these to be four separate variables. Second, the call **mikado(pooh)** conveys the value **(2)** of the actual argument (**pooh** of **main( )**) to the formal argument (**bah** of **mikado( )**). Note that only the value is transferred. The two variables involved (**pooh** of **main( )** and **bah** of **mikado( )**) retain their distinct identities.

We raise the second point because it is not true for all languages. In a FORTRAN subroutine, for example, the subroutine uses the variables in the calling program. The subroutine may call the variables by different names, but the addresses are the same. In C, each function uses its own variables, which is preferable, for it means that the original variables won't be altered mysteriously by some side effect of the called function. But, the C method can make for some difficulties, too, as the next section describes.

9.4 Altering Variables in the Calling Program

Sometimes we want one function to make changes in the variables of a different function. For example, a common task in sorting problems is interchanging the values of two variables. Suppose we have two variables called **x** and **y** and we wish to swap values. The following simple sequence

```
x = y;
y = x;
```

does not work, for by the time the second line is reached, the original value of **x** has already been replaced by the original **y** value. We have to put in an additional line to save the original value of **x**:

```
temp = x;
x = y;
y = temp;
```

We can now use this approach in a function and construct a driver to test it. To make clear which variables belong to **main( )** and which belong to the **interchange( )**, we use **x** and **y** for the **main( )** variables and **u** and **v** for the **interchange( )** variables. See Listing 9.7.

❖ *swap1.c*

Listing 9.7

```
/* swap1.c--1st attempt at a swapping function */
#include <stdio.h>
void interchange(); /* declare function */
main()
{
    int x = 5, y = 10;

    printf("Originally x = %d and y = %d.\n", x , y);
    interchange(x,y);
    printf("Now x = %d and y = %d.\n", x, y);
}
```

**Listing 9.7
(cont'd.)**

```
void interchange(u,v) /* define function */
int u,v;
{
  int temp;

  temp = u;
  u = v;
  v = temp;
}
```

We then run the program and get the following output:

```
Originally x = 5 and y = 10.
Now x = 5 and y = 10.
```

Oops—variables aren't switched! Let's input some printing statements into **interchange( )** to see what has gone wrong. See Listing 9.8.

❖ *swap2.c*

Listing 9.8

```
/* swap2.c--researching swap1.c */
#include <stdio.h>
void interchange();
main()
{
  int x = 5, y = 10;

  printf("Originally x = %d and y = %d.\n", x , y);
  interchange(x,y);
  printf("Now x = %d and y = %d.\n", x, y);
}
void interchange(u,v)
int u,v;
{
  int temp;

  printf("Originally u = %d and v = %d.\n", u , v);
  temp = u;
  u = v;
  v = temp;
  printf("Now u = %d and v = %d.\n", u, v);
}
```

Here is the new output:

```
Originally x = 5 and y = 10.
Originally u = 5 and v = 10.
Now u = 10 and v = 5.
Now x = 5 and y = 10.
```

Well, nothing is wrong with **interchange( )**; it does swap the values of **u** and **v**. The problem is communicating the results back to **main( )**. As we pointed out, **interchange( )** uses different variables from **main( )**, so interchanging the values of **u** and **v** has no effect on **x** and **y**! Can we use **return** somehow? Well, we could finish **interchange( )** with the line

```
return(u);
```

and changing the call in **main( )** to the following:

```
x = interchange(x,y);
```

The outcome gives **x** its new value, but does nothing for **y**. Note that with **return** you can send just one value back to the calling program.

9.5 Pointers: A First Look

To communicate two values, we must use *pointers,* which are symbolic representations of addresses. For example, earlier we used the **&** operator to find the address of the variable **pooh**; therefore, **&pooh** is a pointer-to-**pooh**. The actual address is a number (0xFFD8, in our case), and the symbolic representation **&pooh** is a pointer *constant.* After all, the variable **pooh** will not change addresses while the program is running.

C also has pointer variables. Just as a **char** variable has a character as a value and an **int** variable has an integer as a value, the *pointer variable* has an address as a value. If we give a *particular pointer* the name **ptr**, then we can have statements like

```
ptr = &pooh;    /* assigns pooh's address to ptr */
```

in which we say that **ptr** points to **pooh**. The difference between **ptr** and **&pooh** is that **ptr** is a variable and **&pooh** is a constant. If we want, we can make **ptr** point elsewhere:

```
ptr = &bah;     /* make ptr point to bah instead of pooh */
```

Now the **ptr** value is the **bah** address.

To create a pointer variable, we need to be able to declare its type. For instance, we may declare **ptr** to be a pointer-to-**int**. To make this declaration, we need to use a new operator, the indirection operator.

The Indirection Operator: *

Suppose we know that **ptr** points to **bah**:

```
ptr = &bah;
```

Then we can use the *indirection operator* (*) (also called the *dereferencing operator*) to find the value stored in **bah**:

```
val = *ptr; /* finding the value ptr points to */
```

(Don't confuse this unary indirection operator with the binary * operator of multiplication.) The statements **ptr = &bah;** and **val = *ptr;** taken together amount to the following:

```
val = bah;
```

Using the address and indirection operators is a rather indirect way of accomplishing this result, hence the name "indirection operator."

 Summary: Pointer-Related Operators

The address operator: **&**. When followed by a variable name, **&** gives the address of that variable.

Example.

&nurse *is the address of the variable* **nurse**

The indirection operator: *. When followed by a pointer, * gives the value stored at the pointed-to address.

Example.

```
nurse = 22;
ptr = &nurse;   /* pointer to nurse */
val = *ptr;
```

The net effect is to assign the value **22** to **val**.

Declaring Pointers

Declaring pointers involves a new twist. You might guess that we use the following form:

```
pointer ptr; /* not the way to declare a pointer */
```

But it is not enough to say that a variable is a pointer. We also have to say what kind of variable the pointer points to. The reason is that different variable types take up different amounts of storage, and some pointer operations require knowledge of the storage size. As well, the program has to know what kind of data are stored at the address. A **long** and a **float** may use the same amount of storage, but they store numbers quite differently. Here's how pointers are declared:

```
int *pi;         /* pi is a pointer to an integer variable */
char *pc;        /* pc is a pointer to a character variable */
float *pf,*pg;'  /* pf, pg are pointers to float variables */
```

The type specification identifies the type of variable pointed to, and the asterisk (*)
identifies the variable itself as a pointer. The declaration **int *pi;** therefore says that **pi** is
a pointer and that ***pi** is type **int**. See Figure 9.4.

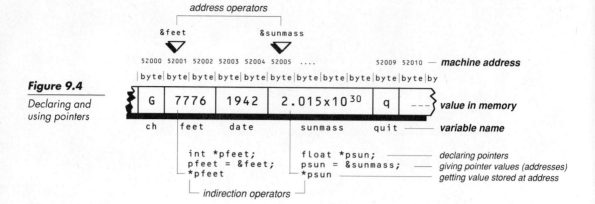

Similarly, the value of what **pc** points to, which is ***pc**, is of type **char**. We describe **pc**
itself as being a pointer to **char**. Because its value is an address, **pc** is an unsigned
integer on most systems. We can thus use the **%u** format to print the **pc** value on those
systems. But this feature need not hold true universally, so ANSI C provides the **%p**
form specifically for pointers.

Using Pointers to Communicate Between Functions

We have touched only the surface of the rich topic of pointers, but our concern here is in
using pointers to solve the communication problem of Listing 9.8. Listing 9.9 shows a
program that uses pointers to make the interchange function work.

❖ *swap3.c*

```
/* swap3.c--using pointers to make swapping work */
#include <stdio.h>
void interchange();
main()
{
    int x = 5, y = 10;

    printf("Originally x = %d and y = %d.\n", x, y);
    interchange(&x,&y);  /* send addresses to function */
    printf("Now x = %d and y = %d.\n", x, y);
}
void interchange(u,v)
int *u, *v;             /* u and v are pointers */
{
```

**Listing 9.9
(cont'd.)**

```
  int temp;

  temp = *u;       /* temp gets value that u points to */
  *u = *v;
  *v = temp;
}
```

The output follows:

```
Originally x = 5 and y = 10.
Now x = 10 and y = 5.
```

Let's now look at how the program works. First, our function call looks like the following:

```
interchange(&x,&y);
```

Instead of transmitting the values of **x** and **y**, we transmit their addresses. Therefore, the formal arguments **u** and **v** that appear in

```
void interchange(u,v)
```

have addresses as values; hence they should be declared as pointers. Since **x** and **y** are integers, we declare **u** and **v** as pointers to integers:

```
int *u, *v;
```

In the body of the function, we declare

```
int temp;
```

to provide the temporary storage we need. We then store the value of **x** in **temp**:

```
temp = *u;
```

Remember, **u** has the value **&x**, so **u** points to **x**. Thus, *****u** gives us the value of **x**, which is what we want. We *don't* want to write

```
temp = u; /* NO */
```

for that will store the address of **x** rather than its value; and we are trying to interchange values, not addresses.

Similarly, to assign the **y** value to **x**, we use

```
*u = *v;
```

which translates to

```
x = y;
```

Let's summarize: We want a function that alters the values **x** and **y**. By telling the function the addresses of **x** and **y**, we give **interchange( )** access to those variables. Using pointers and the * operator, the function can examine the values stored at those locations and change them.

More generally, we can communicate two kinds of information about a variable to a function. If we use a call of the form

```
function1(x);
```

we transmit the value of **x**. If we use a call of the form

```
function2(&x);
```

we transmit the address of **x**. The first form requires that the function definition include a formal argument of the same type as **x**:

```
function1(num)
int num;
```

The second form requires that the function definition include a formal argument that is a pointer to the correct type:

```
function2(ptr)
int *ptr;
```

We use the first form if the function needs a value to perform some calculation or action. We use the second form if the function needs to alter variables in the calling program. We have been doing this all along with the **scanf( )** function. That is, when we want to read in a value for a variable **num,** we use **scanf("%d", &num)**. That function reads a value, then uses the address we give it when it stores the value.

Pointers let us get around the fact that the **interchange( )** variables are local. They let our function reach into **main( )** and alter what is stored there. See Figure 9.5.

Figure 9.5

Names, addresses, and values in a byte-addressable system such as the IBM PC

```
        52000 52001 52002 52003 52004 52005  . . .          52009 52010 ── machine address
        e|byte|byte|byte|byte|byte|byte|byte|byte|byte|byte|byte|by
```

G	7776	1942	2.015x10³⁰	q	---

value in memory

```
        ch      feet     date         sunmass       quit ──── variable name
```

&ch = 52000
&feet = 52001
&date = 52003
&sunmass = 52005
&quit = 52009
│
address operator

"float" *type variable*
takes 4 bytes

Pascal and Modula-2 users may recognize the first form of function argument as being the same as Pascal's value parameter and the second form as being similar (but not identical) to Pascal's variable parameter. BASIC users may find the whole setup unsettling. If this section seems strange to you, be assured that a little practice will make at least some uses of pointers seem simple, normal, and convenient.

▶ **Variables: Names, Addresses, and Values**

Our discussion of pointers hinges on the relationships between the names, addresses, and values of variables, so let's discuss these matters further. When we write a program we think of a variable as having two attributes: a name and a value. (There are other attributes, including type, but these attributes don't concern us here.) After the program has been compiled and loaded, the computer also thinks of the same variable as having two attributes: an address and a value. An address is the computer's version of a name.

In many languages, the address is the computer's business, concealed from the programmer. In C, however, we can learn and use the address through the **&** operator. For example:

&barn is the address of the variable **barn**

We can get the value from the name just by using the name, for instance:

printf(" %d\n", barn) prints the value of **barn**

We can get the value from the address by using the ***** operator: Given **pbarn = &barn;**, then ***pbarn** is the value stored at address **&barn**

Although we can print out an address to satisfy our curiosity, that use is not the primary function of the **&** operator. More important, using **&**, *****, and pointers lets us manipulate addresses and their contents symbolically, as we did in Listing 9.9.

9.6 Recursion

C also permits a function to call itself, which is called *recursion*. Recursion is a sometimes tricky, sometimes convenient tool. One of the tricks is to get recursion to end, for a function that calls itself tends to keep doing so indefinitely unless the programming includes a conditional test to terminate recursion.

Recursion Revealed

To see what's involved, let's look at an example. The function **main( )** in Listing 9.10 calls the **up_and_down( )** function. We term this call the first level of recursion. Then **up_and_down( )** calls itself, which we term the second level of recursion. The second level calls the third level, and so on. The example program is set up to have four recursion levels.

Listing 9.10

```
/* recur.c--recursion illustration */
#include <stdio.h>
void up_and_down(int);
main()
{
  up_and_down(1);
}

void up_and_down(n)
int n;
{
  printf("Level %d\n", n);    /* print #1 */
  if ( n < 4 )
    up_and_down(n+1);
  printf("LEVEL %d\n", n);    /* print #2 */
}
```

The output follows:

```
Level 1
Level 2
Level 3
Level 4
LEVEL 4
LEVEL 3
LEVEL 2
LEVEL 1
```

In the program, **main( )** first calls **up_and_down( )** with an argument of **1**. As a result, the formal argument **n** in **up_and_down( )** has the value **1**, so print statement #1 prints **Level 1**. Then because **n** is less than **4**, **up_and_down( )** (level 1) calls **up_and_-down( )** (level 2) with an argument of **n + 1**, or **2**. This action causes **n** in the level 2 call to be assigned the value **2**, so print statement #1 prints **Level 2**. Similarly, the next two calls lead to the printing of **Level 3** and **Level 4**.

Once level 4 is reached, **n** is **4**. The **if** test now fails, and the **up_and_down( )** function is not called again. Instead, the level 4 call proceeds to print statement #2, which prints **LEVEL 4**, since **n** is **4**. It then reaches the **return** statement. At this point, the level 4 call ends, and control passes back to the function that called it, the level 3 call. The last statement executed in the level 3 call was the call to level 4 in the **if** statement. Therefore, level 3 resumes with the following statement, which is print statement #2. This action causes **LEVEL 3** to be printed. Then level 3 ends, passing control to level 2, which prints **LEVEL 2**, and so on.

There are several important points to understand about recursion. First, each level of function call has its own variables. The **n** of level 1 is a different variable from the **n** of level 2. So our program creates four separate variables, each called **n**, but each having a distinct value. When the program finally returns to the level 1 call of **up_and_down( )**, that **n** still had the value **1** it started with. See Figure 9.6.

Figure 9.6

Recursion variables

variables:	n	n	n	n
after level 1 call	1			
after level 1 call	1	2		
after level 1 call	1	2	3	
after level 1 call	1	2	3	4
after return from level 4	1	2	3	
after return from level 3	1	2		
after return from level 2	1			
after return from level 1	1			
	(all gone)			

Second, each function call is balanced with a **return**. When program flow reaches the **return** at the end of the last recursion level, control passes to the previous recursion level. The program does not jump all the way to the original call. Instead, it must move back though each recursion level.

Third, statements in a recursive function that precede the recursive call are executed in the same order that the functions are called. For instance, in Listing 9.10 print statement #1 precedes the recursive call. It is executed four times in the order of the recursive calls: Level 1, Level 2, Level 3, and Level 4.

Next, statements in a recursive function that follow the recursive call are executed in the opposite order from which the functions are called. For instance, print statement #2 follows the recursive call, and it is executed in this order: LEVEL 4, LEVEL 3, LEVEL 2, and LEVEL 1. This feature of recursion is useful for programming problems involving reversals of order. (We study such an example shortly.)

Finally, although each level of recursion has its own set of variables, the code itself is not duplicated. The code is a sequence of instructions, and a function call really is an instruction to go to the beginning of that set of instructions. So a recursive call returns the program to the beginning of the instruction set. Aside from the fact that recursive calls create new variables with each call, they are much like a loop. Indeed, sometimes recursion can be used instead of loops, and vice versa.

The simplest form of recursion has the recursive call at the end of the function, just before the **return** statement. This type of call is termed *tail recursion* or *end recursion*. This type of recursion is the simplest form because it acts like a loop.

Let's look at a loop version and a tail recursion version of a function to calculate factorials. The factorial of an integer is the product of the integers from 1 through that number. For instance, 3 factorial (written 3!) is 1 x 2 x 3. 0! is taken to be 1. The function isn't defined for negative numbers. Listing 9.11 presents a function that uses a **for** loop to calculate factorials.

❖ *factor.c*

Listing 9.11

```
/* factor.c--use loops to calculate factorials */
#include <stdio.h>
main()
{
   int num;
   long fact();

   while (scanf("%d", &num) == 1)
   {
      if (num < 0 )
         printf("No negative numbers, please.\n");
      else if (num > 15)
         printf("Keep input under 16.\n");
      else
         printf("%d factorial = %ld\n", num, fact(num));
   }
}
long fact(n) /* loop finds factorial */
int n;
{
   long ans;

   for ( ans = 1; n > 1; n--)
      ans *= n;
   return ans;
}
```

The test driver program limits input to the integers 0–15. 15! is slightly over 2 billion, which makes 16! much larger than **long** on our system. To go beyond 15!, we must use a type **double** function.

The loop initializes **ans** to **1**, then multiplies it by the integers from **n** down to **2**. Technically, we should multiply by **1**, but such multiplication doesn't change the value. Here's a sample run:

```
3
3 factorial = 6
10
10 factorial = 3628800
q
```

Now let's try a recursive version. The key here is that $n! = n \times (n-1)!$, which follows because $(n-1)!$ is the product of all the positive integers through $n-1$. Therefore, multiplying by n gives the product through n. This fact suggests a recursive approach. If we call the function **rfact( )**, then **rfact(n)** is **n * rfact(n–1)**, so we can evaluate **rfact(n)** by having it call **rfact(n–1)**. See Listing 9.12. Of course, we have to end the recursion at some point, and we do so by setting the return value to **1** when **n** is **0**. The output is the same as that for Listing 9.11.

❖ *rfactor.c*

Listing 9.12

```
/* rfactor.c--use recursion to calculate factorials */
#include <stdio.h>
main( )
{
   int num;
   long rfact();

   while (scanf("%d", &num) == 1)
   {
     if (num < 0 )
        printf("No negative numbers, please.\n");
     else if ( num > 15)
        printf("Keep input under 16.\n");
     else
        printf("%d factorial = %ld\n", num, rfact(num));
   }
}
long rfact(n)  /* recursive function */
int n;
{
   long ans;

   if (n > 0)
     ans = n * rfact(n-1);
   else
      ans = 1;
   return ans;
}
```

Recursion and Reversal

Let's look at a problem in which recursion's ability to reverse order is handy. The problem: Write a function that prints out the binary equivalent of an integer. Binary notation represents numbers in terms of powers of two and uses only the digits 0 and 1. Therefore, 101 in binary means $1 \times 2^2 + 0 \times 2^1 + 1 \times 2^0$, just as 234 in decimal means $2 \times 10^2 + 3 \times 10^1 + 4 \times 10^0$.

First, we need a method. How can we, say, find the binary equivalent of 5? Well, odd numbers must have a binary representation ending in 1. Even numbers end in 0. For our example, we can find if the last digit is a 1 or 0 by evaluating 5 % 2. If the result is 1, then 5 is odd, and the last digit is 1. In general, if n is a number, the final digit is n % 2. Therefore, the last digit is what we want to print first, which suggests using a recursive function in which n % 2 is calculated before the recursive call and is printed after the recursive call.

To get the next digit, we divide the original number by 2. This action is the binary equivalent of moving the decimal point one place to the left so that we can examine the next binary digit. If the value is even, the next binary digit is 0; if it's odd, the next binary digit is 1. For example, 5/2 is 2 (integer division), so the next digit is 0. Thus far we have 01 for our example. Now we repeat the process: Divide 2 by 2 to get 1; evaluate 1 % 2 to get 1. The next digit is thus 1, giving us 101. We stop the procedure only when the result of dividing by 2 is less than 2, for as long as it is 2 or greater, there is one more binary digit. Each division by 2 lops off one more binary digit until we reach the end. (If this logic seems confusing, try working through a decimal analogy. The remainder of 628 divided by 10 is 8, so 8 is the last digit. Integer division by 10 yields 62, and the remainder from dividing 62 by 10 is 2, so that's the next digit. And so on.)

❖ binary.c

```
/* binary.c--print integer in binary form */
#include <stdio.h>
void to_binary(int n);
main()
{
   int number;

   while (scanf("%d", &number) == 1)
   {
      to_binary(number);
      putchar('\n');
   }
}
void to_binary(n)      /* recursive function */
int n;
{
   int r;

   r = n % 2;
   if ( n >= 2 )
      to_binary( n / 2);
   putchar('0' + r);
   return;
}
```

Listing 9.13

Listing 9.13 implements our approach using ANSI C prototyping. You'll have to change the declaration for **to_binary( )** if your compiler doesn't support this feature.

The expression **'0' + r** evaluates to the character **'0'** if **r** is **0** and to the character **'1'** if **r** is **1**. This outcome assumes the numeric code for the **1** character is one greater than the code for the **'0'** character; both the ASCII and the EBCDIC codes satisfy the assumption. Here's a sample run:

```
5
101
255
1111111
256
10000000
q
```

▶ Summary: Functions

Form. A typical function definition has this form:

name (argument list)
argument declarations
function body

The presence of *argument list* and *argument declarations* is optional. Variables other than the arguments are declared within the body, which is bounded by braces.

ANSI C encourages the following form:

name (argument declaration list)
function body

The *argument declaration list* is a comma-separated list of variable declarations.

Example.

```
diff(x,y)            /* function name and argument list */
int x,y;             /* declare arguments */
{                    /* begin function body */
   int z;            /* declare local variable */

   z = x - y;
   return z;
}                    /* end function body */
diff(int x,int y)    /* ANSI version */
{                    /* begin function body */
   int z;            /* declare local variable */

   z = x - y;
   return z;
}                    /* end function body */
```

Communicating values. Arguments are used to convey values from the calling program to the function. If variables **a** and **b** have the values 5 and 2, then the call

```
c = diff(a,b);
```

transmits 5 and 2 to the variables **x** and **y**. The values 5 and 2 are called actual arguments, and the **diff( )** variables **x** and **y** are called formal arguments. The keyword **return** communicates one value from the function to the calling program. In the preceding example, **c** receives the value of **z**, which is 3. A function ordinarily has no effect on the variables in a calling program. Use pointers as arguments to affect variables directly in the calling program. This procedure may be necessary if you wish to communicate more than one value back to the calling program.

Function type. Functions must have the same type as the value they return. Functions are assumed to be of type **int**. If a function is of another type, it must be declared in the calling program and in the function definition.

Example.

```
main()
{
  double q, x, duff(); /* declare in calling program */
  int n;
  ...
  q = duff(x,n);
  ...
}
double duff( u, k )     /* declare in function definition */
double u;
int k;
{
  double tor;
  ...
  return tor;           /* returns a double value */
}
```

9.7 All C Functions Are Created Equal

Each C function in a program is on equal footing with the others. Each can call any other function or be called by any other function. This feature makes the C function somewhat different from Pascal and Modula-2 procedures, for those procedures can be nested within other procedures. In those languages, procedures in one nest are ignorant of procedures in another nest.

The function **main( )** is a little special, in that when a program of several functions is put together, execution starts with the first statement in **main( )**. But that capability is the limit of its preference. Even **main( )** can be called by other functions, as the example in Listing 9.14 shows.

```
/* re_main.c--another program calls main() */
#include <stdio.h>
main()
{
   char ch;
   void more();

   printf("Enter any character you want. ");
   printf("A Q will end things.\n");
   ch = getchar();
   printf("Aha! That was a %c!\n", ch);
   if (ch != 'Q')
      more();
}
void more()
{
   main();
}
```

Listing 9.14

The function **main( )** calls **more( )**, and **more( )** calls **main( )**. When **main( )** is called, it starts at the beginning, so we have made a sneaky loop. Not only does this program illustrate that **main( )** can be called like any other function, it also demonstrates *mutual recursion,* in which two programs call each other.

Some sample output shows how the program works. Note how it even processes the newline character that is transmitted when we press the Enter key.

```
Enter any character you want. A Q will end things.
I[return]
Aha! That was a I!
Enter any character you want. A Q will end things.
Aha! That was a            ⟸ Prints  newline
!
Enter any character you want. A Q will end things.
Q[return]
Aha! That was a Q!
```

9.8 Compiling Programs with Two or More Functions

The simplest approach to using several functions is to place them in the same file. We then compile that file just as you do a single-function file. Other approaches are more system dependent, as we illustrate in the next few sections.

Suppose **file1.c** and **file2.c** are two files containing C functions. The command

```
cc file1.c file2.c
```

thus compiles both files and produces an executable file called **a.out**. In addition, two object files called **file1.o** and **file2.o** are produced. If you later change **file1.c** and not **file2.c**, you can compile the first and combine it with the object code version of the second file using the following command:

```
cc file1.c file2.o
```

Microsoft C 4.0–5.1

You can use the **cl** command to compile the two files:

```
cl file1.c file2.c
```

which produces two object code files called **file1.obj** and **file2.obj** and the executable file called **file1.exe**. The basename of the first file in the list is used for the executable file. If you need to edit only **file2.c**, you can recompile using this command:

```
cl file1.obj file2.c
```

QuickC

You can use the **Set Program List** entry from the File menu to create a **.mak** file that indicates which files belong to the program. You can use the **Edit Program List** entry to modify this list. QuickC compiles the files in the current program list.

Turbo C

You can create a text file with a **.prj** extension (for project) and put in the names of the files used for the program. For instance, the file **file1.prj** can contain the following text:

```
file1.c
file2.c
```

Use the Project menu to select the desired project file, then select the Run or Compile menu.

Using Header Files

Often you use the C preprocessor to define constants used in a program. Such definitions hold only for the file containing the **#define** directives, so if you place the program functions into separate files, you also must make the **#define** directives available to each file. The most direct way is to retype the directives for each file, but this task is time-consuming and increases the possibility for error. Also, it poses a maintenance problem, for if you revise a value, you have to remember to do so for each file.

A better solution is to place the **#define** directives in a header file, then use the **#include** directive in each source code file. For instance, in Chapter 7, Programming Exercise 7 asked you to write a program that computed gross pay, net pay, and taxes for a set of hourly rates. Following the precepts of top-down programming, we can organize the program as follows:

while *menu selection is not quit*
    assign hourly pay rate
    get hours worked
    compute and display pay and taxes

Next, we can translate this plan to C, using functions to implement the different modules. For simplicity, we use just two files: one for **main( )** and one for the supporting functions. See Listings 9.15 and 9.16.

❖ *payroll1.c*

Listing 9.15

```
/* payroll1.c--a payroll program. Continued in payroll2.c */
#include <stdio.h>
#include "payroll.h"
          /* defines constants, declares functions */
main()
{
   double hours, payrate;
   int code;

   while ( (code = menu() ) != QUIT )
   {
     switch(code)
     {
       case 1 : payrate = PAYRATE1;
                break;
       case 2 : payrate = PAYRATE2;
                break;
       case 3 : payrate = PAYRATE3;
                break;
       case 4 : payrate = PAYRATE4;
                break;
       default: payrate = 0;
                printf("Oops!\n");
                break;
     }
     hours = gethours();
     showtax(payrate, hours);
   }
}
```

```
/* payroll2.c--rest of payroll program */
#include <stdio.h>
#include "payroll.h"
int menu()
{
  int code, status;

  printf("\n%s%s\n", STARS, STARS)
  printf("Enter the number corresponding to the desired ");
  printf("pay rate or action:\n");
  printf("1) $%5.2f2) $%5.2f\n", PAYRATE1, PAYRATE2);
  printf("3) $%5.2f4) $%5.2f\n", PAYRATE3, PAYRATE4);
  printf("5) quit\n");
  printf("%s%s\n", STARS, STARS);
  while ( (status = scanf("%d", &code)) != 1 ||
          (code < 1 || code > 5) )
  {
    if (status != 1)
      scanf("%*s");
    printf("Enter an integer from 1 to 5, please.\n");
  }
  return code;
}
double gethours()
{
  double hours;

  printf("How many hours did the employee work ");
  printf("this week?\n");
  while (scanf("%lf", &hours) != 1)
  {
    scanf("%*s");
    printf("Please enter a number, such as 37.5.\n");
  }
  return hours;
}
void showtax(payrate, hours)
double payrate, hours;
{
  double gross, net, tax;

  if ( hours <= WEEK)
    gross = payrate * hours;
  else
    gross = payrate * WEEK +
      OVERTIME * payrate * (hours - WEEK);
  if (gross <= BREAK1)
    tax = RATE1 * gross;
  else if (gross <= BREAK2)
    tax = CHUNK1 + (gross - BREAK1) * RATE2;
```

Listing 9.16

**Listing 9.16
(cont'd.)**

```
  else
     tax = CHUNK2 + (gross - BREAK2) * RATE3;
  net = gross tax;
  printf("Gross = $%.2f, Net = $%.2f, Tax = $%.2f\n", gross,
         net, tax);
}
```

The various constants the program uses are defined in the header file **payroll.h**. Recall that in UNIX and DOS environments, the double quotation marks in the directive **#include "payroll.h"** indicate that the **#include** file is in the current working directory, which typically is the directory containing the source code. We also can use the **#include** file to provide declarations for the functions used in the program. Listing 9.17 shows the header file.

❖ *payroll.h*

Listing 9.17

```
/* payroll.h--constants and declarations for payroll.c */
#define QUIT     5
#define PAYRATE1 8.75
#define PAYRATE2 9.33
#define PAYRATE3 10.00
#define PAYRATE4 11.20
#define WEEK 40
#define OVERTIME 1.5
#define BREAK1 300
#define BREAK2 450
#define RATE1 0.15
#define RATE2 0.20
#define RATE3 0.25
#define CHUNK1 (BREAK1 * RATE1)
#define CHUNK2 (CHUNK1 + (BREAK2 - BREAK1) * RATE2)
#define STARS "*********************************"
int menu();
double gethours();
void showtax();
```

As well, the program itself (Listings 9.15 and 9.16) has some interesting features. In particular, the **menu( )** and **gethours( )** functions skip over nonnumeric data by noting the **scanf( )** return value and using the **scanf(" %*s")** call to skip to the next whitespace. Note how **menu( )** checks for both nonnumeric input and out-of-limits numeric input:

```
while ( (status = scanf("%d", &code)) != 1 ||
        (code < 1 || code > 5) )
```

This example uses C's guarantee that logical expressions are evaluated from left to right and that evaluation ceases the moment the statement is clearly false. In this instance, the values of **code** are checked only after it is determined that **scanf( )** has succeeded in reading an integer value.

Assigning separate tasks to separate functions encourages this sort of refinement. A first pass at **menu( )** or **gethours( )** may use a simple **scanf( )** without the data verification features we've added. Once the basic version works, you can try to improve each module.

9.9 Summary

You should use functions as building blocks for larger programs. Each function should have a single, well-defined purpose. The function is a natural tool to use to provide modularity to a program.

Use arguments to communicate values to a function, and use the keyword **return** to communicate a value back to the calling program. If the function returns a value not of type **int**, then you must specify the function type in the function definition and in the declaration section of the calling program. If you want the function to affect variables in the calling program, you should use addresses and pointers. A C function can also call itself, which is called recursion.

ANSI C offers function prototyping. This feature is a powerful C enhancement that allows compilers to verify that the proper number and types of arguments are used in a function call.

Review Questions

1. What's the difference between an actual argument and a formal argument?

2. Write function headings (K & R style and the new ANSI C style) for the functions described (note that we are asking for headings only, not the body):

a. **donut( )** takes an **int** argument and prints that number of **0**s

b. **gear( )** takes two **int** arguments and returns type **int**

c. **stuff_it( )** takes a **double** argument and the address of a **double** variable and stores the first value in the given location

3. Write function headings (K & R style and the new ANSI C style) for the functions described (note that we are asking for headings only, not the body):

a. **n_to_char( )** takes an **int** argument and returns a **char**

b. **digits( )** takes a **double** argument and an **int** argument and returns an **int**

c. **random( )** takes no argument and returns an **int**

4. Devise a function that returns the sum of two integers.

5. What changes, if any, do you need to make to have the function of Question 4 add two **double** numbers instead?

6. Devise a function **alter( )** that takes two **int** variables **x** and **y** and changes their values to their sum and their difference, respectively.

7. Is there anything incorrect about this function definition?

```
void salami(num)
{
    int num, count;

    for(count = 1; count <= num; num++)
        printf(" O salami mio!\n");
}
```

8. Write a function that returns the largest of three integer arguments.

9. a. Write a function that displays a menu of four numbered choices and asks you to choose one. That is, the output should look like the following:

```
Please choose one of the following:
1) copy files        2) move files
3) remove files      4) quit
Enter the number of your choice:
```

b. Write a function that has two **int** arguments, a lower limit and an upper limit. The function should read an integer from input. If the integer is outside the limits, the function should print a menu (using the function from Question 9a) and get a new value. When an integer in the proper limits is entered, the function should return that value to the calling program.

c. Write a minimal program using the functions from Questions 9a and 9b. By "minimal," we mean that your program need not actually perform the promised actions from the menu; it should just show the choices and get a valid response.

Programming Exercises

1. Devise a function **min(x,y)** that returns the smaller of two **double** values and test it with a simple driver.

2. Devise a function **chline(ch, i, j)** that prints the requested character in columns **i** through column **j**. Test it in a simple driver.

3. Write a function that takes three arguments: a character and two integers. The character is to be printed. The first integer specifies the number of times that the character is to be printed on a line. The second integer specifies the number of lines to be printed. Write a program that makes use of this function.

4. The harmonic mean of two numbers is obtained by taking the inverses of the two numbers, averaging them, and taking the inverse of the result. Write a function that takes two **double** arguments and returns the harmonic mean of the two numbers.

5. Write a program that reads characters from the standard input to the end of the file. For each character, have the program report whether or not it is a letter. If it is a letter, the program should also report its numerical location in the alphabet. For example, c and C are both letter 3. Incorporate a function that takes a character as an argument and returns the numerical location if the character is a letter and returns –1 otherwise.

6. In Chapter 6, Listing 6.18, we wrote a **power( )** function that returned the result of raising a type **double** number to a positive integer value. Improve the function so that it correctly handles negative powers. Also build into the function that 0 to any power is 0 and that any number to the 0 power is 1. Use a loop. Test the function in a program.

7. Rewrite the program for Exercise 5 using a recursive function.

8. Generalize the **to_binary( )** function of Listing 9.13 so that it takes a second argument in the range 2–10. It should then print the number that is its first argument to the number base given by the second argument.

9. The payroll program organization shown in Listings 9.15 though 9.17 is not the only possible model. For example, we can envision the program working this way:

while *another set of data is gathered*
    calculate and show the results

That is, the **while** loop can be controlled by a function that gathers data and reports whether the program should continue. This function reports three values: the pay rate, the hours worked, and whether or not to continue. Since functions return just one value, you must use pointers to provide the other two.

10

Arrays and Pointers

Contents

Objectives

Declaring a one-dimensional array

Initializing a one-dimensional array

Previewing external and static storage classes

Getting the address of a variable

Learning about pointers

Using the indirection operator to access the value a pointer points to

Using array names as pointers

Learning array-pointer correspondences

Knowing the five operations you can apply to pointer variables

Using pointers in functions operating on arrays

Declaring a two-dimensional array

Writing functions to process two-dimensional arrays

rrays and pointers have an intimate relationship to each other, so traditionally they are discussed together. Before we explore that relationship, however, we review and augment our knowledge of arrays. We will then study the connection with pointers.

10.1 Arrays

By now you are familiar with the fact that an array is composed of a series of elements of one data type. We use declarations to tell the compiler when we want an array. To set up an array properly, the compiler needs to know how many elements the array contains and what the type is for these elements. Array elements can have the same types as ordinary variables. Consider the following example of array declarations:

```
/* some array declarations */
main()
{
    float rain[365];    /* array of 365 floats */
    char code[12];      /* array of 12 chars */
    int states[50];     /* array of 50 ints */
    ...
}
```

Recall, too, that brackets ([ ]) identify arrays and that the enclosed number indicates the number of elements in the array. We identify an individual element by using its subscript number, also called an *index*. The numbering starts with 0. Hence, **rain[0]** is the first element of **rain** array, and **rain[364]** is the 365th and last element.

Initialization and Storage Classes

Often we use arrays to store data needed for a program. For instance, a 12-element array can store the number of days in each month. In cases such as these, there is a convenient way to initialize the array at the beginning of a program. Let's describe the process.

We know that we can initialize scalar (single-valued) variables in a declaration with expressions like

```
int fix = 1;
float flax = PI*2;
```

in which we assume **PI** was defined earlier as a macro. Can we conduct a similar operation with arrays? Yes and maybe: Yes for ANSI C; maybe for K & R C. If the array is an external array or a static array, it can be initialized. If it is an automatic array, it can be initialized under the ANSI C standard but not under the older K & R definition of the language. We cover these terms in Chapter 13, but we preview them now.

The terms *external, static,* and *automatic* describe different storage classes that C allows. The *storage class* determines how widely known a data item is to various functions in a program and for how long it is kept in memory. Until now, we have only used automatic variables. Let's look at these three storage classes.

Automatic Variables and Arrays

An *automatic variable* or *automatic array* is one defined inside a function (including formal arguments). As we've emphasized, a variable defined in a function is private to that function, even if it reuses a name that appears in another function. In addition, such a variable exists only for the duration of a function call to the function using it. When a function finishes and returns to the calling function, the space used to hold its variables is freed.

ANSI C allows us to initialize automatic arrays as shown:

```
main()
{
   int powers[8] = {1,2,4,6,8,16,32,64}; /* ANSI only */
 ...
}
```

Because the array is defined inside **main( )**, it is an automatic array. It's initialized by using a comma-separated list of values enclosed in braces. The first element (**powers[0]**) is assigned the value **1**, and so on.

K & R C, however, does not allow this initialization. The only way to give values to an automatic array in K & R C is to assign values to the elements individually, perhaps by using a loop. We show an example soon.

External Variables and Arrays

An *external variable* or *external array* is one defined outside a function. Here, for example, we define an external variable and an external array:

```
int report;
int sows[5] = {12, 10, 8, 9, 6};  /* ok in ANSI and K&R */
main()
{
   ...
}
int feed(n)
int n;
{
   ...
}
```

External variables and arrays differ from their automatic cousins in three respects. First, they are known to all functions following them in a file. In our example, both **main( )** and **feed( )** can use and modify **report** and the array **sows**. Second, external variables and arrays persist as long as the program runs. Because they are not defined in a particular function, they don't expire when a particular function terminates. Third, external variables and arrays are initialized to zeros by default; therefore **report** is initialized to **0**.

Static Variables and Arrays

You can define a *static variable* or *static array* inside a function by beginning the definition with the keyword **static**:

```
int account(n,m)
int n,m;
{
   static int beans[2] = {343, 332};/* ok in ANSI, K&R */
   ...
}
```

This keyword creates an array that, like an automatic array, is local to the function **account( )**. However, like an external array, a static array retains its values between function calls and is initialized to zeros by default.

Storage Classes: Comments

C offers multiple storage classes to meet different programming needs. In Chapter 13 we investigate the uses of each type. For most cases, automatic variables and arrays are the best choice. But because K & R didn't allow automatic arrays to be initialized, many programs used external or static arrays instead. We, too, often use external and static arrays for that reason. Therefore, our examples work with pre-ANSI compilers as well as with ANSI compilers.

More Array Initialization

Listing 10.1 presents a short program that prints the number of days per month.

❖ *day_mon1.c*

Listing 10.1

```
/* day_mon1.c--prints the days for each month */
#include <stdio.h>
#define MONTHS 12
int days[MONTHS] = {31,28,31,30,31,30,31,31,30,31,30,31};
main()
{
   int index;
   extern int days[];    /* optional declaration */

   for ( index = 0; index < MONTHS; index++)
     printf("Month %d has %d days.\n", index + 1,
            days[index]);
}
```

The output follows (note that the program is incorrect for one month every four years):

```
Month 1 has 31 days.
Month 2 has 28 days.
Month 3 has 31 days.
Month 4 has 30 days.
Month 5 has 31 days.
Month 6 has 30 days.
Month 7 has 31 days.
Month 8 has 31 days.
Month 9 has 30 days.
Month 10 has 31 days.
Month 11 has 30 days.
Month 12 has 31 days.
```

By defining **days[ ]** outside the function, we make it external. We initialize it with a list enclosed in braces; commas are used to separate the members of the list. Inside the function the optional declaration

```
extern int days[];
```

uses the keyword **extern** to remind us that the **days** array is defined elsewhere in the program as an external array. Because the array is defined elsewhere, we needn't give its size here. (See Chapter 13 for more on **extern**.) Note: Omitting this entire declaration statement has no effect on how the program works.

The number of items in the list should match the size of the array. What if we count wrong? Let's modify our example with a list that is too short. See Listing 10.2.

❖ *day_mon2.c*

Listing 10.2

```
/* day_mon2.c--initialize 10 out of 12 elements */
#include <stdio.h>
#define MONTHS 12
int days[MONTHS] = {31,28,31,30,31,30,31,31,30,31};
main()
{
   int index;
   extern int days[];    /* optional declaration */

   for ( index = 0; index < MONTHS; index++)
     printf("Month %d has %d days.\n", index + 1,
            days[index]);
}
```

This time the output looks like the following:

```
Month 1 has 31 days.
Month 2 has 28 days.
Month 3 has 31 days.
Month 4 has 30 days.
Month 5 has 31 days.
Month 6 has 30 days.
Month 7 has 31 days.
Month 8 has 31 days.
Month 9 has 30 days.
Month 10 has 31 days.
Month 11 has 0 days.
Month 12 has 0 days.
```

As you can see, when the compiler runs out of suggestions from the list, it initializes the remaining elements to **0**.

The compiler is not so forgiving if you have too many list members, which it considers an error condition. However, you can let the compiler match the array size to the list. See Listing 10.3.

❖ *day_mon3.c*

Listing 10.3

```
/* day_mon3.c--initialize 10 out of 12 elements */
#include <stdio.h>
int days[] = {31,28,31,30,31,30,31,31,30,31};
main()
{
    int index;
    extern int days[]; /* optional declaration */

    for ( index = 0; index < sizeof days / sizeof (int);
        index++)
      printf("Month %d has %d days.\n", index + 1,
            days[index]);
}
```

There are two main points to note in the program:

1. If you use empty brackets when initializing an array, the program will count the number of items in the list and make the array that large.

2. Notice what we do in the **for** control statement. Lacking faith in our ability to count correctly, we let the computer give us the size of the array. The **sizeof** operator gives us the size, in bytes, of the object or type following it. (See Chapter 3 to review this operator.) On our system, each **int** element occupies two bytes, so we divide the total number of bytes by two to get the number of elements. Other systems may have a different size **int**. Therefore, to be general, we divide by **sizeof (int)**.

Here is the result of running this program:

```
Month 1 has 31 days.
Month 2 has 28 days.
Month 3 has 31 days.
Month 4 has 30 days.
Month 5 has 31 days.
Month 6 has 30 days.
Month 7 has 31 days.
Month 8 has 31 days.
Month 9 has 30 days.
Month 10 has 31 days.
```

Note that we put in just 10 values, but our method of letting the program find the array size keeps us from trying to print beyond the end of the array. This feature points out a potential disadvantage to using automatic counting: Errors in the number of elements may pass unnoticed.

There is also one other short method of initializing arrays that works only for character strings. We discuss this method in Chapter 11.

Assigning Array Values

You can assign values to array members, regardless of storage class. For example, the following fragment assigns even numbers to an automatic array:

```
/* array assignment */
#include <stdio.h>
#define SIZE 50
main()
{
   int counter, evens[SIZE];

   for ( counter = 0; counter < SIZE; counter++)
      evens[counter] = 2 * counter;
   ...
}
```

Note that this assignment is element by element. Unlike some languages, C doesn't let you assign one array to another as a unit. Nor can you use the list-in-braces form except when initializing:

```
/* nonvalid array assignment */
#define SIZE 5
main()
{
  int oxen[SIZE] = {5,3,2,8};   /* ok here */
  int yaks[SIZE];

  yaks = oxen;                  /* not allowed */
  yaks[SIZE] = oxen[SIZE];      /* invalid subscript */
  yaks[SIZE] = {5,3,2,8};       /* doesn't work */
}
```

10.2 Pointers to Arrays

Recall from Chapter 9 that pointers give us a symbolic way of using addresses. Since the hardware instructions of computing machines use addresses heavily, pointers allow us to express ourselves in a way that is close to the way the machine expresses itself. Therefore, programs with pointers are more efficient. In particular, pointers offer a useful way to deal with arrays. Indeed, our array notation is simply a disguised use of pointers.

An example of this disguised use is that an array name is also a pointer to the first element of an array. That is, if **flizny** is an array, then

```
flizny == &flizny[0]
```

and both represent the memory address of that first element. (Recall that **&** is the address operator.) Both are pointer constants, for they remain fixed for the duration of the program. However, they can be assigned as values to a pointer variable, which we can alter. See Listing 10.4. Notice what happens to the value of a pointer when we add a number to it.

❖ *pnt_add.c*

Listing 10.4

```
/* pnt_add.c--pointer addition */
#include <stdio.h>
#define SIZE 4
main()
{
  int dates[SIZE], *pti, index;
  float bills[SIZE], *ptf;

  pti = dates; /* assign address of array to pointer */
  ptf = bills;
  for (index = 0; index < SIZE; index ++)
    printf("pointers + %d: %10u %10u\n",
           index, pti + index, ptf + index);
}
```

Here is the output:

```
pointers + 0:   56014  56026
pointers + 1:   56016  56030
pointers + 2:   56018  56034
pointers + 3:   56020  56038
```

The first line prints the beginning addresses of the two arrays. The next line gives the result of adding 1 to the address, and so on. What?

```
56014 + 1 = 56016?
56026 + 1 = 56030?
```

Pretty dumb? Not so. Our system is addressed by individual bytes, but type **int** uses two bytes and type **float** uses four bytes. What is happening here is that when you say "add 1 to a pointer," C adds one storage unit. For arrays, this addition means the address is increased to the address of the next element, not just the next byte. See Figure 10.1. This situation presents one reason why we have to declare what sort of object a pointer points to; the address is not enough, for the computer needs to know how many bytes are used to store the object. (This fact is true even for pointers to scalar variables; otherwise, the ***pt** operation to fetch the value can't work correctly.)

Now we can define more clearly what is meant by pointer-to-**int** or pointer-to-**float** or pointer-to-any-other-data-object. First, the value of the pointer is the address of the object. How the address is represented internally is hardware dependent. Many computers including the PC and VAX are byte-addressable systems, meaning that each byte in memory is numbered sequentially. In this case, the address of a large object such as a type **double** variable typically is the address of the first byte of the object. Second, applying the * operator to the pointer yields the value represented by the pointed-to

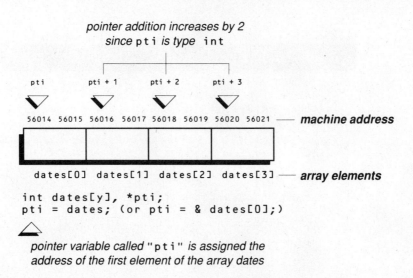

Figure 10.1

An array and pointer addition

object. Third, adding 1 to the pointer increases its value by the size of the pointed-to object.

Pointer addition is an example of *operator overloading;* the meaning of the + operator depends on to what sort of object it is applied. Adding 1 to a type **long** object produces a different result from adding 1 to a type pointer-to-**int** object. The C compiler uses the context to determine how to interpret the + operator. (Note: The C++ language carries operator overloading further by letting the user define new context-dependent meanings for operators.) As a result, we have the following equalities:

```
dates + 2 == &dates[2]    /* same address */
*(dates + 2) == dates[2] /* same value */
```

These relationships sum up the close connection between arrays and pointers. They mean that we can use a pointer to identify an individual element of an array and to get its value. In essence, we have two different notations for the same thing. Indeed, the C language standard describes array notation in terms of pointers.

Incidentally, don't confuse ***(dates+2)** with ***dates+2**. The value operator (*) binds more tightly (has higher precedence) than +, so the latter means **(*dates)+2**:

```
*(dates + 2)    /* value of the 3rd element of dates */
*dates + 2      /* 2 added to the value of the 1st element */
```

The relationship between arrays and pointers also means that we can often use either approach when writing a program. Listing 10.5, for instance, produces the same output as Listing 10.1 when compiled and run.

Here **days** points to the first element of the array; **days + index** points to element **days[index]**; and *(**days + index**) is the value of that element, just as **days[index]** is.

<table>
<tr><td>❖ day_mon4.c</td></tr>
</table>

Listing 10.5

```
/* day_mon4.c--use pointer notation */
#include <stdio.h>
#define MONTHS 12
int days[MONTHS] = {31,28,31,30,31,30,31,31,30,31,30,31};
main()
{
   int index;
   extern int days[];    /* optional declaration */

   for ( index = 0; index < MONTHS; index++)
      printf("Month %d has %d days.\n", index + 1,
             *(days + index));
}
```

10.3 Functions, Arrays, and Pointers

In some cases, however, we have to use pointers. One example is when we have a function with an array as an argument. Let's suppose we wish to write a function that operates on an array. For instance, suppose we want a function that returns the sum of the elements of an array. See Listing 10.6. To point out an interesting fact about array arguments, we also print out the size of the relevant arrays.

❖ *sum_arr1.c*

Listing 10.6

```
/* sum_arr1.c--sum elements of an array */
#include <stdio.h>
#define SIZE 10
long sum();
main()
{
   static int marbles[SIZE] = {20,10,5,39,4,16,19,26,31,20};
   long answer;

   answer = sum(marbles, SIZE);
   printf("The total number of marbles is %ld.\n", answer);
   printf("The size of marbles is %d bytes.\n",
          sizeof marbles);
}

long sum(ar,n)
int ar[];      /* how big an array? */
int n;
{
   int i;
   long total = 0;

   for(i = 0; i < n; i++)
      total +=ar[i];
   printf("The size of ar is %d bytes.\n", sizeof ar);
   return total;
}
```

Recall that the += operator adds the value of the operand on its right to the operand on its left; thus **total** is a running sum of the array elements. The output on our system looks like the following:

```
The size of ar is 2 bytes.
The total number of marbles is 190.
The size of marbles is 20 bytes.
```

The function successfully sums the number of marbles, but what is **ar**? From the function argument declarations, you may expect that **ar** is a new array into which are copied the values found in **marbles**, the actual argument to the function. After all, the formal argument **n** is assigned the value of its corresponding actual argument. Yet **ar** is only 2 bytes, so it can't be assigned the 20 bytes of data in **marbles**. Thus **ar** is not an array of 10 **int**s.

The reason that **ar** is not an array is that C does not allow arrays to be passed as function arguments. Look at the function call:

```
sum(marbles, SIZE);
```

The first argument is **marbles**, the name of an array. Recall that the name of an array is a pointer to the first element of the array. That is, the identifier **marbles** is not an array, it is the address of **marbles[0]**, an **int**. So the function call **sum(marbles,SIZE);** passes two numbers: a pointer and an integer. Therefore the formal arguments to **sum( )** should be a pointer-to-**int** and an **int**, which suggests that the function heading should look like the following:

```
int sum(ar,n)
int *ar;     /* pointer to int */
int n;
```

Indeed, if you replace the heading in Listing 10.6 with the preceding heading, the program works exactly the same as before. When you declare a formal argument in C, the forms

```
int *ar;
```

and

```
int ar[];
```

are exactly equivalent. Both state that **ar** is a pointer-to-**int**. Thus on our system **sizeof** **ar** is **2** because our system uses two-byte pointers.

If **ar** is a pointer, why can we use the expression **ar[i]** in **sum( )**? In C, remember, **ar[i]** is the same as ***(ar + i)**. Both represent the value stored at address **ar + i**. This is true if **ar** is the name of an array, and it is also true if **ar** is the name of a pointer variable. Therefore we can use pointer notation to process an array, and we can use array notation with a pointer variable. In this instance, **ar** starts out pointing to the first element of the **marbles** array. Increasing **i** then makes **ar + i** point to each element in turn. Because we also pass the size of the array, the **sum( )** function knows when the end of the array is reached. In short, when you use an array name as a function argument, you pass a pointer to the function. The function then uses this pointer to effect changes on the original array in the calling program.

Incidentally, note that in Listing 10.6 we design the function to include a parameter representing the array size. This feature lets us use the same function for differently sized arrays. Note that the only way the function can know the array size is if we tell it. As the example shows, applying the **sizeof** operator to an array name yields the size of an array, but applying **sizeof** to a pointer variable yields the size of the pointer, not the size of the object that is pointed to.

Using Pointer Arguments

The fact that **ar** is a variable offers us an alternative way to write the **sum( )** function. Rather than adding **i** to a fixed value **ar**, we can alter the value of **ar** itself. Listing 10.7 illustrates this approach.

Again **ar** starts out pointing to the first element of **marbles**, so the assignment expression **total += *ar** adds the value of the first element (**20**) to **total**. Then the expression **ar++** increments the pointer variable **ar** so that it points to the next element in the array. Since **ar** points to type **int**, C increments the value of **ar** by the size of **int**.

❖ *sum_arr2.c*

```
/* sum_arr2.c--sum elements of an array */
#include <stdio.h>
#define SIZE 10
long sump();
main()
{
   static int marbles[SIZE] = {20,10,5,39,4,16,19,26,
         31,20};
   long answer;

   answer = sump(marbles, SIZE);
   printf("The total number of marbles is %ld.\n", answer);
}

long sump(ar,n)    /* use pointer arithmetic */
int *ar;           /* ar is a pointer */
int n;
{
   int i;
   long total = 0;

   for(i = 0; i < n; i++)
   {
      total += *ar;  /* add value to total */
      ar++;          /* advance pointer to next element */
   }
   return total;
}
```

Listing 10.7

We can condense the body of the loop to one line:

```
total += *ar++;
```

The unary operators * and ++ have the same precedence but associate from right to left. Therefore, the ++ applies to **ar**, not to *ar. That is, the pointer is incremented, not the value pointed to. The fact that we use the postfix form (**ar++** rather than **++ar**) means that the pointer is not incremented until after the pointed-to value is added to **total**. If we use *++**ar**, then the order would be: increment the pointer, then use the value pointed to. But if we use (*ar)++, the program will use the value of **ar**, then increment the value, not the pointer. This case will leave the pointer pointing to the same element, but the element will contain a new number. Listing 10.8 illustrates these niceties of precedence.

❖ order.c

Listing 10.8

```
/* order.c--precedence in pointer operations */
#include <stdio.h>
int data[2] = {100, 300};
int moredata[2] = {100, 300};
main()
{
   int *p1, *p2, *p3;

   p1 = p2 = data;
   p3 = moredata;
   printf("%d %d %d\n", *p1++, *++p2, (*p3)++);
   printf("%d %d %d\n", *p1, *p2, *p3);
}
```

Here is its output:

```
100 300 100
300 300 101
```

The only operation in the program that alters an array value is (*p3)++, which we use to point to a different array from the other pointers so that the **data** array will be unchanged.

Pointers and Arrays: A Comment

As we have seen, functions that process arrays actually use pointers as arguments. But we do have a choice between array notation and pointer notation for writing array-processing functions. Using array notation as we do in Listing 10.6 makes it more obvious that the function is working with arrays. Also, array notation has a more familiar look to programmers versed in other languages such as FORTRAN, Pascal, Modula-2, or BASIC. Still other programmers may be more accustomed to working with pointers and find the pointer notation more natural.

As far as C is concerned, the two notations are equivalent in meaning. Some programmers believe that pointer notation, particularly when used with the increment operator, is closer to machine language and leads to more efficient code. Others feel the programmer's main concerns should be correctness and clarity and that code optimization should be left to the compiler.

10.4 Pointer Operations

C offers five basic operations that we can perform on pointers. See Listing 10.9. To show the results of each operation, we print out the value of the pointer (which is the address it points to), the value stored in the pointed-to address, and the address of the pointer itself. (If your compiler supports the **%p** specifier, use it instead of **%u** for printing the addresses.)

❖ *pt_ops.c*

Listing 10.9

```
/* pt_ops.c--pointer operations */
#include <stdio.h>
main()
{
   static int urn[3] = {100,200,300};
   int *ptr1, *ptr2;

   ptr1 = urn;        /* assign an address to a pointer */
   ptr2 = &urn[2];   /* ditto */
   printf("ptr1 = %u, *ptr1 = %d, &ptr1 = %u\n",
          ptr1, *ptr1, &ptr1)
   ptr1++;              /* increment a pointer */
   printf("ptr1 = %u, *ptr1 =%d, &ptr1 = %u\n",
          ptr1, *ptr1, &ptr1)
   printf("ptr2 = %u, *ptr2 = %d, &ptr2 = %u\n",
          ptr2, *ptr2, &ptr2)
   ++ptr2;              /* going past end of the array */
   printf("ptr2 = %u, *ptr2 = %d, &ptr2 = %u\n",
          ptr2, *ptr2, &ptr2)
   printf("ptr2 - ptr1 = %u\n", ptr2 - ptr1);
}
```

The output follows:

```
ptr1 = 234, *ptr1 =100, &ptr1 = 3606
ptr1 = 236, *ptr1 =200, &ptr1 = 3606
ptr2 = 238, *ptr2 =300, &ptr2 = 3604
ptr2 = 240, *ptr2 =1910, &ptr2 = 3604
ptr2 - ptr1 = 2
```

This example shows the five basic operations that we can perform with or on pointer variables:

1. *Assignment.* We can assign an address to a pointer. Typically we do so by using an array name or by using the address operator (**&**). In our example, **ptr1** is assigned the address of the beginning of the array **urn**; this address happens to be memory cell number 234. (On our system, static variables are stored in low memory locations.) The variable **ptr2** gets the address of the third and last element, **urn[2]**.

2. *Value-finding (dereferencing).* The * operator gives us the value stored in the pointed-to location. Thus, ***ptr1** initially is **100**, which is the value stored at location 234.

3. *Take a pointer address.* Like all variables, pointer variables have an address and a value. The **&** operator tells us where the pointer itself is stored. In our example, **ptr1** is stored in memory location 3606. The content of that memory cell is **234**, the address of **urn**.

4. *Increment-decrement a pointer.* We can increment a pointer by using regular addition or by using the increment operator. Incrementing a pointer to an array element instructs it to move to the next element of an array. Thus, **ptr1++** increases the numerical value of **ptr1** by **2** (two bytes per **int**) and makes **ptr1** point to **urn[1]**. See Figure 10.2. Now **ptr1** has the value **236** (the next array address), and ***ptr1** has the value **200**, which is the value of **urn[1]**. Note that the address of **ptr1** itself remains **3606**. After all, a variable doesn't move around just because it changes value. Of course, we can also decrement a pointer.

   There are some cautions to note, however, when incrementing or decrementing a pointer. The computer does not keep track of whether or not a pointer still points to

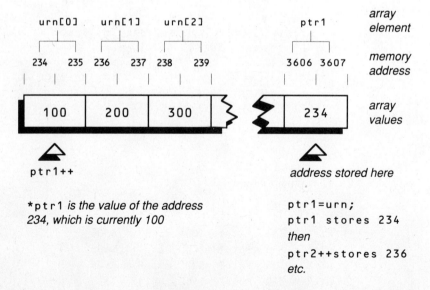

Figure 10.2

*Incrementing a type **int** pointer*

an array element. The operation **++ptr2** in our example causes **ptr2** to move up another two bytes, and now it points to whatever is stored after the array. Also, you can use the increment or decrement operators for pointer variables but not for pointer constants, just as you can't use the increment operator on regular constants. You can use simple addition for pointer variables and constants.

Valid	Invalid
ptr1++;	urn++;
x++;	3++;
ptr2 = ptr1 + 2;	ptr2 = urn++;
ptr2 = urn + 1;	x = y + 3++;

5. *Differencing.* You can find the difference between two pointers. Normally you perform this operation to find out how far apart two pointers to elements are in the same array. Note that the result is in the same units as the type size.

These five pointer operations open many gateways. C programmers create arrays of pointers, pointers to functions, arrays of pointers to pointers, arrays of pointers to functions, and so on. We discuss here only the basic uses we have already mentioned. The first use is to communicate information to and from functions. We have seen that we must use pointers if we want a function to affect variables in the calling function. The second use is in functions designed to manipulate arrays.

10.5 Another Example

Let's look at another programming example using functions and arrays. See Listing 10.10. This time we write a function to display an array and a function that multiplies each element of an array by a given value. The second function emphasizes the fact that array functions operate on the original array, not on a copy. To provide some variety, we use array notation for one function and pointer notation for the other.

❖ *array.c*

Listing 10.10

```
/*array.c--funtions and arrays */
#include <stdio.h>
#define SIZE 5
void show_array(), mult_array();
main()
{
   static double dip[SIZE] = {20.0, 17.66, 8.2, 15.3, 22.22};

   show_array(dip, SIZE);
   mult_array(2.5, dip, SIZE);
   show_array(dip, SIZE);
}
void show_array(ar,n)
double ar[];        /* array notation */
int n;
{
```

```
   int i;

   for (i = 0; i < n; i++)
     printf("%8.3f ", ar[i]);
   putchar('\n');
}
```

Listing 10.10 (cont'd.)

```
/* multiplies each array member by the same multiplier */
void mult_array(mult, ar, size)
double mult; /* multiplier */
double *ar;  /* pointer to first element of array */
int size;
{
   int i;

   for (i = 0; i < size; i++)
     *ar++ *= mult;
}
```

Here is the output:

```
20.000   17.660    8.200   15.300   22.220
50.000   44.150   20.500   38.250   55.550
```

Note that both functions are type **void**. The **mult_array( )** function does provide new values to the **dip** array, but not by using the **return** mechanism.

10.6 Multidimensional Arrays

Tempest Cloud, a weather person who takes her subject cirrusly, wants to analyze five years of monthly rainfall data. One of the first decisions she must make is how to represent the data. One choice is to use 60 variables, one for each data item—which is a senseless choice. Using an array with 60 elements is an improvement, but it will be nicer still if we can keep each year's data separate. We can also use 5 arrays, each with 12 elements, but this method is clumsy and can become quite awkward if Tempest decides to study 50 years' worth of rainfall instead of 5. We need something better.

A good answer is to use an array of arrays. In this case, the master array will have 5 elements, and each element will be a 12-element array:

```
static float rain[5][12];
```

We can also visualize the **rain** array as a two-dimensional array consisting of 5 rows, each of 12 columns. See Figure 10.3. By changing the second subscript we move along a row, and by changing the first subscript we move vertically along a column. For our example, the second subscript takes us through the months, and the first subscript takes us through the years.

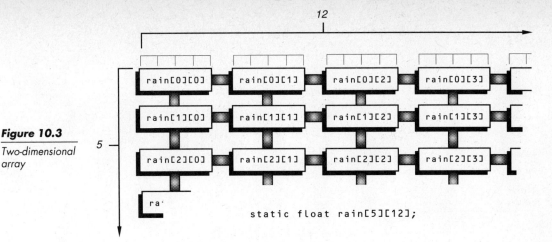

Figure 10.3

Two-dimensional array

```
static float rain[5][12];
```

The two-dimensional view is a way of visualizing an array with two indices. Internally, such an array is stored sequentially, beginning with the first 12-element array followed by the second 12-element array, and so on.

Let's use this two-dimensional array in a weather program. Our goal is to find the total rainfall for each year, the average yearly rainfall, and the average rainfall for each month. To find the total rainfall for a year, we have to add all the data in a given row. To find the average rainfall for a given month, we have to add all the data in a given column. The two-dimensional array makes it easy to visualize and execute these activities. Listing 10.11 shows the program.

❖ *rain.c*

Listing 10.11

```
/* rain.c--finds yearly totals, yearly average, and month-
ly average for several years of rainfall data */
#include <stdio.h>
#define MONTHS 12/* number of months in a year */
#define YRS 5     /* number of years of data */
main()
{
   static float rain[YRS][MONTHS] = {
   {10.2, 8.1, 6.8, 4.2, 2.1, 1.8, 0.2, 0.3, 1.1, 2.3, 6.1,
        7.4},
   {9.2, 9.8, 4.4, 3.3, 2.2, 0.8, 0.4, 0.0, 0.6, 1.7, 4.3,
        5.2},
   {6.6, 5.5, 3.8, 2.8, 1.6, 0.2, 0.0, 0.0, 0.0, 1.3, 2.6,
        4.2},
   {4.3, 4.3, 4.3, 3.0, 2.0, 1.0, 0.2, 0.2, 0.4, 2.4, 3.5,
        6.6},
   {8.5, 8.2, 1.2, 1.6, 2.4, 0.0, 5.2, 0.9, 0.3, 0.9, 1.4,
        7.2}
                        };
```

```
      /* initializing rainfall data for 1970 - 1974 */
      int year, month;
      float subtot, total;

      printf(" YEAR   RAINFALL (inches)\n");
      for ( year = 0, total = 0; year < YRS; year++)
      {   /* for each year, sum rainfall for each month */
        for ( month = 0, subtot = 0; month < MONTHS; month++)
            subtot += rain[year][month];
        printf("%5d %15.1f\n", 1970 + year, subtot);
        total += subtot; /* total for all years */
      }
      printf("\nThe yearly average is %.1f inches.\n\n",
          total/YRS);
      printf("MONTHLY AVERAGES:\n\n");
      printf(" Jan Feb Mar Apr May Jun Jul Aug Sep Oct ");
      printf(" Nov Dec\n");

      for ( month = 0; month < MONTHS; month++ )
      {   /* for each month, sum rainfall over years */
        for ( year = 0, subtot = 0; year < YRS; year++)
            subtot += rain[year][month];
        printf("%4.1f ", subtot/YRS);
      }
      printf("\n");
}
```

*Listing 10.11
(cont'd.)*

The output follows:

```
YEAR      RAINFALL (inches)
1970       50.6
1971       41.9
1972       28.6
1973       32.2
1974       37.8

The yearly average is 38.2 inches.

MONTHLY AVERAGES:

Jan Feb Mar Apr May Jun Jul Aug Sep Oct Nov Dec
7.8 7.2 4.1 3.0 2.1 0.8 1.2 0.3 0.5 1.7 3.6 6.1
```

The main points to notice in this program are the computation scheme and the initialization. The initialization is the more involved of the two, so we look at the computation first.

Computation Scheme

To find the total for a given year, we keep **year** constant and let **month** run its full range. This operation is the inner **for** loop of the first part of the program. We then repeat the process for the next value of **year**, which is the outer **for** loop of the first part of the program. A nested loop structure like this one is natural for handling a two-dimensional array. One loop handles one subscript; the other loop handles the second subscript.

The second part of the program has the same structure, but now we change **year** with the inner **for** loop and **month** with the outer **for** loop. Remember, each time the outer loop cycles once, the inner loop cycles its full allotment. Thus, this arrangement cycles through all the years before changing the months, which gives us a five-year total for the first month, then a five-year total for the second month, and so on.

Initializing a Two-Dimensional Array

For the initialization we include five embraced sets of numbers, all enclosed by another set of braces. The data in the first interior set of braces is assigned to the first row of the array, the data in the second interior set is assigned to the second row, and so on. The rules we discussed earlier in this chapter about mismatches between data and array sizes apply to each row. That is, if the first set of braces encloses 10 numbers, only the first 10 elements of the first row are affected. The last 2 elements in that row receive the standard default initialization to zero. Too many numbers represent an error condition; they do not get pushed into the next row.

We could have left out the interior braces and just retained the two outermost braces. As long as we have the right number of entries, the effect is the same. If we are short of entries, however, the array is filled sequentially without regard to row until the data run out. Then the remaining elements are initialized to 0. See Figure 10.4.

Everything we have said about two-dimensional arrays can be generalized to three-dimensional arrays and further. We declare a three-dimensional array this way:

```
int solido[10][20][30];
```

Figure 10.4

Two methods of initializing an array

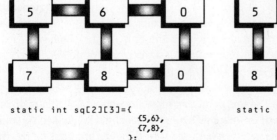

```
static int sq[2][3]={
           {5,6},
           {7,8},
        };
```

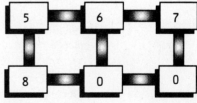

```
static int sq[2][3]={5,6,7, 8};
```

We can visualize this multidimensional array as 10 two-dimensional arrays (each 20 x 30) stacked atop each other. We can also think of it as an array of arrays of arrays. That is, it is a 10-element array, each element of which is a 20-element array. Each of these 20-element arrays has elements that are 30-element arrays. As well, we can simply think of arrays in terms of the number of indices needed. We won't go beyond two dimensions.

10.7 Pointers and Multidimensional Arrays

How do pointers relate to multidimensional arrays? Suppose we have this declaration:

```
int zippo[4][2]; /* an array of arrays of ints */
```

Then **zippo**, being the name of an array, is a pointer. As an array name, **zippo** points to the first element of the array. In this case, the first element of **zippo** is itself an array of two **ints**, so **zippo** points to an array of two **ints**. Let's analyze this situation in terms of pointer properties:

1. The value of a pointer is the address of the pointed-to object. The name of an array is a pointer to its first element. Therefore, as with all array names, **zippo** equals **&zippo[0]**. Next, **zippo[0]** is itself an array of two integers, so **zippo[0]** equals **&zippo[0][0]**, which is the address of its first element, an **int**. In short, **zippo[0]** is the address of an **int**-sized object, and **zippo** is the address of a two-**int**-sized object. Because both the integer and the array of two integers begin at the same location, the **zippo** and **zippo[0]** pointers are the same numerically.

2. Adding one to a pointer yields a value larger by the size of the pointed-to object. In this respect, **zippo** and **zippo[0]** differ, for **zippo** points to an object two **ints** in size, and **zippo[0]** points to an object one **int** in size. Therefore, **zippo + 1** and **zippo[0] + 1** are not the same numerically.

3. Dereferencing a pointer (applying the * operator) yields the value represented by the pointed-to object. Because **zippo[0]** points to its first element, which is **zippo[0][0]**, and ***(zippo[0])** represents the value **zippo[0][0]**, an **int** value. Similarly, ***zippo** represents the value of its first element, **zippo[0]**. But **zippo[0]** itself is a pointer-to-**int**; it's the address **&zippo[0][0]**. So ***zippo**, too, is a pointer-to-**int**. Since ***zippo** is equivalent to **zippo[0]** and since ***(zippo[0])** is equivalent to **zippo[0][0]**, then ****zippo** is also equivalent to **zippo[0][0]**, which is an **int**. In short, **zippo** is a pointer to a pointer and must be dereferenced twice to get an ordinary value. A pointer to a pointer is an example of *double indirection*.

Clearly, increasing the number of array dimensions increases the complexity of the pointer view. It's at this point that most students of C begin realizing why pointers are considered one of the more difficult aspects of the language. You may wish to study the preceding points carefully and see how they are born out by the following examples. First, Listing 10.12 is a program that prints out addresses.

Listing 10.12

```
/* zippo1.c--arrays and addresses */
#include <stdio.h>
main()
{
  int zippo[4][2];

  printf("zippo = %u, zippo[0] = %u, &zippo[0][0] = %u, ",
      zippo, zippo[0], &zippo[0][0] );
  printf("*zippo = %u\n", *zippo);
}
```

Here is the output:

```
zippo = 3512, zippo[0] = 3512, &zippo[0][0] = 3512, *zippo = 3512
```

The output shows that the address of the two-dimensional array **zippo** and the address of the one-dimensional array **zippo[0]** are the same. Each is the address of the corresponding array's first element, which is numerically the same as **&zippo[0][0]**. Also, note that **zippo** and ***zippo** have the same value.

Nonetheless, there is a difference. On our system, **int** is two bytes. So as discussed earlier, **zippo[0]** and ***zippo** point to two-byte data objects. Adding 1 to either should produce a value larger by 2. The pointer **zippo** is the address of an array of two **int**s, so it points to a four-byte data object. Thus, adding 1 to **zippo** should produce an address four bytes larger. Let's modify the program to check this capability. See Listing 10.13.

Listing 10.13

```
/* zippo2.c--more arrays and addresses */
#include <stdio.h>
main()
{
  int zippo[4][2];

  printf("zippo = %u, zippo[0] = %u, &zippo[0][0] = %u\n",
      zippo, zippo[0], &zippo[0][0] );
  printf("*zippo = %u\n", *zippo);
  printf("zippo + 1 = %u, zippo[0] + 1 = %u\n",
      zippo + 1, zippo[0] + 1 );
  printf("&zippo[0][0] + 1 = %u, *zippo + 1 = %u\n",
      &zippo[0][0] + 1, *zippo + 1);
  printf("*(zippo + 1) = %u\n", *(zippo + 1));
}
```

The output follows:

```
zippo = 3512, zippo[0] = 3512, &zippo[0][0] = 3512
*zippo = 3512
zippo + 1 = 3516, zippo[0] + 1 = 3514
&zippo[0][0] + 1 = 3514, *zippo + 1 = 3514
*(zippo + 1) = 3516
```

As predicted, adding **1** to **zippo** moves us from one two-**int** array to the next array, and adding 1 to **zippo[0]** moves us from one **int** to the next. See Figure 10.5. Also note what happens if we add 2 to **zippo[0]** (or equivalently, to ***zippo**). This action will take us beyond the end of the first two-**int** array to the beginning of the next. Both Listings 10.12 and 10.13 illustrate that **zippo[0]**, **&zippo[0][0]**, and ***zippo** are all three different notations for the same array—all are pointers to the same **int**.

Figure 10.5

An array of arrays

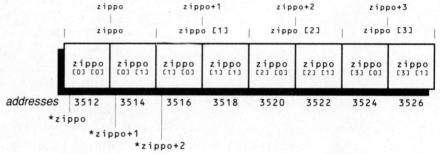

Note the difference between ***zippo + 1** and ***(zippo + 1)**. The first form applies the ***** first, then adds; the second form adds, then dereferences. In the first case, because ***zippo** is a pointer to **int**, adding 1 increases the value by two bytes on our system. In the second case, because **zippo** is a pointer to a two-**int** object, 4 is added. In this case **zippo + 1** points to the second two-**int** array element, and applying the ***** operator yields a pointer to the first element of that array. Thus, ***(zippo + 1)** is a pointer-to-**int**. In particular, ***(zippo + 1)** points to the element **zippo[1][0]**. The ***zippo + 1** expression also is a pointer-to-**int**, but it points to **zippo[0][1]**. In short, dereferencing and then adding moves the pointer along a row (changes the second index), whereas adding and then dereferencing moves the pointer along a column (changes the first index).

Another point to note is that *each* element of **zippo** is an array and hence is a pointer to a first element. Thus we have the following relationships:

```
zippo[0] == &zippo[0][0] == *zippo
zippo[1] == &zippo[1][0] == *(zippo + 1)
zippo[2] == &zippo[2][0] == *(zippo + 2)
zippo[3] == &zippo[3][0] == *(zippo + 3)
```

Applying the ***** operator to each gives these results:

```
*zippo[0] == zippo[0][0] == **zippo
*zippo[1] == zippo[1][0] == *(*(zippo + 1))
*zippo[2] == zippo[2][0] == *(*(zippo + 2))
*zippo[3] == zippo[3][0] == *(*(zippo + 3))
```

More generally, we can represent individual elements using array notation and pointer notation as follows:

```
zippo[m][n] == *(*(zippo + m) + n)
```

The value **m**, being the index associated with **zippo**, is added to **zippo**. The value **n**, being the index associated with the subarray **zippo[m]**, is added to **zippo[m]**, which is ***(zippo + m)** in array notation. Therefore, ***(zippo + m) + n** is the address of element **zippo[m][n]**, and applying the * operator yields the contents at that address.

Now suppose we want to declare a pointer variable **pz** that is compatible with **zippo**. Such a pointer can be used, for example, in writing a function to deal with **zippo**-like arrays. The type pointer-to-**int** won't suffice in this case. That type is compatible with **zippo[0]**, which points to a single **int**, but we want **pz** to point to an array of **int**s. We can use

```
int (*pz)[2];
```

which says that **pz** is a pointer to an array of two **int**s. We include parentheses because under the rules of precedence, [ ] have a higher precedence than *. Using parentheses allows us to apply the * first, creating one pointer to an array of two **int**s. In other words, in a declaration like

```
int *pax[2];
```

we apply the brackets first, making **pax** an array of two somethings. After that we apply the *, making **pax** an array of two pointers. Finally, we use the **int**, making **pax** an array of two pointers to **int**. Thus, this declaration creates two pointers.

Functions and Multidimensional Arrays

Suppose we want to write a function to deal with two-dimensional arrays. We have several choices. We can use a function written for one-dimensional arrays on each subarray. We can use the same function on the whole array, but treat the whole array as one-dimensional instead of two-dimensional. Or we can write a function that explicitly deals with two-dimensional arrays. To illustrate these three approaches, let's take a small two-dimensional array and apply each of the approaches to double the magnitude of each element.

Applying a One-Dimensional Function to Subarrays

To keep matters simple, we declare **junk** to be a **static** array of arrays so that we can initialize it. We write a function that takes an array address and an array size as arguments and doubles the indicated elements. We use a **for** loop to apply this function to each subarray of **junk**. We also print out the array contents. Listing 10.14 shows the program.

Listing 10.14

```
/* dubarr1.c--double array elements */
#include <stdio.h>
main()
{
   static junk[3][4] =  {
                    {2,4,5,8},
                    {3,5,6,9},
                    {12,10,8,6}
                    };
   int i, j;
   void dub();

   for (i = 0; i < 3 ; i++ )
     dub(junk[i], 4);

   for (i = 0; i < 3; i++ )
   {
     for (j = 0; j < 4; j++)
       printf("%5d", junk[i][j]);
     putchar('\n');
   }
}

void dub (ar, size)
int ar[]; /* or int *ar; */
int size;
{
   int i;

   for ( i = 0; i < size; i++ )
     ar[i] *= 2;
}
```

The first **for** loop in **main( )** uses **dub( )** to process subarray **junk[0]**, then **junk[1]**, and so on. This approach works because **junk[0]** and so forth are each one-dimensional arrays. Note that we pass **dub( )** a size parameter of **4**, since that is the number of elements in each subarray.

Here is the output:

```
 4   8  10  16
 6  10  12  18
24  20  16  12
```

Applying a One-Dimensional Function to a Two-Dimensional Array

In Listing 10.14, we looked at **junk** as being an array of 3 arrays of 4 **int**s. We also can look at **junk** as being an array of 12 **int**s. Suppose, for instance, we pass **dub( )** the value **junk[0]** as an argument. This action initializes the pointer **ar** in **dub( )** to the address of **junk[0][0]**, which means **ar[0]** corresponds to **junk[0][0]** and **ar[3]** corresponds to **junk[0][3]**. The element **ar[4]** represents the element following **junk[0][3]**, which is **junk[1][0]**, the first element of the next subarray. In other words, **ar[4]** begins the next row in the array.

The program in Listing 10.15 continues in the preceding fashion to cover the entire array, with **ar[11]** representing **junk[2][3]**.

❖ *dubarr2.c*

Listing 10.15

```
/* dubarr2.c--double array elements */
#include <stdio.h>
main()
{
   static junk[3][4]  =   {
                            {2,4,5,8},
                            {3,5,6,9},
                            {12,10,8,6}
                            };
   int i, j;
   void dub();

   dub(junk[0], 3*4);
   for (i = 0; i < 3; i++ )
   {
     for (j = 0; j < 4; j++)
       printf("%5d", junk[i][j]);
     putchar('\n');
   }
}

void dub (ar, size)
int ar[];        /* or int *ar; */
int size;
{
   int i;

   for ( i = 0; i < size; i++ )
     ar[i] *= 2;
}
```

Note that **dub( )** is unchanged from Listing 10.14; we merely change the limit to **3*4** (or 12) and use one call to **dub( )** instead of three. We write the limit as **3*4** to emphasize that it is the total number of elements calculated by multiplying the number of rows times the number of columns. The output follows:

4	8	10	16
6	10	12	18
24	20	16	12

Applying a Two-Dimensional Function

Both of the approaches so far lose track of the column-and-row information. In this application in which we double each element, that information is unimportant. But suppose each row represents a year and each column a month. Then you may want a function to, say, total individual columns. In that case, the function should have the row and column information available. This task can be accomplished by declaring the correct kind of formal variable so that the function can pass the array properly. In this case, the array **junk** is an array of three arrays of four **int**s. As our earlier discussion has implied, **junk** is thus a pointer to an array of four **int**s. A variable of this type can be declared in the following manner:

```
int (*pj)[4];
```

Alternatively, if **pj** is a formal argument to a function, we can declare it this way:

```
int pj[][4];
```

Such a variable can then be used in the same way as **junk**. See Listing 10.16.

❖ *dubarr3.c*

Listing 10.16

```
/* dubarr3.c--double array elements */
#include <stdio.h>
main()
{
   static junk[3][4] =   {
                          {2,4,5,8},
                          {3,5,6,9},
                          {12,10,8,6}
                          };
   int i, j
   void dub2();

   dub2(junk,3);
   for (i = 0; i < 3; i++ )
   {
      for (j = 0; j < 4; j++)
         printf("%5d", junk[i][j]);
      putchar('\n');
   }
}
void dub2 (ar, size)
int ar[][4];      /* or int (*ar)[4]; */
int size;
```

Listing 10.16 (cont'd.)

```
{
  int i, j;

  for ( i = 0; i < size; i++ )
    for ( j = 0; j < 4; j++)
      ar[i][j] *= 2;
}
```

The output follows:

```
 4   8   10  16
 6   10  12  18
24   20  16  12
```

This time we pass as arguments **junk**, which is a pointer to the first array, and **3**, the number of rows. The **dub2( )** function then treats **ar** as an array of arrays of 4 **int**s. The length of the row is built into the function, but the number of rows is left open. The same function works with, say, a 12-by-4 array if 12 is passed as the number of elements. This situation is true because **size** is the number of elements; but since each element is an array or row, **size** becomes the number of rows.

Note that **ar** is used in the same fashion as **junk** is used in **main( )**. This similarity is possible because **ar** and **junk** are the same type: pointer-to-array-of-four-**int**s. Also note that this declaration will not work properly:

```
int ar[][];    /* faulty declaration */
```

Recall that the compiler converts array notation to pointer notation. For example, **ar[1]** will become **ar+1**. But for the compiler to evaluate this expression, it needs to know what size object **ar** points to.

The following declaration:

```
int ar[][4];
```

says that **ar** points to an array of four **int**s, hence to an object eight bytes long on our system. So **ar+1** means the following: Add eight bytes to the address. With the empty-bracket version, the compiler will not know how to handle the situation. You can also include a size in the other bracket pair, but it is ignored:

```
void dub2(ar, n)
int ar[3][4];  /* the 3 is ignored */
int n;
```

In general, to declare a pointer corresponding to an *n*-dimensional array, you must provide values for all but the first set of brackets.

10.8 Planning a Program

Now that we've seen the mechanics of writing array functions, let's try a more programming-oriented example. Our task is to write a program that reads numbers into an array, prints out the entered numbers, and reports the average. To make the program more realistic, we require that it can terminate input, if desired, before the array is filled. This constraint enables the program to process any number of items up to a maximum determined by the array size. Also, we want to avoid calculating the average if no numbers are entered.

General Plan

Let's take a top-down approach to the problem. Conceptually, we expect the program to perform three major tasks: reading in a set of numbers, printing out the set of numbers, and calculating the average. Now that we know how to process arrays with functions, we can use functions to modularize the work. As a first pass, we can visualize the program as follows:

```
/* first draft of program skeleton */
#include <stdio.h>
#define MAX 25
void read_array();
void show_array();
double mean();
main()
{
   double data[MAX];

   read_array(data);
   show_array(data);
   printf("The average is %.2lf.\n", mean(data) );
}
```

This version reflects the modularity we desire, but it doesn't address data communication satisfactorily. For instance, the **read_array( )** function should know the maximum number of items it's allowed to read; therefore, it should also take **MAX** as an argument. Incidentally, the fact that **data** is a pointer means that the **read_array( )** function can modify directly the **data** array in **main( )**, which is exactly what we want for this function.

Similarly, the **show_array( )** and **mean( )** functions should know the size of an array they are using, so they each need an additional argument. In general, this argument should not be **MAX**, for the user may enter fewer numbers. We can use a variable **size** to represent the actual number of items entered; it can be the second argument to these two functions.

Our plan thus far raises a new problem: How does **main( )** know what **size** is? One solution is to have the **read_array( )** function return that value. That is, **read_array( )** takes as arguments the array to be filled and the maximum number of values the array holds. It then reads data into the array and returns the actual number of items read. If this number is zero, we can skip the rest of the program. This line of thought leads to a second draft:

```c
/* second top-level draft for the program */
#include <stdio.h>
#define MAX 25
int read_array();
void show_array();
double mean();
main()
{
   double data[MAX];
   int size;
   double average;

   size = read_array(data, MAX);
   if ( size == 0 )
     printf("No data. Bye.\n");
   else
   {
     printf("The following numbers were entered:\n\n");
     show_array(data, size);
     printf("\nThe average of these values is %.2f.\n",
         mean(data, size));
   }
}
```

Note that we change the type for **read_array( )** to reflect that it now has a return value.

The read_array *Function*

Now that we have the overall design for the program and its data flow, we can turn to the individual functions. The **read_array( )** function is the most ambitious of the three functions in our program. It should read in values until the array is filled or until the user wants to stop, whichever occurs first. The main question is how to let the user inform the program that he or she wants to terminate the work. We can use the properties of **scanf( )** to help here. Recall that **scanf( )** returns the number of values successfully read. Nonnumeric input or the end of the file cause **scanf( )** to return **0** or **EOF**, respectively. Thus we can terminate input if **scanf( )** doesn't return the value **1**. Also, we can use a counter to track the number of entries, and we terminate input if this number exceeds the size of the array. Here's one approach:

```c
int read_array(ar,limit)
double ar[];
int limit;
{
   int i = 0;
```

```
    printf("Enter up to %d numbers. To terminate\n", limit);
    printf("earlier, enter a letter or EOF.\n");
    while ( i < limit && scanf("%lf", &ar[i]) == 1 ) i++;
    return i;
}
```

Notice some subtle points in this effort. The first is that the test **i < limit** comes first. Recall that the **&&** operator guarantees that the second operand is not evaluated if the first operand is false. Therefore, the expression **scanf(" %lf", &ar[i] == 1** is not evaluated if **i** equals **limit**. Thus the **scanf( )** function is not called, which is good. Suppose we use the opposite order:

```
while ( scanf("%lf", &ar[i]) == 1 && i < limit )
```

In this case **scanf( )** reads a value into **ar[limit]** before finding out it's gone too far. Remember, because array numbering begins with **0**, **ar[limit]** is one position beyond the end of the array. You don't want to put data there!

Another subtle point is that the loop increments **i** after reading a value into **ar[i]**. This action makes **i** one greater than the index of the last array element filled. Because indexing begins with **0**, **i** at that point equals the number of array items, not the array index. This feature is convenient, because the number of array items is the value we wish to return.

The show_array( ) Function

Next we want a function to display the array values. We already wrote one for Listing 10.10. However, this function prints everything on one line. Here we have more data, so we want to insert some newlines. One scheme is to use a **for** loop as before and to print a newline every time, say, six values have been printed. We can achieve this feature by using the modulus operator (%):

```
void show_array(ar, n)
double ar[];
int n;
{
    int i;

    for ( n = 0; i < n; i++)
    {
        printf("%10.2f ", ar[i]);
        if ( i % 6 == 5 )
            putchar('\n');
    }
    if (i % 6 != 0)
        putchar('\n');
}
```

Since **i** starts at **0**, **i % 6** first becomes **5** after six values have been printed. The expression subsequently becomes **5** after each additional six values have been printed.

The **if (i % 6 != 0)** test causes a newline to be printed after all the values have been printed unless the last value printed already was at the end of a line, in which case the loop itself prints a newline. If **i % 6** is **5** inside the loop, the **i++** operation at loop's end makes **i % 6** into **0** after leaving the loop.

The mean( ) *Function*

This function presents only a simple problem. We can use a **for** loop to sum the numbers, then divide by the total number of items to get the average:

```
double mean( ar, n)
double ar[];
int n;
{
   int i;
   double total = 0;

   for ( i = 0; i < n ; i++ )
     total += ar[i];
   return total / n;
}
```

The only potential trouble spot is if **n** is **0**, for dividing by **0** is undesirable. Therefore, we designed the program to shield **mean( )** from this possibility. To build the protection into **mean( )** itself is more involved, since we also will have to design a way for **mean( )** to inform the calling program that it has a problem. One way is to use a pointer argument to **mean( )** to tell it where to place the average value and to use the return value to indicate problems:

```
mean1( ar, n, p_ave)
double ar[];
int n;
double *p_ave;
{
   int i;
   double total = 0;

   if ( i > 0 )
   {
     for ( i = 0; i < n ; i++ )
     total += ar[i];
     *p_ave = total / n;
     return 0;
   }
   else /* i == 0 */
     return -1;
}
```

The Result

Putting the parts together results in the program shown in Listing 10.17.

Listing 10.17

```c
/* mean.c--find the mean of a set of numbers */
#include <stdio.h>
#define MAX 25
int read_array();
void show_array();
double mean();
main()
{
  double data[MAX];
  int size;
  double average;

  size = read_array(data, MAX);
  if ( size == 0 )
    printf("No data. Bye.\n");
  else
  {
    printf("The following numbers were entered:\n\n");
    show_array(data, size);
    printf("\nThe average of these values is %.2f.\n",
        mean(data, size));
  }
}
int read_array(ar,limit)
double ar[];
int limit;
{
  int i = 0;

  printf("Enter up to %d numbers. To terminate\n",
        limit);
  printf("earlier, enter a letter or EOF.\n") ;
  while ( i < limit && scanf("%lf", &ar[i]) == 1 )
        i++;
  return i;
}
void show_array(ar, n)
double ar[];
int n;
{
  int i;

  for ( i = 0; i < n; i++)
  {
```

Listing 10.17
(cont'd.)

```
      printf("%10.2f ", ar[i]);
      if ( i % 6 == 5 )
        putchar('\n');
   }
   if ( i % 6 == 5 )
     putchar('\n');
}
double mean( ar, n)
double ar[];
int n;
{
   int i;
   double total = 0;

   for ( i = 0; i < n ; i++ )
     total += ar[i];
   return totral/n;
}
```

Here's a sample run:

```
Enter up to 25 numbers. To terminate
earlier, enter a letter or EOF.
1 2 3 4 5 6 7 8 9 10
The following numbers were entered:

      1.00      2.00      3.00      4.00    5.00      6.00
      7.00      8.00      9.00     10.00

The average of these values is 5.50.
```

Thanks to top-down programming, the program works exactly as intended.

10.9 Summary

An array is a set of elements all having the same data type. These elements are stored sequentially in memory and are accessed by using an integer index. In C, the first element of an array has an index of **0**, so the final element in an array of **n** elements has an index of **n − 1**.

To declare a simple one-dimensional array, use the following form:

type name [*size*];

Here *type* is the data type, *name* is the name of the array, and *size* is the number of elements.

C interprets the name of an array to be the address of the first element of the array. In other terms, the name of an array is a pointer to the first element. In general, arrays and pointers are closely connected. If **ar** is an array, then the expressions **ar[i]** and ***(ar + i)** are equivalent.

C does not allow entire arrays to be passed as function arguments, but you can pass the address of an array. The function then can use this value to manipulate the original array. You can use either array notation or pointer notation in the function. In either case, you're actually using a pointer variable.

Adding an integer to a pointer or incrementing a pointer changes the value of the pointer by the number of bytes of the object the pointer points to. That is, if **pd** points to an eight-byte **double** value in an array, adding 1 to **pd** increases its value by eight so that it will point to the next element of the array.

Two-dimensional arrays are represented by an array of arrays. For instance, the declaration

```
double sales[5][12];
```

creates an array **sales** having 5 elements. Each of these elements is itself an array of 12 **float**s. The first of these one-dimensional arrays can be referred to as **sales[0]**. Similarly, **sales[1]** is the second array of 12 **int**s. You can use a second index to call up a particular element in these arrays. For instance, **sales[2][5]** is the sixth element of **sales[2]**, and **sales[2]** is the third element of **sales**.

We've used **int** and **double** arrays in this discussion, but the same concepts apply to other types. Character strings, however, have many special rules. The difference stems from the fact that the terminal null character in a string provides a way for functions to detect the end of a string without being passed a size. We look at character strings in detail in the next chapter.

Review Questions

1. What printout does this program produce?

```
#include <stdio.h>
char ref[] = { 'D', 'O', 'L', 'T'};
main()
{
   char *ptr;
   int index;

   for( index = 0, ptr = ref; index < 4; index++, ptr++)
   printf("%c %c\n", ref[index], *ptr);
}
```

2. In Question 1, why was **ref** declared before **main( )**?

3. In Question 1, what does **ref** point to? What does **ref + 1** point to? What does **++ref** point to?

4. What is the value of ***ptr** and of ***(ptr + 2)** in each case?

    a.
```
in *ptr;
static int boop[4] = {12,21,121, 212};
ptr = boop;
```

    b.
```
float *ptr;
static float awk[2][2] = { {1.0, 2.0}, {3.0, 4.0} };
ptr = awk[0];
```

    c.
```
int *ptr;
static int jirb[4] = { 10023, 7};
ptr = jirb;
```

5. What is the value of ***ptr** and of ***(ptr + 2)** in each case?

    a.
```
int *ptr;
static int torf[2][2] = { 12, 14, 16};
ptr = torf[0];
```

    b.
```
int *ptr;
static int fort[2][2] = { {12}, {14,16} };
ptr = fort[0];
```

6. Suppose we have the declaration **static int grid[30][100];**

    a. Express the address of **grid[22][56]** one way

    b. Express the address of **grid[22][0]** two ways

    c. Express the address of **grid[0][0]** three ways

7. Create an appropriate declaration for each of the following variables:

    a. **digits** is an array of 10 **int**s

    b. **rates** is an array of 6 **float**s

    c. **mat** is an array of 3 arrays of 5 integers

    d. **pstr** is a pointer to an array of 20 **char**s

    e. **psa** is an array of 20 pointers-to-**char**

8. a. Declare a static array of six **int**s and initialize it to the values 1,2,4,8,16,32.

    b. Use array notation to represent the third element (the one with the value 4) of the array in Question 8a.

    c. Use pointer notation to represent the third element of the array.

9. Fill in the blanks: for a 10-element array, the index range is _____ through _____.

10. Suppose we have these declarations:

```
float rootbeer[10], things[10][5], *pf, value = 2.2;
int i = 3;
```

Identify each of the following statements as valid or invalid:

	Valid	Invalid
a. `rootbeer[2] = value;`	_____	_____
b. `scanf("%f", &rootbeer);`	_____	_____
c. `rootbeer = value;`	_____	_____
d. `printf("%f", rootbeer);`	_____	_____
e. `things[4][4] = rootbeer[3];`	_____	_____
f. `things[5] = rootbeer;`	_____	_____
g. `pf = value;`	_____	_____
h. `pf = rootbeer;`	_____	_____
i. `rootbeer = pf;`	_____	_____

Programming Exercises

1. Modify Listing 10.11 so that it performs the calculations using pointers instead of subscripts. (Note: You still have to declare and initialize the array.)

2. Write a program that initializes an array and then copies the contents of the array into two other arrays. (All three arrays should be declared in the main program.) To make the first copy, use a function with array notation. To make the second copy, use a function with pointer notation and pointer incrementing. Have each function take as arguments the name of the source array, the name of the target array, and the number of elements to be copied.

3. Write a function that returns the largest value stored in an array. Test the function in a simple program.

4. Write a function that returns the index of the largest value stored in an array. Test the function in a simple program.

5. Write a function that returns the difference between the largest and smallest elements of an array. Test the function in a simple program.

6. Write a program that initializes a two-dimensional array and uses one of the copy functions from Exercise 2 to copy it to a second two-dimensional array. (Note: Since a two-dimensional array is an array of arrays, a one-dimensional copy function can be used with each subarray.)

7. Use a copy function from Exercise 2 to copy the third through the fifth elements of a seven-element array into a three-element array. The function itself need not be altered; just choose the correct arguments. (Note: The actual arguments need not be an array name and array size; they only have to be the address of an array element and a number of elements to be processed.)

8. Write a function that sets each element in an array to the sum of the corresponding elements in two other arrays. That is, if array 1 has the values 2, 4, 5, and 8 and array 2 has the values 1, 0, 4, and 6, the function assigns array 3 the values 3, 4, 9, and 12. The function should take three array names and an array size as arguments. Test the function in a simple program.

9. Write a program that declares a 3 x 5 array and initializes it to some values of your choice. Have the program print out the values, then double all the values, and display the new values. Write functions to accomplish the displaying and the doubling. Have the functions take the array name and the number of rows as arguments.

10. Rewrite Listing 10.11 so that the primary tasks are performed by functions instead of in **main( )**.

11. Write a program that prompts the user to enter three sets of five **double** numbers each. The program should do the following:

a. Store the information in a 3 x 5 array

b. Compute the average of each set of 5 values

c. Compute the average of the values

d. Determine the largest of the 15 values

e. Report the results

Each major task should be handled by a separate function.

11

Character Strings and String Functions

Contents

Objectives

Declaring character arrays
Initializing character arrays
Creating string constants
Initializing pointers to strings
Creating arrays of strings
Using **gets( )** and **puts( )** for string I/O
Using string functions from the C library
Using character functions from the C library
Using command-line arguments
Converting strings to numbers

Character strings form one of the most useful and important data types in C. Although we have been using character strings all along, we still have much to learn about them. Of course, we already know the most basic fact: A character string is a **char** array terminated with a null character (**'\0'**). In this chapter we learn more about the nature of strings, how to declare and initialize them, how to get them into and out of programs, and how to manipulate them.

Listing 11.1 presents a busy program that illustrates several ways to set up strings, read them in, and print them out. We use two new functions: **gets( )**, which fetches a string, and **puts( )**, which prints out a string. (You probably notice a family resemblance to **getchar( )** and **putchar( )**.) The rest should look fairly familiar.

❖ *strings.c*

```
/* strings.c--stringing the user along */
#include <stdio.h>
#define MSG "You must have many talents. Tell me some."
     /* a symbolic string constant */
#define LIM 5
#define LINLEN 81 /* maximum string length + 1 */
char m1[] = "Just limit yourself to one line's worth.";
     /* initializing an external character array */
char *m2 = "If you can't think of anything, fake it.";
     /* initializing an external character pointer */
main()
{
   char name[LINLEN]
   static char talents[LINLEN];
   int i;
   int count = 0;
   char *m3 = "\nEnough about me--what's your name?";
              /* initializing a pointer */
   static char *mytal[LIM] = { "Adding numbers swiftly",
      "Multiplying accurately", "Stashing data",
      "Following instructions to the letter",
      "Understanding the C language"};
              /* initializing an array of strings */

   printf("Hi! I'm Clyde the Computer. ");
   printf("I have many talents.\n");
   printf("Let me tell you some of them.\n");
   puts("What were they? Ah, yes, here's a partial list.");
   for ( i = 0; i < LIM; i++)
      puts( mytal[i] ); /* print list of computer talents */

   puts(m3);
   gets(name);
   printf("Well, %s, %s\n", name, MSG);
```

Listing 11.1

**Listing 11.1
(cont'd.)**

```
    printf("%s\n%s\n", m1, m2);
    gets(talents);
    puts("Let's see if I've got that list:");
    puts(talents);
    printf("Thanks for the information, %s.\n", name);
}
```

To help you see what this program does, here is a sample run:

```
Hi! I'm Clyde the Computer. I have many talents.
Let me tell you some of them.
What were they? Ah, yes, here's a partial list.
Adding numbers swiftly
Multiplying accurately
Stashing data
Following instructions to the letter
Understanding the C language
Enough about me--what's your name?
Nigel Barntwit
Well, Nigel Barntwit, You must have many talents. Tell me some.
Just limit yourself to one line's worth.
If you can't think of anything, fake it.
Fencing, yodeling, malingering, cheese tasting, and sighing.
Let's see if I've got that list: Fencing, yodeling, malingering,
cheese tasting, and sighing.
Thanks for the information, Nigel Barntwit.
```

Let's sift through the program. However, rather than go through it line by line, we take a more organized approach. First, we look at ways of defining a string within a program. Then we look at what is involved in reading a string into a program. Finally, we study methods to output a string.

11.1 Defining Strings Within a Program

You probably noticed when you read Listing 11.1 that there are many ways to define a string. The principal methods are the following: using string constants, using **char** arrays, using **char** pointers, and using arrays of character strings. A program should also make sure there is a place to store a string. We discuss all of these topics in the following sections.

Character String Constants

Whenever the compiler encounters something enclosed in double quotation marks, it recognizes the phrase as a string constant. The enclosed characters, plus a terminating '\0' character automatically provided by the compiler, are stored in adjacent memory locations. The computer counts out the number of characters so it knows how much memory is needed. Our program uses several such character string constants, most often as arguments for the **printf( )** and **puts( )** functions. Note, too, that we can **#define** character string constants.

If you want to include a double quotation mark *in* a string, precede it with the backslash character:

```
printf("\"Run, Spot, run!\" said Dick.\n");
```

which produces the following output:

```
"Run, Spot, run!" said Dick.
```

Character string constants are placed in the static storage class. Therefore, if you use a string constant in a function, the string is stored just once and lasts for the duration of the program, even if the function is called several times. The entire phrase in quotation marks acts as a pointer to where the string is stored. This situation is analogous to the name of an array serving as a pointer to the array's location. If true, what kind of output do you expect the program in Listing 11.2 to produce?

❖ *quotes.c*

Listing 11.2

```
/* quotes.c--strings as pointers */
#include <stdio.h>
main()
{
    printf(" %s, %u, %c\n", "We", "love", *"figs");
}
```

Let's study the program. The **%s** format prints the string, so that should produce a **We**. The **%u** format produces an unsigned integer. If the phrase **"love"** is a pointer, then it should produce the value of the **"love"** pointer, which is the address of the first character in the string. (Type **unsigned** is not guaranteed to be large enough to hold addresses, so newer implementations provide a **%p** specifier specifically for pointers.) Finally, ***"figs"** should produce the value of the address pointed to, which should be the first character of the string **"figs"**. The output follows:

```
We, 3798, f
```

Our success inspires us to make two more predictions: **putchar("Freddy"[2])** should print the letter **e**. So should **putchar(2["Freddy"])**. We leave it to you to check and explain these predictions. (Hint: Use pointer notation instead of subscripts.)

Character String Arrays and Initialization

When we define a character string array, we must let the compiler know how much space is needed. One way to accomplish this is to initialize the array with a string constant. Since automatic arrays cannot be initialized in older C implementations, we use static or external arrays for this purpose. For example:

```
char m1[] = "Just limit yourself to one line's worth.";
```

initializes the external array **m1** to the indicated string. This form of initialization is shorthand for the standard array initialization form:

```
char m1[] = { 'J', 'u', 's', 't', ' ', 'l', 'i', 'm', 'i',
't', ' ', 'y', 'o', 'u', 'r', 's', 'e', 'l',
'f', ' ', 't', 'o', ' ', 'o', 'n', 'e', ' ',
'l', 'i', 'n', 'e', '\"', 's', ' ', 'w', 'o', 'r',
't', 'h', '.', '\0'
};
```

Note the closing null character. Without it, we have a character array, but not a string. For either form—and we do recommend that you use the first—the compiler counts the characters and sizes the array accordingly. Initializing character arrays is one case when it really makes sense to let the compiler determine the array size.

Just as for other arrays, the array name **m1** is a pointer to the first element of the array:

```
m1 == &m1[0] , *m1 == 'J', and *(m1+1) == m1[1] == 'u'
```

Indeed, we can use pointer notation to set up a string, for example:

```
char *m3 = "\nEnough about me--what's your name?";
```

This program line is very nearly the same as saying the following:

```
static char m3[] = "\nEnough about me--what's your name?"
```

These two declarations amount to saying that **m3** is a pointer to the indicated string. In both cases the string itself determines the amount of storage space set aside for the string. Nonetheless, the forms are not identical.

Array Versus Pointer

What is the difference, then, between an array and a pointer form? The array form (**m3[]**) causes an array of 38 elements (one for each character plus one for the terminating **'\0'**) to be created in static storage. Each element is initialized to the corresponding character. Hereafter, the compiler will recognize the name **m3** as a synonym for the address of the first array element, **&m3[0]**. One important point here is that in the array form, **m3** is a pointer constant. You can't change **m3**, because that would mean changing the location (address) where the array is stored. You can use operations like **m3+1** to identify the next element in an array, but **++m3** is not allowed. The increment operator can be used only with the names of variables, not with constants.

The pointer form (***m3**) also causes 38 elements in static storage to be set aside for the string. In addition, it sets aside an additional storage location for the pointer variable

m3. This variable initially points to the first character of the string, but the value can be changed. Thus we can use the increment operator; in this case, **++m3** points to the second character (**E**). Note that we do not have to declare ***m3** as static, because we are not initializing an array of 38 elements. We are initializing a single pointer variable. There are no storage class restrictions for initializing ordinary, nonarray variables, either in K & R C or in ANSI C.

Such differences in form are often unimportant, although it depends on specific instances. See the box entitled "Array and Pointer Differences" for some examples. Meanwhile, we return to the problem of creating storage space for strings.

▶ **Array and Pointer Differences**

Let's examine the differences between initializing a character array to hold a string and initializing a pointer to point to a string. (By pointing to a string, we really mean pointing to the first character of a string.) For example, consider these two declarations:

```
static char heart[] = "I love Tillie!";
char *head = "I love Millie!";
```

The chief difference is that the pointer **heart** is a constant, whereas the pointer **head** is a variable. Let's see what practical difference this makes.

First, both can use pointer addition:

```
for (i = 0; i < 6; i++)
    putchar( *(heart + i) );
putchar('\n');
for (i = 0; i < 6; i++)
    putchar( *(head + i) );
putchar('\n');
```

Here is the output:

```
I love
I love
```

Only the pointer version can use the increment operator:

```
while ( *(head) != '\0' ) /* stop at end of string */
    putchar( *(head++) );
                    /* print character, advance pointer */
```

The output follows:

```
I love Millie!
```

Suppose we want **head** to agree with **heart**. We can say

```
head = heart; /* head now points to the array heart */
```

but we cannot say

```
heart = head;   /* illegal construction */
```

The situation is analogous to **x = 3;** versus **3 = x;**. The lefthand side of the assignment statement must be a variable name. Incidentally, **head = heart;** does not make the **Millie** string vanish; it simply changes the address stored in **head**. But unless you've saved the address of **"I love Millie!"** elsewhere, you won't be able to access the string once **head** points to another location.

You can alter the **heart** message by going into the array itself:

```
heart[7]= 'M';
```

or

```
*(heart + 7) = 'M';
```

The elements of an array are variables, but the name is not a variable.

Specifying Storage Explicitly

Another way to set up storage is to be explicit. In the external declaration of Listing 11.1, we can say

```
char m1[44] = "Just limit yourself to one line's worth.";
```

instead of

```
char m1[] = "Just limit yourself to one line's worth.";
```

Just be sure that the number of elements is at least one more than the length of the string to accommodate the null character. As with other static or external arrays, any unused elements are automatically initialized to 0, which in **char** form is the null character, not the zero digit character. See Figure 11.1.

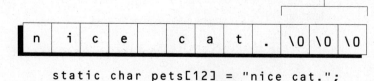

Figure 11.1

Initializing an array

extra elements initialized to \0

```
static char pets[12] = "nice cat.";
```

Note that in our program, we assign a size for the array **name**:

```
char name[81];
```

Since **name** is to be read in when the program runs, the compiler has no way of knowing in advance how much space to set aside unless we tell it. There is no string constant present whose characters the compiler can count. We therefore take a gamble that 80 characters is enough to hold the user's name. Incidentally, the array size must evaluate to an integer constant. You can't use, say, a variable that is set at run time. The array size is locked into the program.

Arrays of Character Strings

Often it is convenient to have an array of character strings. Then you can use a subscript to access several different strings:

```
static char *mytal[LIM] = { "Adding numbers swiftly",
   "Multiplying accurately", "Stashing data",
   "Following instructions to the letter",
   "Understanding the C language"};
```

Let's study this declaration. Recalling that **LIM** is **5**, we can say that **mytal** is an array of five pointers-to-**char**. The first pointer is **mytal[0]**, and it points to the first character of the first string. The second pointer is **mytal[1]**, and it points to the beginning of the second string. In general, each pointer points to the first character of the corresponding string:

```
*mytal[0] == 'A', *mytal[1] == 'M', *mytal[2] == 'S'
```

and so on.

The initialization follows the rules for arrays. The braced portion is equivalent to

```
{{...}, {...},...,{...} };
```

for which the first set of double quotation marks corresponds to a brace-pair and thus is used to initialize the first character string pointer. The next set of double quotation marks initializes the second pointer, and so on. A comma separates neighboring sets.

Again, we can also be explicit about the size of the character strings by using a declaration like:

```
static char mytal_2[LIM][LINLIM];
```

although one difference is that this second choice sets up a "rectangular" array with all the rows the same length. The first declaration,

```
static char *mytal[LIM];
```

however, sets up a "ragged" array, with each row's length determined by the string it is initialized to. The ragged array doesn't waste any storage space.

Also, **mytal** and **mytal_2** are of different types: **mytal** is an array of pointers-to-**char**; **mytal_2** is an array of arrays of **char**. In short, **mytal** holds five addresses, and **mytal_2** holds five complete character arrays.

Pointers and Strings

Perhaps you've noticed an occasional reference to pointers in our discussion of strings. Most C operations for strings actually work with pointers. For example, consider the useless, yet instructive, program shown in Listing 11.3. (Note: Use **%p** instead of **&u** if your compiler supports that form.)

❖ *p_and_s.c*

Listing 11.3

```
/* p_and_s.c--pointers and strings */
#include <stdio.h>
main()
{
   static char *mesg = "Don't be a fool!";
   static char *copy;

   copy = mesg;
   printf("%s\n", copy);
   printf("mesg = %s; value = %u; &mesg = %u\n",
          mesg, mesg, &mesg);
   printf("copy = %s; value = %u; &copy = %u\n",
          copy, copy, &copy);
}
```

Looking at this program, you may think it makes a copy of the string **"Don't be a fool!"** Your first glance at the output may seem to confirm this guess:

```
Don't be a fool!
mesg = Don't be a fool!; value = 14; &mesg = 32
copy = Don't be a fool!; value = 14; &copy = 34
```

But study the **printf( )** output. First, **mesg** and **copy** are printed as strings (**%s**). No surprises here; all the strings are **"Don't be a fool!"** We discuss the second item on each line in a moment.

The third item on each line is the address of the specified pointer. The two pointers **mesg** and **copy** are stored in locations 32 and 34, respectively.

Now let's return to the second item, the one we call **value**. This item is the value of the specified pointer, which is the address it contains. Therefore, we see that **mesg** points to location 14, and so does **copy**. In other words, the string itself is never copied. All that **copy = mesg;** does is produce a second pointer that points to the same string.

Why not just copy the whole string? Well, which is more efficient: copying one address or copying, say, 50 separate elements? Often, the address is all that is needed to get the job done.

11.2 String Input

Now that we have discussed defining strings within a program, let's turn to strings that are read in. Reading a string into a program has two steps: setting aside space to store the string and using an input function to fetch the string.

Creating Space

We first must set up a location to place the string once it is read. As mentioned earlier, we therefore need to allot sufficient storage to hold whatever strings we expect to read. Don't expect the computer to count the string length as it is read and then allot space for it. It won't, unless you write a program to do so. For example, if you try something like

```
static char *name;

scanf("%s", name);
```

it probably will get by the compiler. But when the name is read in, it will be written over data or code in your program. Most programmers regard this as highly humorous, but only in other people's programs.

The simplest method to create storage space is to include an explicit array size in the declaration:

```
char name[81];
```

Another possibility is to use the C library functions that allot memory. We touch on this topic in Chapter 16. In Listing 11.1, we use an automatic array for **name**. We can do so even under K & R C, since we don't have to initialize the array.

Once you have set aside space for the string, you can read the string in. The ANSI C library, recognizing past practice, provides a trio of functions that can read strings: **scanf( )**, **gets( )**, and **fgets( )**. The last is file-oriented, and we defer discussion of it until Chapter 12. Both **gets( )** and **scanf( )** can read in strings, although **gets( )** is the most commonly used.

The gets( ) Function

The **gets( )** (for *get string*) function is handy for interactive programs. It accepts a string from your system's standard input device, which we assume is a keyboard. Since a string has no predetermined length, **gets( )** needs a way to know when to stop taking characters into the string. Its method is to read characters until it reaches a newline (' \n ') character, which you generate by pressing the Enter key. This function accepts the characters before (but not including) the newline, tacks on a null character (' \0 '), and gives the string to the calling program. The newline character itself is read and discarded, so that the next read can begin at the start of the next line. Listing 11.4 shows a simple means of using **gets( )**.

Listing 11.4

```
/* name1.c--read a name */
#include <stdio.h>
#define MAX 81
main()
{
   char name[MAX];  /* allot space */
   printf("Hi, what's your name?\n");
   gets(name);        /* place input in string "name" */
   printf("Nice name, %s.\n", name);
}
```

This program accepts any name (including spaces) up to 80 characters long. (Remember to save one space for **'\0'**.) Note that we want **gets( )** to affect something (**name**) in the calling program. Thus, we should use a pointer as an argument; and of course the name of an array is a pointer.

The **gets( )** function is more sophisticated than this last example suggests. See Listing 11.5.

Listing 11.5

```
/* name2.c--read a name */
#include <stdio.h>
#define MAX 81
main()
{
   char name[MAX];
   char *ptr, *gets();

   printf("Hi, what's your name?\n");
   ptr = gets(name);
   printf("%s? Ah! %s!\n", name, ptr);
}
```

Here is a sample interchange:

```
Hi, what's your name?
Tony de Tuna
Tony de Tuna? Ah! Tony de Tuna!
```

Gets( ) provides two methods for transmitting input to a program:

1. The pointer method, which feeds the string to **name**.

2. The **return** keyword, which returns the address of the string to **ptr**. Notice that **ptr** is a pointer to **char**, which means that **gets( )** must return a value that is a pointer to **char**. In the declaration section of Listing 11.5 you can see that **gets( )** is properly declared.

The declaration form

```
char *gets();
```

says that **gets( )** is a function (hence the parentheses) of type pointer-to-**char** (hence the * and **char**). Note: No such declaration is necessary in Listing 11.4 because we never use the return value of **gets( )**.

ANSI C mandates that the **stdio.h** header file include a declaration for **gets( )**. Thus with newer implementations, you need not declare the function yourself as long as you remember to include the header file.

Incidentally, you can also declare something to be a pointer to a function, such as

```
char (*foop)( );
```

in which **foop** is a pointer to a function of type **char**. We talk a bit more about such declarations in Chapter 14.

The design of the **gets( )** function is something like the following:

```
char *gets(s)
char *s;
{
   ...
   return(s);
}
```

Note that **gets( )** returns the same pointer that is passed to it. Thus there is only one copy of the input string, the one placed at the address passed as a function argument.

The actual design is slightly more complicated, for **gets( )** has two possible returns. If everything works properly, **gets( )** returns the address of the read-in string, as we have said. If something goes wrong or if **gets( )** encounters **EOF**, it returns a null, or zero, address. This null address is called the *null pointer* and is represented in **stdio.h** by the defined constant **NULL**. Thus **gets( )** incorporates a bit of error-checking, which makes it convenient to use constructions like this one:

```
while ( gets(name) != NULL)
```

The pointer aspect provides a value for **name**. The **return** aspect provides a value for **gets(name)** as a whole and allows us to check for **EOF**. If **EOF** is encountered, nothing is read into **name**. This two-pronged approach is more compact than that allowed by **getchar( )**, which has a **return** but no argument:

```
while ( (ch = getchar()) != EOF)
```

Note: Don't confuse the null pointer with the null character. The null pointer is an address; the null character is a type **char** data object with the value zero.

One weakness of **gets( )** is that it doesn't check to see if the input actually fits into the assigned storage area. Extra characters simply overflow into the adjoining memory cells. The **fgets( )** function described in Chapter 12 improves on this behavior by letting you specify an upper limit to the number of characters to be read.

The scanf( ) Function

We've used **scanf( )** with the **%s** format before to read a string. The chief difference between **scanf( )** and **gets( )** lies in how these functions decide they have reached the end of the string. **Scanf( )** is more a "get word" than a "get string" function. The **gets( )** function takes in all the characters up to the first newline. The **scanf( )** function has two choices. For either choice, the string starts at the first nonwhitespace character encountered. If you use the **%s** format, the string runs up to (but not including) the next whitespace character (blank, tab, or newline). If you specify a field width, as in **%10s**, **scanf( )** collects up to 10 characters or to the first whitespace character, whichever comes first. See Figure 11.2.

Recall that the **scanf( )** function returns an integer value that equals the number of items successfully read in or **EOF** if it encounters the end of the file. Listing 11.6 illustrates how **scanf( )** works when you specify a field width.

❖ *scan_str.c*

Listing 11.6

```
/* scan_str.c--using scanf() */
#include <stdio.h>
main()
{
   static char name1[11], name2[11];
   int count;

   printf("Please enter 2 names.\n");
   count = scanf("%5s %10s",name1, name2);
   printf("I read in the %d names %s and %s.\n",
          count, name1, name2);
}
```

Here are three runs:

```
Please enter 2 names.
   Jesse       Jukes
I read in the 2 names Jesse and Jukes.
```

Figure 11.2

Field widths and
scanf( )

Input Statement	Original Input Queue*	Name Contents	Remaining Queue
scanf("%s", name);	Fleebert	Fleebert Hup	□Hup
scanf("%5s", name);	Fleebert□Hup	Fleeb	ert□Hup
scanf("%5s", name);	Ann□Ular	Ann	□Ular

* the □ represents the space character

```
Please enter 2 names.
  Liza Applebottham
I read in the 2 names Liza and Applebotth.

Please enter 2 names.
  Jessica Fitzwillow
I read in the 2 names Jessi and ca.
```

In the first run, both names fall within the allowed size limits. In the second run, only the first 10 characters of **Applebottham** are read because of our **%10s** format. In the third run, the last two letters of **Jessica** are moved into **name2** because the second call to **scanf( )** resumes reading input where the first ended, in this case still inside the word **Jessica**.

If you are obtaining only text from the keyboard, you are best off using **gets( )**, which is easier to use and is a faster, more compact function. The main use for **scanf( )** is for inputting a mixture of data types in some standard form. For example, if each input line contains the name of a tool, the number in stock, and the cost of the item, you may want to use **scanf( )**. Or you may want to create your own, one that does some entry error-checking.

11.3 String Output

Let's now discuss the output process for strings. Again, we use library functions. ANSI recognizes three standard functions for printing strings: **puts( )**, **printf( )**, and **fputs( )**. As already noted, **fputs( )** is file-oriented and is described in Chapter 12.

❖ *put_out.c*

Listing 11.7

```
/* put_out.c--using puts() */
#include <stdio.h>
#define DEF "I am a #defined string."
main()
{
```

Listing 11.7
(cont'd.)

```
      static char str1[] = "An array was initialized to me.";
      char *str2 = "A pointer was initialized to me.";

      puts("I'm an argument to puts().");
      puts(DEF);
      puts(str1);
      puts(str2);
      puts(&str1[4]);
      puts(str2+4);
}
```

The puts( ) Function

The **puts( )** function is quite easy to use; just give it an argument that is a pointer to a string. Listing 11.7 illustrates some of the many ways to accomplish this task.

The output follows:

```
I'm an argument to puts().
I am a #defined string.
An array was initialized to me.
A pointer was initialized to me.
rray was initialized to me.
inter was initialized to me.
```

This example reminds us that phrases in quotation marks are pointers and that the names of character array strings are pointers. Note, too, the final two output phrases. The pointer **&str1[4]** points to the fifth element of the array **str1**. That element contains the character **'r'**, which is what **puts( )** uses for its starting character. Similarly, **str2+4** points to the memory cell containing the **'i'** of **pointer**, and output therefore begins at that location.

The **puts( )** function stops accepting characters for output when it encounters the null character. When **puts( )** finally finds the closing null character, it replaces it with a newline character and then sends the string on. Thus each string displayed by **puts( )** is placed on a new line.

Don't try the program in Listing 11.8! Because **dont** lacks a closing null character, it is not a string. Therefore, **puts( )** doesn't know at what point to stop printing when instructed to output characters. In this case, it simply keeps on going into the memory cells following **dont** until it finds a null character. Usually, there are lots of nulls in memory, and if you're lucky, one may be the very next cell, but luck may fail you.

The printf( ) Function

We've already discussed **printf( )** fairly thoroughly elsewhere in this text. Like **puts( )**, it takes a pointer to a string as an argument. The **printf( )** function is slightly less convenient to use than **puts( )**, but it is more versatile.

Listing 11.8

```
/* nono.c--no! */
#include <stdio.h>
main()
{
   static c1 = 'A';
   static char dont[] = {'H', 'I', '!', '!' };
   static c2 = 'B';

   puts(dont);  /* dont not a string */
}
```

One difference is that **printf( )** does not automatically place each string on a new line. You have to indicate where you want new lines, thus

```
printf("%s\n", string);
```

has the same effect as the following:

```
puts(string);
```

As you can see, the first form takes more typing. It also takes longer for the computer to execute. On the other hand, **printf( )** makes it simple to combine strings for one line of printing. For example:

```
printf("Well, %s, %s\n", name, MSG);
```

combines **Well** with the user's name and a symbolic character string, all on one line.

11.4 The Do-It-Yourself Option

You aren't limited to the standard C library options for input and output. You can prepare your own versions, building on **getchar( )** and **putchar( )**.

Suppose you lack a **puts( )** or want to try writing your own version. Here is one way to do it:

```
/* put1.c--prints a string */
#include <stdio.h>
void put1(string)
char *string;
{
   while(*string != '\0')
     putchar(*string++);
   putchar('\n');
}
```

The **char** pointer **string** initially points to the first element of the called argument. After the contents of that element are printed, the pointer increments and points to the next element. This process continues until the pointer points to an element that contains the null character, at which time a newline is tagged on at the end of the string. Remember, the higher precedence of ++ compared to * means that **putchar(*string++)** prints the value pointed to by **string** but increments **string** itself, not the character it points to.

Many C programmers would use the following test for the **while** loop:

```
while ( *string )
```

When **string** points to the null character, ***string** has the value **0**, which terminates the loop. This approach certainly takes less typing than the previous version, and it may result in more efficient code, depending on the compiler. If you are not familiar with C practice, the merits of this version are less obvious. Nevertheless, this use of idiom is widespread.

Suppose you have a **puts( )**, but you want a function that also tells you how many characters are printed. It's easy to add this feature:

```
/* put2.c--prints a string and counts characters */
#include <stdio.h>
int put2(string)
char *string;
{
   int count = 0;
   while(*string != '\0')
     {
     putchar(*string++);
     count++;
     }
   putchar('\n');
   return(count);
}
```

The following call

```
put2("pizza");
```

prints the string **pizza**. The call

```
num = put2("pizza");
```

also delivers a character count to **num**, in this case, the value **5**. Listing 11.9 presents a slightly more elaborate version that shows nested functions.

In this listing, we assume that you place the **put1( )** and **put2( )** functions in the same file. Note that we use **#include stdio.h** because on our system **putchar( )** is defined there, and our new functions use **putchar( )**.

Listing 11.9

```
/* put_put.c--nested functions */
#include <stdio.h>
void put1();
int put2();
main()
{
   put1("If I'd as much money as I could spend,");
   printf("I count %d characters.\n",
   put2("I never would cry old chairs to mend.") );
}
```

Notice that we are using **printf( )** to print the value of **put2( )**, and in the act of finding the **put2( )** value, the computer first must run the value, causing the string to be printed. Here's the output:

```
If I'd as much money as I could spend,
I never would cry old chairs to mend.
I count 37 characters.
```

You should be able to build on your own a working version of **gets( )** by using **getchar( )**.

11.5 String Functions

The ANSI C library supplies several string-handling functions, most of which have been part of the earlier defacto C standard. We look at five of the most useful and common ones: **strlen( )**, **strcat( )**, **strcmp( )**, **strcpy( )**, and **sprintf( )**.

The strlen( ) Function

We have already discussed **strlen( )**, which finds the length of a string. In this next example, we use it to shorten lengthy strings.

```
/* fit.c--procrustean function */
void fit(string,size)
char *string;
int size;
{
   if ( strlen(string) > size)
     *(string +size) = '\0';
}
```

Try it in the test program in Listing 11.10.

```
/* test.c--try the string-shrinking function */
#include <stdio.h>
#include <string.h>
        /* contains string function declarations */
main()
{
   static char mesg[] = "Hold onto your hats, hackers.";
   void fit();

   puts(mesg);
   fit(mesg,10);
   puts(mesg);
}
void fit(string,size)
char *string;
int size;
{
   if ( strlen(string) > size)
       *(string +size) = '\0';
}
```

Listing 11.10

The output follows:

```
Hold onto your hats, hackers.
Hold onto
```

The **fit()** function places a '**\0**' character in the 11th element of the array, replacing a blank. The rest of the array is still there, but **puts()** stops printing output at the first null character and ignores the rest of the array. Also, note that the **string.h** file contains function declarations for the C family of string functions, so we include it in our examples.

The strcat( ) Function

Listing 11.11 illustrates the abilities of the **strcat( )** function.

Listing 11.11

```
/* str_cat.c--join two strings */
#include <stdio.h>
#include <string.h>/* declares the strcat() function */
#define SIZE 80
main()
{
```

**Listing 11.11
(cont'd.)**

```
static char flower[SIZE];
static char addon[] = "s smell like old shoes.";

puts("What is your favorite flower?");
gets(flower);
strcat(flower, addon);
puts(flower);
puts(addon);
}
```

The output follows:

```
What is your favorite flower?
Rose
Roses smell like old shoes.
s smell like old shoes.
```

As you can see, **strcat( )** (for *string* conca*te*nation) takes two strings for arguments. A copy of the second string is tacked onto the end of the first, and this combined version becomes the new first string. The second string is not altered.

Caution: This function does not check to see if the second string will fit in the first array. If you fail to allot enough space for the first array, you will run into problems as excess characters overflow into adjacent memory locations. Of course, you can use **strlen( )** to alert you to any potential space dilemma. See Listing 11.12. Note that we also add **1** to the combined lengths to allow space for the null character.

❖ join_chk.c

Listing 11.12

```
/* join_chk.c--join two strings, check size first */
#include <stdio.h>
#include <string.h>
#define SIZE 80
main()
{
    static char flower[SIZE];
    static char addon[] = "s smell like old shoes.";

    puts("What is your favorite flower?");
    gets(flower);
    if ( (strlen(addon) + strlen(flower) + 1 ) < SIZE )
        strcat(flower, addon);
    puts(flower);
}
```

Strcat( ) is type **char ***, that is, pointer-to-**char**. It returns the value of its first argument, which is a pointer to the first character of the string to which the second string is appended.

The strcmp( ) *Function*

Suppose you wish to compare someone's response to a stored string:

```
/* nogo.c--will this work? */
#include <stdio.h>
#define ANSWER "Grant"
main()
{
   char try[40];

   puts("Who is buried in Grant's tomb?");
   gets(try);
   while ( try != ANSWER)
     {
     puts("No, that's wrong. Try again.");
     gets(try);
     }
   puts("That's right!");
}
```

As nice as this program may look, it will not work correctly. **ANSWER** and **try** are pointers, so what the comparison **try != ANSWER** really asks is not if two strings are the same but if the two addresses pointed to by **try** and **ANSWER** are the same. Since **ANSWER** and **try** are stored in different locations, the two pointers are never the same, and the user is forever told that he or she has given an incorrect answer.

To fix the example program we need a function that compares string contents, not string addresses. We can devise one of our own, but **strcmp( )** (for *str*ing *comp*arison) already

❖ *compare.c*

Listing 11.13

```
/* compare.c--this will work */
#include <stdio.h>
#include <string.h> /* declares strcmp() */
#define ANSWER "Grant"
#define MAX 40
main()
{
   char try[MAX];

   puts("Who is buried in Grant's tomb?");
   gets(try);
   while (( strcmp(try,ANSWER) != 0 ))
     {
     puts("No, that's wrong. Try again.");
     gets(try);
     }
   puts("That's right!");
}
```

accomplishes that task for us. See Listing 11.13. Note: Since nonzero values are interpreted as "true," we can abbreviate the **while** statement to

```
while (strcmp(try, ANSWER))
```

From this example you may deduce that **strcmp( )** takes two string pointers as arguments and returns a value of **0** if the two strings are the same. One of the nice features of **strcmp( )** is that it compares strings, not arrays. Thus although the array **try** occupies 40 memory cells and **"Grant"** only 6 (including one for the null character), the comparison looks only at the part of **try** up to its first null character. Thus, **strcmp( )** can be used to compare strings stored in arrays of different sizes.

But note: If the user answers **GRANT** or **grant** or **Ulysses S. Grant**, that user is told he or she is wrong. To create a more usable program, you have to anticipate other possible correct answers. For instance, you can **#define** the answer as **GRANT** and write a function that converts all input to uppercase characters only. This coding eliminates the problem of capitalization; we leave you the task of solving other potential problems.

What value does **strcmp( )** return if the strings are not the same? Listing 11.14 shows a sample.

❖ *compback.c*

Listing 11.14

```
/* compback.c--strcmp returns */
#include <stdio.h>
#include <string.h>
main()
{
   printf("%d\n", strcmp("A", "A") );
   printf("%d\n", strcmp("A", "B") );
   printf("%d\n", strcmp("B", "A") );
   printf("%d\n", strcmp("C", "A") );
   printf("%d\n", strcmp("apples", "apple") );
}
```

The output on one system follows:

```
0
-1
1
1
1
```

As expected, comparing **"A"** to itself returns a **0**. Comparing **"A"** to **"B"** returns a **−1**, and reversing the comparison returns a **1**. This outcome suggests that **strcmp( )** returns a negative number if the first string precedes the second alphabetically and that it returns a positive number if the order is reversed. Thus, comparing **"C"** to **"A"** gives a **1**. Other systems may return **2**, which is the difference in ASCII code values. The ANSI standard says that **strcmp( )** returns a negative number if the first string precedes the second alphabetically, 0 if the strings are the same, and a positive number if the first string follows the second alphabetically. The exact numerical values, however, are left open to the implementation.

If the first characters are identical, **strcmp( )** generally continued on until it finds the first pair of disagreeing characters. It then returns the corresponding code. For instance, in Listing 11.14 **"apples"** and **"apple"** agree until the final **s** of the first string. This character matches up with the sixth character in **"apple"**, which is the null character, ASCII 0. Since the null character is the first character, **s** follows it, and the function returns a positive value.

The last comparison points out that **strcmp( )** compares all characters, not just letters. So instead of saying the comparison is alphabetic, we should say that **strcmp( )** follows the machine *collating sequence,* which means characters are compared according to their numeric representation, typically the ASCII code. In ASCII, the codes for uppercase letters precede those for lowercase letters, so **strcmp("A", "a")** is negative.

Usually you don't care about the exact value returned. Typically, you just want to know if it is zero or nonzero, that is, whether or not there is a match. Or you may be trying to sort the strings alphabetically, in which case you want to know if the comparison is positive, negative, or zero. We discuss the sorting of strings alphabetically in a later section of this chapter.

We can also use **strcmp( )** to check to see if a program should stop reading input:

```
/* beginning of some program */
#include <stdio.h>
#include <string.h>
#define SIZE 81
#define LIM 100
#define STOP ""   /* a null string */
main()
{
   static char input[LIM][SIZE];
   int ct = 0;

   while( ct < LIM && gets(input[ct]) != NULL &&
     strcmp(input[ct],STOP) != 0)
   {
      ...
      ct++;
   }
}
```

This program quits reading input when it encounters an **EOF** character (**gets( )** returns **NULL** in that case), when you press the Enter key at the beginning of a line (you feed in an empty string), or when you reach the limit **LIM**. Entering the empty line gives the user an easy way to terminate the entry phase. As well, **STOP** can be redefined to be some other string, such as **stop** or **quit**.

We've already said that if **pts1** and **pts2** are both pointers to strings, then the expression

```
pts2 = pts1;
```

copies only the address of the string, not the string itself. If you want to copy the string, you can use the **strcpy( )** function. See Listing 11.15.

❖ *copy1.c*

Listing 11.15

```
/* copy1.c--strcpy() demo */
#include <stdio.h>
#include <string.h>/* declares strcpy() */
#define WORDS "Please reconsider your last entry."
#define SIZE 40
main()
{
    static char *orig = WORDS;
    static char copy[SIZE] = "reserved space";

    puts(orig);
    puts(copy);
    strcpy(copy, orig);
    puts(orig);
    puts(copy);
}
```

Here is the output:

```
Please reconsider your last entry.
reserved space
Please reconsider your last entry.
Please reconsider your last entry.
```

You can see that the string pointed to by the second argument (**orig**) is copied into the array pointed to by the first argument (**copy**). You can remember the order of the arguments by noting that it is the same as the order in the assignment statement: The string receiving a value is on the left. Often the first string is called the *target,* and the second string is called the *source.* Note that **strcpy( )** writes over any existing contents of the target string.

It is the programmer's responsibility to ensure that the destination array has enough storage space for the incoming string. Therefore, we use the declaration

```
static char copy[SIZE];
```

and not

```
static char *copy; /* allots no space for string */
```

In short, **strcpy( )** takes two string pointers as arguments. The second pointer, which points to the original string, can be a declared pointer, an array name, or a string constant. But the first pointer, which points to the copy, should point to a data object, such as an array, of sufficient size to hold the string.

The **strcpy( )** function is type **char** *; it returns the value of its first argument, which is a pointer to a character. The first argument need not point to the beginning of an array. Listing 11.16 illustrates both these points.

❖ *copy2.c*

Listing 11.16

```
/* copy2.c--strcpy() demo */
#include <stdio.h>
#include <string.h>      /* declares strcpy() */
#define WORDS "beast"
#define SIZE 40
main()
{
   static char *orig = WORDS;
   static char copy[SIZE] = "Be the best that you can be.";
   char *ps;

   puts(orig);
   puts(copy);
   ps = strcpy(copy + 7, orig);
   puts(copy);
   puts(ps);
}
```

The output follows:

```
beast
Be the best that you can be.
Be the beast
beast
```

Note that **strcpy( )** includes the null character from the source string when it copies. In this example, the null character overwrites the **t** in **that** in **copy**, so that the new string ends with **beast**. See Figure 11.3. Also note that **ps** points to the eighth element (index of 7) of **copy** because the first argument is **copy + 7**. Therefore, **puts(ps)** starts printing the string at that point.

The sprintf( ) Function

The **sprintf( )** function is declared in **stdio.h** instead of **string.h**. It works like **printf( )**, but instead of writing to a display, it writes to a string. Thus **sprintf( )** provides a method

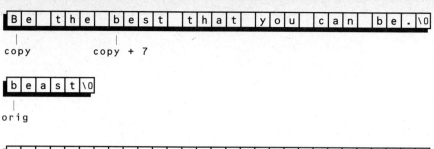

Figure 11.3

The **strcpy( )**
function uses
pointers

the command
strcpy (copy + 7, orig);
means copy string from orig to here

to combine several elements into a single string. The first argument to **sprintf( )** is the address of the destination string. The remaining arguments are the same as for **printf( )**: a conversion specification string followed by a list of items to be written.

One use of **sprintf( )** is to generate a system command. The C library contains a **system( )** function that allows a program to execute operating system commands. For example, you can have a program solicit information from the user about copying a file, then use the **system( )** command to have the operating system do the copying. This command takes a string argument that indicates what command to execute. Listing 11.17 is a simple example using the MS-DOS COPY command; changing **"copy"** to **"cp"** converts the program to the UNIX equivalent.

❖ command.c

```
/* command.c--generate a command string */
#include <stdio.h>
#include <stdlib.h>
                 /* ANSI C: declares the system() function */
#define MAX 20
main()
{
   char source[MAX];
   char target[MAX];
   char command[2*MAX + 5];

   puts("Enter the name of the file you wish to copy:");
   gets(source);
   puts("Enter the desired name for the copy:");
   gets(target);
   sprintf(command, "copy %s %s", source, target);
   printf("Executing the following command: %s\n", command);
   system(command);
}
```

Listing 11.17

A sample run follows:

```
Enter the name of the file you wish to copy:
taxing.c
Enter the desired name for the copy:
taxing1.c
Executing the following command: copy taxing.c taxing1.c
1 File(s) copied
```

The **sprintf( )** command copies the string **"copy taxing.c taxing1.c"** into the **command** array. The **printf( )** command displays the contents of the string. Then the **system( )** call executes the command specified by the string. The final line of output is produced by the operating system after it runs the copy command.

Other String Functions

The ANSI C library includes 16 string-handling functions, including **strchr( )**, which finds the first occurrence of a character in a string, and **strrchr( )**, which finds the last occurrence of a character in a string. Many implementations provide additional functions beyond those required by the ANSI standard. You should check the documentation for your implementation to see what is available.

11.6 A String Example: Sorting Strings

Now that we have outlined some string functions, let's look at a full program that handles strings. We take on the practical problem of sorting strings alphabetically. This task arises in preparing name lists, in making up an index, and in many other situations. One of the main tools in such a program is **strcmp( )**, since it can be used to determine the order of two strings. Our general plan is to read in an array of strings, sort them, and print them out. Earlier in this chapter we presented a scheme for reading in strings, and we start the program using that method. Printing out the strings is no problem, as we use a standard sorting algorithm that we'll explain later. We will do one slightly tricky thing; see if you can spot it. Listing 11.18 presents the program.

❖ *sort_str.c*

Listing 11.18

```
/* sort_str.c--reads in strings and sorts them */
#include <stdio.h>
#include <string.h>
#define SIZE 81  /* size limit for string length with \0 */

#define LIM 20   /* maximum number of lines to be read */
#define HALT ""  /* null string to stop input */
main()
{
   void stsrt();  /* string-sorting function */
   static char input[LIM][SIZE]; /* array to store input */
```

```
    char *ptstr[LIM];          /* array of pointer variables */
    int ct = 0;                     /* input count */
    int k;                          /* output count */

    printf("Input up to %d lines, and I will sort them.\n",
           LIM);

    printf("To stop, press Enter key at a line's start.\n");
    while( ct < LIM && gets(input[ct]) != NULL &&
           strcmp(input[ct],HALT) != 0)
    {
      ptstr[ct] = input[ct];       /* set ptrs to strings */
      ct++;
    }
    stsrt(ptstr, ct);              /* string sorter */
    puts("\nHere's the sorted list:\n");
    for ( k = 0; k < ct; k++)
      puts(ptstr[k]);              /* sorted pointers */
}
/* string-pointer-sorting function */
void stsrt(strings, num)
char *strings[];
int num;
{
  char *temp;
  int top, seek;

  for ( top = 0; top < num-1; top++)
    for( seek = top + 1; seek < num; seek++)
      if ( strcmp(strings[top],strings[seek]) > 0)
      {
          temp = strings[top];
        strings[top] = strings[seek];
        strings[seek] = temp;
      }
}
```

Listing 11.18 (cont'd.)

In this instance, we feed the program an obscure nursery rhyme to test it:

```
Input up to 20 lines, and I will sort them.
To stop, press Enter key at a line's start.
O that I was where I would be,
Then would I be where I am not;
But where I am I must be,
And where I would be I can not.

Here's the sorted list:
And where I would be I can not.
But where I am I must be,
O that I was where I would be,
Then would I be where I am not;
```

The tricky feature we mentioned is that instead of rearranging the strings themselves, we simply rearrange pointers to the strings. Let us explain. Originally, **ptrst[0]** is set to **input[0]**, and so on. Therefore the pointer **ptrst[i]** points to the first character in the array **input[i]**. Each **input[i]** is an array of 81 elements, and each **ptrst[]** is a single variable. The sorting procedure rearranges **ptrst**, leaving **input** untouched. If, for example, **input[1]** precedes **input[0]** alphabetically, the program switches **ptrst**s, causing **ptrst[0]** to point to the beginning of **input[1]** and **ptrst[1]** to point to the beginning of **input[0]**. This method is much easier than using, say, **strcpy( )** to interchange the contents of the two **input** strings. See Figure 11.4 for another view of this process.

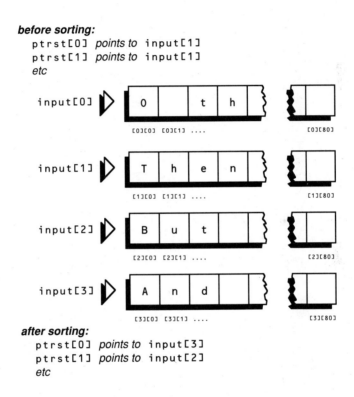

before sorting:
```
ptrst[0] points to input[1]
ptrst[1] points to input[1]
etc
```

Figure 11.4

Sorting string pointers

after sorting:
```
ptrst[0] points to input[3]
ptrst[1] points to input[2]
etc
```

Sorting

To sort the pointers, we use the *selection sort* algorithm. The idea is to use a **for** loop to compare each element in turn with the first element. If the compared element precedes the current first element, the program swaps the two. Thus by the time the program reaches the end of the loop, the first element contains a pointer to whichever string is first in the machine collating sequence. Then the outer **for** loop repeats the process, this time starting with the second element of **input**; when the inner loop completes, the pointer to the second-ranking string is placed as the second element of **ptrst**. The process continues until all the elements have been sorted. We take a more detailed look at this algorithm in Chapter 13.

11.7 The ctype.h Character Functions

ANSI C and many pre-ANSI implementations provide a family of character-related functions that are declared in the **ctype.h** header file. Several of these functions analyze the nature of a character, returning a true (nonzero) value if the character belongs to a particular class and false (zero) otherwise. Table 11.1 lists these functions.

Table 11.1 Character-Testing Functions

Name	True if argument is
isalnum( )	Alphanumeric (alphabetic or numeric)
isalpha( )	Alphabetic
iscntrl( )	A control character, e.g., Control-B
isdigit( )	A digit
isgraph( )	Any printing character other than a space
islower( )	A lowercase character
isprint( )	A printing character
ispunct( )	A punctuation character (any printing character other than a space or an alphanumeric character)
isspace( )	A whitespace character (space, newline, form feed, carriage return, vertical tab, horizontal tab, and possibly other implementation-defined characters)
isupper( )	An uppercase character
isxdigit( )	A hexadecimal-digit character

There also are two character-mapping functions: **toupper( )** maps lowercase characters to uppercase ones, and **tolower( )** maps uppercase characters to lowercase ones. Listing 11.19 presents an program that transforms an input line by reversing the case for letters.

❖ invert.c

Listing 11.19

```
/* invert.c--modify a string */
#include <stdio.h>
#include <string.h>
#include <ctype.h>
#define LIMIT 80
char line[LIMIT];
void modify();
main()
{
   puts("Please enter a line:");
   gets(line);
   modify ( line);
   puts(line);
}
```

Listing 11.19 (cont'd.)

```
void modify(str)
char *str;
{

    while ( *str != '\0')
    {
      if ( isupper(*str) )
        *str = tolower(*str);
      else if ( islower(*str) )
        *str = toupper(*str);
      str++;
    }
}
```

In this program, the **while (*str != '\0')** loop processes each character in the string pointed to by **str** until the null character is reached. Here is a sample run:

```
Please enter a line:
Hello, Mr. Potato Head!
hELLO, mR. pOTATO hEAD!
```

Note: In **modify( )** we use **isupper( )** to check to see if a character is uppercase before trying to convert it to lowercase. Under ANSI C, this function is unnecessary, for **tolower( )** returns the original character if it is not uppercase to begin with. However, not all older implementations offer that protection, so in the interests of maximum portability, we use **isupper( )** as a check.

Incidently, the **ctype.h** functions typically are incremented as macros. These C preprocessor constructions act much like functions but have some important differences. We cover macros in Chapter 16.

11.8 Command-Line Arguments

The *command line* is the line you type in to run your program. Suppose we have a program in a file named **fuss**. The command line may look like

```
% fuss
```

or perhaps

```
A> fuss
```

using two common system prompts.

Command-line arguments are additional items on the same line:

```
% fuss -r Ginger
```

C programs can read in these arguments for their own uses. See Figure 11.5 The mechanism is to use arguments for **main( )**. Listing 11.20 presents a typical example.

Listing 11.20

```
/* echo.c--main() with arguments */
main(argc,argv)
int argc;
char *argv[];
{
  int count;

  for( count = 1; count < argc; count++)
    printf("%s ", argv[count]);  /* process each argument */
  printf("\n");
}
```

If we place this program in an executable file called **echo** and run it, the program can output the following:

```
A> echo I could use a little help.
I could use a little help.
```

You can see why the file is called **echo**, but you may wonder how it works. We explain. C compilers provide for **main( )** having two arguments. The first argument represents the number of strings found on the command line. By tradition (but not necessity), this **int** argument is called **argc**, for *arg*ument *c*ount. The system uses spaces to tell when one string ends and the next begins. Thus our **echo** example has seven strings, and our **fuss** example has three. The second argument is an array of string pointers. Each string on the command line is stored in memory and has a pointer assigned to point to it. By convention, this array of pointers is called **argv**, for *arg*ument *v*alues. When possible, **argv[0]** is assigned the name of the program itself. Note: Some operating systems don't

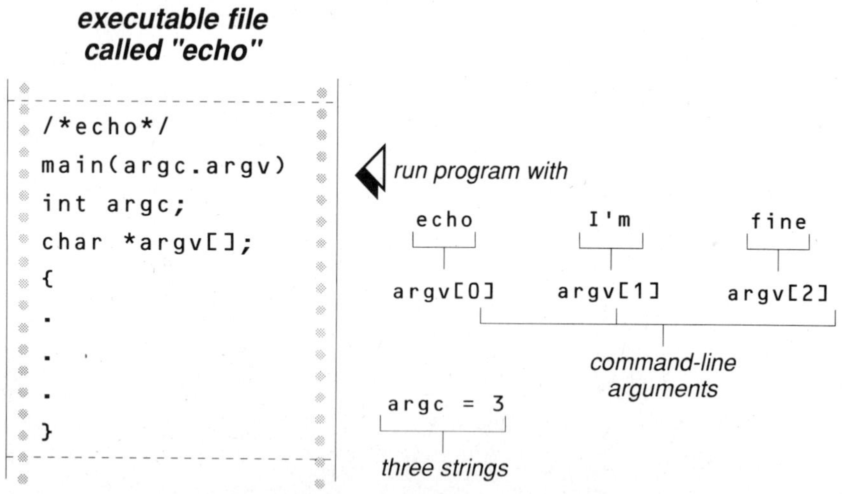

Figure 11.5

Command-line arguments

executable file called "echo"

```
/*echo*/
main(argc.argv)
int argc;
char *argv[];
{
.
.
.
}
```

run program with

echo   I'm   fine
argv[0]   argv[1]   argv[2]

command-line arguments

argc = 3

three strings

allow the **argv[0]** assignment. Then **argv[1]** is assigned the first following string, and so forth. In Listing 11.20, we have the following relationships:

argv[0]	Points to	**echo** (for most systems)
argv[1]	Points to	**I**
argv[2]	Points to	**could**
argv[6]	Points to	**help**

The program uses a **for** loop to print each string in turn. Recall that the **%s** specifier expects the address of a string to be provided as an argument. Each element (**argv[0]**, **argv[1]**, and so on) is just such an address.

Many programmers use a different declaration for **argv**:

```
main(argc, argv)
int argc;
char **argv;
```

This declaration is really equivalent to **char *argv[];**. You read it as saying that **argv** is a pointer to a pointer-to-**char**. Our example program does in essence the same thing. We have an array with seven elements. The name of the array is a pointer to the first element. Thus **argv** points to **argv[0]**, and **argv[0]** is a pointer-to-**char**. Hence even with the original definition, **argv** is a pointer to a pointer-to-**char**. You can use either declaration form, although we feel the one we use in Listing 11.20 more clearly suggests that **argv** represents a set of strings.

Note: Many environments including UNIX let you use quotation marks to lump several words into a single argument. For example, the command

```
echo "I am hungry" now
```

assigns the string **"I am hungry"** to **argv[1]** and the string **"now"** to **argv[2]**.

Command-Line Arguments in Integrated Environments

Integrated environments like QuickC and Turbo C don't use command lines to run programs. However, both have menu selections that let you specify a command-line argument. In QuickC 1.0, open the Run menu, select Set Runtime Options, and enter the argument(s) into the Command Line box. With QuickC 2.0, select Run/Debug from the Options menu. In Turbo C, open the Options menu, select Args, and enter the argument(s).

Command-Line Options

One common use for command-line arguments is to indicate options for a program. For example, you may use the combination **–r** to tell a sorting program to work in reverse order. Traditionally, UNIX options are indicated using a hyphen and a letter, as in **–r**, and MS-DOS options use a slash and a letter, as in **/r**. Such "flags" mean nothing to C; you have to include your own programming to recognize them.

Listing 11.21 presents a modest example showing how a program can check for a flag and make use of it.

❖ flags.c

```
/* flags.c--a modest beginning */
#include <stdio.h>
#define YES 1
#define NO 0
main(argc, argv)
int argc;
char *argv[];
{
    int n;
    int flag = NO;

    if ( argv[1][0] == '-' && argv[1][1] == 'r' )
        flag = YES;
    if (flag == NO)
        puts("Regular sorting was selected.");
    else
        puts("Reverse sorting was selected.");
}
```

Listing 11.21

The program checks the first string after the command file name to see if it begins with a hyphen. Then it checks to see if the next character is the code character **r**. If so, it sets a flag to cause a different sorting routine to be used and ignores any strings thereafter. To handle more than one possible flag, you should use a **while** loop or **for** loop instead of the **if** statement.

If you have used the UNIX system, you probably have noticed the variety of command-line options and arguments that the UNIX commands offer. These are examples of C command-line arguments, for most of UNIX is written in C.

Command-line arguments also can be filenames, and you can use them instead of redirection to tell a program what files to work on. We describe this capability in Chapter 12.

11.9 String-to-Number Conversions

Numbers can be stored either as strings or in numeric form. Storing a number as a string means storing the digit characters. For instance, the number 213 can be stored in a character array as the digits **'2'**, **'1'**, **'3'**, **'\0'**. Storing in numeric form means storing it as, say, an **int**.

C requires numeric forms for numeric operations such as addition and comparison. But displaying numbers on, say, a screen, requires a string form, for there we want the digits printed. The **printf( )** and **sprintf( )** functions, through **%d** specifiers and the like, convert numeric forms to string forms. C also has functions to convert string forms to numeric forms.

Suppose, for example, we have a program read a command-line argument representing a number. Command-line arguments, however, are read as strings, so to use the numeric value, we first must convert the string to a number. If the number is an integer, we can use the **atoi( )** function (for **a**lphanumeric **to** **i**nteger). This function takes a string as an argument and returns the corresponding integer value. Listing 11.22 shows a sample use.

❖ hello.c

Listing 11.22

```
/* hello.c--convert command-line argument to number */
#include <stdio.h>
#include <stdlib.h>
main(argc, argv)
int argc;
char *argv[];
{
   int i, times;

   if ( argc < 2 || (times = atoi(argv[1])) < 1)
      printf("Usage: %s positive-number\n", argv[0]);
   else
      for (i = 0; i < times; i++)
         puts("Hello, good looking!");
}
```

Here's a sample run:

```
% hello 3
Hello, good looking!
Hello, good looking!
Hello, good looking!
```

The **%** is a UNIX prompt. The command-line argument of **3** is stored as the string **'3'** **'\0'**. The **atoi( )** function converts this string to the integer value **3**, which is assigned to **times**. This process then determines the number of **for** loop cycles executed.

If you run the program without a command-line argument, the **argc < 2** test aborts the program and prints a usage instruction. The same occurs if **test** is 0 or negative. C's order-of-evaluation rule for logical operators guarantees that if **argc < 2**, then **atoi(argv[1])** is not evaluated.

What if the command line is something like **hello what?**. On the implementations we've used, the **atoi( )** function returns a value of **0** if its argument is not recognizable as a number. However, the ANSI standard does not require that behavior.

We include the **stdlib.h** header because, under ANSI C, it contains a function declaration for **atoi( )**. This file also includes declarations for **atof( )** and **atol( )**. The **atof( )** function converts a string to a type **double** value. The **atol( )** function converts a string to a type **long** value. Both functions work analogously to **atoi( )**, so they are type **double** and **long**, respectively.

Many implementations also have **itoa( )** and **ftoa( )** functions for converting integers and floating point values to strings. However, they are not part of the ANSI C library, so you should use **sprintf( )** for greater compatibility.

11.10 Summary

A C string is a series of **char** values terminated by the null character (**'\0'**). A string can be stored in a character array. It can be represented by a string constant by enclosing the characters, aside from the null character, in double quotation marks; the null character is understood to be present. Thus, **"joy"** is stored as the four characters **j, o, y,** and **\0**. The length of a string, however, doesn't include the null character.

String constants can be used to initialize character arrays. In pre-ANSI C implementations, only external and static arrays can be initialized, but ANSI C permits automatic arrays to be initialized, too. The array size should be at least one greater than the string length to accommodate the terminating null character. String constants also can be used to initialize pointers of type pointer-to-**char**.

Functions use pointers to the first character of a string to identify which string to act on. Typically, the corresponding actual argument is an array name, a pointer variable, or a quoted string; in each case, the address of the first character is passed. In general, it is not necessary to pass the length of the string, for the function can use the terminating null character to locate the string's end.

The **gets( )** and **puts( )** functions fetch a line of input and print a line of output, respectively. They are part of the **stdio.h** family of functions.

The C library includes several string-handling functions. Under ANSI C, these functions are declared in the **string.h** file. The library also has several character-processing functions that are declared in the **ctype.h** file.

By providing the proper two formal variables to the **main( )** function, you can give a program access to command-line arguments. The first argument, traditionally called **argc**, is an **int** and is assigned the number of command-line arguments. The second argument, traditionally called **argv**, is, in essence, a pointer to an array of pointers-to-**char**. Each pointer-to-**char** points to one of the command-line argument strings, with **argv[0]** pointing to the command name, **argv[1]** pointing to the first command-line argument, and so on. The **atoi( )**, **atol( )**, and **atof( )** functions convert string representations of numbers to type **int**, **long**, and **double** forms, respectively.

Review Questions

1. What's wrong with this attempted declaration of a character string?

```
main()
{
   char
name[] = {'F', 'e', 's', 's' };
   ...
}
```

2. What does this program print?

```
#include <stdio.h>
main()
{
   static char note[] = "See you at the snack bar.";
   char *ptr;

   ptr = note;
   puts(ptr);
   puts(++ptr);
   note[7] = '\0';
   puts(note);
   puts(++ptr);
}
```

3. What does this program print?

```
#include <stdio.h>
#include <string.h>
main()
{
   static char food[] = "Yummy";
   char *ptr;

   ptr = food + strlen(food);
   while ( --ptr >= food)
     puts(ptr);
}
```

4. What does the following program print?

```
#include <stdio.h>
#include <string.h>
main()
{
   static char goldwyn[40] = "art of it all ";
   static char samuel[40] = "I read p";
   char *quote = "the way through.";
```

```
      strcat(goldwyn, quote);
      strcat( samuel, goldwyn);
      puts(samuel);
}
```

5. This exercise provides practice with strings, loops, pointers, and pointer incrementing. First, suppose we have this function definition:

```
#include <stdio.h>
char *pr (str)
char *str;
{
   char *pc;

   pc = str;
   while (*pc)
     putchar(*pc++);
   do {
      putchar(*--pc);
      } while (pc-str);
   return (pc);
}
```

Consider the following function call:

```
x = pr("Ho Ho Ho!");
```

a. What is printed?

b. What type should **x** be?

c. What value does **x** receive?

d. What does the expression ***– – pc** mean? How is it different from **– –*pc**?

e. What is printed if *** – –pc** is replaced with ***pc– –?**

f. For what do the two **while** expressions test?

g. What happens if **pr( )** is supplied with a null string as an argument?

h. What must be done in the calling function so that **pr( )** can be used as shown?

6. How many bytes does **'$'** use? What about **"$"**?

7. What does the following program print?

```
#include <stdio.h>
#include <string.h>
#define M1 "How are ya, sweetie? "
char M2[40] = "Beat the clock.";
char *M3 = "chat";
main()
{
   char words[80];
   printf(M1);
   puts(M1);
   puts(M2);
   puts(M2 + 1);
   strcpy(words,M2);
   strcat(words, " Win a toy.");
   puts(words);
   words[4] = '\0';
   puts(words);
   while(*M3)
     puts(M3++);
     puts(--M3);
     puts(--M3);
     M3 = M1;
     puts(M3);
}
```

8. What does the following program print?

```
#include <stdio.h>
main()
{
   static char str1[] = "gawsie";
   static char str2[] = "bletonism";
   char *ps;
   int i = 0;

   for (ps = str1; *ps != '\0'; ps++) {
     if ( *ps == 'a' || *ps == 'e')
       putchar(*ps);
     else
       (*ps)--;
     putchar(*ps);
     }
   putchar('\n');
   while (str2[i] != '\0' ) {
     printf("%c", i % 3 ? str2[i] : '*');
     ++i;
     }
}
```

9. The **strlen( )** function takes a pointer to a string as an argument and returns the length of the string. Write your own version of this function.

10. Design a function that takes a string pointer as an argument and returns a pointer to the first blank in the string on or after the pointed-to position. Have it return a null pointer if it finds no blanks.

Programming Exercises

1. Design a function that takes a string pointer as an argument, fetches the next **n** characters from input (including blanks, tabs, and newlines), and stores them in the string.

2. Modify the function in Exercise 1 so that it stops after **n** characters or after the first blank, tab, or newline, whichever comes first. Note: Although the blank, tab, or newline is read and removed from the input queue, it shouldn't be stored as part of the string.

3. Design a function that fetches the first word from a line of input and discards the rest of the line. Define a word as a sequence of characters with no blanks, tabs, or newlines in it.

4. Design a function that searches the specified string for the first occurrence of a specified character. Have the function return a pointer to the character if successful and a null pointer if the character is not found in the string. (Note: This function duplicates the way the **strchr( )** function works.)

5. Write a function **is_within( )** that takes a character and a string pointer as arguments. Have the function return a nonzero value (true) if the character is in the string and zero (false) otherwise.

6. The **strncpy(s1,s2,n)** function copies exactly **n** characters from **s2** to **s1**, truncating **s2** or padding it with extra null characters as necessary. The target string may not be null-terminated if the length of **s2** is **n** or more. The function returns **s1**. Write your own version of this function.

7. Write a function **string_in( )** that takes two string pointers as arguments. If the second string is contained in the first string, have the function return the address at which the contained string begins. For instance, **string_in("hats"," at")** returns the address of the **a** in **hats**. Otherwise, have the function return the **NULL** pointer.

8. Write a function that replaces the contents of a string with the string reversed.

9. Write a program that reads in up to 10 strings or to **EOF**, whichever comes first. Have it offer the user a menu with 5 choices: Print the original list of strings, print the strings in ASCII collating sequence, print the strings in order of increasing length, print the strings in order of the length of the first word in the string, and quit. Have the menu recycle until the user enters the quit request. The program, of course, should actually perform the promised tasks.

10. Write a program that reads input up to **EOF** and reports the number of words, the number of uppercase letters, the number of lowercase letters, the number of punctuation characters, and the number of digits. Use the **ctype.h** family of functions.

11. Write a program that echoes the command-line arguments in reverse word order. That is, if the command-line arguments are **see you later**, the program should print **later you see**.

12. Write a program that calculates powers as specified by the command line. The first command-line argument should be the type **double** number to be raised to a power. The second command-line argument should be the integer power.

13. Write a program that reads input until the end of the file and echoes it to the display. Have the program recognize and implement the following command-line arguments:

− **p**	Print input as is
− **u**	Map input to all uppercase
− **l**	Map input to all lowercase

Let − **p** be the default option. If there are multiple arguments, have the program use the last one given.

14. Use the character classification functions to prepare an implementation of **atoi( )**.

12

File Input/Output

Contents

Objectives

Knowing what a file is

Understanding text modes and binary modes

Using low-level I/O services

Buffered and nonbuffered I/O

Using the standard I/O library

Knowing the advantages of the standard I/O library

Using random access in a file

Understanding text and binary data formats

F iles are essential to today's computer systems. They are used to store programs, documents, data, correspondence, forms, and the like. As a programmer, you may have to write programs that create files, write into files, and read from files. This chapter shows you how. We investigate two levels of file communications: low-level I/O and stream I/O. We introduced these levels conceptually in Chapter 8; here we look at the specifics.

12.1 Communicating with Files

Often we need a program to get information from a file or to place results into a file. One form of program/file communication is file redirection, as we saw in Chapter 8. This method is simple, but it is limited. For instance, suppose you wish to write an interactive program that asks you for book titles and saves the complete listing in a file. If you use redirection, as in

```
books > bklist
```

your interactive prompts also are redirected to the file named bklist. Not only does this redirection place unwanted text into bklist, it prevents the user from seeing the questions he or she is supposed to answer. As well, remember that not all operating systems allow redirection.

Fortunately, C offers more powerful methods of communicating with files. It lets you open a file from within a program, and then use special I/O functions to read from or write to that file. Before investigating these methods, however, we review briefly the nature of a file.

What Is a File?

To us, a file is a section of storage, usually on disk, with a name. For instance, we think of **stdio.h** as the name of a file that contains some useful information. To the operating system, a file is a bit more complicated. For instance, a large file may be stored in several scattered fragments. Or a file may contain data that allow the operating system to determine what kind of file it is. But these concerns belong to the operating system, not us (unless we are writing operating systems). Our concern is how a file looks to a C program.

C sees a file as a sequence of bytes, each of which can be read individually. This view corresponds to the file structure in the UNIX environment, which is where C began. Because other environments may not correspond exactly to this model, ANSI C provides for two ways to view files.

The Text View and the Binary View

The two mandated views of a file are binary and text. In the *binary view,* each byte of the file is accessible to a program. In the *text view,* what the program sees can differ from what is in the file. With the text view, the local environment's representation of such things as the end of a line is mapped to the C view when a file is read. Similarly, the C view is mapped to the local representation for output. For instance, MS-DOS text files represent the end of a line with the carriage return, line feed combination: **\r\n**. C programs represent the end of a line with **\n**. Therefore when a C program takes the text view of an MS-DOS text file, it converts **\r\n** to **\n** when reading from a file, and it converts **\n** to **\r\n** when writing to a file.

You aren't restricted to using only the text view for an MS-DOS text file. You can also use the binary view of the same file. In that case, the program sees both the **\r** and the **\n** characters in the file; no mapping takes place. See Figure 12.1. MS-DOS distinguishes between text and binary files, and C provides for text and binary views of those files. Normally, you use the text view for text files and the binary view for binary files, but you can use either view of either type file, although a text view of a binary file will work poorly.

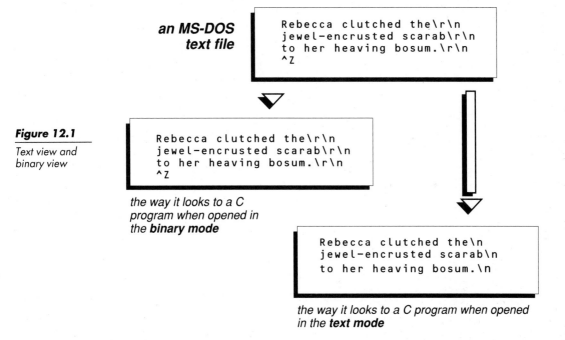

Figure 12.1

Text view and binary view

an **MS-DOS** text file

```
Rebecca clutched the\r\n
jewel-encrusted scarab\r\n
to her heaving bosum.\r\n
^Z
```

```
Rebecca clutched the\r\n
jewel-encrusted scarab\r\n
to her heaving bosum.\r\n
^Z
```

*the way it looks to a C program when opened in the **binary mode***

```
Rebecca clutched the\n
jewel-encrusted scarab\n
to her heaving bosum.\n
```

*the way it looks to a C program when opened in the **text mode***

ANSI C provides for both a binary view and a text view, but these views can be implemented identically. For instance, since UNIX uses just one file structure, both views are the same for UNIX implementations.

Levels of I/O

In addition to selecting which view you wish to have of a file, you can, in most cases, choose between two levels of I/O, that is, between two levels of handling access to files. Remember from Chapter 8 that low-level I/O uses the basic I/O services provided by the operating system. Standard I/O uses a standard package made up from a set of C library functions and definitions in the **stdio.h** file. ANSI C supports only the standard I/O package because there is no way to guarantee that all operating systems can be represented by the same low-level I/O model. However, two of the most popular environments, UNIX and MS-DOS, do offer similar low-level services. We discuss both levels in the next sections. As well, looking at low-level I/O provides a background for understanding why the standard I/O package was developed.

The main difference between the two levels is that low-level I/O is unbuffered; each call to an input or output routine reads from or writes to the file. On the other hand, the standard I/O package is buffered. Input and output routines read from or write to an intermediate buffer. When a buffer is filled on output, its contents are transferred to the file. When a buffer is emptied of input, it is refilled from the file. By reducing the number of times files are accessed, buffered I/O can achieve significant time savings compared to unbuffered I/O.

Standard Files

C programs automatically open three files: the standard input, the standard output, and the standard error. The *standard input,* by default, is the normal input device for the system. We assume that the standard input is a keyboard. Both the *standard output* and the *standard error,* by default, are the normal output device for the system. We assume the standard output and standard error are a display screen.

The standard input provides input to a program. It's the file that is read by **getchar( )**, **gets( )**, and **scanf( )**. The standard output is where normal program output goes; it's used by **putchar( )**, **puts( )**, and **printf( )**. Redirection, as discussed in Chapter 8, causes other files to be recognized as the standard input or standard output. The purpose of the standard error file is to provide a logically distinct place to send error messages. If, for example, you use redirection to send output to a file instead of to the screen, output sent to the standard error still goes to the screen. This feature is a good one, because if the error message were routed to the file, you might not see it.

12.2 Low-Level I/O

To see how low-level I/O works, we examine a short program that opens a file, displays it on the screen, and counts the number of bytes in it. We present it in a form compatible with UNIX System V and then discuss the changes necessary to adapt it to Berkeley (BSD) UNIX and to MS-DOS. We use a command-line argument to specify which file to open and read. Listing 12.1 shows the program.

❖ *count1.c*

Listing 12.1

```
/* count1.c--use low-level I/O */
#include <fcntl.h>        /* low-level I/O info */
#include <stdio.h>
#include <stdlib.h>       /* declares exit() */
main(argc, argv)
int argc;
char *argv[];
```

**Listing 12.1
(cont'd.)**

```
{
   char ch;        /* place to store each character as read */
   int fd;         /* "file descriptor" number */
   long count = 0;

   if (argc != 2)
   {
     printf("Usage: %s filename\n", argv[0]);
     exit(1);
   }
   if ( (fd = open(argv[1], O_RDONLY )) < 0 )
   {
     printf("Can't open %s\n", argv[1]);
     exit(1);
   }
   while ( read(fd,&ch,1) > 0 )
   {
     write(1,&ch,1); /* first 1 is standard output */
     count++;
   }
   close(fd);
   printf("File %s has %ld characters\n", argv[1], count);
}
```

The program first checks the value of **argc** to see if there is a command-line argument. If there isn't, the program prints a usage message; **argv[0]** is the name of the program. Using **arv[0]** instead of the program name explicitly causes the error message to change automatically if you change the name of the executable file. This feature also is handy in environments like UNIX that permit multiple names for a single file. However, note that some operating systems such as pre MS-DOS 3.0 don't recognize **argv[0]**, so this usage is not completely portable.

The **exit( )** function causes the program to terminate, closing any open files. The argument to **exit( )** is passed on to the UNIX operating system, where it can be used by some of the UNIX commands. The UNIX convention is to pass a value of 0 for programs that terminate normally and to pass nonzero values for abnormal termination. Different exit values can be used to distinguish between different causes of failure.

The program uses the **open( )** function to open the file. The first argument to **open( )** should be a pointer to a string that identifies the file by name. Here, **argv[1]** points to the memory location in which the first command-line argument is stored. The second argument indicates the mode in which the file is to be opened. The modes are identified by manifest constants defined in the **fcntl.h** file. The common modes and their meanings follow:

O_CREAT	Create a new file
O_RDONLY	Open the file for reading only
O_WRONLY	Open the file for writing only
O_RDWR	Open the file for reading and writing

This program counts bytes in the file, so we chose the read-only mode. Some older implementations of C lack the **fcntl.h** file; the documentation for those versions should list numeric values that specify the different modes.

The **open( )** function returns a small integer termed a *file descriptor*. If it cannot open the file, **open( )** returns a value of **−1**. This situation can arise, for instance, if there is no file listed under the specified name. The importance of the file descriptor is that the other low-level I/O functions use it to identify the file. Again, the combination of an **if** statement and the **exit( )** function aborts the program if there is a problem. Under ANSI, the **stdlib.h** file declares **exit( )**,

Next, the **read( )** function reads characters a byte at a time, and the **while** loop counts them. The **read( )** function takes three arguments. The first is a file descriptor that identifies which file to read. The second is the address of a memory location in which to place the data that are read. The third is an integer that specifies the number of bytes to be read at a time. Thus, the call **read(fd,&ch,1)** means to read one byte from the file identified by **fd** and to place the byte in the **ch** variable.

The **read( )** function returns the number of bytes read, which is usually **1** in this program. However, when **read( )** reaches the end of the file, it returns the value **0**. And if there is some sort of input error, such as a disk failure, **read( )** returns the value **−1**. Thus, the **while** loop terminates when the end of the file is reached or when a read error occurs.

The **write( )** function writes data to the indicated file. It takes the same types of arguments as **read( )**. The first argument is a file descriptor that identifies the file to be written to. Here we use **1**, which in this case identifies the standard output (the screen by default) that is opened automatically. The second argument is the address where the information is to be printed. The final argument is the number of bytes to be written.

Finally, the **close( )** function severs the connection to the file. It takes the file descriptor as an argument, which frees the file descriptor to be reused if the program opens additional files. A sample run follows:

```
$ count1 prose
I think that I shall never see
a program more lovely than one in C.
The prose file contains 70 characters
```

Berkeley (BSD) UNIX

To run the program on BSD UNIX, use the **sys/file.h** file instead of **fcntl.h**. Presumably, this difference will disappear as the UNIX community moves toward standardization.

MS-DOS

Actually, Listing 12.1 will run under both Turbo C and Microsoft C, but you can make some additions and modifications. First, you should include the file **io.h**. This file contains function prototypes for the low-level I/O functions.

Second, with MS-DOS, you have to choose between the binary view and the text view. By default, Turbo C and Microsoft C choose the text view. Therefore, for example, the \n\r combination in a text file is mapped to \n and is counted as a single character by our program. You can, however, use the **open( )** mode argument to choose the binary view and count \n\r as two characters. The **fnctl.h** file contains the following defined constants:

O_BINARY	Open file in binary mode
O_TEXT	Open file in text mode
O_CREAT	Create a new file

To indicate that you want to open a file in read-only, binary mode, use C's bit-wise OR operator (|) to combine constants. (See Chapter 15 for more about bit-wise operators.) Thus to call up the binary mode, use **open(argv[1], O_RDONLY | O_BINARY)**.

Incidentally, other approaches exist for handling these views under MS-DOS. Borland follows the Microsoft method so that Turbo C can compile source code originally written for Microsoft C, but other implementors do follow other paths. This situation illustrates the problems that can arise when there is no standard.

Standard File Descriptors

The standard files that C opens are assigned file descriptor numbers as follows:

Standard File	**Descriptor**	**Default**
Standard input	0	Keyboard
Standard output	1	Display screen
Standard error	2	Display screen

You can use these descriptors with the **read( )** and **write( )** functions. For instance, in Listing 12.1, we use **1** for **write( )**.

Using a Buffer

Although low-level I/O is unbuffered, you can create your own buffer within a program. To do so, simply declare an array to serve as a buffer, then have **read( )** and **write( )** use larger chunks of data. See Listing 12.2.

❖ *count2.c*

Listing 12.2

```
/* count2.c--low-level I/O with buffer */
#include <fcntl.h>
#include <stdio.h>
#include <stdlib.h>
#define BUFSIZE 512
char buf[BUFSIZE];      /* a buffer */
main(argc, argv)
int argc;
char *argv[];
```

```
{
    int fd;               /* "file descriptor" number */
    long count = 0;
    long nbytes;          /* number of bytes each read */

    if (argc != 2)
    {
        printf("Usage: %s filename\n", argv[0]);
        exit(1);
    }
    if ( (fd = open(argv[1], O_RDONLY )) < 0 )
    {
        printf("Can't open %s\n", argv[1]);
        exit(1);
    }
    while ( ( nbytes = read(fd,buf,BUFSIZE)) > 0 )
    {
        write(1,buf,nbytes);
        count += nbytes;
    }
    close(fd);
    printf("File %s has %ld characters\n", argv[1], count);
}
```

Instead of reading data into the 1-byte variable **ch** in this program, we read it into the 512-byte array **buf**. We declare the array externally so that if we define other functions in the file, they can use the same buffer. By using **BUFSIZE** as the final argument to **read( )**, we instruct the program to read in chunks of 512 bytes. Normally, then, **nbytes** is set to 512. But the file size is unlikely to be an exact multiple of 512. When fewer than 512 bytes are left to be read, **read( )** returns the actual number read. So the expression **count += nbytes** keeps an exact running total of the number of bytes read.

Performance Considerations

Using the buffer speeds up the program considerably. We ran the programs in Listings 12.1 and 12.2 and timed them. To get a truer measure of file access time, we removed the **write( )** statement and timed the read loop. On an MS-DOS system on an AT clone, the version in Listing 12.2 ran about 80 times faster than the version in Listing 12.1 in counting a 20-kilobyte file. On a VAX 750 computer using UNIX, the improvement was 300-fold for the same size file. Reading in larger chunks is clearly beneficial as far as speed is concerned.

The exact gain is influenced by many factors. One is how the functions are implemented. Another is how the operating system functions. For instance, the operating system may do its own buffering. In other words, the "unbuffered" program in Listing 12.1 may make its single-character reads from a system buffer rather than from the original file. *Caching,* in which the system temporarily copies a file into a cache area, also affects access times. Regardless of the exact numeric differences, however, the buffered version outperforms the unbuffered version.

Note: There is a negative side to buffering. Suppose we want to access individual characters in the file, as we do in a word-counting program. With the unbuffered version, we can examine each character as it's read. With the buffered version, we have to read a block into the buffer, then have the program examine each element of the buffer. In short, we may add to the programming load and increase our chances for error. The standard I/O package, however, combines the advantages of buffered I/O and individual byte access.

Commentary

For most applications, you're better off using the standard I/O package, especially if you wish to write portable code. However, some programmers prefer to use the low-level I/O functions for particular situations. Such code is more compact, and with careful programming, it may run faster. A good rule of thumb, though, is that good implementations of the standard library match good low-level programming.

12.3 Standard I/O

The standard I/O package has several advantages over low-level I/O. First, it has many specialized functions for handling various I/O problems. For instance, **printf( )** converts various forms of data to string output suitable for terminals. Second, it is part of the ANSI standard library, thus providing a highly portable solution to I/O programming needs. As well, the standard I/O package is buffered, making file access rapid. The buffering is handled behind the scenes, so you have the convenience of character-by-character access. Listing 12.3 shows the standard I/O alternative to Listing 12.1. The overall look is rather similar, so let's look at the new features.

❖ *count3.c*

Listing 12.3

```
/* count3.c--using standard I/O */
#include <stdio.h>
main(argc, argv)
int argc;
char *argv[];
{
    int ch;    /* place to store each character as read */
    FILE *fp;  /* "file pointer" */
    long count = 0;

    if (argc != 2)
    {
        printf("Usage: %s filename\n", argv[0]);
        exit(1);
    }
```

```
        if ( (fp = fopen(argv[1], "r" )) == NULL )
        {
          printf("Can't open %s\n", argv[1]);
          exit(1);
        }
        while ( (ch = getc(fp)) != EOF )
        {
          putc(ch,stdout);
          count++;
        }
        fclose(fp);
        printf("File %s has %ld characters\n", argv[1], count);
}
```

Listing 12.3 (cont'd.)

The fopen( ) Function

First, we use **fopen( )** instead of **open( )** to open the file. This function is declared in **stdio.h**. The first argument is the name of the file to be opened; more exactly, it's a pointer to a string that contains the name. The second argument is a string that identifies the mode in which the file is to be opened. ANSI C provides for several possibilities:

Mode String	Means
"r"	Open text file for reading.
"w"	Open text file for writing, truncating existing file to zero length, or creating file if it does not yet exist.
"a"	Open text file for writing, appending to the end of existing file, or creating file if it does not yet exist.
"r+"	Open text file for update, that is, for both reading and writing.
"w+"	Open text file for update (reading and writing), first truncating file to zero length if it exists or creating file if it does not yet exist.
"a+"	Open text file for update (reading and writing), appending to the end of existing file, or creating file if it does not yet exist; the whole file can be read, but writing can only be appended.
"rb", **"wb"**, **"ab"**, **"ab+"**, **"a+b"**, **"wb+"**, **"w+b"**, **"ab+"**, **"a+b"**	Like the preceding modes, except using binary mode instead of text mode.

For systems like UNIX that have just one file type, the modes with the **b** are equivalent to the corresponding modes lacking the **b**. Caution: If you use any of the **w** modes for an existing file, the old version is erased so that your program starts with a clean slate.

Like **open( )**, **fopen( )** returns a file identifier. Instead of returning an integer file descriptor, however, **fopen( )** returns a *file pointer*. The **FILE** type is a derived type defined in **stdio.h**. The pointer **fp** doesn't point to the actual file. Instead, it points to a *structure,* which is a data object that can contain several data items of diverse types. The structure set up by the standard I/O package contains information about the file being read and about the buffer that has been automatically set up. Since the I/O functions in the standard package use a buffer, they need to know where the buffer is. They also need to know how full the buffer is and which file is being used. This knowledge enables the functions to refill or empty the buffer when necessary; the structure pointed to by **fp** has all that information. See Chapter 14 for a more detailed discussion of structures and data objects.

The **fopen( )** function returns the **NULL** pointer (also defined in **stdio.h)** if it cannot open the file. Our program in Listing 12.3 exits if **fp** is **NULL**. The **fopen( )** function may fail because the disk is full, the name is illegal, or because of a hardware problem or for some other reason. Remember: Proper error-checking can go a long way toward avoiding problems.

The getc( ) and putc( ) Functions

The two functions **getc( )** and **putc( )** work much like **getchar( )** and **putchar( )**. The difference is that you must tell these newcomers which file to use. Thus

```
ch = getchar();
```

means get a character from the standard input, but

```
ch = getc(fp);
```

means get a character from the file identified by **fp**.

Similarly,

```
putc(ch, fpout);
```

means put the character **ch** into the file identified by the **FILE** pointer **fpout**. In the **putc( )** argument list, the character comes first, then the file pointer.

In Listing 12.3, we use **stdout** for the **putc( )** second argument. It's defined in **stdio.h** as being the file pointer associated with the standard output. So **putc(ch,stdout)** is the same as **putchar(ch)**; indeed, the latter function normally is defined as being the former. Similarly, **getchar( )** is defined as being **getc( )** using the standard input.

The fclose( ) Function

Finally, the **fclose(fp)** closes the file identified by **fp**, flushing buffers as needed. For a program less casual than this one, we would check to see if the file were closed successfully. The function **fclose( )** returns a value of **0** if successful, and **EOF** if not:

```
    if (fclose(fp) != 0)
        printf("Error in closing file %s\n", argv[1]);
```

Standard Files

The **stdio.h** file associates three file pointers with the three standard files opened by C programs:

Standard File	File Pointer
Standard input	**stdin**
Standard output	**stdout**
Standard error	**stderr**

These pointers are all type pointers-to-**FILE**, so they can be used as arguments to the standard I/O functions just as **fp** is in our example program.

12.4 A Simple File-Condensing Program

Let's now look at an example that creates a new file and writes to it. This time we copy selected data from one file to another, so we open two files simultaneously, using the **"r"** mode for one and the **"w"** mode for the other. The program in Listing 12.4 condenses the contents by the brutal expedient of retaining only every third character. Finally, it places the condensed version in a new file whose name consists of the old name plus **.red** (for reduced) appended. Command-line arguments, opening more than one file, and filename appending are quite useful generally, although this particular form of condensing is of more limited appeal. However, this form has its uses, which we discuss.

❖ reducto.c

Listing 12.4

```
/* reducto.c--reduce your files by 2/3rds */
#include <stdio.h>
main(argc,argv)
int argc;
char *argv[];
{
    FILE *in, *out;  /* declare two FILE pointers */
    int ch;
    char name[40];   /* storage for output filename */
    int count = 0;

    if ( argc < 2)   /* check if there is an input file */
    {
        fprintf(stderr,
            "Sorry, I need a filename argument.\n");
        exit(1);
    }
    if ( (in = fopen(argv[1], "r")) == NULL)
```

Listing 12.4 (cont'd.)

```
{
    fprintf(stderr, "I couldn't open the file \"%s\".\n",
            argv[1]);
    exit(2);
}
strcpy(name,argv[1]);    /* copy filename into array */
strcat(name,".red");     /* append .red to name */
if ( (out = fopen(name, "w")) == NULL)
{ /* open file for writing */
    fprintf(stderr,"Can't create output file.\n");
    exit(3);
}
while ( (ch = getc(in)) != EOF)
    if ( count++ % 3 == 0 )
        putc(ch, out);       /* print every 3rd char */
fclose(in);
fclose(out);
}
```

First, we place the program in a file called **reducto**. We apply it to a file called **eddy**, which contains a single line:

```
So even Eddy came oven ready.
```

The command

```
reducto eddy
```

and the output then produce a file called **eddy.red**, which contains the following:

```
Send money
```

In the next few paragraphs we discuss some program notes. The **fprintf( )** function is like **printf( )** except that it requires a file pointer as its first argument. We use the **stderr** pointer to send our error messages to the standard error; this use is a standard C practice.

To construct the new name for the output file, we use **strcpy( )** to copy the name **eddy** into the array **name**. Then we use the **strcat( )** function to combine that **eddy** with **.red**, producing the new filename **eddy.red**. We also check to see if the program succeeds in opening a file by that name. This step is especially important in the DOS environment since a filename like, say, **strange.c.red** is invalid; you can't add extensions to extensions. (The proper MS-DOS approach is to replace an existing extension with **.red**, so that the reduced version of **strange.c** becomes **strange.red**.)

Listing 12.4 involves having two files open simultaneously, so we declare two **FILE** pointers. Note that each file is opened and closed independently of the other. There are limits to how many files you can have open at one time. This limit depends on the system and implementation, but it often is in the range of 10 to 20. You can use the same pointer for different files providing the files are not open at the same time.

12.5 File I/O: fprintf( ), fscanf( ), fgets( ), and fputs( )

The I/O functions we have used in the preceding chapters all have file I/O analogs. The main distinction between those and the functions we describe now is that you need to use a **FILE** pointer to tell the new functions which file to work with. Like **getc( )** and **putc( )**, these functions are used after **fopen( )** opens a file and before **fclose( )** closes it.

The I/O functions we describe here, together with those you are already familiar with, should give you tools aplenty for reading and writing text files. Thus far in the text and throughout this section, we use I/O functions for *sequential access,* that is, processing the file contents in order. In the following section, we look at *random access,* that is, accessing the contents in any desired order.

The fprintf( ) and fscanf( ) Functions

These two file I/O functions work just like **printf( )** and **scanf( )**, except that they require an additional argument to point to the proper file. This argument is the first in the argument list. We've already used **fprintf( )**. Listing 12.5 illustrates both of these file I/O functions along with the **rewind( )** function.

This program lets you add words to a file. By using the **"a+"** mode, the program can both read and write in the file. The first time the program is used, it creates the **words** file and lets you place words in it. When you use the program subsequently, it lets you

❖ *addaword.c*

Listing 12.5

```
/* addaword.c--use fprintf(), fscanf(), and rewind() */
#include <stdio.h>
#include <stdlib.h>
#define MAX 20
main()
{
   FILE *fp;
   char words[MAX];

   if ( (fp = fopen("words", "a+") ) == NULL)
   {
      fprintf(stdin,"Can't open \"words\" file.\n");
      exit(1);
   }
   puts("Enter words to add to the file; type the Enter");
   puts("key at the beginning of a line to terminate.");
   while ( gets(words) != NULL && words[0] != '\0')
      fprintf(fp, "%s ", words);
   puts("File contents:");
   rewind(fp);  /* go back to beginning of file */
   while ( fscanf(fp,"%s",words) == 1)
      puts(words);
   fclose(fp);
}
```

add words to the prior contents. The append modes only let you add material to the end of the file, but the "a+" mode does let you read the whole file. The **rewind( )** command takes the program to the file beginning so that the final **while** loop can print the file contents. Note that **rewind( )** takes a file pointer argument.

If you enter an empty line, **gets( )** places a null character in the first element of the array. We use that fact to terminate the loop. Here's a sample run from a DOS environment:

```
C> addaword
Enter words to add to the file; type the Enter
key at the beginning of a line to terminate.
See the canoes
[enter]
File contents:
See
the
canoes
C> addaword
Enter words to add to the file; type the Enter
key at the beginning of a line to terminate.
on the
sea
[enter]
File contents:
See
the
canoes
on
the
sea
```

The fgets( ) and fputs( ) Functions

The **fgets( )** function takes three arguments, whereas the **gets( )** takes only one. The first argument, as with **gets( )**, is a pointer-to-**char** to indicate where the input should be stored. The second argument is an integer that represents the upper limit to the size of the input string. The final argument is the file pointer that identifies the file to be read.

The **fgets( )** function reads input through the first newline character, until one less than the upper limit of characters is read, or until the end of the file is found; **fgets( )** then adds a terminating null character. Thus, the upper limit represents the maximum number of characters plus the null character.

Note that if **fgets( )** reads in an entire line before running into the character limit, it places the newline character that marks the end of the line into the string. Here **fgets( )** differs from **gets( )**, which reads the newline but discards it.

Like **gets( )**, **fgets( )** returns the value **NULL** when it encounters **EOF**. This feature lets you check for the end of a file. Otherwise, it returns the value of the string pointer passed to it.

The **fputs( )** function takes two arguments: a pointer-to-**char** and a file pointer. It then writes the string found at the pointed-to location into the indicated file. Unlike **puts( )**, **fputs( )** does not append a newline when it prints.

Because **fgets( )** keeps the newline and **fputs( )** doesn't add one, they work well in tandem. Listing 12.6 shows an echo program using these two functions.

❖ *echo.c*

Listing 12.6

```
/* echo.c--using fgets() and fputs() */
#include <stdio.h>
#define MAXLINE 20
main()
{
   char line[MAXLINE];

   while ( fgets(line, MAXLINE, stdin) != NULL &&
           line[0] != '\n')
     fputs(line, stdout);
}
```

When you press the Enter key at the beginning of a line, **fgets( )** reads the newline and places it in the first element of the array. We use that fact to terminate the input loop. Encountering **EOF** also terminates the loop. (Note: In Listing 12.5 we test for '\0' instead of '\n' because **gets( )** discards the newline.)

Here is a sample run:

```
It is Spring.
It is Spring.
The hills are green and the sea is sparkling.
The hills are green and the sea is sparkling.
[enter]
```

The program works fine, but do you notice something odd? The second line we enter contains 45 characters, and the **line** array holds only 20, including the newline character! What is happening here? When **fgets( )** reads the second line, it reads just the first 19 characters, through the second e in **green**. These characters are copied into **line**, and **fputs( )** prints the 19-character line. Because **fgets( )** hasn't reached the end of a line, **line** does not contain a newline character, so **fputs( )** doesn't print a newline. The third call to **fgets( )** resumes where the second call leaves off. Thus, it reads the next 19 characters into **line** beginning with the **n** in **green**. This next block replaces the previous contents of **line**, and in turn, is printed on the same line as the output (remember, the last output didn't have a newline). In short, **fgets( )** reads the second line in chunks of 19 characters, and **fputs( )** prints it in the same size chunks.

You may wonder why the program doesn't print the first 19 characters of the second line as soon as we type them. That's where keyboard buffering comes in (Chapter 8). The second line isn't sent to the program until the entire line is entered.

Commentary: gets( ) and fgets( )

Because **fgets( )** can be used to prevent storage overflow, it's a better function than **gets( )** for serious programming. Because it reads a newline into a string and because **puts( )** appends a newline to output, **fgets( )** should be used with **fputs( ),** not with **puts( ).** Otherwise, one newline in input can become two in output.

12.6 Random Access: fseek( ) and ftell( )

The **fseek( )** function lets you treat a file like an array and move directly to any byte in a file opened by **fopen( ).** To see how it works, we create a program that displays a file in reverse order. See Listing 12.7. Borrowing from our earlier examples, it uses a command-line argument to obtain the name of the file that it affects. Note that **fseek( )** has three arguments and returns an **int** value. The **ftell( )** function returns the current position in a file.

❖ *reverse.c*

Listing 12.7

```
/* reverse.c--display file in reverse order */
#include <stdio.h>
#include <stdlib.h>
#define CNTL_Z '\032'   /* eof marker in DOS text files */
main(argc,argv)
int argc;
char *argv[];
{
   char ch;
   FILE *fp;
   long count, last;

   if ( argc != 2)
     {
     printf("Usage: reverse file\n");
     exit(1);
     }
   if ( ( fp = fopen(argv[1],"rb") ) == NULL )
     { /* read-only and binary modes */
     printf("reverse can't open %s\n", argv[1]);
     exit(1);
     }
   fseek(fp,0L,SEEK_END); /* go to end of file */
   last = ftell(fp);
   for ( count = 1L ; count <= last; count++)
```

**Listing 12.7
(cont'd.)**

```
      {
      fseek(fp, -count, SEEK_END);     /* go backwards */
      ch = getc(fp);
      if ( ch != CNTL_Z && ch != '\r')
        putchar(ch);
      }
    fclose(fp);
}
```

Here is the output using the file named **prose** from the beginning of the chapter:

```
.C ni eno naht ylevol erom margorp a
ees reven llahs I taht kniht I
```

We now discuss three topics: how **fseek( )** and **ftell( )** work, using a binary stream, and portability.

How fseek( ) and ftell( ) Work

The first of the three **fseek( )** arguments is a **FILE** pointer that points to the file being searched. The file should have been opened using **fopen( )**.

The second argument is called the *offset,* which tells us how far to move from the starting point (discussed with regard to the third argument). This argument must be a **long** value. It can be positive (move forward) or negative (move backward).

The third argument is the *mode,* and it identifies the starting point. The ANSI standard specifies the following manifest constants for the mode:

Mode	Measure Offset From
SEEK_SET	Beginning of file
SEEK_CUR	Current position
SEEK_END	End of file

Under ANSI C, the modes are defined in **stdio.h**. Older implementations may lack these definitions and, instead, use the numeric values **0L**, **1L**, and **2L**, respectively, for these modes. Recall that the **L** suffix identifies these modes as type **long** values.

The value returned by **fseek( )** is **0** if the program works properly. It returns a **–1** if there is an error such as attempting to move beyond the file bounds.

The **ftell( )** function is type **long**, and it returns the current file location. Under ANSI C, it's declared in **stdio.h.** As originally implemented in UNIX, **ftell( )** specifies the file position by returning the number of bytes from the beginning, with the first byte being byte 0, and so on. Under ANSI C, this definition applies to files opened in the binary mode, but it does not necessarily apply to files opened in the text mode. This fact represents one reason why we use the binary mode for Listing 12.7.

Let's look at how **fseek( )**and **ftell( )** are used in the sample program.

We use the statement

```
fseek(fp,0L,SEEK_END);
```

to take us to an offset of zero bytes from the end of the file. That is, the statement takes us to the end of the file. Next, the statement

```
last = ftell(fp);
```

assigns to **last** the number of bytes from the beginning of the file to the end.

Next, we have a loop:

```
for ( count = 1L ; count <= last; count++)
{
   fseek(fp, -count, SEEK_END);      /* go backward */
   ch = getc(fp);
   ...
}
```

The first cycle positions the program at the first character before the end of the file, that is, at the final character of the file. Then the program prints it. The next loop positions the program at the preceding character and prints it. This process continues until the first character is printed.

Binary Mode Versus Text Mode

The program is written so that it works in both the UNIX and the MS-DOS environments. With UNIX, there is only one file format, so no special adjustments are needed. MS-DOS, however, requires extra attention. First, many MS-DOS editors mark the end of a text file with the character Control-Z. When such a file is opened in the text mode, C recognizes this character as marking the end of the file. When the same file is opened in the binary mode, however, the Control-Z character is just another character in the file, and the actual end of the file comes later. It may come immediately after the Control-Z, or the file may be padded with null characters to make the size a multiple of, say, 256. Null characters don't print, and we included code to prevent the program from trying to print the Control-Z character.

A second difference is one we've mentioned before: MS-DOS represents a text file newline with the \r\n combination. A C program opening the file in a text mode "sees" \r\n as a simple \n. But when using the binary mode, the program sees both characters. Therefore, we include coding to suppress the printing of \r.

The **ftell( )** function may also work differently in the text mode than in the binary mode. Many systems have text file formats that are different enough from the UNIX model that a byte count from the beginning of the file is not a meaningful quantity. ANSI C states that for the text mode, **ftell( )** returns a value that can be used as the second argument to **fseek( )**. For MS-DOS, for example, **ftell( )** can return a count that sees \r\n as a single byte. Note: Because a UNIX text file normally contains neither Control-Z nor \r, this extra coding therefore does not affect most UNIX text files.

Ideally, **fseek( )** and **ftell( )** should conform to the UNIX model. However, differences in real systems sometimes make such a case impossible. Therefore, ANSI C provides lowered expectations for these functions. Here are some limitations:

1. In the binary mode, implementations need not support the **SEEK_END** mode. (Thus Listing 12.7 is not guaranteed to be portable.)

2. In the text mode, the only calls to **fseek( )** that are guaranteed to work are the following:

fseek(*file*, **0L, SEEK_SET**)	Go to file beginning
fseek(*file*, **0L, SEEK_CUR**)	Stay at current position
fseek(*file*, **0L, SEEK_END**)	Go to file end
fseek(*file*,*ftell-pos*, **SEEK_SET**)	Go to position *ftell-pos* from the beginning, in which *ftell-pos* is a value returned by **ftell( )**

Fortunately, many common environments allow stronger implementations of these functions. Let's look at a text mode example.

12.7 Using Random Access in a Text Mode

Listing 12.8 uses the function approach to write a program that takes a list of file names from the command line and prints the name of each file followed by the last line of that file.

❖ *lastline.c*

Listing 12.8

```
/* lastline.c--prints last lines of files */
#include <stdio.h>
void show_end();
main(argc,argv)
int argc;
char *argv[];
{
   FILE *fp;
   int file;

   if ( argc < 2)
   {
     printf("Usage: %s file(s)\n", argv[0]);
     exit(1);
   }
   for (file = 1; file < argc; file++)
```

```
{
    if ( ( fp = fopen(argv[file],"r") ) == NULL )
        fprintf(stderr,"%s can't open %s\n", argv[0],
            argv[file]);
    else
        show_end(argv[file],fp);
  }
}
void show_end(name,file)
char *name;
FILE * file;
{
  int ch;
  int newlines = 0;
  long count, start, last;

  printf("%s:\n", name);
  start = ftell(file);
  fseek(file,0L,SEEK_END);                    /* go to end of file */
  last = ftell(file);
  for ( count = 1L ; count <= last; count++)
  {
    fseek(file, -count, SEEK_END);  /* go backward */
    ch = getc(file);
    if ( ch == '\n')
      newlines++;
    if ( newlines == 2 )                     /* or maybe 3 */
    {
      start = ftell(file);
      break;
    }
  }
  fseek(file, start, SEEK_SET);
  while ( (ch = getc(file) ) != EOF)
    putchar(ch);
  fclose(file);
}
```

Listing 12.8 (cont'd.)

We let **main( )** handle the command-line arguments and the opening and closing of files. The **show_end( )** function takes care of finding and displaying the final line. Here is a sample run from the MS-DOS environment:

```
C> lastline prose prod produce
a program more lovely than one in C.
lastline can't open prod
red potatoes
C>
```

The **main( )** program contains a loop for processing the command-line arguments. Recall that **argc** includes the command name in the count, so it is one greater than the number of command-line arguments. Also, since **argv[0]** is the command name, **argv[count – 1]** is the last argument. Thus the loop cycles through all the arguments. If the argument is the name of a file the program can open, the file is processed. Otherwise, the loop goes on to the next argument. Note that you can use this form for any program that is expected to handle a list of files.

The **show_end( )** function assumes the text file ends with a newline. It searches backward from the end of the file until it finds a second newline, which marks the end of the next-to-last line. By reading the character, we move to the next character, which is the first character on the final line. The fragment

```
if ( newlines == 2 )  /* or maybe 3 */
{
    start = ftell(file);
    break;
}
```

saves the location of this character and breaks the **for** loop. It's possible, however, that the file has only one line, so that the test **newlines == 2** never becomes true. In that case, the loop runs to completion, examining all the characters in the file. Then the program prints the entire file, using the value of **start** that was set before the loop was entered.

The files are opened in the text mode, so we shouldn't have to worry about detecting the **\r** character. However, with Turbo C 2.0, we find we must use **3** instead of **2** for the number of newlines. The reason: Although this version of Turbo C transforms **\r\n** to **\n** when moving forward through a file, it transforms **\r\n** to **\n\n** when moving backward. Apparently the **\n** is passed as **\n**, and then the **\r** is detected. Turbo C notes that it is immediately followed by a **\n**, so it maps the combination to a second **\n**. Earlier versions of Microsoft C do so also.

The program in Listing 12.8 works in the UNIX and MS-DOS environments, but notice that it goes beyond the ANSI guarantees for **fseek( )**. For example, we use offsets from the file end, and the offsets are not values returned by **ftell( )**.

12.8 Behind the Scenes with Standard I/O

Now that you've seen some of the features of the standard I/O package, let's examine a representative conceptual model. Normally, the first step to using standard I/O is to use **fopen( )** to open a file although the **stdin, stdout,** and **stderr** files are opened automatically. The **fopen( )** function not only opens the file, it sets up a buffer (two buffers for the read and write modes), and it sets up a data structure that contains data about the file and buffer. Also, **fopen( )** returns a pointer to this structure, so other functions will know where to find it; we assume this value is assigned to a pointer variable **fp. Fopen( )** is said to open a stream: If the file is opened in the text mode, we get a *text stream,* and if the file is opened in the binary mode, we get a *binary stream.* The data structure typically includes a *file position indicator* to specify the current position in the stream, indicators for errors and end-of-file, a pointer to the beginning of the buffer, a file identification such as the file descriptor provided by **open( )**, and a holder for the number of bytes actually copied into the buffer.

Let's concentrate on file input. Usually, the next step is to call on one of the input functions declared in **stdio.h**, such as **fscanf( )**, **getc( )**, or **fgets( )**. Calling any one of these functions causes a chunk of data to be copied from the file to the buffer. The buffer size is implementation-dependent, but it typically is 512 bytes or some multiple thereof. In addition to filling the buffer, the initial function call sets values in the structure pointed to by **fp**. In particular, the current position in the stream and the number of bytes copied into the buffer are set. In most cases the current position starts out at character 0.

Once the data structure and buffer are initialized, the input function then reads the requested data from the buffer. As it does so, the file position indicator is set to point to the character following the last character read. Because all the input functions from the **stdio.h** family use the same buffer, calls to any one function resume where the previous call to any of the functions stopped.

When an input function finds that it has read all the characters in the buffer, it requests that the next chunk of data be copied from the file to the buffer. In this manner, the input functions can read all the file contents up to the end of the file. After a function reads the last character of the final buffer's worth of data, it sets the end-of-file indicator to true. The next call to an input function then returns **EOF**.

Output functions write to a buffer in a similar manner. When the buffer is filled, the data are copied to the file.

Comment

It's possible to use low-level I/O and standard I/O simultaneously on the same file, but it is a bad idea to do so. The reason is that input from, say, **read( )** and **getc( )** is not coordinated. **Read( )** reads from the file; **getc( )** reads from the buffer. So **read( )** can be positioned on character 10, and **getc( )** positioned on character 59.

12.9 Other Standard I/O Functions

The ANSI standard library contains over three dozen functions in the standard I/O family, and we don't wish to cover them all. However, we briefly describe a few more to give you a better idea of what is available. We list each function by its ANSI C prototype to indicate its arguments and return values. See Appendix F for the full ANSI C standard I/O package.

int ungetc(int c, FILE *fp)

This function pushes the character specified by **c** back onto the input stream. If you push a character onto the input stream, the next call to a standard input function will read that character. See Figure 12.2. Suppose, for example, you want a function to read characters up to, but not including, the next semicolon. You can use **getchar( )** or **getc( )** to read characters until a semicolon is read, then use **ungetc( )** to place the semicolon back in the input stream. ANSI C standard guarantees only one pushback at a time. If an

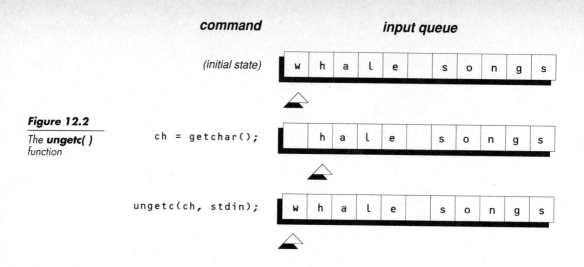

Figure 12.2

The **ungetc( )** function

command

input queue

(initial state)

w h a l e s o n g s

ch = getchar();

h a l e s o n g s

ungetc(ch, stdin);

w h a l e s o n g s

implementation permits you to push back several characters in a row, the input functions will read them in the reversed order of pushing.

int fflush(FILE *fp)

If **fp** points to an output stream, calling this function causes any unwritten data in the buffer to be sent to the output file. This action is called flushing a buffer, as we've mentioned earlier. If **fp** is the **NULL** pointer, all output buffers are flushed.

int setvbuf(FILE *fp, char *buf, int mode, size_t size)

This function sets up an alternative buffer to be used by the standard I/O functions. It's called after the file has been opened and before any other operations have been performed on the stream. The pointer **fp** identifies the stream, and **buf** points to the storage to be used. If the value of **buf** is not **NULL**, it's up to you to create the buffer. For instance, you can declare an array of 1024 **char**s and pass the address of that array. However, if you use **NULL** for the value of **buf**, the function also allocates a buffer. The **size** variable tells **setvbuf( )** how large the array is. (The **size_t** type is a derived type; see Chapter 16.) The **mode** is selected from the following choices: **_IOFBF** for fully buffered, **_IOLBF** for line buffered, and **_IONBF** for nonbuffered. The function returns zero if successful, nonzero otherwise. If a program works with stored data objects having, say, a size of 3000 bytes each, you can use **setvbuf( )** to create a buffer whose size matches that of the data object.

Binary I/O: fread( ) and fwrite( )

Let's look at some background before plunging into the **fread( )** and **fwrite( )** functions. Up to this point, the standard I/O functions we have used have been text-oriented, dealing with characters and strings. What if you want to save numeric data in a file?

True, you can use **fprintf( )** and the **%f** format to save a floating-point value, but such coding saves it as a string. For instance, the sequence

```
double num = 1./3.;
fprintf(fp,"%f", num );
```

saves **num** as the string of 8 characters: **0.333333**. Using a **%.2f** specifier saves it as 4 characters: **0.33**. Using a **%.12f** specifier saves it as 14 characters: **0.333333333333**. Thus, changing the specifier alters the amount of space to store the value; it also can result in different values being stored. Once the value of **num** is stored as **0.33**, there is no way to return to the full precision when reading the file. In general, **fprintf( )** converts numeric values to strings, possibly altering the value.

The most accurate and consistent way to store a number is to use the same pattern of bits that the program does. Thus, a **double** value should be stored in a size **double** container. When data are stored in a file using the same representation the program uses, we say the data are stored in binary form. There is no conversion from numeric forms to strings. In C, the low-level I/O functions **read( )** and **write( )** perform binary I/O; the standard I/O functions **fread( )** and **fwrite( )** perform binary I/O. See Figure 12.3.

Actually, all data are stored in binary form, for characters are stored using the binary representation of the character code. However, if all data in the file are interpreted as being character codes, we say the file contains text data. If some or all of the data are interpreted as being numeric data in binary form, we say the file contains binary data.

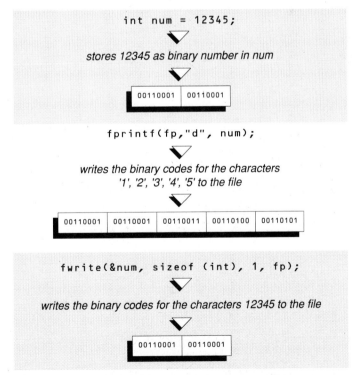

Figure 12.3

Binary and text output

(this figure assumes an integer size of 16 bits)

(Also, note that files in which the data represent machine language instructions are binary files.)

The uses of the terms "binary" and "text" can become a bit confusing. C recognizes two modes for opening files: binary and text. Many operating systems recognize two file formats: binary and text. Information can be stored or read as binary data or as text data. These are all related, but not identical. You can open a text format file in the binary mode. You can store text in a binary format file. You can use **getc( )** to copy files containing binary data. In general, however, you should use the binary mode to store binary data in a binary format file. Similarly, you most often should use text data in text files opened in the text format.

size_t fwrite(void *ptr, size_t size, size_t nmemb, FILE *fp)

This function is the standard I/O counterpart to **write( )**. The **size_t** type is defined in terms of the standard C types. It's the type returned by the **sizeof** operator; typically it is **unsigned int**, but an implementation can choose another type. The pointer **pt** points to the location from which the output should be read. The **size** represents the size, in bytes, of the chunks to be read, and the **nmemb** represents the number of chunks to be read. As usual, **fp** identifies the file to be written to.

For instance, suppose you want to save a data object (such as an array) that is 256 bytes in size. The statements

```
char buffer[256];
  . . .
fwrite(buffer, 256, 1, fp);
```

copy one chunk of 256 bytes to the file. Or to save an array of 10 **double** values, you can use

```
double earnings[10];
  . . .
fwrite(earnings, sizeof double, 10, fp);
```

which copies data from the **earnings** array to the file in 10 chunks of size **double**.

Notice the odd declaration of **void *ptr**. One problem with **fwrite( )** is that its first argument is not a fixed type. For instance, our first example uses **buffer**, which is type pointer-to-**char**. The second example uses **earnings**, which is type pointer-to-**double**. Under ANSI C function prototyping, these actual arguments are converted to the pointer-to-**void** type, which acts as a sort of catch-all type for pointers.

The **fwrite( )** function returns the actual number of items written. Normally, this number equals **nmemb**, but it can be less if there is a write error.

size_t fread(void *ptr, size_t size, size_t nmemb, FILE *fp)

This function takes the same set of arguments that **fwrite( )** does. This time **ptr** points to the memory storage into which file data are copied, and **fp** identifies the file to be read.

Use this function to read data that were written to a file using **fwrite( )**. For example, to recover the array of 10 size **double** chunks of data saved in the last section, use the following call:

```
double earnings[10];
  ...
fread(earnings, sizeof double, 10, fp);
```

This coding copies 10 size **double** values into the **earnings** array.

The **fread( )** function returns the actual number of items read. Normally, this number equals **nmemb**, but it can be less if there is a read error or if the end of the file is reached.

int feof(FILE *fp) *and* int ferror(FILE *fp)

When the standard input functions return **EOF**, that usually means they've reached the end of a file. But it also can indicate that a read error has occurred. The **feof( )** and **ferror( )** functions allow you to distinguish between the two possibilities. The **feof( )** function returns a nonzero value if the last input call detected **EOF** and returns zero otherwise. The **ferror( )** function returns a nonzero value if a reading (or writing) error has occurred.

An Example

Let's use some of the functions we've been describing. Our goal is a program that appends the contents from a list of files to a particular file. One problem is passing the file information to the program. This procedure can be accomplished interactively or by using command-line arguments. We take the second approach, letting the final command-line argument represent the name of the append file. That is, a statement such as

```
append file1 file2 file3
```

appends **file1** and **file2** to **file3**. This command suggests a plan along the following lines:

If *there are fewer than two command-line arguments, quit.*
Open the final command-line file in the append mode.
For *each remaining command-line file, open it in the read mode and copy it to the append file.*

To illustrate **setvbuf( )**, we use it to specify a different buffer size. We can include this function in the next stage of refinement. For instance, consider opening the append file, which we can break down into the following steps:

Open the final command-line file in the append mode.
If *this step cannot be accomplished, quit.*
Establish a 1024-byte buffer for this file.
If *this step cannot be accomplished, quit.*

Similarly, we can refine the copying portion this way:

For *each remaining file in the command-line list:*
  If *it is the same as the append file, skip to the next file.*
  If *it cannot be opened in the read mode, skip to the next file.*
  Append *the contents of the file to the append file.*

Listing 12.9 shows the result.

❖ *append.c*

Listing 12.9

```
/* append.c--appends files to a file */
#include <stdio.h>
#define BUFSIZE 1024
char temp[BUFSIZE];
void append();

main(argc,argv)
int argc;
char *argv[];
{
   FILE *fa, *fr;
   int file;

   if ( argc < 3 )
   {
      fprintf(stderr,
      "Usage: %s source-file(s) destination-file\n",
         argv[0]);
      exit(1);
   }
   if ( (fa = fopen(argv[argc - 1], "a")) == NULL)
   {
      fprintf(stderr, "Can't open %s\n", argv[argc - 1]);
      exit(2);
   }
   if (setvbuf(fa, NULL, _IOFBF, BUFSIZE ) != 0)
   {
      fputs("Can't create output buffer\n", stderr);
      exit(3);
   }
   for (file = 1; file < argc - 1; file++)
   {
      if (strcmp(argv[argc - 1], argv[file]) == 0)
         fputs("Can't append file to itself\n",stderr);
      else if ((fr = fopen(argv[file], "r")) == NULL)
         fprintf(stderr, "Can't open %s\n", argv[file]);
      else
      {
         if (setvbuf(fr, NULL, _IOFBF, BUFSIZE) != 0)
```

Listing 12.9
(cont'd.)

```
            {
                fputs("Can't create output buffer\n",stderr);
                continue;
            }
            append(fr,fa);
            fclose(fr);
        }
    }
}

void append(source, dest)
FILE *source, *dest;
{
    size_t bytes;
    extern char temp[];

    while ((bytes = fread(temp,sizeof(char),BUFSIZE,
            source)) > 0)
        fwrite(temp, sizeof (char), bytes, dest);
}
```

In the program, the code

```
if (setvbuf(fa, NULL, _IOFBF, BUFSIZE ) != 0)
{
    fputs("Can't create output buffer\n", stderr);
    exit(3);
}
```

creates a buffer 1024 bytes in size to be used with the append file. If **setvbuf( )** is unable to meet this requirement, it returns a nonzero value, and the code then terminates the program. Similar coding establishes a 1024-byte buffer for the file currently being copied. By using **NULL** as the second argument, we let the function allocate storage for the buffer.

Another code fragment

```
if (strcmp(argv[argc - 1], argv[file]) == 0)
    fputs("Can't append file to itself\n",stderr);
```

prevents the program from trying to append a file to itself. The argument **argv[argc – 1]** represents name of the final command-line argument, and **argv[file]** represents the name of the file currently being processed.

The **append( )** function does the copying. It uses **fread( )** and **fwrite( )** to copy 1024 bytes at a time, instead of one byte at a time:

```
void append(source, dest)
FILE *source, *dest;
{
  size_t bytes;
  extern char temp[];

  while ((bytes = fread(temp,sizeof(char),BUFSIZE,source)) > 0)
    fwrite(temp, sizeof (char), bytes, dest);
}
```

Because the file specified by **dest** is opened in the append mode, each source file is added to the end of the destination file.

12.10 Summary

Writing to and reading from files is essential for some C programs. Most C implementations offer low-level and standard I/O services for these purposes. Because the ANSI C library includes the standard I/O services and not the low-level ones, the standard package is more portable.

The standard I/O package automatically creates input and output buffers to speed up data transfer. The **fopen( )** function opens a file for standard I/O and creates a data structure designed to hold information about the file and the buffer. This function returns a pointer to the data structure, and the pointer is used by other functions to identify the file to be processed.

ANSI C provides two file-opening modes: binary and text. When a file is opened in the binary mode, it can be read byte for byte. When a file is opened in the text mode, the file contents may be mapped from the system representation of text to the C representation. For UNIX systems the two modes are identical, for the C model for text files is derived from the UNIX file model.

The most common input functions—**getc( )**, **fgets( )**, **fscanf( )**, and **fread( )**—normally read a file sequentially, starting at the beginning of the file.However, the **fseek( )** and **ftell( )** functions let a program move to an arbitrary position in a file, enabling random access.

Review Questions

1. What's wrong with this program?

```
main()
{
  int *fp;
  int k;

  fp = fopen("gelatin");
  for (k = 0; k < 30; k++)
    fputs(fp, "Nanette eats gelatin.");
  fclose("gelatin");
}
```

2. What does the following program do?

```
#include <stdio.h>
#include <ctype.h>
main(argc,argv)
int argc;
char *argv[];
{
  int ch;
  FILE *fp;

  if ( (fp = fopen(argv[1], "r")) == NULL)
    exit(1);
  while ( (ch = getc(fp)) != EOF )
    if( isdigit(ch) )
      putchar(ch);
  fclose (fp);
}
```

3. Suppose we have these statements in a program:

```
#include <stdio.h>
FILE *fp1,fp2;
char ch;

fp1 = fopen("terky", "r");
fp2 = fopen("jerky", "w");
```

Also suppose all files are opened successfully. Supply the missing arguments in the following function calls:

a. ch = getc( );
b. fprintf(, %c\n ,);
c. putc(,);
d. fclose( );   /* close the terky file */

4. Write a program that takes either zero or one command-line argument. If there is one argument, it is interpreted as the name of a file. If there is no argument, the standard input (**stdin**) is to be used for input. Assume that the input consists entirely of floating-point numbers. Have the program calculate and report the arithmetic mean (the average) of the input numbers.

5. Write a program that takes two command-line arguments: The first is a character; the second is a filename. The program should print those lines in the file that contains the given character. Note: File lines are identified by a terminating `'\n'`. Assume that no line is more than 256 characters long. Also, you may wish to use **fgets( )**.

6. What's the difference between binary files and text files on the one hand versus binary streams and text streams on the other?

7. What's the difference between the following:

a. Saving **8238201** using **fprintf( )** and saving it using **fwrite( )**

b. Saving the character **S** using **putc( )** and saving it using **fwrite( )**

8. What's the difference among the following?

```
printf("Hello, %s\n", name);
fprintf(stdout, "Hello, %s, name);
fprintf(stderr, "Hello, %s, name);
```

9. The **"a+"**, **"r+"**, and **"w+"** modes all open files for both reading and writing. Which one is best suited to altering material already present in a file?

Programming Exercises

1. Write a file copy program that uses the original filename and the copy filename as command-line arguments. Use low-level I/O and the binary mode, if possible. Copy in chunks of 512 bytes. To open the copy file, use the mode **O_CREAT | O_WRONLY | O_BINARY**.

2. Write a file copy program that uses the original filename and the copy filename as command-line arguments. Use standard I/O and the binary mode, if possible.

3. Write a program that will take all files given by a series of command-line arguments and print them one after the other on the screen. Use **argc** to set up a loop.

4. Modify the program in Listing 12.8 so that it recognizes an optional flag of the form **–n**, in which **n** is an integer. Have the program print the last **n** lines of listed file(s).

5. Write a program that opens two files whose names are provided by command-line arguments.

a. Have it print line 1 of the first file, line 1 of the second file, line 2 of the first file, line 2 of the second file, and so on, until the last line of the longer file (in terms of lines) is printed.

b. Modify the program so that lines with the same line number are printed on the same line.

6. Write a program that takes as command-line arguments a character and zero or more filenames. If no arguments follow the input character, have the program read standard input. Otherwise, have it open the files in turn. Have the program report on how many times the given character appears in each file; the filename and the character itself should be reported along with the count. Include error-checking for the number of arguments and to see if the files can be opened. If a file can't be opened, have the program report that fact and go on to the next file.

7. Modify Programming Exercise 6 so that it recognizes a **-t** option that causes it to report the cumulative total for all files read.

8. Modify the program in Listing 12.5 so that each word is numbered according to the order in which it is added to the list, with the first word being number 1. Make sure that when the program is run a second time that new word numbering resumes where the previous numbering left off.

9. Write a program that opens a text file whose name is obtained interactively. Set up a loop that asks the user to enter a file position. The program then prints out the part of the file starting at that position and proceeding to the next newline character. Let nonnumeric input terminate the user-input loop.

10. Write a program that reads two command-line arguments:. The first is a string; the second is the name of a file. The program then should search the file, printing all lines containing the string. Because the objective is line-oriented rather than character-oriented, use **fgets( )** rather than **getc( )**. Use a function like **string_in( )** from Chapter 11, Programming Exercise 7, to search each line for the string.

11. Write a function that reads one word from a file, leaving the boundary character (a tab, space, or newline) in the input buffer. The function should skip over initial whitespace. Have it take as arguments a string pointer and a file pointer. Have it return the pointer to the string if successful and the **NULL** pointer if **EOF** is encountered. Don't use **scanf( )** or **fscanf( )**.

12. Programs using command-line arguments rely on the user remembering how to use them correctly. Rewrite the program in Listing 12.9 so that instead of using command-line arguments, it prompts the user for the required information.

13

Storage Classes and Program Development

Contents

Objectives

Understanding automatic, external, static, and register storage classes

Knowing the scope and duration of variables

Understanding the difference between defining declarations and referencing declarations

Learning about the type qualifiers **const** and **volatile**

Practicing top-down programming

Thinking of a function as a black box with information flow

Using data verification

Using the selection sort algorithm

Understanding design differences between interactive and file-oriented programs

ne of C's strengths is that it lets you control the fine points of a program. C's storage classes are an example of such control; they allow you to determine which functions know which variables and how long a variable persists in a program. Storage classes form the first topic of this chapter.

A second topic is that there is more to programming than simply knowing the rules of the language, just as there is more to writing a novel (or even a letter) than knowing the rules of English. In this chapter, we reinforce some of the general principles and concepts of program design that we've introduced earlier. We also develop several useful functions. As we do so, we try to demonstrate some of the considerations that go into the designing of a function. In particular, we emphasize the value of a modular approach.

13.1 Storage Classes and Scope

We gave storage classes passing mention in Chapter 10. We take a longer look now. In Chapter 9, we mentioned that local variables are known only to the functions containing them. C also offers the possibility of global variables known to several functions. Suppose, for example, we want both **main( )** and **critic( )** to have access to the variable **units**. We can accomplish this task by assigning **units** to the external storage class, as shown in Listing 13.1.

❖ *global.c*

Listing 13.1

```
/* global.c */
#include <stdio.h>
int units; /* an external variable */
void critic();
main()
{
   extern int units;

   printf("How many pounds to a firkin of butter?\n");
   scanf("%d", &units);
   while ( units != 56)
      critic();
   printf("You must have looked it up!\n");
}
void critic()
{
   extern int units;

   printf("No luck, chummy. Try again.\n");
   scanf("%d", &units);
}
```

Here is a sample output:

```
How many pounds to a firkin of butter?
14
No luck, chummy. Try again.
56
You must have looked it up!
(We did.)
```

Note how the second value for **units** is read by the **critic( )** function, and **main( )** also knows the new value when it quits the **while** loop.

We made **units** an external variable by defining it outside (external to) any function definition. Then inside the functions that use the variable, we declare the variable by preceding the variable type with the keyword **extern**. This keyword informs the computer to look for the definition of this variable outside the function.

If we omit **extern** (but retain **int units;**) in, say, **main( )**, the computer sets up a separate variable private to **main( )** but also named **units**. The new **units** is visible while **main( )** is running. But when control passes to **critic( )**, the program interprets **units** to be the externally defined variable, and the value assigned to **units** in **main( )** does not affect the value of **units** in **critic( )**.

If we omit any **units** within **main( )**, then **main( )** uses the external definition of **units** by default. Thus, declaring **units** in **main( )** as storage class **extern** primarily is an act of documentation.

As we know, each variable has a type. In addition, each variable has a storage class. Four keywords are used to describe storage classes: **extern** (for external), **auto** (for automatic), **static**, and **register**. Variables declared within a function are considered to be class **auto** unless declared otherwise. The formal arguments to functions necessarily are class **auto**.

The storage class of a variable is determined by where it is defined and by what keyword, if any, is used. The storage class determines two things. First, it controls which functions have access to a variable. The extent to which a variable is available is called its *scope*. Second, the storage class determines how long the variable persists in memory. Let's go over the properties of the four types of storage class.

Automatic Variables

By default, variables declared in a function are automatic. You can, however, make your intentions clear by using the keyword **auto**:

```
main()
{
   auto int plox;
```

You may choose to declare a variable explicitly, for example, to document that you are intentionally overriding an external function definition.

An automatic variable has local scope. Only the function in which the variable is defined knows the variable. (Of course, arguments can be used to communicate the value and the address of the variable to another function, but such communication is partial and indirect knowledge.) Other functions can use variables with the same name, but they are then independent variables stored in different memory locations.

An automatic variable comes into existence when the function that contains it is called. When the function finishes its task and returns control to its caller, the automatic variable disappears. The memory location can then be used for something else.

An additional point about the scope of an automatic variable: the scope is confined to the block (paired braces) in which the variable is declared. We have always declared our variables at the beginning of the function block, so the scope is the entire function. But in principle, one can declare a variable within a subblock. Then that variable would be known only to that subsection of the function. Normally, you don't use this feature when designing a program. However, harried programmers sometimes use this option when trying to make a quick fix.

Initialization of Automatic Variables

Automatic variables are not initialized unless you do so explicitly. Consider the following declarations:

```
main()
{
    int repid;
    int tents = 5;
```

The **tents** variable is initialized to **5**, but the **repid** variables value is determined by whatever bits happen to occupy the space previously assigned to **repid**. Note: You cannot rely on these bits being set to **0**.

External Variables

A variable defined outside a function belongs to the external storage class. As a matter of documentation, an external variable also should be declared in a function that uses it by using the **extern** keyword. Declarations look like the following:

```
int errupt;           /* 2 externally defined variables */
char coal;
double up[100];       /* externally defined array */
main()
{
    extern int errupt;    /* declaring that 2 variables are */
    extern char coal;     /* defined externally */
    extern double up[];   /* plus one array */
```

The group of **extern** declarations may be omitted entirely if the original definitions occur in the same file and before the function that uses them. Including the **extern** keyword allows a function to use an external variable even if it is defined later in a file or in a different file. (Both files, of course, have to be compiled, linked, or assembled together.)

If only the **extern** variable is omitted from the declaration in a function, then a separate, automatic variable is set up by that name. You may want to label this second variable **auto** to show that your coding is a matter of intention and not of oversight.

Three examples show the four possible combinations of **extern** declarations. In the first example, there is one external variable **hocus**, and it is known to both **main( )** and **magic( )**:

```
/* Example 1 */
int hocus;
int magic();
main()
{
   extern int hocus;   /* hocus declared external */
   ...
}
int magic()
{
   extern int hocus;
   ...
}
```

In the second example, there is also one external variable **hocus** known to both functions.

```
/* Example 2 */
int hocus;
int magic();
main()
{
   extern int hocus;   /* hocus declared external */
   ...
}
int magic()
{
   /* hocus not declared at all */
   ...
}
```

This time, **magic( )** knows this information by default.

In the third example, three separate variables are created:

```
/* Example 3 */
int hocus;
int magic();
main()
{
    int hocus;          /* hocus declared, is auto by default */
    ...
}
int magic()
{
    auto int hocus;     /* hocus declared automatic */
    ...
}
```

The **hocus** in **main( )** is automatic by default and is local to **main( )**. The **hocus** in **magic( )** is automatic explicitly and is known only to **magic( )**. The external **hocus** is not known to **main( )** or **magic( )** but is known to any other function in the file that does not have its own local **hocus**.

These examples illustrate the scope of external variables. They persist as long as the program runs, and since they aren't confined to any one function, they don't disappear when a particular function ends its task. Note: If you use just the keyword **extern** without a type, the compiler interprets that as being **extern int**.

Initializing External Variables

Like automatic variables, external variables can be initialized explicitly. Unlike automatic variables, external variables are automatically initialized to zero if you don't initialize them; this feature also applies to elements of an externally defined array.

External Names

The rules for external variable names are more restrictive than those for local variables. The reason is that external names need to comply with the rules of the local environment, which may be more limiting. For local names, the ANSI C standard requires that a compiler distinguish between uppercase and lowercase characters and that it recognize the first 31 characters in a name. For external variables, the compiler need not distinguish between uppercase and lowercase, and it need only recognize the first 8 characters in a name. These rules also apply to function names.

Definitions and Declarations

Consider this example:

```
int tern;
main()
{
    external int tern;
    ...
```

Here **tern** is declared twice. The first declaration causes storage to be set aside for the variable; hence, it constitutes a "definition" of the variable. The second declaration merely tells the compiler to use the **tern** variable that previously has been created; thus, it is not a definition. The first declaration is also called a *defining declaration;* the second form is called a *referencing declaration.* The keyword **extern** *always* indicates that a declaration is not a definition, since it instructs the compiler to look elsewhere. Suppose, for instance, you write the following code:

```
extern int tern;
main()
{

...
```

Then the compiler assumes that the actual definition of **tern** is somewhere else in your program, perhaps in another file. This declaration does not cause space to be allocated; so don't use the keyword **extern** to create an external definition. Use **extern** only to refer to an existing external definition.

An external variable can be initialized only once, and that must occur when the variable is defined. A statement like

```
extern char permis = 'Y';        /* error */
```

is in error, for the presence of the keyword **extern** indicates that this statement is a referencing declaration, not a defining declaration.

Static Variables

The name *static variable* sounds like a contradiction, like a variable that can't vary. Actually, the term "static" means the variable stays put. These variables have the same scope as automatic variables, but they don't vanish when the containing function ends its job. The computer remembers their values from one function call to the next. The example in Listing 13.2 illustrates this point and shows how to declare a static variable.

❖ *static.c*

Listing 13.2

```
/* static.c--using a static variable */
#include <stdio.h>
void trystat();
main()
{
   int count;

   for (count = 1; count <= 3; count++)
   {
      printf("Here comes iteration %d:\n", count);
      trystat();
   }
}
```

Listing 13.2
(cont'd.)

```
void trystat()
{
    int fade = 1;
    static int stay = 1;

    printf("fade = %d and stay = %d\n", fade++, stay++);
}
```

Note that **trystat( )** increments each variable after printing its value. Running the program gives this output:

```
Here comes iteration 1:
fade = 1 and stay = 1
Here comes iteration 2:
fade = 1 and stay = 2
Here comes iteration 3:
fade = 1 and stay = 3
```

The static variable **stay** remembers that its value was increased by 1, and the **fade** variable starts anew each time. This situation points out a difference in initialization: **fade** is initialized each time **trystat( )** is called, whereas **stay** is initialized just once, when **trystat( )** is compiled.

Static Initialization

Like external variables, static variables are initialized to zero if you don't explicitly initialize them to some other value.

External Static Variables

You can also declare a **static** variable outside any function. This act creates an *external static function*. The difference between an ordinary external variable and an external static variable lies in the scope. The ordinary external variable can be used by functions in any file, and the external static variable can be used only by functions in the same file and following the variable definition. To set up an external static variable, place the definition outside any function:

```
static randx = 1;
int rand()
{
```

See Figure 13.1. Later in this chapter we show you an example for which you need this sort of variable.

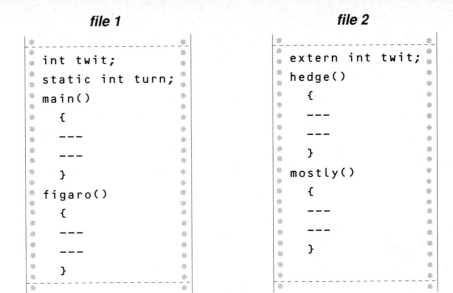

Figure 13.1

External variable versus external static variable

file 1

```
int twit;
static int turn;
main()
    {
    ---
    ---
    }
figaro()
    {
    ---
    ---
    }
```

file 2

```
extern int twit;
hedge()
    {
    ---
    ---
    }
mostly()
    {
    ---
    ---
    }
```

`Twit` *is known to* `main()`, `figaro()`, `hedge()`, *and* `mostly()`

`Turn` *is known to* `main()` *and* `figaro()` *only*

Multiple Files

Complex C programs often use several files of code, and sometimes these files may need to share an external variable. The ANSI C method for accomplishing this task is to have a defining declaration in one file and referencing declarations in the other files using that variable. That is, all but one declaration (the defining declaration) should use the **extern** keyword, and only the defining declaration can be used to initialize the variable.

Note that an external variable defined in one file is not available to a second file unless it is also declared in the second file; external variables are not automatically made available to all files. Historically, however, many compilers have followed different rules in this regard. Many UNIX systems, for example, allow you to declare a variable in several files without using the **extern** keyword, providing that no more than one declaration includes an initialization. If there is a declaration with an initialization, it is taken to be the definition.

Scope and Functions

Functions, too, have storage classes. A function can either be external (the default) or static. An external function can be accessed by other files, and a static function can be used only within the defining file. Consider, for example, a file containing these function declarations:

```
double gamma();        /* external by default */
static double beta();
extern double delta();
```

The functions **gamma( )** and **delta( )** can be used in other files that are part of the program, whereas **beta( )** cannot. Because this **beta( )** is restricted to one file, you can use a different function having the same name in the other files. One reason to use the **static** storage class is to create functions that are private to a particular module, avoiding the possibility of name conflicts.

Under ANSI C the recommended practice is to use the **extern** keyword when declaring functions that are defined in another file. This recommendation is mostly a matter of clarity, since a function declaration is assumed to be **extern** unless the keyword **static** is used.

Register Variables

Variables normally are stored in computer memory. With luck, **register** variables are stored in the CPU registers, where they can be accessed and manipulated more rapidly than in memory. In other respects, **register** variables are the same as automatic variables. They are set up this way:

```
main()
{
    register int quick;
```

We say "with luck," for declaring a variable as **register** class is more a request than a direct order. The compiler has to weigh your demands against the number of registers that are available. Depending on this number, the compiler may designate the variable as an ordinary automatic variable. The types of variables that can be declared **register** may also be restricted. For example, the registers in a processor may not be large enough to hold type **double**. In addition, a processor may not have addresses for its registers, so the **&** operator may not work with **register** variables.

Scope Summary

At this point, let's summarize the scope of the various storage classes. The scope of an automatic variable, including formal arguments to functions, is confined to the defining function. When a variable is declared external to any function in a file, that external variable is known to all functions following it in that file, whether or not those functions explicitly declare the variable as **extern**. If you want a function in a second file to access an external variable in the first file, then you must declare the variable in the second file using the keyword **extern**.

A static variable defined inside a function is local to the function. A static variable defined outside a function is local to that file.

Which Storage Class?

The answer to the question "Which storage class?" most often is "automatic." After all, **auto** is the default. At first glance, external storage is quite alluring: Just make all your variables external, and you'll never have to worry about using arguments and pointers to communicate back and forth between functions. Unfortunately, you do have to worry about function A( ) sneakily altering variables in function C( ), although such was not your intention. The evidence of untold years of collective computer experience is that the latter danger far outweighs the superficial charms of using external storage indiscriminately.

One of the golden rules of protective programming is to observe the "need to know" principle. Keep the workings of each function as private as possible, sharing values only as they are needed.

Since there are times when the other classes are useful, they are available. But ask yourself if it is necessary to use one before doing so.

► Summary: Storage Classes

Keywords: auto, extern, static, and **register**

General Comments. The storage class of a variable determines its scope and how long the variable persists. Storage class is determined by where the variable is defined and by the associated keyword. Variables defined outside a function are external and have global scope. Variables declared inside a function are automatic and local unless one of the other keywords is used. External variables defined before a function are known to it even if not declared internally.

Properties.

Those preceding the dotted line are declared inside a function. Those following the line are defined outside a function.

Storage Class	Keyword	Duration	Scope
Automatic	**auto**	Temporary	Local
Register	**register**	Temporary	Local
Static	**static**	Persistent	Local
External	**extern***	Persistent	Global (all files)
External static	**static**	Persistent	Global (one file)

*The keyword **extern** is used only to redeclare variables that have been defined externally elsewhere; the act of defining the variable outside a function makes it external.

13.2 ANSI C Type Qualifiers

We've seen that a variable is characterized by its type and its storage class. ANSI C adds two more properties to that list: *constancy* and *volatility*. The presence of these properties is indicated by the keywords **const** and **volatile**; these keywords are used in declarations to create *qualified types*.

The **const** keyword in a declaration establishes a variable whose value cannot be modified by assignment, incrementing, or decrementing. On an ANSI-compliant compiler, the code

```
const int nochange;      /* qualifies m as being constant */
nochange = 12;           /* not allowed */
```

should produce an error message. However, you can initialize a **const** variable, therefore the following code is valid.

```
const int nochange = 12;      /* ok */
```

This declaration makes **nochange** a read-only variable; once initialized, it cannot be changed.

Use of the **const** keyword with pointers is more complicated, for we have to distinguish between making the pointer itself **const** and making the value that is pointed to be **const**. The declaration

```
const float *pf;            /* pf points to a constant float value */
```

establishes that **pf** points to a value that must remain constant. The value of **pf** itself can be changed, which means it can be set to point at another **const** value. In contrast, the declaration

```
float * const pt;           /* pt is a const pointer */
```

says that the pointer **pt** itself cannot have its value changed. It must always point to the same address. However, the pointed-to value can change. Finally, the declaration

```
const float * const ptr;
```

means that **ptr** must always point to the same location and that the value stored at that location also must not be changed by the program.

One common use of **const** is to declare pointers that serve as formal function parameters. For example, consider the function **strlen( )**. We pass it a pointer to the beginning of the string whose length it is to find. In general, passing a pointer to a function enables the function to alter data in the calling function. But the declaration

```
int strlen(const char * str)  /* ANSI form */
```

prevents any modification of data, for it says that the data **str** points to cannot be changed. Thus, expressions like ***str = '!'** are not allowed. Yet **str** itself can be altered, so the program can use **str++** in its code.

The ANSI C library follows this practice. If a pointer is passed just to give a function access to values in the calling program, it's declared a pointer to a **const**-qualified type.

If the pointer is passed so the program can alter data in the calling program, then the **const** keyword isn't used. For instance, the ANSI C declaration of **strcat( )** is the following:

```
char *strcat(char *, const char *);
```

Recall that the **strcat( )** function adds a copy of the second string to the end of the first string. The action modifies the first string but leaves the second string unchanged.

The volatile *Type Qualifier*

The **volatile** qualifier indicates that the concerned variable can have its value altered by agencies other than the program. Typically it is used for addresses used by hardware. For instance, an address may hold the current clock time. The value changes as time changes. Or the address may be used to receive information transmitted from, say, another computer.

The **volatile** syntax is the same as the **const**:

```
volatile int loc1;  /* loc1 is a volatile location */
volatile int *ploc; /* ploc points to a volatile location */
```

Actually, a value can be both **const** and **volatile**. For instance, the clock setting should normally not be changed by the program, making it **const**; and it may be changed by an agency other than the program, making it **volatile**. For such a declaration, use both qualifiers in any order.

```
volatile const int loc;
const volatile int *ploc;
```

At this point, you may think that **volatile** is an interesting concept but be wondering why the ANSI committee felt it necessary to make it a keyword. The reason is to facilitate compiler optimization. Suppose, for example, you have code like the following:

```
val1 = x;
...        /* some code not using x */
val2 = x;
```

A smart compiler may notice that you use **x** twice and temporarily store the **x** value in a register. Then when **x** is needed for **val2**, it can save time by reading the value from a register instead of from the original memory location. This procedure is called *caching*. Ordinarily, caching is a good optimization, but it is not if **x** is changed between the two statements by some other agency. If there were no **volatile** keyword, a compiler would have no way of knowing whether this situation might occur. Therefore, to be safe, the compiler couldn't cache. This scenario represents the pre-ANSI situation. Now however, if the **volatile** keyword is not used in the declaration, the compiler can assume a value hasn't changed between mentions, and it can attempt to optimize the code.

Let's now look at a random number function that makes use of an external static variable. The ANSI C library provides a **rand( )** function for random numbers, but it's instructive to make one ourselves. Actually, we create a "pseudorandom" number generator, in which the actual sequence of numbers is predictable although they are spread fairly uniformly over the possible range of values.

The scheme starts with a number called the *seed*. The function uses the seed to produce a new number, which becomes the new seed. Then the new seed can be used to produce a newer seed, and so on. For this scheme to work, the random number function must remember the seed it used the last time it was called, which calls for a static variable.

In the program in Listing 13.3, the static variable **randx** starts out with the value **1** and is altered by the magic formula each time the function is called. The result in systems with a two-byte **short** is a number somewhere in the range of –32768 to 32767. (We use the **short** cast because the size of **short** is more standard than the size of **int**.)

❖ rand0.c

Listing 13.3

```
/* rand0.c--produces random numbers */
rand0()
{
   static int randx = 1;

   randx = (randx * 25173 + 13849) % 65536;
                      /* magic formula */
   return( (short) randx);
}
```

Let's now add a simple driver. See Listing 13.4.

❖ r_drive1.c

Listing 13.4

```
/* r_drive1.c */
#include <stdio.h>
extern int rand0();     /* extern keyword is optional */
main()
{
   int count;

   for(count = 1; count <= 5; count++)
     printf("%d\n", rand0());
}
```

Here's a good chance to practice using multiple files. Use one file for Listing 13.4 and one for Listing 13.3. See Chapter 9 or your compiler manual for guidance. The **extern** keyword reminds us that **rand0( )** is defined in a separate file. The output follows:

```
-26514
-4449
20196
-20531
3882
```

This output seems random enough. Let's run it again:

```
-26514
-4449
20196
-20531
3882
```

The output is the same. This represents the "pseudo" aspect of the function. Each time the main program is run, we start off with the same seed of **1**. We can get around this problem by introducing a second function **srand1( )** that lets you reset the seed. The trick is to make **randx** an external static variable known only to **rand1( )** and **srand1( )**. (The ANSI equivalent to **srand1( )** is called **srand( )**.) Keep **rand1( )** and **srand1( )** in their own file and compile that file separately. See Listing 13.5.

❖ **s_and_r.c**

Listing 13.5

```
/* s_and_r.c--file for rand1() and srand1() */
static int randx = 1;
int rand1()
{
    randx = (randx *25173 + 13849) % 65536;
    return( (short) randx);
}
int srand1(x)
unsigned x;
{
    randx = x;
}
```

Notice that **randx** now is an external static variable, meaning that it can be used by both **rand1( )** and **srand1( )** but not by functions in other files. To test these functions, use the driver in Listing 13.6.

❖ **r_drive2.c**

Listing 13.6

```
/* r_drive2.c */
#include <stdio.h>
extern int srand1(), rand1();
main()
{
```

Listing 13.6

```
    int count;
    int seed;
    printf("Please enter your choice for seed.\n");
    scanf("%d", &seed);
    srand1(seed);   /* reset seed */
    for(count = 1; count <= 5; count++)
      printf("%d\n", rand1());
}
```

Again, use two files. Run the program once:

```
Please enter your choice for seed.
1
-26514
-4449
20196
-20531
3882
```

Using a value of **1** for **seed** yields the same values as before. Let's try a value of **3**:

```
Please enter your choice for seed.
3
23832
20241
-1858
-30417
-16204
```

We now get a different set of numbers. If your system provides a time function, you can use the time value to automate the reseeding of this function.

13.4 Roll 'Em

Let's develop a use for our set of random number functions by simulating dice-rolling. The most popular form of dice-rolling uses two 6-sided dice, although there are other possibilities. Many adventure-fantasy game players use all of the five geometrically possible dice: 4 sides, 6 sides, 8 sides, 12 sides, and 20 sides. (The ancient Greeks cleverly proved that there are but five regular solids having all faces the same shape and size, and these solids are the bases for the dice varieties. One could make dice with other numbers of sides, but the faces would not all be the same, so they wouldn't all have equal odds of turning up.)

Computer calculations aren't limited by geometric considerations, though, and we devise an electronic die that can have any number of sides we want. Let's start with 6 sides, then generalize. We want a random number from 1 to 6, but **rand1( )** produces the range –32768 to 32767, so we must make some adjustments. Here's one approach:

1. Divide the random number by 32768, which results in a number **x** in the range –1 <= **x** < 1. (We have to convert to type **float** so that we can have decimal fractions.)

2. Add 1. Our new number satisfies the relationship 0 <= **x** < 2.

3. Divide by 2. Now 0 <= **x** < 1.

4. Multiply by 6. Now 0 <= **x** < 6. (0 is not a desired value.)

5. Add 1. Now 1 <= **x** < 7. (Note: These are still decimal fractions.)

6. Truncate to an integer. Now we have an integer in the range of 1 to 6.

7. To generalize, just replace 6 in step 4 by the number of sides.

Listing 13.7 shows a function that follows the steps listed previously. We include some explicit type casts to emphasize where type conversions take place.

❖ *diceroll.c*

Listing 13.7

```
/* diceroll.c */
#define SCALE 32768.0
extern int rand1();
int rollem(sides)
int sides;
{
    float roll;

    roll = ( (float) rand1()/SCALE + 1.0) * sides / 2.0 + 1.0;
    return ( (int) roll);
}
```

Listing 13.8 shows a program that uses the tools we've developed thus far.

❖ *manydice.c*

Listing 13.8

```
/* manydice.c--multiple dice roll */
#include <stdio.h>
extern int srand1(), rollem();
main()
{
    int dice, count, roll, seed;
    int sides;

    printf("Enter a seed value.\n");
    scanf("%d", &seed);
    srand1(seed);
```

Listing 13.8
(cont'd.)

```
      printf("Enter the number of sides per die, 0 to stop.\n");
      while (scanf("%d", &sides) == 1 && sides > 0)
      {
         printf("How many dice?\n");
         scanf("%d", &dice);
         for ( roll = 0, count = 1; count <= dice; count ++)
            roll += rollem(sides); /* running total of dice pips */
         printf("You have rolled a %d using %d %d-sided dice.\n",
                roll, dice, sides);
         printf("How many sides? Enter 0 to stop.\n");
      }
      printf("GOOD FORTUNE TO YOU!\n");
}
```

Compile it with the files containing Listings 13.7 and 13.5. Then use it:

```
Enter a seed value.
1
Enter the number of sides per die, 0 to stop.
6
How many dice?
2
You have rolled a 4 using 2 6-sided dice.
How many sides? Enter 0 to stop.
6
How many dice?
2
You have rolled a 7 using 2 6-sided dice.
How many sides? Enter 0 to stop.
0
GOOD FORTUNE TO YOU!
```

You can use **rollem( )** in many ways. With **sides** equal to two, the function simulates a coin toss with "heads" = 2 and "tails" = 1, or vice versa. You can also easily modify the program to show the individual results as well as the total. Or you can construct a craps simulator. If you require a large number of rolls, as may occur in some role-playing games, you can modify the program with little trouble to produce output like the following:

```
Enter a seed value.
10
Enter the number of sets; enter q to stop.
18
How many sides and how many dice?
6 3
Here are 18 sets of 3 6-sided throws.
7 5 9 7 12 10 7 12 10 14 9 8 13 9 10 7 16 10
How many sets? Enter 0 to stop.
q
```

Again, remember that if your C implementation gives you access to some changing quantity such as the system clock, you can use that value (possibly truncated) to initialize the seed value. Another use of **rand1( )** (but not of **rollem( )**) is to create a number-guessing program. In such a program, the computer chooses and you guess.

13.5 Sorting Numbers

Let's develop some more functions. One of the most common tasks for a computer is sorting, therefore our next project is to design a program that reads in a list of integers and sorts them. Let's take a black-box approach and think in terms of input and output. Our overall plan is fairly simple. See Figure 13.2a.

At this point, the program is still too vaguely defined to code. The next step is to identify the main tasks that the program must do to accomplish our goals. We can break down our example into three main tasks:

1. Read in the numbers.

2. Sort them.

3. Print out the sorted numbers.

Figure 13.2b shows this breakdown as we move from the top level of organization down to a more detailed level.

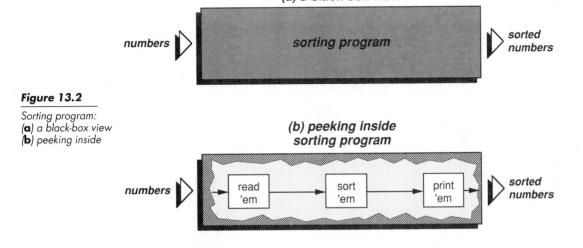

Figure 13.2

Sorting program:
(a) a black-box view
(b) peeking inside

Before designing the individual modules, we need to make some global decisions: We need to choose a data form and decide what information need be passed to the individual modules.

Data Form

How do we represent a collection of numbers? We can use a collection of variables, one for each number—a method that is just too much trouble to even think about. More practically, we can use an array, one element for each number.

But what kind of array? Type **int**? Type **double**? We need to know how the program is going to be used. Let's assume it is to be used with integers, so we develop an array of integers to store the numbers we read.

Information Flow

The first module gathers input. It should know where to place the data it gets, and it should know the maximum number of values that can be accepted. Also, it should report back the actual number of items read. The sorting module should know which array to sort and how many elements are present. The printing module needs to know which array to print and how many elements to print.

These considerations suggest the **main( )** function shown in Listing 13.9, in which we get the overall view of the program.

❖ *sort_int.c*

Listing 13.9

```
/* sort_int.c--sorts integers */
#define MAXSIZE 100/* limit to number of integers to sort */
extern int getarray();
extern void sort(), print();
main()
{
   int numbers[MAXSIZE];   /* array to hold input */
   int size;               /* number of input items */

   size = getarray(numbers, MAXSIZE);
                           /* put input into array */
   sort(numbers, size);    /* sort the array */
   print(numbers, size);   /* print the sorted array */
}
```

The function **getarray( )** places the input into the array **numbers** and reports back how many values are read in; that value is assigned to **size**. Then **sort( )** and **print( )** sort the array and print the results.

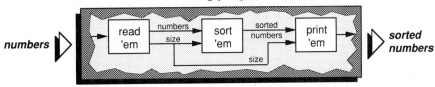

sorting program

Figure 13.3

Sorting program:
adding details

Now that we have refined our picture of the information flow, we should modify our black box sketch. See Figure 13.3. As you can see, we have three black boxes, each with its own input and output. We can assign each part to a different programming team, providing we make sure that the numbers output by "read 'em" are in the same form that they are sorted for input.

We are emphasizing modularity: We have broken the original problem into three smaller, more manageable problems. Now we apply our efforts to each of the three boxes separately, breaking them down into simpler units until we reach a point at which the code is obvious. As we do so, we pay attention to three important points: dataform choice, error-trapping, and information flow.

Reading In Numeric Data

Let's continue with our example, tackling the reading module first. See Figure 13.4.

Many programs involve reading in numbers, so the ideas we develop here will be useful elsewhere. The general form is clear: Use a loop to read in numbers until all the numbers are read. But there is more to it than you may think!

Ending Input

How will the program know how many numbers to read? We faced a similar problem in Chapter 10, in which we had a **read_array( )** function that quit reading numbers when the user simulated **EOF** or entered a nonnumeric value. This time we take a different

Figure 13.4

Sorting program:
the first task

tack. The main change is in the handling of nonnumeric input. Now we instruct the program to alert the user that the input is nonnumeric and then let the user try again.

Why this change? Suppose you are entering data at the keyboard and accidentally enter 1o instead of 10. Would you rather have the program terminate, forcing you to reenter all the data, or have it reject only the one entry and let you continue? Of course, it is simpler to rely on the "perfect user theory," which states that the user makes no entry errors. However, we recognize that this theory may not apply to all users. This checking of input for suitability is termed *data validation*. Here is one approach:

read *a word*
while *not* **EOF**
    if *the word is an integer, assign it to an array*
    else *skip word and request numeric input*
    read *the next word if the array isn't full*

Note that two separate conditions can terminate this section of the program: an **EOF** signal or filling the array.

Further Considerations

Before we set down any C code, we still have decisions to make. The data validation to which we've committed ourselves has two aspects: detecting an error and reporting the error to the user. We can try to code these instructions directly into **getarray( )**, or we can put the code into an input function used by **getarray( )**. We adopt an intermediate approach here that follows a common C style: We give the input function the responsibility to detect errors, and we give the calling function (**getarray( )**) the responsibility to handle the error. This method provides flexibility, for the same input function can be used in programs that process errors differently.

The getarray( ) Function

Let's look at the **getarray( )** function. See Listing 13.10.

❖ *getarray.c*

Listing 13.10

```
/* getarray.c--reads in an array */
#include <stdio.h>
#include "getint.h"/* declares getint(), constants */
int getarray( array, limit)
int array[], limit;
{
    int num, status;
    int index = 0; /* array index */

    printf("This program stops reading numbers ");
    printf("after %d values\n", limit);
```

Listing 13.10
(cont'd.)

```
    while( index < limit && (status = getint(&num)) != EOF )
    {
       if ( status == YESNUM)
       {
          array[index++] = num;
          printf("The number %d has been accepted.\n", num);
       }
       else if ( status == NONUM)
          printf("That was no integer! Try again.\n");
       else
          printf("This can't happen! Something's very wrong.\n");
    }
    if ( index == limit )   /* report if array gets filled */
       printf("All %d elements of the array were filled.\n",
              limit);
    return(index);
}
```

The function is not a simple one, and we have quite a few points to note.

Explanation

The **getarray( )** function is premised on the existence of a **getint( )** function with the following properties:

1. The **getint( )** function returns a status of **YESNUM** if it has read an integer, and it places the value in the location pointed to by its argument, which should be a pointer-to-**int**.

2. It returns a status of **NONUM** if it reads a noninteger, and it discards the invalid input.

3. It returns a value of **EOF** if it encounters end-of-file.

4. The **getint.h** file contains the function declaration and definitions of the status values.

The implementation of this function comes on the next level of our top-down approach. Using the status codes, we set up **getarray( )** to handle each of the possible status values. An **EOF** status causes the reading cycle to end when **getint( )** detects an **EOF** signal. A **YESNUM** status results in the number being stored in the awaiting array. Also, the number is echoed back to the user to let him or her know that it was accepted. A **NONUM** status sends the user back for another try.

But notice in Listing 13.10 that there is also another **else** statement. Logically, the only way that statement can be reached is if **getint( )** returns a value other than –1, 0, or 1. Yet those are the only values that can be returned, so this statement seems useless. We include it as an example of *defensive programming,* the art of protecting a program from future fiddling. We, or someone else, may someday decide to add a few more possible status values to the **getint( )** repertoire. Most likely we will have forgotten, and they may never have known, that **getarray( )** assumes that there are just three possible responses. We therefore include this final **else** statement to trap any new responses that may show up at that time.

We use the keyword **return** to communicate back the number of items read. Thus our function call

```
size = getarray(numbers, MAXSIZE);
```

assigns a value to **size** and gives values to the **numbers** array.

In functions involving counters and limits, like this one, the most likely place to find errors is at the *boundary conditions,* where counts reach their limits. Are we going to read a maximum of **MAXSIZE** numbers, or are we going to be off by one? We need to pay attention to details such as **++index** versus **index++** and **<** versus **<=**. We also have to keep in mind that arrays start their subscripting with **0**, not **1**. Check through Listing 13.10 and see if it works as it should. The easiest way to do so is to imagine that **limit** is **1** and then walk through the procedure step by step.

Finally, the function informs the user when the array is full so that he or she is not taken by surprise.

The getint( ) Function

We need to supply a **getint( )** function, which we can create from the existing library functions. Listing 13.11 shows an implementation based on **scanf( )**.

❖ *getint.c*

Listing 13.11

```
/* getint.c */
#include <stdio.h>
#include "getint.h"
int getint(ptint)
int *ptint;        /* pointer to integer output */
{
   int status;

   status = scanf("%d", ptint);
   if (status == NONUM)
      scanf("%*s");
   return status;
}
```

We also need a **getint.h** file:

```
/* getint.h -- definitions used by getint() */
#define NONUM 0
#define YESNUM 1
extern int getint();
```

Recall that **scanf( )** returns the number of items successfully read. If it finds an **int**, it returns **1**, or **YESNUM**. If it finds a noninteger, it returns **0**, or **NONUM**. And it returns **EOF** on detecting the end of the file. Our **getint( )** function merely passes these return values along. If the return value is **0**, the function skips over the invalid input. Recall that the **%*s** specifier causes **scanf( )** to skip over the next word. If **status** is **0**, then the input is not an integer, so we want to skip it. Otherwise, **scanf( )** remains stuck on that data item.

Often the most difficult part of a program is getting it to interact in a convenient and dependable manner with the user. Such is the case with this program. Now that we have completed **getarray( )** and **getint( )**, we find **sort( )** and **print( )** easier to implement.

Sorting the Data

Let's look at **main( )** again:

```
/* sort_int.c--sorts integers */
#define MAXSIZE 10 /* limit to number of integers to sort */
int getarray();
void sort(), print();
main()
{
    int numbers[MAXSIZE];          /* array to hold input */
    int size;                      /* number of input items */

    size = getarray(numbers, MAXSIZE);
                                   /* put input into array */
    sort(numbers, size);           /* sort the array */
    print(numbers, size);          /* print the sorted array */
}
```

We see that the input to **sort( )** is an array of integers to be sorted and a count of the number of elements to be sorted. The output is the array containing the sorted numbers. We still haven't decided how to accomplish the sorting, so we need to refine this description further. See Figure 13.5.

One obvious point to decide is the direction of the sort: from large to small or small to large. We arbitrarily select to sort from large to small. (We can also make a program sort

Figure 13.5

Sorting program: the second task

numbers

size

sort'em

numbers

in either direction , but then we would have to develop a way to tell the program which choice we want.)

Let's consider our method. Many sorting algorithms have been developed for computers. Here we use one of the simplest, the selection sort we introduced in Chapter 11. Here is our plan in pseudocode:

for n = *first to* **n** = *next-to-last element,*
find largest remaining number and place it in the **n**-*th element*

It works as follows. First, **n** = 1. We look through the entire array, find the largest number, and place it in the first element. Then **n** = 2, and we look through all but the first element of the array, find the largest remaining number, and place it in the second element. We continue this process until we reach the next-to-last element, at which point only two elements are left. We compare these elements and place the larger in the next-to-last position, which leaves the smallest element in the final position. See Figure 13.6.

The procedure looks like a **for** loop task, but we still have to describe the "find and place" process in more detail. One way to select the largest remaining value is to compare the first and second elements of the remaining array. If the second is larger, switch the two values. Now compare the first element with the third. If the third is larger, switch those two. Each time, the larger element floats to the top. Continue in this fashion until you have compared the first with the last element. When you finish, the largest number is now the first element of the remaining array. In essence, we have sorted the array for the first element, but the rest of the array is in a jumble.

In pseudocode

for n = *second element to last element,*
compare **n**th *element with first element;*
if nth is greater, swap values

looks like another **for** loop, which is nested in the first **for** loop. The outer loop indicates which array element is to be filled, and the inner loop finds the value to put there.

Figure 13.6

Sorting program: the third task

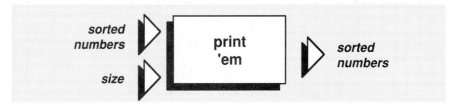

Combining the two pieces of the previously listed pseudocode and translating into C, we achieve the function in Listing 13.12.

Listing 13.12

```
/* sort.c--sorts an integer array in decreasing order */
void sort(array, limit)
int array[], limit;
{
   int top, search, temp;

   for ( top = 0 ; top < limit -1 ; top++)
      for ( search = top + 1; search < limit; search++)
         if ( array[search] > array[top])
         {
            temp = array[search];
            array[search] = array[top];
            array[top] = temp;
         }
}
```

Here we remember that the first element has **0** for a subscript. Also, we use the swapping technique we discussed in Chapter 9. Notice that we use **top** as the subscript for the array element that is to be filled, since it is at the top of the unsorted part of the array. The **search** index roams over the array below the current **top** element.

Printing the Data

The program in Listing 13.13 is fairly straightforward.

Listing 13.13

```
/* print.c--print an array */
#include <stdio.h>
void print(array, limit)
int array[], limit;
{
   int index;

   for ( index = 0; index < limit; index++)
      printf("%d\n", array[index]);
}
```

If we want something a little different, such as printing in rows instead of in one column, we can always alter the function, leaving the other functions untouched. Similarly, if we find a sorting algorithm we like better, we can replace that module. That is one of the nice features about a modular program.

Let's compile and test the package. To make checking the boundary conditions simpler, we temporarily change **MAXSIZE** to **5**. For our first test, we feed numbers into the program until it refuses to take more:

```
This program stops reading numbers after 5 values
or if EOF is encountered.
12 34 54 23 67 232[enter]
All 5 elements of the array were filled.
67
54
34
23
12
```

Our first test is a success; the program halts when five numbers are read, and it sorts the results.

Now we test to see if the program stops when end-of-file is encountered.

```
This program stops reading numbers after 5 values
or if EOF is encountered.
456 928
-23 +16
[control-d]    ⇐(Transmits EOF on UNIX system)
928
456
16
-23
```

The four-element array is sorted, and the program halts input on encountering **EOF**. (Recall that Control-Z transmits **EOF** on MS DOS systems.)

Note: We should point out that the Microsoft C version of this program requires us to press Enter twice if the **EOF** signal (Control-Z) is the first entry on a line. Apparently, the Micosoft version of **scanf( )** works slightly differently from the Turbo C or the UNIX.

13.6 Another Example

Our last example used interactive input from the keyboard. Another common model for programs, especially in the UNIX environment, is the noninteractive program that takes information from a file. We now adapt the last example to this model, examining some of the pertinent differences. The modular approach lends itself to such revision.

Rather than process keyboard input, we let the program process a list of files given in the command line. Because we are not eliciting responses from the user, we drop the user prompts. To process a list of files, we can use a loop that opens each file in turn, and we use standard file I/O functions to read the file contents.

The chief difficulties we face concern the termination of input. Since there may be more than one file, the program can't stop at the first end-of-file marker. Instead, it should test to see that the program has run out of storage space and if it has run out of input files. If the program runs out of space before it runs out of files, it should let the user know. The program should also let the user know if it runs out of space in the middle of a file.

A related question is how big an array should be used. The size depends on the intended use of the program. Conceivably, the data files may contain many integers, but using, say, an array of 30,000 elements borders on the wasteful if the program only needs to sort 8 numbers. The best way of handling the problem is to request additional memory as needed. We don't cover memory allocation functions until Chapter 16, therefore we use a 100-integer limit at this time.

Our considerations lead us to the modified **main( )** function shown in Listing 13.14.

❖ sort_file.c

Listing 13.14

```
/* sort_file.c--sorts integers from files */
#include <stdio.h>
#include "fgetarr.h"
#define MAXSIZE 100/* limit to number of integers to sort */
extern void sort(), print();
int part_file = FALSE;          /* an external variable */

main(argc,argv)
int argc;
char *argv[];
{
    int numbers[MAXSIZE];       /* array to hold input */
    int size = 0;               /* number of input items */
    int file;
    FILE *fp;

    if ( argc < 2 )
    {
        fprintf(stderr,"Usage: %s filename[s]\n", argv[0]);
        exit(1);
    }
    for ( file = 1; file < argc && size < MAXSIZE; file++)
    {
        if ( ( fp = fopen(argv[file],"r") ) != NULL)
            size += fgetarray(fp,numbers + size, MAXSIZE - size);
```

Listing 13.14
(cont'd.)

```
    else
      fprintf(stderr,"File %s could not be opened.\n",
          argv[file]);
    }
    if (file < argc)
      fprintf(stderr,"The last file read was %s\n",
          argv[file-1]);
    if (part_file == TRUE)
      fprintf(stderr,"%s: EOF not reached.\n", argv[file-1]);
    sort(numbers, size);    /* sort the array */
    print(numbers, size);   /* print the sorted array */
  }
```

The program is accompanied by a new include file, called **fgetarr.h**:

```
/* fgetarr.h--fgetarr() info */
#define TRUE 1
#define FALSE 0
extern int fgetarr();
```

As usual, we have the program print an error message and terminate if there are no command-line arguments. If there are arguments, the **for** loop processes them in turn. Two conditions can terminate the loop. First, **argc** is one more than the number of command-line arguments, so the loop terminates if the counter **file** reaches **argv**. Second, **size** is the running total of the number of elements read, and the loop terminates once this number reaches **MAXSIZE**.

Note the arguments to the function **fgetarray( )**. First, **fp** tells the function which file to read. Second, **numbers + size** points to the first vacant location in the array. Third, **MAXSIZE – size** tells **fgetarray( )** how much space is left in the array. If a file cannot be opened, the program passes over it and proceeds to the next file.

The **for** loop increments the variable **file** at the end of each cycle, thus when the loop ends, **file** is one greater than the number of files processed. This value makes **file** equal to **argc** if, indeed, all the files have been processed. If this equality is not true, then the program has run out of room before processing all files. The statement

```
if (file < argc)
  fprintf(stderr,"The last file read was %s\n", argv[file-1]);
```

test for this fact. If some files have not been processed, this statement prints the name of the last file that was processed.

The statement

```
if (part_file == TRUE)
  fprintf(stderr,"%s: EOF not reached.\n", argv[file-1]);
```

tests to see if the array is filled before end-of-file is detected. It uses an external variable (**part_file**) that is initialized to **FALSE**, a value defined in the **fgetarr.h** file. It's the responsibility of the **fgetarray( )** function to set **part_file** to **TRUE** if a file is not fully read. Note that we can also create a different variable in **fgetarray( )** to pass this information, but we want to illustrate using an external variable.

The fgetarray( ) *Function*

We make four modifications to **getarray( )** to develop **fgetarray( )**. First, we add a pointer-to-**FILE** argument so that the function can read opened files. Second, we remove the interactive print statements. Third, we use the external variable **part_file** to report if a file is abandoned before **EOF**. Finally, to read files, we use an **fgetint( )** function instead of **getint( )**. Listing 13.15 shows the **fgetarray( )** function.

❖ *inarray.c*

Listing 13.15

```
/* inarray.c--using fgetint() */
#include <stdio.h>
#include "getint.h"
#include "fgetarr.h"
extern int part_file;

int fgetarray(fp, array, limit)
FILE *fp;
int array[], limit;
{
   int num, status;
   int index = 0; /* array index */

   while(index < limit && (status = fgetint(fp,&num)) != EOF)
   {
     if (status == YESNUM)
        array[index++] = num;
   }
   if (status != EOF)
     if (fgetint(fp,&num) != EOF)
        part_file = TRUE;
   return(index);
}
```

Note that we use the **extern** keyword to declare that **part_file** is defined in another file.

If **status** is **EOF** when the function exits the **while** loop, then the entire file has been read. This suggests using the statement

```
if (status != EOF)
   part_file = TRUE;
```

to report that the file is not completely read. However, it can happen that the integer that filled the array is also the last entry in the file. The statement

```
if (status != EOF)
  if (fgetint(fp,&num) != EOF)
    part_file = TRUE;
```

checks for this eventuality by attempting to read one more value.

The fgetint( ) Function

The only changes necessary from **getint( )** to **fgetint( )** are adding a **FILE** pointer argument and switching from **scanf( )** to **fscanf( )**. See Listing 13.16.

❖ *fgetint.c*

Listing 13.16

```
/* fgetint.c */
#include <stdio.h>
#include "getint.h"
int fgetint(fp,ptint)
FILE *fp;
int *ptint;     /* pointer to integer output */
{
  int status;

  status = fscanf(fp,"%d", ptint);
  if (status == NONUM)
    fscanf(fp,"%*s");
  return status;
}
```

The sort( ) Function

The sorting algorithm we've used is one of the simplest, but it also is one of the slowest, particularly for large numbers of items. The ANSI C library implements a much more effective algorithm called quick sort, with the **qsort( )** function. Because this function involves using pointers to functions, we delay covering it until Chapter 16. In the meantime, we continue to use our selection sort function.

The print( ) Function

We alter **print( )** so that it prints seven integers per line. See Listing 13.17.

❖ *print.c*

Listing 13.17

```
/* print.c--print an array */
#include <stdio.h>
void print(array, limit)
int array[], limit;
{
  int index;
```

**Listing 13.17
(cont'd.)**

```
for ( index = 0; index < limit; index++)
{
  printf("%10d ", array[index]);
  if (index % 7 == 6)
    putchar('\n');
}
}
```

The modular approach lends itself to such step-wise refinements.

13.7 Summary

In this chapter we developed a random number generator and an integer-sorting program. In the process we developed a **getint( )** function that we can use in other programs. We also illustrated some general principles and concepts useful in designing programs.

The most fundamental point to note is that programs should be *designed* rather than allowed to evolve through a random process of growth, trial, and error. You should think carefully about the form and content of input and output for a program before sitting down to code it. You should break the program into well-defined tasks, then program these tasks separately, but with an eye to how they interface with one another. The idea is to achieve modularity. When necessary, break a module into smaller modules. Use functions to enhance program modularity and clarity.

When designing a program, try to anticipate what may go wrong, and then program accordingly. Use error-trapping to circumvent potential problems or, at least, to alert the user if a problem occurs. It's much better to give the user a second chance to enter data than to send the program crashing in ignominy.

When designing a function, first decide how it will interact with the calling function. Decide what information flows in and what information flows out. What will the arguments be? Will you use pointers, **return**, or both? Once you have these design parameters in mind, you can turn your attention to the mechanics of the function.

As you put these ideas to use, you'll produce programs with greater reliability. You will acquire a body of functions that you can use in other programs. Your programming will take less time.

Don't forget about storage classes. Variables can be defined outside functions, in which case they are called external (or global) variables and are available to more than one function. Variables defined within a function are local to that function and are not known to other functions. When possible, use the automatic variety of local variables to prevent variables in one function from being contaminated by the actions of other functions.

Review Questions

1. Which storage classes create variables local to the function containing them?

2. Which storage classes create variables that persist for the duration of the containing program?

3. Which storage class creates variables that can be used across several files? restricted to just one file?

4. What may make the selection sort algorithm inefficient?

5. How can you modify the sorting routine to make it sort in increasing order instead of decreasing order?

6. How can you modify **getint( )** to handle strings that represent octal numbers?

7. Which functions know each variable in the following? Are there any errors?

```
/* file 1 */
int daisy;
main()
{
   int lily;
}
int petal()
{
   extern int daisy, lily;
}
/* file 2 */
static int lily;
int rose;
int stem()
{
   int rose;
}
void root()
{
   extern int daisy;
}
```

8. What does the following program print out?

```
#include <stdio.h>
char color= 'B';
main()
{
   extern char color;
   void first(), second();
```

```
        printf("color in main() is %c\n", color);
        first();
        printf("color in main() is %c\n", color);
        second();
        printf("color in main() is %c\n", color);
}

void first()
{
   char color;

   color = 'R';
   printf("color in first() is %c\n", color);
}

void second()
{
   color = 'G';
   printf("color in second() is %c\n", color);
}
```

9. a. What does the following function heading tell you about the intent of the programmer?

```
static int plink;
int value_ct( const int arr[], int value, int n)
```

b. Does replacing **int** value and **int n** with **const int value** and **const int n** enhance the protection of values in the calling program?

Programming Exercises

1. Some users may be daunted by being asked to enter an **EOF** character. Modify **getarray( )** and **getint( )** so that a # character also terminates input.

2. Create a program that sorts **float** numbers in increasing order.

3. Write and test in a loop a function that returns the number of times it has been called.

4. Write a program that generates a list of 100 random numbers in the range 1–10 in sorted, decreasing order.

5. Write a program that generates 1000 random numbers in the range 1–10. Don't save or print the numbers out, but do print out how many times each number appears. Have the program use 10 different seed values. Do the numbers appear in equal amounts? You can use this chapter's functions or the ANSI C **rand( )** and **srand( )** functions, which follow the same format our functions do. This is one way to test the randomness of a particular random number generator.

6. Write a program that behaves like the modification of Listing 13.8 that we discuss after showing its output.

7. Write an interactive program that lets the user enter up to 20 words. Have the program display the words in sorted order (recall the string-sorting example in Chapter 11) and then ask the user if he or she wishes to save the sorted words in a file. If the user responds "yes," have the program request a name for the file, then write the words into a file by that name.

8. Write a function that skips over input until encountering a digit. It then stores that digit and subsequent digits in a string until encountering a nondigit. The nondigit is placed back in the input string, and the function converts the digit string to a numeric value. The function should use a pointer argument to provide the numeric value to the calling program. Use the function return value to return **EOF** if the function encounters end-of-file. It should return **1** otherwise. Use **getc( )** and **ungetc( )**. In short, this function finds the next integer in output, whether it be isolated or embedded in text. For example, the function can locate the integer **22** in **be22again**.

9. Modify Exercise 8 so that the function recognizes an optional minus sign. That is, confronted with input of **be–22now**, it extracts the value **–22**.

10. Construct a text file that contains 20 lines of a name, a colon, and three integers each. Write a program that reads the file and prints the lines in order of increasing average value of the line. That is, the line **Shalla Booger: 80 70 84** should precede the line **Hagar Joe Plinty: 70 90 80** because the average of its three values is less than the second average. Also have the program append the average to each line when it is printed. Note that the name part of the input need not consist of exactly two names.

14

Structures and Other Data Forms

Contents

Objectives

Defining a structure template
Creating structure variables
Using structure tags and accessing structure members
Using pointers to structures to access structure members
Writing functions that use pointers to structures
Passing structures as arguments and using structures as return values
Defining and using nested structures and arrays of structures
Setting up a union
Using **typedef** to create type synonyms, and using pointers to functions

*O*ften a program's success depends on finding a good way to represent the data with which the program must work. Through design, C possesses a powerful means to represent complex data. This data form, called a *structure*, not only is flexible enough in its basic form to represent a diversity of data, but it also allows the user to invent new forms. If you are familiar with Pascal "records," you should be comfortable with structures.

14.1 Example Problem: Creating an Inventory of Books

Let's study an example to see why a structure may be needed and how to create and use one. Gwen Glenn wishes to print out an inventory of her books. There is a variety of information she would like for each book: its title, author, publisher, copyright date, number of pages, number of copies, and dollar value. Some of these items, such as the titles, can be stored in an array of strings. Other items require an array of **int** or **float** values. Keeping track of so many different arrays can become quite hectic, especially if Gwen wishes to have several complete lists sorted by various criteria (a list sorted by title, one sorted by author, one sorted by value, and so on). A much better solution is to use one array, in which each member contains all the information about one book.

We therefore need a data form that can contain both strings and numbers and somehow keep the information separate. We use the C structure for this purpose. To see how a structure is set up and how it works, we start with a limited example. To simplify the problem, we impose two restrictions: First, we include only title, author, and value; second, we limit the inventory to one book. We extend the program later in the chapter.

Let's look at the program in Listing 14.1 and its output.

❖ *book.c*

Listing 14.1

```
/* book.c--one-book inventory */
#include <stdio.h>
#define MAXTIT 41   /* maximum length of title + 1 */
#define MAXAUT 31
            /* maximum length of author's name + 1 */
struct book { /* first structure template: tag is book */
        char title[MAXTIT];
        char author[MAXAUT];
        float value;
        };     /* end of structure template */
main()
{
    struct book libry;
            /* declare libry as book-type variable */

    printf("Please enter the book title.\n");
    gets(libry.title);   /* access to the title portion */
    printf("Now enter the author.\n");
    gets(libry.author);
```

**Listing 14.1
(cont'd.)**

```
      printf("Now enter the value.\n");
      scanf("%f", &libry.value );
      printf("%s by %s: $%.2f\n",libry.title,
             libry.author, libry.value );
      printf("%s: \"%s\" \($%.2f\)\n", libry.author,
             libry.title, libry.value );
}
```

Here is a sample run:

```
Please enter the book title.
Urban Swine Raising
Now enter the author.
Godfrey Porcelot
Now enter the value.
27.50
Urban Swine Raising by Godfrey Porcelot: $27.50
Godfrey Porcelot: "Urban Swine Raising" ($27.50)
```

The structure consists of three parts, called *members* or *fields:* one to store the title, one to store the author, and one to store the value. We describe three main points in detail in the following sections:

1. How to set up a template (format) for a structure

2. How to declare a variable to fit that template

3. How to gain access to the individual components of a structure variable

14.2 Setting Up the Structure Template

The *structure template* is the master plan that describes how a structure is put together. Our template looks like this:

```
struct book  {
       char title[MAXTIT];
       char author[MAXAUT];
       float value;
       };
```

This template describes a structure made up of two **char** arrays and one **float** variable. Let's look at the details. First comes the keyword **struct**, which identifies that which comes next as a structure. Then comes an optional *tag,* the word **book**. The tag is a shorthand label we can use later to refer to this structure. Thus, later on we declare

```
struct book libry;
```

which declares **libry** to be a structure of the **book** type.

Next we find the list of structure members enclosed in a pair of braces. Each member is described by its own declaration. For instance, the **title** portion is a **char** array with **MAXTIT** elements. The members can be any data types, including other structures.

Finally, a semicolon ends the template definition. The template may be placed outside any function (externally), as we have done, or it may be placed inside a function definition. If the template is defined inside a function, then it can be used only inside that function. If the template is external, it is available to all the functions that follow the definition in the program. For example, in a second function, you can define

```
struct book dickens;
```

and that function would have a variable **dickens** that follows the form of our template.

Note: We earlier said that the tag name is optional, but you must use one when you set up structures as we have done here, with the template defined one place and the actual variables defined elsewhere. We return to this point shortly.

14.3 Defining a Structure Variable

The word "structure" is used in two senses. One is the sense "structure template," which we just discussed. The template is a plan; it tells the compiler how to represent the data, but it doesn't cause the computer to allocate space for the data. The next step is to create a *structure variable,* which is the second sense of the word. The following line in Listing 14.1 causes a structure variable to be created:

```
struct book libry;
```

On receiving this instruction, the computer creates the variable **libry**. Following the plan laid down by **book**, the computer allots space for a **char** array of **MAXTIT** elements, for a **char** array of **MAXAUT** elements, and for a **float** variable. See Figure 14.1. This storage is lumped together under the single name **libry**. (In the next section we describe how to access the structure members as needed.)

```
struct stuff {
              int number;
              char code[4]
              float cost;
              };
```

Figure 14.1

Memory allocation for a structure

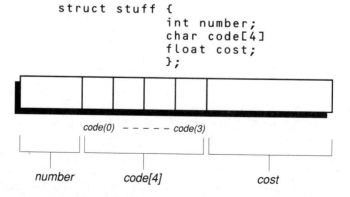

In this declaration, **struct book** plays the same role that **int** or **float** does in a declaration. For example, we can declare two variables of the **struct book** type or even a pointer to that kind of structure:

```
struct book doyle, panshin, *ptbook;
```

In this case, the structure variables **doyle** and **panshin** each have **title**, **author**, and **value** parts. The pointer **ptbook** can point to **doyle**, **panshin**, or any other **book** structure.

As far as the computer is concerned,

```
struct book libry;
```

is short for

```
struct book {
        char title[MAXTIT];
        char author[MAXAUT];
        float value;
        } libry;
        /* follow template with variable name */
```

In other words, the process of defining a structure template and the process of defining a structure variable can be combined into one step. Combining the template and the variable definitions is the one circumstance in which a tag need not be used:

```
struct    {      /* no tag */
        char title[MAXTIT];
        char author[MAXAUT];
        float value;
        } libry;
```

However, note that the tag form is handy if you use a structure template more than once.

Initializing a Structure

One aspect of defining a structure variable has not come up in our example: initialization. Let's take a quick look at this topic. We've seen how to initialize variables and arrays:

```
int count = 0;
static int fibo[] = {0,1,1,2,3,5,8};
```

Can a structure variable also be initialized? Yes, although many pre-ANSI implementations limit initialization to external or static structure variables. The point here is that whether or not a structure variable is external depends on where the variable is defined, not on where the template is defined.

In our example program, the template **book** is external, but the variable **libry** is not, for it is defined inside the function and is, by default, placed in the automatic storage class. Suppose, though, that we make the following declaration:

```
static struct book libry;
```

Then the storage class is static, and we can initialize the structure this way (pre-ANSI or ANSI):

```
static struct book libry = {
  "The Pirate and the Damsel",
  "Renee Vivotte",
  1.95
  };
```

Each member is given its own line of initialization, and all the compiler needs are commas to separate one member's initialization from the next.

14.4 Gaining Access to Structure Members

Let's now continue with our study of structure properties. A structure is like a superarray in which one element can be **char**, the next element **float**, and the next an **int** array. We access the individual array elements by using a subscript. We access the individual members of a structure by using a period (.), which is the structure member operator. For example, **libry.value** is the **value** portion of **libry**. You can use **libry.value** exactly as you use any other **float** variable. Similarly, you can use **libry.title** exactly as you use a **char** array. Thus, we can use expressions like the following:

```
gets(libry.title);
```

and

```
scanf("%f", &libry.value);
```

In essence, **.title**, **.author**, and **.value** play the role of subscripts for a **book** structure.

Note that although **libry** is a structure, **libry.value** is a **float** type and is used like any other **float** type. For example, **scanf(" %f ", ...)** requires the address of a **float** location, which is what **&libry.float** is. The period has higher precedence here, so the expression is the same as **&(libry.float)**.

If you have a second structure variable of the identical type, you can use the same system:

```
struct book spiro, gerald;

gets(spiro.title);
gets(gerald.title);
```

The **.title** refers to the first member of the **book** structure. Notice how in our initial program in Listing 14.1 we print out the contents of the **libry** structure in two different formats to illustrate our freedom when using the members of a structure.

The preceding discussion takes care of the basics. Now we explore several ramifications of structures, including arrays of structures, structures of structures, pointers to structures, and functions and structures.

14.5 Arrays of Structures

Let's extend our book program to handle a greater number of books. Clearly each book can be described by one structure variable of the **book** type. To describe two books, we use two variables, and so on. To handle several books, we use an array of such structures. See Listing 14.2. (Note: With Microsoft C, either set the stack size to 9000 to accommodate the array of structures or else make the array static.)

❖ *manybook.c*

Listing 14.2

```
/* manybook.c--multiple book inventory */
#include <stdio.h>
#define MAXTIT 40
#define MAXAUT 40
#define MAXBKS 100 /* maximum number of books */
#define STOP ""     /* null string, ends input */
struct book {       /* set up book template */
        char title[MAXTIT];
        char author[MAXAUT];
        float value;
        };
main()
{
   struct book libry[MAXBKS];
                    /* array of book structures */

   int count = 0;
   int index;

   printf("Please enter the book title.\n");
   printf("Press [enter] at the start of a line to stop.\n");
   while ( count < MAXBKS &&
     strcmp(gets(libry[count].title),STOP) != 0)
   {
     printf("Now enter the author.\n");
     gets(libry[count].author);
     printf("Now enter the value.\n");
     scanf("%f", &libry[count++].value );
     while ( getchar() != '\n')
        ;               /*clear input line */
     if ( count < MAXBKS )
```

**Listing 14.2
(cont'd.)**

```
        printf("Enter the next title.\n");
    }
    printf("Here is the list of your books:\n");
    for( index = 0; index < count; index++)
    printf("%s by %s: $%.2f\n",libry[index].title,
            libry[index].author, libry[index].value );
}
```

A sample program run follows:

```
Please enter the book title.
Press [enter] at the start of a line to stop.
My Life as a Budgie
Now enter the author.
Mack Zackles
Now enter the value.
12.95
Enter the next title.
    ...more entries...
Here is the list of your books:
My Life as a Budgie by Mack Zackles: $12.95
Thought and Unthought by Kindra Schlagmeyer: $33.50
The Anatomy of an Ant by Salome Deschamps: $9.99
Power Tiddlywinks by Jack Deltoids: $13.25
UNIX Primer Plus by Waite, Martin, & Prata: $19.95
Coping with Coping by Dr. Rubin Thonkwacker: $10.00
Delicate Frivolity by Neda McFey: $29.99
Fate Wore a Bikini by Mickey Splats: $8.95
A History of Buvania by Prince Nikoli Buvan: $50.00
Mastering Your Digital Watch by Miklos Mysz: $13.95
A Foregone Confusion by Phalty Reasoner: $25.66
```

The two main points to note about an array of structures are how to declare them and how to access individual members. Let's look at both of these topics. Following this discussion, highlight several aspects of the program.

Declaring an Array of Structures

The process of declaring a structure array is analogous to declaring any other kind of array:

```
struct book libry[MAXBKS];
```

This statement declares **libry** to be an array with **MAXBKS** elements. Each element of the array is a structure of **book** type. Thus, **libry[0]** is a **book** structure, **libry[1]** is a second **book** structure, and so on. Figure 14.2 may help you visualize this concept. The name **libry** itself is not a structure name; it is the name of the array that holds the structures.

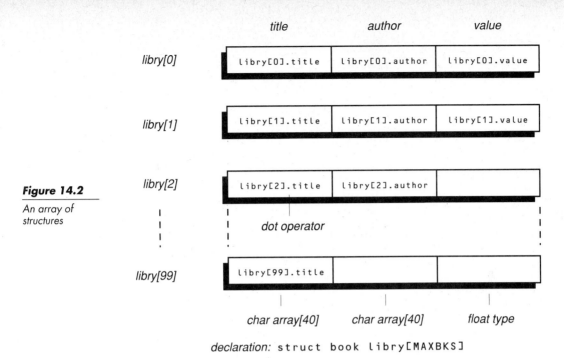

Figure 14.2

An array of
structures

title   author   value

```
libry[0]    libry[0].title    libry[0].author    libry[0].value

libry[1]    libry[1].title    libry[1].author    libry[1].value

libry[2]    libry[2].title    libry[2].author

                              dot operator

libry[99]   libry[99].title
```

char array[40]   char array[40]   float type

declaration: `struct book libry[MAXBKS]`

Identifying Members of a Structure Array

We identify members of a structure array by applying the same rule we use for individual structures: Follow the structure name with the member operator and the member name:

```
libry[0].value   /* the value associated with the first array
                    element */
libry[4].title   /* the title associated with the fifth array
                    element */
```

Note that the array subscript is attached to **libry** and not to the end of the name:

```
libry.value[2] /* WRONG */
libry[2].value /* RIGHT */
```

The reason we use **libry[2].value** is that **libry[2]** is the structure variable name, just as **libry[1]** is another structure variable name, and our earlier **doyle** was also a structure variable name.

Incidentally, what do you suppose

```
libry[2].title[4]
```

represents? It's the fifth element in the title (**title[4]**) of the book described by the third structure (**libry[2]**). In our sample run, this would be the character **A**. This example points out that subscripts found to the right of the **.** operator apply to individual members, whereas subscripts to the left of the operator apply to arrays of structures.

Program Details

Let's now return to the major points of the program. The main difference between Listing 14.1 and Listing 14.2 is that the new program incorporates a loop to read in successive books. We begin the loop with the following **while** condition:

```
while ( count < MAXBKS &&
          strcmp(gets (libry[count].title),STOP) != 0)
```

The expression **gets(libry[count].title)** reads an input string for the title of a book. The **strcmp( )** function compares this string to **STOP**, which is just " ", the empty string. If the user presses the Enter key at the beginning of a line, the empty string is transmitted, and the loop ends. We also have a check to keep the number of books read in under the size limit of the array. Then we have these lines:

```
while ( getchar( ) != '\n')
   ;             /* clear input line */
```

As you may recall from earlier chapters, this code handles the fact that the **scanf( )** function ignores spaces and newlines. When you respond to the request for the book's value, you type something like

```
12.50[enter]
```

which transmits the following sequence of characters:

```
12.50\n
```

The **scanf( )** function collects the **1**, **2**, **.**, **5**, and **0**, but it leaves the **\n** alone, awaiting whatever read statement is to follow. If the preceding code were missing, the next read statement is **gets(libry[count].title)** in the loop control statement. So it would read the leftover newline character as its *first* character, and the program would think we had sent a stop signal. The code we did insert collects characters until it finds the newline. It doesn't do anything with that character except remove it from the input queue, which gives **gets( )** a fresh beginning.

14.6 Nested Structures

Sometimes it is convenient for one structure to nest within another. For example, Shalala Pirosky is building a structure containing information about her friends. One member of the structure, naturally enough, is the friend's name. The name, however, can be represented by a structure itself, with separate entries for first and last name. Listing 14.3 is a condensed example of Shalala's work.

```
/* friend.c--example of a nested structure */
#include <stdio.h>
#define LEN 20
#define M1 " Thank you for the wonderful evening, "
#define M2 "You certainly prove that a "
#define M3 "is a special kind of guy. We must get together"
#define M4 "over a delicious "
#define M5 " and have a few laughs."
struct names {                    /* first structure template */
        char first[LEN];
        char last[LEN];
        };
struct guy {                      /* second template */
        struct names handle;  /* nested structure */
        char favfood[LEN];
        char job[LEN];
        float income;
        };
main()
{
   static struct guy fellow = {
                                /* initialized a variable */
        { "Franco", "Wathall" },
        "eggplant",
        "doormat customizer",
        15435.00
        };
   printf("Dear %s, \n\n", fellow.handle.first);
   printf("%s%s.\n", M1, fellow.handle.first);
   printf("%s%s\n", M2, fellow.job);
   printf("%s\n", M3);
   printf("%s%s%s\n\n", M4, fellow.favfood, M5);
   printf("%40s%s\n", " ", "See you soon,");
   printf("%40s%s\n", " ", "Shalala");
}
```

Listing 14.3

Here is the output:

```
Dear Franco,
   Thank you for the wonderful evening, Franco.
You certainly prove that a doormat customizer
is a special kind of guy. We must get together
over a delicious eggplant and have a few laughs.

                        See you soon,
                        Shalala
```

The first point to note is how the nested structure is set up in the template. It is simply declared, just as an **int** variable would be:

```
struct names handle;
```

This statement says that **handle** is a variable of the **struct names** type. Of course, the file should also include the template for the **names** structure.

The second point to note is how we gain access to a member of a nested structure. We simply use the . operator twice:

```
fellow.handle.first == "Franco"
```

We interpret the construction this way, going from left to right:

```
(fellow.handle).first
```

That is, first find **fellow**, then find the **handle** member of **fellow**, and finally find the **first** member of member.

14.7 Pointers to Structures

Pointer lovers will be glad to know that you can have pointers to structures. This is useful for at least three reasons. First, just as pointers to arrays are easier to manipulate (in a sorting problem, say) than the arrays themselves, so are pointers to structures easier to manipulate than structures themselves. Second, in some older implementations, a structure can't be passed as an argument to a function, but a pointer to a structure can be. Third, many data representations are actually structures containing pointers to other structures.

The next example shows how to define a pointer to a structure and how to use it to access structure members. See Listing 14.4.

❖ friends.c

Listing 14.4

```
/* friends.c--uses pointer to a structure */
#include <stdio.h>
#define LEN 20
struct names {
        char first[LEN];
        char last[LEN];
        };
struct guy   {
        struct names handle;
        char favfood[LEN];
        char job[LEN];
        float income;
        };
```

```
main()
{
   static struct guy fellow[2] = {
      { { "Franco", "Wathall" },
         "eggplant",
         "doormat customizer",
         15435.00
      },
      { { "Rodney" , "Swillbelly" },
         "salmon mousse",
         "interior decorator",
         35000.00
      }
   };
   struct guy *him;       /* a pointer to a structure */

   printf("address #1: %u #2: %u\n", &fellow[0], &fellow[1] );
   him = &fellow[0];      /* tell the pointer where to point */
   printf("pointer #1: %u #2: %u\n", him, him + 1);
   printf("him->income is $%.2f: (*him).income is $%.2f\n",
            him->income, (*him).income);
   him++;                       /* point to the next structure */
   printf("him->favfood is %s: him->handle.last is %s\n",
            him->favfood, him->handle.last);
}
```

Listing 14.4

The output follows:

```
address #1: 12 #2: 96
pointer #1: 12 #2: 96
him->income is $15435.00: (*him).income is $15435.00
him->favfood is salmon mousse: him->names.last is Swillbelly
```

Let's look first at how we create a pointer to a **guy** structure. Then we study how to specify individual structure members by using the pointer.

Declaring and Initializing a Structure Pointer

Declaration is an easy process:

```
struct guy *him;
```

First is the keyword **struct**, then the template tag **guy**, then an * followed by the pointer name. The syntax is the same as for the other pointer declarations we have seen.

The pointer **him** now can be made to point to any structures of the **guy** type. We initialize **him** by making it point to **fellow[0]**. Note that we use the address operator:

```
him = &fellow[0];
```

The first two output lines show the success of this assignment. Comparing the two lines, we see that **him** points to **fellow[0]** and **him + 1** points to **fellow[1]**. Note that adding **1** to **him** adds **84** to the address. This situation occurs because each **guy** structure occupies 84 bytes of memory: **names.first** is 20, **names.last** is 20, **favfood** is 20, **job** is 20, and **income** is 4 (the size of the **float** type on our system).

Member Access by Pointer

We have **him** pointing to the structure **fellow[0]**. How can we use **him** to get a value of a member of **fellow[0]**? The third output line shows two methods.

The first and most common method uses a new operator, **->**. This operator is formed by typing a hyphen (-) followed by the "is greater than" symbol (>). The example helps make the meaning clear:

```
him->income is fellow[0].income if him == &fellow[0]
```

In other words, a structure pointer followed by the **->** operator works the same as a structure name followed by the **.** operator. (We can't properly say **him.income** because **him** is not a structure name.)

It is important to note that **him** is a pointer but **him->income** is a member of the pointed-to structure. Thus in this case, **him->income** is a **float** variable.

The second method for specifying the value of a structure member follows from this sequence: If **him == &fellow[0]**, then ***him == fellow[0]**. The conclusion is true because **&** and ***** are reciprocal operators. Hence

```
fellow[0].income == (*him).income
```

by substitution. Note that the parentheses are required because the **.** operator has higher precedence than *****.

In summary, if **him** is a pointer to the structure **fellow[0]**, then the following are all equivalent:

```
fellow[0].income == (*him).income == him->income
```

14.8 Telling Functions About Structures

Recall that function arguments pass values to the function. Each value is a number, perhaps **int**, **float**, ASCII character code, or an address. A structure is a bit more complicated than a single value, so it is not surprising that older implementations do not allow a structure to be used as an argument for a function. This limitation has been removed in newer implementations, however, and ANSI C states that structures can be used as arguments. Thus modern implementations give us a choice between passing structures as arguments or passing pointers to structures as arguments. Or if we are concerned with just part of a structure, we can pass structure members as arguments. Let's look at each of these methods.

Using Structure Members

As long as a structure member is a variable with a single value (that is, an **int** or one of its relatives, a **char**, a **float**, a **double**, a pointer, or in modern C, another structure), it can be passed as a function argument. A primitive financial analysis program that adds the client's bank account to his or her savings and loan account illustrates this point. See Listing 14.5. (Incidentally, note that we combine the template definition, the variable declaration, and the initialization into one statement.)

❖ *funds1.c*

Listing 14.5

```
/* funds1.c--passing structure members as arguments */
#include <stdio.h>
struct funds {
   char *bank;
   float bankfund;
   char *save;
   float savefund;
   } stan =   {
           "Garlic-Melon Bank",
           1023.43,
           "Snoopy's Savings and Loan",
           4239.87
           };
main()
{
   float total, sum();
   extern struct funds stan;      /* optional declaration */
   printf("Stan has a total of $%.2f.\n",
      sum(stan.bankfund, stan.savefund) );
}
   /* adds two float numbers */
float sum(x,y)
float x, y
{
   return(x + y);
}
```

The result of running this program follows:

```
Stan has a total of $5263.30.
```

Notice that the function **sum( )** neither knows nor cares whether or not the actual arguments are members of a structure; it only just requires that they be type **float**.

Of course, if you want a program to affect the value of a member in the calling program, you can transmit the address of the member:

```
modify(&stan.bankfund);
```

Such a statement is a function that can alter Stan's bank account.

Using the Structure Address

The next approach to telling a function about a structure involves letting the summing function know that it is dealing with a structure. To illustrate, we solve the same problem as before, but this time we will use the address of the structure as an argument. Since the function must work with the **funds** structure, it too must use the **funds** template. See Listing 14.6.

❖ *funds2.c*

Listing 14.6

```
/* funds2.c--passing a pointer to a structure */
#include <stdio.h>
struct funds {
   char *bank;
   float bankfund;
   char *save;
   float savefund;
   } stan = {
        "Garlic-Melon Bank",
        1023.43,
        "Snoopy's Savings and Loan",
        4239.87
        };
main()
{
   float sum();

   printf("Stan has a total of $%.2f.\n", sum( &stan) );
}
float sum(money)
struct funds *money;
{
   return( money->bankfund + money->savefund );
}
```

The output follows:

```
Stan has a total of $5263.30.
```

The **sum( )** function uses a pointer **money** to a **fund** structure. Passing the address **&stan** to the function causes **money** to point to the **stan** structure. We then use the **->** operator to gain the values of **stan.bankfund** and **stan.savefund**.

Note that the **sum( )** function also has access to the institution names, although it doesn't use this information. Also note that we must use the **&** operator in the function call to get the structure address. Unlike the array name, the structure name alone is *not* a synonym for its address.

Passing a Structure as an Argument

For compilers that permit you to pass structures as arguments, we can rewrite the last example as shown in Listing 14.7.

❖ *funds3.c*

Listing 14.7

```
/* funds3.c--passing a pointer to a structure */
#include <stdio.h>
struct funds {
   char *bank;
   float bankfund;
   char *save;
   float savefund;
   } stan =  {
          "Garlic-Melon Bank",
          1023.43,
          "Snoopy's Savings and Loan",
          4239.87
          };
main()
{
   float sum();

   printf("Stan has a total of $%.2f.\n", sum( stan) );
}
float sum(moolah)
struct funds moolah;
{
   return( moolah.bankfund + moolah.savefund );
}
```

Again, we get the same output:

```
Stan has a total of $5263.30.
```

In this example, we replace **money**, which points to the **struct funds** variable in Listing 14.6, with **moolah**, which is a **struct funds** variable. When **sum( )** is called, an automatic variable **moolah** is created according to the **funds** template. The members of this structure are then initialized to the values held in the corresponding members of the **stan** structure. Thus the computations are performed using a copy of the original structure, whereas the preceding program uses the original structure itself. Because **moolah** is a structure, we use **moolah.bankfund**, not **moolah->bankfund**. In Listing 14.6, we use **money->bankfund** because **money** is a pointer, not a structure.

More on the New, Improved Structure Status

Under modern C, including ANSI C, not only can structures be passed as function arguments, they also can be returned as function values. To make the return mechanism workable, the values in one structure can be assigned to another. That is, if **n_data** and **o_data** are both structures of the same type, you can do the following:

```
o_data = n_data;
```

This statement causes each member of **o_data** to be assigned the value of the corresponding member of **n_data**.

The fact that structures can be used as function arguments lets us convey structure information to a function. The fact that functions can return structures lets us convey structure information from a function to the calling program. Structure pointers also allow two-way communication, so often you can use either approach to solve programming problems. Let's look at two examples that illustrate these approaches.

To contrast the approaches, we write a simple program that handles structures by using pointers; we then rewrite it to use structure-passing and structure returns. The program itself asks for your first and last name and reports the total number of letters. This project hardly requires structures, but it provides a simple framework for seeing how they work. Listing 14.8 presents the pointer form.

❖ *nameln1.c*

Listing 14.8

```
/* nameln1.c--uses pointers to a structure */
#include <stdio.h>
struct namect {
            char fname[20];
            char lname[20];
            int letters;
            };
main()
{
   struct namect person;
   void getinfo(), makeinfo(), showinfo();

   getinfo(&person);
   makeinfo(&person);
   showinfo(&person);
}

void getinfo ( pst )
struct namect *pst;
{
```

Listing 14.8
(cont'd.)

```
    printf("Please enter your first name:\n");
    gets(pst->fname);
    printf("Please enter your last name.\n");
    gets(pst->lname);
}

void makeinfo ( pst )
struct namect *pst;
{
    pst->letters =    strlen(pst->fname) +
            strlen(pst->lname);
}

void showinfo ( pst )
struct namect *pst;
{
    printf("%s %s, your name contains %d letters.",
         pst->fname, pst->lname, pst->letters);
}
```

Compiling and running the program produce results like the following:

```
A> nameln1
Please enter your first name:
Nathan
Please enter your last name:
Hale
Nathan Hale, your name contains 10 characters.
```

We allocate the work of the program to three functions. In each case, we pass the address of the **person** structure to the function. The **getinfo( )** function transfers information from itself to **main( )**. In particular, it obtains names from the user and places them in the **person** structure, using the **pst** pointer to locate the structure. Recall that **pst->lname** means the **lname** member of the structure pointed to by **pst.** Thus, **pst->lname** is equivalent to the name of a **char** array, hence a suitable argument for **gets( )**. Note that although **getinfo( )** feeds information to the main program, it does not use the return mechanism, so it is type **void.**

The **makeinfo( )** function performs a two-way transfer of information. By using a pointer to **person**, it locates the two names stored in the structure. It uses the C library function **strlen( )** to calculate the total number of letters and then uses the address of **person** to store the datum. Again, the type is **void.** The third function, the **showinfo( )** function, uses a pointer to locate the information to be printed.

In all of these operations, there has been but one structure variable, **person**, and each of the functions uses the structure address to access it. One function transfers information from itself to the calling program; one transfers information from the calling program to itself; and one does both.

Now let's see how we can program the same task using structure arguments and return values. First, to pass the structure itself, we use the argument **person** rather than **&person**. The corresponding formal argument is then declared type **struct namect** instead of being a pointer to that type. Second, when we need to provide structure values to the main program, we can return a structure. Listing 14.9 presents the nonpointer version.

❖ *nameln2.c*

Listing 14.9

```
/* nameln2.c--passes and returns structures */
#include <stdio.h>
struct namect {
            char fname[20];
            char lname[20];
            int letters;
            };
main()
{
  struct namect person;
  struct namect getinfo(), makeinfo();
  void showinfo();

  person = getinfo();
  person = makeinfo(person);
  showinfo(person);
}

struct namect getinfo ( )
{
  struct namect temp;
  printf("Please enter your first name.\n");
  gets(temp.fname);
  printf("Please enter your last name.\n");
  gets(temp.lname);
  return temp;
}
struct namect makeinfo ( info )
struct namect info;
{
  info.letters = strlen(info.fname) + strlen(info.lname);
  return info;
}

void showinfo ( info )
struct namect info;
{
  printf("%s %s, your name contains %d letters.\n",
         info.fname, info.lname, info.letters);
}
```

This version produces the same final result as the preceding one, but it proceeds in a different manner. Each of the three functions creates its own copy of **person**, so this program uses four distinct structures instead of just the one.

Consider the **makeinfo( )** function, for example. In the first program, the address of **person** is passed, and the function fiddles with the actual **person** values. In the second program, a new structure called **info** is created. The values stored in **person** are copied into **info**, and the function works with the copy. So when the number of letters is calculated, that datum is stored in **info**, but not in **person**. However, the line

```
return info;
```

and the line

```
person = makeinfo(person);
```

copy the values stored in **info** into **person**. Also note that the **makeinfo( )** function must be declared type **struct namect** because it returns a structure.

Structures or Pointers to Structures?

Suppose you have to write a structure-related function. Should you use structure pointers as arguments? Or should you use structure arguments and return values? Each approach has its strengths and weaknesses.

The two primary advantages of using pointers as arguments are that this method works on older as well as newer C implementations and is quick—you pass a single address. The disadvantage is that you have less protection for your data. Some function operation may inadvertently affect data in the original structure.

The ANSI C addition of the **const** qualifier offers the means to protect against accidental changes. For example, the pointer version of **showinfo( )** (Listing 14.8) prints the structure contents and should not alter them. Therefore, we would use the following function heading:

```
void showinfo( pst )
const struct namect *pst;
```

This states that **pst** points to a structure whose values cannot be changed.

One advantage of passing structures as arguments is that having the function work with copies of the original data is safer than working with the original data itself. Also, this method tends to make for a clearer programming style. Suppose, for instance, we define the following structure type:

```
struct vector = { double x; double y;} ;
```

Suppose we want to set the vector **ans** to the sum of the vectors **a** and **b.** We can write a structure-passing and returning function that creates a program like the following:

```
struct vector ans, a, b, sum_vect();
  ...
ans = sum_vect(a,b);
```

This code is more natural looking to an engineer than a pointer version is, which may look as follows:

```
struct vector ans, a, b;
void sum_vect();
  ...
sum_vect(&a, &b, &ans);
```

Also, the user has to remember whether the address for the sum should be the first or the last argument.

The two main disadvantages to structure-passing are that older implementations may not handle the code and that it's wasteful of time and space to pass large structures. It's especially wasteful to pass large structures to a function that uses only one or two members of the structure. In such a case, it makes more sense to pass a pointer or else to pass only the required members as individual arguments.

Functions Using an Array of Structures

Suppose we have an array of structures that we wish to process with a function. The name of an array is a synonym for its address, so it can be passed to a function. Again, the function needs access to the structure template. Listing 14.10 expands our monetary program to two people, so that we have an array of two **funds** structures.

❖ *funds4.c*

Listing 14.10

```
/* funds4.c--passing an array of structures to a function */
#include <stdio.h>
#define N 2
struct funds {
            char *bank;
            float bankfund;
            char *save;
            float savefund;
            } jones[N] =    {
                            {
                            "Garlic-Melon Bank",
                            1023.43,
                            "Snoopy's Savings and Loan",
                            4239.87
                            },
                            {
                            "Honest Jack's Bank",
                            976.57,
```

Listing 14.10
(cont'd.)

```
                              "First Draft Savings",
                              1760.13
                              }
                         };
main()
{
   float total, sum();

   printf("The Joneses have a total of $%.2f.\n",
          sum(jones,N));
}

float sum(money,n)
struct funds *money;
int n;
{
   float total;
   int i;

   for( i = 0, total = 0; i < n; i++, money++)
       total += money->bankfund + money->savefund;
   return(total);
}
```

The output follows:

```
The Joneses have a total of $8000.00.
```

The array name **jones** is a pointer to the array. In particular, it points to the first element of the array, which is the structure **jones[0]**. Thus initially, the pointer **money** is given by this expression:

```
money = &jones[0];
```

Using the **->** operator lets us add the two funds for the first Jones. This is really very much like the Listing 14.6. The **for** loop then increments the pointer **money** by 1. Now it points to the next structure, **jones[1]**, and the rest of the funds can be added to **total**.

These are the two main points:

1. We can use the array name to pass a pointer to the first structure in the array to a function.

2. We then can use pointer arithmetic to move the pointer to successive structures in the array. Note that the function call

```
sum(&jones[0].N)
```

has the same effect as using the array name, since both refer to the same address. Using the array name is simply an indirect manner of passing the structure address.

14.9 Saving Structure Contents in a File

Because structures can hold a wide variety of information, they are an important tool for constructing databases. For example, you can use a structure to hold all the pertinent information about an employee or an auto part. Ultimately, you want to be able to save this information in a file and to retrieve it from a file. A database file contains a number of such data objects. The entire set of information held in a structure is termed a *record,* and the individual items are called **fields**. Let's investigate these topics.

Perhaps the most obvious, and least efficient, method to save a record is to use **fprintf( )**. For example, recall the **book** structure we introduced in Listing 14.1:

```
#define MAXTIT 40
#define MAXAUT 40
struct book  {
        char title[MAXTIT];
        char author[MAXAUT];
        float value;
        };
```

If **pbooks** identifies a file stream, we can save the information in a **struct book** variable called **primer** with the following statement:

```
printf("pbooks, %s %s %.2f\n",primer.title,primer.author,
    primer.value);
```

Such a setup becomes unwieldy for structures with, say, 30 members. It also poses a retrieval problem, for the program still needs some way of telling where one field ends and another begins. This difficulty can be fixed by using fixed-size fields, for example, **%39s%39s%8.2f**, but the awkwardness remains.

A better solution is to use **fread( )** and **fwrite( )** to read and write in structure-sized units. Recall that these functions read and write using the same binary representation the program uses. For example,

```
fwrite(&primer, sizeof (struct book), 1, pbooks);
```

moves to the beginning address of the **primer** structure and copies that structure to the file associated with **pbooks**. The **sizeof (struct book)** term tells the function how large a block to copy, and the **1** indicates it should copy just one block. The **fread( )** function with the same arguments copies a structure-sized chunk of data from the file to the location pointed to by **&primer.** In short, these functions read and write a record at a time instead of a field at a time. Also, **fread( )** returns the number of structure-sized items read.

To show how these functions can be used in a program, we modify the program in Listing 14.2 so that the book titles are saved in a file called **book.dat**. Also, if the file already exists, the program shows you its current contents, then lets you add to the file. Listing 14.11 presents the new version.

```
/* savebook.c--save structure contents in a file */
#include <stdio.h>
#define MAXTIT 40
#define MAXAUT 40
#define MAXBKS 10   /* maximum number of books */
#define STOP ""     /* null string, ends input */
struct book {       /* set up book template */
        char title[MAXTIT];
        char author[MAXAUT];
        float value;
        };
main()
{
   struct book libry[MAXBKS];
                   /* array of book structures */

   int count = 0;
   int index, filecount;
   FILE *pbooks;
   int size = sizeof (struct book);

   if ( (pbooks = fopen("book.dat", "a+b")) == NULL)
   {
     fputs("Can't open book.dat file\n",stderr);
     exit(1);
   }
   rewind(pbooks);  /* go to start of file */
   while ( count < MAXBKS && fread(&libry[count], size,
        1, pbooks) == 1)
   {
     if (count == 0)
       puts ("Current contents of book.dat:");
     printf("%s by %s: $%.2f\n",libry[count].title,
            libry[count].author, libry[count].value );
     count++;
   }
   filecount = count;
   if (count == MAXBKS)
   {
     puts("The book.dat file is full.");
     exit(2);
   }
   puts("Please add new book titles.");
   puts("Press [enter] at the start of a line to stop.");
   while ( count < MAXBKS &&
          strcmp(gets(libry[count].title),STOP) != 0)
   {
     puts("Now enter the author.");
     gets(libry[count].author);
     puts("Now enter the value.");
```

Listing 14.11

**Listing 14.11
(cont'd.)**

```
        scanf("%f", &libry[count++].value );
        while ( getchar() != '\n')
            ;                /* clear input line */
        if ( count < MAXBKS )
            puts("Enter the next title.");
    }
    puts("Here is the list of your books:");
    for( index = 0; index < count; index++)
      printf("%s by %s: $%.2f\n",libry[index].title,
            libry[index].author, libry[index].value );
    fseek(pbooks, 0L, SEEK_END);  /* go to end of file */
    fwrite(&libry[filecount], size, count - filecount, pbooks);

    fclose(pbooks);
}
```

Let's look at a couple of sample runs:

```
% booksave
Please add new book titles.
Press [enter] at the start of a line to stop.
Metric Merriment
Now enter the author.
Polly Poetica
Now enter the value.
18.99
Enter the next title.
Epicurean Dreams
Now enter the author.
Waldo Snid
Now enter the value.
15.99
Enter the next title.
[enter]
Here is the list of your books:
Metric Merriment by Polly Poetica: $18.99
Epicurean Dreams by Waldo Snid: $15.99
% booksave
Current contents of book.dat:
Metric Merriment by Polly Poetica: $18.99
Epicurean Dreams by Waldo Snid: $15.99
Please add new book titles.
Nit for Gnat
Now enter the author.
Nellie Nicely
Now enter the value.
21.99
Enter the next title.
[enter]
```

```
Here is the list of your books:
Metric Merriment by Polly Poetica: $18.99
Epicurean Dreams by Waldo Snid: $15.99
Nit for Gnat by Nellie Nicely: $21.99
%
```

Running the program again shows all three books as current file members.

Program Points

First, we use the **"a+b"** mode for opening the file. The **a+** portion lets the program read the entire file and append data to the end of the file. The **b** is the ANSI way of signifying that the program will use the binary file format. For UNIX systems that don't accept the **b**, you can omit it, since UNIX only has one file form anyway. For other pre-ANSI implementations, you may need to find the local equivalent to using **b**.

We choose the binary mode because **fread( )** and **fwrite( )** are intended for binary files. True, some of the structure contents are text, but the **.value** member is not. If you use a text editor to look at **book.dat**, the text portion appears all right, but the numeric part is unreadable. The **rewind( )** command ensures that the file position pointer is situated at the start of the file, ready for read operations.

The initial **while** loop reads a structure at a time into the array of structures, stopping when the array is full or when the file is exhausted. The variable **filecount** keeps track of how many structures are read.

The next **while** loop takes user input. As in Listing 14.2, this loop quits when the array is full or when the user strikes the Enter key at the beginning of a line. Note that the **count** variable starts off with the value it has after the preceding loop. This action causes the new entries to be added to the end of the array. The **for** loop then prints out the data from the file and from the user.

The **fseek( )** call places the file position pointer at the end of the file, ready to append new data. Note that ANSI C specifies that **SEEK_END** is defined in **stdio.h**. If you use a pre-ANSI system, you may have to use the numerical value **2** instead.

To append the new data to the file, we could have used a loop to add one structure at a time. However, we use the **fwrite( )** function's ability to write more than one block at a time. The term **count – filecount** represents the number of new book titles added, and the call to **fwrite( )** writes that number of structure-sized blocks to the file. The expression **&libry[filecount]** is the address of the first new structure in the array, so copying begins from that point.

This example is perhaps the simplest way to save structures to a file and to retrieve them. However, it can waste space, as the unused parts of a structure also are saved. The size of this structure is 2 x 40 x **sizeof (char)** + **sizeof (float)**, which totals 84 bytes on our system. None of our entries actually needs all that space. However, the fact that each data chunk is the same size makes it simple to retrieve the data.

Another approach is to use variably sized records. To facilitate reading such records from a file, each record can begin with a numerical field that specifies the record size. This method is a bit more complex. It normally involves "linked structures," which we describe next and follow up with an example in Chapter 16, and using dynamic memory allocation, which we also discuss in Chapter 16.

14.10 Structures—What Next?

We won't take the explanation of structures any further, but we want to mention one of the more important uses of structures: creating new data forms. Computer users have developed data forms much more efficient for certain problems than the arrays and simple structures we have presented. These forms have names such as queues, binary trees, heaps, hash tables, and graphs. Many such forms are built from *linked structures*. Typically, each structure contains one or two items of data plus one or two pointers to other structures of the same type. The pointers serve to link one structure to another and to furnish a path to let you search through the overall structure. For example, Figure 14.3 shows a binary tree structure with each individual structure (or "node") connected to two below it.

Figure 14.3

A binary tree structure

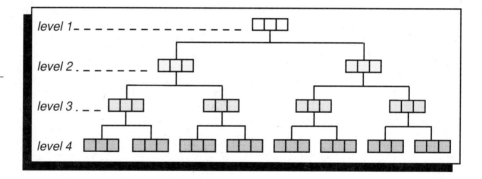

Is such a hierarchical or tree structure more efficient than an array? Consider the case of a tree with 10 levels of nodes. It has $2^{10} - 1$, or 1023, nodes in which you can store, say, 1023 words. If the words are arranged according to some sensible plan, you can start at the top level and find any word in at most 9 moves as your search moves down one level to the next. If your words are housed in an array, you may have to search all 1023 elements before finding the word.

You can consult a computer science text on data structures if you are interested in more advanced material. With the C structure feature, you will be able to create virtually every form presented in these texts.

14.11 Unions—A Quick Look

Let's now take a quick look at two other C features for dealing with data: the union and **typedef**. A *union* is a device that lets you store different data types in the same memory space (but not simultaneously). A typical use is in creating a table to hold a mixture of types in some order that is neither regular nor known in advance. The union allows you to create an array of equal-sized units, each of which can hold a variety of data types.

Unions are set up in much the same way as structures, with a union template and a union variable. They can be defined in one step or, by using a union tag, in two. The following illustrates a template with a tag:

```
union holdem {
        int digit;
        double bigfl;
        char letter;
        };
```

Next is an example of defining union variables of the **holdem** type:

```
union holdem fit;        /* union variable of holdem type */
union holdem save[10];   /* array of 10 union variables */
union holdem *pu;        /* pointer to a variable of holdem type */
```

The first declaration creates a single variable **fit**. The compiler allots enough space so that it can hold the largest of the described possibilities. In this case, the largest possibility listed is **double**, which requires 64 bits (8 bytes) on our system. The array **save** has 10 elements, each 8 bytes large.

We use unions in the following manner:

```
fit.digit = 23;      /* 23 is stored in fit; 2 bytes used */
fit.bigfl = 2.0;     /* 23 cleared, 2.0 stored; 8 bytes used */
fit.letter = 'h';    /* 2.0 cleared, h stored; 1 byte used */
```

The membership operator shows which data type is being used. Only one value is stored at a time; you can't store a **char** and an **int** at the same time, even though there is enough space to do so. It is your responsibility to keep track of the data type currently being stored in a union. The next sequence shows what not to do:

```
fit.letter = 'A';
flnum = 3.02*fit.bigfl;     /* ERROR ERROR ERROR */
```

This sequence is incorrect because a **char** type is stored, but the next line assumes the content of **fit** is a **double** type.

However, sometimes it can be useful to use one member to place values into a union and then to use a different member for viewing the contents. We show an example in Listing 15.4.

You can also use the **->** operator with unions in the same fashion you do with structures:

```
pu = &fit;
x = pu->digit;       /* same as x = fit.digit */
```

The Membership operator. The **.** operator is used with a structure or union name to specify a member of that structure or union. If **name** is the name of a structure and **member** is a member specified by the structure template, then

```
name.member
```

identifies that member of the structure. The type of **name.member** is the type specified for **member**. The membership operator can also be used in the same fashion with unions.

Example. The following program fragment assigns a value to the **code** member of the structure **item**:

```
struct {
    int code;
    float cost;
    } item;

item.code = 1265;
```

Indirect membership operator. This operator is used with a pointer to a structure or union to identify a member of that structure or union. Suppose **ptrstr** is a pointer to a structure and that **member** is a member specified by the structure template. Then

```
ptrstr->member
```

identifies that member of the pointed-to structure. The indirect membership operator can be used in the same fashion with unions.

Example. The following program fragment assigns a value to the **code** member of **item**:

```
struct {
      int code;
      float cost;
      } item, *ptrst;
ptrst = &item;
ptrst->code = 3451;
```

These three expressions are equivalent:

```
ptrst->code    item.code    (*ptrst).code
```

14.12 typedef—A Quick Look

The **typedef** feature lets you create your own name for a type. It is a lot like **#define** in that respect, but with three differences:

1. Unlike **#define**, **typedef** is limited to giving symbolic names only to data types.

2. The **typedef** function is performed by the compiler, not the preprocessor.

3. Within its limits, **typedef** is more flexible than **#define**.

To see how **typedef** works, let's suppose you want to use the term **real** for **float** numbers. In this case, you define **real** as if it were a **float** variable and precede the definition by the keyword **typedef**:

```
typedef float real;
```

From then on, you can use **real** to define variables:

```
real x, y[10], *z;
```

The scope of this definition depends on the location of the **typedef** statement. If the definition is inside a function, the scope is local, confined to that function. If the definition is outside a function, then the scope is global.

Sometimes, uppercase letters are used for **typedef** definitions to remind the user that the type name is really a symbolic abbreviation:

```
typedef float REAL;
```

This last example can also be duplicated with a **#define**:

```
#define REAL float
```

Here is one that can't be duplicated with **#define**:

```
typedef char *STRING;
```

Without the keyword **typedef**, this example identifies **STRING** itself as a pointer-to-**char**. With the keyword, it makes **STRING** an *identifier* for pointers-to-**char**. Thus:

```
STRING name, sign;
```

means

```
char *name, *sign;
```

We can also use **typedef** with structures. Here is an example:

```
typedef struct {
      float real;
      float imag;
} COMPLEX;
```

We then can use type **COMPLEX** to represent complex numbers. One reason to use **typedef** is to create convenient, recognizable names for types that turn up often. For instance, many people prefer to use **STRING** or its equivalent.

A second reason for using **typedef** is that **typedef** names are often used for complicated types. For example, the declaration

```
typedef char (*FRPTC ()) [5];
```

makes **FRPTC** represent a type that is a function that returns a pointer to a five-element array of **char**. (See the box entitled "Fancy Declarations.")

A third reason for using **typedef** is to make programs more portable. Suppose, for instance, that your program needs to use 16-bit numbers. On some systems, this requires type **short**; on others, it is type **int**. If you use just **short** or **int** in your declarations, you must then alter all the declarations when you move from one system type to the other. Instead, insert in an **#include** file the following definition:

```
typedef short TWOBYTE;
```

Use **TWOBYTE** in your programming for those **short** variables that must be 16 bits. Then when you move the program to a system that requires type **int**, simply change the single definition in your **#include** file:

```
typedef int TWOBYTE;
```

This example illustrates how portable C is.

When using **typedef**, bear in mind that it does not create new types; it creates convenient labels. For example, variables of the **STRING** type can be used as arguments for functions expecting type pointer-to-**char**.

▶ *Fancy Declarations*

C allows us to create elaborate data forms. In this text we try to stick to simpler forms, but here we point out the potentialities. When we make a declaration, the name (or identifier) we use can be modified by tacking on a modifier:

Modifier	Significance
*	Indicates a pointer
( )	Indicates a function
[ ]	Indicates an array

C lets us use more than one modifier at a time, which allows us to create a variety of types:

```
int board[8][8];     /* an array of arrays-of-int */
int **ptr;           /* a pointer to a pointer-to-int */
int *risks[10];
                     /* a 10-element array of pointers-to-int */
int (*rusks)[10];    /* a pointer to an array of 10 ints */
int *oof[3][4];      /* a 3 x 4 array of pointers-to-int */
int (*uuf)[3][4];    /* a pointer to a 3 x 4 array of ints */
int (*uof[3])[4];    /* a 3-element array of pointers to a
                        4-element array-of-int */
```

The trick to unravel these declarations is figuring out the order in which to apply the modifiers. You can use the following precedence rules as a guide.

1. The [ ] to indicate an array and the ( ) to indicate a function have the same precedence, which is higher than the precedence of the * indirection operator. Therefore,

```
int *risks[10];
```

makes **risks** an array of pointers rather than a pointer to an array.

2. The [ ] and ( ) associate from left to right. Thus,

```
int goods[12][50];
```

makes **goods** an array of 12 arrays of 50 **int**s, not an array of 50 arrays of 12 **int**s.

3. Parentheses used for grouping have the highest precedence. For example,

```
int (*rusks)[10];
```

makes **rusks** a pointer to an array of 10 **int**s.

Let's apply these rules to the following code:

```
int *oof[3][4];
```

The [3] has a higher precedence than the *, and because of the left-to-right rule, it has a higher precedence than the [4]. Hence **oof** is an array with three elements. Next in order is [4], so the elements of **oof** are arrays of four elements. The * then tells us these elements are pointers. The **int** completes the picture: **oof** is a three-element array of four-element arrays of pointers-to-**int**, or for short, a 3 x 4 array of pointers-to-**int**.

Now look at this declaration:

```
int (*uuf)[3][4];
```

The parentheses cause the * modifier to have first priority, making **uuf** a pointer to a 3 x 4 array-of-**int**s.

These rules also yield the following types:

```
char *fump();          /* function returning pointer-to-char */
char (* frump)();
          /* pointer to a function that returns type char */
char (*flump[3]) ();
                    /* array of 3 pointers to functions that
                          return type char */
```

When you bring structures into the picture, the possibilities for declarations grow truly baroque. And the applications—well, we leave that for more advanced texts.

14.13 Functions and Pointers

As the box entitled "Fancy Declarations" illustrated, it's possible to declare pointers to functions. Naturally, you probably wonder what is the use of a function pointer. Typically, a function pointer is used as an argument to another function, telling the second function which function to use. In Chapter 16 we show an example using the **qsort( )** sorting function from the C library. Thus far, we've used one sorting function for integers and another for strings. The algorithm was the same, but we used > for comparing integers and **strcmp( )** for strings. The **qsort( )** function takes a more general approach. You pass it a pointer to a comparison function appropriate to the type you wish to sort, and **qsort( )** then uses that function to sort the type, whether it be integer, string, or structure.

To show the essential ideas, the program in Listing 14.12 uses function pointers to print a command-line argument in normal and in reverse order.

❖ *func_ptr.c*

Listing 14.12

```
/* func_ptr.c--uses function pointers */
#include <stdio.h>
int rputs();
void show();
main(argc, argv)
int argc;
char *argv[];
{
   if (argc < 2)
       exit(1);
   show(puts, argv[1]);   /* use puts() */
   show(rputs, argv[1]);  /* use rputs() */
}
int rputs(str)
char *str;
```

Listing 14.12
(cont'd.)

```
{
   char *start = str;

   while (*str != '\0')
       str++;              /* go to end of string */
   while ( str != start)
       putchar(*--str);
   return putchar('\n');
}
void show ( fp, str)
int (*fp)();          /* fp points to function returning int */
char *str;
{
   (*fp)(str);          /* pass str to the pointed-to function */
}
```

Here are two sample runs:

```
C> funct_ptr pretty polly
pretty
ytterp
C> funct_ptr "fabulous duo"
fabulous duo
oud suolubaf
```

As we mentioned in an earlier chapter, some operating systems allow you to use quotes to group several words into a single command-line argument.

The first point to make about this program is that the name of a function used without parentheses acts as a pointer to a function. So the function call **show(puts, argv[1])** passes a pointer to the **puts( )** function, and **show(rputs, argv[1])** passes a pointer to the **rputs( )** function. Both also pass a pointer to a string. Incidentally, you also can use function names in assignment statements. For instance, if **pfun** is declared to be a pointer to a function that returns **double**, you can do the following:

```
pfun = atof;
```

Second, the **show( )** function definition must declare its argument types. Both **puts( )** and **rputs( )** return an **int**, so the proper declaration for **fp** is this one:

```
int (*fp)();
```

In ANSI C, you also can (and should) indicate what type arguments the pointed-to function takes:

```
int (*fp)(char *);    /* ANSI C prototyping */
```

Note that we define **rputs( )** so that it has the same type arguments and return value as **puts( )**. Passing pointers of different types of functions can cause problems; the ANSI C function prototyping helps catch this sort of error.

Third, the example shows how to use a function pointer. Because **fp** points to a function, the expression ***fp** represents the function that is pointed to, and **(*fp)(str)** is a call to that function, passing **str** as an argument to it. Similarly, given the definition

```
pfun = atof();
```

you can use this call to invoke the **atof( )** function:

```
(*pfun)(string);
```

Some C compilers have allowed the following usage when **pfun** is a pointer:

```
pfun(string);          /* rogue usage */
```

Note: Neither ANSI C nor K & R C supports this form.

14.14 Summary

The structure provides a means to store several data items, usually of different types, in the same data object. You can use a tag to identify a specific structure template and to declare variables of that type. The membership operator (**.**) lets you access the individual members of a structure by using labels from the structure template.

If you have a pointer to a structure, you can use the pointer and the **->** operator instead of a name and the **.** operator to access individual members. To obtain the address of a structure, use the **&** operator. Unlike the case for arrays, the name of a structure does not serve as a pointer to the structure.

Traditionally, structure-related functions have used pointers to structures as arguments. Modern C, including ANSI C, permits structures to be passed as arguments, to be used as return values, and to be assigned to structures of the same type.

Unions use the same syntax as structures. However with unions, the members share a common storage space. Instead of storing several data types simultaneously, the union chooses which single data item type from a list of choices is stored. That is, a structure can hold, say, an **int**, a **double**, *and* a **char**, whereas the corresponding union can hold an **int**, a **double**, *or* a **char**.

The **typedef** facility enables you to establish aliases or shorthand representations of standard C types.

The name of a function can be used as a pointer to a function. Such pointers can be passed as arguments to functions which then use the pointed-to function. Figure 14.4 illustrates the four uses of function names: in defining a function, in declaring a function, in calling a function, and as a pointer.

Figure 14.4

Function name uses

```
function name used in a prototype declaration: int comp(int x, int y);
             function name used in a function call: status = comp(q,r);
      function name used in a function definition: int comp(x,y)
                                                    int x,y;
                                                    { ...
      function name used as a pointer in assignment: pfunct = comp;
            function name used as pointer argument: slowsort(arr,n,comp);
```

Review Questions

1. What's wrong with this template?

```
structure {
        char itable;
        int num[20];
        char *togs
        }
```

2. What does the following program portion print?

```
struct house    {
                float sqft;
                int rooms;
                int stories;
                char *address;
                };
main()
{
   static struct house fruzt = { 1560.0, 6, 1, "22 Spiffo Road"};
   struct house *sign;

   sign = &fruzt;
   printf("%d %d\n", fruzt.rooms, sign->stories);
   printf("%s \n", fruzt.address);
   printf("%c %c\n", sign->address[3], fruzt.address[4]);
}
```

3. Devise a structure template that holds the name of a month, a three-letter abbreviation for the month, the number of days in the month, and the month number.

4. Define an array of 12 structures of the sort in Question 3 and initialize it for a nonleap year.

5. Write a function that when given the month number returns the total days in the year up through that month. Assume that the structure template and array developed in Questions 3 and 4 are declared externally.

6. Given the following **typedef**, declare a 10-element array of the indicated structure:

```
typedef struct {          /* lens descriptor */
          float foclen;   /* focal length, mm */
          float fstop;    /* aperture */
          char *brand;    /* brand name */
          } LENS;
```

Then, using individual member assignment, let the third element describe a Remarkatar lens of focal length 500 mm and aperture f/2.0.

7. Consider the following programming fragment:

```
struct name { char first[20];
        char last[20];
        };
struct bem   { int limbs;
        struct name title;
        char type[30];
        };
struct bem *pb;
struct bem deb = { 6,
                { "Berbnazel", "Gwolkapwolk"},
                "Arcturan"
                };
pb = &deb;
```

a. What does each of the following statements print?

```
printf("%d", deb.limbs);
printf("%s", pb->type);
printf("%s", pb->type + 2);
```

b. How can you represent "Gwolkapwolk" in structure notation (two ways)?

c. Write a function that takes the address of a **bem** structure as an argument and prints out the contents of the structure in the form shown:

```
Berbnazel Gwolkapwolk is a 6-limbed Arcturan.
```

Assume that the structure definitions are in a file called **starfolk.h**.

8. Consider the following declarations:

```
struct fullname   {
        char fname[20];
        char lname[20];
        };
struct bard     {
        struct fullname name;
        int born;
        int died;
        };
struct bard willie;
struct bard *pt = &willie;
```

a. Identify the **born** member of the **willie** structure using the **willie** identifier.

b. Identify the **born** member of the **willie** structure using the **pt** identifier.

c. Use a **scanf( )** call to read in a value for the **born** member using the **willie** identifier.

d. Use a **scanf( )** call to read in a value for the **born** member using the **pt** identifier.

e. Construct an identifier for the third letter of the first name of someone described by the **willie** variable.

f. Construct an expression that represents the total number of letters in the first and last names of someone described by the **willie** variable.

9. Define a structure template that is suitable for holding the following items: the name of an automobile, its horsepower, its EPA city-driving mpg rating, its wheelbase, and a pointer to another structure of the same type. Use **car** as the template tag.

10. Suppose we have this structure:

```
struct gas   { float distance;
         float gals;
         float mpg;
         };
```

Define a function that takes a pointer to a **gas** structure, computes miles per gallon from the **distance** and **gals** members, places the answer in the **mpg** member, and also returns that value.

11. Accomplish the main objective of Question 10 (getting a miles-per-gallon value into the **mpg** member) using a function that doesn't take pointers.

12. a. In Listing 14.5, can we use **char bank[30]** and **char save[30]** as structure members instead of **char *bank** and **char *save**?

b. What effect does this change in structure members have on the structure?

c. Can either form be used if the names are to be read from the keyboard instead of being supplied as initialization data?

13. Declare a pointer to a function that returns a pointer-to-**char**.

14. Declare four type **void** functions and initialize an array of pointers to point to them.

Programming Exercises

1. Redo Review Question 5, but have the argument be the spelled-out name of the month instead of the month number. (Note: Don't forget about **strcmp( )**.)

2. Write a program that asks the user to input the day, month, and year. The month can be a month number, a month name, or a month abbreviation. The program then returns the total number of days in the year up through the given day. It should use the year information to identify and handle leap years correctly.

3. Revise Listing 14.2 so that it prints out the book descriptions alphabetized by title and the total value of the books.

4. a. Write a program that creates a structure template with two members. The first element is a Social Security number. The second element is a structure with three members. Its first member contains a first name; the second member contains a middle name; and the final element contains a last name. Create and initialize an array of five such structures. Have the program print out the data in this form:

```
Dribble, Flossie M. 302039823
```

Note that only the initial of the middle name is used and that a period is added. Neither the initial nor the period should be printed if the middle name member is empty. Write a function to do the printing; pass the structure address to the function.

   b. Modify a by passing the structure value instead of its address.

5. Write a program that fits the requirements listed in parts a–c.

   a. Externally define a **name** structure template with two members: a string to hold the first name and a string to hold the second name.

   b. Externally define a **student** structure template with three members: a **name** structure, a grade array to hold three floating-point scores, and a variable to hold the average of the three scores.

   c. Have the **main( )** function declare an array of **CSIZE** (with **CSIZE = 4**) student structures and initialize the name portions to names of your choice.

   Use functions to perform the tasks described in d–g.

   d. Interactively acquire scores for each student by prompting the user with a student name and a request for scores. Place the scores in the grade array portion of the appropriate structure. The required looping may be performed in **main( )** or in the function, whichever you prefer.

   e. Calculate the average score value for each structure and assign it to the proper location.

   f. Print out the information in each structure.

   g. Print out the class average for each of the numerical structure elements.

6. Modify Listing 14.11 so that as each record is read from the file and shown to you, you are given the chance to delete the record or modify its contents. If you delete the record, use the vacated array position for the next record to be read.

To accomplish this assignment, you should alter several aspects of the original program. First, you should modularize the program further. Second, you need a way to indicate that a structure is deleted. You can do so by, say, using a special title such as "ZZZXXXZZ" or by adding a new member to the structure to indicate its deletion status. Your program will then check for the special title or the status member before displaying and saving the structure contents. Third, the **"a+b"** mode no longer is appropriate, for it doesn't let you alter existing parts of a file.

Probably the simplest approach is first to open the file in the **"rb"** mode to report the current contents and then to close the file and reopen it in the **"wb"** mode when it's time to save the array of structures. Opening the file in the **"rb"** mode truncates the current contents, giving you a clean slate with which to work. Thus the approach: Copy the file to the array of structures, modify and extend that array as desired, and save the new array contents to the file.

7. The Colossus Airlines fleet consists of one plane with a seating capacity of 12. It makes one flight daily. Write a seating reservation program with the following features.

  a. It uses an array of 12 structures. Each structure should hold a seat identification number, a marker that indicates whether or not the seat is assigned, the last name of the seat holder, and the first name of the seat holder.

  b. It displays the following menu:

```
To choose a function, enter its letter label:
a) Show number of empty seats
b) Show list of empty seats
c) Show alphabetical list of seat assignments
d) Assign a customer to a seat
e) Delete a seat assignment
f) Quit
```

  c. It successfully executes the promises of its menu. Choices d and e require additional input, and each should allow the user to abort entry.

  d. After executing a function (other than choice f), the program redisplays the menu.

  e. Data are saved in a file between runs. When the program is started up, it first loads in the data, if any, from the file.

For programs of this sort, you should follow top-down programming practices, developing the overall structure first, using a modular approach, and using simple stub functions (functions that do nothing but act as placeholders) initially. Once the overall design works, start replacing the stub functions with working functions.

8. Colossus Airlines now acquires a second plane also with a seating capacity of 12 and expands its service to four flights daily (flights 102, 311, 444, and 519). Expand the program you developed in Exercise 7 to handle the four flights. Have a top level menu that offers a choice of flights and quitting. Selecting a particular flight then should bring up a menu similar to that of Exercise 7. However, one new item should be added: confirming a seat assignment. Also, the quit choice should be replaced with the choice of exiting to the top-level menu. Each display should indicate which flight is currently being handled. The seat assignment display should also indicate the confirmation status.

9. Write a program that implements a menu by using an array of structures. Each structure contains a type **char** member, a pointer-to-**char** member, and a pointer-to-type-**void** function member. The **char** member is initialized to a menu label; the pointer-to-**char** member is initialized to point to a string to attach to the label; and the function pointer is initialized to point to a function to be executed if the user selects the corresponding label.

The program should pass over invalid label selections, prompting the user to try again. One approach is to pass the array of structures and the array size to a **menu( )** function in a **while** loop. This function shows the menu, reads the response, runs the corresponding function, and returns a value indicating whether or not the loop should continue.

15

Bit Fiddling

Contents

Objectives

Understanding binary representation of values

Using octal and hexadecimal number bases

Using the bitwise operators

Using bit fields

*T*he C programming language has the ability to manipulate individual bits in a byte or word. This facility endears C to programmers who find it necessary, or at least desirable, to do precisely that. For example, many a hardware device is controlled by sending it a byte in which each bit has special meaning to the device. Also, often operating system information about, say, files is stored using particular bits to indicate specific items. In this chapter, we investigate C's bit powers, but first we supply you with some background about bits, bytes, binary notation, and other number bases.

15.1 Binary Numbers, Bits, and Bytes

The way we usually write numbers is based on the number 10. For instance, 3652 has a 3 in the thousand's place, a 6 in the hundred's place, a 5 in the ten's place, and a 2 in the one's place. Therefore, we can think of 3652 as being the following:

```
3 x 1000 + 6 x 100 + 5 x 10 + 2 x 1
```

But 1000 is 10 cubed, 100 is 10 squared, 10 is 10 to the first power, and by convention, 1 is 10 (or any positive number) to the zero power. So we also can write 3652 in this way:

$$3 \times 10^3 + 6 \times 10^2 + 5 \times 10^1 + 2 \times 10^0$$

Because our system of writing numbers is based on powers of ten, we say that 3652 is written in *base 10*.

Presumably, the decimal system evolved because we have ten fingers. A computer bit, in a sense, has only 2 fingers, for it can be set only to 0 or 1, which is off or on. Thus *base 2* system is a natural number for a computer. It uses powers of 2 instead of powers of 10. As we mentioned in earlier chapters, numbers expressed in base 2 are termed binary numbers. For instance, a binary number such as 1101 means

$$1 \times 2^3 + 1 \times 2^2 + 0 \times 2^1 + 1 \times 2^0$$

which becomes

```
1 x 8 + 1 x 4 + 0 x 2 + 1 x 1 = 13
```

in decimal numbers. The binary system lets us express any number (if we have enough bits) as a combination of 1s and 0s. This facility is convenient for digital computers, which express information in combinations of on and off states that can be interpreted as 1s and 0s. Let's see how this system works for a one-byte integer.

Binary Integers

By modern definition, a byte contains eight bits. (A few, rare, older systems use a bigger byte.) We can think of these eight bits as being numbered from 7 to 0, left to right. Bit 7

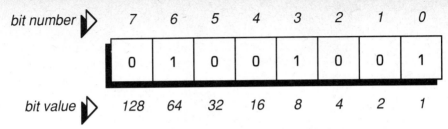

Figure 15.1

Bit numbers and values

bit number ▷ 7 6 5 4 3 2 1 0

0	1	0	0	1	0	0	1

bit value ▷ 128 64 32 16 8 4 2 1

This example show bits 6, 3, and 0 set to 1.
The value of this byte is 64 + 8 + 1 or 73.

is called the *high-order bit;* bit 0 is the *low-order bit.* The bit number corresponds to an exponent of 2.

Imagine a byte as looking like Figure 15.1. Here, 128 is 2^7, and so on. The largest number this byte can hold is one with all bits set to 1: 11111111. The value of this binary number follows:

```
128 + 64 + 32 + 16 + 8 + 4 + 2 + 1 = 255
```

The smallest binary number this byte can hold is 00000000, or a simple 0.

A byte can store numbers from 0 to 255 for a total of 256 possible values. Or by changing the interpretation, a byte can store numbers from −128 to +127, again a total of 256 values.

Signed Integers

The representation of signed numbers is determined by the hardware, not by C. Probably the simplest way to represent signed numbers is to reserve one bit, such as the high-order bit to represent the sign. In a one-byte value, seven bits are therefore left for the number itself. In such a *sign-magnitude representation,* 10000001 is −1 and 00000001 is 1. The total range, then, is −127 to +127.

One disadvantage of this approach is that it has two zeros: +0 and −0. This situation is confusing, and it also uses up two bit patterns for just one value.

The *two's-complement method* avoids the preceding problem and is the most common system used today. Let's discuss it as it applies to a one-byte value. In that context, the values 0 through 127 are represented by the last seven bits, with the high-order bit set to 0. So far, the setup is the same as for the sign-magnitude method. Also, if the high-order bit is 1, the value is negative. The difference between the two representations comes in determining the value of that negative number. Subtract the bit pattern from the nine-bit pattern 100000000 (256 in binary), and the result is the magnitude of value. For example, suppose the pattern is 10000000. As an unsigned byte, this pattern represents 128. As a signed value, it is negative (bit 7 is 1) and has a value of 100000000 − 10000000, or 10000000 (128). Thus the number is −128. Similarly, 10000001 is −127, and 11111111 is –1. The two's-complement method represents numbers in the range –128 to 127.

The *one's-complement method* forms the negative of a number by inverting each bit in the pattern. For instance, 00000001 is 1, and 11111110 is –1. This method also has a –0: 11111111. Its range for a one-byte value is –127 to +127.

Binary Floating Point

Floating-point numbers are stored in two parts: a binary fraction and a binary exponent.

Binary Fractions

The ordinary fraction .324 represents

$3/10$ + $2/100$ + $4/1000$

with the denominators representing increasing powers of 10. In a binary fraction, we use powers of 2 for denominators. Thus the binary fraction .101 represents

$1/2$ + $0/4$ + $1/8$

which in decimal notation is

0.50 + 0.00 + 0.125

or 0.625.

Many fractions, such as $1/3$, cannot be represented exactly in decimal notation. Similarly, many fractions cannot be represented exactly in binary notation. Indeed, the only fractions that can be represented exactly are combinations of multiples of powers of $1/2$. Thus $3/4$ and $7/8$ can be represented exactly as binary fractions, but $1/3$ and $2/5$ cannot be.

Floating-Point Representation

To represent a floating-point number in a computer, a certain number (system-dependent) of bits is set aside to hold a binary fraction. Additional bits hold an exponent. In general terms, the actual value of the number consists of the binary fraction multiplied by 2 to the indicated exponent. Thus multiplying a floating-point number by, say, 4, increases the exponent by 2 and leaves the binary fraction unchanged. Multiplying by a number that is not a power of 2 changes the binary fraction and if necessary, the exponent.

15.2 Other Bases

Computer workers often use number systems based on 8 and on 16. Since 8 and 16 are powers of 2, these systems are more closely related to a computer's binary system than the decimal system is.

Octal

Octal refers to a base 8 system, as noted in earlier chapters. In this system, the different places in a number represent powers of 8. We use the digits 0 to 7. For example, the octal number 451 (written 0451 in C) is represented by the following:

```
4 x 8² + 5 x 8¹ + 1 x 8⁰ = 297 (base 10)
```

A handy thing to know about octal numbers is that each octal digit corresponds to three binary digits. Table 15.1 shows this correspondence, which makes it simple to translate between the two systems. For example, the octal number 0377 is 11111111 in binary; we replace the 3 with 011, drop the leading 0, then replace each 7 with 111. The only awkward part is that a 3-digit octal number may take up to nine bits in binary form, so an octal value larger than 0377 requires more than a byte. Note that internal 0s are not dropped: 0173 is 01 111 011, not 01 111 11.

Table 15.1 Comparison of Octal Digits and Binary Equivalents

Octal Digit	Binary Equivalent
0	000
1	001
2	010
3	011
4	100
5	101
6	110
7	111

Hexadecimal

Also as noted in earlier chapters hexadecimal or hex, refers to a base 16 system. Here we use powers of 16 and the digits 0 to 15. But since we don't have single digits to represent the values 10 to 15, we use the letters A to F for that purpose. For instance, the hex number A3F (written 0xA3F in C) represents

```
10 x 16² + 3 x 16¹ + 15 x 16⁰ = 2623 (base 10)
```

since A represents 10 and F represents 15.

Each hexadecimal digit corresponds to a four-digit binary number. Thus, two hexadecimal digits correspond exactly to an eight-bit byte. The first digit represents the first four bits; the second digit represents the last four bits. Therefore, the hexadecimal system is a natural choice for representing byte values. Table 15.2 shows the correspondence. For example, the hex value 0xC2 translates to 11000010.

Table 15.2 Comparison of Decimal and Hexadecimal Digits and Their Binary Equivalents

Decimal Digit	Hexadecimal Digit	Binary Equivalent	Decimal Digit	Hexadecimal Digit	Binary Equivalent
0	0	0000	8	8	1000
1	1	0001	9	9	1001
2	2	0010	10	A	1010
3	3	0011	11	B	1011
4	4	0100	12	C	1100
5	5	0101	13	D	1101
6	6	0110	14	E	1110
7	7	0111	15	F	1111

Now that we've seen what bits and bytes are, let's examine what C can do with them. We discuss the two facilities that help you manipulate bits. The first is a set of six bitwise operators that act on bits. The second is the **field** data form, which gives you access to bits within an **int**.

15.3 C's Bitwise Operators

C offers bitwise logical operators and shift operators. In the following sections, we write out values in binary notation so that you can see the mechanics. In an actual program, you should use integer variables or constants written in the usual forms. For instance, instead of 00011001, you should use 25, 031, or 0x19. For our examples, we will use eight-bit numbers, with the bits numbered 7 to 0, left to right.

Bitwise Logical Operators

The four *bitwise logical operators* work on integer-class data, including **char**. They are termed bitwise because they operate on each bit independently of the bit to the left or right.

One's Complement, or Bitwise Negation: ~

This unary operator changes each 1 to a 0 and each 0 to a 1, for example:

```
~(10011010) == (01100101)
```

Suppose, for instance, that **val** is an **unsigned char** that has been assigned the value **2**. In binary, this number is 00000010. With ~**val**, the value is 11111101, or **253**. Note that the operator does not change the value of **val**, just as **3 * val** does not change the **val** value; **val** is still **2**. But this operator does create a new value that can be used or assigned elsewhere:

```
newval = ~val;
printf("%d", ~val);
```

If you want to change the value of **val** to **~val**, use simple assignment:

```
val = ~val;
```

Bitwise AND: &

This binary operator produces a new value by making a bit-by-bit comparison between two operands. For each bit position, the resulting bit is 1 only if both corresponding bits in the operands are 1. (In terms of true–false, the result is true only if each of the two bit operands is true.) Thus,

```
(10010011) & (00111101) == (00010001)
```

since only bits 4 and 0 are 1 in both operands.

C also has a combined AND-assignment operator: **&=**. For example,

```
val &= 0377;
```

produces the same final result as the following:

```
val = val & 0377;
```

Bitwise OR: |

This binary operator produces a new value by making a bit-by-bit comparison between two operands. For each bit position, the resulting bit is 1 if either of the corresponding bits in the operands is 1. (In terms of true–false, the result is true if one or the other bit operands are true or if both are true.) Thus,

```
(10010011) | (00111101) == (101111111)
```

since all bit positions but bit 6 have the value 1 in one or the other operands.

C also has a combined OR-assignment operator: **|=**. The statement

```
val |= 0377;
```

produces the same final result as the following:

```
val = val | 0377;
```

Bitwise EXCLUSIVE OR: ^

This binary operator makes a bit-by-bit comparison between two operands. For each bit position, the resulting bit is 1 if one or the other (but not both) of the corresponding bits in the operands is 1. (In terms of true–false, the result is true if one or the other bit operands—and not both—are true.) Thus,

```
(10010011) ^ (00111101) == (10101110)
```

Note that since bit position 0 has the value 1 in both operands, the resulting 0 bit has value 0.

C also has a combined OR-assignment operator: ^=. The statement

```
val ^= 0377;
```

produces the same final result as the following:

```
val = val ^ 0377;
```

Usage: Masks

The AND operator often is used in conjunction with a *mask,* which is a bit pattern with some bits on (1) and some bits off (0). To see why a mask is so named, let's see what happens when a quantity is ANDed with a mask. For example, suppose we **#define MASK** to be **2**, that is, binary 00000010, with only bit number 1 being nonzero. Then the statement

```
flags = flags & MASK;
```

causes all the bits of **flags** (except bit 1) to be set to 0, since any bit combined with 0 via the **&** operator yields 0. Bit 1 is left unchanged. (If the bit is 1, then **1 & 1** is 1; if the bit is 0, then **0 & 1** is 0.)

This scenario is called using a mask because the zeros in the mask hide the corresponding bits in **flags**. Extending the analogy, we can think of the 0s in the mask as being opaque and the 1s as being transparent. The expression **flags & MASK** is like covering the **flags** bit pattern with the mask; only the bits under the **MASK** 1s are visible. See Figure 15.2.

We can also shorten the code by using the AND-assignment operator:

```
flags &= MASK;
```

One common C usage of masks is the following:

```
ch &= 0377;
```

The value 0377, recall, is 11111111 in binary. This mask leaves the final 8 bits of **ch** alone and sets the rest to 0. Thus regardless of whether the original **ch** is 8 bits, 16 bits, or more, the final value is trimmed down to something that fits into a single byte.

Usage: Turning Bits On

Sometimes you may need to turn on particular bits in a value while leaving the remaining bits unchanged. For instance, the IBM PC controls its hardware through

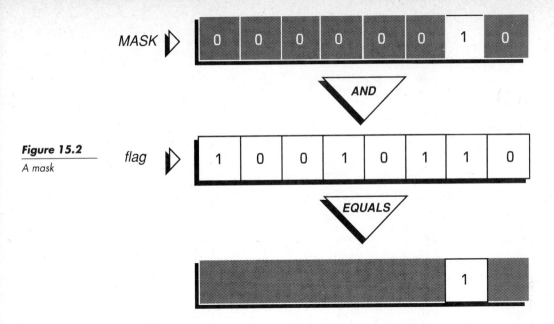

Figure 15.2

A mask

MASK

AND

flag

EQUALS

values sent to ports. To turn on, say, the speaker, you may have to turn on one bit while leaving the others unchanged. This task can be accomplished using the OR operator.

For example, consider our **MASK**, which has bit 1 set to 1. The statement

```
flags = flags | MASK;
```

sets bit number 1 in **flags** to 1 and leaves all the other bits unchanged. This action follows because any bit combined with 0 via the | operator is itself, and any bit combined with 1 via the | operator is 1. For short, you can also use the OR-assignment operator

```
flags |= MASK;
```

which sets to 1 those bits in **flags** that also are on in **MASK**, leaving the other bits unchanged.

Note: Recall from our discussion of **open( )** in Chapter 12 that we use the combination **O_RDONLY | O_BINARY** to open a file in the binary mode. This expression uses the OR operator to set to 1 the bits corresponding to the 1 bits of the defined constants.

Usage: Turning Bits Off

Just as it is useful to be able to turn particular bits on without disturbing the other bits, it's sometimes useful to be able to turn them off. Suppose, for instance we want to turn off bit 1 in the variable **flags**. Once again **MASK** has just the 1 bit on. We can do the following:

```
flags = flags & ~MASK;
```

Since **MASK** is all 0s except for bit 1, then **~MASK** is all 1s except for bit 1. A 1 AND any bit is that bit, so our statement leaves all the bits other than bit 1 unchanged. Also, a 0 AND any bit is 0, so bit 1 is set to 0 regardless of its original value.

You can also use the short form:

```
flags &= ~MASK;
```

Usage: Toggling Bits

Toggling a bit means turning it off if it is on or turning it on if it is off. You can use the EXCLUSIVE OR operator to toggle a bit. The idea is that if **b** is a bit setting (1 or 0), then **1 ^ b** is 0 if **b** is **1** and is **1** if **b** is 0. Also, **0 ^ b** is **b**, regardless of its value. Thus if we EXCLUSIVE OR a value with a mask, values that correspond to 1s in the mask are toggled, and values that correspond to 0s in the mask are unaltered. So to toggle bit 1 in **flag**, we can do either of the following:

```
flags = flags ^ MASK;
flags ^= MASK;
```

Usage: Checking the Value of a Bit

We've seen how to change the values of bits. Suppose, instead, that you want to check the value of a bit. For example, does **flags** have bit 1 set to 1? You shouldn't simply compare **flag** to **MASK**:

```
if ( flags == MASK )
  puts("Wow!");    /* doesn't work right */
```

Even if bit 1 in **flags** is set to 1, the other bit setting in **flags** can make the comparison untrue. Instead, we must first mask the other bits in **flags** so that we compare only bit 1 of **flags** with **MASK**:

```
if ( (flags & MASK) == MASK)
  puts("Wow!");
```

We use parentheses around **flags & MASK** because the bit-wise operators have lower precedence than ==.

Bitwise Shift Operators

Now let's look at C's shift operators. The *bitwise shift operators* shift bits to the left or right. Again, we use binary numbers explicitly to show the mechanics.

Left Shift: <<

This operator shifts the bits of the value of the left operand to the left by the number of places given by the right operand. The vacated positions are filled with 0s, and bits moved beyond the end of the left operand are lost. Thus, in the statement

```
(10001010) << 2 == (00101000)
```

each bit is moved two places to the left.

This operation produces a new bit value, but it doesn't change its operands. For example, suppose **stonk** is **1**. Then **stonk<<2** is **4**, but **stonk** still is **1**. You can use the left-shift-assignment operator (<<=) to change the variable's value. This operator shifts the bit in the variable to its left by the number of places given by the righthand value. For instance:

```
int stonk = 1;
int onkoo;

onkoo = stonk << 2;        /* assigns 4 to onkoo */
stonk <<= 2;               /* changes stonk to 4 */
```

Right Shift: >>

This operator shifts the bits of the value of the left operand to the right by the number of places given by the right operand. Bits moved beyond the right end of the left operand are lost. For **unsigned** types, the places vacated at the left end are replaced by 0s. For an unsigned value, in the statement

```
(10001010) >> 2 == (00100010)
```

each bit is moved two places to the right. For **signed** types, the result is machine dependent. The vacated places may be filled with 0s, or they may be filled with copies of the sign (leftmost) bit.

The right-shift-assignment operator (>>=) shifts the bits in the lefthand variable to the right by the indicated number of places. For example:

```
int sweet = 16;
int ooosw;

ooosw = sweet >> 3;        /* ooosw = 4, sweet still 16 */
sweet >>= 3;               /* sweet changed to 4 */
```

Usage

The bitwise shift operators provide swift and efficient multiplication and division by powers of 2:

number << n	Multiplies **number** by **2n**
number >> n	Divides **number** by **2n** if **number** is not negative

This system is analogous to the decimal system procedure of shifting the decimal point to multiply or divide by 10.

In Chapter 9 we used recursion to write a program to convert numbers to a binary representation. Now we solve the same problem using bitwise operators. The program in Listing 15.1 reads an integer from the keyboard and passes it along with a string address to a function called **itobs( )** (for integer **to** binary string). This function then uses bit-wise operators to select the correct pattern of 1s and 0s to put into the string.

❖ *binary.c*

Listing 15.1

```
/* binary.c--using bit operations to display binary */
#include <stdio.h>
main()
{
   char bin_str[1 + 8 * sizeof(int)];
   char *itobs();
   int number;

   puts("Enter integers and see them in binary.");
   puts("Nonnumeric input terminates the program.");
   while ( scanf("%d", &number) == 1)
     printf("%d is %s\n", number, itobs(number,bin_str));
}

char *itobs(n, ps)
int n;
char *ps;
{
   int i;
   static int size = 8 * sizeof(int);

   for ( i = size - 1; i >= 0; i--, n >>= 1)
     ps[i] = (01 & n) + '0';
   ps[size] = '\0';
   return ps;
}
```

This program assumes the system uses eight bits to a byte. Thus, the expression **8 * sizeof(int)** is the number of bits in an **int**. The **bin_str** array has that many elements plus one to allow for the terminating null character.

The **itobs( )** function returns the same address passed to it so that we can use the function as, say, an argument to **printf( )**. In **itobs( )** we make **size** a **static** variable so that it is initialized just once instead of every time the function is called.

The first time through the **for** loop, the function evaluates the quantity **01 & n**. The term **01** is a mask with all but the zero bit set to 0. Therefore **01 & n** simply just the value of the final bit in **n**. This value is a 0 or a 1, but for the array, we need the *character* **'0'** or the *character* **'1'**. Adding the ASCII code for **'0'** accomplishes this conversion.

The result is placed in the next-to-last element of the array, the last element being reserved for the null character.

Then the loop executes the statements **i--** and **n >>= 1**. The first moves us one element earlier in the array, and the second shifts the bits in **n** over one position. Thus the next time through the loop, we find the value of the bit that used to be next to the end. The corresponding digit character then is placed in the element preceding the final digit. In this fashion, the function fills the array from right to left. Here is a sample run:

```
Enter integers and see them in binary.
Nonnumeric input terminates the program.
7
7 is 0000000000000111
255
255 is 0000000011111111
30000
30000 is 0111010100110000
-1
-1 is 1111111111111111
q
```

Another Example

Let's work through one more example. Our goal this time is to write a function that inverts the last **n** bits in a value, in which both **n** and the value are function arguments.

The ~ operator inverts bits, but it inverts all the bits in a byte, not just a select few. But, the EXCLUSIVE OR operator can be used to toggle bytes. Suppose we create a mask with the last **n** bits set to 1 and the remaining bits set to 0. Then EXCLUSIVE OR-ing that mask with a value toggles, or inverts, the last **n** bits, leaving the other bits unchanged. See Listing 15.2.

Listing 15.2

❖ *invert.c*

```
/* invert.c */
int invert_end(num,bits)
int num, bits;
{
   int mask = 0;
   int bitval = 1;

   while (bits-- > 0)
   {
      mask |= bitval;
      bitval <<= 1;
   }
   return num ^ mask;
}
```

The **while** loop creates the mask. Initially, **mask** has all its bits set to **0**. The first pass through the loop sets bit 0 to **1** and then increases the value of **bitval** to **2**. That is, this pass sets bit 0 to **0** and bit 1 to **1**. The next pass through then sets bit 1 of **mask** to **1**, and so on. Finally, the **num ^ mask** operation produces the desired result.

To test the function, we can slip it into Listing 15.1. See Listing 15.3.

❖ *invert4.c*

```
/* invert4.c--invert last 4 bits of integers */
#include <stdio.h>
main()
{
   char bin_str[1 + 8 * sizeof(int)];
   char *itobs();
   int invert_end();
   int number;

   puts("Enter integers and see them in binary.");
   puts("Nonnumeric input terminates the program.");
   while ( scanf("%d", &number) == 1)
   {
     printf("%d is %s\n", number, itobs (number,bin_str));
     printf("Inverting the last 4 bits gives %s\n",
            itobs( invert_end(number,4)));
   }
}
```

Listing 15.3

```
char *itobs(n, ps)
int n;
char *ps;
{
   int i;
   static int size = 8 * sizeof(int);

   for ( i = size - 1; i >= 0; i--, n >>= 1)
       ps[i] = (01 & n) + '0';
   ps[size] = '\0';
   return ps;
}
int invert_end(num,bits)
int num, bits;
{
   int mask = 0;
   int bitval = 1;
   while (bits-- > 0)
   {
     mask |= bitval;
     bitval <<= 1;
   }
   return num ^ mask;
}
```

A sample run follows:

```
Enter integers and see them in binary.
Nonnumeric input terminates the program.
7
7 is 0000000000000111
Inverting the last 4 bits gives 0000000000001000
255
255 is 0000000011111111
Inverting the last 4 bits gives 0000000011110000
q
```

15.4 Bit Fields

The second method of manipulating bits is to use a *bit field*, which is simply a set of neighboring bits within an **unsigned int**. A bit field is set up via a structure definition that labels each field and determines its width. The following definition sets up four one-bit fields:

```
struct   {
      unsigned autfd : 1;
      unsigned bldfc : 1;
      unsigned undln : 1;
      unsigned itals : 1;
      } prnt;
```

The variable **prnt** now contains four one-bit fields and is stored in an **int**-sized memory cell, although only four bits are used in this example.

The structure membership operator can be used to assign values to individual fields:

```
prnt.itals = 0;
prnt.undln = 1;
```

Because each field is just 1 bit, **1** and **0** are the only values we can use for assignment. However, fields aren't limited to one-bit sizes. For example,

```
struct   {
      unsigned code1 : 2;
      unsigned code2 : 2;
      unsigned code3 : 8;
      } prcode;
```

creates two two-bit fields and one eight-bit field. We can make assignments such as:

```
prcode.code1 = 0;
prcode.code2 = 3;
prcode.code3 = 102;
```

Just make sure that the value doesn't exceed the field's capacity.

If the total number of bits you declare exceeds the size of an **int**, then the next **int** storage location is used. A single field is not allowed to overlap the boundary between two **int**s; the compiler automatically shifts an overlapping field definition so that the field is aligned with the **int** boundary. If this compiler shift occurs, it leaves an unnamed hole in the first **int**.

You can "pad" a field structure with unnamed holes by using unnamed field widths. Using an unnamed field width of 0 forces the next field to align with the next integer:

```
struct   {
        field1   : 1;
                 : 2;
        field2   : 1;
                 : 0;
        field3   : 1;
        } stuff;
```

Here, there is a two-bit gap between **stuff.field1** and **stuff.field2**; and **stuff.field3** is stored in the next **int**.

One important machine dependency is the order in which fields are placed into an **int**. On some machines the order is left to right; on others it is right to left. Also, machines differ in the location of boundaries between fields. For these reasons, bit fields tend not to be very portable. Typically, however, they are used for nonportable purposes such as putting data in the exact form used by a particular hardware device.

Bit Field Example

As mentioned, bit fields typically are used in programs dedicated to a specific piece of hardware. Our example is IBM PC–based, but if you aren't using that platform, you still can read through the example to see how it works.

Table 15.3 Equipment Word for the Original IBM PC

Bit(s)	Meaning	Value
0	Diskette drive	1 if present
1	Not used	
2–3	Motherboard memory	00 = 16k, 01 = 32k, 10 = 48k, 11 = 64k
4–5	Initial video setup	01 = 40x25, 10 = 80x25, 11 = mono
6–7	Number of drives	Number of diskette drives −1
8	Not used	
9–11	Number of command cards	Number of cards
12	Game port	1 if present
13	Not used	
14–15	Number of printers	Number of printers

The original IBM PC has various configuration switches that have to be set on the motherboard. When the computer is turned on, it copies information from these switch settings to a two-byte memory location. Within that two-byte word, the bits have the meaning shown in Table 15.3.

We can use a structure with bit fields to represent the data:

```
struct equip_word {unsigned has_drive    : 1;
                   unsigned              : 1;
                   unsigned mother_bd    : 2;
                   unsigned vid_setup    : 2;
                   unsigned num_drives   : 2;
                   unsigned              : 1;
                   unsigned num_comcds   : 3;
                   unsigned gameio       : 1;
                   unsigned              : 1;
                   unsigned num_ptrs     : 2;
                   };
```

Note that we use the unnamed bit fields to represent the unused bits in the equipment word.

To find if, say, a game I/O card is present, we can test if the **gameio** member is 1 or not. The tricky part is getting the correct values into the structure. Listing 15.4 shows one way.

❖ *ibmchk.c*

Listing 15.4

```
/* ibmchk.c--check IBM PC equipment word */
#include <stdio.h>
#include <dos.h>              /* MS-DOS specific declarations */
#define DSKTE 0x0001          /* diskette drives are present */
#define DRV_MASK 0x00C0       /* drive count bits */
#define DRV_SHFT 6            /* shift drive bits to right end */
#define GAMES 0x1000          /* game I/O ?*/
#define PRN_SHFT 14           /* printer count shift */
#define EQCK 0x11             /* equipment check interrupt */
struct equip_word {unsigned has_drive         : 1;
                   unsigned                    : 1;
                   unsigned mother_bd          : 2;
                   unsigned vid_setup          : 2;
                   unsigned num_drives         : 2;
                   unsigned                    : 1;
                   unsigned num_comcds         : 3;
                   unsigned gameio             : 1;
                   unsigned                    : 1;
                   unsigned num_ptrs           : 2;
                   };
```

```
main()
{
    union REGS rin, rout;
    unsigned int equip;
    union {
        struct equip_word s_view;
        unsigned int i_view; } eq_data;

    equip = int86 ( EQCK, &rin, &rout);
    eq_data.i_view = equip;
    if ( equip & DSKTE != DSKTE )
        printf("No disk drives\n");
    else
    {
      printf ("Bit operations: %u floppy drive(s)\n",
            ( (equip & DRV_MASK) >> DRV_SHFT) + 1 );
      printf ("Bit fields: %u floppy drive(s)\n",
            eq_data.s_view.num_drives + 1 );
    }
    printf("Bit operations: %u printer(s) attached\n",
            equip >> PRN_SHFT );
    printf("Bit fields: %u printer(s) attached\n",
            eq_data.s_view.num_ptrs);
}
```

Listing 15.4 (cont'd.)

The **int86( )** function, found both in MS C and Turbo C, uses interrupts to obtain information. Interrupts, more or less, are subroutines built into the IBM PC. The **int86( )** function, then, is implementation specific and is not part of any general C library. The particular interrupt we use here, represented by **EQCK**, causes **int86( )** to return the value of the equipment word in integer form.

To convert this integer to a structure, we used a trick. The union **eq_data** has two members, an **equip_word** structure and an unsigned integer:

```
union {
    struct equip_word s_view;
    unsigned int i_view; } eq_data;
```

On a PC, both members are 16-bit data objects. We make the following assignment:

```
eq_data.i_view = equip;
```

The **i_view** member views the union as an unsigned **int**, and we read in the equipment word in that form. Then by using **eq_data.s_view**, we can look at the same data as a structure. That is, bit 0 of the integer **eq_data.i_view** also is the **has_drive** member of the structure **eq_data.s_view.** Thus the **eq_data** union lets us view the equipment word two ways: as a structure with bit fields and as an **unsigned int**. This correspondence depends on the implementation-dependent feature that structures are loaded into

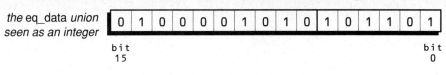

eq_data. i_view

the eq_data *union*
seen as an integer

| 0 | 1 | 0 | 0 | 0 | 0 | 1 | 0 | 1 | 0 | 1 | 0 | 1 | 1 | 0 | 1 |

bit
15

bit
0

eq_data.s_view

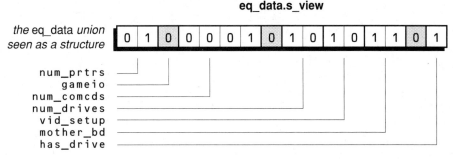

Figure 15.3

*A union as an
integer and as a
structure*

the eq_data *union*
seen as a structure

| 0 | 1 | 0 | 0 | 0 | 0 | 1 | 0 | 1 | 0 | 1 | 0 | 1 | 1 | 0 | 1 |

```
num_prtrs
  gameio
num_comcds
num_drives
vid_setup
mother_bd
has_drive
```

memory from the low-bit end to the high-bit end of a byte. That is, the first bit field in the structure goes into bit 0 of the word. See Figure 15.3. Incidentally, the type **REGS** union (defined in **dos.h**) uses a similar approach to provide both word view and a byte view of the CPU registers.

The program then proceeds to use both the bit-operator approach and the bit-field method for examining the contents of the equipment word. Once the bit fields are set up, they are easier to use. For example, **eq_data.s_view.num_drives** represents the value stored in the two bits that represent the number of floppy drives. Using bit operations, we first evaluate **equip & DRV_MASK** to turn off all other bits. At this point we have a value in the form 00000000bb000000. We then use a right-shift operator to move these two bits to the low end of the word: 00000000000000bb. Now we can evaluate the expression numerically to determine the number of drives.

15.5 Summary

Computing hardware is closely tied to the binary number system because the 1s and 0s of binary numbers can be used to represent the on and off states of bits in computer memory and registers. Although C does not allow us to write out numbers in binary form, it does recognize the related octal and hexadecimal notations. Just as each binary digit represents 1 bit, each octal digit represents three bits, and each hexadecimal digit represents four bits. This correspondence makes it relatively simple to convert binary numbers to octal or hexadecimal form.

C features several bitwise operators, so called because they operate independently on each bit within a value. The bitwise negation operator (~) inverts each bit in its operand, converting 1s to 0s and vice versa. The bitwise AND operator (**&**) forms a value from two operands. Each bit in the value is set to 1 if both corresponding bits in the operands are 1; otherwise the bit is set to 0. The bitwise OR operator (|) also forms a value from two operands. Each bit in the value is set to 1 if either or both corresponding bits in the operands are 1; otherwise the bit is set to 0. The bitwise EXCLUSIVE OR operator (^)

acts similarly, except that the resulting bit is set to 1 only if one or the other, but not both, corresponding bits of the operands is 1.

C also has a left-shift (<<) and a right-shift (>>) operator. Each produces a value formed by shifting the bits in a pattern the indicated number of bits to the left or right. For the left-shift operator, the vacated bits are set to 0. For the right-shift operator, the vacated bits are set to 0 if the value is **unsigned**. The behavior of the right-shift operator is implementation dependent for **signed** values.

Bit fields in a structure let you address individual bits or group of bits in a value. The details are implementation independent.

All of the bit tools discussed in the chapter assist C programs in dealing with various hardware matters. Therefore, they most often appear in implementation-dependent contexts.

Review Questions

1. Convert the following decimal values to binary values:

   a. 3

   b. 13

   c. 59

   d. 119

2. Convert the following binary values to decimal, octal, and hex values:

   a. 00010101

   b. 01010101

   c. 01001100

   d. 10011101

3. Evaluate the following expressions, assuming all values are one byte:

   a. ~3

   b. 3 & 6

   c. 3 | 6

   d. 1 | 6

   e. 3 ^ 6

f. 7 >> 1

g. 7 << 2

4. Evaluate the following expressions, assuming all values are one byte:

a. ~0

b. !0

c. 2 & 4

d. 2 && 4

e. 2 | 4

f. 2 || 4

g. 65 << 3

5. Because the ASCII code uses only the final seven bits, sometimes it is desirable to mask off the other bits. Explain the appropriate masks for use in binary, decimal, octal, and hexadecimal.

6. In Listing 15.2, we can replace

```
while (bits-- > 0)
{
   mask |= bitval;
   bitval <<= 1;
}
```

with

```
while (bits-- > 0)
{
   mask += bitval;
   bitval *= 2;
}
```

and the program still works. Does this fact mean that the operation *= **2** is equivalent to <<= **1**? What about |= and +=?

7. In Listing 15.4, we mask **equip** with **drive_mask** before using the right-shift operator to obtain the drive number. Yet we don't mask **equip** before using the right-shift operator to obtain the number of printers. Why doesn't this omission cause problems?

8. a. The Tinkerbell computer has a drive byte with the following bit assignments:

Bit(s)	Meaning
0–1	Number of 1.4M floppy drives
2	Not used
3–4	Number of 1.2M drives
5	Not used
6–7	Number of hard drives

Like the IBM PC, the Tinkerbell fills in structure bit fields from right to left. Create a bit field template suitable for holding the information.

b. The Klinkerbell, a near Tinkerbell clone, fills in structures from left to right. Create the corresponding bit field template for the Klinkerbell.

Programming Exercises

1. Write a function that converts a binary string to a numeric value. That is, if we have

```
char *pbin = "01001001";
```

then we can pass **pbin** as an argument to the function and have the function return an **int** value of **25**.

2. Write a program that reads two binary strings as command-line arguments and prints out the results of applying the ~ operator to each number and the results of applying the **&, |,** and ^ operators to the pair. Show the results as binary strings.

3. Write a function that takes an **int** argument and returns the number of on bits in the argument.

4. Write a function that takes two **int** arguments: a value and a bit position. Have the function return **1** if that bit position is 1; have it return **0** otherwise.

5. Write a function that returns the result of rotating the bits of an **unsigned int** by a specified number of bits to the left. For instance, **rotate_l(x,4)** should move the bits in **x** four places to the left, and the bits lost off the left end should reappear at the right end. That is, the bit moved out of the high-order position is placed in the low-order position.

16

The C Preprocessor and the C Library

Contents

Objectives

Defining symbolic constants

Defining macro functions

Understanding the advantages and disadvantages of macros

Including files

Using conditional compilation

Using the C library

Using math functions

Using **qsort( )**

Allocating memory with **malloc( )** and **calloc( )**

Creating linked lists

C was developed to meet the needs of working programmers, and working programmers like having a preprocessor. This useful aid looks at your program before it gets to the compiler (hence the term "preprocessor"), and following your preprocessor directives, replaces the symbolic abbreviations in your program with the directions they represent. It looks for other files you request. It can also alter the conditions of compilation. However, this description does not do justice to the true utility and value of the preprocessor, so let's turn to examples.

16.1 Manifest Constants: #define

We've already introduced the **#define** preprocessor directive in earlier chapters to define symbolic, or manifest, constants in our programs. But this directive also has greater range. Listing 16.1 illustrates some of the possibilities and properties of the **#define** directive.

❖ *preproc.c*

Listing 16.1

```
/* preproc.c--simple preprocessor examples */
#include <stdio.h>
#define TWO 2   /* you can use comments if you like */
#define MSG "The old grey cat sang a merry \
        song."
/* a backslash continues a definition to the next line */
#define FOUR TWO*TWO
#define PX printf("X is %d.\n", x)
#define FMT "X is %d.\n"
main()
{
   int x = TWO;

   PX;
   x = FOUR;
   printf(FMT, x);
   printf("%s\n", MSG);
   printf("TWO: MSG\n");
}
```

Like all preprocessor directives, **#define** begins with a # symbol in the left-most column. (Note: ANSI C permits the # symbol to be preceded by spaces or tabs, and it allows for space between the # and the remainder of the directive.) It can appear anywhere in the source file, and the definition holds from its place of appearance to the end of the file.

Preprocessor directives run until the first newline is encountered following the #. That is, a directive is limited to one line in length. However, the combination back-

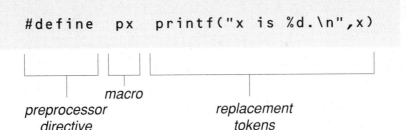

```
#define  px  printf("x is %d.\n",x)
```

Figure 16.1

Parts of a macro
definition

*preprocessor
directive*

macro

*replacement
tokens*

slash/newline is treated as a space, so that the one "logical line" can use more than one physical line in the file.

Each logical line consists of three parts. The first part is the **#define** directive. The second part is our chosen abbreviation, known as a *macro*. The macro must have no spaces in it. Its name must conform to the same rules that C variables follow: Only letters, digits, and the _ character can be used, and the first character cannot be a digit. The remainder of the line is termed the *body*. See Figure 16.1. When the preprocessor finds one of your macros within the program, it almost always replaces it with the body. (There is one exception, which we describe shortly.) This process of going from a macro to a final replacement is called *macro expansion*. Note that we can insert comments in standard C fashion, as they are ignored by the preprocessor. Also, as just mentioned, most systems (and the ANSI C standard) allow you to use the backslash (\) to extend a definition over more than one line.

Let's run the example program from Listing 16.1 and see how it works.

```
X is 2.
X is 4.
The old grey cat sang a merry song.
TWO: MSG
```

Here's what is happening. The statement

```
int x = TWO;
```

becomes

```
int x = 2;
```

as **2** is substituted for **TWO**. Then the statement

```
PX;
```

becomes

```
printf("X is %d.\n", x);
```

as the entire substitution is made. This feature represents a new wrinkle in our programming abilities, since up to now we've used macros only to represent constants. Here we see that a macro can express any string, even an entire C expression. Note, though, that this string is a constant string; **PX** can print only a variable named **x**.

The next line of the program also represents something new. You may think that **FOUR** is replaced by **4**, but the actual process is that

```
x = FOUR;
```

becomes

```
x = TWO*TWO;
```

which becomes

```
x = 2*2;
```

The macro expansion process ends at this point. The actual multiplication then takes place, not while the preprocessor works but during compilation, for the C compiler evaluates all constant expressions (expressions consisting only of constants). The preprocessor does no calculation; it simply makes the substitutions. Note also that a macro definition can include other macros (although some compilers do not support this "nesting" feature).

In the next line

```
printf (FMT, x);
```

becomes

```
printf("X is %d.\n",x);
```

as **FMT** is replaced by the corresponding string. This approach can be handy if you have a lengthy control string that you use several times.

In the next line **MSG** is replaced by the corresponding string. The quotation marks make the replacement string a character string constant; that is, once the program gets hold of it, it is stored in an array terminated with a null character. Thus

```
#define HAL 'Z'
```

defines a character constant, but

```
#define HAP "Z"
```

defines a character string: **Z\O**.

In the example program, we use a backslash immediately before the end of the line to extend the string to the next line:

```
#define MSG "The old grey cat sang a merry \
song."
```

The space between the **y** and the \ is so that we don't print **merrysong**. Also note that **song** is flush left. Suppose, instead, that we use the following:

```
#define MSG "The old grey cat sang a merry \
            song."
```

Then the output becomes as follows:

```
The old grey cat sang a merry          song.
```

The space between the beginning of the line and **song** counts as part of the string.

In general, wherever the preprocessor finds a macro in your program, it literally replaces it with the equivalent replacement string. If that string also contains macros, they, too, are replaced. The one exception to this replacement rule is a macro found within double quotation marks. Thus,

```
printf("TWO: MSG");
```

prints **TWO: MSG** instead of

```
2: The old grey cat sang a merry song.
```

If you want this last line printed, you must use the following:

```
printf("%d: %s\n", TWO, MSG);
```

Here, the macros are outside the quotation marks.

When should you use symbolic constants? You probably should use them to represent most numbers. If the number is some constant used in a calculation, a symbolic name makes its meaning clearer. If the number is an array size, a symbolic number makes it simpler to alter your program to handle a larger array. If the number is a system code for, say, **EOF**, a symbolic representation makes your program much more portable, as you must change only the one **EOF** definition to move between systems. Mnemonic value, easy alterability, and portability all make symbolic constants worthwhile.

Tokens

Technically, the body of a macro is considered to be a string of *tokens* rather than a string of characters. C preprocessor tokens are the separate "words" in the body of a macro definition. They are separated from one another by whitespace. For example, the definition

```
#define FOUR 2*2
```

has one token, the sequence **2*2**. But the definition

```
#define SIX 2 * 3
```

consists of three tokens: **2**, *****, and **3**.

One difference between character strings and token strings is in how multiple spaces in a body are treated. Consider this definition:

```
#define EIGHT 4  *   8
```

A preprocessor that interprets the body as a character string replaces EIGHT with the following: **4   *   8**. That is, the extra spaces are part of the replacement. But a preprocessor that interprets the body as tokens replaces **EIGHT** with three tokens separated by single spaces: **4 * 8**. In other words, the character string interpretation views the spaces as part of the body, whereas the token interpretation views the spaces as separators between the tokens of the body. In practice, some C compilers view macro bodies as strings rather than as tokens. The difference is of practical importance only for usages more intricate than those we attempt here.

Incidentally, the C compiler takes a more complex view of tokens than the preprocessor does, for the compiler understands the rules of C and doesn't necessarily require spaces to separate tokens. For instance, the C compiler views **2*2** as three tokens, for it recognizes that the **2**s are constants and the ***** is an operator.

Redefining Constants

Suppose you define **LIMIT** to be **20**, and then later in the same file define it again to be **25**. This action is called *redefining a constant*. Implementations differ on redefinition policy. Some consider it an error unless the new definition is the same as the old one. Others allow redefinition, perhaps issuing a warning. The ANSI standard takes the first view, allowing redefinition only if the new definition duplicates the old.

Having the same definition means the bodies must have the same tokens in the same order. Thus, these two definitions agree:

```
#define SIX 2 * 3
#define SIX 2  *   3
```

Both have the same three tokens, and the extra spaces are not part of the body. But the next definition is considered different:

```
#define SIX 2*3
```

It has just one token, not three, so it doesn't match.

If you want to redefine a **macro**, use the **#undef** directive. We discuss this directive later in the chapter.

16.2 Using Arguments with #define

By using arguments, we can create macros that look and act much like functions. A macro with arguments looks much like a function, since the arguments are enclosed within parentheses. Listing 16.2 illustrates how such "macro functions" are defined and used. Some of the examples also point out possible pitfalls, so read them carefully.

❖ mac_arg.c

```
/* mac_arg.c--macros with arguments */
#include <stdio.h>
#define SQUARE(x) x*x
#define PR(x) printf("x is %d.\n", x)
main()
{
   int x = 4;
   int z;

   z = SQUARE(x);
   PR(z);
   z = SQUARE(2);
   PR(z);
   PR(SQUARE(x));
   PR(SQUARE(x+2));
   PR(100/SQUARE(2));
   PR(SQUARE(++x));
}
```

Listing 16.2

Wherever **SQUARE(x)** appears in our program, it is replaced by **x*x**. What is different from our earlier examples is that we are free to use symbols other than **x** when we use this macro. The **x** in the macro definition is replaced by the symbol used in the macro call in the program. Thus, **SQUARE(2)** is replaced by **2*2**; the **x** really does act as an argument.

However, as we shall soon see, a macro argument does not work exactly like a function argument. Here are the results of running the program with a K & R style preprocessor:

```
z is 16.
z is 4.
SQUARE(x) is 16.
SQUARE(x+2) is 14.
100/SQUARE(2) is 100.
SQUARE(++x) is 30.
```

Note that some of the answers are different from what you may expect. The first two lines are predictable. However, notice that even the **x** inside the double quotation marks of the **PR** definition is replaced by the corresponding argument. *All* arguments in the definition are replaced.

The third line is interesting. Under K & R rules

```
PR(SQUARE(x));
```

becomes

```
printf("SQUARE(x) is %d.\n", SQUARE(x));
```

after the first stage of macro expansion. The second **SQUARE(x)** is expanded to **x*x**, but the first is left as is, for it is now inside double quotation marks in a program statement and thus is immune to further expansion. The final program line

```
printf("SQUARE(x) is %d.\n", x*x);
```

produces this output:

```
SQUARE(x) is 16.
```

Let's review the consequences of double quotation marks one more time. If your macro definition includes an argument within double quotation marks, then that argument is replaced by the corresponding string in the macro call. After that, it is not expanded further, even if the string is another macro. In our example, **x** becomes **SQUARE(x)** and stays that way.

ANSI C, however, does not allow substitution within double quotation marks. However, under ANSI C if **x** is a macro argument, then **#x** is that argument in string form. That is, if **x** is, say, **SQUARE (y)**, then **#x** is replaced by **"SQUARE(y)"**.

Returning to the output of Listing 16.2, we come to some peculiar results. Recall that **x** has the value **4**. This fact may lead you to expect that **SQUARE(x+2)** will be **6*6** or **36**. But the printout says it is **14**. There is a simple explanation: As we've already stated, the preprocessor doesn't make calculations; it only substitutes strings. Wherever our definition shows an **x**, the preprocessor substitutes the string **x+2**. Thus

```
x*x
```

becomes

```
x+2*x+2
```

The only multiplication is **2*x**. If **x** is **4**, then the value of this expression is:

```
4+2*4+2 = 4 + 8 + 2 = 14
```

This example pinpoints an important difference between a function call and a macro call. A function call passes the value of the argument to the function while the program is running. A macro call passes the argument string to the program before compilation; it's a different process at a different time.

Can our definition be fixed to make **SQUARE(x+2)** equal to 36? Sure. We simply need more parentheses:

```
#define SQUARE(x) (x)*(x)
```

Then **SQUARE(x+2)** becomes **(x+2)*(x+2)**, and we obtain our desired multiplication as the parentheses carry over in the replacement string.

However, such modification doesn't solve all our problems. Consider the events leading to the next output line:

```
100/SQUARE(2)
```

becomes

```
100/2*2
```

By the laws of precedence, the expression is evaluated from left to right: **(100/2)*2**, or **50*2**, or **100**. This mix-up can be cured by defining **SQUARE(x)** as:

```
#define SQUARE(x) (x*x)
```

which produces **100/(2*2)** and eventually evaluates to **100/4**, or **25**.

To handle both of the last two examples, we need the following definition:

```
#define SQUARE(x) ((x)*(x))
```

The lesson here is to use as many parentheses as necessary to ensure that operations and associations are done in the correct order.

Even these precautions fail to save the final example:

```
SQUARE(++x)
```

becomes

```
++x*++x
```

and **x** is incremented twice, once before the multiplication and once afterward:

```
++x*++x = 5*6 = 30
```

(Because the order of operations is left open, some compilers render the product **6*5**, but the end result is the same.)

The only remedy for this last problem is to avoid using **++x** as a macro argument. In general, don't use increment or decrement operators with macros. Note, however, that **++x** will work as a function argument, for it evaluates to **5** and then the value **5** is sent to the function.

16.3 Macro or Function?

Many tasks can be accomplished by using a macro with arguments or by using a function. Which one should you use? There is no hard-and-fast rule, but here are some considerations.

Macros are somewhat trickier to use than regular functions, for they can have odd side effects if you are unwary. Some compilers limit the macro definition to one line, and it is probably best to observe that limit even if your compiler does not.

The macros-versus-function choice represents a trade-off between time and space. A macro produces *in-line code;* that is, a statement is inserted in your program. If you use the macro 20 times, then 20 lines of code are inserted in your program. If you use a function 20 times, you have just one copy of the function statements in your program, so less space is used. On the other hand, program control must shift to where the function is and then return to the calling program, which takes longer to run than in-line code.

Macros have an advantage in that they don't worry about variable types because they deal with character strings, not with actual values. Thus, our **SQUARE(x)** macro can be used equally well with **int** or **float** values.

Programmers typically use macros for simple functions like the following:

```
#define MAX(X,Y) ( (X) > (Y) ? (X) : (Y))
#define ABS(X)    ((X) < 0 ? -(X) : (X))
#define ISSIGN(X)( (X) == '+' || (X) == '-' ? 1 : 0 )
```

(The last macro has value 1—true—if **x** is an algebraic sign character.) Here are some points to note:

1. Remember that no spaces are used in the macro name, including in the argument list, but spaces can appear in the replacement string. The preprocessor thinks the macro ends at the first whitespace, so anything after that space is lumped into the replacement string. See Figure 16.2.

2. Use parentheses around each argument and around the definition as a whole. This procedure ensures that the terms are grouped properly in an expression like **forks = 2 * MAX(guests + 3, last);**

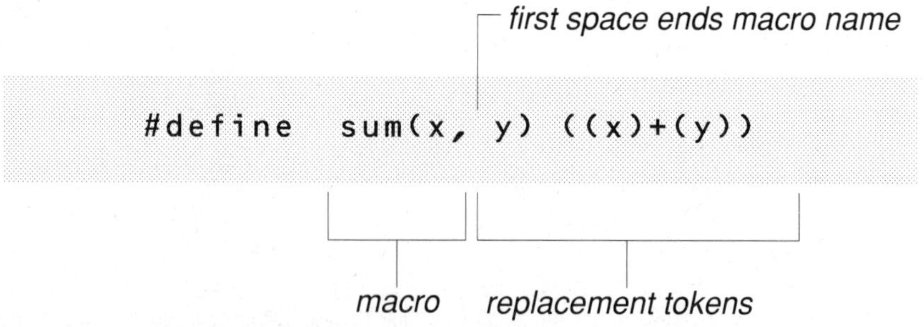

Figure 16.2

Faulty spacing in a
macro definition

first space ends macro name

```
#define  sum(x, y) ((x)+(y))
```

macro   *replacement tokens*

3. Use uppercase letters for macro function names. This convention is not as widespread as that of using uppercase letters for macro constants, but one good reason for using it is that it reminds you to be alert to possible macro side effects.

4. If you intend to use a macro instead of a function primarily to speed up a program, see if you can first determine if it is likely to make a significant difference. A macro that's used once in a program most likely will make no noticeable improvement in running time. A macro inside a nested loop is a much better candidate for speed improvements. Many systems offer program profilers to help pin down where a program uses the most time.

16.4 File Inclusion: #include

Suppose you have developed some macro functions you like. If you use the **#include** directive, you do not have to retype these macros each time you write a new program. We review **#include** now.

When the preprocessor spots an **#include** directive, it looks for the following filename and includes it with the current file. The **#include** directive in your source code file is replaced with the text from the included file; it's as if you sat down and typed in the entire contents at that particular location in your file. The directive comes in two varieties:

```
#include <stdio.h>          ⇐Filename in angle brackets
#include "mystuff.h"        ⇐Filename in double quotation marks
```

On a UNIX system, the angle brackets tell the preprocessor to look for the file in one or more standard system directories. The quotation marks tell it to look first in your directory (or some other directory, if you specify it in the filename) and then in the standard places. For example:

```
#include <stdio.h>          ⇐Searches system directories
#include "hot.h"            ⇐Searches your current working directory
#include "/usr/biff/p.h"    ⇐Searches the /usr/biff directory
```

Depending on the implementation, the two forms of the directive may be synonymous, and the preprocessor looks through the indicated disk drive:

```
#include "stdio.h"          ⇐Searches the default disk drive
#include <stdio.h>          ⇐Searches the default disk drive
#include "a:stdio.h"        ⇐Searches disk drive a
```

However, many newer microcomputer implementations use conventions similar to UNIX's. Consult your compiler manual.

ANSI C doesn't demand adherence to this directory model for files, for not all computer systems are organized similarly. In general, the method used to name files is system dependent, but the use of angle brackets and quotation marks is not.

We **#include** files because they have information the compiler needs. The **stdio.h** file, for example, typically includes definitions of **EOF**, **NULL**, **getchar( )**, and **putchar( )** (the last two are defined as macro functions). The **.h** suffix conventionally is used for header files, which we've earlier defined as information files that are placed at the head of your program. Header files usually consist of preprocessor statements. Some, like **stdio.h**, come with the system, but you are free to create your own.

Note that including a large file doesn't necessarily add much to the size of your program. The contents of **#include** files, for the most part, are information used by the compiler to generate the final code, not material to be added to the final code.

Header Files: An Example

Suppose, for instance, that you like using Boolean values. That is, instead of having **1** be true and **0** be false, you like to use the actual words **TRUE** and **FALSE**. You can create a file called, say, **bool.h**, which contains these definitions:

```
/* bool.h file */
#define BOOLEAN int
#define TRUE 1
#define FALSE 0
```

Listing 16.3 is an example of a program that includes this header file:

Listing 16.3

❖ *cnt_sp.c*

```
/* cnt_sp.c--counts whitespace characters */
#include <stdio.h>
#include "bool.h"
main()
{
   int ch;
   int count = 0;
   BOOLEAN whitesp();

   while ( (ch = getchar() ) != EOF)
      if ( whitesp(ch) )
         count++;
   printf("There are %d whitespace characters.\n", count);
}
BOOLEAN whitesp(c)
char c;
{
   if ( c == ' ' || c == '\n' || c == '\t')
      return(TRUE);
   else
      return(FALSE);
}
```

Note the following points about this program:

1. If the **main( )** and **whitesp( )** functions are to be compiled separately, you use the #include "bool.h" directive with each.

2. The expression **if (whitesp(ch))** is the same as **if (whitesp(ch) == TRUE)**, since **whitesp(ch)** itself has the value **TRUE** or **FALSE**.

3. We have not created a new type **BOOLEAN**, since **BOOLEAN** is simply **int**. The purpose of labeling the function **BOOLEAN** is to remind the user that the function is being used for a logical (as opposed to arithmetic) calculation.

4. Using a function for involved logical comparisons can make a program clearer. It also can save effort if the comparison is made in more than one place in a program.

5. We can use a macro instead of a function to define **whitesp( )**.

Header File Uses

A look through a standard header can give you a good idea of what kinds of information are found in a header. Typical header contents include the following:

1. Manifest constants: A typical **stdio.h** file, for instance, defines **EOF**, **NULL**, and **BUFSIZE** (the size of the standard I/O buffer).

2. Macro functions: For example, **getchar( )** usually is defined as **getc(stdin)**, and **getc( )** usually is defined as a rather complex macro. The **ctype.h** header typically contains macro definitions for the **ctype** functions.

3. Function declarations: The **string.h** header, for instance, contains function declarations for the family of string functions. Under ANSI C, the declarations are in function prototype form.

4. Structure template definitions: The standard I/O functions make use of a structure containing information about a file and its associated buffer. The **stdio.h** file contains the template for this structure.

5. Type definitions: You may recall that the standard I/O functions use a pointer-to-**FILE** argument. Typically, **stdio.h** uses a **#define** or a **typedef** to make **FILE** represent a structure type.

Many programmers develop their own standard header files to use with their programs. Some files may be for special purposes; others may be used with almost every program. Since included files can incorporate **#include** directives, you can create concise, well-organized header files if you like.

Consider this example:

```
/* header file mystuff.h */
#include <stdio.h>
#include "bool.h"
#include "funct.h"
#define YES 1
#define NO 0
```

First, it's a good idea to use a comment to identify the name of the header file. Second, we **#include** three files. Presumably the third one contains some macro functions we use often. Third, we define **YES** to be **1**, whereas in **bool.h** we define **TRUE** to be **1**. There is no conflict here, as we can use **YES** and **TRUE** in the same program. Each is replaced by a **1**.

Also, you can use header files to declare external variables to be shared by several files. Some programmers think it's okay to do so. Others think it is a poor style, since you have to check another file to see if a variable is declared or not.

16.5 Other Directives

The **#include** and **#define** directives are the most heavily used C preprocessor features. We treat the other directives in less detail.

The **#undef** directive cancels an earlier definition. The **#if**, **#ifdef**, **#ifndef**, **#else**, **#elif**, and **#endif** directives are typically used with larger blocks of programming. They allow you to produce files that can be compiled in more than one way.

The #undef Directive

This directive *undefines* a given macro. That is, suppose we have this definition:

```
#define LIMIT 400
```

Then the directive

```
#undef LIMIT
```

removes that definition. Now if you like, you can redefine **LIMIT** so that it has a new value. Even if **LIMIT** is not specifically defined, it still is valid to undefine it. Thus if you want to use a particular name and you are unsure whether it has been used previously, you can undefine it to be cautious.

Some compilers allow you to redefine a defined name and to nest **#define**s and **#undef**s so that undefining a name causes it to revert to its original value. However, such practice is not standard, and it is not part of the ANSI standard. More typically, you get a warning or error message if you redefine a name. So use **#undef** first if you wish to redefine.

Conditional Compilation

The other directives we mentioned previously let you set up *conditional compilations*. That is, they allow you to tell the compiler to accept or ignore blocks of information or code according to conditions at the time of compilation.

The #ifdef, #else, and #endif Directives

A short example may clarify the concept of conditional compilation. Consider the following:

```
#ifdef MAVIS
    #include "horse.h"      /* gets done if MAVIS is #defined */
    #define STABLES    5
#else
    #include "cow.h"        /* gets done if MAVIS isn't #defined */
    #define STABLES   15
#endif
```

Here we've used the indentation allowed by newer implementations and by the ANSI standard. If you have an older implementation, you may have to move all the directives to flush left.

The **#ifdef** directive says that if the following identifier (**MAVIS**) has been defined by the preprocessor, then follow all the directives up to the next **#else** or **#endif**, whichever comes first. If there is an **#else**, then everything from the **#else** to the **#endif** is done if the identifier isn't defined. Incidentally, an "empty" definition like

```
#define MAVIS
```

is sufficient to define **MAVIS** for the purposes of **#ifdef**.

The structure is much like that of the C **if else**. The main difference is that the preprocessor doesn't recognize the { } method of marking a block, so it uses the **#else** (if any) and the **#endif** (which must be present) to mark blocks of directives. These conditional structures can be nested.

You can also use **ifdef**, **#else**, and **#endif** to mark blocks of C statements. See Listing 16.4.

Listing 16.4

❖ *checking.c*

```
/* checking.c */
#include <stdio.h>
#define JUST_CHECKING
#define LIMIT 4
main( )
{
    int i;
    int total = 0;
    for (i = 1; i <= LIMIT; i++)
```

**Listing 16.4
(cont'd.)**

```
    {
        total += 2*i*i + 1;
#ifdef JUST_CHECKING
        printf("i=%d, running total = %d\n", i, total);
#endif
    }
    printf("Grand total = %d\n", total);
}
```

Compiling and running the program produces this output:

```
i=1, running total = 3
i=2, running total = 12
i=3, running total = 31
i=4, running total = 64
Grand total = 64
```

If you omit the **JUST_CHECKING** definition and compile the program, only the final line is displayed. You can use this approach, for instance, to help in program debugging. To do so, define **JUST_CHECKING** and use a judicious selection of **#ifdef**s. The compiler will include program code for printing out intermediate values for debugging. Once everything is working, you can remove the definition and recompile. If, later, you find you need the information again, you can reinsert the definition and avoid having to retype all the extra print statements. Another possible use for **#ifdef** is to select among alternative chunks of codes suited for different C implementations.

The #ifndef Directive

The **#ifndef** directive can be used with **#else** and **#endif** in the same way. This directive asks if the following identifier is *not* defined; it is the negative of **#ifdef**. The **#ifndef** often is used to define a constant if it is not already defined:

```
#ifndef SIZE
    #define SIZE 100
#endif
```

(Again, older implementations may not permit you to indent the **#define** directive.) Suppose this preprocessor code were in an **#include** file called **arrays.h**. Placing the line

```
#include "arrays.h"
```

at the head of a file results in **SIZE** being defined as **100**. But placing

```
#define SIZE 10
#include "arrays.h"
```

at the head sets **SIZE** to 10. Because **SIZE** is defined before the lines in **arrays.h** are reached, the **#define SIZE 100** line is skipped. You may use this procedure to test a program with a smaller array size, for example. Once it worked to your satisfaction, you can remove the **#define SIZE 10** statement and recompile. In this way, you don't have to worry about modifying the header array itself.

The #if and #elif Directives

The **#if** directive is more like the regular C **if**. It is followed by a constant integer expression that is considered to be true if nonzero. You can use C's relational and logical operators:

```
#if SYS == 1
#include "ibm.h"
#endif
```

The **#elif** (not available in some older implementations) directive allows you to extend an **if else** sequence. For example:

```
#if SYS == 1
   #include "ibmpc.h"
#elif SYS == 2
   #include "vax.h"
#elif SYS == 3
   #include "mac.h"
#else
   #include "general.h"
#endif
```

Also, many newer implementations offer a second way to test whether a name is defined. Instead of using

```
#ifdef VAX
```

we can use this form:

```
#if defined (VAX)
```

Here **defined** is a preprocessor operator that returns **1** if its argument is **#define**d and **0** otherwise. The advantage of this newer form is that it can be used with **#elif**. Using it, we can reexpress the last example this way:

```
#if defined (IBMPC)
   #include "ibmpc.h"
#elif defined (VAX)
   #include "vax.h"
#elif defined (MAC)
   #include "mac.h"
#else
   #include "general.h"
#endif
```

Therefore, if we are inputting this code on, say, a VAX, we must include the following line earlier in the file:

```
#define VAX
```

One use for these conditional compilation features is to make a program more portable. By changing a few key definitions at the beginning of a file, we can set up different values and include different files for different systems.

The #error and #pragma Directives

The ANSI standard creates two new directives designed to increase control over the compilation process. The **#error** directive provides a mechanism for printing a message and terminating compilation when certain errors occur, and the **#pragma** directive provides a mechanism for modifying the behavior of a compiler.

To use the **#error** directive, you follow the directive with an error message. On encountering the directive, the system prints a diagnostic message that includes the error message you've provided. The framers of the standard recommend that compilation stop when an **#error** directive is encountered, but that is not yet a requirement.

Normally, you use **#error** following a preprocessor **if** statement so that the **#error** directive is acted upon only in the event of some test failing. For instance, you can code like the following:

```
#if (FILES < 20)
#error FILES must be set to 20 or greater
#endif
```

This checks if the manifest constant **FILES** has been set to an acceptable value.

To use the **#pragma** directive, you follow the directive with a directive name specific to the compiler being used. For example, with Turbo C 2.0, the directive

```
#pragma inline
```

instructs the Turbo C compiler to expect in-line assembly code. With Microsoft C 5.1, the directive

```
#pragma linesize(132)
```

causes the source listing to have 132 characters per line.

In general, different implementations offer different pragmas, and a compiler ignores a pragma if it doesn't recognize it.

16.6 Enumerated Types

The *enumerated type* lets us define symbolic names to represent integer constants, and it is a common C extension that has been incorporated into the ANSI C standard. By using the **enum** keyword, we can create a new "type" and specify the values it may have. (Actually, **enum** is type **int**, so we really create a new name for an existing type.)

The purpose of enumerated types is to enhance program readability. The syntax is similar to that used for structures. For example, we can make these declarations:

```
enum spectrum {red, orange, yellow, green, blue, violet};
enum spectrum color;
```

The first declaration establishes **spectrum** as a type name; the second declaration makes **color** a variable of that type. The identifiers within the braces enumerate the possible values that a **spectrum** variable can have. Thus, the possible values for **color** are **red**, **orange**, **yellow**, and so on. We can therefore use statements like the following:

```
color = blue;
if (color == yellow)
    ...;
```

enum *Constants*

Just what are **blue** and **red**? Technically, they are type **int** constants. For instance, given the preceding enumeration declaration, we can try the following:

```
printf("red = %d, orange = %d\n", red, orange);
```

Here is the output:

```
red = 0, orange = 1
```

What has happened is that **red** has become a *named constant* that represents the integer **0**. Similarly, the other identifiers are named constants that represent the integers **1** through **5**. The process is similar to using defined constants, except that these definitions are set up by the compiler rather than the preprocessor.

Default Values

By default the constants in the enumeration list are assigned the integer values **0, 1, 2,** and so on. Thus, the declaration

```
enum kids {nippy, slats, skippy, nina, liz};
```

results in **nina** having the value **3**.

Assigned Values

You can choose the integer values you want the constants to have simply by including the desired values in the declaration:

```
enum levels {low = 100, medium = 500, high = 2000};
```

If you assign a value to one constant but not to the following constant, then the following constant is numbered sequentially. For example, suppose we have this declaration:

```
enum feline {cat, lynx = 10, puma, tiger};
```

Then **cat** is **0**, by default, and **lynx**, **puma**, and **tiger** are **10**, **11**, and **12**, respectively.

Usage

As we said earlier, the purpose of enumerated types is to enhance the program readability. For example, if you are dealing with colors, using **red** and **blue** is much more obvious than using **0** and **1**. Note that the enumerated types are for internal use. If you want to input a value of **orange** for **color**, you must read in a **1**, not the word **orange**. Otherwise, you can read in the string **"orange"** and have the program convert it to the value **orange**.

The ANSI C standard provides that enumerated variables be considered type **int** variables. Therefore, compliance with the standard implies that **enum** variables can be used in expressions in the same manner as **int** variables.

16.7 The C Library

Originally, there was no official C library, but a de facto standard emerged based on the UNIX implementation of C. The ANSI C committee, in turn, developed an official standard library based largely on the de facto standard. However, recognizing the expanded C universe, the committee sought to define the library so that it can be implemented on a wide variety of systems.

We've already discussed several I/O functions and string functions from the library. In this chapter we browse through other areas. First, however, let's discuss how to use the library.

Gaining Access to the C Library

How you gain access to the C library depends on your implementation, so you must check to see how our more general statements apply to your system. First, there are often several different places to find library functions. For example, **getchar( )** is usually defined as a macro in the file **stdio.h**, and **strlen( )** is usually kept in a library file. Second, different systems have different ways to reach these functions. We describe three possibilities in the following sections. Clearly, we can't go through all the specifics for all systems, but these discussions should alert you to what you should look for.

Automatic Access

On many systems, library access is automatic. You simply compile your program and the more common library functions are made available automatically.

But keep in mind that you should declare explicitly the function type for functions you use. Usually you can do so by including the appropriate header file. User manuals describing library functions tell you which files to include. On some older systems, however, you may have to enter the function declarations yourself. Again, the user manual indicates the function type.

In the past, the header filenames have not been consistent among different implementations. The ANSI C standard groups the library functions into families, with each family having a specific header file for its function prototypes.

File Inclusion

If a function is defined as a macro, then you can **#include** the file containing the definition. Often, similar functions are collected in an appropriately titled header file. For example, many systems have a **ctype.h** file that contains several macros that determine the nature of a character: uppercase, digit, and so forth.

Library Inclusion

At some stage in compiling or linking a program, you may have to specify a library option. Even a system that checks its standard library automatically may have other libraries of less frequently used functions, and these libraries must be requested explicitly by using a compile-time option. Note that this process is distinct from including a header file. A header file provides a function declaration or prototype. The library option tells the system where to find the function code.

Using the Library Descriptions

We haven't the space to discuss the complete C library, but we can discuss some representative examples. First, though, let's take a look at documentation.

You can find function documentation in a number of places. Your system may have an on-line manual. As well, C implementors supply printed user guides to library functions. Several publishers have also issued reference manuals for C library functions. Some are generic in nature; some are targeted toward specific implementations.

The key skill you need in reading the documentation is the interpretation of function headings. The idiom has changed with time. Here, for instance, is how **fread( )** is listed in older UNIX documentation:

```
#include <stdio.h>

fread(ptr, sizeof(*ptr), nitems, stream)
FILE *stream;
```

First, the proper **#include** file is given. No type is given for **fread( )**, **ptr**, **sizeof(*ptr)**, or **nitems**. By default, then, these are taken to be type **int**. But the context makes it clear that **ptr** is a pointer. However, in C's early days, pointers were handled as integers. The **stream** argument is declared as a pointer-to-**FILE**. The declaration makes it look as if you are supposed to use the **sizeof** operator as the second argument. Actually, it's saying that the value of this argument should be the size of the object pointed to by **ptr**. Often, you use **sizeof** as illustrated, but any type **int** value satisfies the syntax.

Later, the form changed to the following:

```
#include <stdio.h>

int fread(ptr, size, nitems, stream);
char *ptr;
int size, nitems;
FILE *stream;
```

Now all types are given explicitly, and **ptr** is treated as a pointer-to-**char**.

The ANSI C standard provides the following description:

```
#include <stdio.h>
size_t fread(void *ptr, size_t size, size_t nmemb, FILE *stream);
```

First, it uses the new prototype format. Second, it changes some types.

The **size_t** type is defined to be the unsigned integral type that the **sizeof** operator returns. Usually this type is either **unsigned int** or **unsigned long**. The **stddef.h** file contains a **typedef** or a **#define** for **size_t**. So do several other files, including **stdio.h**. Many functions, including **fread( )**, often use the **sizeof** operator as part of an actual argument. The **size_t** type makes the formal argument match this common usage.

Also, ANSI C uses pointer-to-**void** as a kind of generic pointer for situations in which pointers of different types may be used. For instance, the actual first argument to **fread( )** may be a pointer to an array of **double** or to a structure of some sort. The idea is that if the actual argument is, say, a pointer-to-array-of-20-**double** and the formal argument is pointer-to-**void**, then the compiler will make the appropriate type version without complaining about any type clash.

Let's now turn to some specific libraries and their functions.

16.8 The Math Library

The math library contains many useful mathematical functions. The **math.h** header file provides the function declarations or prototypes for these functions.

To show some of the features of the library, we calculate the motion of a weight on the end of a spring. Physics tells us that such a system oscillates in sinusoidal motion. Thus the position of the mass can be described by this equation:

$x = A \sin (w\ t)$

Here x is the displacement of the mass from its equilibrium position, A is the maximum displacement (called the amplitude), t is time, and w is a constant that depends on the mass and the strength of the spring. Physics also tells us that if m is the mass of the weight and k is the spring constant (a measure of its strength), w is the square root of k/m. Also, the velocity of the mass is given by the following:

$$y = -w\, A \cos (w\, t)$$

We're not going to try to teach you physics here; we just want to show how to use the math library to represent these equations. We need a sine function, a cosine function, and a square root function. Looking through the documentation, we find that the C math library answers our needs. The **sin( )**, **cos( )**, and **sqrt( )** functions are all type **double**, and all require one type **double** argument. Listing 16.5 uses these functions. The **math.h** file contains the function declarations or prototypes for these functions, so we've included it.

❖ *spring.c*

Listing 16.5

```
/* spring.c--mass on a spring */
#include <stdio.h>
#include <math.h>
#ifndef PI
#define PI 3.141592654
#endif
#define DIVISIONS 20
main()
{
    float mass;
    float k_spring;
    float amp;
    double w, t, tmax;

    puts("Enter the object's mass in grams:");
    scanf("%f", &mass);
    if (mass <= 0 )
        exit(1);
    puts("Enter the spring constant in dynes/cm:");
    scanf("%f", &k_spring);
    if (k_spring <= 0)
        exit(1);
    puts("Enter the amplitude in cm:");
    scanf("%f", &amp);
    w = sqrt(k_spring/mass);
    tmax = 2 * PI / w;
    printf("%5s %10s %10s\n", "Time", "Position", "Velocity");
    for ( t = 0; t <= tmax; t += tmax/DIVISIONS )
        printf("%5.2f %10.2e %10.2e\n", t, amp * sin (w*t),
                -w * amp * cos(w*t));
}
```

The time needed for one complete cycle (**tmax**) equals **2 * PI / w**. The program computes that number, then calculates data for increments of 1/20 that size. Some implementations may provide a pi value as a courtesy, so we use **#ifndef PI** to avoid redefining it. Compiling and running the program on our system produces these results:

```
Enter the object's mass in grams:
1000
Enter the spring constant in dynes/cm:
100
Enter the amplitude in cm:
10
```

Time	Position	Velocity
0.00	0.00e+000	−3.16e+000
0.99	3.09e+000	−3.01e+000
1.99	5.88e+000	−2.56e+000
2.98	8.09e+000	−1.86e+000
3.97	9.51e+000	−9.77e−001
4.97	1.00e+001	6.49e−010
5.96	9.51e+000	9.77e−001
6.95	8.09e+000	1.86e+000
7.95	5.88e+000	2.56e+000
8.94	3.09e+000	3.01e+000
9.93	−4.10e−009	3.16e+000
10.93	−3.09e+000	3.01e+000
11.92	−5.88e+000	2.56e+000
12.91	−8.09e+000	1.86e+000
13.91	−9.51e+000	9.77e−001
14.90	−1.00e+001 −	1.95e−009
15.90	−9.51e+000 −	9.77e−001
16.89	−8.09e+000	−1.86e+000
17.88	−5.88e+000	−2.56e+000
18.88	−3.09e+000	−3.01e+000
19.87	8.20e−009	−3.16e+000

If you receive a message like

```
Undefined:
  _sqrt
```

or

```
'sqrt': unresolved external
```

or something similar, then your compiler/linker is not finding the math library. For instance, UNIX systems require that you instruct the linker to search the math library. Use the **-lm** flag after the filename to accomplish this task:

```
cc spring.c -lm
```

In QuickC, creating a program list file for the program will cause QuickC to search the math library.

The equations we use in the sample program for position and velocity assume that the quantity **wt** is measured in an angular unit called a *radian*. The trigonometric functions in the C library make the same assumption, so there was no problem. But if you want to use degrees with these functions, you should convert angles in degrees to radians before using them as arguments. To convert degrees to radians, multiply by pi, then divide by 180.

If we calculate **tmax** exactly correctly, the final output line should show **x** as being **0**, for one full cycle brings the system to its starting point. However, the calculation is limited by the precision to which we specify pi.

The close but not exact correspondence of an answer to an expected result is a common event in floating-point calculations. Indeed, when we run this program on a VAX, the program stops one line short of **tmax**. In adding increments of **tmax/DIVISIONS**, a slight rounding error causes the presumed final value of **t** to slightly exceed **tmax** instead of equaling it. That is, adding **tmax/20** 20 times can produce a value not exactly identical to **tmax**. With floating-point values, you shouldn't rely on tests of equality. Rather, you should test if a value obtained is within an acceptable amount of a particular range.

16.9 The General Utilities Library

This family contains a general grab bag of functions including a random number generator, searching and sorting functions, conversion functions, and memory management functions. Under ANSI C, prototypes for these functions exist in the **stdlib.h** header file. Let's now look closely at the **qsort( )** function and two memory management functions.

The qsort( ) Function

The *quick sort method* is one of the most effective sorting algorithms, especially for larger arrays. Developed by C. A. R. Hoare in 1962, it uses a recursive approach to partition arrays into ever smaller sizes until the element level is reached. First the array is divided into two parts, with every value in one partition being less than every value in the other partition. This process continues until the array is fully sorted.

We look at **qsort( )** because it exemplifies a function that uses function pointers. To keep the example short and to the point, we have it generate an array of random strings, then sort it. Also, we use **#ifdef** to provide for differences between ANSI and pre-ANSI C. Listing 16.6 presents the program.

Listing 16.6

❖ *qsort_str.c*

```
/* qsort_str.c--string functions, qsort */
#include <stdio.h>
#include <string.h>
#define LEN 8
#define NUM 40
#define ANSI          /* omit for non-ANSI implementation */
#ifdef ANSI
```

```
#include <stdlib.h>
#define VOID void
#define SIZE_T size_t
void fillstrings(char (*ar)[LEN], int n);
void showstrings(char (*ar)[LEN], int n);
int comp(char (*str1)[LEN], char (*str2)[LEN]);

#else
#define VOID char
#define SIZE_T int
int rand();
void qsort();
void fillstrings( );
void showstrings( );
int comp( );

#endif
char things[NUM][LEN];

main()
{
  fillstrings(things, NUM);
  showstrings(things, NUM);
  qsort((VOID *)things, (SIZE_T) NUM,(SIZE_T)( LEN*
      (sizeof(char))), comp);
  putchar('\n');
  showstrings(things, NUM);
}
void fillstrings(ar, n)
char (*ar)[LEN];
int n;
{
  int word, letter;

  for( word = 0; word < n; word++)
  {
    for(letter = 0; letter < LEN 1; letter++)
        ar[word][letter] = 'a' + rand() % 26;
    ar[word][LEN - 1] = '\0';
  }
}
void showstrings(ar, n)
char (*ar)[LEN];
int n;
{
  int word;
  for (word = 0; word < n; word++)
  {
    printf("%s ", ar[word]);
    if ( word % 8 == 7)
      putchar('\n');
  }
```

Listing 16.6 (cont'd.)

Listing 16.6
(cont'd.)

```
   if (word % 8 != 0 )
       putchar('\n');
}

int comp(str1,str2)
char (*str1)[LEN], (*str2)[LEN];
{
   return strcmp(*str1, *str2);
}
```

A sample run follows:

```
phqghum eaylnlf dxfircv scxggbw kfnqdux wfnfozv srtkjpr epggxrp
nrvystm wcysyyc qpevike ffmznim kkasvws renzkyc xfxtlsg ypsfadp
ooefxzb coejuvp vaboygp oeylfpb npljvrv ipyamye hwqnqrq pmxujjl
oovaowu xwhmsnc bxcoksf zkvatxd knlyjyh fixjswn kkufnux xzrzbmn
mgqooke tlyhnko augzqrc ddiutei ojwayyz pvscmps ajlfvgu bfaaovl

ajlfvgu augzqrc bfaaovl bxcoksf coejuvp ddiutei dxfircv eaylnlf
epggxrp ffmznim fixjswn hwqnqrq ipyamye kfnqdux kkasvws kkufnux
knlyjyh mgqooke npljvrv nrvystm oeylfpb ojwayyz ooefxzb oovaowu
phqghum pmxujjl pvscmps qpevike renzkyc scxggbw srtkjpr tlyhnko
vaboygp wcysyyc wfnfozv xfxtlsg xwhmsnc xzrzbmn ypsfadp zkvatxd
```

Let's look at three main areas: the ANSI/pre-ANSI adjustment, the use of **qsort( )**, and the definition of **comp( )**.

ANSI Differences

The **qsort( )** and **rand( )** functions have prototypes in the **stdlib.h** file; older implementations don't include that file. Therefore, if **ANSI** is not defined, the program provides old-fashioned function declarations for **qsort( )** and **rand( )**. If **ANSI** is defined, then the program uses the prototypes in **stdlib.h**.

The ANSI library uses the **size_t** type for some of the **qsort( )** arguments, whereas pre-ANSI uses **int**. Also, ANSI uses pointer-to-**void** as the type for the first argument, and pre-ANSI uses pointer-to-**char**. Our program uses type casts to **VOID** and **SIZE_T**. These are defined as **void** and **size_t** if **ANSI** is defined and as **char** and **int** if **ANSI** is not defined. As well, the program uses function prototypes if **ANSI** is defined and the older function declarations if it isn't.

Listing 16.6 shows **ANSI** being defined, so that version can be used in an ANSI implementation. Remove the definition, and you can compile the program on an older implementation.

Using qsort( )

The **qsort( )** function sorts an array of data objects. Its first argument is a pointer to the beginning of the array to be sorted. In our case, **things** is a pointer to an array of arrays of characters. We type cast the pointer to agree with the declared pointer type for the qsort( ) first argument: pointer-to-**char** for pre-ANSI implementations or pointer-to-**void** for ANSI implementations.

The second argument is the number of items to be sorted. In this case, **N** is the number of strings. Again, we use a type cast to achieve type agreement.

One consequence of the **qsort( )** pointer type for its first argument is that **qsort( )** can't tell just from the pointer what size object is being pointed to. If you write your own function to sort an array of structures, you can declare the formal argument of the function to be a pointer to the structure type, and the function will then know with what it is dealing. By being more general, **qsort( )** loses that insight. To compensate, we must tell **qsort( )** explicitly the size of the data object, which is the third argument. We use the number of array elements multiplied by the size of an individual array element to represent the size of each string.

Finally, **qsort( )** requires a pointer to the function to be used to determine the sorting order. The comparison function should take two arguments: pointers to the two items being compared. The function should return a positive integer if the first item should follow the second value, zero if the two items are the same, and a negative integer if the second item should follow the first. The **qsort( )** function uses the comparison function, passing it pointer values that it calculates from the other information given to it.

Defining comp( )

In this case, we are comparing elements of the **things** array. Each element of this array is itself an array of **LEN char** elements, so **comp( )** should take pointers-to-**char** arrays of that size as arguments. Hence the declaration **char (*str1)[LEN];**. Therefore, ***str1** is syntactically the same as the name of a **char** array, and we can thus use it and ***str2** as arguments to **strcmp( )**. The **strcpy( )** function returns a positive value if the second string follows the first, a negative value if the first string follows the second, and zero if the strings are the same. This behavior is the exact one we need for **comp( )**, so we use **strcmp( )** to calculate the return value.

Memory Allocation: malloc( ) and calloc( )

Now let's look at memory management. All programs have to set aside enough memory to store the data they use. Some of this *memory allocation* is achieved automatically. For example, we can declare

```
char place[] = "Pork Liver Creek";
```

and enough memory to store that string is set aside. Or we can be more explicit and ask for a certain amount of memory:

```
int plates[100];
```

This declaration sets aside 100 memory locations, each able to store an **int** value.

C goes beyond such simplistic memory management. It lets you allot more memory as a program runs. The main tool is the **malloc( )** function, which takes one argument: the number of bytes of memory desired. Then **malloc( )** finds a suitable block of free memory and returns the address of the first byte of the block. Since **char** represents a byte, **malloc( )** has traditionally been defined as type pointer-to-**char**. The ANSI C standard, however, uses a new type: pointer-to-**void**. This type is intended to be a "generic pointer." The **malloc( )** function can be used to return pointers to arrays, structures, and so on, so normally the return value is type-cast to the proper value. Under ANSI C you still should type cast for clarity, but assigning a pointer-to-**void** value to a pointer of another type is not considered a type clash. If **malloc( )** fails to find the required space, it returns a **NULL** pointer.

Listing 16.7 presents an unsophisticated program showing how **malloc( )** can be used. It creates an array of 100 pointers, and it reads in strings. The **malloc( )** function is used to set aside storage for each string, and the addresses of the strings are stored in the array.

❖ *memsym.c*

Listing 16.7

```
/* memsym.c--memorize symphony orchestras */
#include <stdio.h>
#define ANSI
#ifdef ANSI
#include <stdlib.h>    /* ANSI C header for malloc() */
#else
char *malloc();        /* pre-ANSI declaration */
#endif
#define LINE 81        /* maximum line length for input */
#define MAX 100        /* maximum number of symphonies */
main()
{
    char temp[LINE];   /* temporary input storage */
    char *ps[MAX];     /* array of ptrs to strings */
    int index = 0;     /* number of input lines */
    int count;         /* for loop counter */

    puts("Name some symphony orchestras.");
    puts(
      "Enter them one at a time; press [enter] at the start");
    puts("of a line to end your list. Okay, I'm ready.");
    while ( index < MAX && fgets(temp,LINE,stdin) != NULL
          && temp[0] != '\n' )
    {
      ps[index] = (char *)malloc( strlen(temp) + 1 );
      strcpy (ps[index], temp);
      if ( ++index < MAX )
        printf("That's %d. Continue if you like.\n",
               index);
    }
    puts("Okay, here is what I've got.");
    for ( count = 0; count < index; count++)
        fputs(ps[count], stdout);
}
```

Here is a sample run:

```
Name some symphony orchestras.
Enter them one at a time; press [enter] at the start
of a line to end your list. Okay, I'm ready.
San Francisco Symphony
That's 1. Continue, if you like.
Chicago Symphony
That's 2. Continue, if you like.
Berlin Philharmonic
That's 3. Continue, if you like.
The Concertgebouw
That's 4. Continue, if you like.
London Symphony
That's 5. Continue, if you like.
Vienna Philharmonic
That's 6. Continue, if you like.
Pittsburgh Symphony
That's 7. Continue, if you like.
[enter]
Okay, here is what I've got:
San Francisco Symphony
Chicago Symphony
Berlin Philharmonic
The Concertgebouw
London Symphony
Vienna Philharmonic
Pittsburgh Symphony
```

Let's look at the coding. The input is controlled by these lines:

```
while (index < MAX && fgets(temp,LINE,stdin) != NULL
  && temp[0] != '\n')
```

First, the program checks to see if any more string pointers are left by comparing **index** to **MAX**. Next, it attempts to read the input into a temporary storage area; if the end-of-file (indicated by a return value of **NULL**) is reached, the loop quits. Finally, the program checks to see if the first character in **temp** is the newline character. This occurs if the user presses the Enter key with no other input; the program responds by quitting the loop.

Next, suppose input has been placed in **temp**. Then the following line allocates enough space to hold the string:

```
ps[index] = (char *) malloc( strlen(temp) + 1 );
```

The **strlen( )** function gives the length of the input string, which most likely is significantly less than the length of the **temp** array. The program adds 1 for the null character and stores the beginning address of the still empty storage block in **ps[index]**. The **malloc( )** function now finds a chunk of memory large enough to hold the string and returns a pointer to its beginning. We then type cast the pointer to agree with the lefthand side. (In pre-ANSI C, **malloc( )** already returns pointer-to-**char**, but in ANSI C it returns pointer-to-**void**.)

The next program line copies the contents of **temp** into the allocated storage. This action frees **temp** to be reused for the next input string:

```
strcpy (ps[index], temp);
```

What have we gained by using this approach? Well, suppose we do not use **malloc( )**. Instead of declaring an array of 100 pointers-to-**char**, we could declare an array of 100 character arrays, with each character array capable of holding 81 characters. Therefore, we allocate 8100 bytes of memory, much of which never would be used, since most of the strings are smaller than the maximum size and since we are not likely to enter the full 100 symphonies. With the **malloc( )** approach, we only use the amount of memory that is needed. We allocate 281 bytes to hold **ps[ ]** and **temp[ ]**, but this amount is more than made up if we have a large number of input values.

Now suppose you want to use **int** memory, not **char**. You still can use **malloc( )**. Here is the procedure:

```
int *newmem;

newmem = (int *) malloc(100);       /* use cast operator */
```

Again, 100 bytes are set aside. The cast operator converts the returned value from a **char** pointer to an **int** pointer. If, as on our system, **int** takes 2 bytes of memory, then **newmem + 1** increments the pointer by 2 bytes, just right to move it to the next integer. As well, the 100 bytes can be used to store 50 integers.

Another option for memory allotment is to use **calloc( )**. A typical use looks like the following:

```
long *newmem;

newmem = (long *) calloc( 100, sizeof (long) );
```

Like **malloc( )**, **calloc( )** returns a pointer-to-**char** in its pre-ANSI version and a pointer-to-**void** under ANSI. You must use the cast operator if you want to store a different type. The **calloc( )** function has two arguments, both of which should be unsigned integers (type **size_t** under ANSI). The first argument is the number of memory cells desired. The second argument is the size of each cell in bytes. In our case, **long** uses 4 bytes, so the preceding instruction sets up 100 4-byte units, using 400 bytes in all for storage. By using **sizeof (long)** instead of **4**, we make this coding more portable. In other words, our code can work on systems on which **long** is some size other than **4**.

The **calloc( )** function throws in one additional feature. It sets all the bits in the block to zero. (Note, however, that on some hardware systems, a floating-point value of 0 is not represented by all bits set to 0.)

Another common memory function is **free( )**, which takes as an argument the address of a memory block previously allocated by **malloc( )** or **calloc( )**. It then returns the block of memory to the *free memory pool*, so that it can be used by future calls to **malloc( )** and **calloc( )**. The various assignments expire with the program. Your C library probably offers several other memory-management functions, and you may wish to check on them.

16.10 Linked Lists

We mentioned earlier that the example in Listing 16.7 is unsophisticated. One reason is because we still use an array to store the pointers. Thus, the maximum capacity of the program is limited by the array size. A less limiting approach is to use **malloc( )** to allocate space for the pointers as well as for the strings. To keep track of the pointers, you can define a structure that holds two pointers. Then each structure can hold a pointer to a string and a pointer to the next structure, which holds a pointer to the next string and a pointer to the next structure, and so on. Such systems of structures are called *linked lists*. A second example of the program's naivete is that it fails to check if **malloc( )** succeeds in finding more space. This problem can be remedied by using an **if** to check the **malloc( )** return value.

Let's apply the linked list approach and add the missing **if**. At the same time, let's use functions to modularize the program. First, we need to design an appropriate structure. We can have each structure hold a string and a pointer to the next structure, but it's better to have each structure hold a pointer to a string and a pointer to the next structure. This way, each structure doesn't need to have enough space for the longest string. That is, instead of using

```
struct symp  {
        char name[81];
        struct symp *next;
        };
```

we can use the following:

```
struct symp  {
        char *name;
        struct symp *next;
        };
```

We use **malloc( )** to store the strings themselves elsewhere in memory. See Figure 16.3. Note that the **next** member is a pointer to a **struct symp** and not a **struct symp** itself. A C structure cannot contain a member of the same type as itself, but it can contain a pointer to its own type.

The program uses the **symp** structure and pointers to that structure. We can use **typedef** to create convenient synonyms for those types:

```
typedef struct symp SYM;
typedef SYM *PT_SYM;    /* type PT_SYM is pointer-to-struct symp */
```

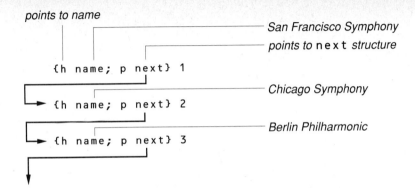

Figure 16.3

Linked structures

points to name

San Francisco Symphony

points to **next** structure

{h name; p next} 1

Chicago Symphony

{h name; p next} 2

Berlin Philharmonic

{h name; p next} 3

Now we can put together the essential features of the **main( )** function:

```
main()
{
    PT_SYM start;

    start = fill_list();
    if (start == NULL)
        puts("No symphonies");
    else
        show_list(start);
}
```

The **fill_list( )** function reads in the symphonies and creates the linked list of structures. Also, it returns a pointer to the first structure in the list. The way we've written **main( )** implies that **fill_list( )** should return the **NULL** pointer if there is no input. The **show_list( )** function takes a pointer to the beginning of the list and prints out the associated strings.

The next step is to write these functions and to fill in other details. Listing 16.8 shows the result.

❖ *linked.c*

Listing 16.8

```
/* linked.c--memorize symphony orchestras with linked
   list*/
#include <stdio.h>
#include <string.h>
#define ANSI
#ifdef ANSI
#include <stdlib.h>    /* ANSI C header for malloc() */
#else
char *malloc();
#endif
#define LINE 81        /* maximum line length for input */
struct symp {
        char *name;
        struct symp *next;
        };             /* linked structure template */
```

```
typedef struct symp SYM;
typedef SYM *PT_SYM;
void show_list();
PT_SYM fill_list();

main()
{
  PT_SYM start;

  puts("Name some symphony orchestras.");
  puts(
    "Enter them one at a time; press [enter] at the start");
  puts("of a line to end your list. Okay, I'm ready.");
  start = fill_list();
  if (start == NULL)
    puts("No symphonies");
  else
    show_list(start);
}

PT_SYM fill_list()
{
  char temp[LINE]; /* temporary input storage */
  PT_SYM pfirst, pprev, pnow;
  int count = 0;

  pfirst = pprev = NULL;
  while ((fgets(temp, LINE, stdin) != NULL)
      && temp[0] !='\n')
  {
    pnow = (PT_SYM) malloc( sizeof (SYM) );
    if (pnow == NULL)
    {
      fputs("Unable to allocate more memory", stderr);
      exit(2);
    }
    if (pprev == NULL)
      pfirst = pnow;
    else
      pprev->next = pnow;
    pnow->name = (char *) malloc(strlen(temp) + 1);
    if (pnow->name == NULL)
    {
      fputs("Unable to allocate more memory", stderr);
      exit(2);
    }
    strcpy(pnow->name, temp);
    pnow->next = NULL;
    pprev = pnow;
    printf("That's %d. Continue if you like.\n", count);
  }
  return pfirst;
```

Listing 16.8
(cont'd.)

Listing 16.8
(cont'd.)

```
}
void show_list( ps)
PT_SYM ps;
{
  puts("Okay, here is what I've got.");
  do
  {
    printf("%s", ps->name);
    ps = ps->next;
  } while (ps != NULL);
```

From the user's vantage, this program runs the same as that of Listing 16.7 except that there is no 100-symphony limit. Now you can keep adding symphonies until the system runs short of memory. Let's look at the **fill_list** and **show_list** functions.

The fill_list( ) Function

This function begins by declaring an array for temporary storage of input. Then it declares three pointers to structures. The pointer **pfirst** is intended to save the address of the first structure in the list. The **pnow** pointer points to the structure currently being processed. The **pprev** pointer points to the previous structure.

The **pfirst** and **pprev** pointers are set to the **NULL** pointer initially. Eventually, the function returns the value of **pfirst**. If there is no input, **pfirst** never receives another value, and the function returns **NULL**, as expected by **main( )**. The **pprev** pointer is set to **NULL** to indicate that initially there is no previous structure.

The **while** loop uses **fgets( )** to read a line of input. Once the program determines that there is, in fact, an input line, it calls on **malloc( )** to create storage for a type **struct symp** structure. The address is assigned to **pnow**. The first time through the loop, **pprev** still is **NULL**. In this case, **pfirst** is set to the address of the first structure created. Later, **pprev** is set to **pnow** so that the next loop cycle will know the address of the previous structure. This information is used to set **pprev->next** to the new **pnow** value. That is, during the second passage through the loop, the **next** member of the first structure is set to the address of the second structure. In this manner, each structure winds up containing the address of the next structure in the line. The most recent structure has its **next** member set to **NULL**. Thus, the structure with its **next** member set to **NULL** is the last structure in the linked list.

The loop also uses **malloc( )** to create storage for the input string. The address of the string is stored in the **name** member of the structure. The end result is that each structure holds the address of a string and the address of the next structure. The program keeps track of the first structure with the pointer **pfirst**. This value is assigned to the **start** structure in **main( )**. Each structure is linked to the next by storing its address, and the end of the list is marked by a structure having its **next** member set to **NULL**.

The show_list( ) Function

The program passes the address of the first structure to **show_list( )**. This action causes the actual argument **ps** in **show_list( )** to be set to that address. Then the structure member **ps->name** contains the address of the first input string. The program uses this address to print the string. To go to the next structure, the program does the following:

```
ps = ps->next;
```

Because the **ps->next** member holds the address of the next structure, this statement causes **ps** to point to the next structure. Note that something like **ps++** doesn't work because there is no guarantee that the structures are stored sequentially. The loop continues until **ps->next** is **NULL**. Since **NULL** marks the end of the list, the loop goes no further.

16.11 Other Directions

In this book we've covered the essential features of C, but we've only touched on the library. The ANSI C library contains scores of useful functions. Most implementations additionally offer extensive libraries of functions specific to particular systems. Microsoft C and Turbo C, for instance, offer functions to facilitate hardware control, keyboard input, and the generation of graphics for IBM PCs and clones. You should take the time to explore what your system has to offer. If it doesn't have what you want, you can create your own functions. That's part of C. If you think you can do a better job on, say, an input function, do it!

And as you refine and polish your programming technique, you will go from C to shining C.

Once you are comfortable with C, you may wish to investigate C++ or Objective C. These *object-oriented languages* have their roots in C. C includes the use of data objects. These range in complexity from a simple **char** variable to large and intricate structures. Object-oriented programming systems (OOPs), such as C++ and Objective C, carry the idea of the object further. For instance, the properties of an object include not only what kinds of information it can hold but also what kinds of operations can be performed on it. As well, objects can inherit properties from other objects. OOPs carry modularization to a higher level of abstraction and facilitate the writing of large programs.

16.12 Summary

The C preprocessor and the C library are two important adjuncts to the C language. The C preprocessor, following preprocessor directives, adjusts your source code before it is compiled. The C library provides many functions designed to help with tasks such as input, output, file handling, memory management, sorting and searching, mathematical calculations, and string processing, to name a few.

Review Questions

1. Here are groups of one or more macros followed by a source code line that uses them. What code results in each case? Is it valid code?

   a. ```
      #define FPM 5280   /* feet per mile */
      dist = FPM * miles;
      ```

   b. ```
      #define FEET 4
      #define POD FEET + FEET
      plort = FEET * POD;
      ```

   c. ```
      #define SIX = 6;
      nex = SIX;
      ```

   d. ```
      #define NEW(X) X + 5
      y = NEW(y);
      berg = NEW(berg) * lob;
      est = NEW(berg) / NEW(y);
      nilp = lob * NEW(-berg);
      ```

2. Correct the definition in Question 1d to make it more reliable.

3. Define a macro function that returns a minimum of two values.

4. Replace the **whitesp( )** function of Listing 16.3 with a macro of your own devising.

5. Define a macro function that prints the representations and the values of two integer expressions. For example, it may print

   ```
   3+4 is 7 and 4*12 is 48
   ```

   if its arguments are **3+4** and **4*12**.

6. Create **#define** statements to accomplish the following goals:

   a. Create a named constant of value 25.

   b. Have **SPACE** represent the space character.

   c. Have **PS( )** represent printing the space character.

   d. Have **BIG(X)** represent adding 3 to **X**.

   e. Have **SUMSQ(X,Y)** represent the sums of the squares of **X** and **Y**.

7. Define a macro that prints out the name, value, and address of an **int** variable in the following format:

   ```
   name: fop; value: 23; address: 4016
   ```

8. Suppose you have a block of code you wish to skip over temporarily while testing a program. How can you do so without actually removing the code from the file?

9. a. How can you create an enumerated type **days** that makes the abbreviations **sun, mon, tue, wed, thu, fri**, and **sat** stand for the integers 0–6?

b. How can you create a variable **visit** of that type?

10. What's wrong with this program?

```
#include <stdio.h>
main(argc, argv)
int argc;
char argv[];
{
   printf("The square root of %f is %f\n", argv[1],
          sqrt(argv[1]) );
}
```

11. Suppose **scores** is an array of 1000 **double** values that you wish to sort into descending order. You use **qsort( )** and a comparison function called **comp( )**.

a. What is a suitable call to **qsort( )**?

b. What is a suitable definition for **comp( )**?

12. How can you allot space to hold an array of structures?

13. Why can't the **symp** structure used in Listing 16.8 allow the symphonies to be listed in reverse order? What change could you make in the definition of **symp** to allow the list to be traversed in both directions?

Programming Exercises

1. Start developing a header file of preprocessor definitions that you wish to use.

2. The harmonic mean of two numbers is obtained by taking the inverses of the two numbers, averaging them, and taking the inverse of the result. Use a **#define** directive to define a macro function that performs this operation.

3. Polar coordinates describe a vector in terms of magnitude and the counterclockwise angle from the x-axis to the vector. Rectangular coordinates describe the same vector in terms of x and y components. See Figure 16.4. Write a program that reads as input the magnitude and angle (in degrees) of a vector and then displays the x and y components. The relevant equations are these:

$$x = r \cos A$$

$$y = r \sin A$$

To perform the conversion use a function that takes a structure containing the polar coordinates and returns a structure containing the rectangular coordinates. (Or use pointers to such structures, if you prefer.)

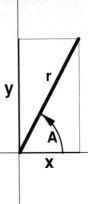

Figure 16.4

Rectangular and polar coordinates

4. Modify the program in Listing 16.7 so that it uses **qsort( )** to sort the array of pointers so that the final list is displayed in alphabetical order. Keep in mind that the pointers should be sorted according to the strings they point to, not according to their own values.

5. Modify the program in Listing 16.8 so that it uses a doubly-linked list as described in Review Question 13. Have the program print the list both in normal and reversed order.

6. Modify the program in Listing 16.8 so that it saves the symphony names in a file. Also, if the file already exists when the program is run, have it first load the contents into memory and then display them. Keep in mind that you should store the strings, not the contents of the structures, which are just addresses. Use a fixed-size record for storing each string, and use **fread( )** and **fwrite( )**.

7. This exercise is the same as Exercise 5, except you should use variable-sized records to store the strings. Each string should be preceded in storage by a byte that holds the length of the string. On input, the program should first read the byte number and then use that information to determine the number of bytes to read for the string.

8. The ANSI library features a **clock( )** function with this description:

```
#include <time.h>
clock_t clock (void);
```

Here **clock_t** is a type defined in **time.h**. The function returns the processor time, which is given in some implementation-dependent units. (If the processor time is unavailable or cannot be represented, the function returns a value of **–1**.) However, **CLK_TCK**, which is also defined in **time.h**, is the number of processor time units per second. Thus, dividing the difference between two return values of **clock( )** by **time.h** provides the number of seconds elapsed between the two calls. Type casting the values to **double** before division lets you obtain fractions of a second. Write a function that takes a **double** argument representing a desired time delay and then runs a loop until that amount of time has passed.

9. Write a function that takes as arguments the name of an array of type **int** elements, the size of an array, and the value that represents the number of items picked. The function should then select the indicated number of items at random from the array and print them. No array element is to be picked more than once. (This scenario simulates picking lottery numbers or jury members.) Also, if your implementation has available **clock( )** or a similar function, use its output in conjunction with **srand( )** to initialize the **rand( )** random number generator.

Additional Reading

If you wish to learn more about C and programming, the following references may be useful.

The C Language

BYTE **8, no. 8 (August 1983).** This issue of BYTE magazine is devoted to C. It includes articles that discuss the history, philosophy, and uses of C. Also included is an extensive bibliography of books and articles on C. Each bibliographic entry contains a short summary of the book or article.

Feuer, A. R. *The C Puzzle Book*. **Englewood Cliffs, N. J.: Prentice-Hall, 1982.** This book contains a large number of programs whose output you are supposed to predict. It gives you a good opportunity to test and expand your understanding of C. The book includes answers and explanations.

Kernighan, B. W., and D. M. Ritchie. *The C Programming Language*. **Englewood Cliffs, N. J.: Prentice-Hall, 1978.** This book is the first text on C. (Note that the creator of C, Dennis Ritchie, is one of the authors.) It constitutes the definition of K & R C, the unofficial standard for many years. The book includes many interesting examples. It does, however, assume that the reader is familiar with systems programming.

Kernighan, B. W., and D. M. Ritchie. *The C Programming Language*. **2d ed. Englewood Cliffs, N. J.: Prentice-Hall, 1988.** This second edition incorporates ANSI changes based on the ANSI draft standard at the time the book was written.

Koenig, A. C *Traps and Pitfalls*. **Reading, Mass.: Addison-Wesley, 1988.** The title says it all.

Ritchie, D. M., S. C. Johnson, M. E. Lesk, and B. W. Kernighan. "The C Programming Language." *The Bell System Technical Journal* **57, no. 6 (July\August 1978).** This article discusses the history of C and provides an overview of its design features.

Stroustrup, B. *The C++ Programming Language*. **Reading, Mass.: Addison-Wesley, 1986.** This book, by the creator of C+, presents the C++ language and includes the reference manual for C++.

Programming

Kernighan, B. W., and P. J. Plauger. *The Elements of Programming Style.* **2d ed. New York: McGraw-Hill, 1978.** This slim classic draws on examples from other texts to illustrate the do's and don'ts of clear, effective programming.

Kernighan, B. W., and P. J. Plauger. *Software Tools.* **Reading, Mass.: Addison-Wesley, 1976.** This book develops several useful programs and systems of programs, while emphasizing good program design. It comes in a RATFOR (rationalized FORTRAN) and in a Pascal version. Since RATFOR represents an attempt to make FORTRAN work like C, the first version is the choice of C users.

C Operators

C is rich in operators. The following table lists them in order of decreasing precedence and indicates how they associate. All operators are binary (two operands) unless otherwise indicated. Note that some binary and unary operators such as ***** (multiplication) and ***** (indirection) share the same symbol but have different precedence. The text following the table summarizes what each operator does.

Operators (from high to low precedence)	Associativity
( ) [ ] . ->	L–R
– + ~ ! * & ++ -- sizeof (*type*) (all unary)	R–L
* / %	L–R
+ –	L–R
<< >>	L–R
< > <= >=	L–R
== !=	L–R
&	L–R
^	L–R
|	L–R
&&	L–R
||	L–R
?: (trinary operator)	L–R
= *= /= %= += –= <<= >>= &= |= ^=	R–L
,	L–R

Arithmetic Operators

+   Adds value at right to value at left

–   Subtracts value at right from value at left

–   As a unary operator, changes sign of value at right

*   Multiplies value at right by value at left

/   Divides value at left by value at right; answer is truncated if both operands are integers

%   Yields the remainder when value at left is divided by value at right (integers only)

++   Adds 1 to value of variable to right (prefix mode) or to value of variable to left (postfix mode)

--   Like ++, but subtracts **1**

Relational Operators

Each of these operators compares the value at its left to the value at its right.

<   Is less than

<=   Is less than or equal to

==   Is equal to

>=   Is greater than or equal to

>   Is greater than

!=   Is unequal to

Relational Expressions

A simple relational expression consists of a relational operator with an operand on each side. If the relation is true, the relational expression has the value 1. If the relation is false, the relational expression has the value 0.

Examples

5 > 2   is true and has the value 1

(2 + a) == a   is false and has the value 0

Assignment Operators

=	Assigns value at right to lvalue at left

Each of the following assignment operators updates the lvalue at its left by the value at its right, using the indicated operation. We use r-h for righthand, and l-h for lefthand.

+=	Adds r-h quantity to l-h variable
−=	Subtracts r-h quantity from l-h variable
*=	Multiplies l-h variable by r-h quantity
/=	Divides l-h variable by r-h quantity
%=	Gives the remainder from dividing l-h quantity by r-h quantity
&=	Assigns l-h **&** r-h to l-h quantity
|=	Assigns l-h | r-h to l-h quantity
^=	Assigns l-h ^ r-h to l-h quantity
>>=	Assigns l-h >> r-h to l-h quantity
<<=	Assigns l-h << r-h to l-h quantity

Example

rabbits *= 1.6; is the same as **rabbits = rabbits * 1.6;**

Logical Operators

Logical operators normally take relational expressions as operands. The **!** operator takes one operand. The rest take two: one to the left, one to the right.

&&	And
||	Or
!	Not

Logical Expressions

expression1 && expression2	is true if and only if both expressions are true
expression1 || expression2	is true if either one or both expressions are true
!expression	is true if the expression is false, and vice versa

Order of Evaluation for Logical Expressions

Logical expressions are evaluated from left to right; evaluation stops as soon as something is discovered that renders the expression false.

Example

6 > 2 && 3 == 3	is true
! (6 > 2 && 3 == 3)	is false
x != 0 && 20/x < 5	the second expression is evaluated only if **x** is nonzero

The Conditional Operator

?:   This operator takes three operands, each of which is an expression. They are arranged this way:

expression1 **?** *expression2* **:** *expression3*

The value of the expression equals the value of *expression2* if *expression1* is true. It equals the value of *expression3* otherwise.

Examples

(5 > 3) ? 1 : 2	has the value **1**
(3 > 5) ? 1 : 2	has the value **2**
(a > b) ? a : b	has the value of the larger of **a** or **b**

Pointer-Related Operators

&   (Address Operator) When followed by a variable name, **&** gives address of that variable.

*   (Indirection or Dereferencing Operator) When followed by a pointer, ***** gives value stored at pointed-to address.

Examples

&nurse is the address of the variable **nurse**.

```
nurse = 22;
ptr = &nurse;        /* pointer to nurse */
val = *ptr;
```

The net effect is to assign the value **22** to **val**.

Sign Operators

–   Minus sign: reverses sign of operand

+   Plus sign: leaves sign unchanged

Structure and Union Operators

The Membership Operator: .

.   This operator is used with a structure or union name to specify a member of that structure or union. If **name** is the name of a structure and **member** is a member specified by the structure template, then

```
name.member
```

identifies that member of the structure. The type of **name.member** is the type specified for **member**. The membership operator can also be used in the same fashion with unions.

Example

```
struct    {
          int code;
          float cost;
          } item;
item.code = 1265;
```

This program fragment assigns a value to the **code** member of the structure **item**.

The Indirect Membership Operator: ->

->   This operator is used with a pointer to a structure or union to identify a member of that structure or union. Suppose **ptrstr** is a pointer to a structure and **member** is a member specified by the structure template. Then

```
ptrstr->member
```

identifies that member of the pointed-to structure. The indirect membership operator can be used in the same fashion with unions.

```
struct    {
          int code;
          float cost;
          } item, *ptrst;
ptrst = &item;
ptrst->code = 3451;
```

This program fragment assigns a value to the **code** member of **item**.

The following three expressions are equivalent:

```
ptrst->code   item.code   (*ptrst).code
```

Bitwise Operators

All but ~ are binary operators.

~   (Unary Operator) Produces a value with each bit of the operand inverted.

&   (AND) Produces a value in which each bit is set to 1 only if both corresponding bits in the two operands are 1.

| (OR) Produces a value in which each bit is set to 1 if either or both corresponding bits of the two operands are 1.

^   (EXCLUSIVE OR) Produces a value in which each bit is set to 1 only if one or the other (but not both) of the corresponding bits of the two operands is 1.

<<   (Left-Shift) Produces a value obtained by shifting the bits of the left hand operand to the left by the number of places given by the righthand operand; vacated slots are filled with zeros.

>>   (Right-Shift) Produces a value obtained by shifting the bits of the left hand operand to the right by the number of places given by the righthand operand. For unsigned integers, the vacated slots are filled with zeros; the behavior for signed values is implementation dependent.

Examples

Suppose we have the following:

```
int x = 2;
int y = 3;
```

Then **x & y** has the value **2**, for only bit 1 is on for both **x** and **y**. Also, **y<<x** has the value **12**, for that is the value obtained when the bit pattern for **3** is shifted two bits to the left.

Miscellaneous Operators

sizeof   Yields the size, in bytes, of the operand to its right. The operand can be a type-specifier in parentheses, as in **sizeof (float)**, or it can be the name of a particular variable, array, and so forth as in **sizeof foo**.

(type)   (Cast Operator) Converts following value to the type specified by the enclosed keyword(s). For example, **(float) 9** converts the integer **9** to the floating-point number **9.0**.

,   (Comma Operator) Links two expressions into one and guarantees that the leftmost expression is evaluated first. The value of the entire expression is the value of the righthand expression. It is typically used to include more information in a **for** loop control expression.

Example

```
for ( step = 2, fargo = 0; fargo < 1000; step *= 2)
        fargo += step;
```

Basic Types and Storage Classes

Basic Data Types

Keywords:

The basic data types are set up using the following eight keywords: **int**, **long**, **short**, **unsigned**, **char**, **float**, **double**, **signed** (**signed** is new with ANSI C).

Signed Integers

These can have positive or negative values:

int   The basic integer type for a given system.

long or **long int**   Can hold an integer at least as large as the largest **int** and possibly larger.

short or **short int**   The largest **short** integer is no larger than the largest **int** and may be smaller. Typically, **long** is bigger than **short**, and **int** is the same as one of the two. For example, Turbo C and MicroSoft C for the IBM PC provide 16-bit **short** and **int** and 32-bit **long**. It all depends on the system.

Unsigned Integers

These have zero or positive values only and extend the range of the largest possible positive number. Use the keyword **unsigned** before the desired type: **unsigned int**, **unsigned long**, **unsigned short**. A lone **unsigned** is the same as **unsigned int**.

Characters

These are typographic symbols such as A, &, and +. Typically, just one byte of memory is used.

char: The keyword for this type.

Some implementations use a **signed char**; others use an **unsigned char**. ANSI C allows you to use the keywords **signed** and **unsigned** to specify which form you want.

Floating Point

These can have positive or negative values:

float: The basic floating-point type for the system.

double: A (possibly) larger unit for holding floating-point numbers. It may allow more significant figures and perhaps larger exponents than **float** does.

long double: A (possibly) even larger unit for holding floating-point numbers. It may allow more significant figures and perhaps larger exponents than **double** does. (**Long double** is new with ANSI C.)

How to Declare a Simple Variable

1. Choose the type you need.

2. Choose a name for the variable.

3. Use the following format for a declaration statement:

type-specifier variable-name;

The *type-specifier* is formed from one or more of the type keywords. Here are some examples: **int erest;** and **unsigned short cash;**

4. You may declare more than one variable of the same type by separating the variable names with commas, for example: **char ch, init, ans;**.

5. You can initialize a variable in a declaration statement, for example: **float mass = 6.0E24;**.

Storage Classes

Keywords

The storage classes are set up using the following keywords: **auto, extern, static, register**.

General Comments

The storage class of a variable determines its scope and how long the variable persists. Storage class is determined by where the variable is defined and by the associated keyword. Variables defined outside a function are external and have global scope. Variables declared inside a function are automatic and local unless one of the other keywords is used. External variables defined before a function are known to it even if not declared internally. The following table summarizes the use of storage classes. Those above the dotted line are declared inside a function; those below the line are defined outside a function.

Storage Class	Keyword	Duration	Scope
Automatic	**auto**	Temporary	Local
Register	**register**	Temporary	Local
Static	**static**	Persistent	Local
External	**extern***	Persistent	Global (all files)
External static	**static**	Persistent	Global (one file)

*The keyword **extern** is used only to redeclare variables that have been defined externally elsewhere; the act of defining the variable outside a function makes it external.

Expressions, Statements, and Program Flow

Expressions

An expression is a combination of operators and operands. The simplest expression is a constant or a variable with no operator, such as **22** or **beebop**. More complex examples are **55 + 22** and **vap = 2 * (vip + (vup = 4))**.

Statements

A statement is a command to the computer. There are simple statements and compound statements. Simple statements terminate in a semicolon:

Declaration statement:	**int toes;**
Assignment statement:	**toes = 12;**
Function call statement:	**printf(" %d\n", toes);**
Control statement:	**while (toes < 20)**
	toes = toes + 2;
Null statement:	**; /* does nothing */**

Compound statements, or blocks, consist of one or more statements (which themselves can be compound) enclosed in braces. The following **while** statement contains an example:

```
while ( years < 100 )
   {
   wisdom = wisdom + 1;
   printf("%d %d\n", years, wisdom);
   years = years + 1;
   }
```

The while Statement

Keyword: while

General Comments

The **while** statement creates a loop that repeats until the test *expression* becomes false, or zero. The **while** statement is an entry-condition loop; the decision to make another pass through the loop is made before the loop is traversed. Thus, it is possible that the loop is never traversed. The *statement* part of the form can be a simple statement or a compound statement.

Form

```
while ( expression )
    statement
```

The *statement* portion is repeated until the *expression* becomes false, or zero.

Examples

```
while ( n++ < 100 )
    printf(" %d %d\n",n, 2*n+1 );

while ( fargo < 1000 )
    {
    fargo = fargo + step;
    step = 2 * step;
    }
```

The for Statement

Keyword: for

General Comments

The **for** statement uses three control expressions, separated by semicolons, to control a looping process. The *initialize* expression is executed once, before any of the loop statements are executed. If the *test* expression is true, or nonzero, the loop is cycled through once. Then the *update* expression is evaluated, and the *test* expression is checked again. Like the **while** statement, the **for** statement is an entry-condition loop; the decision to make another pass through the loop is made before the loop is traversed. Thus, it is possible that the loop is never traversed. The *statement* part of the form can be a simple statement or a compound statement.

Form

```
for ( initialize ; test ; update )
    statement
```

The loop is repeated until *test* becomes false, or zero.

Example

```
for ( n = 0; n < 10 ; n++ )
    printf(" %d %d\n", n, 2*n+1 );
```

The do while *Statement*

Keywords: do, while

General Comments

The **do while** statement creates a loop that repeats until the test *expression* becomes false, or zero. The **do while** statement is an exit-condition loop; the decision to make another pass through the loop is made after the loop is traversed. Thus, the loop must be executed at least once. The *statement* part of the form can be a simple statement or a compound statement.

Form

```
do
    statement
        while ( expression );
```

The *statement* portion is repeated until the *expression* becomes false, or zero.

Example

```
do
    scanf("%d", &number)
        while( number != 20 );
```

Using if Statements for Making Choices

Keywords: if, else

General Comments

In each of the following forms, the *statement* can be either a simple statement or a compound statement. A true expression, more generally, means an expression with a nonzero value.

Form 1

```
if ( expression )
    statement
```

The *statement* is executed if the *expression* is true.

Form 2

```
if ( expression )
    statement1
else
    statement2
```

If the *expression* is true, *statement1* is executed; otherwise *statement2* is executed.

Form 3

```
if ( expression1 )
    statement1
else if ( expression2 )
    statement2
else
    statement3
```

If *expression1* is true, then *statement1* is executed. If *expression1* is false but *expression2* is true, *statement2* is executed. Otherwise, if both expressions are false, *statement3* is executed.

Example

```
if (legs == 4)
    printf("It might be a horse.\n");
else if (legs > 4)
    printf("It is not a horse.\n");
else      /* case of legs < 4 */
    {
    legs++;
    printf("Now it has one more leg.\n")
    }
```

Multiple Choice with switch

Keyword: switch

General Comments

Program control jumps to the statement bearing the value of *expression* as a label. Program flow then proceeds through the remaining statements unless redirected again. Both *expression* and labels must have integer values (type **char** is included), and the labels must be constants or expressions formed solely from constants. If no label matches the expression value, control passes to the statement labeled **default**, if present. Otherwise, control passes to the next statement following the **switch** statement.

Form

switch (*expression*)
   {
   case label1 : *statement1*
   case label2 : *statement2*
   default   : *statement3*
   }

There can be more than two labeled statements, and the **default** case is optional.

Example

```
switch ( letter )
   {
   case 'a' :
   case 'e' : printf("%d is a vowel\n", letter);
   case 'c' :
   case 'n' : printf("%d is in \"cane\"\n", letter);
   default : printf("Have a nice day.\n");
   }
```

If **letter** has the value **'a'** or **'e'**, all three messages are printed; **'c'** and **'n'** cause the last two to be printed. Other values print only the last message.

Program Jumps

Keywords: break, continue, goto

General Comments

These three instructions cause program flow to jump from one location of a program to another location.

The break Command

The **break** command can be used with any of the three loop forms and with the **switch** statement. It causes program control to pass over the rest of the loop or **switch** that contains the **break** and to resume program flow with the next command following the loop or **switch**.

Example

```
switch ( number )
   {
   case 4:   printf("That's a good choice.\n");
             break;
   case 5:   printf("That's a fair choice.\n");
             break;
   default:  printf("That's a poor choice.\n");
   }
```

The continue Command

The **continue** command can be used with any of the three loop forms but not with a **switch**. It causes program control to skip the remaining statements in a loop. In a **while** or **for** loop, the next loop cycle is started. In a **do while** loop, the exit condition is tested and then, if necessary, the next loop cycle is started.

Example

```
while ( (ch = getchar()) != EOF )
   {
   if ( ch == ' ' )
      continue;
   putchar(ch);
   chcount++;
   }
```

This fragment echoes and counts nonspace characters.

The goto Command

A **goto** statement causes program control to jump to a statement bearing the indicated label. A colon is used to separate a labeled statement from its label. Label names follow the rules for variable names. The labeled statement can precede or follow the **goto.**

Form

goto *label*;
   ...
label : *statement*

Example

```
top : ch = getchar();
    ...
if ( ch != 'y' )
    goto top;
```

ASCII Table

DEX X_{10}	HEX X_{16}	OCT X_8	Binary X_2	ASCII	Key
0	0	00	000 0000	NUL	CTRL/1
1	01	01	000 0001	SOH	CTRL/A
2	02	02	000 0010	STX	CTRL/B
3	03	03	000 0011	ETX	CTRL/C
4	04	04	000 0100	EOT	CTRL/D
5	05	05	000 0101	ENQ	CTRL/E
6	06	06	000 0110	ACK	CTRL/F
7	07	07	000 0111	BEL	CTRL/G
8	08	10	000 1000	BS	CTRL/H, BACKSPACE
9	09	11	000 1001	HT	CTRL/I, TAB
10	0A	12	000 1010	LF	CTRL/J, LINE FEED
11	0B	13	000 1011	VT	CTRL/K
12	0C	14	000 1100	FF	CTRL/L
13	0D	15	000 1101	CR	CTRL/M, RETURN
14	0E	16	000 1110	SO	CTRL/N
15	0F	17	000 1111	SI	CTRL/O
16	10	20	001 0000	DLE	CTRL/P
17	11	21	001 0001	DC1	CTRL/Q
18	12	22	001 0010	DC2	CTRL/R
19	13	23	001 0011	DC3	CTRL/S
20	14	24	001 0100	DC4	CTRL/T
21	15	25	001 0101	NAK	CTRL/U
22	16	26	001 0110	SYN	CTRL/V
23	17	27	001 0111	ETB	CTRL/W
24	18	30	001 1000	CAN	CTRL/X
25	19	31	001 1001	EM	CTRL/Y

DEX X_{10}	HEX X_{16}	OCT X_8	Binary X_2	ASCII	Key
26	1A	32	001 1010	SUB	CTRL/Z
27	1B	33	001 1011	ESC	ESC, ESCAPE
28	1C	34	001 1100	FS	CTRL <
29	1D	35	001 1101	GS	CTRL/
30	1E	36	001 1110	RS	CTRL/=
31	1F	37	001 1111	US	CTRL/-
32	20	40	010 0000	SP	SPACEBAR
33	21	41	010 0001	!	!
34	22	42	010 0010	"	"
35	23	43	010 0011	#	#
36	24	44	010 0100	$	$
37	24	45	010 0101	%	%
38	26	46	010 0110	&	&
39	27	47	010 0111	'	'
40	28	50	010 1000	(	(
41	29	51	010 1001	)	)
42	2A	53	010 1010	*	*
43	2B	53	010 1011	+	+
44	2C	54	010 1100	,	,
45	2D	55	010 1101	-	-
46	2E	56	010 1110	.	.
47	2F	57	010 1111	/	/
48	30	60	011 0000	0	0
49	31	61	011 0001	1	1
50	32	62	011 0010	2	2
51	33	63	011 0011	3	3
52	34	64	011 0100	4	4
53	35	65	011 0101	5	5
54	36	66	011 0110	6	6
55	37	67	011 0111	7	7
56	38	70	011 1000	8	8
57	39	71	011 1001	9	9
58	3A	72	011 1010	:	:
59	3B	73	011 1011	;	;
60	3C	74	011 1100	<	<
61	3D	75	011 1101	=	=
62	3E	76	011 1110	>	>
63	3F	77	011 1111	?	?
64	40	100	100 0000	@	@
65	41	101	100 0001	A	A

DEX X_{10}	HEX X_{16}	OCT X_8	Binary X_2	ASCII	Key
66	42	102	100 0010	B	B
67	43	103	100 0011	C	C
68	44	104	100 0100	D	D
69	45	105	100 0101	E	E
70	46	106	100 0110	F	F
71	47	107	100 0111	G	G
72	48	110	100 1000	H	H
73	49	111	100 1001	I	I
74	4A	112	100 1010	J	J
75	4B	113	100 1011	K	K
76	4C	114	100 1100	L	L
77	4D	115	100 1101	M	M
78	4E	116	100 1110	N	N
79	4F	117	100 1111	O	O
80	50	120	101 0000	P	P
81	51	121	101 0001	Q	Q
82	52	122	101 0010	R	R
83	53	123	101 0011	S	S
84	54	124	101 0100	T	T
85	55	125	101 0101	U	U
86	56	126	101 0110	V	V
87	57	127	101 0111	W	W
88	58	130	101 1000	X	X
89	59	131	101 1001	Y	Y
90	5A	132	101 1010	Z	Z
91	5B	133	101 1011	[	[
92	5C	134	101 1100	\	\
93	5D	135	101 1101	]	]
94	5E	136	101 1110	^	^
95	5F	137	101 1111	—	—
96	60	140	110 0000	`	`
97	61	141	110 0001	a	a
98	62	142	110 0010	b	b
99	63	143	110 0011	c	c
100	64	144	110 0100	d	d
101	65	145	110 0101	e	e
102	66	146	110 0110	f	f
103	67	147	110 0111	g	g
104	68	150	110 1000	h	h
105	69	151	110 1001	i	i

DEX X_{10}	HEX X_{16}	OCT X_8	Binary X_2	ASCII	Key
106	6A	152	110 1010	j	j
107	6B	153	110 1011	k	k
108	6C	154	110 1100	l	l
109	6D	155	110 1101	m	m
110	6E	156	110 1110	n	n
111	6F	157	110 1111	o	o
112	70	160	111 0000	p	p
113	71	161	111 0001	q	q
114	72	162	111 0010	r	r
115	73	163	111 0011	s	s
116	74	164	111 0100	t	t
117	75	165	111 0101	u	u
118	76	166	111 0110	v	v
119	77	167	111 0111	w	w
120	78	170	111 1000	x	x
121	79	171	111 1001	y	y
122	7A	172	111 1010	z	z
123	7B	173	111 1011	{	{
124	7C	174	111 1100				
125	7D	175	111 1011	}	}
126	7E	176	111 1110	~	~
127	7F	177	111 1111	DEL	DEL, RUBOUT

Standard I/O Functions (ANSI C)

The ANSI C Standard library includes several standard I/O functions associated with streams and the stdio.h file. The following list presents the ANSI prototypes for these functions along with a brief explanation of what they do. For complete descriptions, consult the documentation for your implementation or a reference manual.

ANSI Prototypes	Description
void clearerr(FILE *)	Clears end-of-file and error indicators
int fclose(FILE *)	Closes indicated file
int feof(FILE *)	Tests for end-of-file
int ferror(FILE *)	Tests error indicator
int fflush(FILE *)	Flushes indicated file
int fgetc(FILE *)	Gets next character from indicated input stream
int fgetpos(FILE *, fpos_t *)	Store current value of file position indicator
char * fgets(char *, int, FILE *)	Gets next line (or indicated number of characters) from indicated stream
FILE * fopen(const char *, const char *)	Opens indicated file
int fprintf(FILE *, const char *, ...)	Writes formatted output to indicated stream
int fputc(int, FILE *)	Writes indicated character to indicated stream
int fputs(const char *, FILE *)	Writes indicated character to indicated stream

```
size_t fread(void *, size_t, size_t, FILE *)
```
Reads binary data from indicated stream

```
FILE * freopen(const char *, const char *, FILE *)
```
Opens indicated file and associates it with indicated stream

```
int fscanf(FILE *, const char *, ...)
```
Reads formatted input from indicated stream

```
int fsetpos(FILE *, const fpos_t *)
```
Sets file position pointer to indicated value

```
int fseek(FILE *, long, int)
```
Sets file position pointer to indicated value

```
long ftell(FILE *)
```
Gets current file position

```
size_t fwrite(const void *, size_t, size_t, FILE *)
```
Writes binary data to indicated stream

```
int getc(FILE *)
```
Reads next character from indicated input

```
int getchar( )
```
Reads next character from standard input

```
char * gets(char *)
```
Gets next line from standard input

```
void perror(const char *)
```
Writes system error messages to standard error

```
int printf(const char *, ...)
```
Writes formatted output to standard output

```
int putc(int, FILE *)
```
Writes indicated character to indicated output

```
int putchar(int)
```
Writes indicated character to standard output

```
int puts(const char *)
```
Writes string to standard output

```
int remove(const char *)
```
Removes named file

```
int rename(const char *, const char *)
```
Renames named file

```
void rewind(FILE *)
```
Sets file position pointer to start of file

```
int scanf(const char *, ...)
```
Reads formatted input from standard input

```
void setbuf(FILE *, char *)
```
Sets buffer size and location

```
int setvbuf(FILE *, char *, int, size_t)
```
Sets buffer size, location, and mode

```
int sprintf(char *, const char *, ...)
```
Writes formatted output to indicated string

```
int sscanf(const char *, const char *, ...)
```
Reads formatted input from indicated string

`FILE * tmpfile(void)`   Creates temporary file

`char * tmpnam(char *)`   Generates unique name for temporary file

`int ungetc(int, FILE *)`   Pushes indicated character back into input stream

```
int vfprintf(FILE *, const char *, va_list)
```
Like **fprintf( )**, except uses single list argument instead of variable argument list

```
int vprintf(const char *, va_list)
```
Like **printf( )**, except uses single list argument instead of variable argument list

```
int vsprintf(char *, const char *, va_list)
```
Like **sprintf( )**, except uses single list argument instead of variable argument list

Answers to Odd-Numbered Review Questions

Chapter 1

1. A perfectly portable program is one whose source code can, without modification, be compiled into a successful program on a variety of different computer systems.

3. (1) Defining program objectives; (2) designing the program; (3) coding the program; (4) compiling the program; (5) running the program; (6) testing and debugging the program; (7) maintaining and modifying the program.

5. Top-down programming means to break down a program into modular form and to write the code for the top-level modules first, then write the code for the next level, and so on.

7. A linker combines object code from several sources into a single, executable program.

Chapter 2

1. They are called functions.

3. A syntax error is a violation of the rules governing how sentences or programs are put together. Here's an example in English: Me speak English good. Here's an example in C: **printf "Where are the parentheses?"**

5. *Line 1:* Begin the line with a **#**; spell the file **stdio.h**; place the filename within angle brackets.

Line 2: Use ( ), not { }; end comment with */, not /*.

Line 3: Use { , not (.

Line 4: Complete the statement with a semicolon.

Line 5: Mr. IBM got this one (the blank line) correct!

Line 6: Use = and not := for assignment (apparently Mr. IBM knows a little Pascal); use **52**, not **56**, weeks per year.

Line 7: Should be **printf("There are %d weeks in a year.\n", s);**.

Line 8: There isn't a line 8, but there should be; it should consist of the closing brace (}).

7. a. `Baa Baa Black Sheep.Have you any wool?`

(Note that there is no space after the period. We could have had a space by using **" Have** instead of **"Have.**)

b. `Begone!`
`O creature of lard!`

(Note that the cursor is left at the end of the second line.)

c. `What?`
`No/nBonzo?`

(Note that the slash (/) does not have the same effect as the backslash (\ ).)

d. `2 + 2 = 4`

(Note how each **%d** is replaced by the corresponding variable value from the list. Also note that + means addition and that calculation can be performed inside a **printf( )** statement.)

9. **int** and **char**

11. `printf("There were %d words and %d lines.\n", words, lines);`

13. After line 5, **a** is **5** and **b** is **2**. After line 6, both **a** and **b** are **5**. After line 7, both **a** and **b** are **5**. Note that **a** can't be **2** because by the time we say **a = b;**, **b** has already been changed to **5**.

Chapter 3

1. a. **int**, possibly **short** or **unsigned** or **unsigned short**; population is a whole number

b. **float**; it's unlikely the average will be an exact integer

c. **char**

d. **int**, possibly **unsigned**

3. *Line 1:* Fine.

Line 2: Should have a parentheses pair following **main**; that is, **main( )**.

Line 3: Use { , not (.

Line 4: Should be a comma, not a semicolon, between **g** and **h**.

Line 5: Fine.

Line 6: (blank) Fine.

Line 7: Should be at least one digit before the **e**; either **1e21** or **1.0e21** is okay.

Line 8: Fine.

Line 9: Use **}** , not **)** .

Missing lines: First, **rate** is never assigned a value. Second, the variable **h** is never used. Also, the program never informs us of the results of its calculation. Neither of these errors will stop the program from running (although you may be given a warning about the unused variable), but they do detract from its already limited usefulness.

5. a. **int, %o**

  b. **long double, %Le**

  c. **char, %c**

  d. **int, %d** or **long, %ld**, depending on the size of the **int** type

  e. **char, %c**

  f. **float, %f**

  g. **int, %x**

7. *Line 0:* It's better form to use **#include <stdio.h>**

  Line 1: Use **/*** and ***/**

  Line 3: **int cows, legs;**

  Line 5: **count?\nÜ);**

  Line 6: **%d**, not **%c**

  Line 6: **&legs**

  Line 8: **%d**, not **%f**

Chapter 4

1. The program bombs. The first **scanf( )** statement reads only your first name, leaving your last name untouched but still stored in the input "buffer" (a temporary storage area used to store the input). When the next **scanf( )** statement looks for your weight, it picks up where the last reading attempt ended, and it reads your last name as your weight. This produces garbage. On the other hand, if you respond to the name request with something like **Lasha 144**, the program uses **144** as your weight even though you typed it before your weight was requested.

3. Remember the escape sequences discussed in Chapter 3 and try the following:

```
printf("\"%s\"\nhas %d characters.\n", Q, strlen(Q));
```

5. Recall the %% construction for printing %:

```
printf("This copy of \"%s\" sells for $%0.2f.\n", BOOK, cost);
printf("That is %d%% of list.\n", percent);
```

7. a. **%15lu**   b. **%#4x**   c. **%–12.2E**   d. **%+10.3f**   e. **%8.8s**

9. a
```
int dalmations;
scanf("%d", &dalmations);
```

b.
```
float kgs, share;
scanf("%f%f", &kgs, &share);
```

(Note that for input, **e**, **f**, and **g** can be used interchangeably. Also, for all but **%c**, it makes no difference if you leave spaces between the conversion specifiers.)

c.
```
char name[20];
scanf("%s", name);
```

d.
```
char action[20];
int value;
scanf("%s %d", action, &value);
```

e.
```
int value;
scanf("%*s %d", &value);
```

11. The substitutions would take place. Unfortunately, the preprocessor cannot discriminate between those parentheses that should be replaced with braces and those that should not. So

```
main()
(
    printf("Hello, O Great One!\n");
)
```

becomes

```
main{}
{
    printf{"Hello, O Great One!\n"};
}
```

Chapter 5

1. a. **30**

b. **27** (not 3). **(12 + 6)/(2*3)** would give 3.

c. **x = 1, y = 1** (integer division)

d. **x = 3** (integer division), and **y = 9**

3. *Line 3:* Should end in a semicolon, not a comma.

Line 8: The **while** statement sets up an infinite loop, for the value of **i** remains **1** and is always less than **30**. Presumably we meant to write **while(i++ < 30)**.

Lines 8\10: The indentation implies we wanted lines 9 and 10 to form a block, but the lack of braces means the **while** loop includes only line 9. Braces should be added.

Line 9: Since **1** and **i** are both integers, the result of the division is **1** when **i** is **1**, and **0** for all larger values. Using **n = 1.0/i;** would cause **i** to be converted to floating point before division and yield nonzero answers.

Line 10: We omitted a newline character (**\n**) in the control statement, which would cause the numbers to be printed on one line, if possible.

5. Here is the output:

```
%s is a string
is a string
1
1
2
1
```

Let us explain. The first **printf( )** statement is the same as the following:

```
printf("%s is a string\n","%s is a string\n");
```

The second print statement first increments **num** to **1**, then prints the value. The third print statement prints **num**, which is **1**, then increments it to **2**. The fourth print statement prints the current value of **n**, which still is **2**, then decrements **n** to **1**. The final print statement prints the current value of **n**, which is **1**.

7. It prints the digits 1 through 10 in five-column-wide fields on one line and then starts a new line:

```
    1    2    3    4    5    6    7    8    9    10
```

9. Here is the output for each example:

a.   1   2

(Note that **x** is incremented, then compared. The cursor is left on the same line.)

b. 101
102
103
104

(Note that this time **x** is compared, then incremented. In both this case and in part a, **x** is incremented before printing takes place. Note, too, that indenting the second **printf( )** statement does not make it part of the **while** loop. Thus, it is called only once, after the **while** loop ends.)

c. stuvw

(Here there is no incrementing until after the first **printf( )**.)

11. a. x = x + 10;

b. x++;

c. c = 2 * (a + b);

d. c = a + 2* b;

Chapter 6

1. 2, 7, 70, 64, 8, 2

3. a. **x > 5**   b. **scanf(" %lf", &dnum) != 1**   c. **x == 5**

5. For style, should start with **#include <stdio.h>**.

Line 3: Should be **list[10]**.

Line 5: Commas should be semicolons.

Line 5: Range for **i** should be from **0** to **9**, not **1** to **10**.

Line 8: Commas should be semicolons.

Line 8: >= should be <=. Otherwise, when **i** is **1**, the loop never ends.

Line 10: Should be another closing brace between lines 9 and 10. One brace closes the compound statement; one closes the program.

7. a. Hi! Hi! Hi! Bye! Bye! Bye! Bye! Bye!

b. ACGM

9. Here is the output:

```
11121314
***
1
4
7
***
1 5
2 7
4 9
8 11
***
+++++
++++
+++
++
```

11. Because the first element has index **0**, the loop range should be **1** to **SIZE – 1**, not **1** to **SIZE**. Making that change, however, causes the first element to be assigned the value **0** instead of **2**. Therefore, rewrite the loop this way:

```
for( index = 0; index < SIZE; index++)
      by_twos[index] = 2 * (index + 1);
```

Similarly, the limits for the second loop should be changed. Also, an array index should be used with the array name:

```
for( index = 0; index < SIZE; index++)
      printf("%d ", by_twos[index]);
```

13.
```
long square(num)
int num;
{
    return num * num;
}
```

Chapter 7

1. True: b

3. *Line 5:* Should be **scanf(" %d %d", &weight, &height);** (don't forget the **&** for use with **scanf( )**). Also, this line should be preceded by a line prompting input.

Line 9: What is meant is **(height > 72 && height > 64)**. However, the first part of the expression is unnecessary, since **height** must be less than **72** for the **else if** to be reached in the first place. Thus, a simple **(height > 64)** will serve.

Line 11: The condition is redundant; the second subexpression (**weight** not less than or equal to **300**) means the same as the first. A simple (**weight > 300**) is all that is needed. But there is more trouble. Line 11 gets attached to the wrong **if**! Clearly this **else** is meant to go along with line 6. By the most recent **if not** rule, however, it is associated with the **if** of line 9. Thus, line 11 is reached when **weight** is less than **100** and **height** is **64** or under. It is therefore impossible for **weight** to exceed **300** when this statement is reached.

Lines 7–9: Should be enclosed in braces. Then line 11 will become an alternative to line 6, not to line 9.

Line 12: Simplify the expression to (**height > 48**).

Line 14: This **else** associates with the last **if**, the one on line 12. Enclose lines 12 and 13 in braces to force this **else** to associate with the **if** of line 11. Note that the final message is printed only for those weighing between 100 and 300 pounds.

5. The program prints the following:

```
*#%*#%$#%*#%*#%$#%*#%*#%$#%*#%*#%
```

(Despite what the indentation suggests, the # is printed during every loop since it is not part of a compound statement.)

7. The comments on lines 5–7 should be terminated with */. The expression
'a' <= ch >= 'z' should be replaced with **ch >= 'a' && ch <= 'z'**

Incidentally, **'a' <= ch >= 'z'** is valid C; it just doesn't have the right meaning. Since relational operators associate from left to right, the expression is interpreted as (**'a' <= ch) >= 'z'**. The expression in parentheses has the value **1** or **0** (true or false), and this value is checked to see if it is equal to or greater than the numeric code for **'z'**. Neither **0** nor **1** satisfies that test, so the entire expression always evaluates to **0** (false).

In the second test expression, || should be **&&**. Also, although **!(ch < 'A')** is both valid and correct in meaning, **ch >= 'A'** is simpler. The **'Z'** should be followed by two closing parentheses, not one. The **oc++;** statement should be preceded by an **else**. Otherwise, it is incremented every character. The control expression in the **printf( )** call should be enclosed in double quotes.

9. Here is the resulting run using the given input:

```
q
Step 1
Step 2
Step 3
c
Step 1
```

```
g
Step 1
Step 3
b
Step 1
Done
```

(Note that both **b** and **#** terminate the loop, but that entering **b** elicits the printing of **Step 1** whereas entering **#** doesn't.)

Chapter 8

1. The statement **putchar(getchar( ));** causes the program to reach the next input character and to print it; the return value from **getchar( )** is the argument to **putchar( ).** No, **getchar(putchar( ))** is invalid because **getchar( )** doesn't use an argument and **putchar( )** needs one.

3. **count <essay >essayct** or **count >essayct <essay**

5. It's a signal returned by **getchar( )** and **scanf( )** to indicate that an **EOF** has been detected.

7. C's standard I/O library maps diverse file forms to uniform streams that can be handled equivalently.

Chapter 9

1. A formal argument is a variable defined in the function being called. The actual argument is the value appearing in the function call; this value is assigned to the formal argument.

3. a.
```
char n_to_char(n)
    int n;
```
or
```
char n_to_char(int n)
```

b.
```
int digits(x,n)
    double x;
    int n;
```
or
```
int digits(double x, int n)
```

```
    c. int random()

       or

       int random(void)
```

5.
```
float sum(j,k)
float j, k;
```

(Also, declare **float sum( )** in the calling program.)

7. Yes; **num** should be declared before the first brace, not after. Also, it should be **count++**, not **num++**.

9. Here is the minimal program; the **showmenu( )** and **getchoice( )** functions are possible solutions to parts a and b:

```
void showmenu();    /* declare functions used */
int getchoice();
main()
{
    int res;

    showmenu();
    res = getchoice(1,4);
    printf ("I don't know how to do choice %d: bye!\n", res);
}

void showmenu()
{
    printf("Please choose one of the following:\n");
    printf("1) copy files      2) move files\n");
    printf("3) remove files    4) quit\n");
    printf("Enter the number of your choice:\n");
}

int getchoice(low, high)
int low, high;
{
    int ans;

    scanf("%d", &ans);
    while ( ans < low || ans > high )
{
        printf("%d is not a valid choice; try again\n", ans);
        showmenu();
        scanf("%d", &ans);
    }
    return ans;
}
```

Chapter 10

1. The printout follows:

```
D D
O O
L L
T T
```

3. The array name **ref** points to the first element of the array, the character **D**. The expression **ref + 1** points to the second element, the character **O**. The construction **++ref** is not a valid C expression; **ref** is a constant, not a variable.

5. a. 12 and 16

   b. 12 and 14 (just the 12 goes in the first row because of the braces)

7. a. **int digits[10];**

   b. **float rates[6];**

   c. **int mat[3][5];**

   d. **char (*pstr)[20];** (Note that **char pstr[20];** is incorrect. This statement would make **pstr** a constant pointer (not a variable) to a single **char**, the first member of the array; **pstr + 1** would point to the next byte. With the correct declaration, **pstr** is a variable, and **pstr + 1** points 20 bytes beyond the initial byte.)

   e. **char *pstr[20];** (Note that the [ ] have higher precedence than *, so in the absence of parentheses, the array descriptor is applied first, then the pointer descriptor. Hence, this declaration is the same as **char *(pstr[20]);**.)

9. 0–9

Chapter 11

1. Storage class should be external or static for pre-ANSI implementations; initialization should include a **'\0'**.

3.
```
y
my
mmy
ummyYummy
```

5. a. `Ho Ho Ho!!oH oH oH`

   b. pointer-to-**char**

   c. The address of the initial **H**

d. ***--pc** means decrement the pointer by 1 and use the value found there. **--*pc** means take the value pointed to by **pc** and decrement that value by **1** (for example, **H** becomes **G**).

e. `Ho Ho Ho!!oH oH o`

(Note that a null character comes between **!** and **!**, but it produces no printing effect.)

f. **while(*pc)** Check that **pc** does not point to a null character (that is, to the end of the string). The expression uses the value at the pointed-to location.

while(pc – str) Check that **pc** does not point to the same location that **str** does (the beginning of the string). The expression uses the values of the pointers themselves.

g. After the first **while** loop, **pc** points to the null character. On entering the second loop, **pc** is made to point to the storage location before the null character (that is, to the location just before the one **str** points to). That byte is interpreted as a character and is printed; the pointer then backs up to the preceding byte. The terminating condition (**pc == str**) never occurs, and the process continues until you or the system gets tired.

h. **pr( )** must be declared in the calling program: **char *pr( );**

7. Here is what we get:

```
How are ya, sweetie? How are ya, sweetie?
Beat the clock.
eat the clock.
Beat the clock. Win a toy.
Beat
chat
hat
at
t
t
at
How are ya, sweetie?
```

9. Here is one solution:

```
int strlen(s)
char *s;
{
    int ct = 0;

    while (*s++ != '/0')        /* or while (*s++) */
        ct++;
    return(ct);
}
```

Chapter 12

1. It should have **#include <stdio.h>** for its file definitions. It should declare **fp** a file pointer: **FILE *fp; . The function fopen( )** requires a mode: **fopen("gelatin", "w",)** or perhaps the **"a"** mode. The order of the arguments to **fputs( )** should be reversed. The **fclose( )** function requires a file pointer, not a filename: **fclose(fp); .**

3. a. `ch = getc(fp1);`

b. `fprintf(fp2,"%c",ch);`

c. `putc(ch,fp2);`

d. `fclose(fp1);        /* close the terky file */`

(Note that **fp1** is used for input operations, since it identifies the file opened in the read mode. Similarly, **fp2** was opened in the write mode, so it is used with output functions.)

5. Here is one approach:

```
#include <stdio.h>
#define BUF 256
main(argc,argv)
int argc;
char *argv[];
{
FILE *fp;
char ch;
char line [BUF];
char *fgets();

if (argc != 3)
{
    printf("Usage: %s character filename\n", argv[0]);
    exit(1);
}
ch = argv[1][0];
if ( (fp = fopen(argv[2], "r")) == NULL)
{
    printf("Can't open %s\n", argv[2]);
    exit(1);
}
while (fgets(line,BUF,fp) != NULL)
{
    if (has_ch(ch,line) )
            fputs(line,stdout);
    }
    fclose(fp);
}
```

```
int has_ch(ch,line)
char ch;
char *line;
{
    while (*line)
        if (ch == *line++)
            return(1);
    return(0);
}
```

(The **fgets( )** and **fputs( )** functions work together, for **fgets( )** leaves the **\n** produced by Enter in the string, and **fputs( )** does not add in a **\n** the way **puts( )** does.)

7. a. When **8238201** is saved using **fprintf( )**, it's saved as seven characters stored in seven bytes. When saved using **fwrite( )**, it's saved as a four-byte integer using the binary representation of that numeric value.

   b. No difference; in each case it's saved as a one-byte binary code.

9. The **"r+"** mode lets you read and write anywhere in a file, so it's best suited. The **"a+"** mode only lets you append material to the end of the file. The **"w+"** mode starts with a clean slate, discarding prior file contents.

Chapter 13

1. The automatic and the static storage classes

3. The external storage class; the external static storage class

5. Replace **array[search] > array[top]** with **array[search] < array[top]**.

7. **daisy** is known to **main( )** by default and to **petal( )** and **root( )** because of the **extern** declaration. The **extern int daisy;** declaration in **root( )** makes **daisy** known to all the functions in file 2. The first **lily** is local to **main( )**: the reference to **lily** in **petal( )** is an error, because there is no external **lily** in either file. There is an external static **lily**, but it is known only to functions in the second file. The first external **rose** is known to **root( )**, but **stem( )** has overridden it with its own local **rose**.

9. a. It tells us the program will use a variable **plink** that is local to the file containing the function. The first argument is a pointer to an integer, presumably the first element of an array of **n** members. The important point here is that the program will not be allowed to use the pointer **arr** to modify values in the original array.

   b. No. Already **value** and **n** are copies of original data, so there is no way for the function to alter the corresponding values in the calling program. What these declarations do accomplish is to prevent the function from altering **value** and **n** within the function. For example, the function can't use the expression **n++** if **n** is qualified as **const**.

Chapter 14

1. The proper keyword is **struct**, not **structure**. The template requires either a tag before the opening brace or a variable name after the closing brace. Also, there should be a semicolon after ***togs** and at the end of the template.

3.
```
struct month {
              ch
              char name [10];
              char abbrev[4];
              int days;
              int monumb;
              };
```

5.
```
extern struct month months[];
int days(month)
int month;
{
    int index, total;
        if ( month < 1 || month > 12 )
            return(-1);          /* error signal */
        else
            for ( index = 0, total = 0; index < month; index ++)
                    total += months[index].days;
            return( total);
}
```

(Note that **index** is one less than the month number, since arrays start with the subscript 0; hence we use **index < month** instead of **index <= month**.)

7. a. 6
```
Arcturan
cturan
```

b. Use the structure name and the pointer:
```
deb.title.last
pb->title.last
```

c. Here is one version:
```
#include <stdio.h>
#include "starfolk.h"    /* make the struct defs available */
void prbem ( pbem )
struct bem *pbem;
{
    printf("%s %s is a %d-limbed %s.\n", pbem->title.first,
        pbem->title.last, pbem->limbs, pbem->type);
}
```

9. Here is one possibility:

```
struct car    {
                char name[20];
                float hp;
                float epampg;
                float wbase;
                struct car *pcar;
              };
```

11. The function can be set up like the following:

```
struct gas    {  float distance;
                 float gals;
                 float mpg;
              };

struct gas mpgs (trip)
struct gas trip;
{
    if (trip.gals > 0)
        trip.mpg = trip.distance / trip.gals) ;
    else
        trip.mpg = -1.0;
    return trip;
}
```

Note that this function cannot directly alter values in the calling program, so we must use the return value to convey the information:

```
struct gas idaho, ;
...
idaho = mpgs(idaho);
```

13. `char * (*pfun)();`

Chapter 15

1. a. 00000011

  b. 00001101

  c. 00111011

  d. 01110111

3. a. 252   b. 2   c. 7   d. 7   e. 5   f. 3   g. 28

5. In binary, the mask is 1111111. In decimal, it's 127. In octal, it's 0177. In hexadecimal, it's 0xFF.

7. The two printer number bits are the leftmost bits of an unsigned quantity. When they are right-shifted to bit positions 1 and 0, all the vacated bits are replaced with 0s, so there is no need for further masking.

Chapter 16

1. a. **dist = 5280 * miles;** is valid.

   b. **plort = 4 * 4 + 4;** is valid, but if the user really wanted **4 * (4 + 4),** he or she should have used **#define POD (FEET + FEET)**

   c. **nex = = 6;;** is not valid; apparently the user forgot that he or she was writing for the preprocessor, not writing in C.

   d. **y = y + 5;** is valid.

   berg = berg + 5 * lob; is valid but is probably not the desired result.

   est = berg + 5/ y + 5; is valid but is probably not the desired result.

   nilp = lob *–berg + 5; is valid but is probably not the desired result.

3. `#define MIN(X,Y) ( (X)<(Y) ? (X) : (Y) )`

5. `#define PR2(X,Y) printf("X is %d and Y is %d.\n",X,Y)`

   (Since **X** and **Y** are never exposed to any other operatons such as multiplication in this macro, we don't have to cocoon everything in parentheses.)

7. Try this:

   `#define PR(X) printf("name: X; value: %d; address: %u\n",X,&X)`

   Or, if your implementation allows, use the **%p** specification for the address.

9. a. `enum days {sun, mon, tue, wed, thu, fri, sat};`

   b. `enum days visit;`

11. a. We show it using the ANSI C type casts:

   `qsort( (void *)scores, (size_t) 1000, sizeof(double), comp);`

   (Note that the **sizeof** expression, by definition, is type **size_t**.

   b.
```
   int comp()
   double *p1, *p2;
   {
      if ( *p1 > *p2 )
         return -1;
      else if ( *p2 > *p1)
         return 1;
```

```
            else
                return 0;
        }
```

or for admirers of compactness,

```
int comp (double *p1, double *p2)   /* ANSI form */
{
    return *p1==*p2?0:(*p1>*p2?-1:1);
}
```

13. Each structure contains the address of the next structure but has no knowledge of where
the preceding structure is located. To remedy this problem, we can have each structure
hold the addresses of both the preceding structure and the following structure:

```
struct symp {
            char *name;
            struct symp *next;
            struct symp *prec;
            };
```

Index

Hosted environment, 28

IBM PCs, 12
    compiling C on, 17
    editing on, 16–17
    and end of file marker, 244
    equipment words for, 522
    sizes for data types, 67
#if directive, 545–546
If else, 200–201, 202
    compared with **if**, 202
    compared with **switch**, 225
If statements, 198–211, 586–587
    else if, 204–207
    nested, 206, 207–212
#ifdef directive, 543–544
#ifndef directive, 544–545
Imax( ) function, 285–287, 288
Imin( ) function, 281–283, 285
In-line code, 538
    and **#pragma** directive, 546
#include directive, 27, 539–542, 549
    with **#define**, 87, 307–309
Incrementing operator (++), 128–131, 141, 326
    avoid, in macros, 537
    and pointers, 328–329
    and precedence, 132–134
Indefinite loops, 166
Indentation in code, 138
Indices for arrays, 183, 314
Indirect membership operator (–), 493, 494, 575–576
Indirection operator (*), 292–293, 297, 326, 328
Initializing
    arrays, 314, 316–319, 359
    automatic variables, 432
    character data, 59–60
    character string arrays, 356–357, 358
    external variables, 434
    pointers, 360
    static variables, 436
    structure pointers, 477–478
    structure variables, 469
    structures, 469–470
    two-dimensional arrays, 333–334
    variables, 53, 69
Input, inputting
    buffered, 241–242, 252–254
    do-it-yourself, 368–370
    of files, 396–424
    mixing character and numeric data, 255–257, 265–268
    redirecting, 247–248
    with **scanf( )**, 104

    skipping over, 106–107
    strings, 362–366
    terminating, 242–246, 457
Input/output (I /O)
    formatting functions, 78–108
    functions, 88, 240–268, 397–398, 403–406, 417–424, 595–597
    levels of, 397–398
    low-level, 243, 398–403
    simultaneous low-level and standard, 417
    standard package of functions, 243, 397–398, 403–406, 417– 424, 595–597
    See also Functions
Int86( ) function, 524
Int feof( ) function, 421
Int ferror( ) function, 421
Int fflush( ) function, 418
Int setvbuf( ) function, 418
Int ungetc( ) function, 417–418
Integer (**int**) data, 29, 47, 49, 68–69
    adjective keywords for, 55–56
    compared to floating-point, 49, 51
    constants, 53–54, 57–58, 61, 546–548
    and division, 121–122
    hexadecimal, 54, 60
    int, 52–55, 68
    long, 56, 68
    octal, 54, 60
    overflow, 57
    printing, 54–55, 58
    raising numbers to, 186
    short, 55, 68
    signed, 52, 68, 97, 509–510, 579
    size allowable, 56, 67
    unsigned, 55–69, 579–580
Interchange( ) function, 290–292, 296
Interface, user, 252–257
    with menus, 263–268
Interpreted languages, 4
Interrupts, 524
Io.h header file, 400
Isalnum( ) function, 382
Isalpha( ) function, 382
Iscntrl( ) function, 382
Isdigit( ) function, 382
Isgraph( ) function, 382
Islower( ) function, 382
Isprint( ) function, 382
Ispunct( ) function, 382
Isspace( ) function, 382
Isupper( ) function, 382
Isxdigit( ) function, 382
Iteration cycles, 155

The Waite Group

100 Shoreline Highway, Suite A-285   Mill Valley, CA 94941   (415) 331-0575

Compuserve: 75146,3515   usenet: hplabs!well!mitch   AppleLink: D2097

Dear Reader:

Thank you for considering the purchase of our book. Readers have come to know products from **The Waite Group** for the care and quality we put into them. Let me tell you a little about our group and how we make our books.

It started in 1976 when I could not find a computer book that really taught me anything. The books that were available talked down to people, lacked illustrations and examples, were poorly laid out, and were written as if you already understood all the terminology. So I set out to write a good book about microcomputers. This was to be a special book—very graphic, with a friendly and casual style, and filled with examples. The result was an instant best-seller.

Over the years, I developed this approach into a ''formula'' (nothing really secret here, just a lot of hard work—I am a crazy man about technical accuracy and high-quality illustrations). I began to find writers who wanted to write books in this way. This led to co-authoring and then to multiple-author books and many more titles (over seventy titles currently on the market). As The Waite Group author base grew, I trained a group of editors to manage our products. We now have a team devoted to putting together the best possible book package and maintaining the high standard of our existing books.

We greatly appreciate and use any advice our readers send us (and you send us a lot). We have discovered that our readers are detail nuts: you want indexes that really work, tables of contents that dig deeply into the subject, illustrations, tons of examples, reference cards, and more.

I think you will find that **C: Step-by-Step** is a good example of The Waite Group formula for a computer book. You'll find facts, tips, boxes, quizzes, projects, icons, warnings, and much more. This book has been specially designed to make your learning of C as painless as possible and hopefully enjoyable too. We have gone to lengths to make the book follow a structured approach and to present C in a problem-solving manner so that you learn the best programming habits from the start. If you'd like to extend your C programming experience further, you'll want to study our book **Advanced C Primer ++**. If you are interested in a specific implementation of C, you'll want to examine our best sellers **Microsoft C Programming for the PC** and **Turbo C Programming for the PC**. Finally, if you need a comprehensive reference to the C libraries, check out our Microsoft, Turbo, and QuickC Bibles. A list of all our titles can be found in the back of this book. In fact, let us know what you want and we'll try to write about it.

Thanks again for considering the purchase of this title. If you care to tell me anything you like (or don't like) about the book, please write or send email to the addresses on this letterhead.

Sincerely,

Mitchell Waite
The Waite Group

The Waite Group Library

If you enjoyed this book, you may be interested in these additional subjects and titles from **The Waite Group** and Howard W. Sams & Company. Reader level is as follows: ★ = introductory, ★★ = intermediate, ★★★ = advanced. You can order these books by calling 800-428-SAMS.

Level	Title	Catalog #	Price	
	C and C++ Programming Language			
Tutorial, UNIX & ANSI				
★	C Primer Plus, Revised Edition, Waite, Prata, & Martin	22582	$24.95	
★★	C++ Programming, Berry	22619	$24.95	
★★★	Advanced C Primer ++, Prata	22486	$24.95	
Tutorial, Product Specific				
★	Microsoft C Programming for the PC, Revised Edition, Lafore	22661	$24.95	NEW
★	Turbo C Programming for the PC, Revised Edition, Lafore	22660	$22.95	NEW
★★	Inside the Amiga with C, Second Edition, Berry	22625	$24.95	
Reference, Product Specific				
★★	Microsoft C Bible, Barkakati	22620	$24.95	NEW
★★	Quick C Bible, Barkakati	22632	$24.95	NEW
★★	Turbo C. Bible, Barkakati	22631	$24.95	NEW
★★	Essential Guide to ANSI C, Barkakati	22673	$7.95	NEW
★★	Essential Guide to Turbo C, Barkakati	22675	$7.95	NEW
★★	Essential Guide to Microsoft C, Barkakati	22674	$7.95	NEW
	DOS and OS/2 Operating System			
Tutorial, General Users				
★	Discovering MS-DOS, O'Day	22407	$19.95	
★	Understanding MS-DOS, O'Day & Angermeyer	27067	$17.95	
Tutorial/Reference, General Users				
★★	MS-DOS Bible, Second Edition, Simrin	22617	$22.95	
Tutorial/Reference, Power Users				
★★	Tricks of the MS-DOS Masters, Angermeyer & Jaeger	22525	$24.95	
Tutorial, Programmers				
★★	MS-DOS Papers, Edited by The Waite Group	22594	$26.95	
★★	OS/2 Programmer's Reference, Dror	22645	$24.95	NEW
★★★	MS-DOS Developer's Guide, Revised Edition, Angermeyer, Jaeger, et al.	22630	$24.95	NEW
	UNIX Operating System			
Tutorial, General Users				
★	UNIX Primer Plus, Waite, Prata, & Martin	22028	$22.95	
★	UNIX System V Primer, Revised Edition, Waite, Prata, & Martin	22570	$22.95	
★★	UNIX System V Bible, Prata and Martin	22562	$24.95	
★★	UNIX Communications, Henderson, Anderson, Costales	22511	$24.95	
★★	UNIX Papers, Edited by Mitchell Waite	22570	$26.95	
Tutorial/Reference, Power Users and Programmers				
★★	Tricks of the UNIX Masters, Sage	22449	$24.95	
★★★	Advanced UNIX—A Programmer's Guide, Prata	22403	$24.95	
	Macintosh			
Tutorial, General Users				
★	HyperTalk Bible, The Waite Group	48430	$24.95	NEW
Tutorial/Reference, Power Users and Programmers				
★★	Tricks of the HyperTalk Masters, Edited by The Waite Group	48431	$24.95	NEW